ABSTRACT BODIES

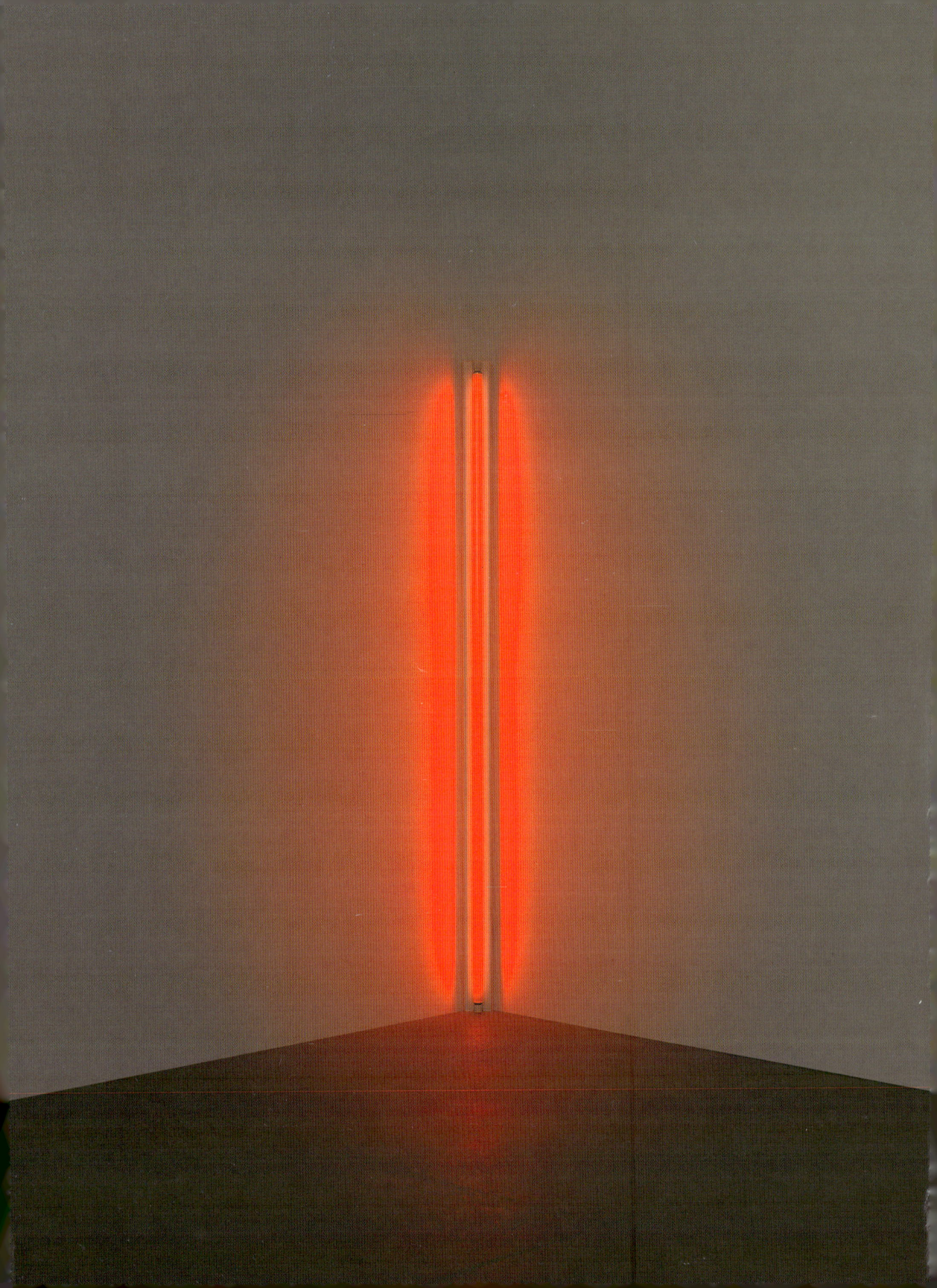

ABSTRACT BODIES

SIXTIES SCULPTURE IN THE EXPANDED FIELD OF GENDER

DAVID J. GETSY

YALE UNIVERSITY PRESS
NEW HAVEN AND LONDON

Copyright © 2015 by David Getsy.
All rights reserved.

This book may not be reproduced, in whole or in part, in any form (beyond that copying permitted by Sections 107 and 108 of the U.S. Copyright Law and except by reviewers for the public press), without written permission from the publishers.

Designed by Charlotte Grievson.
Printed in China.

Library of Congress Cataloging-in-Publication Data

Getsy, David.
Abstract bodies : sixties sculpture in the expanded field of gender/David J. Getsy.
pages cm
Includes bibliographical references and index.
ISBN 978-0-300-19675-7 (hardback)
1. Sculpture, Abstract--United States--Themes, motives. 2. Sex role in art. 3. Flavin, Dan, 1933-1996--Criticism and interpretation. 4. Grossman, Nancy--Criticism and interpretation. 5. Chamberlain, John, 1927-2011--Criticism and interpretation. 6. Smith, David, 1906-1965--Criticism and interpretation. I. Title.
NB212.5.A2G48 2015
730.973--dc23
2015019376

Frontispiece: Dan Flavin, *red out of a corner (to Annina)*, 1963/70 (detail of fig. 116).
Page vi: Detail of Nancy Grossman, *For David Smith*, 1965 (fig. 82).

CONTENTS

Acknowledgments		VII
Preface		VII
Introduction:		I
	"New" Genders and Sculpture in the 1960s	
1	On Not Making Boys: David Smith, Frank O'Hara, and Gender Assignment	43
2	Immoderate Couplings: Transformations and Genders in John Chamberlain's Work	97
3	Second Skins: The Unbound Genders of Nancy Grossman's Sculpture	147
4	Dan Flavin's Dedications	209
Conclusion:		267
	Abstraction and the Unforeclosed	
Notes		281
Bibliography		329
Index		356
Illustration Credits		371

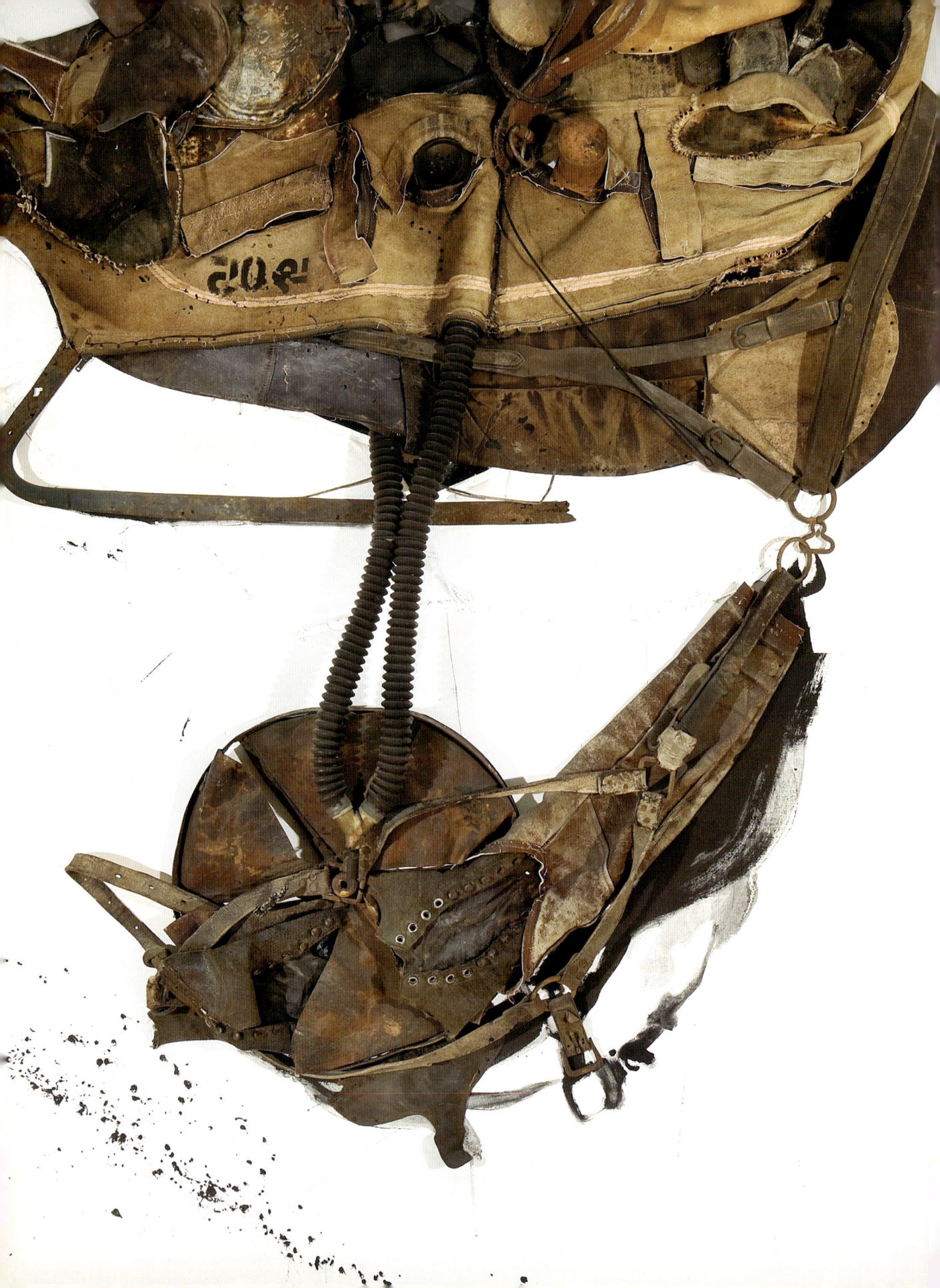

ACKNOWLEDGMENTS

This book is the result of innumerable conversations through which the ideas were developed. Many smart questions and generous listeners helped me to think through the arguments and to understand their stakes, and my best memories of this work are primarily about those formative discussions. With this project, I shifted my attention drastically, from nineteenth-century statues to postwar abstraction, and I could not have done this without the encouragement I received and the sense of purpose that my interlocutors helped me to realize.

First and foremost, I would like to thank the artists and their families, estates, and representatives, all of whom facilitated my work on this project. I owe much to the encouragement and generosity of Susan Cooke of the Estate of David Smith, Maureen Granville-Smith, Alexandra Fairweather, Prudence Fairweather, Angelo Piccozi, halley k harrisburg, Michael Rosenfeld, and Heather Cassils. Nancy Grossman has been nothing less than an inspiration, and it was one of the great pleasures of the research for this book to be able to get to know her and her remarkable work. Overall, I conclude this project with a great respect for the work of each of the artists, and I hope this book stands as both a testament to their practices as well as a proposition for how they can be viewed anew.

This book's form was first conceptualized during my time as an Ailsa Mellon Bruce Senior Fellow at the Center for Advanced Study in the Visual Arts at the National Gallery of Art in Washington, D.C. I learned much from the intellectual community of the Center and my cohort during that year. In particular, Elizabeth Cropper, Peter Lukehart, Therese O'Malley, Suzanne Preston Blier, Evonne Levy, Ruth Iskin, and Michael Schreffler asked important questions that helped me to formulate the ambitions of the project. A fellowship from the Sterling and Francine Clark Art Institute further supported the research, and it was in Williamstown that discussions with Rachel Haidu, Michael Ann Holly, Richard Brettell, Keith Moxey, and David Breslin were formative. I would especially like to thank Nanette Salomon for her smart questions and enthusiasm during my time at the Clark. The School of the Art Institute of Chicago provided sabbatical leave and a Faculty Research Grant, and I am grateful to Dean Lisa Wainwright for her encouragement of this work.

Much time was spent in archives and collections for this project, and I benefited greatly from the assistance provided by Marisa Bourgoin of the Archives of American Art, Melissa Watterworth of the Thomas J. Dodd Research Center at the University of Connecticut, the staff of the Museum of Modern Art (MoMA) Archives, the staff of the Getty Research Institute, the staff of the Henry Moore Institute, Charles Silver of the Department of Film at MoMA, Danielle King of the Department of Painting and Sculpture at MoMA, Alexandra Whitney and Lauren Knighton of David Zwirner Gallery, Eugenia Bell, Rob Weiner of the Chinati Foundation, Mary Richardson of the Museum of Contemporary Art Chicago, and Ian Berry and Megan Hyde of the Tang Museum at Skidmore College. Interviews with Mac McGinnes and Michael Harwood were exceedingly helpful and enjoyable.

The chapters have benefited from close readings and public presentations. In particular, I am very grateful to Jason Edwards, Julian B. Carter, Jenni Sorkin, Michael Brenson, Amy Sillman, Sarah Betzer, Jennifer Doyle, and David Raskin for their comments on drafts of parts of this book. The first and fourth chapters were workshopped in extremely helpful seminars at the University of Chicago – first at the Center for the Study of Gender and Sexuality and second at the Society of Fellows in the Liberal Arts (during which time I had a useful formal response from Lisa Lee). Chapter 2 was first presented at the Chinati Foundation, and it was the initial invitation to speak on John Chamberlain by Marianne Stockebrand that prompted me to work on this material. An earlier version was published in the proceedings of the Chinati's symposium on Chamberlain in 2009. A turning point for me in realizing that there was a larger project to be undertaken occurred through discussions with Gregg Bordowitz about the initial Chamberlain essay. This culminated in a conversation recorded as a podcast for *Bad at Sports* in May 2007. That podcast has proven to be useful to many since it aired, and it was also instrumental in my early thinking about this research and its stakes. Part of Chapter 3 was published in the catalogue to the retrospective exhibition prepared by Ian Berry at the Tang Museum. I am grateful for the ability to update these writings and to republish my keyword essay for *TSQ: Transgender Studies Quarterly* in the introduction to this volume and, in the conclusion, a short piece written to accompany Orlando Tirado's exhibition *FLEX* at Kent Fine Art, New York, in 2014. With regard to public presentations, I received many useful comments and questions when parts of this book were presented as lectures at Washington & Lee University, the School of the Art Institute of Chicago (SAIC), Human Resources Los Angeles, the Chinati Foundation, the Universities Art Association of Canada Conference, the College Art Association Conference, the University of Illinois at Chicago, the University of York, the University of Virginia, George Washington University, and the "Transsomatechnics" Conference in 2008 at Simon Fraser University.

Many institutions and individuals assisted with the acquisitions of images and copyright. I thank Stephen Flavin, the David Smith Estate, Fairweather & Fairweather Ltd, Michael Rosenfeld Gallery (with special thanks to Marjorie Van Cura), David Zwirner Gallery (and, in particular, Lauren Knighton), the Tang Museum and Teaching Gallery, the Richard Avedon Foundation, the Felix Gonzalez-Torres Foundation, the Guggenheim Museum, Meredith Potts of the Dan Budnik Studio, Gregory Most and Meg Melvin of the Department of Image Collections at the National Gallery of Art, Selena Bartlett of the Allen Memorial Art Museum, Stacey Sherman of the Nelson-Atkins Museum of Art, Heather Monahan of the Pace Gallery, the Des Moines Art Center, the Philadelphia Museum of Art, the Margulies Collection, the Chinati Foundation, the Dan Flavin Art Institute, the Dia Foundation, Ronald Feldman Gallery, Allen Stone Gallery, Paul Cooper Gallery, Gagosian Gallery, Galerie Karsten Greve, and Robyn Farrell and Aimee Marshall of the Art Institute of Chicago. Both Artists Rights Society and VAGA have been helpful.

I would also like to thank the staff of Yale University Press, and especially Gillian Malpass, whose enthusiasm for and commitment to this project have been constant sources of encouragement. This book also owes a great deal to Katharine Ridler's careful eye and good suggestions, as well as to Charlotte Grievson for the beautiful design.

My colleague Terry Myers and I co-taught a graduate seminar on Frank O'Hara that allowed for many productive discussions of his poetry and criticism. Also, my research assistants at the SAIC were crucial to this project, and I am grateful for the hard work and keen eyes of Beth Capper, Bryce Dwyer, and Rebecca Henderson. Many students in other graduate seminars at SAIC have heard early versions of these ideas. While I cannot mention each conversation, questions from the following continue to come to mind: Danny Orendorff, Rachel Wolff, Kate Pollasch-Thames, Gordon Hall, Zach Blas, Marc Adelman, Antje Gamble, Aiden Simon, Jules Rosskam, and again, Beth Capper.

Many interlocutors have assisted me with thinking through this project, and it could not have been realized without their help. In addition to those thanked above, I am grateful for conversations about these ideas with Jennifer Doyle, Gregg Bordowitz, Whitney Davis, Frédéric Moffet, Barbara DeGenevieve, Lisa Wainwright, James Elkins, James Rondeau, Kate Nesin, Mary Jane Jacob, Susan Stryker, Michael Golec, Jonathan D. Katz, Tirza Latimer, James Meyer, Alex Potts, Harry Cooper, Jo Applin, Gavin Butt, Dieter Schwarz, Hollis Clayson, Anne Collins Goodyear, Christopher Bedford, Elise Archias, Elliot King, Amy Sillman, Ernesto Pujol, and Doug Ischar.

And finally, I would like to thank my family and friends for listening to endless variations on this book. Without them, nothing would be possible. My parents, David and Donna Getsy, are a constant source of strength. Many friends have encouraged and assisted me throughout, and I am especially thankful for Matthew Harvat, Warren Davis, Paul Moffat, Sean Fader, Adam Colangelo, Hugo Eyre-Varnier, Corin Baird, Rob Bondgren, Andrew Kain Miller, Tom Glassic, Dennis Mendoza, Murtaza Nemat Ali, Ron Wittman, Jeanette Hanna-Ruiz, Kate Zeller, Emi Winter, Pierre Scott, and Dwight McBride. Throughout this exploration of abstraction, Jude Hansen has kept me grounded, and this book owes much to his love and support.

PREFACE

> In a sense, what is most important is what an artist *does*, rather than what he *is*, what the object *does* – in terms of response – rather than what it *is*.
>
> Gregory Battcock, 1968[1]

Transformation was the norm in American sculpture of the 1960s. The decade saw thoroughgoing attacks on sculptural representation and on the very idea of the statue. In the wake of sculpture's reconfiguration, modes such as assemblage, the reductive object, and earthworks proliferated. Rosalind Krauss famously dubbed the new conditions of sculpture that emerged in the 1960s as entering an "expanded field" and wrote of the medium's diffusion and dispersal.[2] Even though sculpture (as well as the format of the statue) did not end as widely foretold, in this contentious decade it was inexorably altered and multiplied.

The 1960s in America also saw a fundamental shift in the ways that persons were understood. This was the decade in which gender identities and their distinction from biological sex began to be more publically contested.[3] A key development driving these debates was the realization that sex could be changed, and 1960s America witnessed the emergence of public and institutional acknowledgments of transsexuality. In popular culture, evidence had already been mounting since the 1950s about the lived diversity of transformable and multiple genders. The media discourse around transsexuality had begun in 1952 when Christine Jorgensen made international headlines for being the first publicly disclosed case of sex reassignment surgery.[4] In 1954, the American magazine *People Today* would report, "Next to the recurrent hydrogen bomb headlines, reports of sex changes are becoming the most persistently startling world news."[5] By the 1960s, gender research clinics began to be founded across the country, starting with the University of California Los Angeles in 1962 and growing to include such institutions as Johns Hopkins University, Northwestern University, the University of Washington, and Stanford University. In 1966, the groundbreaking book by Harry Benjamin, *The Transsexual Phenomenon*, was published.[6] That same year, the *New York Times* ran a front-page story about sex-change operations, soon followed by articles in *Esquire*, *Time*, *Newsweek*, and *U.S. News & World Report*.[7] In 1968, the Olympic Games held in Mexico City were the first formally to introduce gender confirmation testing, Jorgensen went on a twenty-city book tour to publicize her just-released autobiography, and Gore Vidal published his bestselling novel featuring its eponymous transsexual heroine, *Myra Breckinridge*. In 1969, the Stonewall Riots that launched Gay Liberation were sparked by the resistance of transwomen and drag queens to police harassment. In the 1960s, definitions of gender, sex, and the human body also moved into an expanded field.

This book questions what these two concurrent histories might have to say to each other. How, in other words, does the emerging public recognition of the presence of transformable genders and bodies in the 1960s correlate with sculpture's contentious relationship to figuration and the body in that decade? Questions of gender often accompanied sculpture's struggle to dispense with recognizable figures while maintaining abstract and non-referential objects' relationships to human bodies and human lives. Whether it was the metaphors of bodily couplings in the work of John Chamberlain, the transformed skins and garments of Nancy Grossman's assemblages, or Dan Flavin's affectionate dedications of literalist objects to friends and mentors, even the most abstract and non-representational sculpture nevertheless kept allusions to persons and bodies near. An attention to transformable genders, mutable morphologies, and successive states of personhood illuminates these positions in sculpture, showing how abstraction produced less determined and more open ways of accounting for bodies and persons.

Sculpture in the 1960s sought finally to free itself from the statue and its allusions to conventional human figures. The decade increasingly became characterized by abstract sculptures that repudiated the conventions and format of the freestanding statue but were nevertheless still discrete human-scale objects. Instead, new materials and new configurations emerged around the goal of making sculpture that neither fell back on conventional materials nor imaged the human figure or shared its proportions. David Smith was the key transitional figure in this, and his final years of sculpture were taken up with the battle to overcome the lingering statuary format that had characterized his major works of the 1950s. In his wake, sculptors moved more decisively into alternative materials, new formats, and higher degrees of abstraction and non-reference. At the same time, this embrace of total abstraction fueled the long-running anxiety about the differences between sculptures, everyday objects, and furniture. Caught between their flight from the conventional statue and their fear of having abstract sculptures dissolve into the world of everyday functional things, sculptors in the 1960s developed a mode between these two options of the statue and the object. By the end of the decade, modes such as conceptual art, earthworks, and the like would overcome this issue by moving out of the gallery and away from the discrete object, but the first half of the 1960s was caught up with making what one could call non-statues on a human scale.

Artists as different as Smith, Chamberlain, Grossman, and Flavin all wrestled with how to make abstract works. They did so through relying on metaphors of the human body and of personhood. That is, even though their works did not image the human, they invoked it. Smith's welded steel constructions, Chamberlain's dense but delicate compositions made from crushed automobile parts, Grossman's de-constructed leather garments remade into writhing abstract reliefs, or Flavin's cool electrified light tubes all aimed to confront viewers with new entities, new bodies. In their work, the non-correlation between these objects and the metaphors the artists' applied to them produced questions – for viewers, for critics, and for the artists themselves – about how and where gender could be mapped onto the works and, more broadly, what gender's relationships to embodiment could be. What happens, in other words, when artists such as these refuse to present the human form but demand that their sculptures be seen as related to human bodies and persons?

This book begins to answer that question by drawing on the interdisciplinary field of transgender studies. Its methods and priorities inform the questions I ask of Sixties sculpture. I take as axiomatic that the ever-growing literature on the history of transgender experience in the twentieth century demands reconsiderations of larger accounts of the body, of normalcy, of personhood, of representation, and of the human. Accordingly, this book offers the first sustained, book-length use of transgender studies in the field of art history.[8] I show how this perspective enhances clarity about the terms, history, and implications of sculpture's relationship to definitions of the human, to the figure, and to abstraction in this decade. I have not sought an iconography of transgender in this project, nor is this book about transgender artists or even artists who were in direct dialogue with the emerging popular discourse of transsexuality and gender nonconformity in the 1960s. Rather, I have used the methods and theories of transgender studies to approach anew and in depth a small group of artists in order to show how their anxious, excited, and fearless invocations of the body in relation to abstract and non-referential objects can be understood to produce accounts of gender's plurality and mutability. In examining these artists and their archives, I pursued fundamental historical and conceptual questions that transgender studies poses: that is, how non-binary genders are articulated and acknowledged, how human morphologies could be valued for their mutability, and how to do justice to successive states of personhood or embodiment. The accounts of human experience and potential that underwrite transgender studies demand a broad critique and a fundamental remapping of the ways we understand societies and individuals. In keeping with this, the long history of figural representation (and its opponents) looks different when we attend to the reality of transformable genders and bodies.

Both the history of figuration and of abstraction's repudiation of it are inextricably bound up with sex and gender. Images of the human form generally incite a desire to categorize that form according to its sex and, in turn, to align it with assumptions about how gender should relate to that sex. In order for many to see a body (or an image of a body) as human, its relation to gender needs to be settled. Gender "figures as a precondition for the production and maintenance of legible humanity," as Judith Butler has maintained.[9] From the first, the determination of gender operates as a predicate for integration into the social. For instance, the negotiation of pronoun usage becomes, for many, the obligatory first step in conversations and interactions, and any ambiguity or mobility of pronoun usage will quickly derail or arrest interactions. Or, more fundamentally, one could think of the primal nomination of personhood at birth. No matter if it is cliché or ritual, the performative assignment of sex and gender to a newborn ("It's a girl!") has immediate effects. This performative utterance (whether said out loud or inscribed on a birth certificate) alters how that child is understood by others, determines such things as what colors many will think are appropriate for its garments, and produces a set of expectations with regard to gender identity.[10]

Ambiguous or ambivalent images of the human form trouble these taxonomic impulses. Anything that does not simply and clearly reflect presumptions about the dimorphism of human bodies is ignored or rejected, and those figures that exceed binary categories are considered inadequate or incomplete renderings of the human. Attempts at simplifying representation to its basics as a means of offering the generic or the universal image have limited scope, for soon enough the question will be raised about "what kind" of person such a humanoid form actually implies. Even stick figures incite questions of gender assignment. This book goes even further than such simplified figurative images to investigate how sculptures that refused to image the human form were nevertheless caught up with nominations of gender for non-representational objects. A transgender studies perspective provides a basis for examining the political and ethical implications of such arbitrations. It allows, on the one hand, for a wider recognition of gender's contestations and alternatives (which would otherwise be renounced or go unrecognized). On the other, it calls for a critical reassessment of normative accounts of the human that take dimorphism as absolute and binaries as immutable truths.[11]

The term "transgender" has been used to bring into alliance a wide range of nonascribed genders, and I discuss its use in historical analysis further in the Introduction. Viviane K. Namaste described "transgender" as "an umbrella term used to refer to all individuals who live outside of normative sex/gender relations – that is, individuals whose gendered self-presentation (evidenced through dress, mannerisms, and even physiology) does not correspond to the behaviors habitually associated with members of their biological sex."[12] In this, the history of transsexuality was foundational to the later expansion and formulation of "transgender" as an inclusive category for a range of lived experiences of gender and embodiment.[13] Transformation and temporality are central to definitions of transgender's conjugation of non-binary, unique, or recombined gender potentialities. Susan Stryker has nominated this idea of transformative movement as crucial to wider applications of "transgender," taking the term's defining trait as "the movement across a socially imposed boundary away from an unchosen starting place – rather than any particular destination or mode of transition."[14]

Neither the transformability of genders and bodies nor their variability and plurality are contemporary developments. There is extensive evidence for a broad and diverse history of gender nonconformity, successively adopted genders, and mutable bodily morphologies that decisively refutes the assumption that gender is binary and static.[15] Similarly, there is an extensive (but silenced) history of intersex lives that discredits the misconception that the human species is absolutely dimorphic.[16] The 1950s and 1960s saw long-running scientific debates about sex and gender cross over into popular culture. Gender's variability, complexity, and mutability began to be more publically discussed as part of the wide-ranging cultural upheavals of these years. As Paul B. Preciado has argued, "In the 1950s, which were confronted with the political rise of feminism and with homosexuality, as well as with the desire of 'transvestites,' 'deviants,' and 'transsexuals' to escape or transform birth sex assignment, the dimorphism epistemology of sexual difference was simply crumbling."[17] By the 1960s, this process had accelerated. New medical and social institutions were spawned, and evidence of nonascribed and transformed genders began to be featured regularly in the press, in popular culture, and in the work of artists and writers. As I discuss in the Introduction, Stryker nominated the 1960s as the era of "transgender liberation" because of the widespread cultural and institutional acknowledgment of gender mutability and multiplicity that emerged in those years.[18]

A transgender history attends not just to the evidence of gender nonconforming lives but also — as this study does — shows how accounts of transgender capacity are produced (sometimes inadvertently) through attempts to reconsider how bodies and persons can be imaged or evoked. It also asks its questions broadly with the understanding that all genders must be characterized differently once mutability and temporality are recognized among their defining traits.[19] Once personhood is valued for its transformations and gender is understood as workable beyond conventional static and binary norms, any account of the human or of its representations looks different and more complex. Such is the case with the contentious role of the human form in the history of sculpture, and this book discusses the history of postwar sculpture for the ways it proposed "successive states" of personhood and unforeclosed accounts of genders' inhabitations in works that evoked but did not image the human body. (I encountered this phrase "successive states" in Donald Judd's writing on the formal character of Chamberlain's reworked components, and it has stuck with me as a particularly apt way of characterizing the hard-won reworking of gender and personhood that transgender studies values.[20])

In bringing to light the ways in which abstract sculpture of the 1960s came to posit gender's mutability and multiplicity, I see this book as taking up the challenge that Butler put to historical inquiry when she wrote of the need to provide new accounts of the long history of the complexity and diversity of genders:

> I would say that it is not a question merely of producing a new future for genders that do not exist. The genders I have in mind have been in existence for a long time, but they have not been admitted into the terms that govern reality. So it is a question of developing within law, psychiatry, social, and literary theory a new legitimating lexicon for the gender complexity that we have been living with for a long time. Because the norms governing reality have not admitted these forms to be real, we will, of necessity, call them "new."[21]

The present book pursues this call to action from the perspective of the history of art, which has a long tradition of debating the human form and attending to its vicissitudes. In this, I see art history as offering a particularly rich resource for transgender studies – for example, in its methods for interpreting the allegorical deployments of the human form or for critically engaging with visual abstractions. In turn, the perspective of transgender studies is energizing as a means to re-view art-historical episodes in which the human body and its metaphors were at issue. American abstract sculpture in the 1960s – with its paradoxical combination of a refusal to represent the human body and a reliance on it as analogue – offers an exemplary site at which to bring these modes of inquiry into productive dialogue. Accordingly, I have committed to gender's historical plurality and mutability, and I have pursued the ways in which artists' practices reward attention to transforming genders and successive personhood. The complexity of Sixties sculpture becomes more apparent and generative when one attends to the accounts of genders, of the body, and of persons that underwrote it.

During the decade characterized by the atomization of the statue into specific objects and expanded fields, abstract bodies emerged from the sculpture's refusal of the figure. The human form could no longer be taken for granted or treated as universal. Gender became an open question, and it was mapped variably and successively onto abstraction. In these same years, genders and bodies came into question more widely, and nonascribed genders became visible as potentialities and actualities. Transgender lives presented a challenge to the authority given to the normative image of the human. Challenging this authority was also sculpture's preoccupation in the 1960s.

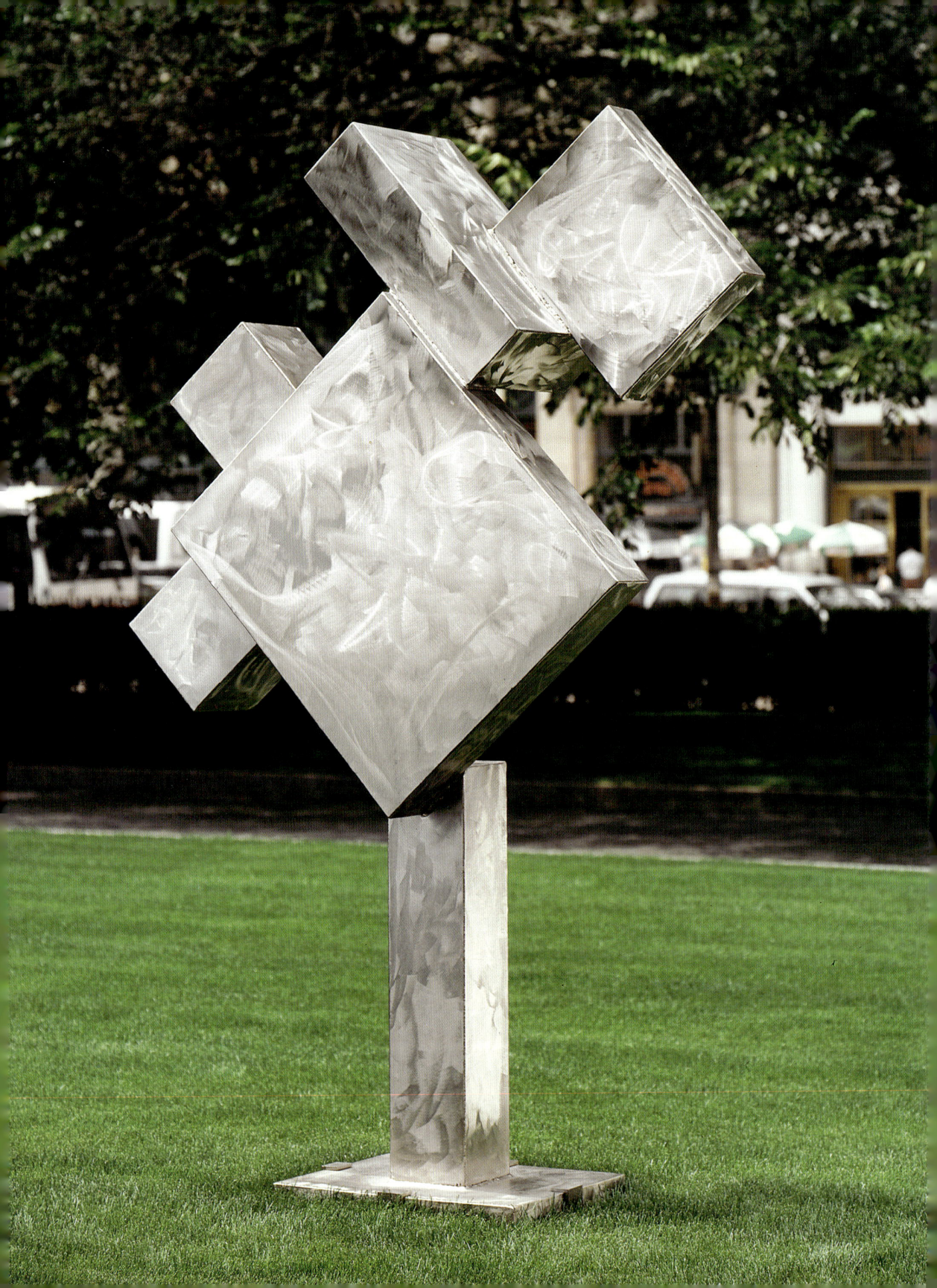

INTRODUCTION

"NEW" GENDERS AND SCULPTURE IN THE 1960S

An epiphany for this project, which helped me envision its shape, occurred when I was leaving the David Smith retrospective at Tate Modern a number of years ago. One of the final rooms was the media room, and the 1964 televised interview between Smith and Frank O'Hara I discuss in Chapter 1 was being projected on a large wall. I had not intended to watch this didactic and was walking through the room when I was arrested by Smith's line, "I don't make boy sculptures." How bizarre, I thought, that such a negative designation was a necessary or useful term for Smith. This line continued to nag at me, and I began to realize how perniciously gender functioned as the predicate for nominating works of art in relation to the human. Further, I began to question how sculpture in the 1960s often returned to this scene of facing gender multiplicity created through pursuits of abstraction or literalism. I started conceiving of this project as a book once I investigated that casual comment and realized how much it crystalized a larger set of issues confronting sculpture during the decade when the statuary format dissolved into the expanded field. Other comments, such as John Chamberlain's that "everybody's both" genders or Nancy Grossman's that each individual was fundamentally bi-sexed, led me to see a wider complex of issues that these individual artists helped to clarify.

My central contention in this book is that sculpture of the 1960s gains greater historical resonance and wider interdisciplinary relevance through attention to how the human was mapped onto objects that patently refused to image even the most basic traits of the human figure. More so than in

OPPOSITE 1   David Smith, *Cubi VII*, 1963. Stainless steel, 281.9 × 175.3 × 58.4 cm (111 × 69 × 23 in.). Art Institute of Chicago, Grant J. Pick Purchase Fund, 1964.1141.

the long tradition of abstracted, simplified, and stylized figures from the preceding decades of modernism, sculpture in the 1960s shattered the expectations of the medium, expanded its material practices, left the format of the freestanding statue behind, and made decisive moves to achieve non-reference and objecthood. At the same time, these innovations increasingly sought to activate the viewer's bodily and affective relations with those abstract sculptural objects. As with the four artists on whom I focus in this volume, such propositions for abstract sculpture were often animated by references direct and indirect to sexuality and gender. To be clear: this book is not about the genders of the sculptors discussed in it. On the contrary, I have chosen my case studies deliberately to show how accounts of genders as multiple and mutable erupt in the work of artists for whom gender and sexuality were not necessarily stated or primary terms of investigation. Accordingly, I reveal no secrets about the artists' lives nor are their biographies used as the main tools for interpretation of their practices. My focus is on their artistic practices, repeated methods, and the rhetorics they employed to communicate their priorities. These provide the basis for an extrapolation of gender multiplicity and transformability fostered by their pursuit of abstract bodies and persons. I argue that transgender capacity was inadvertently realized out of abstract sculpture's coupling of objecthood and personhood as it negotiated what would come after the statuary tradition.

"Sculpture" is an open and contested category in this book. Any examination of the tumultuous transformations in three-dimensional art-making in the 1960s could have it no other way. I have intentionally chosen objects that vary in their definitions of the sculptural object, from the accumulated compositions of Chamberlain through Grossman's relief assemblages to Flavin's modular light tubes. Flavin's work, in particular, has been appropriated as sculpture in this book because of the ways in which it signals an expansion into spatial practices. Early on, Flavin rejected the singular category of sculpture for his work (as did many Minimalists), but his early fluorescent work nevertheless was taken to be sculpture and participated in the debates about the medium's future or ruin. In all of the case studies, I draw on the three-dimensionality of these artists' works and the ways that their attempts at abstraction, non-reference, or literalism activated bodily identifications in the viewer precisely because of their physicality.

Fluorescent tubes, welded steel planes and cubes, and discarded autobody parts or leather garments – these are the materials used by Flavin, Smith, Chamberlain, and Grossman in their pursuit of abstract sculptural objects. Despite their aim to refuse or befuddle reference and signification, they

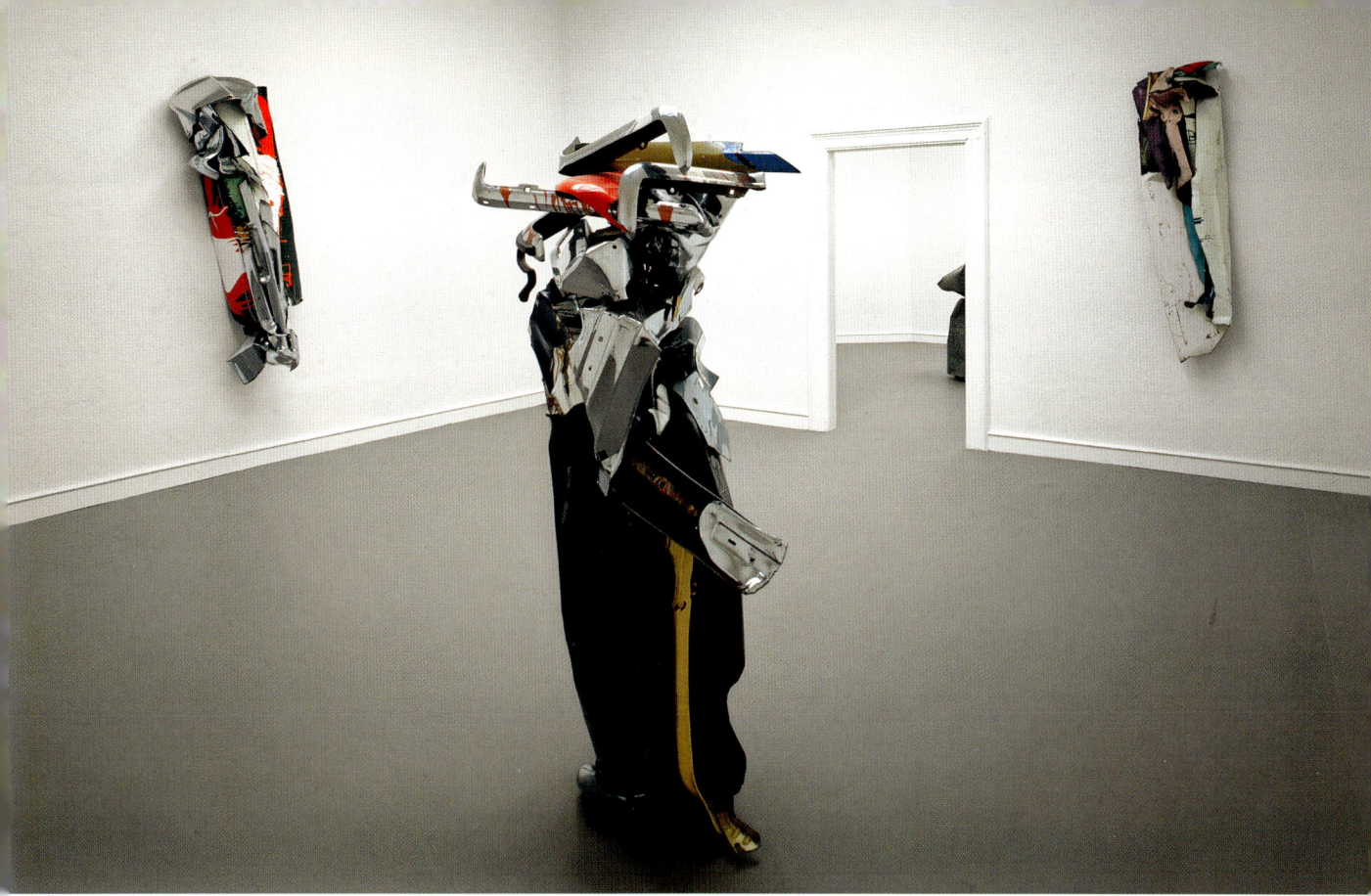

2   John Chamberlain, *Flavin Flats*, 1977. Painted and chromium-plated steel, 195.5 × 95.5 × 94 cm (77 × 37½ × 37 in.). Installed at Staatliche Kunsthalle Baden-Baden, 1991, in foreground.

nevertheless couched these moves in allusions to bodies, in practices of naming, in evocations of orifices and skins, in desire, and in the intermingling of bodies in sexuality. I focus on these issues in order to explore the gaps created when bodies are evoked but not imaged and when their transformability becomes valued. My analyses follow the development of their perspectives in the 1960s and track them through larger trajectories and, when possible, into their work of the 1970s and beyond. I use these four artists as representative of that broader preoccupation in the 1960s with colliding two seemingly contradictory priorities: on the one hand, commitments to complete abstraction and non-reference and, on the other, metaphors of the body, of sexuality, and of personhood. These four artists were also chosen for their differences in the ways in which abstraction was embraced (and sometimes contested) in the long trajectories of their practices. Loosely, the selection speaks to some of the major positions in abstract sculpture of the first half of the 1960s, such as Abstract Expressionist (Smith), Chamberlain's almost Pop embrace of the auto industry's lurid colors as a means to update the tradition of abstract steel sculpture, assemblage and found objects (Grossman's reliefs), and Minimalist (Flavin). None of these categories are adequate to the artists' work, obviously, and they bleed into each other. Naming them so bluntly, however, gives a sense of abstract options for sculpture in the first half of the 1960s. In addition, I have chosen to focus this book on artists conventionally associated with Sixties sculpture before Postminimalism – heralded by Lucy Lippard's 1966 exhibition *Eccentric Abstraction*. Within the study of that sculpture, it is Postminimalism that has received the most attention to date with regard to issues of gender, as I discuss shortly. I chose to redirect questions of gender to artists and movements that have, previously, been seen as less amenable to it than the more expected example of Postminimalism.

The questions pursued in my case studies expand on and explore the importance given to abstraction in Jack Halberstam's formative proposition of an aesthetics of the transgender body emerging in art after modernism.[1] As I shall be discussing, there are many more artists and art-historical periods (both before and after the 1960s) that abstracted the body and made gender ambiguous. My contention is not that the artists in this study are wholly unprecedented. To the contrary, they represent episodes in a much longer history of the ways in which abstracted bodies facilitate capacities for seeing the human otherwise. These four artists were chosen because I believe that the sophistication of their practices and the complexity of the issues they raise reward sustained investigation and, in turn, mark crucial tensions in the shift from the statuary tradition to sculpture's expanded field. In their negotiations of gender mutability, their cases offer more general models for how we articulate transgender capacities in other such artworks that – like theirs – were neither created by transgender artists nor made with the primary intention of envisioning mutable and multiple genders.

These chapters do not aim at a negative critique of these artists. In this study, I work primarily with these artists' artworks and the textual productions with which they buttressed them. I closely examine archives, objects, and statements in order to show how we can recognize new meanings and new accounts of the human in their struggle with the body in the abstract. I have been committed to explicating the driving concerns of their practices while, at the same time, arguing for the semantic and identificatory possibilities that expand out from those concerns. Such generative aims drive the book's analyses, and they respond to Eve Kosofsky Sedgwick's call for "reparative" interventions that multiply avenues of identification and cathexis, that offer tactics of survival, and that proliferate possibilities. As she urged about reparative readings, "What we can best learn from such practices are, perhaps, the many ways selves and communities succeed in extracting sustenance from the objects of a culture – even of a culture whose avowed desire has often been not to sustain them."[2] Accordingly, the invested but self-consciously rogue readings I offer in this book demonstrate that a deep engagement with these artists' priorities and practices unfolds to reveal unforeseen reparative potential in their accounts of personhood and gender.

In the sections that follow, I outline some of the key contexts for this study. First, I focus on the parameters of sculpture, followed by a discussion of how questions of figuration were displaced into debates about anthropomorphism, one of the central questions for sculpture criticism of the 1960s. I then discuss the emergence of abstract eroticism and bodily evocations in the middle of the decade, followed by a brief summary of the role of ambiguity and androgyny in twentieth-century art. I then offer a comparison to the history of transgender issues in the 1960s and an examination of the conceptual framework of transgender capacity.

STATUES, SCULPTURE, AND PHYSICALITY

Sculpture has an activated relationship to the human body that differs significantly from pictorial and other two-dimensional modes of representation. Its physicality and three-dimensionality necessarily invoke bodily relations – even in the most patently abstract of sculptures. Of course, other media such as paintings, textiles, and photographs do this in their own ways, but sculpture has historically been patterned after and scaled in relation to the human body. When sculptures are representational, that "image" occurs in three dimensions rather than two and, consequently, shares space with the viewer who can circumambulate it and physically interact with its real volumes. A result of this is that there is not the same physical boundary as there is with a two-dimensional image. Pictorial representation involves a translation of the three-dimensional world to a new world untouchable behind the picture plane. By contrast, the condition of sculptural representation is that it is boundaryless in its physical proximity and real tactility.[3] There is an immediacy and implied equivalency between the mass and volume of the sculptural object and the mass and volume of the viewer's encounter of it in shared space. Standing before a sculpture, the viewer is prompted to negotiate a series of bodily engagements, judgments of scale, incitements to tactility, and perceptions of shared environmental conditions between the sculptural body and their own. (This physical and spatial engagement is another reason why I have considered Flavin's immersive light fields in the realm of sculpture, as he himself did initially.)

The potentials and limitations of sculpture's physicality have long confronted those who would make statues. Commonly, they have navigated these parameters by focusing on discrete bodies rather than on the representation of fully contextual scenes in which those bodies operate. Consequently, the history of sculptural production has tended to center on representations of persons, and in conventional freestanding sculpture there is no equivalent of such options for pictorial representation as landscape or still life in which figures might be absent. By contrast, sculptors focused on the human figure alone or in small groups, with the single figure dominating the sculptural genres of the ideal statue, the portrait, and the monument. For most of its history, that is, sculpture had been primarily an art of the human form in both its physical relationality and its content.[4]

Sculpture in the twentieth century explored new options, and the human figure's centrality was questioned and supplemented during the decades of modernism.[5] Despite the fact that figuration increasingly became labeled as conservative and unmodern, versions of the human form persisted, and the formats of the statue and statuette retained their coherence after being overtaken by abstraction. Even during the highest periods of modernist abstraction there were relatively few modes of sculpture that did not somehow rely on the form and format of figuration (except for the most radical departures such as those of Vladimir Tatlin or Katarzyna Kobro and, debatably, the readymades of Marcel Duchamp). Animal bodies were adopted by artists such as Constantin Brancusi and Henri Gaudier-Brzeska as alternatives to the human form but, by and large, European and American traditions of sculpture continued to allude to or find equivalents for the human figure and its proportions. As Frances Colpitt noted, "Traditional sculpture depends on anthropomorphism to strike a bond between the spectator and the object, which accounts for the nonabstractness of most sculpture prior to the sixties."[6]

In the 1950s, the recognizable human figure was successively attacked and suppressed in sculpture. Nevertheless, the statue format continued to underwrite all but the most rigorously abstract sculpture. Even as mimetic representation was banished, sculptures continued to exhibit other defining parameters of statues: they were still predominantly freestanding, human-scale sculptural objects that shared the proportions, frontality, and structure of the human body. One can look to Rosalind Krauss's 1977 groundbreaking book, *Passages in Modern Sculpture*, for a narrative of the struggle in the medium of sculpture to defeat the statue format and its figurative valences.[7]

The teleology of her account culminated in installation, earthworks, and the Minimal and Postminimal options best represented for her by Robert Morris. This triumphal narrative was built through her careful discussions of sculptors' attempts to move beyond the coherence of the statue and its reliance on an organizing core (both formally and semantically). In that story, Smith served as the crucial transitional figure to the 1960s (an opinion I share, demanding his inclusion in this book).[8] Krauss's polemical and magisterial account of modern sculpture evidenced the ways in which conventions and meanings of the statue continued to shadow sculpture as it moved to embrace abstraction, objects, and new materials and formats.

While the summary history of sculpture provided in the preceding paragraphs is necessarily brief and over-simplifying, it nevertheless encapsulates what I see as the predominant patterns that led up to the beginnings of sculpture's more thoroughgoing revision that started in the 1950s and exploded in the 1960s. Despite the vicissitudes of style and degrees of representation and abstraction, however, across this history of modern sculpture it was the material object's physical co-presence and spatial relations with the viewer (as both object and, potentially, image) that were defining issues.[9] A consequence of this is that sculpture – even at its most abstract – necessarily invokes the motile body of the viewer in a direct and immediate way. As Lucy Lippard said in 1967, "Sculpture, existing in real space and physically autonomous, is *realer* than painting."[10] This invocation of real bodily relations meant that even as sculptors in the 1960s started to make non-statues, bodily metaphors and equivalencies were still operative. No matter how assiduous the pursuit of abstraction and non-reference, the body still haunted sculpture as its denominator. This study focuses on sculpture for the reason that such bodily resonances and invocations accompanied abstraction in a manner more pervasive and powerful than in two-dimensional media.

The nearness of bodies to even the most adventurous departures from traditional sculpture was remarked on by Krauss in her 1977 history of modern sculpture. Writing about Minimalism, often taken to be the apogee of abstraction, and other developments such as earthworks, Krauss reminded readers:

> The abstractness of minimalism makes it less easy to recognize the human body in those works and therefore less easy to project ourselves into the space of that sculpture with all of our settled prejudices left intact. Yet our bodies and our experience of our bodies continue to be the subject of this sculpture – even when a work is made of several hundred tons of earth.[11]

The image of the human body had been left behind, perhaps, but this move opened up a wider range of modes of address to multiple bodies across the 1960s. In this decade, the human body itself became an abstraction to be evoked and activated through sculptural objects.

LATENT ANTHROPOMORPHISMS, ECCENTRIC ABSTRACTIONS, AND OTHER "VEHICLES OF THE UNFAMILIAR" IN THE 1960s

This book is not about ambiguous human figures or generic bodies so much as the ways in which artists and viewers mapped bodily or personifying metaphors onto patently un-figurative, non-representational sculptural objects. It was in the 1960s that abstraction and non-reference became central to sculpture, and artists sought to leave any traces of the human form behind.

At the beginning of the decade, many had increasingly become disdainful of sculpture's dependence on the human figure. For instance, in 1963, Lawrence Alloway decried the state of recent sculpture, seeing its conventions as "cliché." Explaining the long tradition of modern sculpture, he argued:

> One reason that the 20th century sculptors rely so heavily, and so placidly, on the human image, is that if they don't, their work may look like furniture and hardware. Because sculpture has a more substantial and literal physical existence than paint on a canvas (which has an inveterate sign-making capacity and an unquenchable potential for illusion – and these are the medium's main carriers of meaning) it is prone to object-status.[12]

He quipped that the statues of the 1950s and early years of the 1960s were "commanding symbols of almost nothing" and called for a renewed engagement with the spatial characteristics of sculpture. In a statement that could be understood to presage Minimalism's spatial address (and Alloway's own burgeoning interest in systematic art), he argued: "One of the great problems (i.e., opportunity) in sculpture, which painting does not have in the same way, is the relation of the object to our physical space."[13] At the beginning of the 1960s, abstract sculpture struggled to be neither objects nor statues. The representation of the body – or even any bipedal figure – increasingly became suspect even as sculpture's opportunity was seen to be its activation of spatial and bodily relations.

A contradiction emerged forcefully in the 1960s between the push toward ever more extreme abstraction and sculpture's continued reliance on and evocation of the human body. As James Meyer has recently discussed, this manifested itself most strongly in the accusations of anthropomorphism that characterized critical discourse on sculpture in that decade. Anthropomorphism became a central term of derision from all sides.[14] Underlying such charges, he argued, was an attempt to retain and enhance sculpture's association with the body even as its image was banished. Summarizing this situation, Meyer contended that "During the 1960s, then, critiques of anthropomorphism and anthropocentrism typically went hand in hand. A third term was subsequently introduced into the discursive field, which I will call the *bodily*. The seminal critical debates of this period centered on the dialectic of the anthropomorphic and the bodily."[15] As part of a broader antihumanist critique that informed debates on 1960s art (and Minimalism more specifically), both figuration and the attribution of human traits to objects were elided with the anthropocentric. Consequently, more extreme versions of abstraction and non-reference were pursued, and anthropomorphism became equivalent to a charge of outmoded and deluded conservativism. In the expanding field, there was little room for figures.

The hunt to eradicate the anthropomorphic among abstract artists was animated by the resurgence of representational modes among abstraction's competitors in the decade. Sculptural figuration was embraced by such artists as Paul Thek, George Segal, Edward Kienholz, and Bruce Conner. Pop Art, too, challenged the idea of abstraction and the avoidance of the figurative, most notably in the non-human anthropomorphisms resulting from Claes Oldenburg's soft giganticism.[16] Faced with a burgeoning range of such representational sculptural practices, those artists who privileged abstraction or non-reference reacted by seeking to purge figural allusions and anthropomorphisms at all costs. This came to a head in debates centered on Minimalism, as Donald Judd and others attempted finally to transcend representation, convention, and allusion.

Michael Fried famously undercut Minimalism's claims that it had purged the anthropomorphic in his 1967 essay "Art and Objecthood."[17] Despite the seriality and impassivity of the literalist object, Fried outlined how its human scale and obdurate presence before the viewer evoked another human: "[T]he beholder knows himself to stand in an indeterminate, open-ended – and unexacting – relation *as subject* to the impassive object on the wall or floor. In fact, being distanced by such objects is not, I suggest, entirely unlike being distanced, or crowded, by the silent presence of another *person*."[18] Fried then proceeded to call out Minimalism for its anthropomorphism, using Tony Smith's human-scale, six-foot steel cube *Die* (1962) as his example (fig. 3). Fried concluded, "One way of describing what Smith

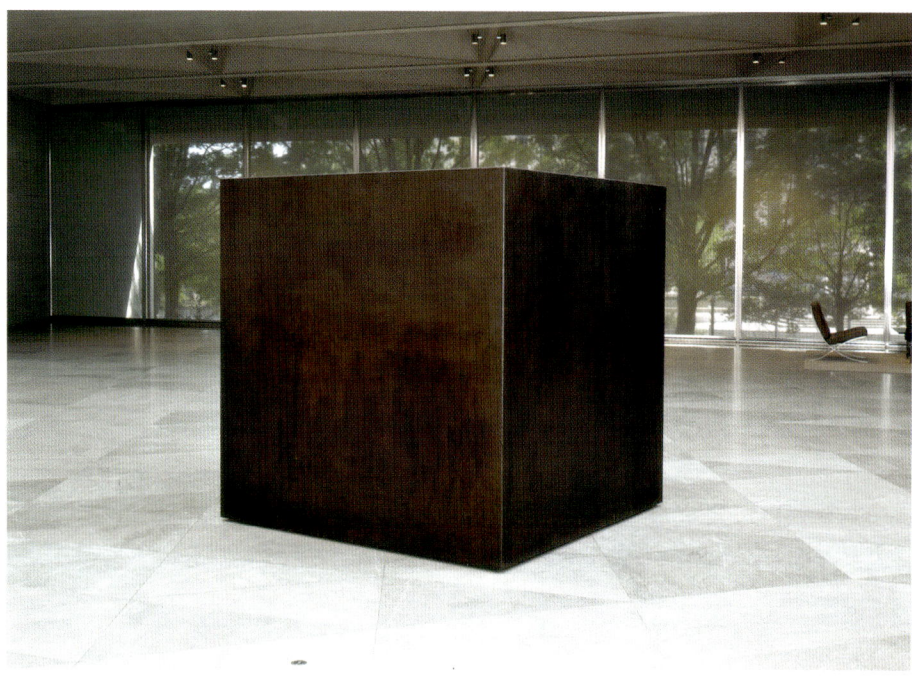

3   Tony Smith, *Die*, 1962 (fabricated 1968). Steel with oiled finish, 182.9 × 182.9 × 182.9 cm (72 × 72 × 72 in.). National Gallery of Art, Washington, D.C.; gift of the Collectors Committee 2003.77.1.

was making might be something like a surrogate person – that is, a kind of *statue*."[19] Recalling the ways in which Clement Greenberg elided the sculptural with the figurative, Fried cast the literalist object as a "statue" in order to show how its lack of resemblance to the human form nevertheless prompted the projection of the human onto it.[20] He quipped, "I am suggesting, then, that a kind of latent or hidden naturalism, indeed anthropomorphism, lies at the core of literalist theory and practice. The concept of presence all but says as much."[21]

Such back-and-forth about anthropomorphism was a way of negotiating sculpture's invocation of the bodily. As Colpitt characterized this situation, "The fact of the total abstractness of Minimal art resulted in a personification of its objects. The objects are not formally similar to human beings, yet their complete self-sufficiency encouraged the critic and spectator to treat them as other beings."[22] Writers from different positions in these debates claimed that the resemblance to the body and the statue had been finally eradicated, but they did so by arguing about how other bodily valences could be mapped onto abstract sculpture. As Meyer later remarked, "Minimalist sculpture alludes to and evokes the body in order to critique the anthropomorphic. A latent anthropomorphism would seem to inhabit *any* sculpture, including those works that we take to most strenuously undermine such associations."[23]

In an essay following "Art and Objecthood" by two years, Fried argued that the work of Anthony Caro achieved what Minimalism could not: an evocation of the bodily in works that bore no vestiges of the freestanding statue. Unlike literalist seriality, however, Caro captured the dynamic and lived experience of embodiment, according to Fried. He argued: "I am suggesting that it is *our* uprightness, frontality, axiality, groundedness and symmetry – as these determine our perceptions, our purposes, the very meanings we make – which, rendered wholly abstract, are the norms of Caro's art."[24] In these, the "bodily" itself became abstracted and open-ended, producing unforeclosed assignments of it to the sculptural encounter. Again, even as the format of the freestanding statue receded and new structures were proposed as alternatives, the bodily still found itself addressed and reflected in rigorously abstract sculpture.

From a far different standpoint, Jack Burnham similarly attempted to articulate the bodily capacities of entirely un-figural forms. Reflecting on the debates about anthropomorphism, he wrote in 1969:

> It is important to remember that most modern abstractionist movements have rejected their predecessors on the grounds of anthropomorphism. This has consistently undercut the humanistic intention of figurative work; and it has provided new abstraction with the appearance of greater detachment and objectivity. Yet the absurdity of who is less anthropomorphic soon ends in its own logical *cul-de-sac*. The *more* obvious truth is that all art is anthropomorphic – that is, if it is interpreted not solely through appearance but as one of many extensions of human need and thought. In reality, the argument over anthropomorphism is one concerned with the priorities of different sign and symbol systems, not over the limits of mimetic imagery.[25]

Burnham was advocating interactive structures (his example was the work of Mowry Baden) that – unlike Caro's – literalized the experience of sculpture as tactile and motile rather than just optical. In the end, he saw how even Baden's structures facilitated an equation of sculpture's physical potentiality with embodiment. "Comprehension of sculpture becomes the act of being sculpture," he concluded. Like Fried's account of Caro's poised abstractions, Burnham too saw how the sculpture's three-dimensionality necessarily opened the door for such porous identifications between body and sculpture. As Briony Fer has remarked, such questions relied on "a notion of bodily empathy that, in the language of the 1960s, was called 'anthropomorphism'."[26]

This position was extended by Robert Morris, whose "Notes on Sculpture" essays were definitive for the 1960s. Whereas his early essays had called for an embodied spectator,[27] the fourth of this series, published in April 1969, argued for an end to sculpture as a medium. Sculpture had, for Morris, been "terminally diseased with figurative allusion" and he sketched a narrative of how even the most abstract – but still discrete and specific – objects could not escape the analogies to human bodies:

> There is no question that so far as an image goes, objects removed themselves from figurative allusions. But, in a more underlying way, in a perceptual way, they did not. Probably the main thing we constantly see all at once, or as a thing, is another human figure. Without the concentration of a figure, any given sector of the world is a field.[28]

Morris was setting the stage for his anti-form installation works and, more broadly, for a conception of artistic practice that left discrete objects behind. In this and the other "Notes on Sculpture" essays, Morris adopted a rhetorical strategy in which he pushed a logic to hyperbolic levels and adopted the absurdity of the resulting extreme position as the next evolutionary step to be promoted. The reductive or Minimalist object was not abstract or non-referential enough from this perspective. The non-statue or the abstract body offered too many allusions, and Morris consequently called for a move "Beyond Objects" (his subtitle for the essay). He continued:

> The specific art object of the '60s is not so much a metaphor for the figure as it is an existence parallel to it. It shares the perceptual response we have toward figures. This is undoubtedly why subliminal, generalized, kinesthetic responses are strong in confronting object art. Such responses are often denied or repressed since they seem so patently inappropriate in the face of non-anthropomorphic forms, yet they are there. Even in subtly morphological ways, object-type art is tied to the body.[29]

In this and the other essays from the series, Morris offered deadpan analysis that is simultaneously perspicacious and coolly parodic. Although less confrontationally than Fried, Morris took aim at Judd's sweeping claims for his own work and, in the end, agreed with Fried's argument about the latent anthropomorphism of Minimalist sculpture. Morris contended that discrete sculptures and objects should be abandoned in favor of a more formless and inclusive installation-based art. Ten years later, Krauss retrospectively characterized this as a generative move into sculpture's expanded field. That move, however, was predicated on the debates about freestanding sculpture's inability to avoid the figure, in all its forms.

For my purposes, however, the important point to draw from these debates is the way in which those artists and critics who were proponents of sculptural abstraction and non-representation continued to find themselves arguing for sculpture's bodiliness. The level and breadth of this discourse on sculpture sets this decade apart from earlier moments in modernism when abstract sculptures presented ambiguous bodies, as I shall discuss later. Instead, the 1960s was committed to varieties of abstraction that sought to leave the imaging of the human form behind as it nevertheless activated the body as its analogue.

Gender and sexuality were a recurring part of these debates and nowhere is that clearer than in the influential role of Lucy Lippard in advocating a more affective account of object-based abstraction. In particular, two essays outlined the potentials for seeing the bodily in relationship to genders and sexualities. In the fall of 1966, Lippard curated a much-discussed exhibition titled *Eccentric Abstraction* at Fischbach Gallery, New York, and, in November, published an essay of the same title in *Art International*.[30] A few months later, in spring 1967, her article on the erotic potential of abstract art, "Eros Presumptive," was released in *Hudson Review* and subsequently revised for Gregory Battcock's 1968 anthology *Minimal Art*.[31]

It is surprising that Lippard's "Eros Presumptive" is rarely discussed in the literature on the writer or the decade. This is perhaps because it makes direct claims for the capacity of abstract art to activate sexuality and sensuality (in a manner, Lippard suggests, more effective than representational art). Indeed, with its focus on eroticism and bodily activations, "Eros Presumptive" sits uncomfortably among the essays in Battcock's anthology on Minimalism. As Anne Wagner noted in her account of Battcock's compilation, the artists whom Lippard discussed – such as Claes Oldenburg, Yayoi Kusama, Lucas Samaras, Hannah Wilke, and Jean Linder – are largely unrelated to Minimalism. Instead, she contends, "[Lippard's inclusion of these artists] point[s] to a moment when Minimalism could be defined differently, when fantasy – even erotic fantasy – was one word for the viewer's share."[32] It is this emphasis on the viewer's engagement with sensuous components of abstract art and its activated internal relations that Lippard explored in her text. She argued that, "from an esthetic point of view, abstraction is capable of broader formal power, since the shapes are not bound to represent any particular thing or coincide in scale with other forms. The experience provoked may relate to, but is not dependent upon the realistic or symbolic origins of the form."[33] The majority of Lippard's positive examples of the eroticism made possible by abstraction are sculpture, and her essay registers the ways in which abstract sculpture at its most extreme invoked the body even as it refused to image it. She pursued this idea of abstraction widely, and argued that non-figurative eroticism could be incited by fully formal means. This, in turn, led her (via a too-casual and problematic reference to Hindu temple sculpture) to propose that some abstract work transcended or fused gender difference:

> As in the classic Indian yoni and lingam sculptures, momentary excitement is omitted in favor of a double-edged experience; opposites are witnesses to the ultimate union or the neutralization of their own opposing characteristics. Hannah Wilke's androgynous terra cotta at the Nycata [Gallery] show, though conceptually less advanced than other works mentioned here, might also serve to illustrate this principle.[34]

Lippard's text, while focused on the erotic potential of abstraction, nevertheless points to larger reconsiderations of gender, here signaled through her idea of the bi-sexed or the androgynous. One must understand Lippard's formulations as part of a larger attempt to come to terms with the ways in which abstract sculpture provided an open-ended question about how bodies and bodiliness could be related to the non-representational object. Recasting Lippard's observations through the lens of transgender studies, one can discern an awareness that the abstract yet erotic forms that she discussed also prompted a variable and mobile account of how (and how many) genders could be mapped onto those same objects. The emphasis on the "viewer's share," in other words, produced the capacity for a plurality of responses to the questions of the erotic and the gendered that these sculptures posed.

In the initial publication of "Eros Presumptive" in *Hudson Review*, Lippard included the 1966 exhibition she had curated for Fischbach Gallery as one its framing examples.[35] Both it and the eponymous essay "Eccentric Abstraction" focused on the ways in which artists used a high degree of abstraction to incite visceral and bodily reactions. As she defined it: "The makers of what I am calling, for semantic convenience, eccentric abstraction, refuse to eschew imagination and the extension of sensuous experience while they also refuse to sacrifice the solid formal basis demanded of the best in current non-objective art."[36] Relating these practices to an earlier history of Surrealism's emphasis on eroticism, Lippard discussed a number of New York-based and West Coast artists who continued to explore abstract, regularized forms but who allowed those forms to be modified by variable repetitions, pliable materials, and appeals to irregularity and sensuosity. For Lippard, these artists aimed to produce bodily affect – a "mindless, near visceral identification with form," as she called it – without alluding to the human form.[37]

As has been much discussed in the literature on this essay, Lippard followed the critical protocols of Sixties abstraction by denying the presence of any allusive or figural imagery in this work. While she later came to reject this position (and these lines), she argued in 1966:

> [A] more complete acceptance by the senses – visual, tactile, and "visceral" – the absence of emotional interference and literary pictorial association, is what the new artists seem to be after. They object to the isolation of biological implications and prefer their forms to be felt, or sensed, instead of read or interpreted. Ideally, a bag remains a bag and does not become a uterus, a tube is a tube and not a phallic symbol, a semi-sphere is just that and not a breast.[38]

These lines are most often discussed in relation to Lippard's nascent feminism and seen as a complicit moment of denial in which sexual difference was erased.[39] In a later revision of her thought, Lippard came to argue that it was precisely such figurative allusions that animated the visceral engagements with object-based abstraction. It was these allusions that must be accounted for differently, she argued, if they were made by artists identified as female or male: "[T]he image of the breast used by a woman artist can now be the subject as well as object."[40] For Lippard, this later reconsideration emerged as part of her desire to value women artists' difference and to support imagery and themes that spoke directly to women's experience. Rooted in the feminism of the 1970s, such an aim made sense, but – as Briony Fer has argued – the higher degree of variability and potentiality of her initial position is lost in this move.[41] It was, after all, not only allusions to reproductive organs on which abstract eroticism and Eccentric Abstraction turned. These were just one part of what Lippard praised as a more open set of erotic and bodily potentials that emerged when no such part-objects were imaged. As she wrote in 1966, "I doubt that more pictures of legs, thighs, genitalia, breasts and new positions, no matter how 'modernistically' portrayed, will be as valid to modern experience as this kind of sensuous abstraction. Abstraction is a far more potent vehicle of the unfamiliar than figuration."[42]

My contention in this book is that the particular context of Sixties sculpture allowed it to be precisely such a "vehicle of the unfamiliar" with regard to the questioning of conventional genders. It emerged from the recurring debates around anthropomorphism, figural allusions, and bodily empathies. The discourse of Sixties sculpture centered on the body in the abstract, and it produced proliferative and unruly accounts of gender in which static states and binary distinctions could not be assumed. Lippard's texts from 1966 and 1967 register such an open-endedness with regard to gender assignments that might emerge from the viewer's encounter with these objects. But Lippard's texts took as their starting point the supersession of other modes of Sixties sculpture that form the basis of this book's case studies, and she cited the drawing-in-space sculpture of David Smith, assemblage, and primary structures as the movements that Eccentric Abstraction was leaving behind. Lippard herself came to recognize how her essay marked a fundamental shift in expectations for sculpture. When she revised the essay in 1971, she retracted her statements about Eccentric Abstraction and its relation to the category of sculpture. Reflecting on the rapid reconfiguration of sculpture that had accompanied the new decade, she remarked: "I no longer think that either "nonsculptural" or "antisculptural" make sense as adjectives. At the time this was written, these terms seemed the only ones to imply the radicality of the moves being made away from traditional sculpture. Now, only four years later, this radical nature can be taken for granted."[43] This retraction registered how pliable and open the category of sculpture had quickly become. Her initial nomination of it as "nonsculptural," however, was meant to signal a rejection of the traditional equation of sculpture with the statue and the figure. It is for this reason that I have preferred the term "non-statue" in characterizing the discrete human-scale sculptural object in the wake of David Smith.

Eccentric Abstraction was, in many ways, one of the most significant of watersheds in the 1960s. (In 1972, Robert Pincus-Witten remarked that "*Eccentric Abstraction*…is one of the most influential group exhibitions in recent history."[44]) It heralded, as Lippard realized just a few years later, the explosion of Postminimalism and the more radical reconfiguration of sculpture that superseded Minimalism's reductive objects.[45] This is the same shift that Morris later declared with "Beyond Objects" and that Krauss looked back on as the emergence of the expanded field. While Minimalism has often been seen as the pivotal break in the 1960s, at the time the developments of Postminimalism seemed, to many, to be the more fundamental move away from the traditions of sculpture.[46] Postminimalism's attitude toward reactive materials, environmental conditions of the scene of viewing, variability in the face of seriality, and more visceral addresses to the viewer combined to make it a highly generative development that reconfigures fundamentally the expectations of sculpture "beyond objects."

Lippard's texts also mark a break in relation to the issues of gender and sexuality. Beyond ushering in a reprieve from the regular and uninflected forms of Minimalism, they also presaged the eruption of feminism, gender, sexuality, and embodiment – all of which became major themes of art of the next decade.[47] In regard to this book's case studies, I placed focus on artists whose initial works (and the art-historical positions they represent) could be understood to precede the developments of Eccentric Abstraction and Postminimalism. While it would be productive to follow Lippard's examples, I chose to address artists who might not at first seem to be related to issues of gender and who have not undergone sustained critiques of gender and sexuality in their work.[48] This has also been the reason that I have left to one side those artists associated with Lippard's essays who have extensive art-historical literatures that deal with gender – namely, Louise Bourgeois and Eva Hesse, both of whom have come to dominate accounts of genders and bodies in Sixties sculpture.

Undoubtedly, the work of Bourgeois, Hesse, and many other sculptors of the 1960s could productively be analysed in relation to the themes of this book. For instance, both Bourgeois and Hesse vexed gender assignments with their sculptural works that evoke bodies and corporeal processes.[49] In the 1940s and 1950s, Bourgeois had a practice of making minimally anthropomorphic sculptures in which the thin sculptural bodies were given almost no articulating traits. Like Smith (and earlier than him), she often referred to these as "personages."[50] These gave way, throughout the 1960s, to works that brought representation and figuration back into her work in the form of "part-objects."[51] Hesse's work, too, has been discussed by Halberstam as able to "stand in here for a long tradition of work on embodiment by women that, in a way, predicted the aesthetic and physical phenomenon of transgenderism."[52] For Halberstam, Hesse's sculptures are "able to make the provisionality of identity, subjectivity, and gender a universal or at least generalizable condition."[53] This relates to how Hesse, as James Meyer put it, "consistently despecified the body."[54] With such histories and descriptions in mind, both Bourgeois and Hesse could undoubtedly by re-viewed productively with the analytic framework of transgender that I use in this book, since both evidence a kind of proliferative gender assignment and unforeclosed morphological potential that is my main topic.

I have chosen, however, to avoid these two most expected examples in Sixties sculpture. Bourgeois and Hesse have become restrictively synonymous with questions of gender in the study of art of this period.[55] Interrogations of the relationship between sculpture and gender from the perspective of these artists have been historiographically transformative and productive, but their prominence in this regard has narrowly concentrated into their literatures the majority of examinations of gender for the entire decade. In short, it has been only a select few women sculptors whose critical reception has carried the lion's share of the discussion of gender in the study of the 1960s. My decision not to include Bourgeois and Hesse as case studies was influenced by the often reflex invocation of their names when any topic of gender in Sixties art arises. They are without a doubt important, but a claim I make in this book is that there are other artists who might not at first appear to have anything to do with gender (let alone transgender) but who also reward sustained investigation from its perspective. That is, while gender has been mentioned in relation to artists such as Smith, Chamberlain, and Flavin, it is rarely a fundamental axis of interpretation and in-depth discussions of gender are largely absent in writing about their work. This is, in fact, the case with many men artists of the decade, whose literatures often go uncomplicated by such questions. (Such an imbalance was not rectified with the fad for masculinity studies that emerged in the 1990s and that tended to reify an essentialist account of masculinity by attending to its "crisis" rather than engage in a wider analysis of gender.[56]) In addition to moving beyond binary and static accounts of gender, my intention in this book has been to pursue unexpected case studies as a means to challenge the too easy concentration of questions of gender (of any kind) in the literature on the decade.

This approach has also meant that I have chosen some artists for whom such issues seem extra-intentional or unexpected. That is, they are not artists who, as Halberstam said, "adapt the nonnarrative potential of abstract art into an oppositional practice" with regard to gender and embodiment.[57] Rather, my interest in artists such as Smith, Chamberlain, and Flavin lies in their inadvertent theorization of gender's mutability and multiplicity. While committed to explicating the artists' own priorities for their work, my readings go on to supplement discussions of their professed intentions and to demonstrate how their practices can be viewed otherwise. As I demonstrate in the chapters themselves, the histories of these artists benefit from an account of gender that moves beyond binary formulations and embraces the wider set of positions and potentials that we might now refer to as transgender.

As a counterpoint to these anti-intentionalist readings, I include the chapter on Grossman both to address the relative paucity of writing on the artist and because of the particular complexity of her version of abstracting the body as material to be remade. If her abstract relief assemblages had been better known, they could well have contributed to the literature on part-objects and gender that takes Hesse, Bourgeois, and Kusama as its organizing figures. Paradoxically, however, she returned to figuration in the late 1960s, producing the work for which she is most known – leather-bound heads. These leave the body behind to focus on the head, obscured underneath its leather coverings. I included Grossman's work because of her contradictory place in feminist histories of the 1960s and 1970s. Late in the 1960s and early in the 1970s, she was upheld as one of few successful women artists and seen as an important example for a feminist art history. Within a decade, however, she had come to occupy a somewhat uncomfortable position in feminist art histories because of her turn to figuration and her engagement with physiognomies that were taken to be male – despite her own claims that they were self-portraits. In short, the cross-gender identification that characterized her practice conflicted with the dominant trends of 1970s feminism in a way paralleled by the anxious and often combative attitude that feminism had to transsexuality and transgender positions in that decade. So, much like the men artists that I read against the grain, I found that the extrapolation of the transgender affinities of Grossman's work bring to light issues from the archive that had previously gone unrecognized.

All four of the case studies have been written with the recognition that the Sixties was also a period of transformation with regard to the idea of gender. Each of the four made work and made statements that reflected an understanding of gender as potentially detachable from the body and able to be transformed. This drew not only on a long history of bodily ambiguity in the history of modern sculpture but also the popular understanding emerging in the 1960s that gender was workable.

FROM AMBIGUITY TO OPENNESS IN MODERN SCULPTURE

Ambiguous figures and simplified morphologies are recurring features of abstraction in the visual arts. Evident from the earliest explorations in modernism, they necessarily raise questions about how such abstract figures worked in relation to gender. Abstract portraits that befuddle or code gender (think Marsden Hartley, Georgia O'Keeffe, or Pablo Picasso), hybrid bodies or couplings (like Jacob Epstein's *Rock Drill* or Rudolf Belling's *Erotik*), and attempts at figuring non-human entities (such as in Marcel Duchamp's work or Mark Rothko's "organisms") were among the ways in which gender had been complicated in earlier modes of abstraction. In fact, modernism's stylized bodies are just one episode in a longer history of the ambiguous figure that stretches from Cycladic art through the Borghese Hermaphrodite to Aestheticism and modernism. (It is worth noting that Harry Benjamin's 1966 book *The Transsexual Phenomenon* compared photographs of patients to ancient statues of hermaphrodites in order to discuss a history of representational confusion of intersex and transsexual.[58]) Within modernism, examples such as Cubist portraiture, the streamlined forms of Arp, Noguchi, or Hepworth, or the emblematic portraits of the Stieglitz Circle all similarly vexed the correlation between the nomination of the figure and non-verisimilar art.

Another aspect of this longer history of nonconforming genders in modernism may be seen in the self-fashioning of the modern artist. It has been argued that androgyny and cross-gender identification were important aspects of modernism from Aestheticism and Symbolism onward.[59] One could look to Duchamp's or Apollinaire's artistic strategies of adopting other genders or the complex genders of figures in the work of Salvador Dalí or Francis Picabia. In fact, the range and sophistication of Duchamp's use of gender in his works is still being uncovered – in particular, in relation to Duchamp's complication of authorship through his alter ego Rrose Sélavy.[60]

For the present study, however, the most important precedent within modernist sculpture is Constantin Brancusi. His attempts to simplify form to its most basic organic shapes (such as the egg) often relied on allusions to gender and sexuality. With his simplified figures, gender assignment was a key concern for Brancusi, and he often chose to fix gender rather than let his human forms be read as ambiguous or generic bodies. For instance, while the form of his *Torso of a Young Man* (1917–22) could be read as either totemic phallic symbol or a human figure without external genitalia, he identified it as male (fig. 4). Similarly, the simpler form of *Torso of a Young Girl* (c. 1923; fig. 5) is made figural by virtue of the titular assignment of gender to this form (it too does not have depicted external genitalia). As Anna Chave has discussed, Brancusi also sometimes sought to combine male and female into one form, as in *Adam and Eve* (1921), *Leda* (1920), or the famously phallic form of his portrait of *Princess X* (1916). This was most successful when animal and avian subjects were chosen, and Chave saw his bird sculptures as exemplary of this (fig. 6). She concluded:

> In doubling, confounding, and fusing the markers of sexual identity, Brancusi breached the imposed rigidity of the gender divide and conjured the vision of an inclusive, nonhierarchical sexuality. By destabilizing

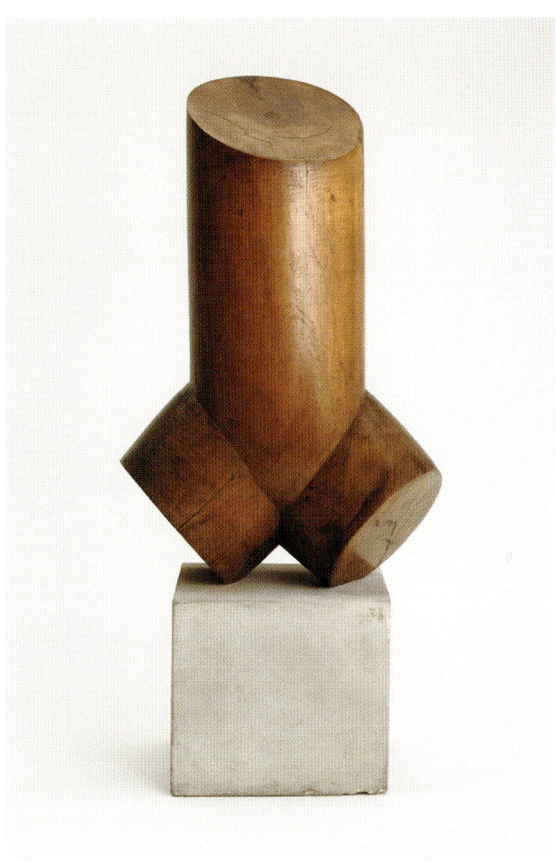

4 Constantin Brancusi, *Torso of a Young Man [I]*, 1917–22. Maple on limestone block, 48.3 × 31.5 × 18.5 cm (19 × 12⅜ × 7⅞ in.) on 21.5 cm (8⅜ in.) base.

the supposed fixities of sexual positioning, he left his viewers in a vertiginous position: peering at the terrifying or exhilarating symbolic possibility of a non- or a dual sexual identity.[61]

Chave's account is suggestive and points to the ways in which such ideas as bisexuality, hermaphroditism, and androgyny were operative in European modernism of the early decades of the twentieth century. With his idealism, Brancusi sought to transcend the mundane, and gender was associated with human bodies and their carnality. The blunt fusion of the sexes in *Adam and Eve* tells much about the ways in which Brancusi conceived of gender as a primary trait tied to bodies and sexuality. He successfully transcended this, however, only when his idealism led him to non-human bodies (such as birds) for whom gender, at least for their human viewers, was less consequential. Brancusi's example reminds us that, for many, the nomination of the "human" has long been predicated on gender assign-

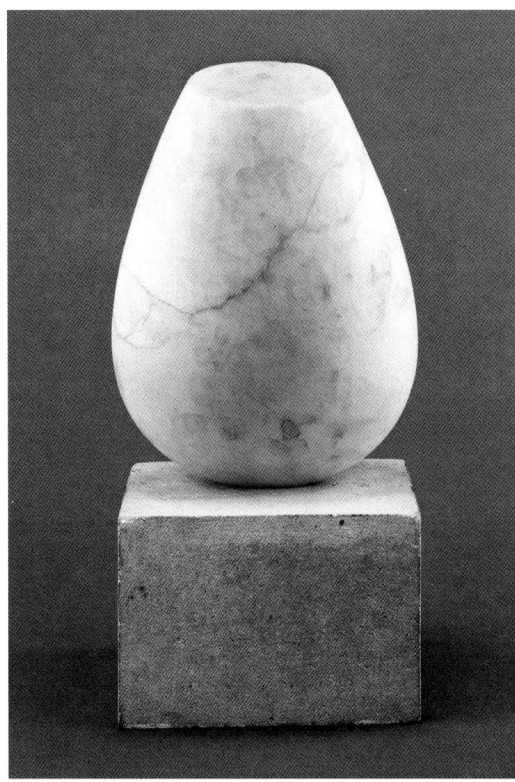

5 Constantin Brancusi, *Torso of a Young Girl [II]*, c. 1923. White marble on limestone block, 34.9 × 24.8 × 15.2 cm (13¾ × 9¾ × 6 in.) on 15.6 × 22.9 × 22.5 cm (6⅛ × 9 × 8¾ in.) base.

ment. Thus, despite the availability of *Torso of a Young Man* to readings of it as female or phallic, Brancusi reminded us that it was a young man. *Princess X*'s conflation of female portrait and phallic shape operates as a joke (as the story goes, on the sitter) or, at best, as an oscillation between two opposed readings. Despite the volleying of gender in his works depicting humans, they ultimately relied on binary definitions and domesticated ambiguity. More complex and mobile forms of genders were left for the birds.

Keeping such examples from earlier in the twentieth century in mind, this book does not argue that the 1960s was the first time that sculpture had problematized gender assignment. Rather, I show that the particular pursuits of abstraction, non-reference, and objecthood that characterize this decade amplified that complication of gender. What makes these sculptors of the 1960s especially productive for such a study are the ways in which sexuality and gender are at play in some of these practices and the ways in which that play prompts multiple, successive, non-binary, and open-ended accounts of how genders could be defined and inhabited. By con-

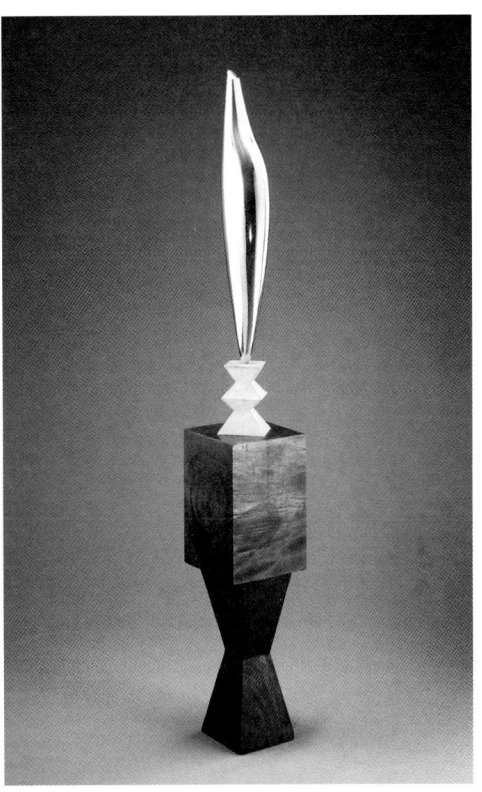

6   Constantin Brancusi, *Golden Bird*, 1919/1920 (base c. 1922). Bronze, stone, and wood, 217.8 × 29.9 × 29.9 cm (86 × 11¾ × 11¾ in.). Art Institute of Chicago, partial gift of The Arts Club of Chicago, restricted gift of various donors; through prior bequest of Arthur Rubloff; through prior restricted gift of William E. Hartmann; through prior gifts of Mr. and Mrs. Carter H. Harrison, Mr. and Mrs. Arnold H. Maremont through the Kate Maremont Foundation, Woodruff J. Parker, Mrs. Clive Runnells, Mr. and Mrs. Martin A. Ryerson, and various donors, 1990.88.

trast, many (but not all) of the modernist precedents rested on figural ambiguity or proposed androgyny. Such earlier instances relied, in the end, on the representation of the figure, however stylized. And when a de-sexed androgyny was not the aim, many sought to fix ambiguity and establish a conventional gender for an unconventional (but still recognizably "human") figure. At mid-century, the ambiguous sculptural figure fed directly into humanist discourses of the post-Second World War era and into sculptors' attempts to refashion monumentality to account for a newly activated global international political frame. Sculptors such as Barbara Hepworth and Henry Moore rose to ascendance owing to the potential of the generic figure as a vehicle for universalist aims. In their work, as well, the ambiguous body raised questions of gender assignment.[62]

The issues of gender mutability that had previously been anchored in ambiguous or stylized human forms were joined, in the 1950s and 1960s, by other artistic investigations into nonconforming genders and bodies. Such work by artists contributed to the larger, but as yet inadequately acknowledged, history of gender's mutability and multiplicity in the postwar decades. One could look to the recent wave of interest in the remarkable work and life of Forrest Bess, whose abstract paintings visualized hybrid genders and hermaphroditism through ideographs. He started showing with Betty Parsons Gallery in 1950, and his work contributed to the story of Abstract Expressionism as well as to medical discourses of gender and sexuality in subsequent years.[63] He kept up extensive correspondences with the likes of Meyer Schapiro and John Money, and he had a retrospective at Parsons's gallery in 1962. By 1968, he was well known enough among medical professionals to be mentioned by Robert Stoller in his groundbreaking 1968 book *Sex and Gender*.[64]

Other such nonconforming practices in the art world precipitated discussions of gender in larger public discourses. A particularly interesting example of this, which bears on the questions of sculpture that are the focus of this study, is offered by the American reception of the British-based sculptor Fiore de Henriquez, who had her New York debut exhibition at Sagittarius Gallery in 1957. Born intersex, de Henriquez acknowledged this in conversation with sitters and friends, and she thematized being "two sexes," as she called it, in her sculpture.[65] For her exhibition in New York, her appearance became a main topic of press discussion because of her short haircut and androgynous clothing. Perhaps because of this unconventional self-fashioning, she quickly became a media sensation, appearing on Jack Paar's *Tonight Show* a few times, first in 1957. She was taken on by the W. Colston Leigh Agency, which booked a U.S. lecture tour for her. Since her English was not fluent, the appearances entailed mostly the demonstration of clay modeling. She traveled the country with her tour manager, Jennifer Paterson, a motorcycle-riding former girls' school matron (who later became famous as a food writer and co-host of the 1990s cooking show *Two Fat Ladies* on British television). The two did a series of U.S. lecture tours in the 1950s and early in the 1960s, and de Henriquez lived part of the year in New York at this time. During these years, de Henriquez increasingly became known for her unconventional dress and attitude more than for her sculpture. This was regularly discussed in press coverage, and she was bold in her responses, as when she told a reporter (who had commented on her hands): "A sculptor is a man, not a woman. I've become the image of a man."[66]

As with the artists in this study, these articulations of nonascribed and nonconforming genders were part of the discourse of Sixties art, and a few examples can give a sense of the ways in which this was manifested. Hesse remarked that her *Ringaround Arosie* was both "like breast and penis."[67] In 1967, Oldenburg said of his *Drum Set*:

> The Drum Set is the image of the human body. It is a body of both sexes, a bisexual subject. Anyone who has traveled with a drum set knows that it must always be disassembled and assembled, packed in boxes. The organ of the pedal, for example, the masculine appendage, is detachable, and so are the "breasts" (cymbals), and the bass (womb) has its own box. The set is like a doll.[68]

These, and other examples ranging from Frank O'Hara's 1955 poem "Hermaphrodite" to Diane Arbus's 1960s photographs of gender performers, run through these decades.[69]

Similarly, in the 1970s, such possibilities proliferated. Lynda Benglis produced many works in the 1970s that addressed these questions, most notably the 1976 video *The Amazing Bow Wow*, with its depiction of an intersex anthropomorphized dog. As she later said, "The idea of combining the sexes, of a hermaphrodite was not new. I wasn't presenting myself as a hermaphrodite but presenting myself as an object of humanism, so that the sexes would be considered equal."[70] Just two years before, in 1974, Louise Bourgeois said: "We are all vulnerable in some way, and we are all male-female."[71]

Gender nonconformity, drag, and transsexuality all had been regularly discussed in both popular and art press throughout the 1960s and 1970s, as I discuss later. One need only recall Charles Ludlam's Ridiculous Theater Company and Andy Warhol's Factory as two of the more visible examples of this within the art world. Warhol's films, in particular, began regularly to feature transgender actresses, so that, by the early years of the 1970s, they had become equally famous for their involvement with Warhol and for their gender nonconformity. In 1971, for instance, Jackie Curtis was already replacing the terminology of transsexuality for something that might today be called transgender or genderqueer, saying: "I never claimed to be a man, a woman, an actor, an actress, a homosexual, a heterosexual, a transsexual, a drag queen, an Academy Award winner."[72] Curtis and the other Warhol stars were of great interest to the press and their fame helped to provide further media exposure for transsexuality and gender nonconformity.[73] By the 1970s, questions of genders' mutability were frequent in contemporary art, and it is my hope that the present study will prompt reconsideration of such varied works as Vito Acconci's sex-change video performances, the work of Marisol, Adrian Piper's 1972–6 *Mythic Being*, Robert Morris's plays with gender (such as the 1963 *Cock/Cunt* or 1973–4 *Voice*), or Ana Mendieta's 1972 *Untitled (Facial Hair Transplants)*.[74] While many of these works have contributed to a feminist retelling of these decades, a transfeminist approach could bring to light the ways in which they reconsider not just hegemonic gender difference but binary modes altogether.[75]

Through its focus on deep readings of its artists' practices, this book tracks the ways in which their trajectories came to raise issues of transformable genders analogous to those that were increasingly debated in popular culture and the art world throughout the decade. Whether in the late work of Smith or the early work of Flavin, Grossman, and Chamberlain, all of these artists called on metaphors of gender and sexuality in the new practices they developed in the first half of the 1960s. With the last three artists, I examine the longer trajectory of their work into the 1970s, focusing on the ways in which they developed terms for their own practices that carried forward, mutated, and proliferated those early attachments to issues of gender and sex. That is, the book is not strictly about the early to mid-1960s alone. Rather, it grapples with the ways in which the intense period of experimentation in Sixties sculpture helped to forge these artists' particular long-term practices and their accounts of gender's plurality and mutability.

THE TRANSGENDER PHENOMENON OF THE 1960s

As the selection of artists' statements here indicates, questions about the unhinging of gender from the sexed body were circulating widely by the 1960s. This built on a longer history of these issues in American culture from the nineteenth century onward. An ever-growing literature has established that larger social, scientific, and political developments were influenced by the eruption of transgender and intersex politics and concerns over the course of the twentieth century. For instance, Halberstam has argued that female-bodied masculinities inflected and helped to define mainstream conceptions of masculinity throughout the modern era.[76] Elizabeth Reis has shown that the medical establishment's concern about how to locate gender in the body of intersex infants underwrote the advances in the science of gender and spurred larger cultural accounts of gender from the nineteenth century onward.[77] Similarly, Joanne Meyerowitz has established that transsexuality was fundamental in developing a popular discourse that distinguished sexuality from sex and gender.[78] Drawing on these studies, Paul B. Preciado has offered a damning account of the pharmaceutical and medical technologies of gender in the second half of the twentieth century.[79] Leslie Feinberg has championed a long history of activists and "transgender warriors."[80] Stryker has proven, in her groundbreaking *Transgender History*, that transgender issues have been at the core of many social movements in the postwar decades.[81] These studies also contribute to a body of literature that is bringing to light transgender and intersex histories that had been subsumed into lesbian and gay histories or overlooked or obscured altogether.[82] Indeed, a galvanizing issue for the academic discipline of transgender studies has been a resistance to the uncritical appropriation of transgender experience into queer studies and queer theory.[83]

In American culture, as I have already suggested in the Preface, transsexuality became a part of popular discourse in the wake of the international headlines of the Christine Jorgensen story in 1952. As Stryker remarked, "In a year when hydrogen bombs were being tested in the Pacific, war was raging in Korea, England crowned a new queen, and Jonas Salk invented the polio vaccine, Jorgensen was the most written-about topic in the media."[84] Popular culture continued to feature transsexuality, culminating in such milestones as the *New York Times* front-page story in 1966 or the formal instatement of gender testing at the 1968 Mexico City Olympics. These mainstream stories were fueled by pulp novels and tabloid papers, both of which kept transsexuality in their headlines throughout the 1950s, 1960s, and 1970s. As Meyerowtiz noted about these attempts to whip up sensationalism and scandal, "From the early 1960s on, tabloid newspapers and pulp publishers produced a stream of articles and cheap paperback books on mtfs [male-to-female transsexuals] who had worked as female impersonators, strippers, or prostitutes."[85] The transsexual performer Hedy Jo Star had published her memoirs in 1962 and wrote an advice column for the *National Insider*. Nancy Bernstein, who ran a "charm school for transsexuals" on the Upper East Side in New York, later told the *Village Voice* that she had been doing such work since 1959.[86] The cultural fascination with transgender potential did not just fuel interest in Warhol's stars but also centered on such bestselling novels as Hubert Selby Jr.'s *Last Exit to Brooklyn* (1957, republished in 1961 and 1964) or Gore Vidal's *Myra Breckinridge* (1968).[87] What these events make clear is that a general, and continuing, concern emerged in the 1960s around the newly publicized ability to change sex and to unhinge gender from it.

Nevertheless, this history is still often suppressed or inadequately known in many accounts of the decade, and certainly within art history. For the benefit of readers, I have compiled a selective and partial list of events punctuating transgender history based on the required reading that is Stryker, Meyerowitz, and Reis's more extensive narratives. This abbreviated list demonstrates how popular, scientific, and political arenas registered a newly visible transgender presence in American culture. For convention's sake, I start at the Jorgensen headlines, include just a few events of the 1950s, then focus on the 1960s, ending in 1970. This is just one slice of a longer and ongoing history (and historical revision).

1952
- 1 Dec: Christine Jorgensen makes international front-page news for having sex reassignment surgery. The *New York Daily News* headline is "Ex-GI Becomes Blonde Beauty." Her story was propagated by *American Weekly*, which paid Jorgensen $20,000 for an exclusive interview that became a feature story. She becomes one of the most famous people of the 1950s.

1953
- Harry Benjamin publishes his groundbreaking article "Transvestism and Transsexuality" in the *International Journal of Sexology*.[88]
- Ed Wood releases his exploitation film *Glen or Glenda?* (originally titled *I Changed My Sex!*), featuring Bela Lugosi.

1955
- John Money begins to develop the term "gender role." This is taken up in subsequent articles by him and Joan and John Hampson.[89]

1957
- Fiore de Henriquez makes appearances on Jack Paar's *Tonight Show*.

1959
- May: in Los Angeles, the late-night coffeehouse Cooper's Donuts is raided by police who start arresting the drag queens who frequented it. These and other patrons resist and the incident ends with a conflict between police and protesters in the street. The novelist John Rechy was among the patrons.

1962
- The Gender Identity Research Clinic is founded at University of California Los Angeles.
- *The National Insider* runs a series of autobiographical writings by transsexual nightclub entertainer Hedy Jo Star; published the following year as a book titled *"I Changed My Sex!"*; Star starts writing an advice column for the tabloid.[90]

1964
- The novel *Last Exit to Brooklyn*, by Hubert Selby, Jr., is republished to critical acclaim and controversy for its depiction of lower-class life in the 1950s. It features a transgender character, Georgette. The novel had previously appeared in 1957 and 1961 but received a wider critical and popular reception on its 1964 release.
- Robert Stoller and Ralph Greenson of the University of California at Los Angeles coin the term "gender identity."
- Reed Erickson, an industrial magnate and female-to-male transsexual, establishes Erickson Educational Foundation, which

becomes a major funding source for medical and social research into transsexuality.[91]

1965
- In April and May, protesters stage picket lines and sit-ins at Dewey's coffeehouse in Philadelphia because of its refusal to serve the transgender and gay clientele that had been frequenting it since the 1940s.
- Doctors at Johns Hopkins University, long a center for the study of intersex conditions, form a committee on gender reassignment and agree to perform their first surgery, on Phyllis Avon Wilson. By November 1966, they had performed ten such surgeries (five transsexual men and five transsexual women).

1966
- Harry Benjamin publishes his book *The Transsexual Phenomenon*, which has an immediate impact on medical and social fields.[92]
- The Compton's Cafeteria Riot occurs in San Francisco in response to police harassment of drag queens and transwomen.
- Johns Hopkins Medical School Gender Identity Clinic (GIC) is founded.
- 4 Oct: Johns Hopkins GIC's first patient, Phyllis Avon Wilson, is written about in *New York Daily News* gossip column: "Making the rounds of the Manhattan clubs these nights is a stunning girl who admits she was male less than a year ago…"
- 21 November: *The New York Times* runs front-page story: "A Changing of Sex by Surgery Begun at Johns Hopkins." This story is followed by major articles in *Time* on 2 December and, on 5 December, in *Newsweek* and *U.S. News & World Report*.[93]

1967
- Jorgensen's long-anticipated memoir is published.[94] She begins to publicize it with a radio interview (conducted in 1966) with Richard Lamparski for New York's radio station WBAI. The 1968 paperback edition sells more than 400,000 copies.[95]
- *Esquire*'s April issue includes a nine-page article on "The Transsexual Operation."[96]
- Northwestern University begins a gender treatment and study program.

1968
- The International Olympic Committee formally adopts gender testing for Olympians at the Mexico City Games. It had used testing on a more experimental basis for the Winter Games in Grenoble.
- To publicize the paperback release of her autobiography, Jorgensen goes on a twenty-city book tour of the U.S., which

includes appearances on the Steve Allen Show and the Merv Griffin Show.
- Gore Vidal publishes his bestselling novel *Myra Breckinridge*.
- Candy Darling and Jackie Curtis make their film debuts in Andy Warhol's movie *Flesh*, directed by Paul Morrissey.
- Stanford University Gender Reorientation Program (later called the Gender Identity Clinic) is established.
- Robert Stoller's *Sex and Gender* is published. This book leads to the popularization of the notion of "gender identity."[97]
- Esther Newton completes a dissertation at the University of Chicago on drag queens and gender performance, focusing on drag shows she studied in New York City, Chicago, and Kansas City from 1965. It was published in 1972 as the groundbreaking *Mother Camp: Female Impersonators in America*.[98]

1969
- Richard Green and John Money's field-establishing anthology, *Transsexualism and Sex Reassignment*, is published by Johns Hopkins University Press.[99]
- Transgender patrons of the Stonewall Inn are the first to resist a police raid, sparking a riot in the streets of Greenwich Village, New York. The Stonewall Riots became the central catalysing event for the gay rights movement.

1970
- After a sit-in at New York University, Sylvia Rivera and Marsha P. Johnson found Street Transvestite Action Revolutionaries (STAR) to organize transgender youth.[100]
- Transsexual Action Organization (TAO) is founded in Los Angeles.
- Jointly with the Florida Transvestite-Transsexual Action Organization and the New York Femmes Against Sexism, STAR issues a manifesto demanding such action as the abolition of laws prohibiting cross-dressing (some in place since the nineteenth century), free access to hormone treatment and surgery, and the legal right to live as a gender of one's choosing.

Stryker has called the Sixties the decade of "transgender liberation" because of the explosion of social movements, medical research, and political action that centered on transgender issues during these years. As she has remarked, "By the early 1970s, transgender political activism had progressed in ways scarcely imaginable when the 1960s had begun."[101] She also argues that a widespread backlash occurred in 1973 when the American Psychiatric Association removed homosexuality from its list of disorders in its *Diagnostic and Statistical Manual of Mental Disorders* (DSM). This event, combined with other cultural moves to retract the progressivism of the 1960s, resulted in the suppression of transgender visibility and politics. Mainstream forms of feminism became increasingly anxious about trans and queer forms of gender expression. In addition to the homophobia in the ranks, a transphobia extended to MTF transsexuals who were cast as enemies to cisgendered women's struggles.[102] The seeds were sewn for decades of divisive debates in feminist communities about the participation of butches, transmen, and transwomen.[103] In addition, the gay liberation movement of the 1970s distanced itself from gender variance in its quest to argue that homosexuality was normal and deserving of legal protection. With this move, the transsexual and gender variant members of what was an obstensibly more inclusive "gay" community became ostracized precisely for their complication of normative gender roles (which gay and lesbian assimilationists supported in their attempts to prove the equality of recombined, but still binary, sexual orientations). In many ways, the widespread belief in the "newness" of transgender issues in the late twentieth century derives from the period of backlash and suppression in the 1970s when more varied accounts of the recent past were recast or edited. To recall Butler's words from the Preface, "Because the norms governing reality have not admitted these forms to be real, we will, of necessity, call them 'new.'"[104] It is for good reason that Stryker nominates the 1960s until 1973 as the period of transgender liberation and political flourishing. This study also follows that period in seeing the open questions about gender's relationship to figures and bodies as characterizing the 1960s.

My reason for going into such depth about this larger cultural context is to refute the misconceptions that transgender issues are new or that questions of mutable genders were unknown to Americans of the 1960s. Quite the contrary, popular stories of transsexuality eroded conventional beliefs in the immutability of sexual difference and contributed to the decade's cultural upheavals. In a decade when the idea of gender emerged and was transformed radically, why would one not see in art's history of negotiating the figure and of personhood a parallel openness or unfixity? I do not make the claim that there is a smoking gun or direct link between the popular or specialized discourses of transsexuality and the artists' practices under consideration (though I should mention that Grossman, in conversations with me, has brought up Christine Jorgensen and *Myra Breckinridge* independently and unprompted[105]). My point is, I hope, a larger one: that the perspective of transgender history compels us to look widely to moments when genders and bodies were conceived of as mutable and multiple. It is exactly this capaciousness that emerged from the particular history of abstraction's collisions with metaphors of the body and personhood in this tumultuous decade. The sculpture of the 1960s offers one of many episodes in a larger story of the ways in which genders, bodies, and persons were considered otherwise.

The one admitted anachronism is my usage of the term "transgender." As has been discussed by such scholars as Stryker and David Valentine, this term gained currency only in the 1990s.[106] It came into usage to refer more broadly to the range of gender variance, including but not limited to transsexuality. The term's popularity grew because it was argued to be more inclusive.[107] Also, it enabled (as with Stryker's formulation of it as "away from an unchosen" gender) an affirmation of those lives that did not accord with binary or dimorphic models.[108] Such an inclusivity, however, invariably leads to a leveling of individuality and difference, and the term continues to be debated for its adequacy to the range of options it is said to describe.[109] Given its limitations, it has nevertheless proven both politically and intellectually efficacious as a formation under which diverse modes of gender nonconformity can coalesce. In this, I again follow Stryker's justification for its use in American history before the 1990s. As she argued in the introduction to *Transgender History*:

> I use the word "transgender" as a shorthand way of talking about a wide range of gender variance and gender atypicality in periods before the word was coined, and I sometimes apply it to people who might not apply it to themselves. Some butch women or queeny men will say that they are not transgender because they do not want to change sex. Some transsexuals will say that they are not transgender because they do. There is no way of using the word that doesn't offend some people by including them where they don't want to be included or excluding them from where they do not want to be included. And yet, I still think the term is useful as a simple word for indicating when some practice or identity crosses gender boundaries that are considered socially normative in the contemporary United States. Calling all of these things transgender is a device for telling a story about the political history of gender variance that is not limited to any one particular experience.[110]

Similarly, this study uses the term "transgender" to highlight and refine accounts of genders' mutabilities, pluralities, and temporalities as they were proposed in the practices of the artists under consideration here.

The necessary (and enabling) anachronism of mobilizing "transgender" to bring to light a long-running history of gender variance has been widely discussed in transgender studies. In one of the founding texts of the field, Halberstam's *Female Masculinity*, the idea of "perverse presentism" was proposed as a willing embrace of anachronism in the service of bringing lived diversity and complexity in history to light. Halberstam's groundbreaking book sought to tell the history of masculinities adopted by female-bodied individuals. This history was distinguished from that of a history of sexuality, and Halberstam examined such roles as the tribade and the female husband – among others present in both literature and history – as recognizable and repeated historical phenomena that demanded to be understood primarily in terms of gender rather than sexuality. Halberstam argued for a model "that avoids the trap of simply projecting contemporary understandings back in time, but one that can apply insights from the present to conundrums of the past."[111] This study is inspired by the historical approach offered by Halberstam in this formulation, and I use the term "transgender" to register moments of gender's plurality and temporality as they are manifested in the historical record. As Halberstam has written elsewhere in *Female Masculinity*, "Transgender discourse in no ways argues that people should just pick up new genders and eliminate old ones or proliferate at will because gendering is available as a self-determining practice; rather, transgender discourse asks only that we recognize the nonmale and nonfemale genders already in circulation and presently under construction."[112]

Transgender lives are already present and already historical, and it should be remembered that the recognition of the mutability and multiplicity of genders in academic discourse is a response to and an activation of that history. Similarly, Gayle Salamon has argued in support of the lived plurality of genders in history and at the present moment, writing that "Genders beyond the binary of male and female are neither fictive nor futural, but are presently embodied and lived."[113] This book does not presume to write a history of transgender art, but I do claim that the history of art is fundamentally enriched and clarified when we put into action the recognition that gender has a complex, temporal, and exponential relationship to individual human bodies.

Transgender, in these new developments and in the present book, signals a commitment to do justice to narratives of variance and specificity in the lived experience of gender and in its deployments as an axis of meaning around which norms are debated. Energized by the wider community and more capacious critique that this term afforded, the discipline of transgender studies has grown rapidly in recent decades to offer a dynamic and broad recasting of biopolitics.[114] Similarly, the emergence of a distinctly intersex history and politics has paralleled transgender history in its critique of the historical record's blindness to and willful erasure of non-dimorphic bodies and atypical sexual development. In keeping with these historical revisions, this book sees in the particularities of abstract sculpture accounts of gendered embodiment that exceed binary and dimorphic models. It is both methodologically and historiographically urgent to allow such capacities present in the historical record to be identified and cultivated.

TRANSGENDER CAPACITY

A central aim of this book is to argue for the transgender capacity of abstract sculpture through detailed engagements with the archive of artists' works and statements.[115] Through an analysis of their art-theoretical priorities and their stated engagements with gender and sexuality, I show how artists arrived at positions where their work offered accounts of multiplying genders, mutable morphologies, and successive states of personhood – even if these accounts might be alien or anathema to them in their own lives. Because I believe that transgender studies demands a widespread revision of the ways in which genders, bodies, and figures must be viewed historically, I have concerned myself not with artists' expressed intentions with regard to these issues but rather with the capaciousness that their practices affords.

A capacity is both an "active power or force" and an "ability to receive or maintain; holding power" (*OED*). A capacity manifests its power as potentiality, incipience, and imminence. Only when exercised do capacities become fully apparent, and they may lie in wait to be activated.

Transgender capacity is the ability or the potential for making visible, bringing into experience, or knowing genders as mutable, successive, and multiple. It can be located or discerned in texts, objects, cultural forms, situations, systems, and images that support an interpretation or recognition of proliferative modes of gender nonconformity, multiplicity, and temporality. In other words, transgender capacity is the trait of those many things that support or demand accounts of gender's dynamism, plurality, and expansiveness.

The dimorphic model of sex and the binary account of gender – not to mention the assertion of their static natures – are never adequate ways of knowing the sophisticated and divergent modes of existence that people enact. Such strictures always encode their own possibilities for collapse and deconstruction, and transgender capacity erupts at those moments when such reductive norms do not hold.

The most important feature of transgender capacity is that it can be an unintended effect of many divergent decisions and conditions. That is, a transgender critique can be demanded of a wide range of texts, sites, systems, and objects – including those that, at first, seem unrelated to transgender concerns and potentialities. A capacity need not be purposefully planted or embedded (though of course it may be), and it does not just result from the intentions of sympathetic or self-identified transgender subjects. It may emerge at any site where dimorphic and static understandings of gender are revealed as arbitrary and inadequate. Transgender phenomena can be generated from a wide range of positions and competing (even antagonistic) subjects, and it is important to recognize that a transgender hermeneutic can and should be pursued at all such capacitating sites.

This concept's usefulness is primarily methodological and is meant as a tool for resisting the persistent erasure of the evidence of transgender lives, gender diversity, non-dimorphism, and successive identities. Its questions are valid to many areas of scholarly inquiry, including such different fields as biology, sociology, and economics. It is a retort to charges of anachronism and a reminder to search widely for the nascence of transgender critique. With regard to historical analysis, transgender capacity poses particularly urgent questions, since it is clear that there is a wealth of gender variance and nonconformity that has simply not been registered in the historical record. Without projecting present-day understandings of transgender identities into the past, one must recognize and make space for all of the ways in which self-determined and successive genders, identities, and bodily morphologies have always been present throughout history as possibilities and actualities.[116] Dimorphic and static definitions of gender and sexual difference obscure such diversity and facilitate the obliteration of the complex and infinitely varied history of gender nonconformity and strategies for survival. To recognize transgender capacity is not to equate all episodes of potential but rather to allow the recognition of their particularity and to resist the normative presumptions that have enforced their invisibility.

Transgender epistemologies and theoretical models fundamentally remap the study of human cultures. Their recognition of the mutable and multiple conditions of the apparatus we know as gender has wide-ranging consequences. That is, once gender is understood to be temporal, successive, or transformable, all accounts of human lives look different and more complex. It would be a mistake to limit this powerful epistemological shift to clearly identifiable transgender topics and histories. While transgender subjects and experience must remain central and defining, the lessons of transgender critique demand to be applied expansively.

Across the disciplines, there is much evidence of the limitations of static and dimorphic models of genders, identities, and relations. One must search for and be attentive to transgender capacities in both expected and unexpected places. Tracking them is a hermeneutic rather than an iconographic task, and the conceptual space of gender transformability erupts anywhere that dimorphism is questioned, mutability becomes a value, or self-creation becomes a possibility. While they are most readily located in the study of the representation of human bodies and experiences, transgender capacities can be located in such topics as abstract art, rhetorical forms, digital cultures, technologies of complex systems, economic ecologies, and histories of scientific discovery. In these areas and beyond, there are innumerable forms and modes of transgender capacity still to be found, imagined, or realized.

The concept of transgender capacity provides a supple and adaptive model through which to re-interrogate archives and artworks, and it is particularly helpful when accounting for abstract art's potentiality and openness. It is in accord with Butler's position that "critique is understood as an interrogation of the terms by which life is constrained in order to open up the possibility of different modes of living; in other words, not to celebrate difference as such but to establish more inclusive conditions for sheltering and maintaining life that resists models of assimilation."[117] Excavating transgender capacity is a means of cultivating such expanded semantic spaces and proliferative identificatory sites in the historical record and in current methodological debates.

SEXUALITY AND GENDERS' MULTIPLICATION

While the central aim of this book is focused on gender and on demonstrating how abstract sculpture can support and call for accounts of it as successive and multiple, this is also a book about sexuality. These two categories through which we make sense of lived experience and habitual embodiments are inextricably intertwined. Indeed, as David Valentine has noted, their distinction as separate and discrete categories is a historical development of the twentieth century that "results in a substitution of an analytic distinction for actual lived experience."[118] A critique of queer politics and queer theory has been that both largely seek to trouble sexuality while leaving binary and deterministic models for gender largely intact. By contrast, transgender, as Stryker has argued, disrupts this homonormativity just as much as it does heteronormativity, and sexualities become widened and remapped when genders are understood as mutable and multiple.[119]

Nevertheless, it is also important to resist the view that transgender is merely equivalent to non-normative sexualities, since gender's transformations and the particularity of transgender experience both have a history of being co-opted (and made invisible) by queer politics.[120]

Keeping these historical and historiographic issues in mind, I nevertheless came to realize how much my historical cases demanded attention to sexuality. As I investigated the history of these artists' practices and statements about gender, I realized that all of them had been catalysed by a recognition of sexuality. That is, the narratives about these artists' production of accounts of gender's mutability and plurality began with a confrontation with sexual themes and metaphors. For this reason, this book also deals extensively with questions of sexuality and sexual identities (of many kinds), and its methodological and theoretical touchstones come from both transgender studies and queer studies. I found that non-normative sexualities were themselves figured (in the rhetorical sense) as a means of grappling with gender's multiplicity and mutability. Further, while transgender studies was galvanized by a rejection of the appropriation of trans lives in queer theory of the 1990s, subsequent positions in both transgender studies and queer studies have sought to attend to the shared issues and overlapping communities without equating them or, for that matter, sexuality and gender more broadly. As Salamon has argued,

> Insisting on the radical separability and separateness of sexual orientation and gender identity overlooks the ways in which these two categories are mutually implicated, even when they are not mutually constituting. That is, even when the trajectory of one's desire cannot be predicted by one's gender, it surely is the case that my desire is experienced through my gender and that a strict parsing runs the risk of impoverishing both categories.[121]

Owing to this mutual constitution, sexuality often (though not exclusively) invokes the image and the idea of the relations of genders and bodies. As Stryker has argued, "Gendering practices are inextricably enmeshed with sexuality. The identity of the desiring subject and that of the object of desire are characterized by gender. Gender difference undergirds the homo/hetero distinction. Gender conventions code permissible and disallowed forms of erotic expression, and gender stereotyping is strongly linked with practices of bodily normativization."[122] Many invocations of sexuality imply the possibility of multiplicity or, at least, coupling. Queer and divergent sexualities usher in a disruption by asking the question of how and why same genders could couple. Especially when attached to works of sculpture that evoked but refused to image human bodies, the injection of sexuality set in play a hypothesizing of genders and their relations.

The narratives in the case studies were often sparked by the recognition or invocation of sexuality or sexual relations: Flavin's allegorization of the homosexual as the figure of illusionism, Chamberlain's reliance on an orgiastic and polymorphous sexuality as a metaphor for his artistic practice, Grossman's autopenetrating *Ali Stoker*, or Smith differentiating himself from O'Hara's personification of his own works. While, ultimately, the trajectories of these artists' practice center on gender as the key element for personhood and propose its multiplications, it was the initial confrontation with sexuality – often, a non-normative sexuality – that set in motion a calculus of where and how conventional genders fit.

The effects of the negotiation of sexuality in relation to the abstract body, in other words, produced multiple, competing, and possibly infinite propositions for the ways in which genders could be imagined in that relation. Transgender capacity does not derive from sexuality. Rather, the categorical disruption caused by queer or polyamorous sexualities produces a need to account for gender's already existing multiplicity and potentiality. Especially in the formative decade of the 1960s when the discourse of transgender politics was differentiating itself from the politics of sexuality, the axes of gender and sexuality often allowed each other to be seen as complex and varied rather than simple or singular. For me, this is one reason why I believe that the cisgendered artists on whom I focus in this book found themselves making works that spoke of genders' non-binary multiplicity and transformability. Non-normative sexualities demanded a new conjugation of relations and recombinations of genders, none of which could be secured to an image of the human form with the abstract bodies offered by non-representational sculpture. It was this catalysing potential of the erotic that Lippard, in "Eros Presumptive," first attempted to articulate for Sixties abstraction and its activation of bodily empathies.

As I show in the case studies, it is the departure from a focus on sexuality, however, that affords the potential to make bigger claims about personhood's successive states and gender's exponential multiplication. For instance, despite Flavin's concern with the figure of the homosexual in 1962 and 1963, his subsequent practice arrived at an account of transformable personhood by engaging more broadly with how literalist objects could be personalized and made adaptive. Chamberlain came to admit that "everybody's both" genders, in part, because he had proposed a thoroughgoing mash-up and multiplication of genders as the best way to describe his patently abstract "fit." These examples point to a more general issue for the study of nonascribed and transformable genders: namely, that sexuality (and, in particular, disagreements or distinctions between individuals' sexualities) can serve as a catalyst for proposing or recognizing the possibility of other, multiple, or successive genders. A focus solely on sexuality (even queer sexuality) cannot adequately describe those genders, those lives, or those transformations, but it does illuminate the need for new accounts of personhood that can.

AN EXPANDED FIELD

Rather than attempt to survey the divergent paths of sculpture in this decade, this book charts one trajectory through in-depth case studies of individual artists. Smith, as the widely accepted leader of American sculpture at the end of the 1950s, begins the book, and it is his continued negotiation of the statuary tradition in the face of his increasingly abstract and unmonolithic constructions that set the tone for the 1960s. Focusing on a 1964 interview with the poet and curator O'Hara, I discuss how Smith found himself viewing his own sculptures through O'Hara's eyes, forcing him to face (and reject) their gender ambiguity. I examine how a seemingly minor joke from this televised interview was recast as a recurring (and erroneous) explanatory statement in subsequent accounts of his work. I then turn to Chamberlain, the abstract sculptor who is often understood to have taken up Smith's mantle as the sculptor of metal. His brash accumulated sculptures signaled a further leap from the artisanal sculptural materials into the found and the mass-produced, and I expand on the gendered and sexualized metaphors he provided as an explanation of his process of fitting parts together to make new forms. From there, I move to another artist, Grossman, who used everyday materials, old leather garments, to produce abstract assemblages that ultimately led her to turn to figuration. I discuss Grossman's many statements about cross-gender identification and use them to assess her process of reworking parts – that is, making sculptures from old garments made from the skins of animals. I then analyse her turn to "figuration" late in the 1960s as another means of abstracting the body. Giving an account of her contentious reputation in the 1970s, I discuss how Grossman's work was characterized by an open account of genders' multiplicity that went misrecognized as male-identified. And, finally, I examine the logics of interchangeability and naming in Dan Flavin's work. While not conventionally "sculpture" (like most Minimalism), Flavin's works nevertheless continue with the adoption of the mass-produced objects (fluorescent lights) redeployed as art objects. More importantly, however, I look at the development of installation practices in Flavin's work, signaling one of the major examples of the new practices that ultimately produced the richness of example on which Krauss drew for her essay in the late 1970s. My focus in that chapter is on Flavin's use of titling and its effects on his modular interchangeable medium. Naming calls up a question of personhood and its nominations, and Flavin's work developed its systemic interchangeability out of a performative usage of the dedication as title.

As for the title of this book, I adopt Krauss's term "expanded field" both for its specificity and its allusiveness. While the term is often applied to other areas, I use it to invoke the particular conditions for which Krauss's essay sought to account – namely, the dissolution of the statuary tradition into a moment where sculpture could no longer be defined by recourse to a tradition but rather through a coordination of its contemporary negations and counter-terms.[123] While the intention of her essay was to derail historicist attempts to explain new formations as effects of a lineage of the medium of sculpture, it has come, as well, to characterize a particular historical moment at which such transformations were retrospectively described.[124] My deployment of this term in the title points to this as the condition of sculpture throughout the 1960s and into the 1970s. The abstract body, the non-statue, the dedicated literalist object, and other contenders for sculpture's successor all contributed to the movement into the field that Krauss described.

In her compelling analysis of the text and the receptions of it, Eve Meltzer has argued that the appeal of Krauss's "expanded field" exceeds the terms of its argument and that its users often ignore its methodological aims.[125] I agree with her reservations about the vulgar overuse of the term. Nevertheless, I could think of no more succinct way to describe what happened to gender in the 1960s. After years of erosion of their boundaries, the binary categories of male and female became, in this decade, newly visible as porous, mutually defining, and productive of unforeseen positions through their selective combinations or negations. Gender, like sculpture in Krauss's analysis, was definitively revealed to be not an essential category or transhistorical constant. Rather, it was shown to be contingent, workable, and defined in relation to an open topography of mutually defining and interdependent positions. As Krauss said about sculpture, "What is important here is that we are not dealing with an either/or…but with both/and."[126] The value of Krauss's structuralist description is that it demands that we see, in other historical moments, the particular set of synchronic exclusions, negations, and affinities through which categories were understood, defined, and performed. The historical phenomenon of a more open-ended, available, and expansive field of options that happened to both sculpture and gender in the 1960s, in other words, was made visible by – and, in turn, was accelerated by – an approach that attended to hybrids, double negations, synergies, and other non-binary proliferations.

This book offers deep readings of its artists' practices, statements, works, and archives in order to draw out both their historical complexity in relation to genders and sexualities and, perhaps more importantly, to cultivate from them a set of potentialities about how art can view gender and personhood otherwise. These two aims are not at cross-purposes, and I show how these artists' engagements with abstraction prompted them to offer their works as more capacious (and capacitating) accounts of the human and of art. Rooted in the archive and reparative in attitude, these case studies argue for these artists' practices as well as for their contemporary relevance as theoretical objects that posit openness and possibility for conceiving of genders. With regards to such a goal of expanding accounts of potential, Butler once remarked: "Some people have asked me what is the use of increasing possibilities for gender. I tend to answer: Possibility is not a luxury; it is as crucial as bread. I think we should not underestimate what the thought of the possible does for those for whom the very issue of survival is most urgent."[127]

The cultivation of possibility is an ethical and political, not just a theoretical, aim. The artists I discuss offered abstract bodies and, with them, open accounts of personhood's variability and possibility. Their sculptures do this by moving away from the human form and the rendering of the body. Rather, they figure it in the abstract. That is, these works evoke the concept of the body without mimesis, producing a gap between that calling forth of the human and the presentation of artworks that resolutely refuse to provide an anchoring *image* of a body. In that gap, there grew new versions of genders, new bodily morphologies, and a new attention to the shifting and successive potentials of these categories. Activated by the conventions of sculpture's attachment to the human body, these abstractions posited unforeclosed sites for identifying and cultivating polyvalence. As the predicate for nominating the human, gender was the operative question that these artists arrived at in their attempts to make sense of these abstractions of the body and of personhood. Each of these artists pursued this spaciousness as part of the development of their practices, and their individual trajectories mirror and contribute to the widening awareness in popular culture of gender's mutability and multiplicity. Both sculpture and gender moved into fields that were, by the end of the decade, expanded.

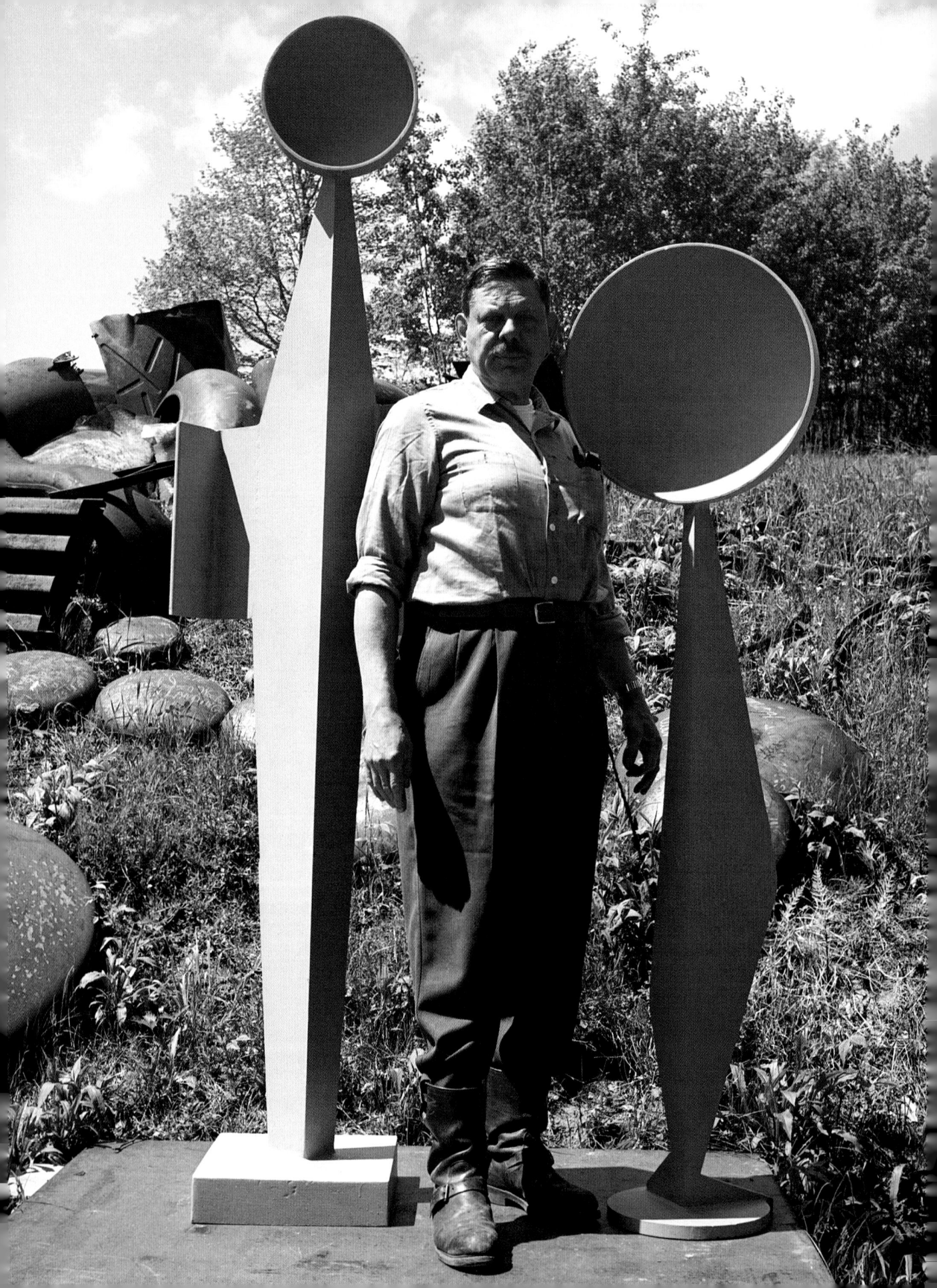

1

ON NOT MAKING BOYS

DAVID SMITH, FRANK O'HARA, AND GENDER ASSIGNMENT

David Smith once said starkly about his sculptures, "Well, they're all girls, Frank....I don't make boy sculptures." The "Frank" in question was the poet and curator Frank O'Hara, and the context of this enigmatic claim was an interview with Smith in 1964 for the public television series *Art New York*.[1] Smith's assertion that he did not make "boy sculptures" runs counter to what one might expect of his work, especially that of the 1960s. He had risen to prominence as the most important American sculptor of the past two decades, becoming known for his predominantly abstract, welded metal sculptures. Given his sustained advocacy of abstraction, his repeated claims that words fail or limit art, and his insistent strategies for achieving formal and semantic openness and variability, it might at first seem easy to dismiss this casual and reductive statement as inconsequential.[2] It was, after all, made as an off-the-cuff remark in playful banter with O'Hara, whom Smith had known for years and who was in the process of curating his third exhibition of the sculptor's work.

This comment, however, has not been disregarded. Quite the contrary, it repeatedly resurfaces in the Smith literature, where it is frequently taken as a self-evident and uncomplicated statement of intentionality.[3] Its applicability to Smith's work has been propagated ever since its first publication in 1966, when it was singled out for inclusion in *Art in America*'s special issue commemorating Smith after his accidental death in 1965.[4] Subsequently, it has been a recurring epigram in the writing about the sculptor,

OPPOSITE 7 David Smith, with *Ninety Father*, 1961 (unfinished state), and *Ninety Son*, 1961 (unfinished state). Photograph by the artist, Bolton Landing, New York, 1961.

and many treatments of this comment attempt, directly or obliquely, to prove that its comprehensiveness fits his works.

Smith's sculpture, to the contrary, does not fit. Both his works and his many other statements on artistic practice evidence a far more sophisticated agenda that the reductiveness of "I don't make boy sculptures" fails to accommodate. His sculpture was astonishingly complex in the ways it sought to reconfigure the statuary tradition, struggling with how the figural could be rendered without resemblance to actual human bodies.[5] "My concept as an artist is a revolt against the well-worn beauties in the form of a statue," he asserted.[6] Smith's works willfully eschew mimesis of the body as a means of creating new, previously unimagined, configurations, which nevertheless allude to or invoke the human figure. As Alex Potts has remarked, these new images are "incongruous yet compelling ciphers of subjectivity."[7] Why then, has this complexity been made to conform with an offhand jest made in a televised interview?

In what follows, I shall examine the history and conditions of this statement and how it has come to assume such a central place in the literature on Smith. Crucial in this story is the role of O'Hara as interviewer and friend of Smith. Even though O'Hara curated three exhibitions of Smith's work and wrote essays for journals and catalogues on the sculptor, his contribution to Smith's career has rarely, if ever, been acknowledged. Grounded in the history of O'Hara's ongoing engagement with Smith's artistic practice, this chapter dissects the dialogic situation of Smith's statement: namely, its taking place as part of a conversation, in front of a camera, with O'Hara on 6 November 1964. As an object of historical inquiry, the back and forth between Smith and O'Hara offers an opportunity for what Jane Gallop has called anecdotal theory – in which a minor incident registers or reframes broader conceptual questions.[8] Despite the quick and jovial nature of this exchange and its over-simplification, this episode exposes larger questions about gender assignment to abstract statues. Such questions are fundamental to Smith's work and determining of its reception in postwar art and criticism.

In attempting to dethrone the assumption of uncomplicated intentionality attributed to Smith's statement, I am not seeking to prove him right or wrong, nor am I attempting to figure out if, when we are confronted with a Smith sculpture, we really are seeing a boy or a girl. Rather, by tracking the long-running investments in Smith's work by O'Hara as they informed the intersubjective dynamic of the interview, I hope to demonstrate how the compulsion to assign gender to his statues points to a larger problematic for the rendering of the abstract body in the postwar era. This not only

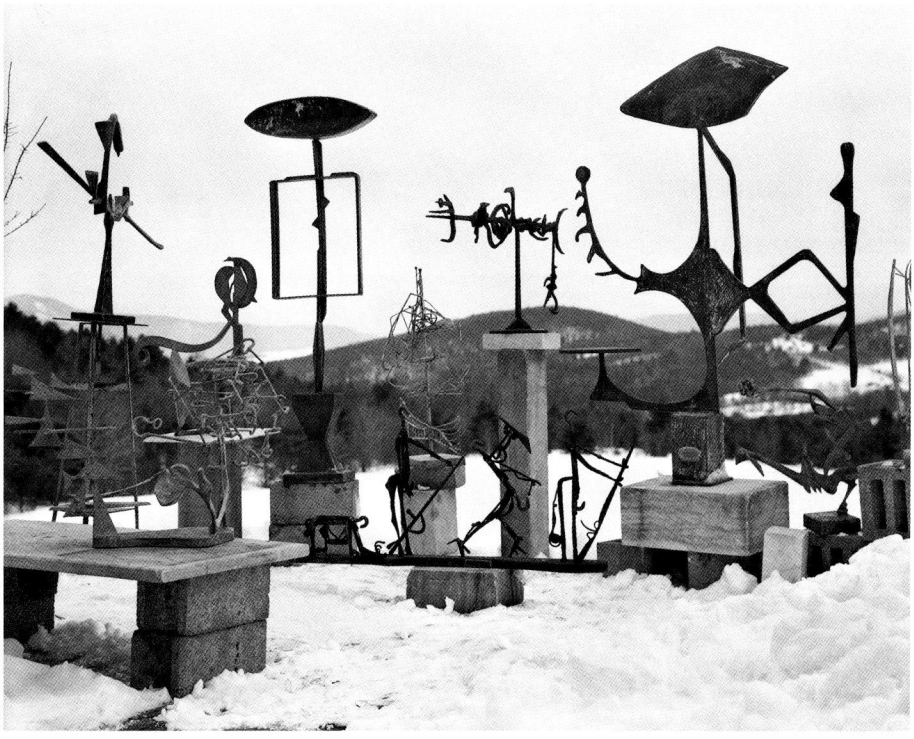

8 David Smith, sculptures from 1951 and 1952. Photograph by the artist, Bolton Landing, New York, c. 1952.

provides a better historical and historiographic understanding of this overdetermined epigram and of Smith's artistic agenda. It also offers an opportunity to examine the often overlooked role of O'Hara in Smith's career, and the following provides the first sustained art-historical account of their professional relationship. Through the lens offered by O'Hara and his interest in the sculptor's work, I shall argue that Smith's artistic practice was more complex and more interesting than he himself claimed in this bad joke that subsequently became a cipher for his work.

MULTIPLE PROFILES: O'HARA AS A CURATOR AND CRITIC OF SMITH'S SCULPTURE

Frank O'Hara had his first substantive encounter with Smith's sculpture in 1961 as part of his duties at the Museum of Modern Art (MoMA) in New York. At that time, he was an Assistant Curator in the International Program at MoMA. In that role (and in his later promotion to Associate Curator in the Department of Painting and Sculpture) he organized a number of major traveling exhibitions, including those of the work of Jackson Pollock (1957), Franz Kline (1963–64), and Robert Motherwell (1965–68), as well as such large exhibitions as *New Spanish Painting and Sculpture* (1960–62) and *Modern Sculpture U.S.A.* (1965–66). At the time of his death in 1966, O'Hara was working on retrospectives of Pollock and Willem de Kooning, the latter having agreed to a retrospective only if O'Hara would curate it.[9] As for Smith, O'Hara oversaw touring exhibitions of his sculpture in 1961 and his drawings in 1963. While his first Smith exhibition was an assignment, he quickly became a major advocate. By the time of the 1964 interview, O'Hara was already working on Smith's first major European retrospective, which opened in the Netherlands in 1966 and traveled throughout Europe in 1967.

O'Hara was also a central figure in the New York literary scene of the 1950s and became one of the key players in the so-called New York School of poets. His open-ended, conversational-style poems contained a dense array of private references to his social networks, splicing emotional and allusive content with the mundane, the overheard, and the observed. The full range of O'Hara's poetic practice is not the topic of this discussion: suffice it to say that his advocates have considered him everything from a latter-day Walt Whitman to a forerunner of post-structuralist accounts of meaning and identity.[10] O'Hara's poetry was also tightly interwoven with his engagement with visual art, and he wrote poems to or about de Kooning, Larry Rivers, Joan Mitchell, Grace Hartigan, Jasper Johns, Robert Rauschenberg, Smith, and Pollock (the Pollock poem was infamously included in his 1959 monograph on the painter, blurring the lines between poet and curator).[11] Most famously, O'Hara was known to have written poems after his lunch hours at MoMA, leading to the publication of his book *Lunch Poems* in 1964.[12]

The poems in the late 1950s and early 1960s were permeated with O'Hara's social world, and he adopted a chatty tone, leaning on the mode of gossip in his poetic voice.[13] Showcased among the multiple, overlapping social and professional networks that featured in O'Hara's poetry were his friends, lovers, and relationships within the artistic circles of 1950s New York. O'Hara's poetry consequently registered the non-traditional sexual identities and unorthodox romantic relationships that became increasingly common and visible in the art world of the time despite the prevailing conformity and homophobia of the Cold War era.[14] His published poems at the time were laced with references both overt and veiled to homosexu-

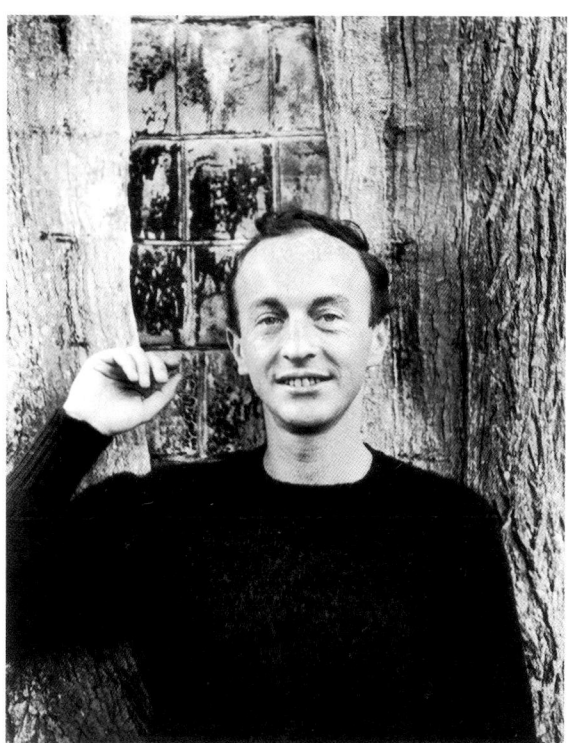

9 Frank O'Hara, Southampton, New York, 1961.

ality and to the new social formations coalescing in relation to its increasing visibility.[15] This community was central to the personal and professional life of O'Hara, who unabashedly pursued affairs and forged friendships within it.[16] Beyond the much gossiped-over entanglements with the otherwise straight Larry Rivers or the love for the dancer Vincent Warren that forged O'Hara's 1965 book *Love Poems (Tentative Title)*, the letters and memoirs from O'Hara and his circle indicate a wide and influential network of artists, curators, poets, and critics who adopted homosexual and other non-heterosexual identities. As has been well-argued by Gavin Butt, Jonathan D. Katz, and Richard Meyer, among others, a strong network of disavowals prevented full and open disclosure of these affiliations.[17] Nevertheless, such networks had a paradoxical centrality to the 1950s art world, constituting what Maggie Nelson has called "an artistic gay male brotherhood at the heart of a heterosexist, homophobic culture....And despite the real and often dangerous problems faced by gay men in the period, and despite (or because of) their air of insouciance, the male New York School poets [such as O'Hara] most definitely found comfortable – and occasionally power-ful – positions at the center of the New York art world."[18]

O'Hara's professional careers as both a poet and a curator were exemplary of this open secret of homosexuality in the art world, which informed his collaborations with Joe Brainard, Johns, Rauschenberg and others, his being scandalously painted with an erection by Rivers in 1954, his sometimes bold poems themselves, and his engagement in public critical debate about the emerging body of homosexual fiction, such as in his 1963 review of John Rechy's *City of Night*, the novel that heralded a new wave of explicitly gay writing.[19] O'Hara's work was not solely about these topics.[20] Quite the contrary, his primary concerns within his art criticism and curation were centered on straight artists such as de Kooning, Pollock, and Smith. To these and others, however, his homosexuality and social circles were no secret. Overall, there is much evidence as to the general awareness and unremarkability of O'Hara's sexuality, but there were also, of course, negative registrations of it, as with the well-known story of Pollock calling O'Hara a "fag" in the Cedar Tavern.[21] All of this is to say that Smith would have known, neutrally or not, of O'Hara's non-normative sexuality, as it was central to both the poet's life and work.[22] However, the general recognition of O'Hara's sexuality in his circle did not overshadow the energy, artistic credentials, and curatorial enthusiasm that made him a key player in the art world in the early 1960s. As one commentator later wrote, "His was the spirit which held together a whole group of artists and poets – gay and straight – in New York in the fifties and early sixties."[23] Without a doubt, his engagement with contemporary art was complex in its commitments and wide-ranging in its support.

O'Hara's friendship with Smith began in August 1961 when he visited the sculptor's studio at Bolton Landing in upstate New York in preparation for the American touring exhibition.[24] The experience of viewing Smith's sculpture over the course of two days infused O'Hara with enthusiasm about the work. It was a good time to visit Smith. The sculptor had just that summer made a leap forward with work and was more ambitiously painting his works. As he wrote to Kenneth Noland at the end of June 1961, "I'm making bigger & better sculpture. The colors I'm less sure of, but progress is challenge and challenge is always less sure. Some day I'll get it by the ass."[25] His two young daughters were visiting for the summer, and they were preparing for a birthday party for Candida, the younger daughter, a few days later on the 12th. Smith had been separated from his wife, Jean Freas, for three years, and their divorce was made final that year. The presence of his daughters always lightened Smith's mood, and he wrote in his telegraph style in a postcard to Frankenthaler in July: "Happyest [sic] I've been sometime with my dolls."[26] Smith's happiness no doubt aided O'Hara.

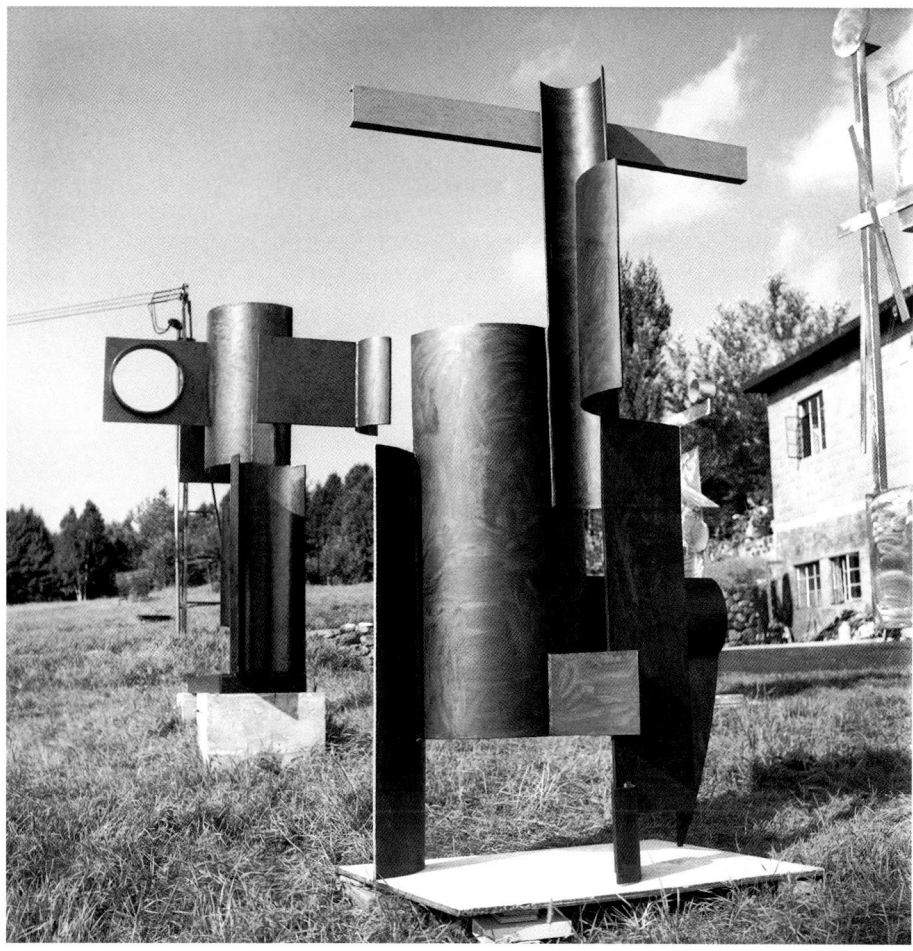

10   David Smith, *Zig III* and *Zig II*, both 1961, outside the artist's house, Bolton Landing, New York. Photograph by the artist, c. 1961.

In the weeks before, O'Hara had been assigned the potentially unpleasant task of organizing the American touring exhibition on short notice following the ouster of his superviser, Porter McCray.[27] After two days in Bolton Landing, however, the last-minute selection for the exhibition was well along, and Smith demonstrated his appreciation of O'Hara by giving him a painting.[28] This is significant, as Smith publicly voiced throughout his career a deep distrust of curators, art historians, and collectors. Such dislike could manifest itself in gendered terms for Smith. For instance, when Andrew Ritchie and Sam Hunter had visited Smith a few years before, in 1957, to pick work for an earlier MoMA exhibition, Smith wrote to his

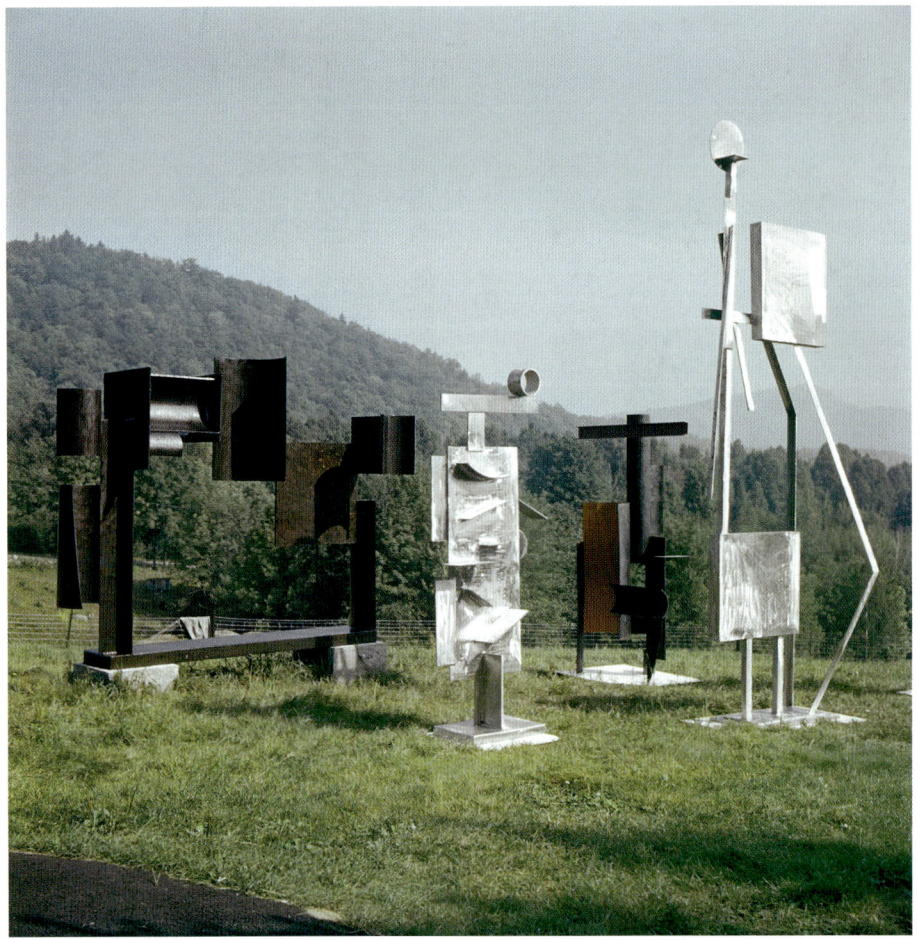

11   David Smith, *Zig III*, *Two Circle Sentinel*, *Zig II*, and *Two Box Structure*, all 1961. Photograph by the artist, Bolton Landing, New York.

good friend Frankenthaler, "I liked Ritchie. He seems a solid, characterful type, masculine *for once in that world*. He even loves to fish."[29] Overcoming such resistance, O'Hara also seems to have won over Smith on this first visit, leaving Bolton Landing with a completed exhibition checklist and the gift of the painting from the sculptor.

This trip made an immediate impact on the poet. On the day of his leaving Bolton Landing, 10 August 1961, O'Hara wrote the poem "Mozart Chemisier" about the experience.[30] The recurring imagery in the non-sequitur lines of dialogue that make up the poem revolve around drinking (a favored activity of both Smith and O'Hara), the topography of Bolton

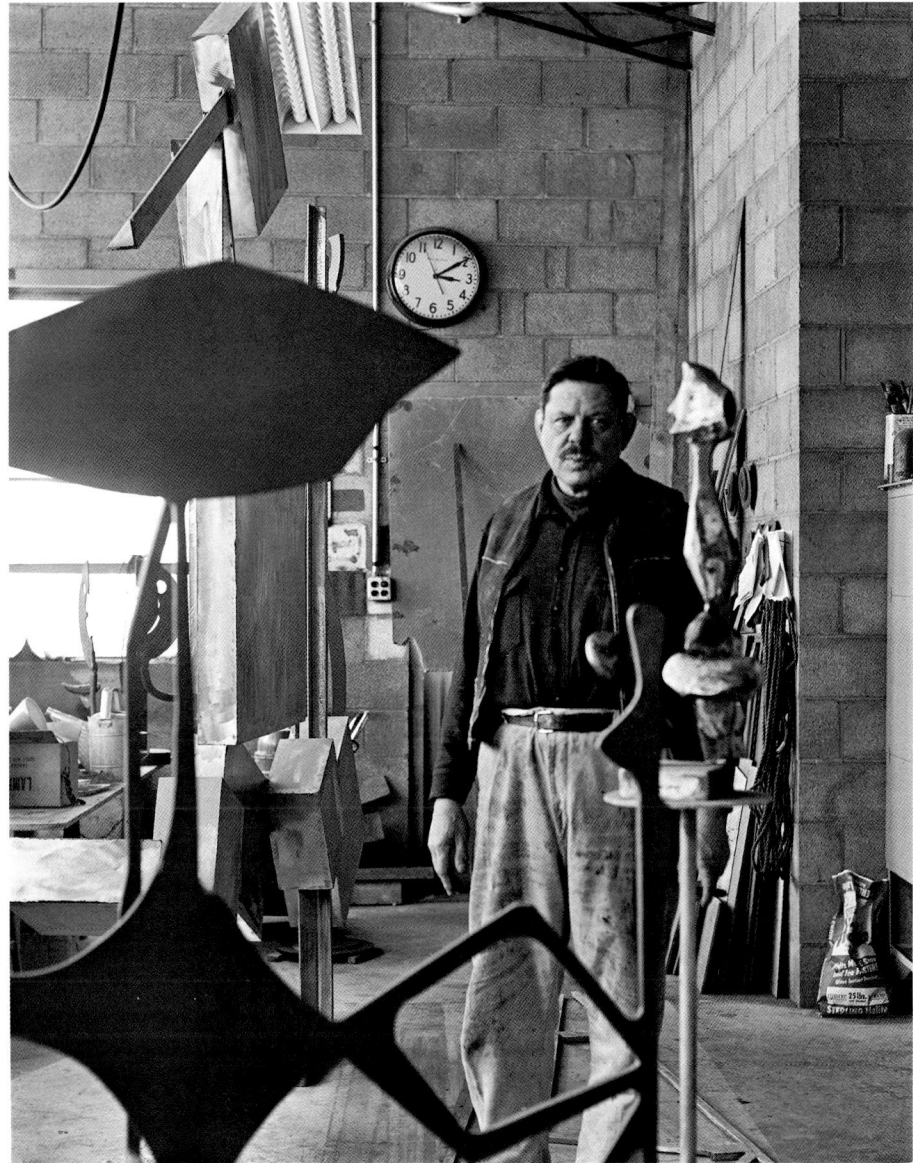

12 David Smith with *Agricola I*, 1951–2, *Cube Totem 7 and 6*, 1961–2, and *Tahstvaat*, 1946, Bolton Landing Shop, New York. Photograph by the artist, c. 1962.

Landing with its "unexperienced lake" (Lake George) and its poplars that "looked like aspidistra." Smith and his daughters make appearances in the shifting address of lines of the poem such as "put in your earrings we're going to the railroad station" (Smith to one of his daughters) as do other

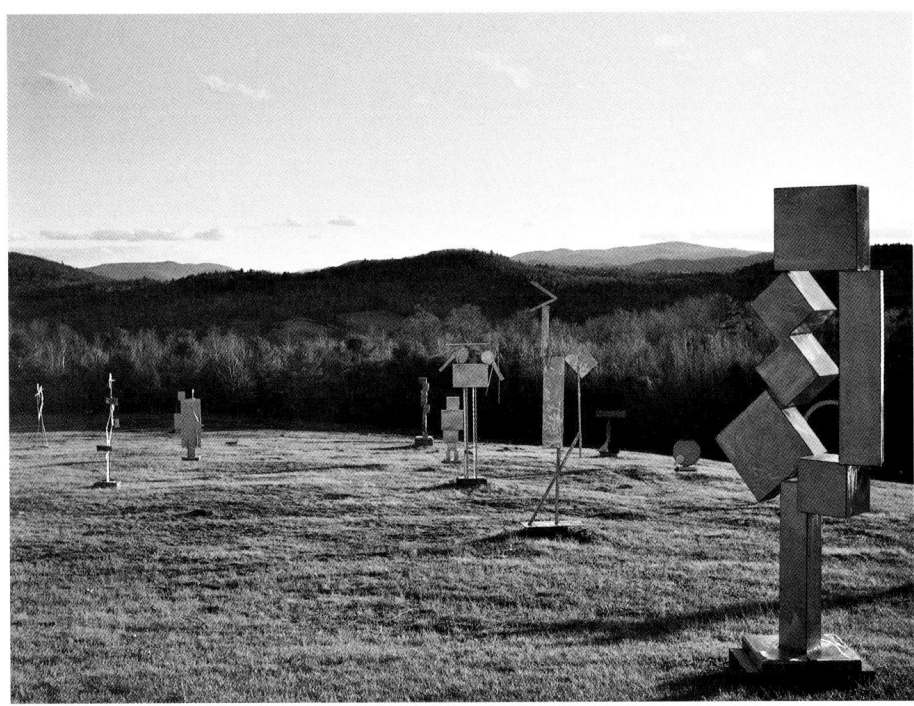

13 David Smith, sculptures in the fields at Bolton Landing, New York. Photograph by the artist, c. 1963.

voices, with vernacular phrases including "everyone thinks they're going up/ in these here America." O'Hara would sometimes write poems to mark important locations and conversations in his memory, weaving remembered phrases, observations, and overheard comments into a poem that evoked the place and the experience. "Mozart Chemisier" was significant enough for O'Hara to use it as the opening poem for the short documentary film on his work, *USA Poetry* (directed by Richard O. Moore, 1966), mentioning both Smith and Bolton Landing in his introduction to the poem.[31] In addition, in his collaboration with the painter Alfred Leslie on the film *The Last Clean Shirt*, the poem was among those from which O'Hara appropriated a line to be used as part of the dialogue.[32] In other words, O'Hara's poetic practice, as well as his curatorial and critical work, demonstrated the importance of this trip for him.

Within a week of returning to New York, O'Hara wrote a personal letter to the sculptor after further reflecting on his trip to Bolton Landing. Not using the MoMA letterhead, this less formal letter expressed his appreciation, talked about Smith's daughter's party, and thanked him for the gift of

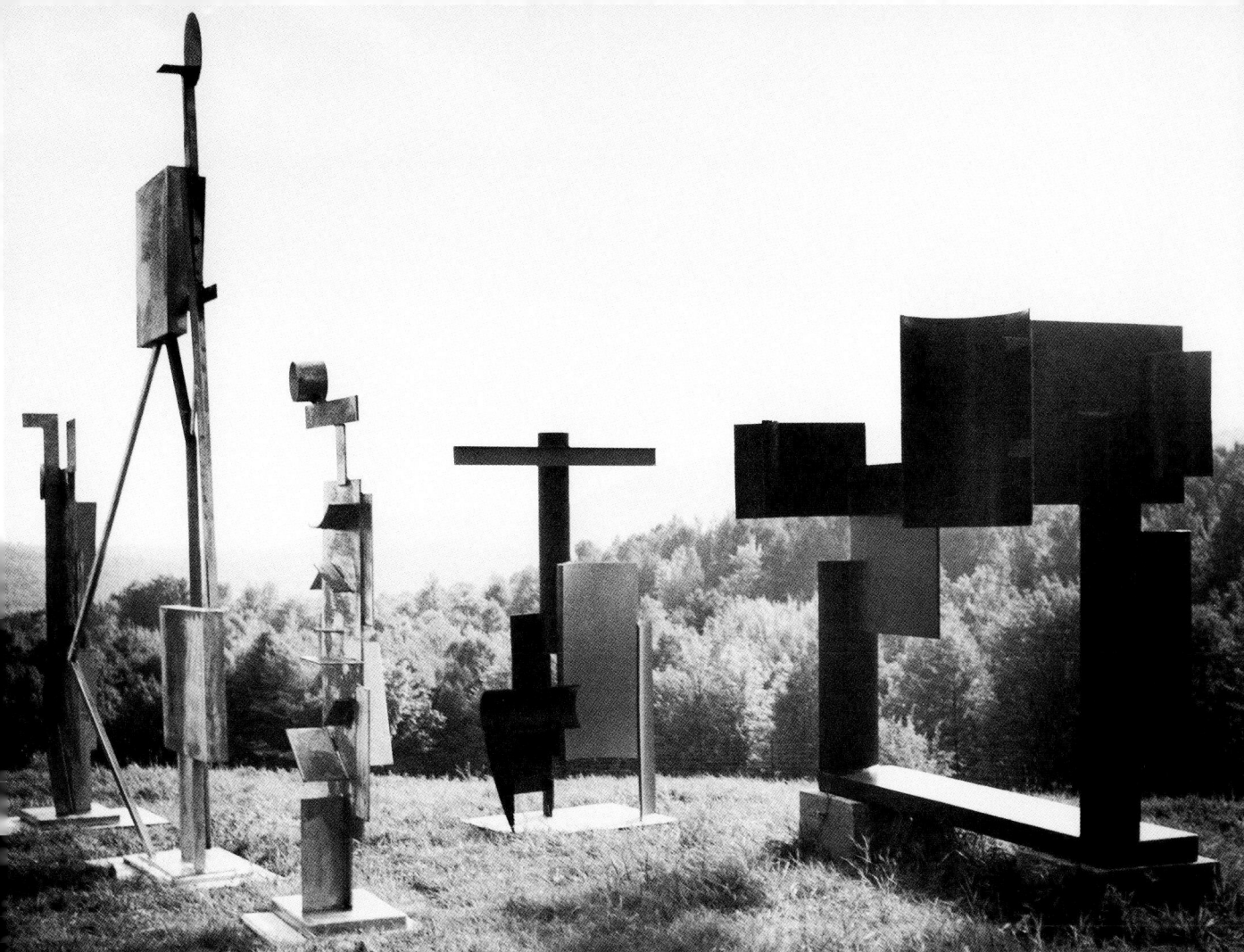

14 David Smith, *March Sentinel (Stainless Steel Planes)*, *Two Box Structure*, *Two Circle Sentinel*, *Zig II*, and *Zig III*, all 1961. Photograph by the artist, Bolton Landing, New York, c. 1961.

a painting. He continued, "I think we have a terrific show lined up and I've been elated just thinking about it. Also I've been thinking about the new work ever since leaving, and it's staggering."[33]

The Spring and Summer of 1961 was a pivotal time for Smith because he had, in the previous months, completed such important works as the transitional work *Cubetotem* that inaugurated the *Cubi* series, *Ninety Father* and *Ninety Son* (fig. 7), and *Zigs I* to *IV* – which made an appearance in another of O'Hara's poems begun in August that year, the major work "Biotherm (for Bill Berkson)" completed in January 1962.[34] In fact, The *Zigs*, *March Sentinel*, and *Two Circle Sentinel* were among the works O'Hara featured in an article written for the December 1961 issue of *ARTnews* on

Smith's work, one of the first major assessments of Smith's work of the early 1960s.[35]

O'Hara's *ARTnews* article is historically significant for its argument about the importance of color in Smith's sculptural practice (its subtitle was "The color of steel"). In particular, it offers evidence that proved crucial in the debates about Smith's use of polychromy and the scandal of the removal of paint on Smith's sculptures by Clement Greenberg in his capacity as one of the executors of Smith's estate.[36] Later discussions of O'Hara's article largely refer to its author solely in terms of his reported observations of Smith's sculptures and what colors they were painted. The content of his art-critical take on Smith, however, has been – like O'Hara in histories of Smith's career more generally – dismissed or simply unaddressed. O'Hara's art criticism was idiosyncratic, there is no doubt. Yet, as in the poetic voice he developed, his wry incorporation of observed details, knowing asides, and perceptive quips into his art criticism only masquerade as casual and uncommitted. They perform a certain lightness, more accurately, as a means to articulate the sophistication, ineffability, and variability of the artwork.[37]

This strategy is clearly evident in O'Hara's 1961 *ARTnews* article, which served as the foundational synthesis of his views on the sculptor's work. Written in O'Hara's breezy and perceptive style, its ostensible goal was to discuss Smith's process of painting his sculptures. The issue that he pursued most emphatically in this article is not, however, color or paint. Rather, O'Hara's article attempted to cast Smith's sculptures as figural presences and to discuss their effects on the viewer. It put forth an almost relentless personification of the sculptures in which he characterized them as human. In this, O'Hara highlighted the figural valences of Smith's sculptures and extrapolated from their anthropomorphic echoes an account of the works not just as figures but as attentive subjects.[38]

More than anything else, that is, O'Hara was struck by the ways in which the highly abstract constructions nevertheless compelled him to think of them as evocative of persons. The figure had, after all, served as a constant denominator and a recurring foil in Smith's artistic practice. From the sculptor's Surrealist-informed work of the 1930s and 1940s to the welded diagrammatic constructions which brought him to national prominence in the 1950s, Smith's work had become increasingly abstract without, however, fully abandoning its reference to the human form and the statuary format.[39] As William Tucker noted, often Smith's sculptures "create the effect of a human figure, not through imitation but through the evocation of uprightness, frontality, general separation into parts, and size."[40] Smith quite regu-

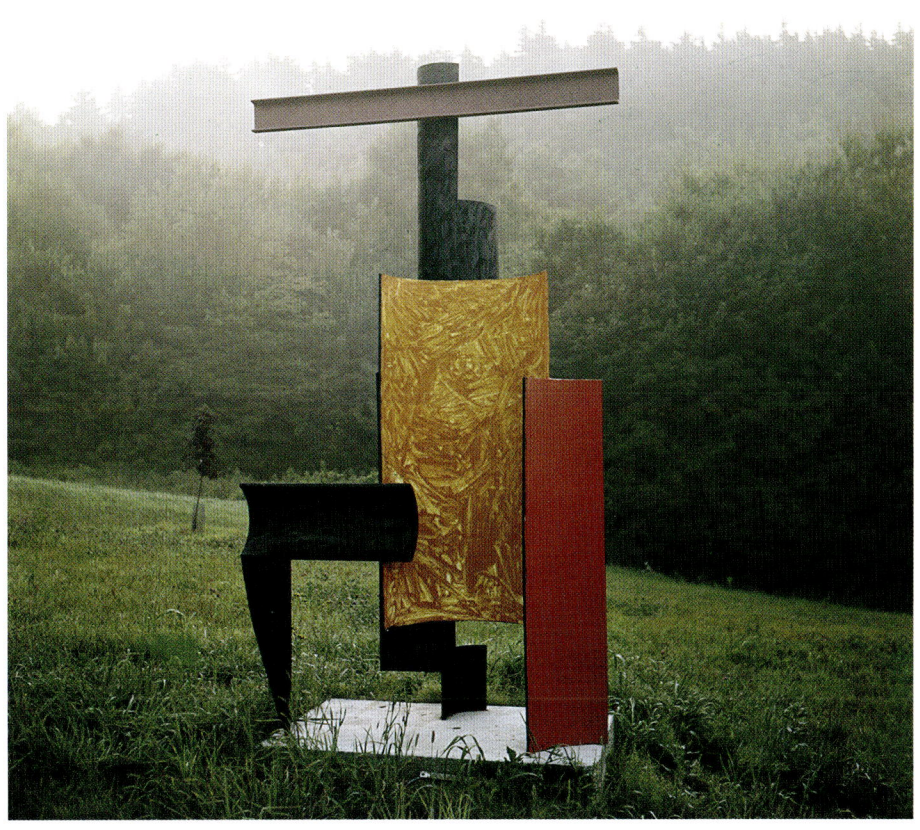

15 David Smith, *Zig II*, 1961 (unfinished state). Painted steel, 255.3 × 85.1 × 150.5 cm (100½ × 33½ × 59¼ in.). Photograph by the artist, Bolton Landing, New York, c. 1960–1.

larly underscored anthropomorphic references with blatantly figural titles, such as "sentinel," "personage," "father," "son," "girl," and "man."[41] That the human body retained crucial importance in his work of these years is attested by the 140 enamel paintings he created after photographs of female nudes in 1964, some of which became the source images for *Cubi* sculptures.[42] As Clement Greenberg wrote in the 1966 memorial issue of *Art in America*, "But as [Smith] turned increasingly abstract in latter years, in the conception and scheme, not to mention execution, the human figure became more and more the one constant attaching him to nature."[43] That

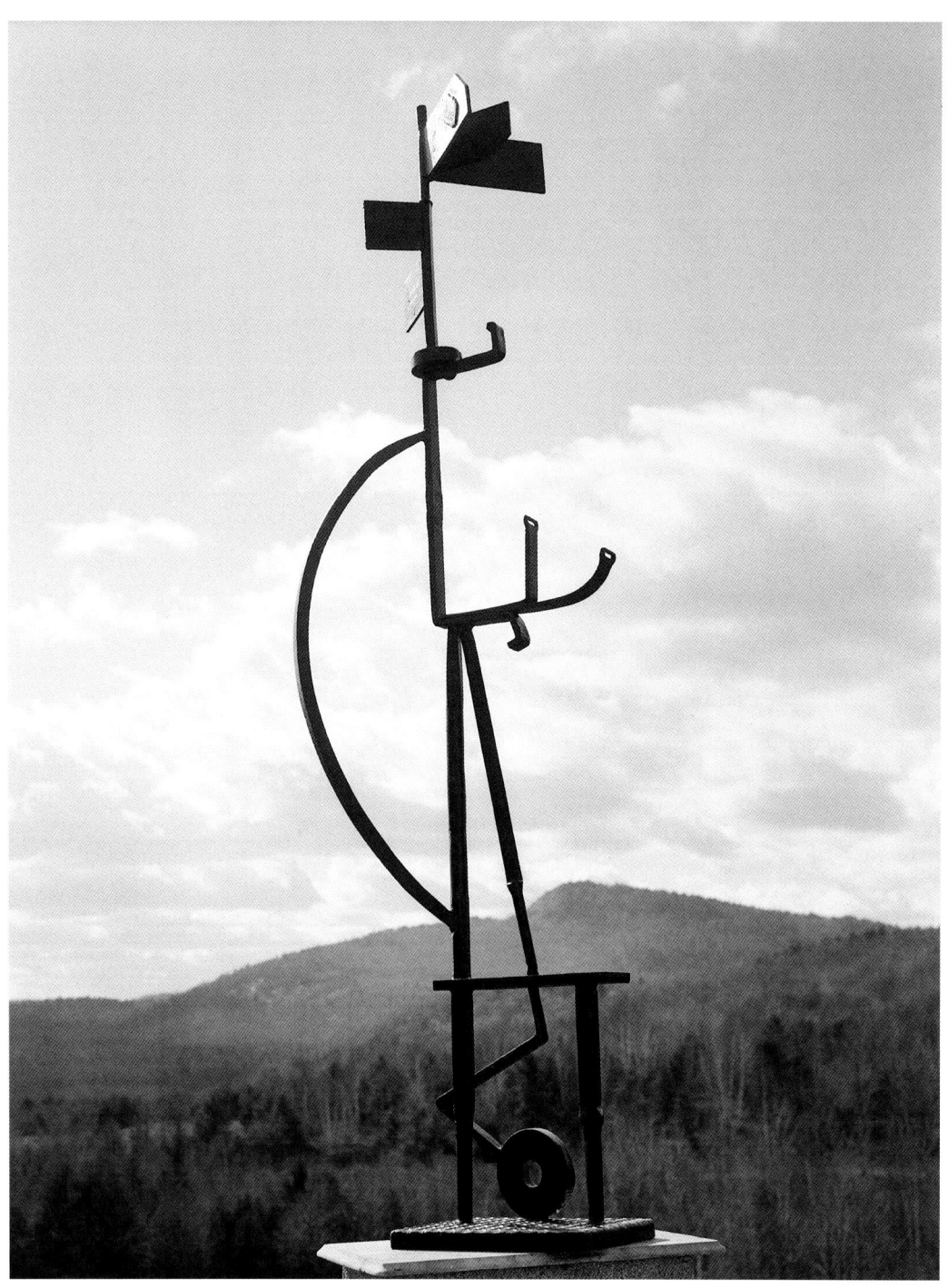

16   David Smith, *Sentinel I*, 1956. Steel, 227.6 × 42.9 × 57.5 cm (89⅝ × 16⅞ × 22⅝ in.). Photograph by the artist, Bolton Landing, New York, c. 1956.

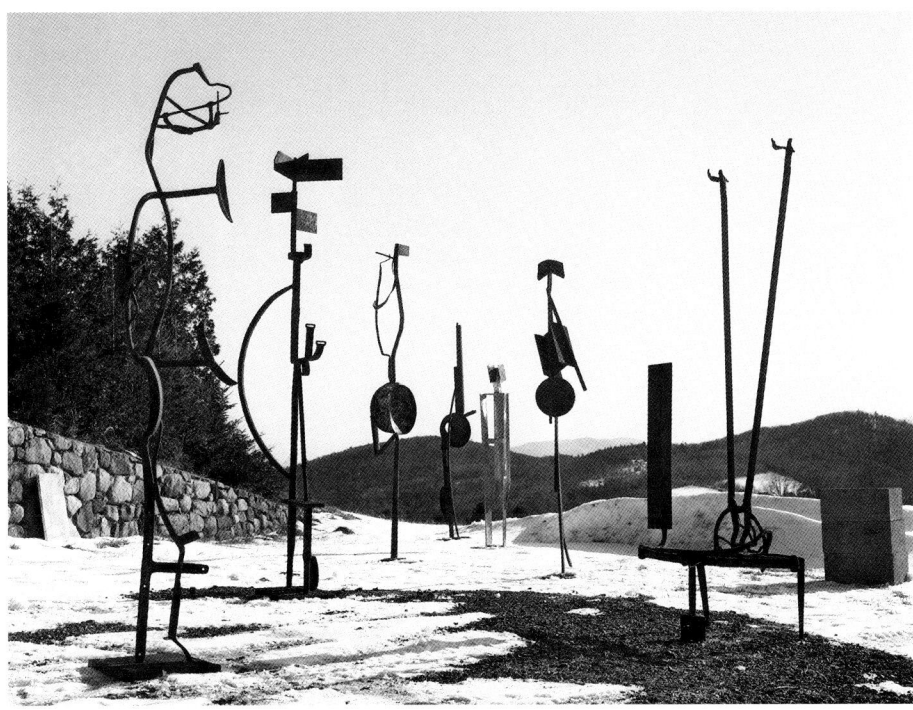

17   David Smith, *Personage of August*, 1956, *Sentinel I*, 1956, *Running Daughter*, 1956–60 (unfinished state), *Tanktotem VI*, 1957, *Sentinel II*, 1957, *Pilgrim*, 1957, and *The Five Spring*, 1956. Photograph by the artist, Bolton Landing, New York, c. 1958.

is, despite the subsequent reputation of the Smith of the Sixties as the quintessential abstract sculptor, one of the continuing concerns into the last decade of his career was the degree to which his sculpture stood in relation to the human figure.

O'Hara perceived this quickly, and his personification of Smith's work is evident from the start of the *ARTnews* article, which begins with a description of the drive into Bolton Landing. O'Hara remarked that "along the road up to the house a procession of new works, in various stages of painting, stood in the attitudes of some of Smith's characteristic titles: they stood there like a *Sentinel* or *Totem*, or *Ziggurat*, not at all menacing, but very aware".[44] Repeatedly throughout the piece, O'Hara continues to refer to the sculptures as if they were people, aware both of themselves and of O'Hara's presence. In one such passage, he wrote: "The effect of all these works along the road and around the house was somewhat that of people who are awaiting admittance to a formal reception and, while they wait, are thinking about their roles when they join the rest of the guests already

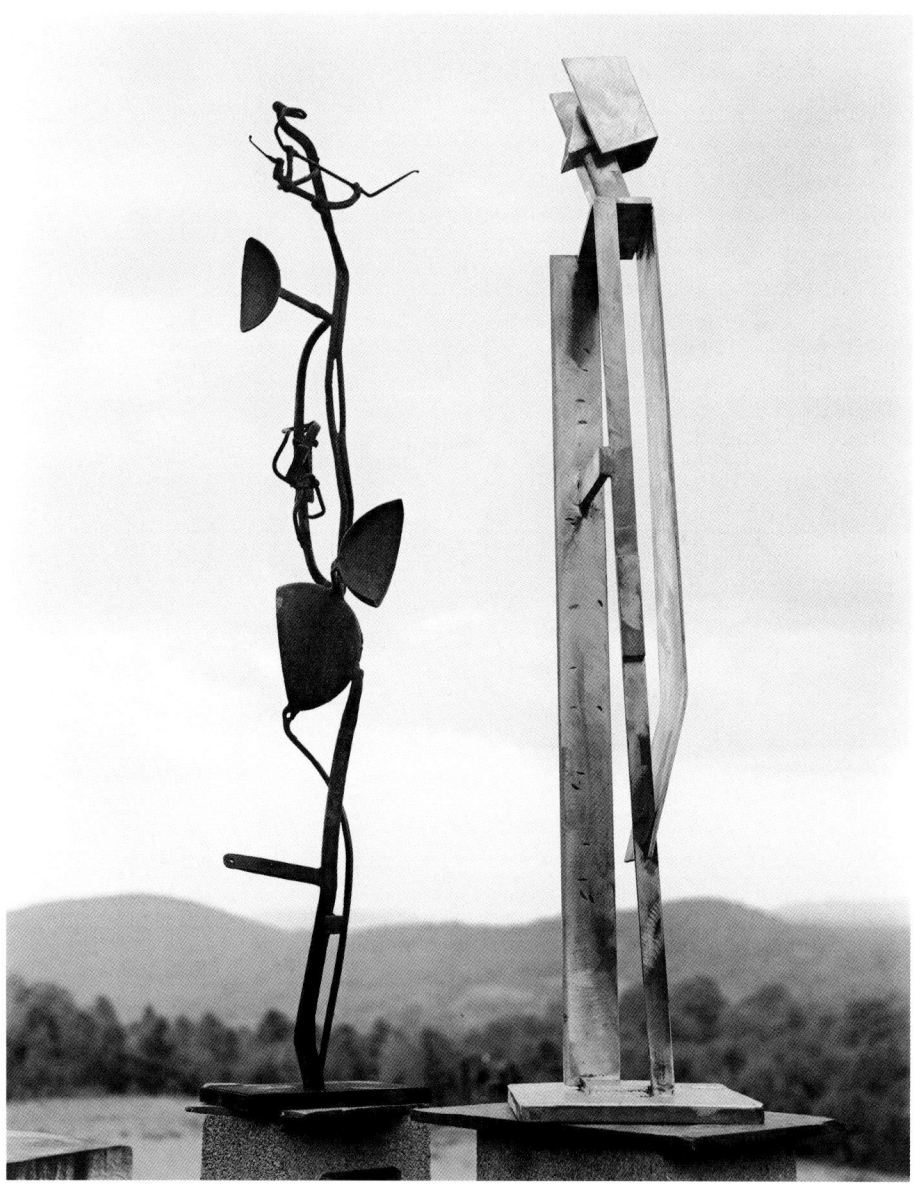

18 David Smith, *Personage of August*, 1956 and *Sentinel II*, 1957. Photograph by the artist, Bolton Landing, New York, c. 1957.

in the meadow."[45] For O'Hara, Smith's sculptures were attentive and self-possessed. In that personal letter to Smith, he had said something similar: "They get to me but I don't get to them. They make me feel like the world going round and round and not knowing what's going on, or, in a word, alive."[46] In the published article, he continued this tack, writing of the sculptures' "authoritative presence" and "insistence of their individual personalities."[47] Rarely was there a direct discussion of anthropomorphism or figural resemblance, save for the occasional adjective like "leggy" or "dashing." Instead, Smith's works were, more importantly, the kind of people you want to know. In O'Hara's account, they registered the art critic's staring at them and reacted in turn. He wrote: "to continue the meadow-party idea, they are the sort of people who are about to walk away because you just aren't as interesting as they are, but they're not quite mean enough to do it."[48] Throughout the article, there was a thoroughgoing attempt playfully to characterize Smith's sculptures as persons to aspire to and be mutually recognized by.[49] This identification with Smith's sculptures as subjects culminates in the last line of the article with O'Hara writing, "The best of the current sculptures didn't make me feel I wanted to *have* one, they made me feel I wanted to *be* one."[50] No off-hand remark, this same sentiment infused his initial elation with the works. The postscript to the letter to Smith of 17 August said, "What I think I mean by the above is I'd like to *be* one of those sculptures!"[51]

Alive, attentive, aloof, alluring – this is how O'Hara saw Smith's sculptures, transforming them into urbane party-guests whom you wanted to be introduced to and approved by. Indeed, as he had repeated at least twice to the sculptor, they were like the multifaceted person one wanted to be. Smith, himself, must have known well just how O'Hara saw his work. In addition to receiving that letter, Smith also read and told O'Hara that he approved of the *ARTnews* article. As O'Hara wrote to his then-partner Vincent Warren, "David Smith told me he was crazy about my piece on him in *Art News*, so I feel quite cheered about my prose writing, knock on wood."[52] Similarly self-effacing, he wrote to Smith to thank him for his "kind words," saying "I'm so relieved you thought it was okay."[53]

I have placed such emphasis on this first intense beginning of O'Hara and Smith's professional relationship because it provided the basis for both Smith's continued trust in O'Hara as a curator and O'Hara's attitude toward Smith's work. In particular, this emphatic identification of O'Hara with Smith's sculptures infused their later interactions. More, there is much evidence that the friendship between Smith and O'Hara continued and was deeply felt.[54] After the sculptor's untimely death in a car crash in 1965, O'Hara's colleague at MoMA, Waldo Rasmussen, recalled how painful the task was to select works for the 1966 Smith European retrospective that O'Hara organized, saying "Both Frank and I were particularly close to Smith....Before [Smith's death], [he] and Frank had worked together very

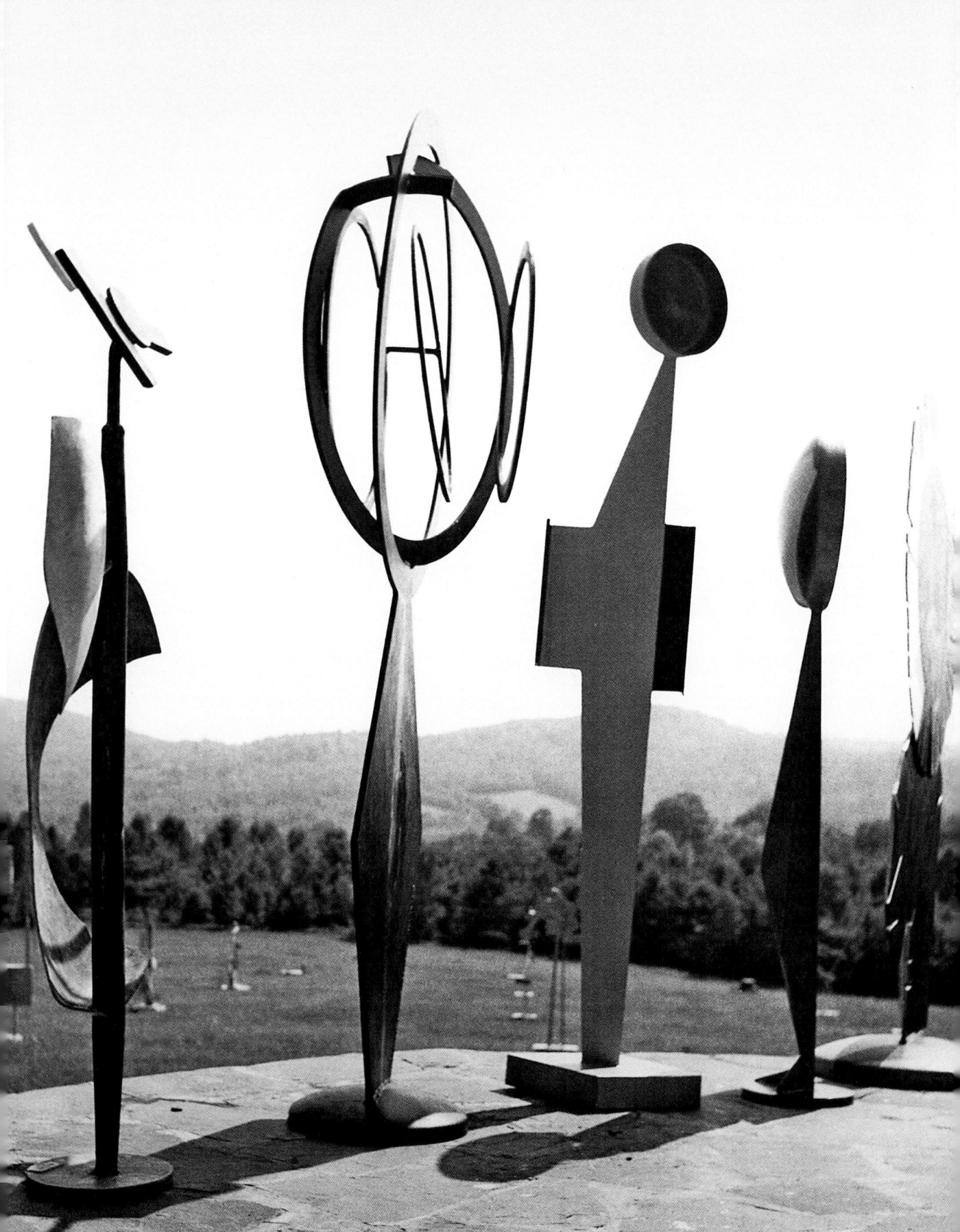

closely on the selection, and David was exuberant about the challenge this first major exhibition of his work in Europe would provide."[55] O'Hara even repaired the damaged surfaces of some of Smith's sculptures after they traveled to the Netherlands for the retrospective.[56] As he wrote to Joan Mitchell, "The Smiths all arrived in good condition except for chips on some of the big painted Zigs which had to be touched up (I'd brought David's own paint – that part was quite melancholy)."[57] Before his own death, O'Hara was advocating a catalogue raisonné of the sculptor's work, "if we ever find anyone to do it."[58] Smith's death had hit O'Hara hard. The writer and one-time de Kooning bodyguard Erje Ayden remembered how O'Hara talked about Smith:

> I had never heard before a man who could describe a fellow artist so fully, making you think you knew David Smith all your life, played marbles with him, went to school with him, drank, suffered with him, shared the same women with him...And when Frank cried at the death of David Smith, self-consciously letting his tears drop into the cognac, I did the same thing.[59]

In short, when Smith sat down to be interviewed by O'Hara in 1964, they were close and mutually sympathetic. In the three years since 1961, Smith would have become familiar with O'Hara's personification of and identification with his sculptures, as this was evident in both O'Hara's personal and published accounts of the sculptor's work.

"ON GUARD": THE 1964 TELEVISED INTERVIEW WITH SMITH

The November 1964 interview with O'Hara happened in the context of a major exhibition of Smith's new work that October organized by the Marlborough-Gerson gallery.[60] Smith received the invitation from Bill Berkson, who was at that time an associate producing the television series *Art New York* for the Educational Broadcasting Corporation and WNDT in New York.[61] The young poet Berkson was a friend and the subject of many

---

OPPOSITE 19   David Smith, *Tanktotem VIII*, 1960, *Noland's Blues*, 1961, *Ninety Father*, 1961, *Ninety Son*, 1961, *Rebecca Circle*, 1961, 1960. Photograph by the artist, Bolton Landing, c. 1962.

of O'Hara's poems, including "Biotherm" in which Smith's *Zigs* make an appearance. By this time, Smith was also familiar with Berkson, whose chatty letter to the sculptor about the taping of the interview reminded him to not wear a white shirt (he had scrawled a similar note on O'Hara's copy of the voiceover script).[62]

Smith's episode of *Art New York* was titled "Sculpting Master of Bolton Landing" (fig. 20). The interview with O'Hara took place on the afternoon of Friday, 6 November 1964, in a New York television studio. Smith had traveled down to the city for the weekend for the taped interview, but there was also extensive footage of Smith taking O'Hara around the grounds of Bolton Landing (fig. 21). It also seems that Frankenthaler, at one point, was going to share the stage with O'Hara to talk about Smith's work, but this did not transpire.[63] The program was aired a week later on 11 November and took the form of a visual retrospective of Smith's career with commentary on individual sculptures as the introduction to the interview between Smith and O'Hara. The two had been in regular contact over the preceding months, as O'Hara continued preparations for the retrospective and as MoMA installed three Smith sculptures in their garden that autumn. O'Hara had been up to Bolton Landing again that October.[64]

The interview was characterized by the deliberate and rather gruff Smith and the verbally nimble O'Hara going back and forth throughout, casually talking with the occasional laugh on both sides. They both smoked throughout – Smith a cigar and O'Hara an always-lit cigarette. It took them a while to warm up. The camera made them both slightly self-conscious at first, though they relaxed during the twenty-minute interview. O'Hara later wrote jokingly to the painter Michael Goldberg, "Did I tell you I did a TV show with David Smith? Everybody seemed to like it, and not everybody who said so likes me or David so much that they'd have to lie."[65] The majority of the conversation concerned Smith's practice of painting the sculptures and his attitude toward color. This was, of course, one of O'Hara's main themes from his 1961 *ARTnews* article. Finishing up a line of discussion about the surface of the stainless steel sculptures, Smith remarked: "But the polishing is not so important – any more than the brushstroking is important in a picture. It's the concept of the form or the concept of the content." O'Hara then asked a somewhat innocuous and stumbling question:

> O'Hara: "Well, then, you know, conceiving of form. Let's say, when you look at these things and study them – I mean, you study them, since you've created them – I study them and you look at them. But do you

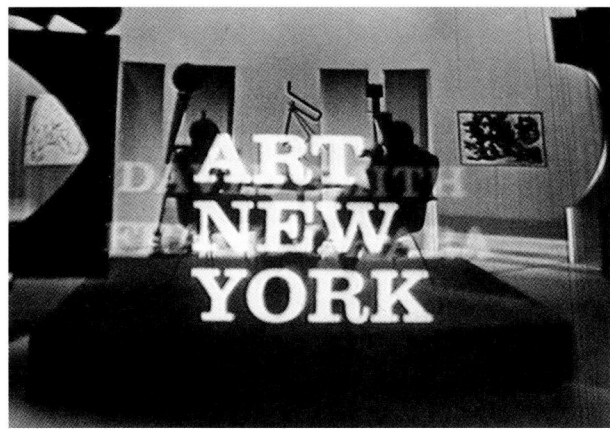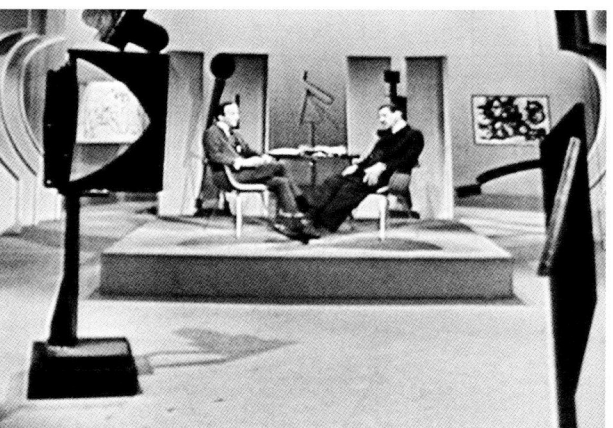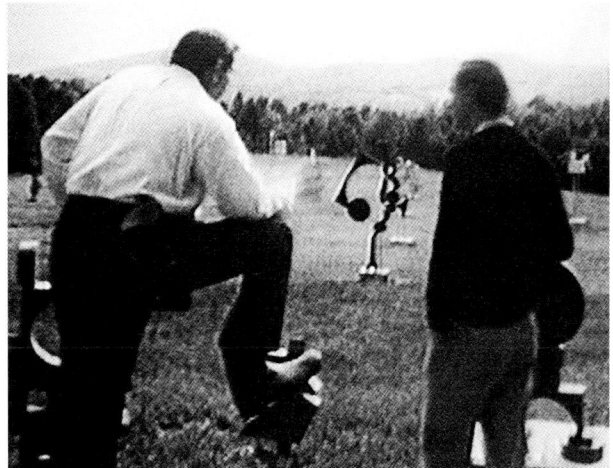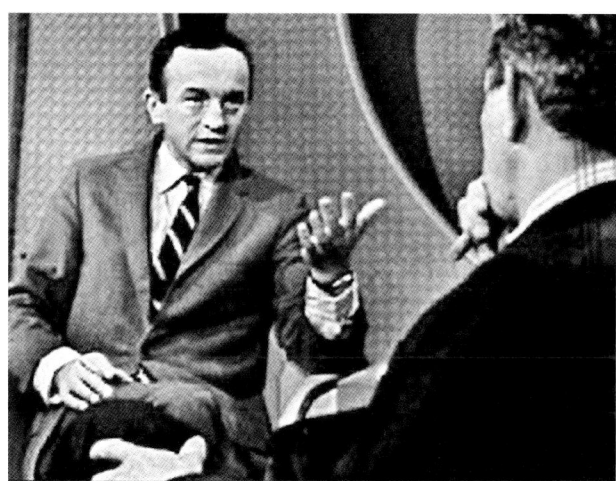

20   Stills from *Art New York: The Sculpting Master of Bolton Landing*, 6 November 1964.

feel like they're people around your house? Are they aesthetic things? What are they? I mean, you must feel that they're all these, um, strange objects surrounding your whole studio – "

[At which point, Smith broke in saying,] "Well, they're all girls, Frank."

O'Hara: "They're all girls?"

Smith: "Yeah, they're all female sculptures."

[Laughing, O'Hara replied:] "Oh, they are."

Smith: "I'm sure."

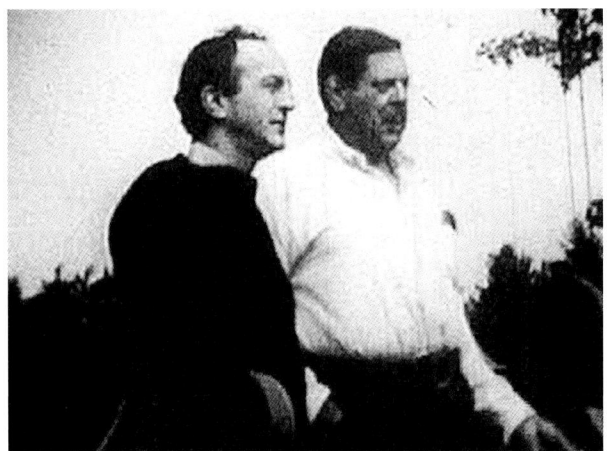 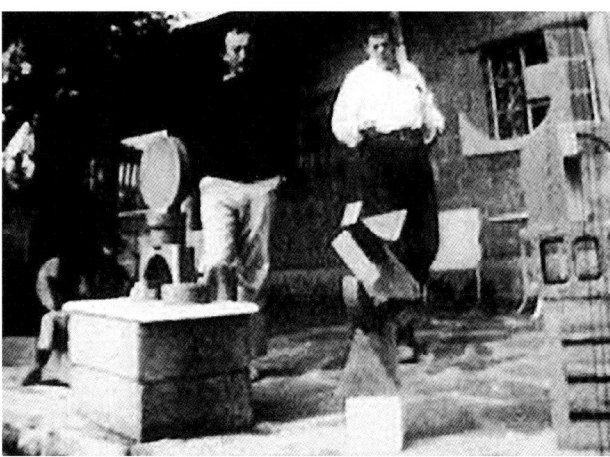

21 Stills from *Art New York: The Sculpting Master of Bolton Landing*, 6 November 1964.

[O'Hara followed up, asking,] "Very angular girls?" [to which Smith replied:]

"I don't make boy sculptures."⁶⁶

This interchange lasted only a few seconds, with O'Hara and Smith speaking over each other's lines as they both attempted to adapt to Smith's interjection. Smith's initial comment in this exchange was meant as a joke and was said with a smile, and both parties chuckle throughout. The exchange was rapid, with Smith having to repeat his "I don't make boy sculptures" line twice under O'Hara's question of "Very angular girls?" Camaraderie rather than antagonism characterized the back and forth, but both wanted their reaction to this line of thinking to be voiced and heard. After the "boy sculpture" line, Smith tried to recoup the seriousness of the conversation, saying "But they become kind of personages. And sometimes they point out to me that I should have been better or bigger. And, mostly, they tell me that I should have done that 10 years before – or 20 years before."⁶⁷ O'Hara did not let this line of conversation go, however, asking, "Well, don't they ever tell you that they're very glad you did them?" Smith replied, "I like their presence – yes."⁶⁸

Throughout the second half of the interview after Smith's quip about them all being "female sculptures," O'Hara chidingly returned a few times to his central characterization – that of Smith's sculptures as people – and the sculptor resisted, deflecting comments from O'Hara such as "Well, they do seem like friends who came to New York, I must say – having seen

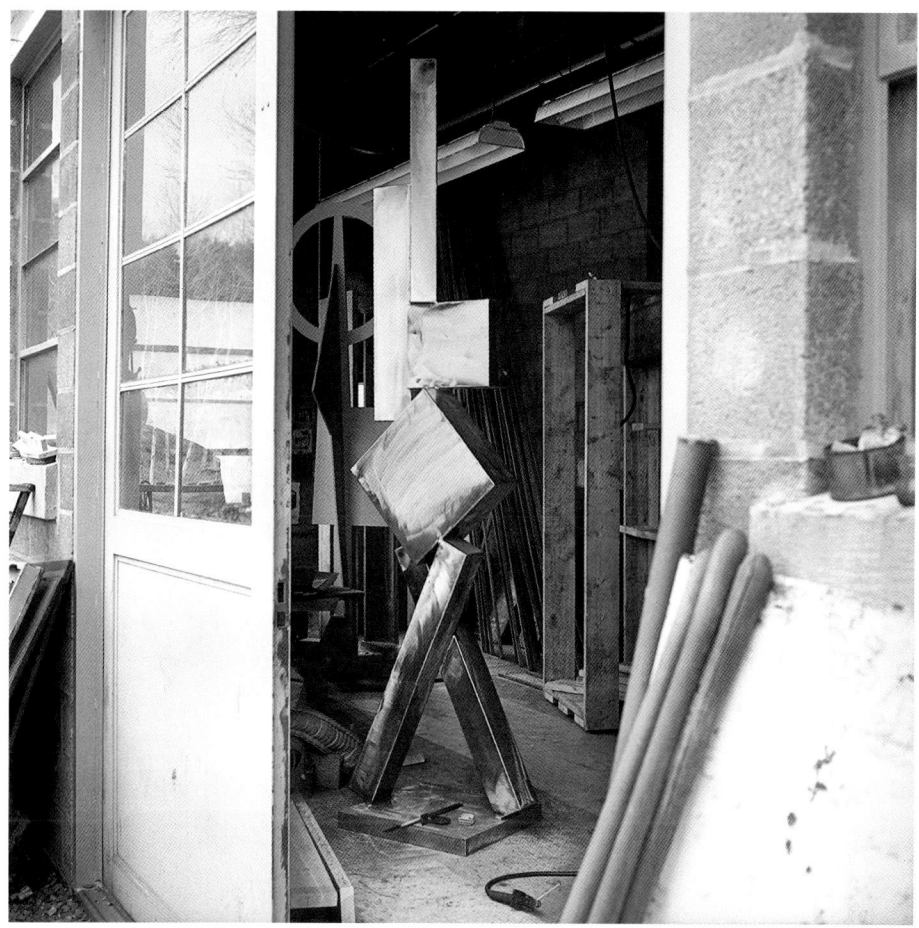

22 David Smith, *Cubi VI*, 1963, with *Circle and Box (Circle and Ray)*, 1963, in the background, Bolton Landing Shop. Photograph by the artist, c. 1963.

them at your house and then seeing them in town…in the gallery."[69] In response to such remarks, Smith would instead emphasize their object-nature or how they were made. It is as if the sculptor's reluctance to continue the metaphor he himself had introduced grew from a recognition of that joke's limitations and reductiveness. For its impact, the quip had drawn directly on and responded to the ways in which O'Hara's question to Smith was, itself, representative of his long-standing account of Smith's sculptures as ideal people. In making his joke, however, Smith had literalized it to the point of absurdity, and he resisted O'Hara's coy attempts to keep this metaphor going. For instance, as O'Hara closed the interview, he thanked Smith for coming from Bolton Landing, hoping he had had fun, and remarked

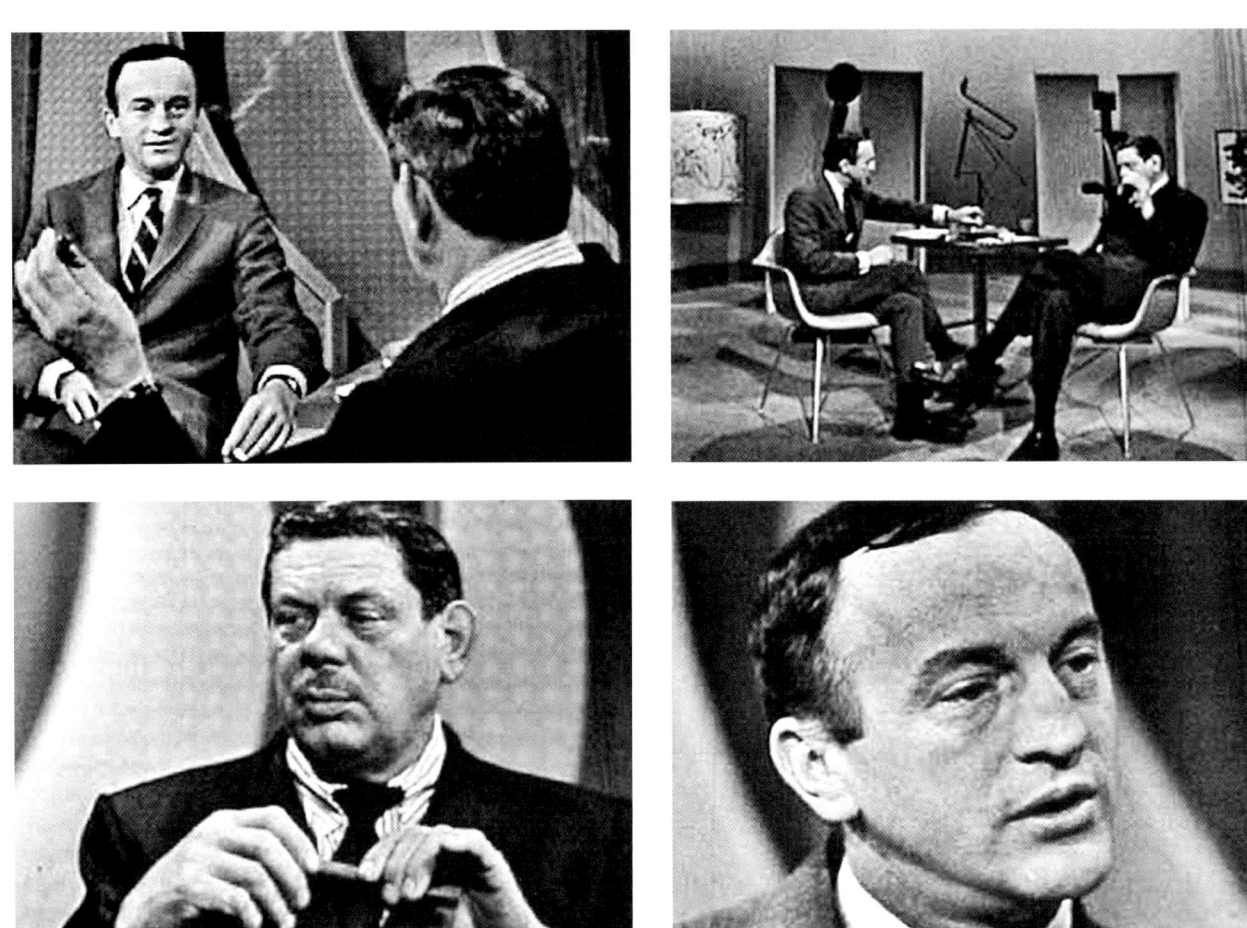

23 Stills from *Art New York: The Sculpting Master of Bolton Landing*, 6 November 1964.

that "It is really very kind of you to come down from Bolton Landing and *abandon* the work in order to be here."[70] With a smile, O'Hara laid stress on this word "abandon," further pushing the back-and-forth about personification and subtly giving one last reply to Smith's joke. Smith understood only too well and replied with a similarly sly but off-topic in-joke, saying "Oh, I've had fun in New York. After all, I've heard some nice music, and seen dancing girls and things like that, you know."[71] O'Hara smiled broadly in response and said "Well, thank you very much, and I hope to see you in Bolton Landing very soon." Smith jovially responded, "Come back." After this chummy interchange, O'Hara concluded the interview by reading the closing narrative voiceover from the teleprompter.

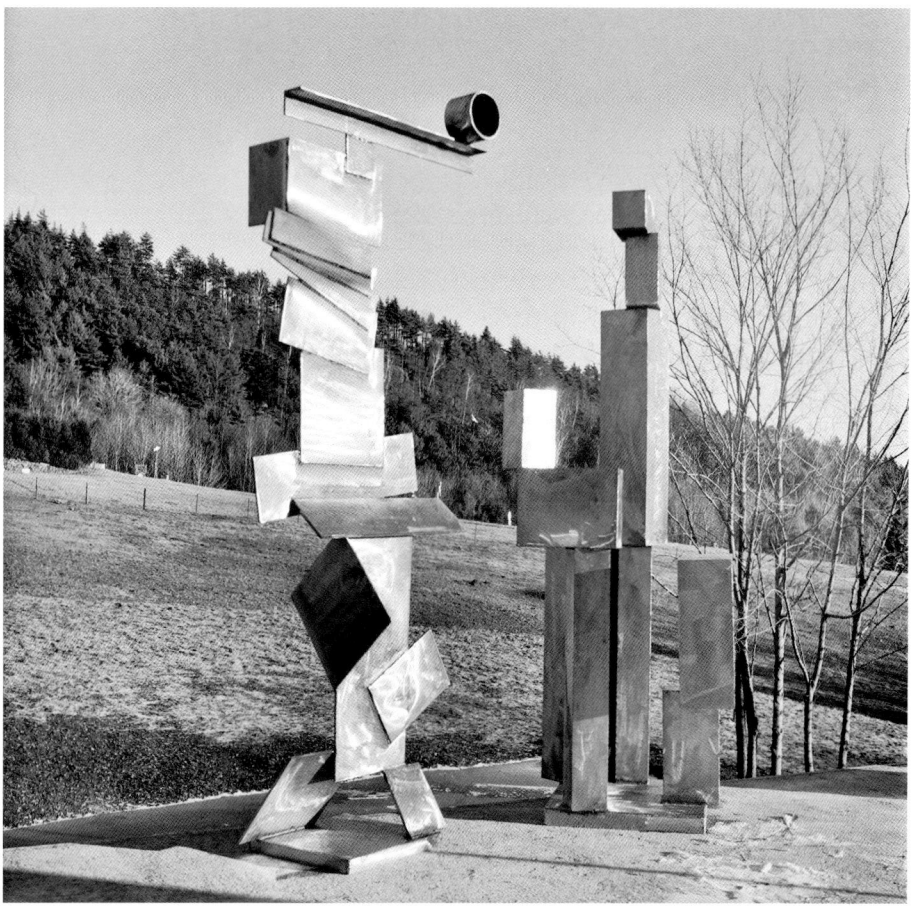

24   David Smith, *Lectern Sentinel*, 1961 and *Cubi VIII*, 1962. Photograph by the artist, Bolton Landing, New York.

Nowhere is O'Hara's take on Smith's work clearer than in that closing voiceover narrative, scripted by him before the interview was taped. It deserves to be quoted at length:

> It is the nature of sculpture to be there. If you don't like it, you wish it would get out of the way, because it occupies space which your body could occupy. David Smith's sculptures are, big or small, figurative or abstract, very complete, very attentive to your presence. They are generous. They have no boring views; circle them as you may, they are never napping. They present a total attention and they are telling you that *that* is the way to be. On guard. In a sense they are benign, because they

offer themselves for your pleasure. But beneath that kindness is a warning: don't be bored, don't be lazy, don't be trivial, and don't be proud. The slightest loss of attention leads to death. The primary passion in these sculptures is to avert catastrophe, or to sink beneath it in a grand way. So, as with the Greeks, Smith's is a tragic art.[72]

In and among its camp grandiosity, this summary by O'Hara offers another manifestation of his admiring personification of Smith's works and of his continued identification with them. For him, Smith's sculpture was "very complete, very attentive to your presence" and "On guard."

This attentiveness that O'Hara admired and aspired to in Smith's sculpture was not empty praise, and it is worth pausing to consider this central theme of the voiceover text. The idea of the works being "attentive" was a concise description of the formal and compositional complexity of Smith's sculptures that, in turn, related to some of O'Hara's main priorities. Attention, as he wrote in another context, "equals Life, or is its only evidence."[73] This is what he saw reflected in Smith's work.

Smith's famously graphic welded steel surpassed logical or rational structure and held divergent elements in the air in a carefully balanced dynamic instability (fig. 25). Even though static, Smith's works do not rest. They sometimes appear top-heavy or precarious, but this is merely evidence of their abandonment of the conventional ways in which structures (and bodies) are engineered. It is the weld – Smith's Abstract Expressionist gesture – that holds the steel elements together in the air (fig. 26). Combined with Smith's ability to create works that cohered yet varied from each viewing angle, Smith mobilized his "drawing in space" practice to defy the limitations of conventional load-bearing structures and their solidity.[74] This is especially true of the standing works of the 1950s (especially the *Tanktotem* and *Sentinel* series) and 1960s (the *Zigs* and *Cubi*) that were some of O'Hara's main points of reference (see figs 10, 14, 19, 31).[75]

The aliveness, alertness, and engagement that O'Hara attributed to Smith's sculptures stood in direct contrast to how he conceived of traditional statuary, a recurring image in his poetry.[76] Smith's works subverted the frontality that was the basis of that tradition (which was derived from the faciality of the human form).[77] In this subversion of the figure, O'Hara recognized that Smith's work could, as well, be understood to offer an analogous departure from the statuary tradition's organizing presumptions (most notably, the belief in a unified subjectivity).[78] It was variability that Smith's sculptures allegorized and that made them party guests whom he wanted to know and to be like. For O'Hara, conventional statuary was

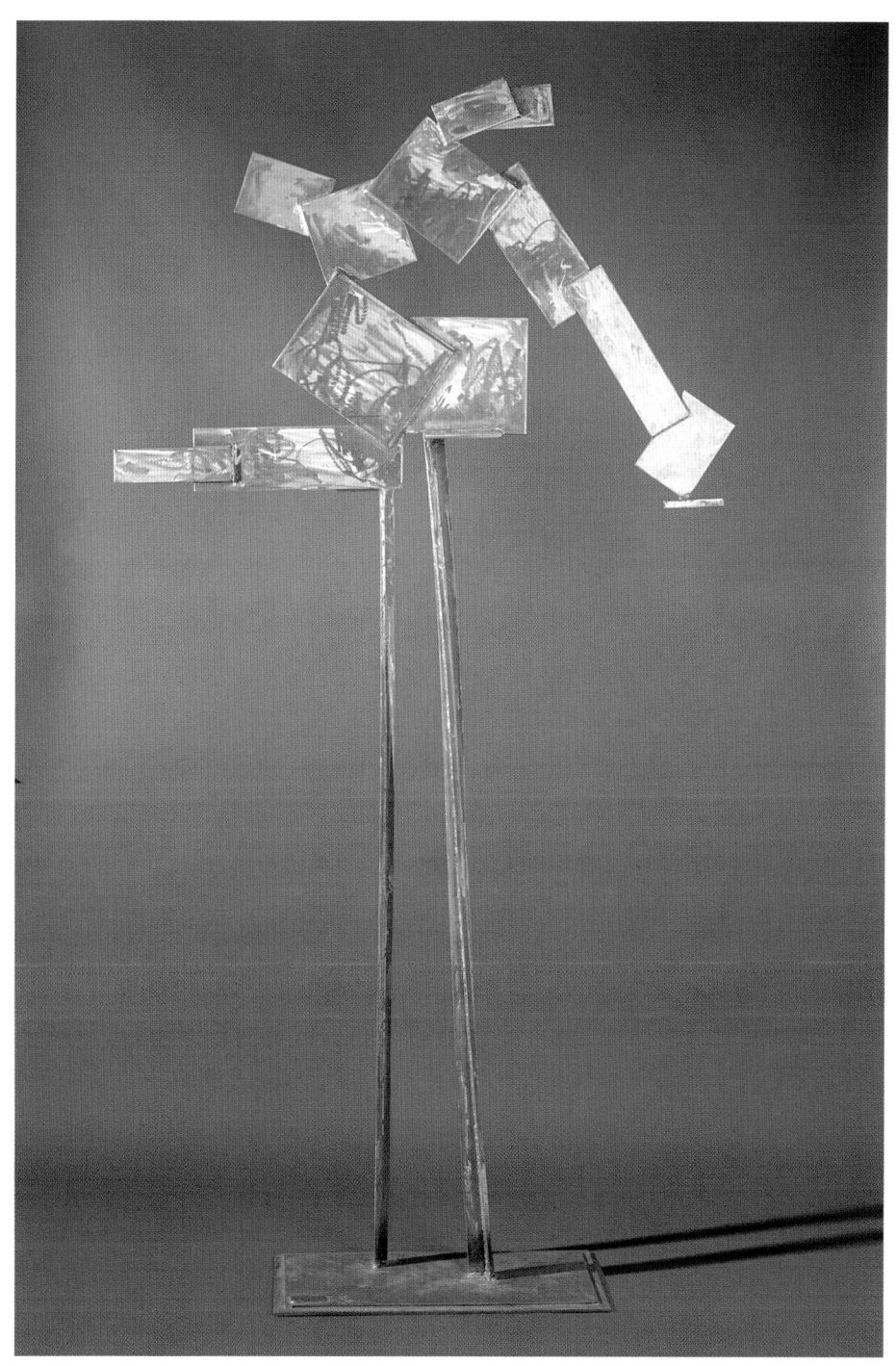

25 David Smith, *Fifteen Planes*, 1958. Stainless steel, 289 × 150 × 40.7 cm (113¾ × 59⅛ × 16 in.). Seattle Art Museum, gift of the Virginia Wright Fund, 74.1.

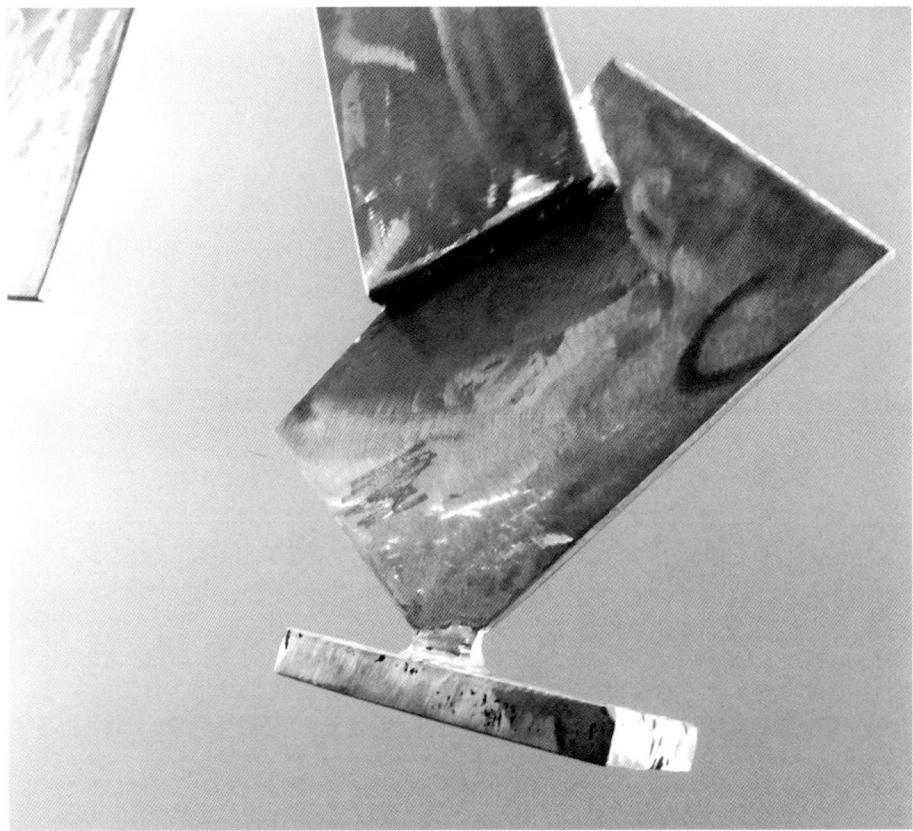

26   Detail of David Smith, *Fifteen Planes*.

implacable and cold, despite its potential for beauty or evocation of memory.[79] In the exemplary poem "Having a Coke with You," written in 1960, O'Hara wrote "it is hard to believe when I'm with you that there can be anything as still / as solemn as unpleasantly definitive as statuary when right in front of it."[80] This was what he saw Smith's sculptures as overcoming with their dynamic balances and divergent profiles. Not only do Smith's works demand attention to their varying facets, but they also seem in their multifaciality to address multiple viewers' vantage points concurrently. They greet you from every angle, establishing the reciprocal alertness that O'Hara praised.

This multiplicity was also a priority for his poetry. One of the characteristic traits of O'Hara's practice was the way in which his poems mobilized fleeting, contradictory, and seemingly inconsequential details. His later works, in particular, often subvert the conventional definition of a well-

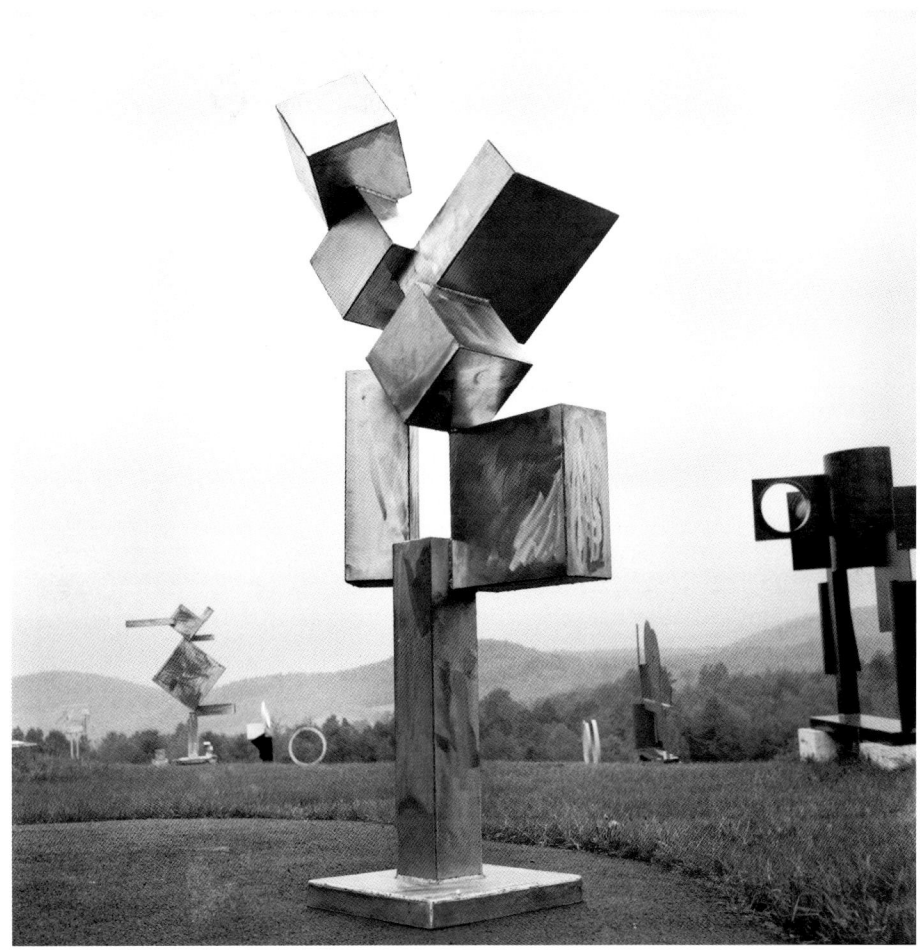

27 David Smith, *Cubi XI*, 1963. Stainless steel, 233.7 × 73.7 × 96.5 cm (92 × 29 × 38 in.). Photograph by the artist, Bolton Landing, New York.

crafted poem with its consistent and coherent imagery or settings. Instead, his poems came to be riddled with overheard phrases, distracted glimpses of headlines, and a mixture of memories and quotidian observations. Paul Carroll called this "impure poetry" and Charles Altieri expanded on this idea in his nomination of O'Hara as one of the first postmodern poets.[81] He wrote: "O'Hara then shows how the poet need no longer feel committed to organic unity as a principle of poetic construction."[82] O'Hara himself said it best in his manifesto "Personism": "I just heard that one of my fellow poets thinks that a poem of mine that can't be got at one reading is because I was confused too. Now, come on. I don't believe in god, so I don't have to make elaborately sounded structures."[83] O'Hara eschewed the imperative for consistency in his poems, replacing it with the rapid-fire pace of minute-to-minute experience. (It is for this reason that his staccato poems have sometimes been seen as the analogue to Abstract Expressionist "action painting" in their directness and immediacy.[84]) The concatenated structure of his poems with their interpenetrating memories and observations has, furthermore, been understood as means through which O'Hara articulated a plural self against a conviction in a unified subjectivity.[85] This idea of the self as multiple has been seen as one of the key themes of his work and is often summarized through reference to the earlier, 1956, poem "In Memory of My Feelings" (which Jasper Johns took as a title for one of his paintings) with its lines such as "My quietness has a number of naked selves" and the famous "Grace / to be born and live as variously as possible."[86]

The idea of multiple selves that O'Hara posited through his own work found a visual analogue in Smith's with its multiple profiles and compositional complexity. That is, he found Smith's sculptures resonant because, similarly, they represent an assault on the conventional goals of structural coherence, unity, and consistency. Smith's first major chronicler, Rosalind Krauss, made this attack on the tradition of the statue a central theme of her work on him. She wrote in 1969 that, "For Smith it became clear that he could subvert the coherence of the free-standing object by making each facet of the sculpture radically different from the next."[87] Krauss rightly emphasized this crucial artistic strategy of Smith's, later calling it his "principle of radical discontinuity."[88] Smith's "radical discontinuity" was akin to O'Hara's "impure poetry" (again to use Carroll's apt phrase). Both deny an underlying logic evident in and determining of every part, replacing it instead with the display of variations and inconsistencies that, nevertheless, cohere in a dynamic balance. As O'Hara wrote in his 1961 article on Smith, "Unification is approached by inviting the eye to travel over the complicated surface exhaustively, rather than inviting it to settle on the whole first and then explore details. It is the esthetic of culmination rather than examination."[89]

In its attempt to find a language to express the dynamism and activity of Smith's sculptures, O'Hara's 1964 closing voiceover text pursued what he had meant when he earlier wrote in the 1961 letter to Smith that "I'd like to *be* one of those sculptures!"[90] With regard to such thrilled statements by O'Hara, Lytle Shaw has argued: "In O'Hara's writing, the collapsing boundaries between disciplines [of criticism and poetry] parallels what was perceived, to many readers' anxiety, as a collapsing erotic or social space: his 'poetic' appreciation is frequently an intense affective response to the works of his friends and lovers." Consequently, Shaw argues, O'Hara's criticism is bound up with (and energized by) "the implication of inappropriate closeness."[91] Such an affective intensity underwrote O'Hara's enthusiasm for Smith's sculptures and, indeed, his own projective identification with them. Richard Howard once wrote of O'Hara's criticism: "there is an attempt to find, in his own vocabulary and rhythms, a means of appropriating what he responds to in the work before him – for O'Hara a critical statement is always an *appropriation*."[92] O'Hara's calling the sculptures "on guard" and saying he wanted "to *be*" them was just such an appropriation. It was this close embrace of the sculptures that drove his enthusiasm for Smith and that became a central theme of his engagement with the sculptor's work.

That is, O'Hara was not just consistent in his laudatory personification of the works; he was earnest. It was his way of evoking the perceptual complexity offered by a Smith sculpture and of asserting a closeness and intimacy with Smith's intentions. This was enabling, as it allowed O'Hara to grasp and to articulate the complexity of Smith's departure from the statuary tradition. However, the personification O'Hara called out for Smith's work was – like the sculptures themselves – unforeclosed and endlessly variable. Such potentiality for the sculptures to evoke open-ended personhood is precisely what Smith shut down with his awkward joke that crassly arrested their complexities and blocked O'Hara's identification with them. Nervously or not, Smith's quip made it clear that, in this case, there were nothing but girls.

TO BE OR NOT TO BE: O'HARA'S ASPIRATIONS, SMITH'S ASSIGNMENTS, AND GIRLS

O'Hara's long-running interpretation of and identification with these sculptures were well-known to Smith. The sculptor's interjection of the "girls" barb, in this regard, was not just a response to O'Hara's question about them being people occupying his house. More deeply, Smith's joke was informed by the poet's repeated characterization of the sculptures as people he would like to be. However, O'Hara's overriding concern was not to literalize them as bodies but, rather, make grand claims for them as ideal states of being. With his quick and dismissive joke, however, Smith invoked a gendered hierarchy in which the sculptures were arbitrarily assigned a position subordinate to him. He did not even call them "women." In-

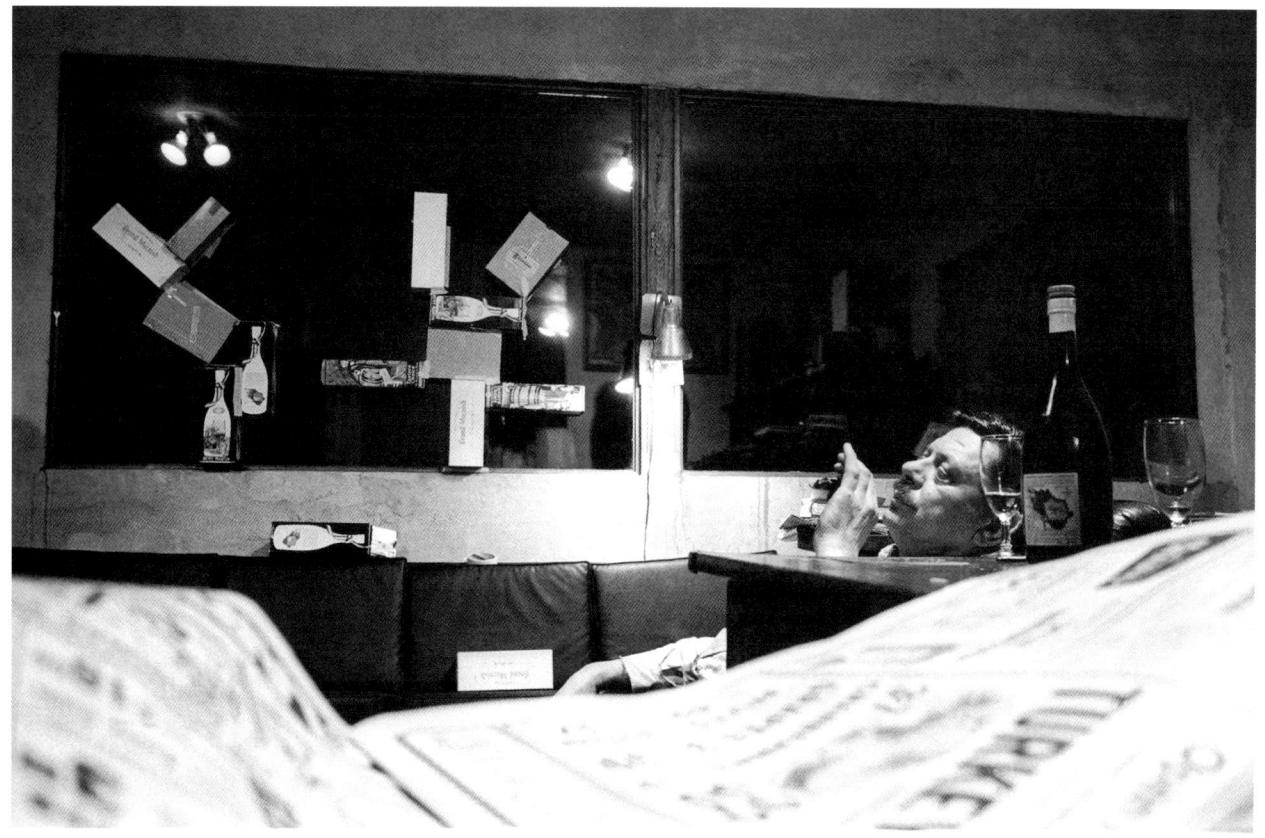

28 David Smith smoking in his studio, Bolton Landing, New York. Photograph: Dan Budnik, 1962.

deed, he made sure to designate their age using the diminutive "girls." This became even more apparent when he then asserted that he did not make "boys." This implication of age in Smith's comments further served to block the idea that his works could be people – adults – with whom one could identify and aspire to be, as O'Hara wished. In Smith's joke, they became gendered bodies, not ideal subjects. In effect, he narrowed the mutability and range of O'Hara's open-ended line of inquiry, blocking the ways in which one could imagine being or having them. His joke was chauvinistic and reductive, and he himself pulled back from its full implications by back-tracking and changing his designation to "personages."[93] Nevertheless, the move served to repossess his own sculpture from O'Hara's framing account of his works while simultaneously dispossessing the poet's claims to aspiration and identification.

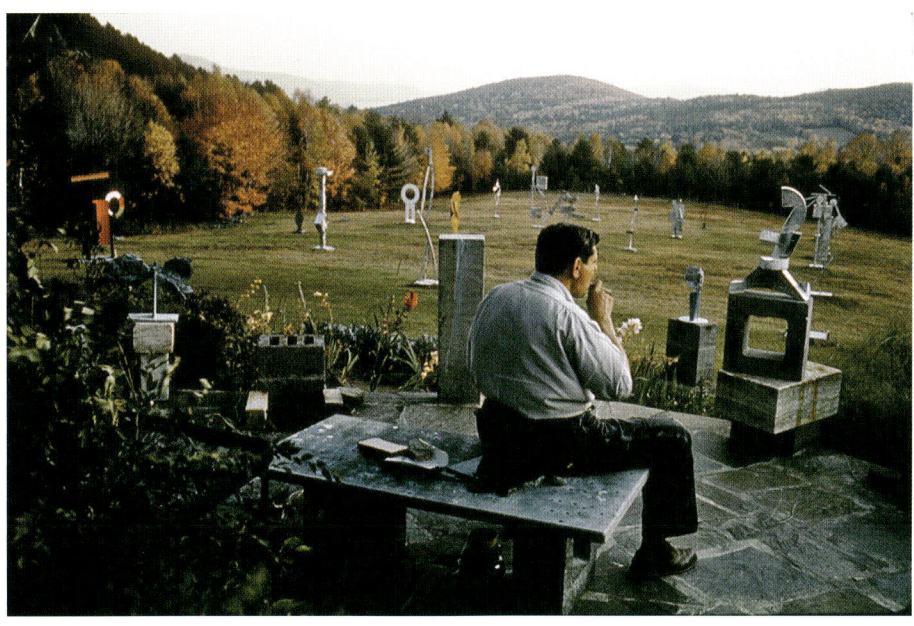

29   David Smith seated on the back terrace of his house, overlooking the south sculpture field, Bolton Landing, New York. Photograph: Dan Budnik, 1962.

The implied ground against which Smith's joke made sense was, of course, his cognizance of O'Hara's sexuality. Smith not only problematized O'Hara's easy identification with the sculptures but also preemptively declared his own erotic interests with his reply. (Remember the "dancing girls" comment a few minutes later.) Under the glare of the camera lights, Smith reacted to O'Hara's innocuous question and its prompting of the artist, the viewers, and himself to see Smith's work as people. The vague invocation of houseguests incited Smith's need to define just what kind of people they were and for whom. Even if just an inside joke shared between friends, Smith's comment about his works all being female asserted his own preferred sexual object.[94] This question of sexual objects was never the content of O'Hara's personifications of or identifications with Smith's sculpture, but Smith made it clear that it was his in making such a reply. In this sense, his was a tactic of preemption of a possible (but not actually declared) threat posed by O'Hara's question.[95] In other words, O'Hara's query incited a compulsion to rein in the variability and multiplicity that Smith's abstract bodies supported. As Brian Massumi has written about threat and preemption, "A threat can have specificity and lead to decisive preemptive actions with a corresponding level of specificity without having

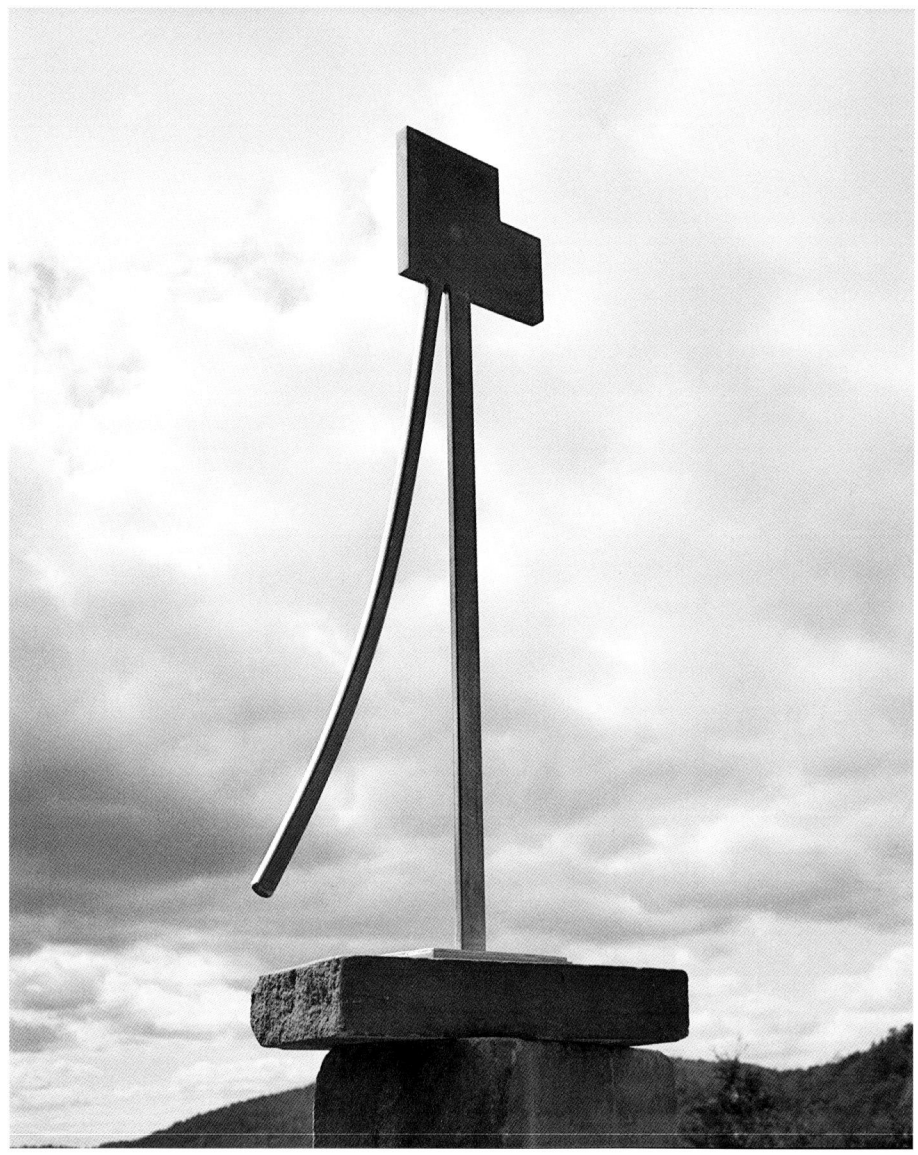

30 David Smith, *Lonesome Man*, 1957. Silver, 71.1 × 24.1 × 11.4 cm (28 × 9½ × 4½ in.). Photograph by the artist, Bolton Landing, New York.

'real substance' or objective 'credibility.'"[96] Such was the case with Smith's awkward joke in reply to O'Hara's (probably initially innocent) open-ended question. Based in Smith's long-term awareness of O'Hara's desire to see his sculptures as people he would like to be, the sculptor's joke forestalled

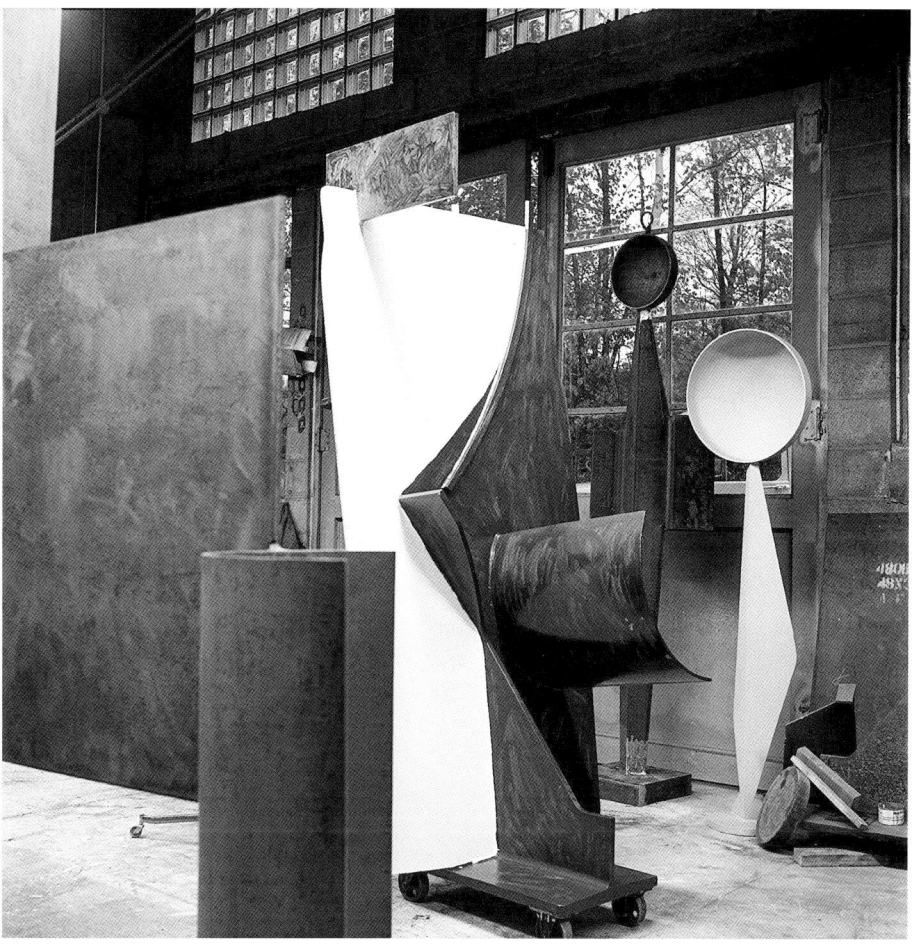

31 David Smith, *Zig III*, 1961 (in progress, partial view), *Black White Forward*, 1961, *Ninety Father*, 1961 (unfinished state), and *Ninety Son*, 1961 (unfinished state), outside Bolton Landing Shop, New York. Photograph by the artist, c. 1961.

any possibility for O'Hara's identification with the sculptures, which were, thenceforth, "only girls."

While sexuality functioned as the ground for this jokey exchange, it was not its main content. The fact that Smith and O'Hara were of different sexualities prompted a sparring about how to personify Smith's abstract statues, but its terms were about the gender of Smith's sculptures. As I shall discuss shortly, this anecdote reveals, more fundamentally, the compulsion to assign gender to these otherwise abstract bodies as a means of qualifying them as persons.

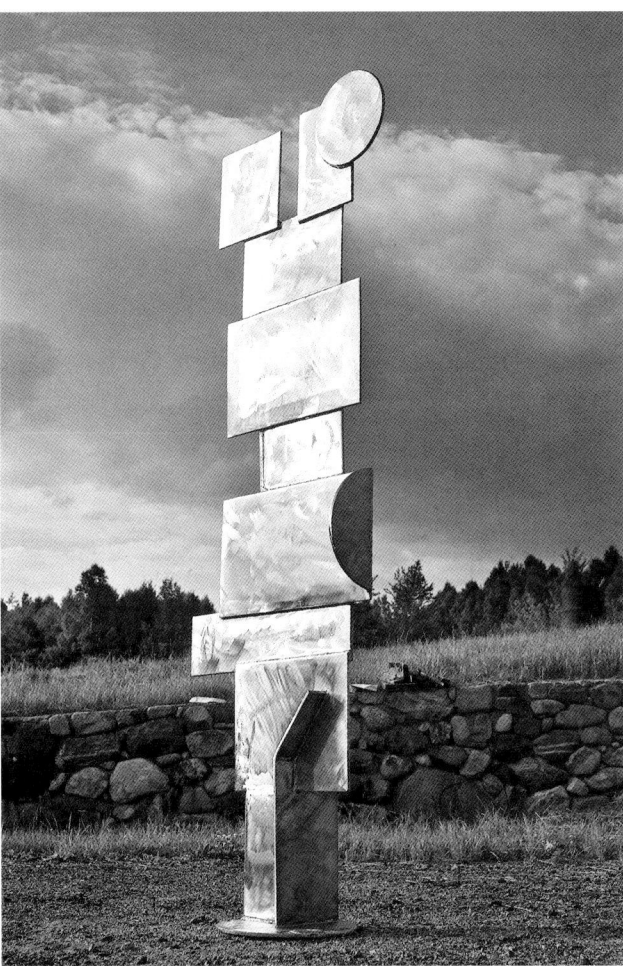

32 David Smith, *XI Books III Apples*, 1959. Stainless steel, 238.8 × 88.9 × 41.3 cm (94 × 35 × 16¼ in.). Photograph by the artist, Bolton Landing, New York, c. 1959.

First, though, it is worth further considering the multiple ways in which Smith might have meant the word "girls," since he pointedly used this word to block and to chide O'Hara. None of these, however, apply to all the sculptures in the way that Smith's unequivocal statement seems to demand. One has to remember the presence of sculptures like *Ninety Father, Ninety Son*, or *Lonesome Man* (see figs 7, 30, 40) in Smith's work as examples of male-gendered sculptures, in addition to the substantial amount of other works with no ostensible link to gender or to the body (fig. 32). As "girls," however, there are a few options. One response in interpreting Smith's joke could be to assume that "girls" could mean Smith's daughters, Candida and Rebecca, who were an important part of Smith's life. They feature in many of the titles, and he would even write inscriptions on some of his sculptures to them. There are certainly many sculptures of this period wrapped up with his daughters. In a reading of Smith's work as autobiographical, Paul Tucker has asserted that Smith's daughters were "cornerstones of his identity" and therefore central to his sculpture of the 1960s.[97] However, such a one-to-one correspondence works only in limited cases, and Tucker himself tempers his own claim. In a footnote, he cites Smith's "I don't make boy sculptures" statement but acknowledges that with regard to calling the sculptures girls "it is difficult to know whether this was a specific reference to his daughters or to girls in general."[98] To return to the 1964 interview with O'Hara, even if "girls" meant "daughters" (and I do not believe the tone of the conversation bears this out), Smith's joke still placed them in a gendered subordinate position and derailed O'Hara's vague aspirations to be them.

Given the context of the interview and the intersubjective dynamic of Smith and O'Hara, however, it is much more likely that this usage of the term "girls" falls in line with the ways in which he used that term to mean lovers or sexual objects. Smith's first wife, Dorothy Dehner, reported that, after he broke with his second wife, the sculptor "referred to the sculptures as 'girls' who would never run away."[99] In its contrast to the departed former spouse, the "girls" of this statement were the lovers who would never themselves flee. Similarly, in the interview with Thomas Hess published in the catalogue to the 1964 Marlborough-Gerson show that was the occasion of the televised interview, Smith talked about the series of paintings of nude models he had been making the previous year. A statement by Smith edited out of the version published in the catalogue referred directly to the genitalia of the "girls" who were posing for him.[100]

It is this sexualized and demeaning usage of the word "girls" that Smith used in another 1964 interview, this one for the radio station WNCN in New York, just two weeks before the televised conversation with O'Hara. Conducted in the gallery on 25 October, Smith's radio appearance was similarly intended to introduce viewers to his work. Marian Horosko, the interviewer, had little of the intimate familiarity that O'Hara had with Smith's work, and the questions were far more basic and pedestrian with Smith being more on guard. At one point, Horosko asked Smith whether he liked viewers to touch his work. Smith replied, "I think sculpture along with any art is a strictly visual response….I touch with the eye. I touch – I think the sensitivity is mostly from the eye. You touch girls but you look at sculpture."[101] Unlike the statement to O'Hara that he would make a fortnight later, Smith's assertion here clearly sexualizes the term "girls" but also makes clear how his sculptures are, by implication, neither girls nor sexual. Not only does this further refute the idea that "girls" meant daughters, but this statement (made close in time to the conversation with O'Hara) also indicates that Smith in this exchange did not feel the need to sexualize or gender his sculpture in the way he would two weeks later.

In his conversations with Hess and Horosko, Smith used "girls" to denote sexual objects and referred to real or imagined human bodies. Speaking to O'Hara, however, Smith applied that term to his sculptures, collapsing the distinction he made to Horosko about touching girls but looking at sculpture. If nothing else, however, it is abundantly clear that, when seen in relation to his sculptures, Smith's joke could not apply equally or comprehensively to his work. Whatever "girls" might have meant at that point to Smith, it was clear that he wanted his personages be interpreted in relation to him, not O'Hara. For, in the rapid interchange, Smith remembered to make the negative assertion (twice) that he "did not make boy sculptures" as means of saying that he only made girls.

O'Hara was not passive in this exchange. His sly question of "very angular girls?" did a lot of work in this regard, for with it he exposed, subtly, the contradictions and larger implications of the jokey exchange. Smith's works rely strongly on an anthropomorphic echo as a point of reference and comparison, even if they do not resemble the organization and components of human bodies. As Krauss once remarked, "one feels confronted not so much by a surrogate for figural presence as by an abstract sign for it."[102] The invocation of the human body and the real gap between it and Smith's sculpture generate what Smith would call "the *image recall* of orders more true than the object itself."[103] It was this tenuous link between the abstract sculpture and the human figure that produced the possibility of visualizing the latter anew. In the face of his realization of O'Hara's potentially different (but never stated) gendering of sculpture as surrogate or as sexual object, Smith used humor to recoil from the very semantic openness he had made a life-long aim for his work. O'Hara understood this reversal and the absurdity of Smith's sudden assignment of gender, and his question about angularity was a fitting riposte, forcing Smith (and the listeners) to map the question of gender back onto the material sculptures and their formal arrays. For his part, O'Hara had never literalized gender assignment in his writings on the sculptor's works or even in his interview questions to the sculptor.[104] However lofty his comments on Smith's sculptures as the stars of meadow cocktail parties, their personification was never as bodies, sexual objects, or as gendered. It was Smith who invoked a binary logic of sexual object choice and a dimorphic account of gender in making a statement that was, for him, uncharacteristically limiting and simplistic.

Throughout his career, Smith emphasized that his conceptual and artistic process involved an open-ended discovery that could not, under any circumstances, be boiled down to words. For instance, he once wrote: "We must revolt against all word authority. Our only language is vision."[105] As early as 1952, Smith asserted that "Words are little limited things, but people are afraid to like things without words" and spoke of the need to "take culture out of the hands of the 'word mongers.'"[106] In another context, he further distinguished art from words, saying: "Art history to the artist is visual. His art is not made up of historian's words of judgments."[107] Similarly, he remarked about his 1951 sculpture *Hudson River Landscape*, "You can reject it, like it, pretend to like it, or almost like it, but its understanding will never come with words, which had no part in its making, nor can they truly explain the wonders of the human sensorium."[108]

This attitude is pervasive and consistent in Smith's writings and statements. It is this agenda that makes the statement "They're all girls, Frank" so contradictory to his practice – not because he declared them all female but, more fundamentally, because of the compulsion, at that moment, to use words to assign a fixed gender category at all and to all. That is, Smith's own joke and the posthumous use of it as iconographic key both ran counter to the sculptor's pursuit of formal and semantic openness in his works and his own dislike for the limitations words imposed on art. Smith prized the ability of his work to defy categorization and direct symbolization. "Nothing is closed – everything is open," he once asserted.[109] In his 1964 interview with O'Hara, however, Smith perpetrated the offense that he regularly criticized others for: simplifying his work through words.

FIXING GENDER: THE HISTORIOGRAPHIC LEGACY OF AN AWKWARD JOKE

With his little question, "Very angular girls?" O'Hara introduced a disturbance in Smith's otherwise easy characterization – a disturbance that was well-supported by the works themselves. He got Smith's joke and laughed as he chided back about how the sculptures contradicted it.[110] In short, O'Hara exposed the gap between the abstract body and the human body. That this question was, in fact, a disturbance is attested by the subsequent publication of this famous exchange. Taken out of context as a nervous and awkward joking, these lines of dialogue have been reprinted in the Smith literature because they seem to clarify a relation between Smith and his sculpture, explaining the persistence of figurative echoes in the work of the exemplary abstract postwar sculptor. Furthermore, these lines have been used to forestall any question of gender variability in Smith's work, and a recurring concern in the Smith literature has been to validate Smith's assignment of gender to his works. Much of the posthumous writing on Smith's sweeping statement has taken its contradiction as something to be explicated and fitted onto his sculptures. Nowhere in the literature is there an acknowledgment that this was a joke nor is there any account of O'Hara's long-running engagement with Smith or of his personifying take on Smith's sculptures. This is because, as the interview was first excerpted and published in the memorial issue of *Art in America* to Smith in 1966, the transcription was different from the actual interview that I have quoted. This version was part of a collection of Smith quotations assembled for the issue by Cleve Gray, who liberally rewrote the statements (a practice that continued in his widely read collection of Smith's writings published in 1968).[111] In the version edited by Gray and initially published in *Art in America* in 1966, O'Hara had been made to agree with Smith. As can be seen, some heavy editing went on:

> O'Hara: You must feel that there are all these strange objects around you, in your whole studio or outside?
>
> Smith: Well, they're all girl sculptures. Oh, they're all girls.
>
> O'Hara: Yeh, they're all female sculptures.
>
> Smith: I don't make boy sculptures…[112]

Whether by intention or error, O'Hara in Gray's published version was made to agree with Smith rather than to question the applicability of Smith's assigning of gender. Gone is the contention of O'Hara's response as well as the implication that Smith's statement might not be taken as valid. The actual interview tells a different story, but it was this altered transcription of the exchange that has been exclusively cited as a key to Smith's sculpture in the subsequent literature.

For his collection of the sculptor's writings, *David Smith by David Smith*, Gray used just one line of edited exchange, further entrenching it as crucial to the understanding of Smith's practice. He juxtaposed "I don't make boy sculptures" with illustrations of Smith's paintings of female nudes in an attempt to make a visual equivalency between Smith's figurative two-dimensional work and the supposed truth of this statement.[113] Beyond this polemical one-line excerpt of the O'Hara–Smith exchange, Gray's 1966 altered version remained the singular source for these statements. These lines have become a touchstone in the writing on the sculptor, recurring throughout the literature and surfacing when the question of his abstract sculptures' relation to figuration is raised.[114] In fact, it is so often rehearsed that its repetition in the literature has sometimes been misconstrued as Smith's own. For instance, Karen Wilkin asserted (again relying on the 1966 transcription) that Smith "*frequently* claimed that he made only 'girl sculptures,' once denying in an interview with Frank O'Hara that he ever made 'boy sculptures.'"[115]

Looking at the first monograph on Smith, Krauss's *Terminal Iron Works*, one can see the effects of this misquotation being installed in the trajectory of the Smith literature. In that book, Krauss argued that Smith's formal complexity amounts to a concerted effort to frustrate the desire for possession.[116] Building on his use of the word "totem" for one series (see figs 33, 37, 39), she then associated this frustration with the prohibition of incest and taboo (*pace* Sigmund Freud's 1913 *Totem and Taboo*[117]), based on Smith's awareness of psychoanalysis. Relying on the 1966 *Art in America* transcript of the O'Hara interview in two instances, she expanded on its mistranscribed claims to argue that works such as *The Hero* and the *Tanktotems* "assert their identity as females."[118] She based this claim on an interpretation of the parts of the sculptures that she could equate to sexed characteristics of the normative human body (fig. 35). Thus, the two asymmetrical triangular forms on *The Hero* become "incipient breasts" and the rounded tank lids that are used throughout the *Tanktotem* series "locate the pelvic region." Such assignments rely on a leap of faith in which select parts of the sculpture are understood to signify specific (gendered) body parts, while the others that do not conform to a conventional human morphology are simply disregarded (such as the repeated jags on the topmost side of the rectangular frame in *The Hero*; fig. 36). The *Tanktotems*, too, only partially seem to fit any such direct gendered reading. While a work such as *Tanktotem IV* might seem more or less to support a reading of the curves as feminine curves (fig. 37), what are we to make of the placement of the boiler lid in *Tanktotem I* (fig. 33) or the lack of bodily curves in the three-legged *Tanktotem IX* (fig. 39)? Indeed, a later reviewer claimed in 1987 (in one of the few comments that break with the historiographic dominance of Smith's 1964 joke), that the *Tanktotems* and *Sentinels* "appear both astonishingly anthropomorphic and androgynous. They play havoc with our unquestioning assumption of the absolute distinction between…masculine and feminine."[119] Krauss, however, mistook the flawed transcription for Smith's word and struggled to make his unruly sculptures conform to the binary logic of his joke about not making boys.[120] This was the case even when faced with contradictory

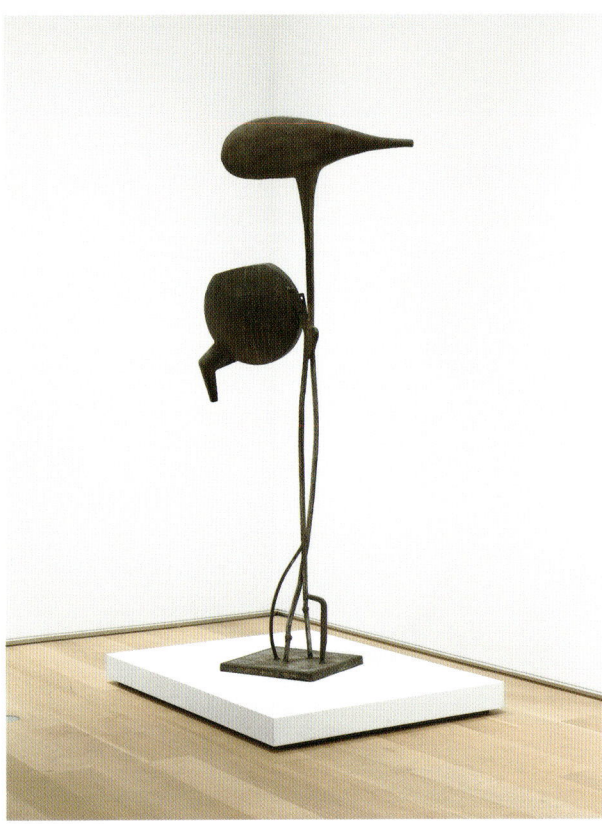

33 David Smith, *Tanktotem I*, 1952. Steel, 228 × 99 × 42 cm (89¾ × 39 × 16½ in.). Art Institute of Chicago, gift of Jay Steinberg and Muriel Kallis Steinberg in memory of her father, Maurice Kallis, 1953.193.

OPPOSITE 34 David Smith, *Cubetotem 7 and 6*, 1961–2. Stainless steel, 313.7 × 230.5 × 56.5 cm (123½ × 90¾ × 22¼ in.). Photograph by the artist, Bolton Landing, New York, c. 1961.

information, as with the poem Smith wrote about *The Hero* in which he claims "the subject is me."[121]

The attempt to force Smith's work into a dimorphic and binary account of gender with an either/or conclusion, misses – like Smith himself did in making that diffusing joke – the divergent, more various accounts of the possibilities of seeing and reviewing bodies nominated as human that Smith's abstract personages offer. As William Tucker noted, it is precisely the lack of correspondence with human bodies that more accurately describes Smith's practice: "Smith was engaged in making sculptures which deliberately convey the presence of human figures, without in any sense being naturalistic, or symbolic, in terms of making reference part by part to elements of the body."[122] Nevertheless, the adherence to the sincerity of Smith's statement leaves little room to account for the openness of the sculptures, as with Krauss's contradictory assertion that a decidedly non-figurative construction such as *Cubetotem 7 and 6* had a "female presence" (fig. 34)[123]

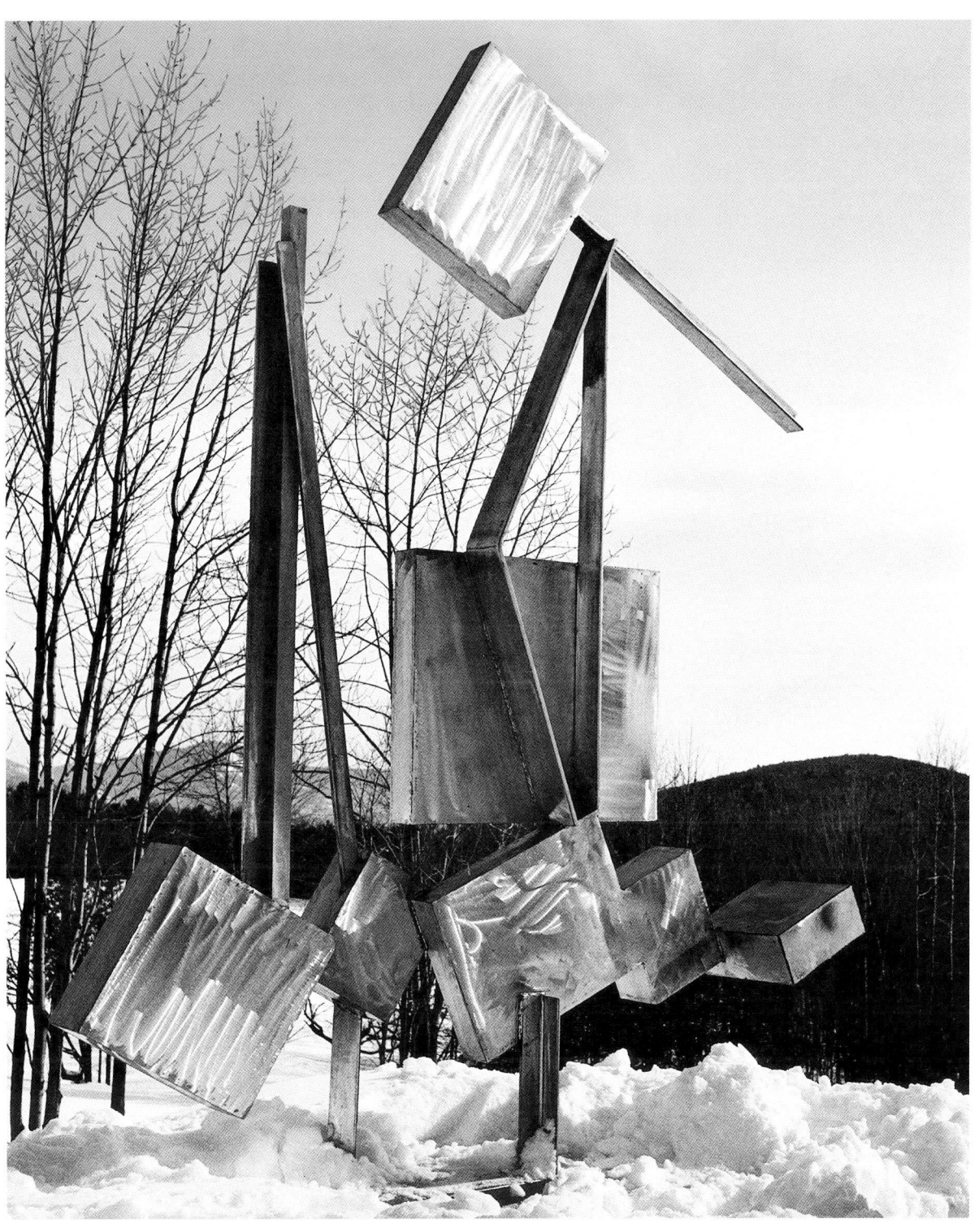

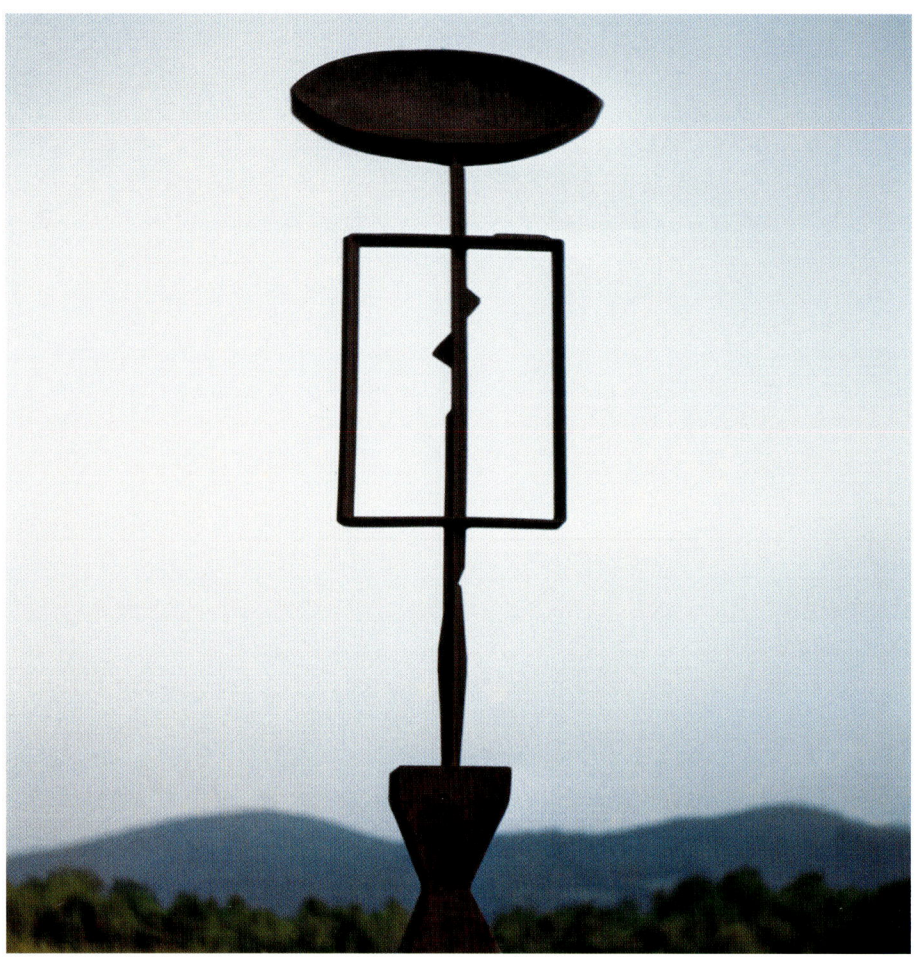

The historiographic legacy of Smith's statement was determined by Gray's flawed (or even falsified) transcription that expunged O'Hara's playful irony and his questioning of the leap from sculptural personage to human body. The actual ambiguity of Smith's sculptures (not to mention the resistance to Smith's joke offered by O'Hara) has been simplified through the recurring reliance on this epigram as sincere and self-explanatory. It is the compulsion to repeat this quotation in the literature that I find interesting. It offers little insight into the formal or semantic complexity of Smith's work and is, blatantly, inaccurate as a sweeping generalization about it. Nevertheless, it has proven reassuring to many, and it has been used to stabilize and domesticate the wildness of Smith's abstract figures.

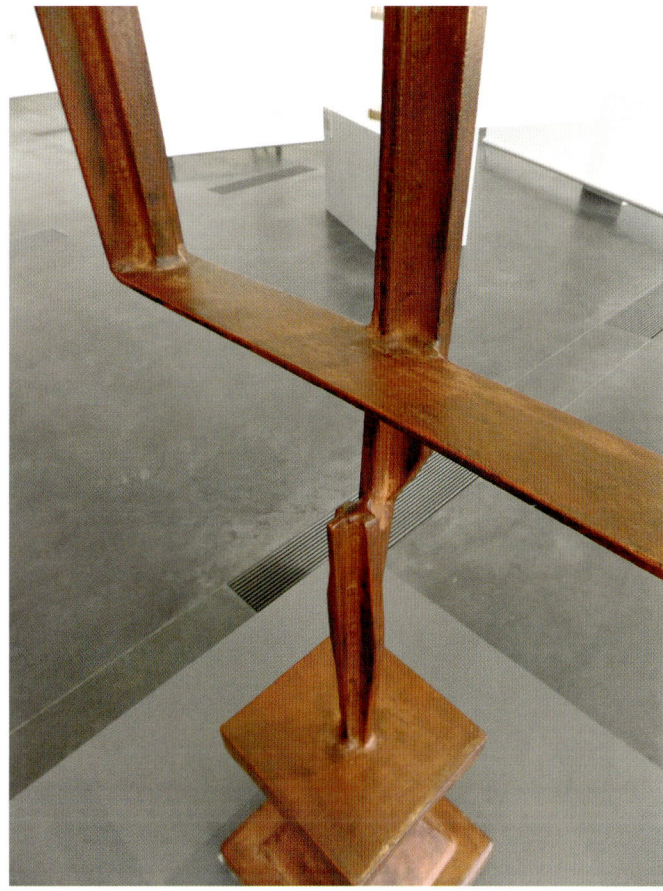

OPPOSITE
35 David Smith, *The Hero (Eyehead of a Hero)*, 1951–2. Painted steel, 187.2 × 64.8 × 29.8 cm (73¾ × 25½ × 11¾ in.). Photograph by the artist, Bolton Landing, New York, c. 1952.

RIGHT 36 Detail of David Smith, *The Hero (Eyehead of a Hero)*.

THE UNRECOGNIZABILITY OF ABSTRACT BODIES

The art-historical elevation and dissemination of Smith's declaration that he did not make "boy sculptures" demands critical assessment, for its posthumous legacy has insured that it became no longer just a joke. Beyond the recovery of this history and the restoration of instability and humor to the epigram, an analysis of this case offers further lessons about the importance of attending to the resistances by works of art to the gendered words used to describe them. That is, the awkwardness of Smith's and O'Hara's interchange points to fundamental questions with regard to the abstract body: namely, how gender assignment predicates the nomination of an abstract or unorthodox morphology as "human" and how that morphology exceeds and calls into question that very nomination. Smith's work is decisive in the dissolution of the statuary tradition via abstraction and its

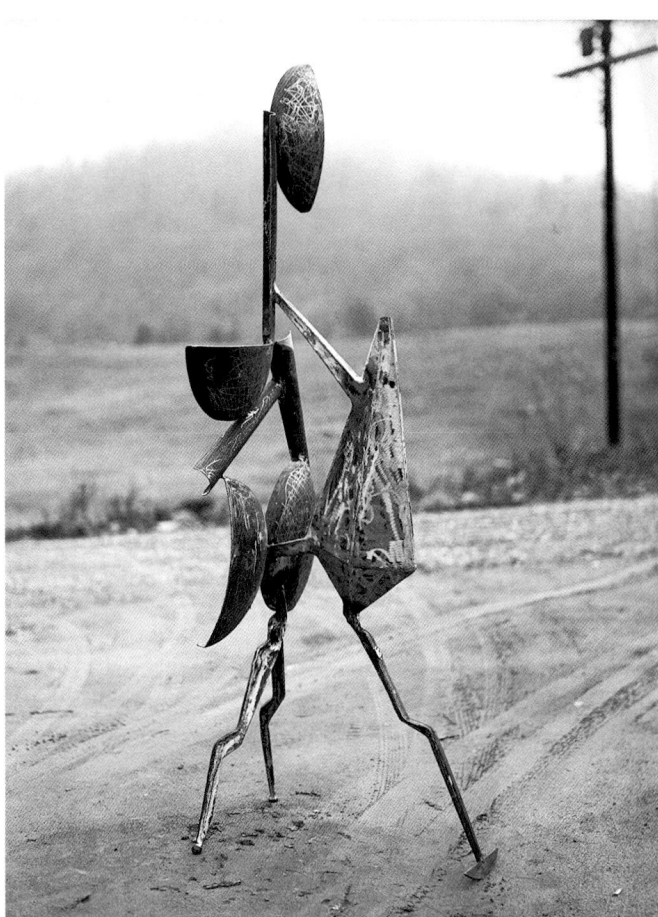

37 David Smith, *Tanktotem IV*, 1953. Steel, 237.5 × 86.4 × 73.7 cm (93½ × 34 × 29 in.). Photograph by the artist, Bolton Landing, New York, c. 1953.

reconstitution (by his successors) as the "expanded field" of objects, spaces, situations, and places. His sculptures represent the final attack on the coherence of the statue (as Krauss has decisively proven in her many writings on the artist). He created new constructions, previously unseen and unimagined, that nevertheless purported to refer, even in the most oblique or incomplete manner, to the human figure. He banished the mimetic human form while nevertheless invoking its palimpsest as the foil for his practice. This has generated great richness and complexity in his work. In turn, that push and pull with the human form has proven a compelling issue in the criticism and history of Smith's work – and it is this issue that the epigram "I don't make boy sculptures" seems to address and to mollify.

Perhaps the central concern for the history of sculpture has been the rendering of the human figure, and Smith's attack on that tradition created,

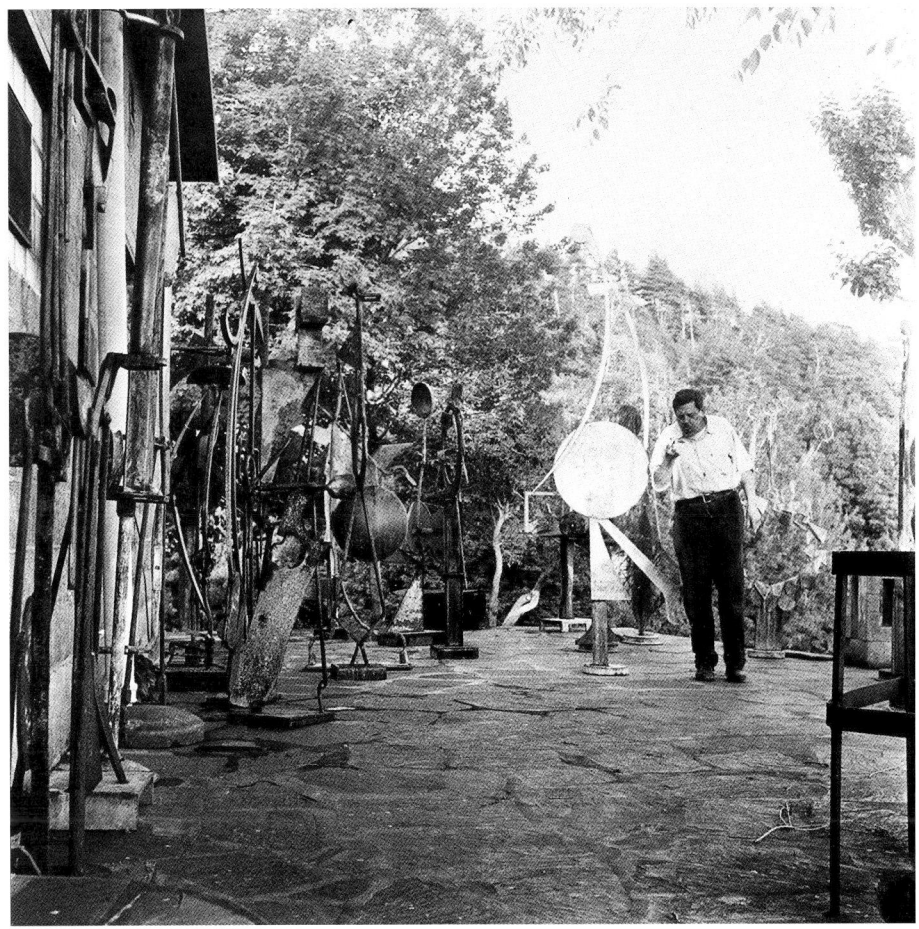

38 David Smith with Voltri-Boltons outside of his studio, n.d. Photographer unknown.

more than any of his contemporaries, unorthodox and novel configurations that demanded to be legible within and yet expansive of that lineage. The sculptures are, as Smith would have it, new images previously unimagined. Rather than see Smith's sculptures for what they are, writings that rely on the joke-turned-epigram instead assign a conventional gender as the means to remake these inhuman forms as human.

As Judith Butler has cogently argued, "Gender figures as a precondition for the production and maintenance of legible humanity."[124] In writing this, Butler was making an argument, in part, about transgender lives and their exclusions from the category of "human." New configurations of genders, bodies, and sexes with multiple and previously unimagined terms challenge

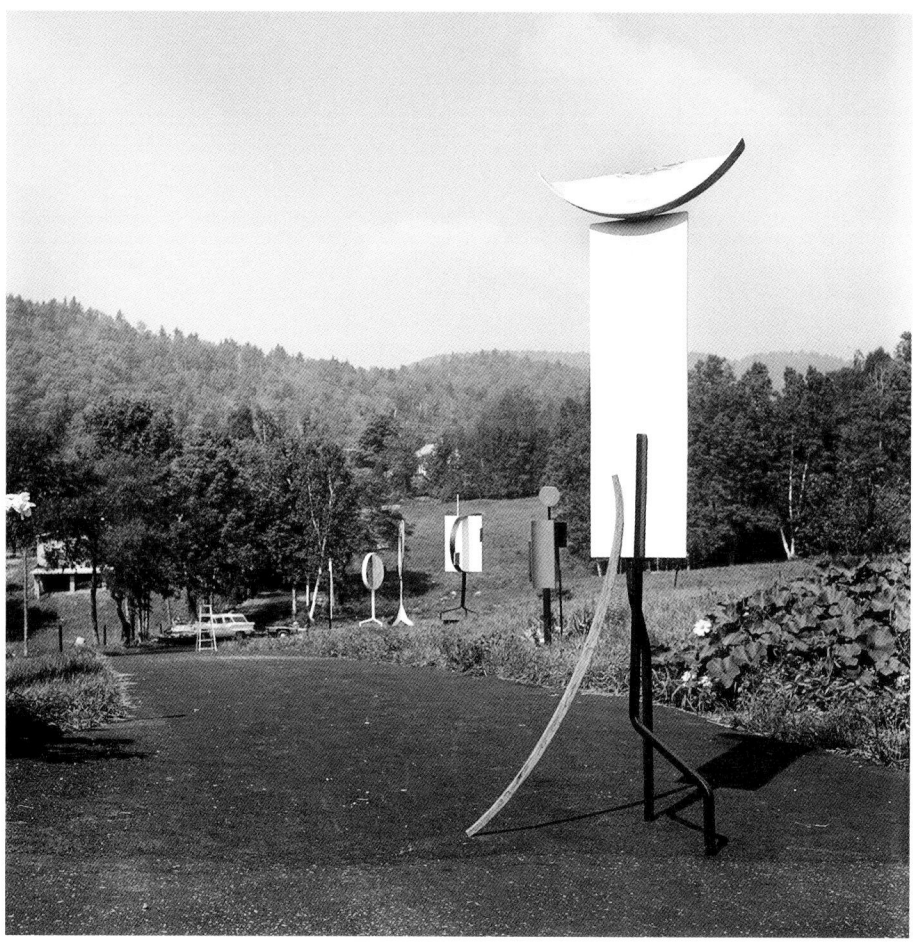

39 David Smith, *Tanktotem IX*, 1960. Steel, painted, 228.6 × 83.8 × 61.3 cm (90 × 33 × 24⅛ in.). Photograph by the artist, Bolton Landing, New York, c. 1961.

the order of dimorphism that determines categories of personhood and of humanity. As she argues,

> To posit possibilities beyond the norm or, indeed, a different future for the norm itself, is part of the work of fantasy when we understand fantasy as taking the body as a point of departure for an articulation that is not always constrained by the body as it is. If we accept that altering these norms that decide normative human morphology give differential "reality" to different kinds of humans as a result, then we are compelled to affirm that transgendered lives have a potential and

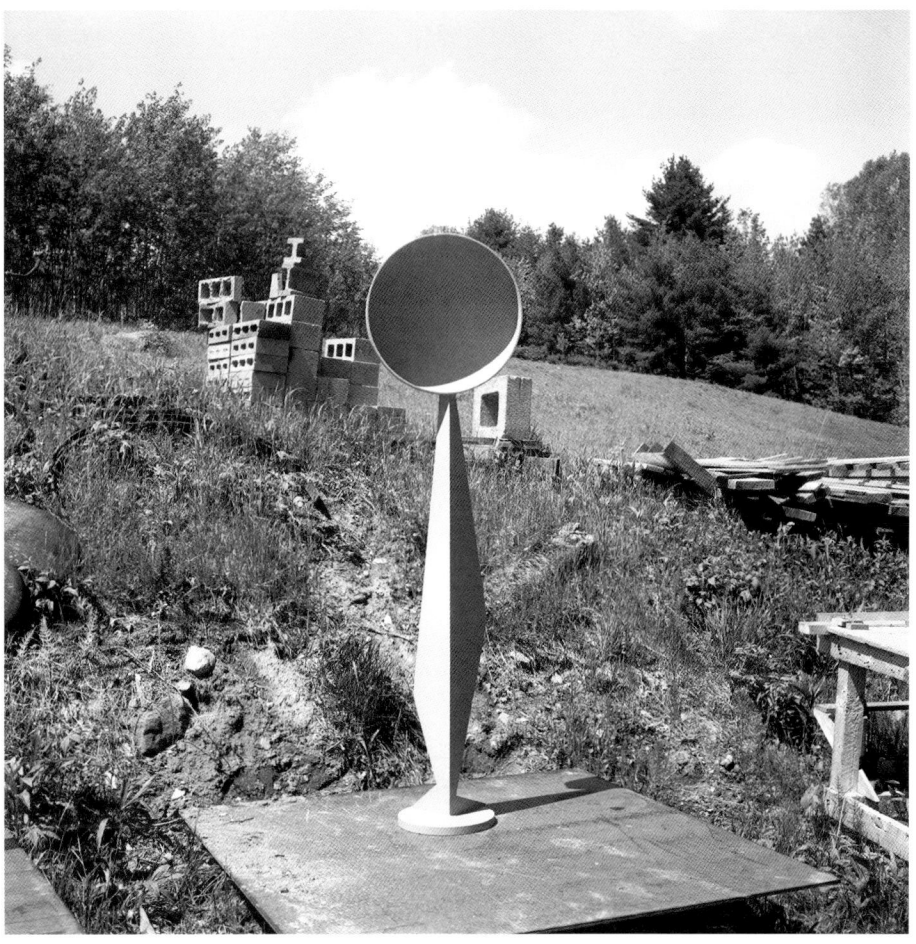

40 David Smith, *Ninety Son*, 1961 (unfinished state). Steel, painted, 188 × 50.8 × 33 cm (74 × 20 × 13 in.). Photograph by the artist, Bolton Landing, New York.

actual impact on political life at its most fundamental level, that is, who counts as human, and what norms govern the appearance of "real" humanness.[125]

In its reference to and utter departure from the human form, the abstract statue does nothing less than offer an analogous visualization of the challenge to the norms that govern humanness. Standing at the crux of modern sculpture's abandonment of the human form and the dissolution of the traditions of the freestanding statue, Smith's sculptures – in all of their contradictions – offer the most cogent and generative case of this. It

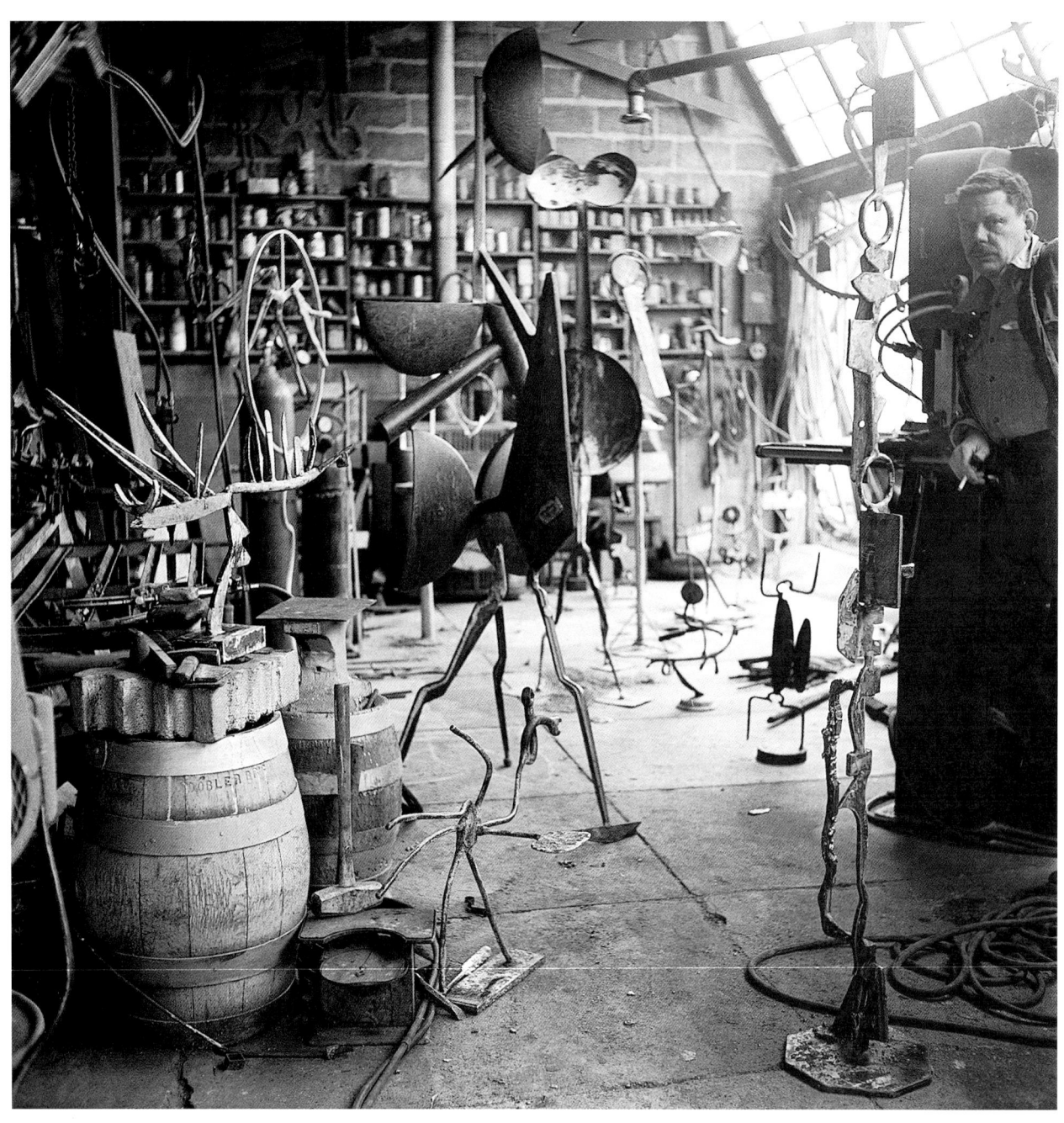

41 David Smith in his Bolton Landing Shop, with sculptures from 1953 and works in progress. Photograph by the artist, c. 1953.

is no surprise that the assignment of gender to these abstract bodies has proven so seductive since Smith made his awkward joke. That assignment forecloses the more open and unprecedented possibility that Smith's sculptures present.

Rather than accept Smith's joke as sincere, it is my claim that the very unruliness of his and O'Hara's exchange (and of Smith's sculpture generally) demonstrates that the unorthodox body – in its unrecognizability – can disrupt the finality of that assignment of gender and of humanity. When the abstract body is reduced to normative linguistic assignments of personhood via dimorphic gender, the results are unsatisfying, aphasic, and scotomatous. I see both the alteration of Smith's joke and the compulsion to propagate it as epigram as symptomatic of an anxiety about the unorthodox body's capacity to resist the assignments laid onto it. The abstract body prompts different and divergent nominations depending on who is doing the assigning and for what reasons. In short, it is not really gender *ambiguity* that the Smith–O'Hara episode reveals. The sculptures' genderings occur after they are made. It happens each time the viewer (even if this viewer is Smith himself) nominates these abstract bodies as human figures. Here, gender is *successively and differently* assigned to these same bodies as the condition for them to be legible as persons or humans – a condition that is nevertheless exceeded and resisted by the abstraction of the works themselves. The posthumous canonization (and sanitization) of the Smith–O'Hara exchange attempted to arrest the capacity for successive and divergent gender assignments for Smith's abstract personages. It was singled out from the interview – and from Smith's voluminous writings and statements – as a means to block the possibility of unforeclosed gendering and to normalize the abstract body. As such, its use as a shorthand answer to the problems of personification and anthropomorphism has served to lock Smith's sculpture to a reductive caricature of his intentions, obscuring the complexity that he more often desired for his sculptures.

Smith's aims were shortcircuited at the moment when they were confronted with O'Hara's own interests in personification (and identification) and in his own version of openness as a means of making works of art "live" for him (both in his criticism and his poetry). In neither case does one learn much about the character or psyche of Smith or O'Hara. Rather, it is the repeated patterns in their public statements about art and in their works themselves that address and privilege a kind of abstract personification or figuration leading to this symptomatic moment of confronting the abstract statue as an abstract human. What one can learn from this episode is not just that Smith's sculptures appear ambiguous. That much has been evident to critics and viewers from the start. Indeed, ambiguity is a long-running and pervasive – yet unacknowledged – condition of any rendering of the human body. What Smith shows us differently, however, is how the furthest reaches of the rendering of abstract bodies results in moments of unintelligibility and retrenchment in which accounts of what makes a body human are brought to light and questioned, even if momentarily.

Again, Butler's later account of intelligibility can serve to highlight the stakes of this struggle to recognize:

> Sometimes the very unrecognizability of the other brings about a crisis in the norms that govern recognition. If and when, in an effort to confer or to receive a recognition that fails again and again, I call into question the normative horizon within which recognition takes place, this questioning is part of the desire for recognition, a desire that can find no satisfaction, and whose unsatisfiability establishes a critical point of departure for the interrogation of available norms.[126]

In short, the unrecognizability of Smith's statues resulted from the dissonance caused by his pursuit of non-mimetic and abstract forms that nevertheless retained the statue format and aspired to invoke the "human," the figure, and personhood. It is this, highly traditional, authority of the freestanding statue – to evoke ideal personhood – that Smith wished to redeploy, especially in the pivotal works of the late 1950s and early 1960s that were the context of O'Hara's writings and of the interview. When confronted with multiplicity through O'Hara's playful and neutered question, however, Smith rushed to fix gender and unrecognizability and to block the perceived threat of O'Hara's having or being his sculptures. The security of the category of "human" had been opened to interrogation, in Butler's sense. Smith had ardently pursued a departure from nature in his work only to face, at this moment, that his more open vision of nature and of the figure got away from him. Presciently, he wrote in a sketchbook in 1962 or 1963 about this vision: "nature is not the same – it varies for everyone by what is seen – rejected by what eyes refuse to see[,] censored[,] blocked out – by what privilege sometimes grants – by what fantasy projects."[127]

Ultimately, the 1964 anecdote is useful because it encapsulates a larger trend in modern sculpture, one that is characterized by a recurring engagement with the human figure combined with increasing degrees of abstraction. More and more, sculptors created abstract bodies that they, their critics, and their publics struggled to see in relation to the category of "human." Gender became the primary question in these negotiations, often – like

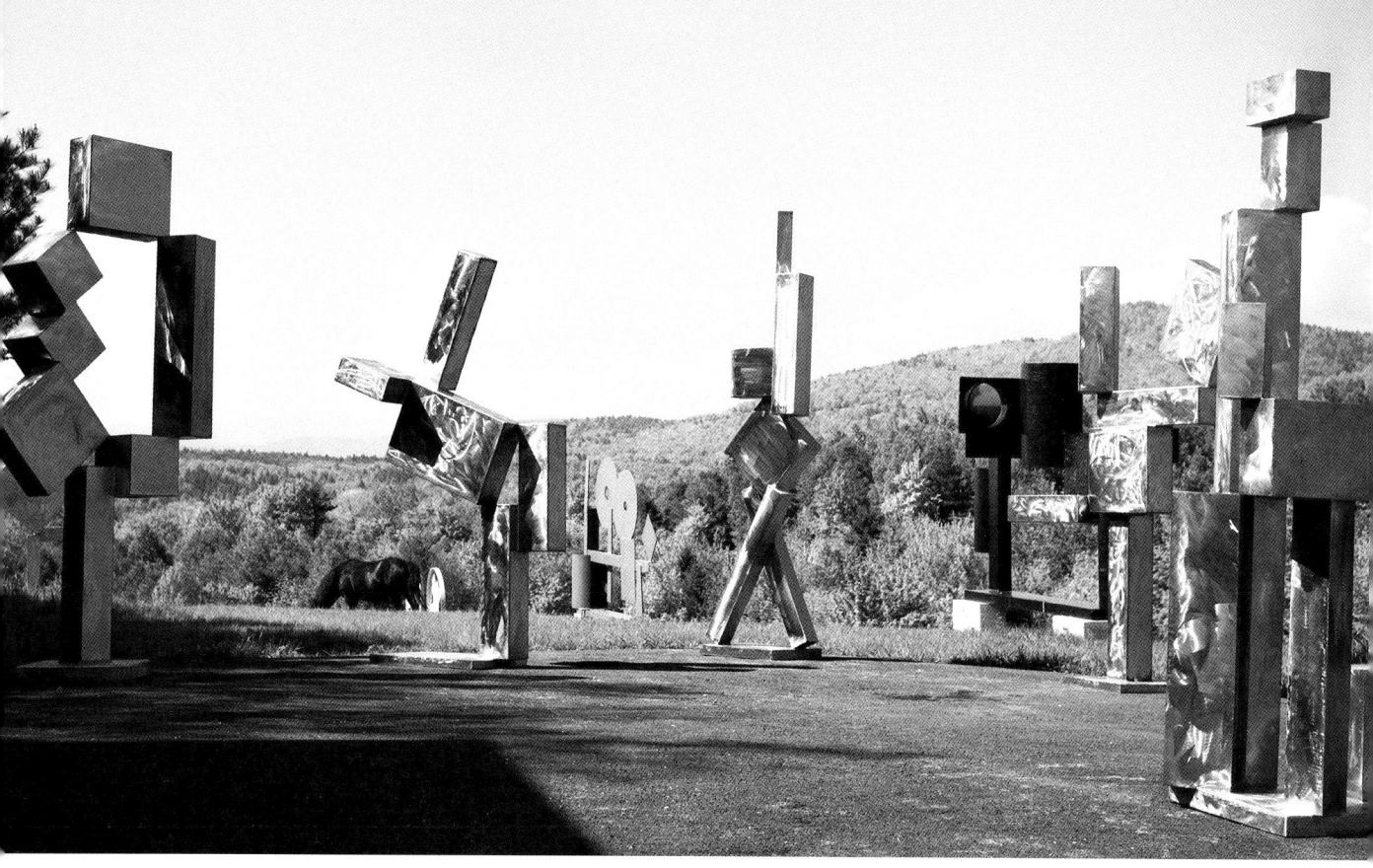

42   David Smith, *Cubi* and other sculptures from 1961 to 1963. Photograph by the artist, Bolton Landing, New York, c. 1963.

Smith in the context of O'Hara – shifting and being agreed on differently depending on the situation and the participants in it. In sum, what one can learn from these negotiations is how the position of abstract sculpture offered the possibility of seeing gendered bodies successively otherwise and anew. Smith may have wanted to see only girls or, even, just wanted to make a joke about wanting only girls as a result of the intersubjective back-and-forth of the public forum of the televised interview. Nevertheless, the fact that this needed to be asserted and could then be called into question points to the capacity of his sculptures to begin to visualize differently, and more variably, the category of the "human."

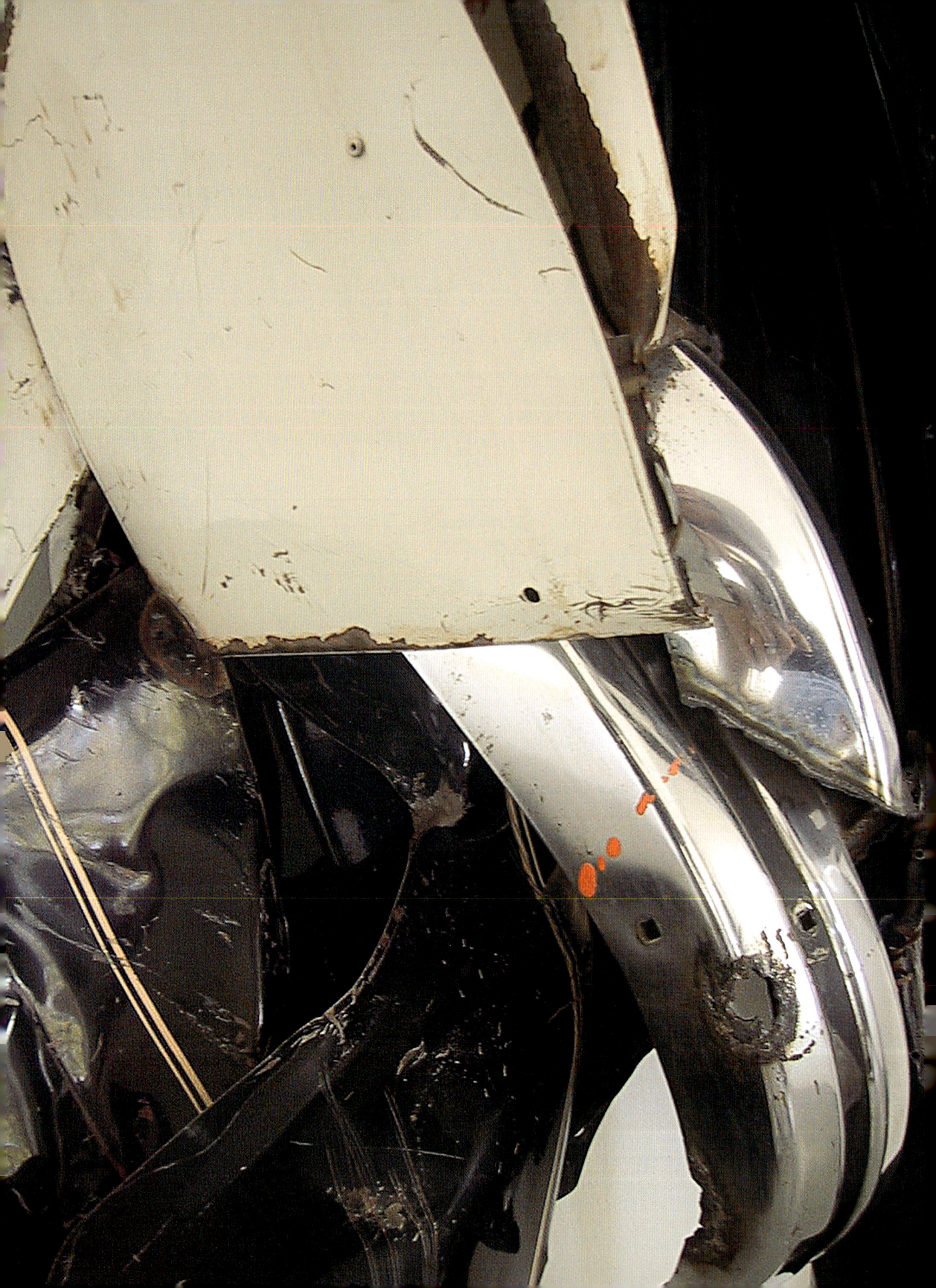

2

IMMODERATE COUPLINGS
TRANSFORMATIONS AND GENDERS IN JOHN CHAMBERLAIN'S WORK

There are two opposed and seemingly irreconcilable tendencies in the critical appraisal of John Chamberlain's sculpture. The first has been to treat the works as if they are simply and purely abstract, attending almost exclusively to their formal traits. The second tack – equally unsatisfying but no less persistent – has been to see the works primarily in terms of allusion: namely, as crushed automobiles commenting obliquely on a notion of the American dream. The critical writing on Chamberlain has been conflicted between these opposed camps since the early 1960s,[1] and both positions emerge as clichés that effectively foreclose the significance of his work at the outset. Neither the formalist nor the pseudo-Pop views of Chamberlain fit fully with the dynamic and poised play between form and reference in his work. The artist himself is often of little help, seeming – as he frequently does – to vacillate between the trivial and the vaguely profound in his statements and in the interviews that he gleefully sabotages. As Elizabeth Baker remarked, "He is, in fact, even as artists go, enigmatic, idiosyncratic, uneven, frustratingly difficult to pin down, and extremely resistant to classification."[2]

As a means to move beyond the standard ways in which Chamberlain's work has been discussed, it is imperative to examine those tactics and concerns that have remained consistent within his tendency to be "frustratingly difficult to pin down" in both his statements and his work. In particular, this chapter pursues the central technical and conceptual operation of Chamberlain's work – fitting. Not just in his sculptures but also in his

OPPOSITE 43 John Chamberlain, *Folded Nude*, 1978 (detail of fig. 67).

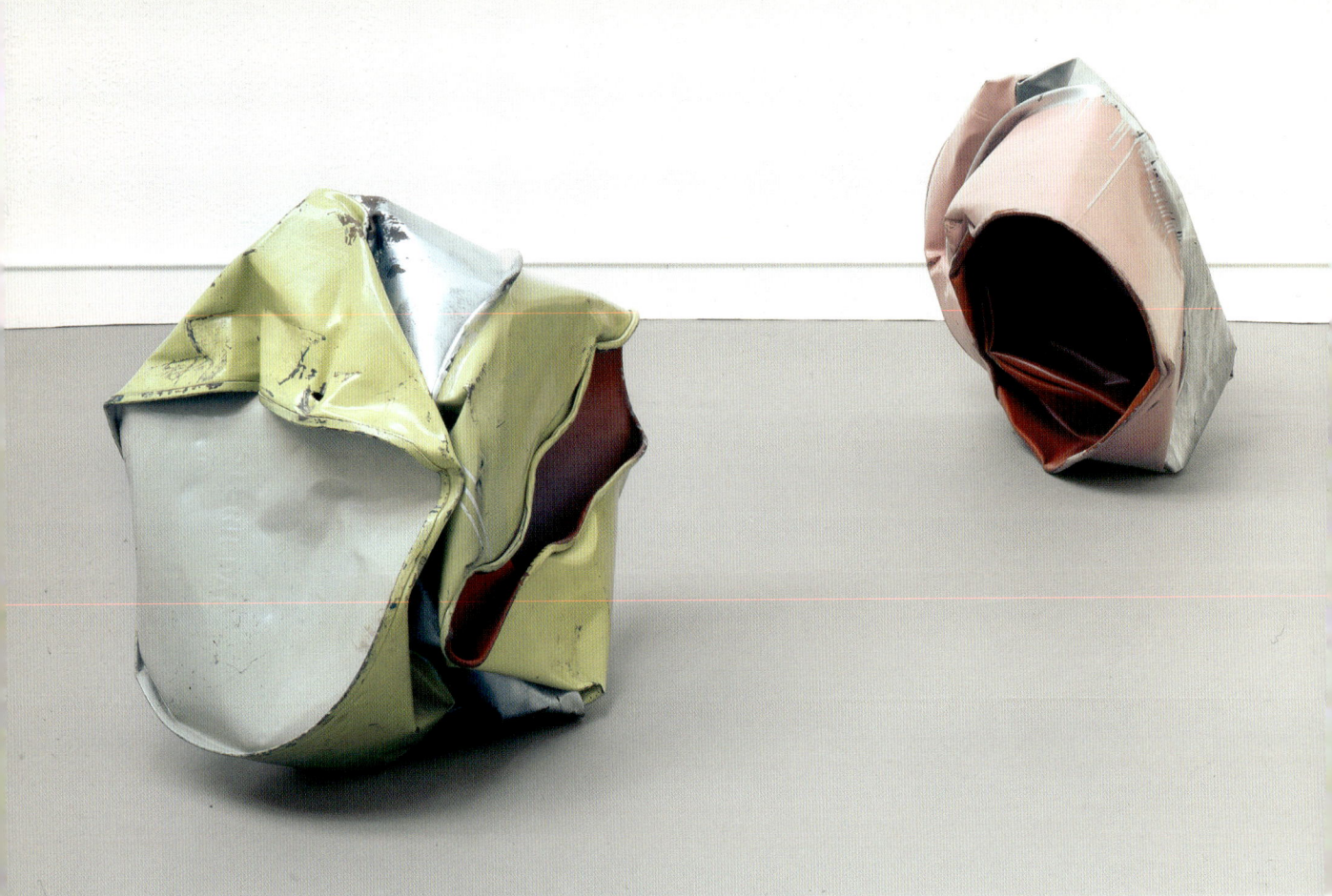

44 John Chamberlain, *Socket*, 1977 (cat. rais. 578) and *Socket*, 1977 (cat. rais. 579). Both painted steel, 68.5 × 82.5 × 48.5 cm (27 × 32½ × 19 in.) and 72.5 × 53.5 × 84 cm (28½ × 21 × 33 in.).

words, Chamberlain interlocked disparate elements that may have previously been discrete, differentiated, unrelated, or distant. Debates about whether his works are simply abstract compositions or patently signifying popular culture, however, often fail to pursue the full implications of what he enigmatically, but regularly, characterizes as this "fit."

In what follows, I focus on the patterns that emerge in the descriptions of Chamberlain's works – by others and, importantly, himself. As I shall argue, his statements provide not so much an explication as a parallel manifestation of his process of fitting, and an analysis of them allows for a better understanding of the material and formal dynamics of the works themselves. Evasive and elliptical, Chamberlain's way of talking about his practice and his sculptures was nevertheless consistent in its reliance on an analogy to which he repeatedly returned, that of sexual activity. His favorite way of discussing fitting was to call it sexual, and he has frequently made such statements as, "With my sculpture the sexual decision comes in the fitting

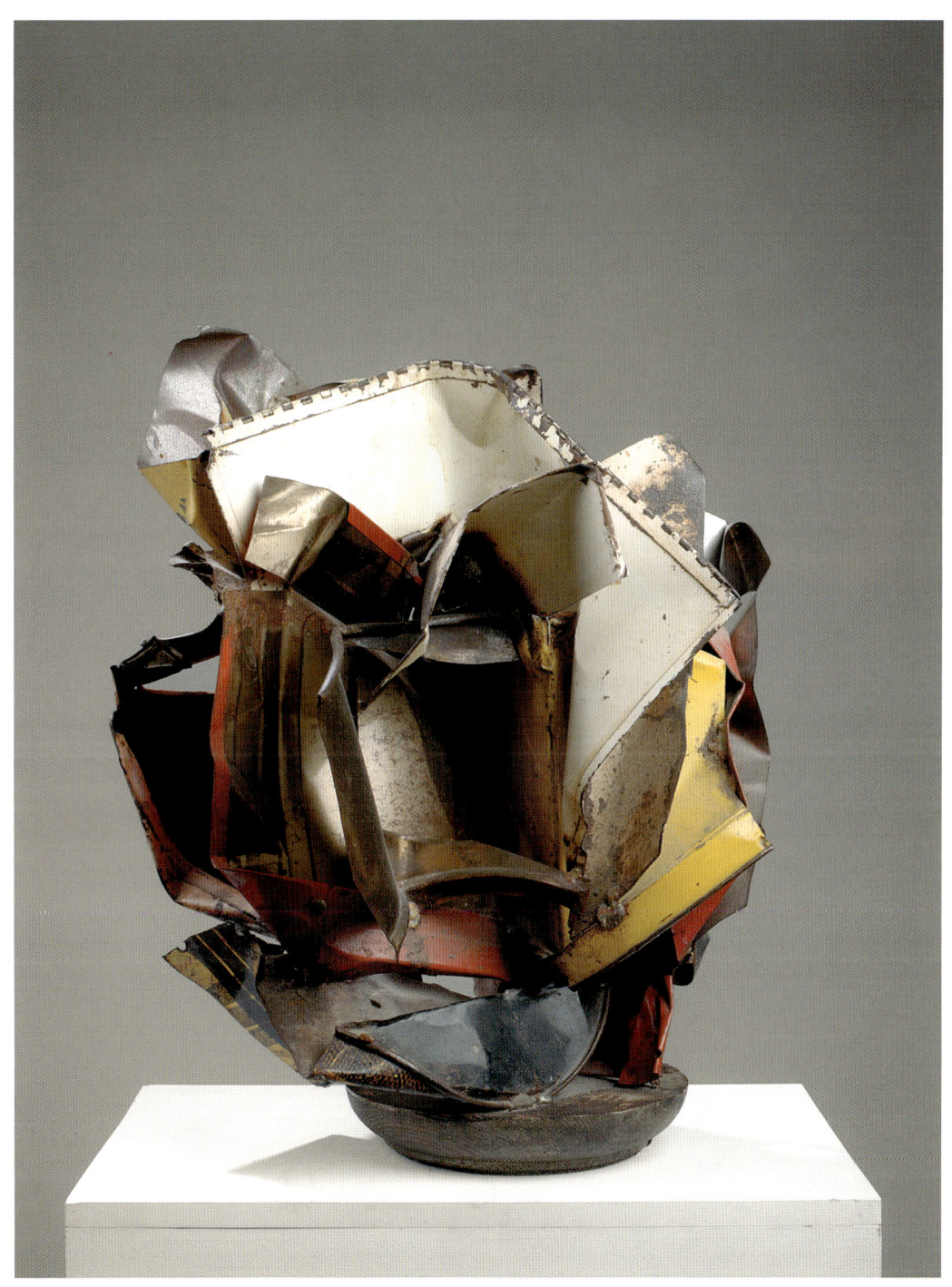

45 John Chamberlain, *Bouquet*, 1960. Painted metal, 40.6 × 33 × 33 cm (16 × 13 × 13 in.). Martin Z. Margulies Collection.

of the parts."[3] Reading through the writing about Chamberlain, one is immediately struck by the pervasiveness of this connection. The sexual always seemed to be invoked by Chamberlain, but the critical assessments of his sculpture often stop short of serious discussion of just what this recurring metaphor for his practice might imply.

To draw out these implications, I want to propose a related term that has also been used to explain Chamberlain's tactics – coupling. "Coupling" is sometimes used interchangeably with "fitting" in the literature on Chamberlain but the former does more than simply offer a substitute for the latter. As Michael Auping noted, "The obvious metaphor for sexual coupling in the work is one that has not escaped the artist."[4] In many ways, "coupling" is more directly suggestive of the range of possible meanings that Chamberlain circulated around his work and, more to the point, it registers the metaphor of sex that he was fond of when talking about his material practice. An analysis of Chamberlain's multiple tactics of coupling offers a means to bridge the gap between the ostensible abstraction of his sculptures and the loaded metaphoric language he and others use to explain them. I am not proposing this as a cipher to any hidden iconography – far from it. Chamberlain's practice, I shall argue, is far more interesting for its derailing of any simplistic iconographic searching for symbols and signs. However, despite the fact that his sculptures largely repudiate any degree of mimetic representation, he has nevertheless insisted on tying his works to sexuality, a topic that has been conventionally registered in art through images of human bodies. This paradox is important. The analogies of sexuality and of gender to his work are crucial to an understanding of his process of generating multiplicity and particularity through fitting, conjoining, and intermingling. By examining how these analogies function both in his practice and in the critical responses to it, one can get not only a better sense of the complexity of Chamberlain's project but also of the capacity of abstract and non-figurative art to propose unforeclosed accounts of genders and sexualities. That is, an investigation into Chamberlain's primary metaphor and its role in his work affords a means to come to terms with the range of implications of such a statement as, "My sculpture is not *calculated* to do anything other than what it looks like it's doing."[5]

So, what does a Chamberlain sculpture look like it's doing? His works have always presented a challenge to description and analysis. They are hyper-composed yet chaotic, massive yet delicate, volumetric yet planar, multipart yet unitary, clearly sculptural but patently pictorial, sharp yet pliable, figural yet abstract, seductive yet demurring, recognizable yet unique,

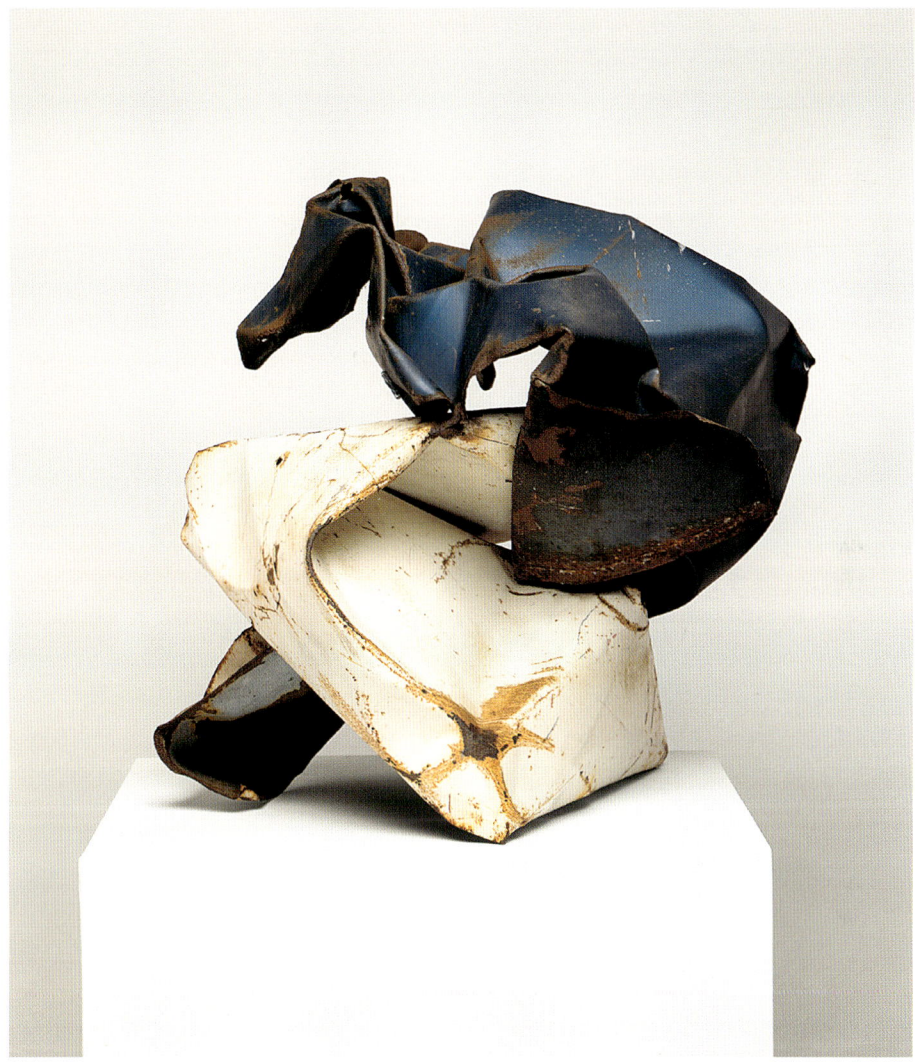

46 John Chamberlain, *M. Junior Love*, 1962. Painted metal, 51 × 51 × 35.5 cm (20 × 20 × 14 in.).

and on and on. In short, they are oxymorons. Chamberlain seems to have fostered a mode of parataxis, relishing the contradictions and inventions that his juxtapositions sometimes engender.[6] Discussions of his sculpture almost always return to the difficulties of pinning it down, and analyses often read like lists of opposed terms, coexisting somehow in the work itself. For instance, Donald Judd in 1964 wrote, "Chamberlain's sculpture is simultaneously turbulent, passionate, cool and hard."[7] Barbara Rose remarked that same year: "These strange mixtures, of tenderness and violence, of elegance and brutality, of patience and recklessness, evoke a complex response that for me is part of the unique beauty of a Chamberlain."[8] Elizabeth Baker, in a 1969 essay on his films, concluded, "But a complex sensibility is there: innocent and cynical, squalid and elegant, highly intelligent and deliberately mindless."[9] In a similar vein to these lists of opposites is Klaus Kertess's sensitive later assessment of the work, which points to the complex play with meaning that it presents: "[Chamberlain's] sculptures invite and desire endless adjectives, but none of them can stick. His configurations are in a referential state, but their constant re-forming slips out of the adjectival grip; ultimately they transcend the language of analysis and description. The ravishing opticality must be its own pleasure and reward."[10] All of these responses are sympathetic to Chamberlain. Nevertheless, they also exemplify the circularity and adjectival accumulation that his work incites in critics. Consistently, writers on Chamberlain have used such descriptive strategies both to evoke but also to evade the oxymoronic multiplicity of his works.

In other words, it is Chamberlain's multiple tactics of coupling that such critical responses register. It is essential to consider not just the choice of adjectives critics use but also the tendency to pile them onto the work because Chamberlain's sculptures resolutely resist straightforward description and analysis. As Gary Indiana astutely confessed, with Chamberlain's sculpture "It's easier to say what it isn't."[11] This inability to decide what a Chamberlain is seems to me to be one of the most important things about it. Is it a crushed car or colored sculpture matter? Is it ironically referential or sincerely abstract?[12] Is it art or is it refuse?[13] Is it sculpture or is it painting? Any possible answer to questions such as these will be circular and slippery, for his coupled works always incorporate a degree of multiple options, fitted together. Once fitted, however, they are greater than the sum of their parts. As Barbara Rose noted in an early review of Chamberlain's work, "The special charge of his works resides largely, I think, in the tension born of contradiction."[14]

Despite the major changes in his work over decades, Chamberlain's foundational questions and tactics remained remarkably consistent. In order to examine the way in which coupling operates on multiple material and conceptual levels for Chamberlain, I will outline below but a few of the ways in which this conceptual and material practice was repeatedly put into play in the works themselves. In multiple ways, the parataxical tendencies of Chamberlain's way of working result in the blurring of boundaries, the conjoining of categories, and the undermining of binaries.

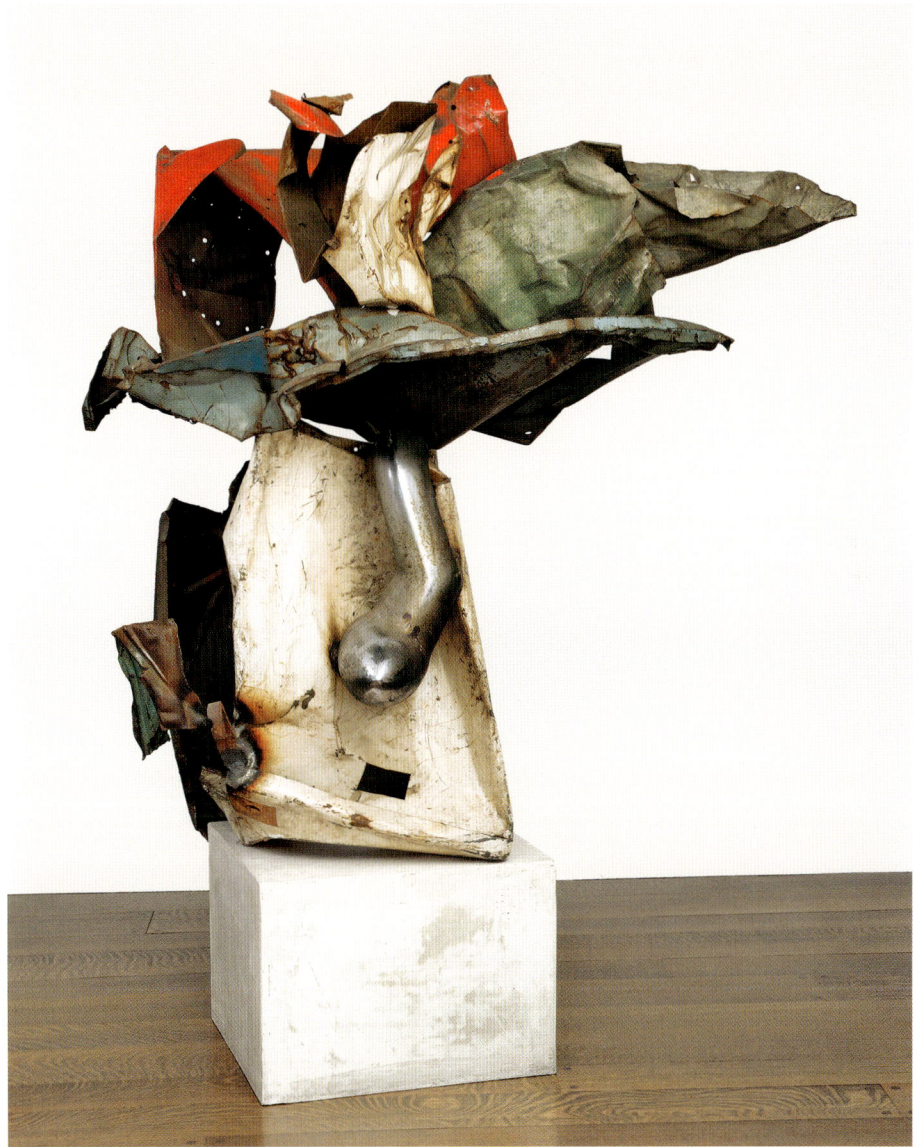

47 John Chamberlain, *Fantail*, 1961. Painted and chromium-plated steel, 178 × 190.5 × 152.4 cm (70 × 75 × 60 in.). Collection of Jasper Johns.

For example, a central characteristic of Chamberlain's work is how volume and mass are differentiated yet hinged together. Chamberlain's metallic works are composed of planar elements that eschew mass in the traditional sculptural sense. They have no solidity, yet they are not hollow. They seem both light and heavy. They enclose and enfold space and thus

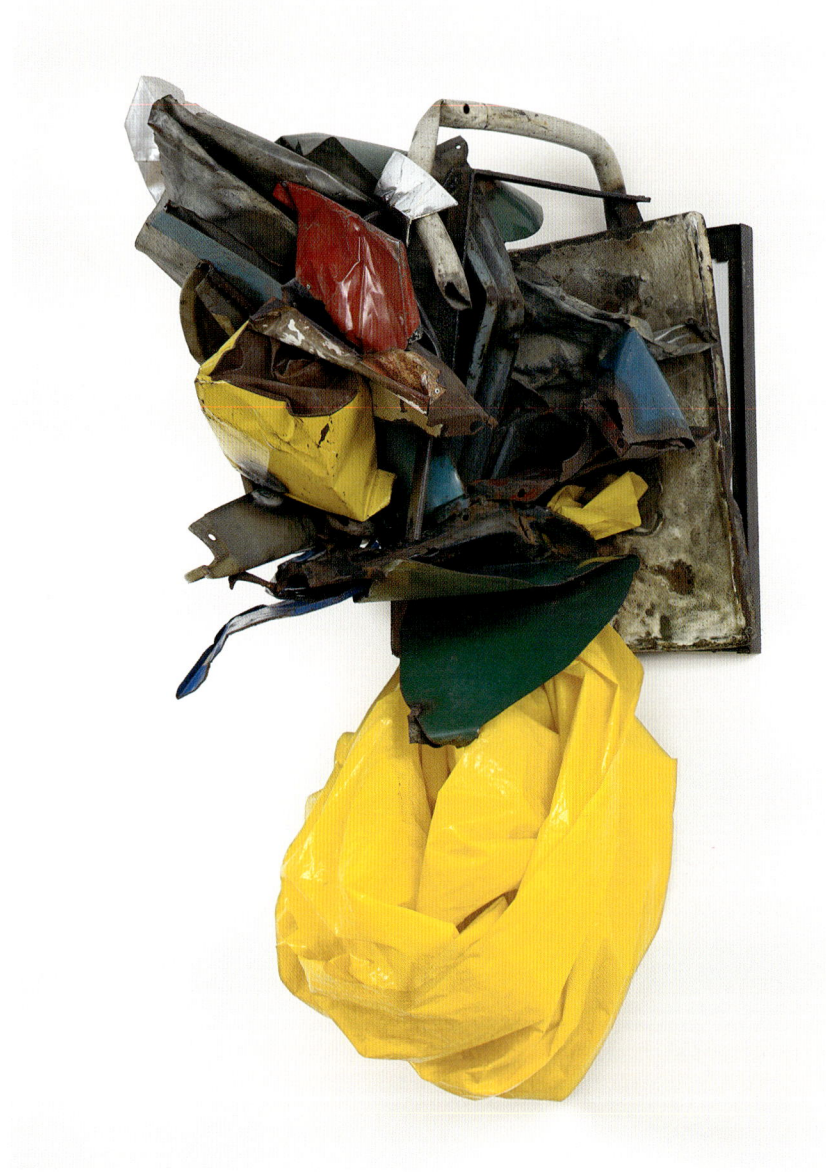

48   John Chamberlain, *Toy*, 1961. Steel, paint, and plastic, 136 × 98 × 77.5 cm (53½ × 38½ × 30½ in.). Art Institute of Chicago, gift of William Hokin, 1969.809.

establish volume, yet it is not clear where that volume starts or dissolves. They are bodies made up of, only, too much skin.

Another example of coupling often brought up in the literature on Chamberlain is the conjoining of sculpture and painting. A large amount of critical energy has been spent trying to figure out into which of these two categories Chamberlain can be more appropriately placed. The raucous use of color arrays combined with a refined understanding of the manipulation of space brings together central criteria for both painting and sculpture. This aspect of Chamberlain's coupling has been widely discussed, and it is generally agreed that Chamberlain is art-historically significant for being one of the first sculptors to use bold color effectively as an integral structural element. Judd argued that Chamberlain was "the first…to use color successfully in sculpture."[15] Kertess perhaps said it best when he wrote: "[his] ability to make roundness into color and color into roundness, pushing the two into an overall unity, is without equal."[16]

Color is, of course, one of the most important features of Chamberlain's art. As Kertess also observed, he "transgressed lavishly the prohibition of color in sculpture, employing hues that ranged from the virginal to the lurid."[17] Beyond praising Chamberlain's use of it, Kertess rightly emphasized that color had traditionally been barred from sculpture proper. When the nineteenth-century sculptor John Gibson exhibited a neoclassical nude Venus with a light, cosmetic tinting at the 1862 International Exhibition in London, its modest polychromy was greeted with accusations of impropriety (fig. 49).[18] Even though color had emerged by the end of the nineteenth century as a viable possibility for sculpture and was used throughout the modern era, there remained an anxiety about its appropriateness. This is not the place to recount the complex story of color and modern sculpture; suffice it to say that even after the examples of such artists as Pablo Picasso and David Smith, color always needed to be justified or explained for sculpture. At the heart of this concern was the conception that color in sculpture was usually applied to sculptural form, rather then integral to it. Since sculpture has been conventionally regarded as an art of space, matter, and form, any coat of color added to those forms has been understood to mitigate, or merely decorate, the spatial and three-dimensional aspects that are conventionally understood to be modern sculpture's basis.

The anxiety about colored sculpture that Gibson's *Tinted Venus* brought to the surface remained implicit into the next century.[19] Applied color was too much like cosmetics, and its application to sculpture seemed, for many, to cheapen it. E. C. Goosen wrote in the 1960s: "The rush to employ painting-type color in sculpture, as refreshing as it might momentarily seem, has more often than not removed the possibility of the sculptural experience from the work at hand. Moreover, all the radiant color in the world cannot camouflage weak form. And the tendency toward camouflage is tantamount to a return to illusionism."[20] A further example of the disdain

106 ABSTRACT BODIES

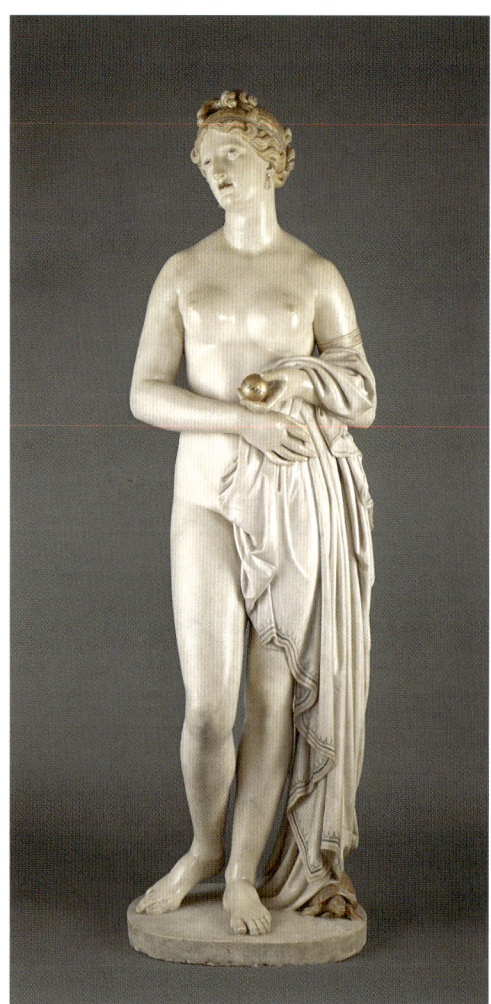

LEFT 49 John Gibson, *Tinted Venus*, c. 1851–6. Tinted marble, h. 175 cm (69 in.). National Museums Liverpool, Walker Art Gallery.

OPPOSITE 50 John Chamberlain, *Mustang Sally McBright*, 1965. Automobile metal, 142.2 × 160 × 111.8 cm (56 × 63 × 44 in.).

for sculptural color can be found in a 1968 essay by Darby Bannard on the legacy of Cubism in sculpture, where he flatly stated that "color is usually so unfortunate in sculpture." Chamberlain, however, seemed to find a way out of this impasse, according to Bannard, who then dismissively continued: "Chamberlain's crushed auto-part sculptures, although they are not great art, use color effectively because his materials are colored to begin with, so we are prepared for it."[21]

The importance of the colored auto bodies in the earlier sculptures, as well as Chamberlain's later processes of painting before crushing metal, have often been marshaled as justifications for the vibrant color central to his art. Perhaps it is not that surprising that Chamberlain would be the one

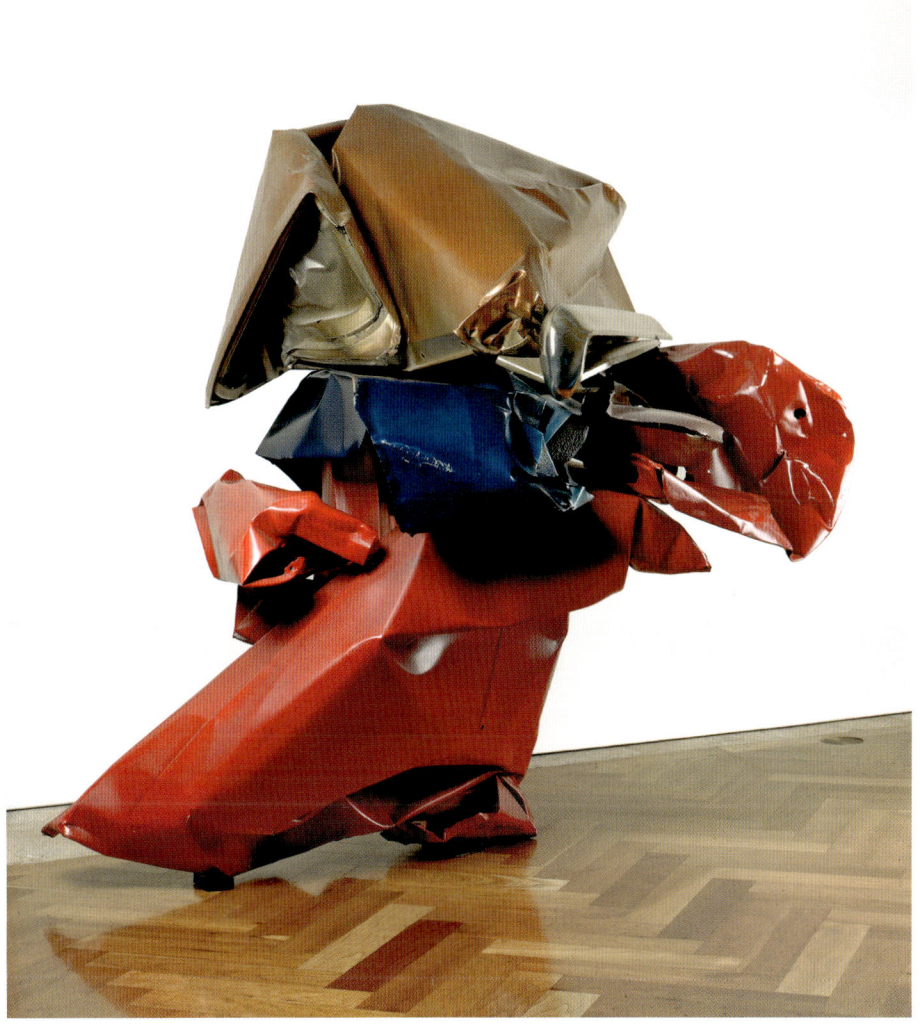

to overturn the negative connotations of color and use it "successfully." In the late 1950s, he worked not only as a hairdresser but also as a make-up artist – both jobs in which he could also capitalize on his grasp of volume and its relation to color.[22] Chamberlain, himself, occasionally voiced the reading of color in sculpture as cosmetics. For instance, speaking of the resin he used in the paper sculptures of the late 1960s, he said: "The color on it became flashy like lipstick or eyeshadow or something for a girl. Whatever people put on as colors, they put on so that somebody sees it."[23] In Chamberlain's work, color is both applied and integral, cosmetic and industrial. That is, color itself is a coupled category in his work. As Judd

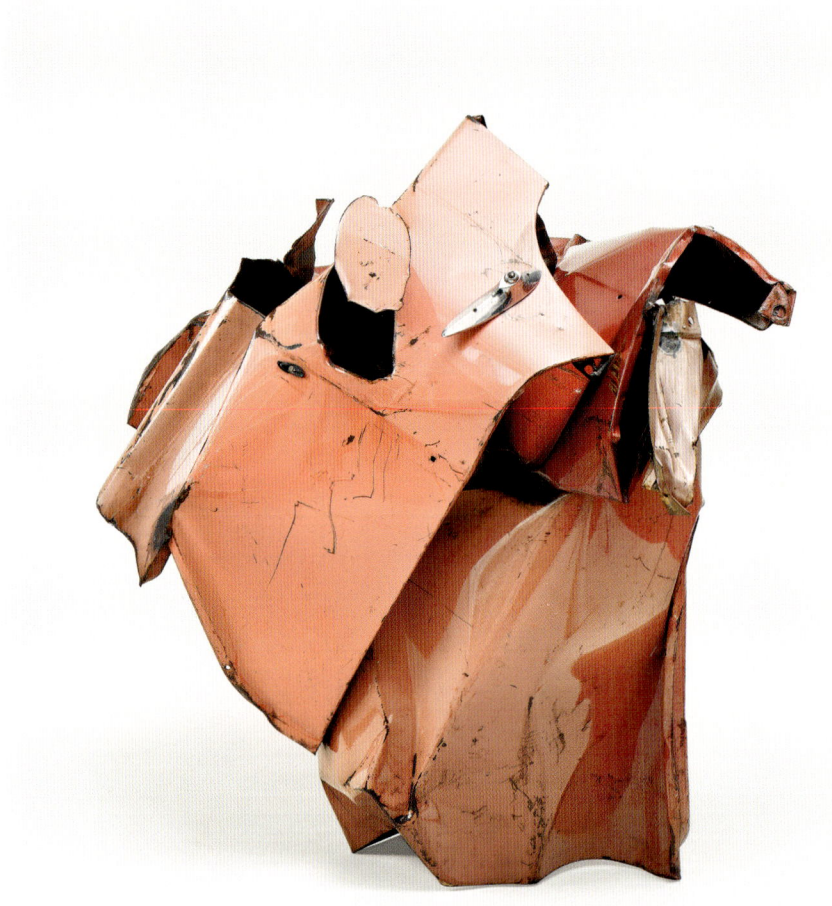

51 John Chamberlain, *Miss Lucy Pink*, 1962. Painted and chromium-plated steel, 119.4 × 106.7 × 99 cm (47 × 42 × 39 in.). Private collection.

remarked about Chamberlain, "The color is also both neutral and sensitive…Color is never unimportant, as it usually is in sculpture."[24]

A third example of Chamberlain's consistent strategy of coupling is the shuttling between reference and abstraction mentioned at the outset. Throughout his career, Chamberlain and his advocates refuted the reading of his sculptures in terms of their source material of automobiles. There is little doubt that the interpretations of his sculptures as commentaries on car culture or violence are limited in their scope. Such readings largely fail

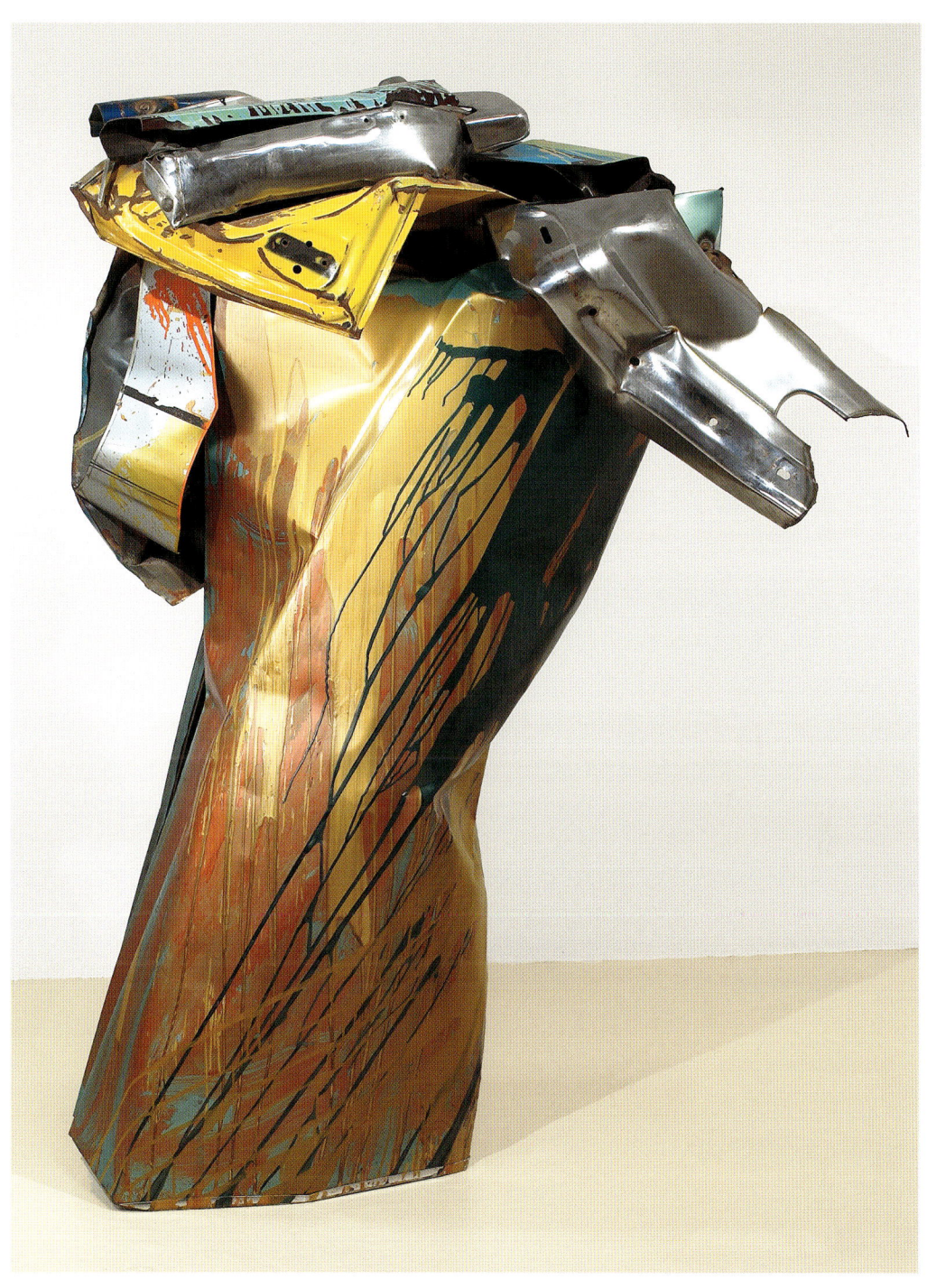

52 John Chamberlain, *Son of Dudes*, 1977. Painted and chromium-plated steel, 182.9 × 132.1 × 96.5 cm (72 × 52 × 38 in.). Collection Christophe de Menil.

to account for the range of traits that makes Chamberlain's works compelling — from the complexity of their composition to the subtle dynamism of their color relations to their quizzical and leading titles. As Robert Creeley once put it, with a Chamberlain, the automobile "was there, but now you are contained in a thing already changing, bringing you into its terms."[25] Or, as Chamberlain more bluntly put it, "people say, 'Oh, that looks like my old Mustang there' or something. It doesn't look like their old Mustang at all."[26]

Some of Chamberlain's would-be supporters, however, have taken this injunction against the car crash interpretation to mean that his sculptures are wholly formal constellations without subject matter or referentiality in any degree. Such a view, as I claimed earlier, also fails to account for the multiple levels on which a Chamberlain sculpture operates. The work is often vigorously non-mimetic yet slyly referential. For instance, a color often sparks an association and/or makes a reference (*Miss Lucy Pink*, *Velvet White*, and so on), materials evoke gendered associations (for example, *Endless Gossip* made from cookie tins and other metal components with floral prints or the *Penthouse* series of sculptures made from brown-paper magazine wrappers; see fig. 58), or are simply descriptive of content (as with perhaps Chamberlain's only figurative or representational sculpture, *Endzoneboogie*; fig. 53). Despite the patent evidence that the titles evoke interpretation of, modify, or connect to the sculptures to which they are attached, some of Chamberlain's advocates have upheld the erroneous belief that not only are his sculptures just formalist but that his titles are also entirely devoid of meaning.[27]

Chamberlain's abstraction emphasized openness and a play with reference. It achieved this by largely refusing representation or recognizable imagery, but Chamberlain nevertheless cultivated generative allusions that were produced through his parataxical process of fitting (in both his sculptures and his titles). That is, Chamberlains never *signify* automobiles, car culture, and so on. Nevertheless, they *refer* to their previous material existence as industrially manufactured automobile parts, whether recycled or new. Even Judd was careful not to discount this level of reference and its role in Chamberlain's work:

> The quality of John Chamberlain's sculpture, in contrast, involves a three-way polarity of appearance and meaning, *successive states* of the same form and material. A piece may appear neutral, *just junk*, casually objective; or redundant, voluminous beyond its structure, obscured by other chances and possibilities; or simply expressive, through its structure and details

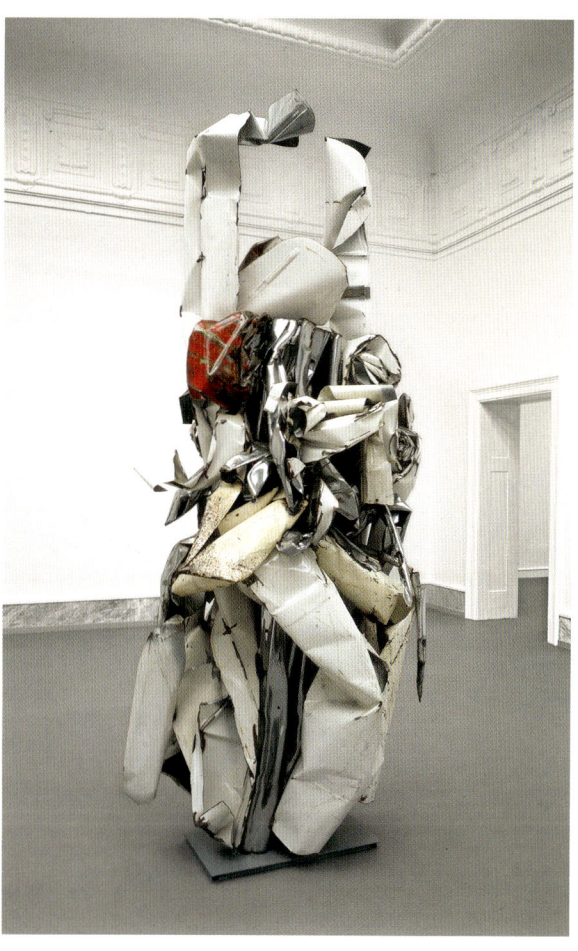

53 John Chamberlain, *Endzoneboogie*, 1988. Painted and chromium-plated steel, 295 × 122.6 × 123.2 cm (116 × 48¼ × 48½ in.). Froehlich Collection, Stuttgart.

and *oblique imagery. The appearance of a mass of colored automobile metal is obviously essential.*[28]

While Chamberlain and others rightly resist the reductive reading of the sculptures in terms of their material sources (that is, cars), the referential vestiges of those materials are nevertheless persistent and crucial, as Judd noted. One sees a Chamberlain not just as abstract but, to repeat Judd, in "successive states of the same form and material." At least one of those circulating states involves seeing the work as referential – even if to "just junk." That is, the material components of a Chamberlain work to establish an extensional reference to a pre-existing thing (an autobody, an oil drum) that has been discarded or scrapped (or, in the case of his later use of van tops, ordered fresh). Even if this level of reference is subsumed as the viewer

112   ABSTRACT BODIES

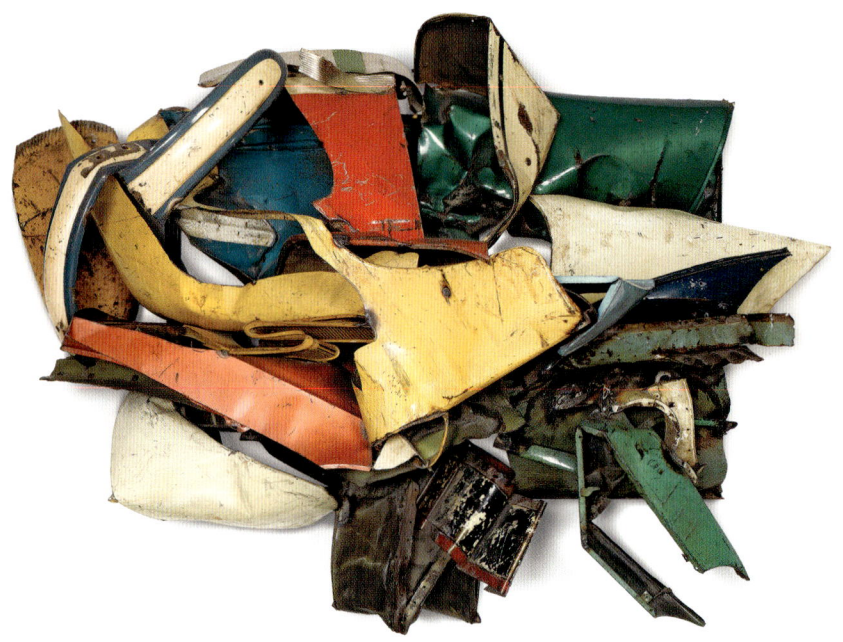

54   John Chamberlain, *Dolores James*, 1962. Painted and chromium-plated steel, 184.2 × 257.8 × 117.5 cm (72½ × 101½ × 46¼ in.). Solomon R. Guggenheim Museum, New York, 70.1925.

OPPOSITE 55   Installation view, Chinati Foundation, Marfa, Texas, with John Chamberlain's *Tongue Pictures*, 1979, in foreground.

cycles through seeing the work's multiplicity, it is never invisible or inconsequential, as Judd was careful to indicate. The engagements produced by the visual encounter with a Chamberlain are fueled by the viewer's recognition of the repurposed nature of his materials that have become delicately poised to establish dynamic volumes exceeding their mass.[29] In this, the referential status of his materials was foundational for they facilitated the aim that Chamberlain prized for his own work – the "discovery angle" in which art showed us something previously unrecognized.[30] Indeed, for much of his career, Chamberlain staged the theme of transformation by facilitating viewers' identifications of his source materials, be they automobiles, bathroom cabinets, women's undergarments, or oil drums.

Like it or not, Chamberlain's materials have never been able to be completely overlooked because he makes their material specificity central to

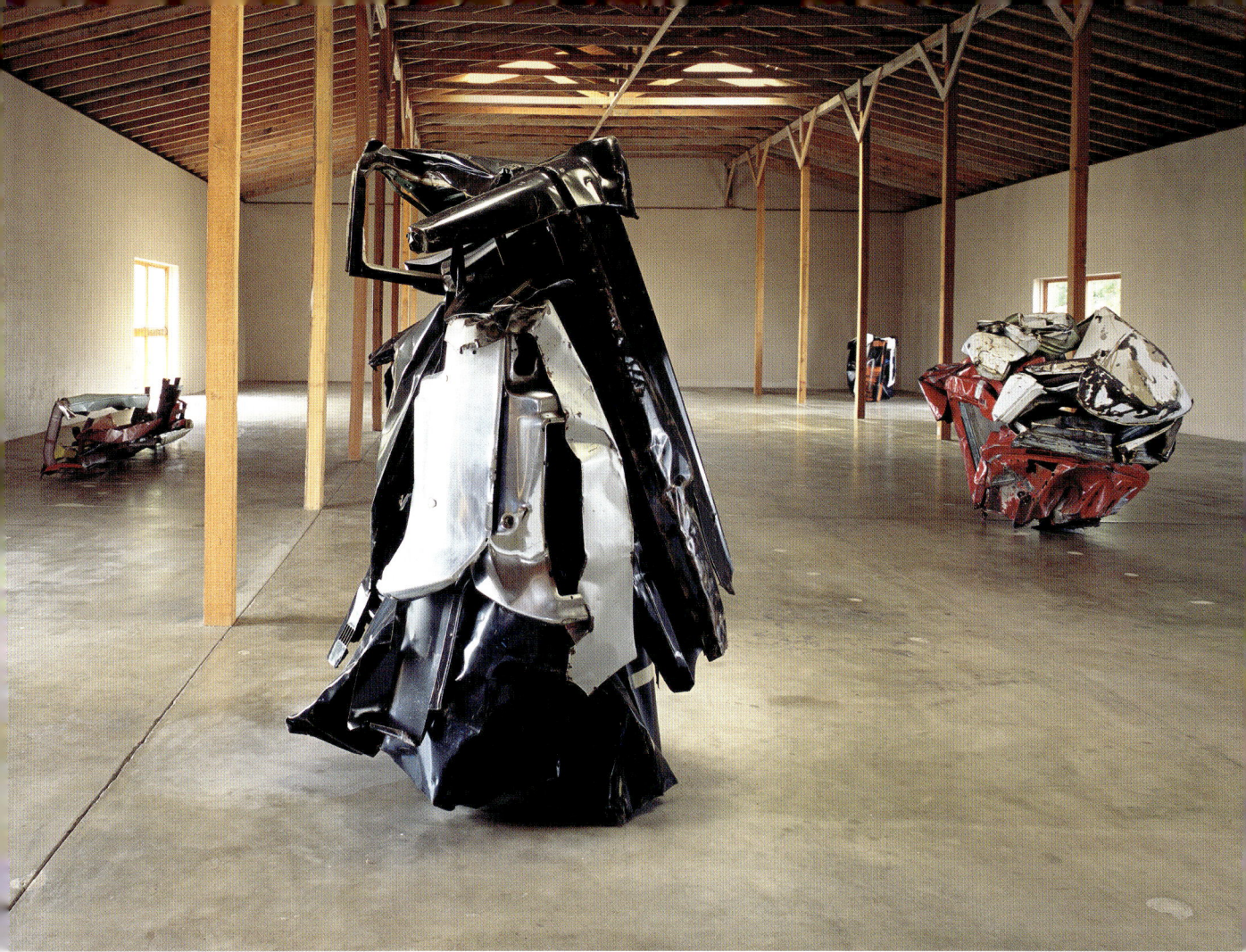

their deployment. That is, his process ensures that we know that the materials have had a previous history, even if it is just his own acts of making his components. Beyond the use of recycled cars, car parts, van tops, oil drums, and the like, Chamberlain's practice of crumpling and cracking of colored surfaces calls attention to the fact that these materials have undergone transformation – that they once were something else, even if we do not know what. We see the present sculpture as the aggregation of the multiple prior stages his materials have undergone – manufactured, used, acquired by him, sometimes painted, crushed, and then fitted together (fig. 54). However much Chamberlain and others stress that his sculptures are abstract and non-signifying, the sculptures themselves are always permeated by and coupled with this level of reference and this intimation of his materials' previous histories. For instance, the subtle yet distinct role played by a woman's slip, ivory colored with black lace trim, in the sculpture titled *Huzzy* is crucial in establishing a relationship between an ostensibly

114 ABSTRACT BODIES

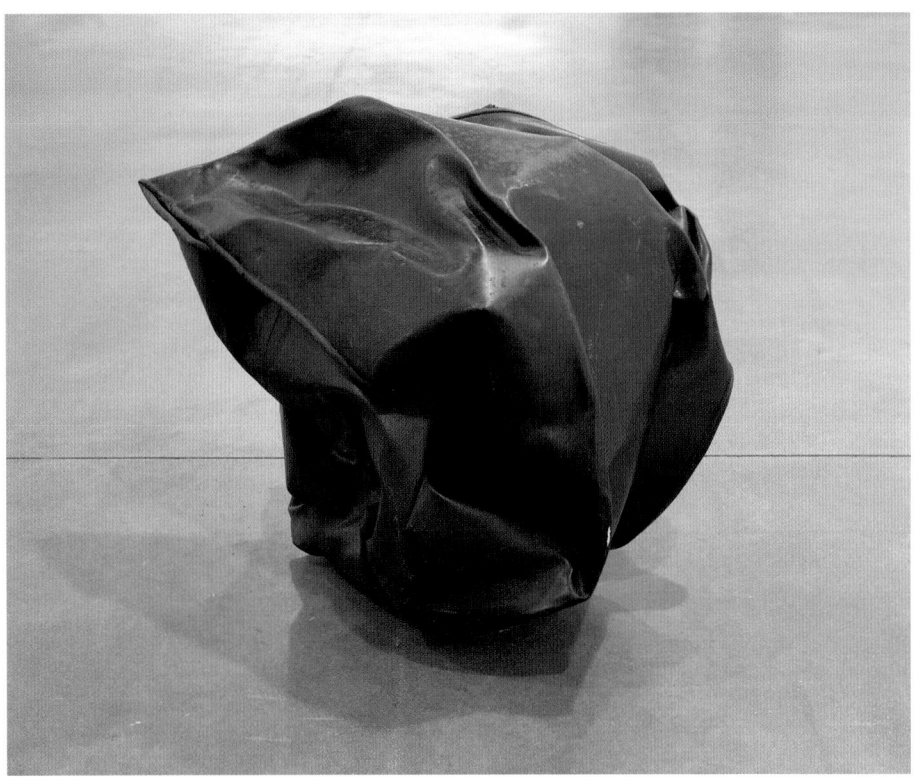

56 John Chamberlain, *Socket*, 1975. Painted steel, 58.7 × 69.9 × 45.7 cm (23 × 27½ × 18 in.).

abstract sculpture and its figural and gendered associations (fig. 57). Clothing infers the human body more directly than many other materials. Combined with a title that is inescapably close to a word for an impudent or immoral woman ("hussy"), a particular gender is overlaid on an otherwise non-figural assemblage. That is, the viewer will probably not experience any noetic resemblance between *Huzzy* and the human form. Nevertheless, the entire assemblage gains an unmistakably gendered valence once the recognition of source materials (women's lingerie) and title are conjoined in the successive states of the viewer's attention. As I shall argue, this emphasis on "successive states" and transformation is a crucial component of Chamberlain's conceptual process and the possibilities for meaning that it effects.

For a final, fourth example of the importance of "fit" or coupling as a wide-ranging strategy, one could look to the treatment for an unrealized film he planned with Viva Auder. In it, he used "fit" to explain how this

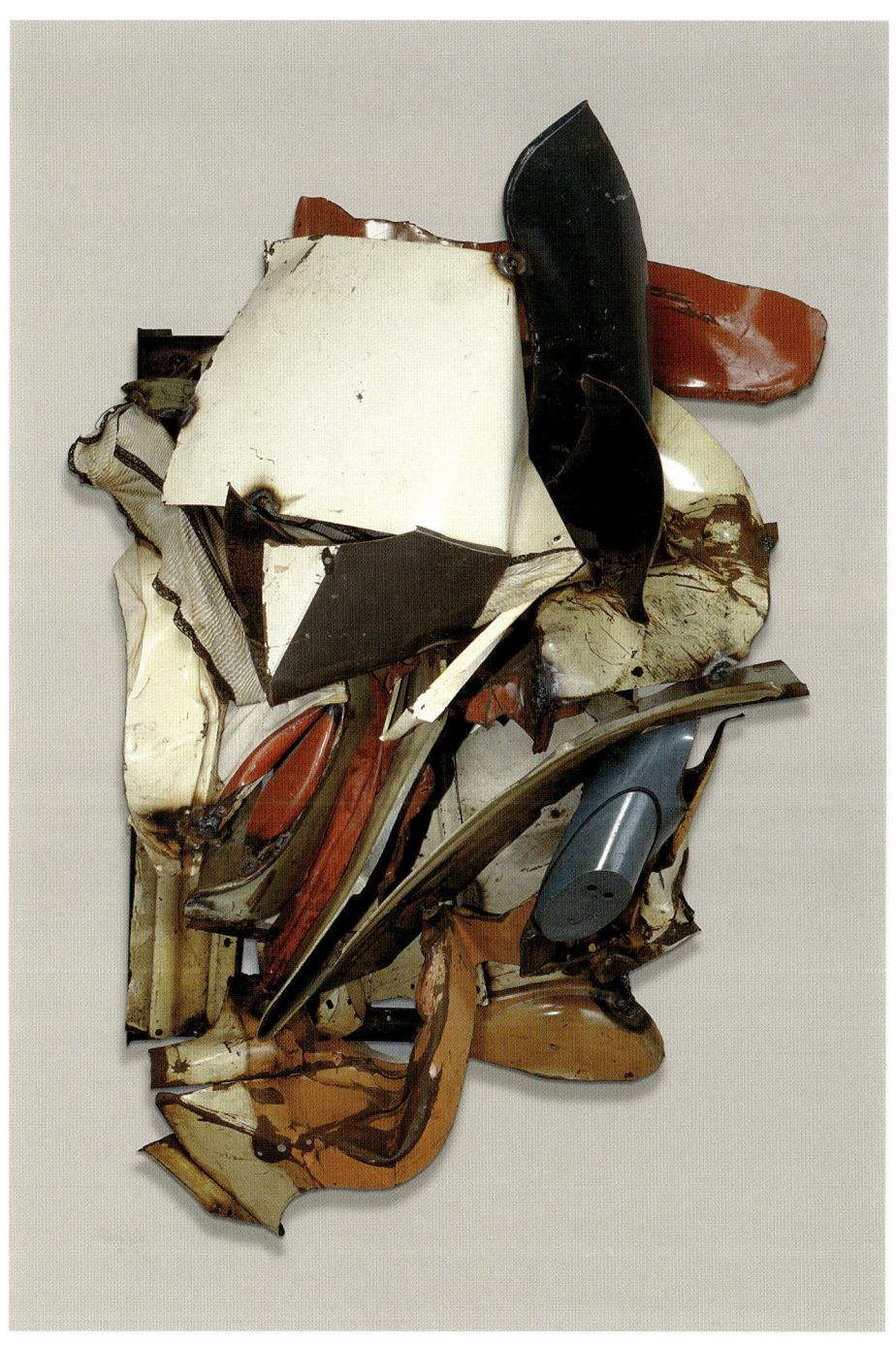

57 John Chamberlain, *Huzzy*, 1961. Steel, paint, and chromium plating with fabric, 137.2 × 83.8 × 53.3 cm (54 × 33 × 21 in.). The Nelson-Atkins Museum of Art, Kansas City, Missouri, gift of Mrs. Charles F. Buckwalter in memory of Charles F. Buckwalter, F64-8.

film's narrative structure would be the result of how "magic moments" could be spliced together. *The Secret Life of William Shakespeare* was to have been Chamberlain's second feature-length film, after his sexually explicit and freeform *The Secret Life of Hernando Cortez* from 1968 that featured Ultra Violet and Taylor Mead.[31] For the Shakespeare film, he and Auder devised a dream cast for this anachronistic take on Elizabethan court drama that included the trans actress Holly Woodlawn along with the gay men Gary Indiana and Truman Capote because, they explained, "it appears that only actors of a certain sexual persuasion are adept at repartee, at gossip, at picking up the thread of an idea and running with it; in other words only those of a certain sexual persuasion would be able today to fit into the Elizabethan court. Why this is we don't know. Suffice to say it exists."[32] (The character of Queen Elizabeth is, in the film, revealed to be a "hermaphrodite."[33]) Following on this question of Elizabethan fit, they explained the process for making their improvisational film:

> *The film ought to evolve as a piece of sculpture*; a Chamberlain sculpture. By this we don't mean the researching, the writing, the casting – we mean the actual filming itself – the recording. The job of the director, like the job of the sculptor, is first to *see* the pieces, then to *put them together*. He isn't going to take each piece and twist it, bend it, direct it, before he adds it to the ensemble, he's going to choose each piece because he knows in advance it will fit....Just as a sculpture dictates its own form, the movie must be allowed to dictate its own direction. *Since the magic moments are to be allowed to happen spontaneously, the direction will mainly lie in the editing.*[34]

As this description makes clear, Chamberlain understood the process of fitting as a general strategy. Derived from parataxis and daily tested in his acts of interlocking and balancing autobody parts and other materials, fitting was also the core Chamberlain's attitude toward art and its effects. As he once told Creeley, "[I]t's that fit which really has importance...a very crucial part of what art is really about."[35]

With the four examples of coupling detailed above – volume and mass, painting and sculpture, abstraction and referentiality, and spontaneity and narrative structure – I have suggested just a few of the ways in which the formal and artistic operations of Chamberlain's work continually return to this strategy of conjoining of differentiated elements to produce new possibilities. Throughout his career, Chamberlain expanded the concept of "fit," seeing it as a general strategy of undermining binaries and categories through conjunction and interpenetration.

Beyond his artistic practice, he also used this strategy relentlessly when discussing his work, persistently undermining any positive assertions with the incorporation of alternative or counter-propositions. He often stressed the ways in which two aspects are distinguished only to be intermingled. Referring again to the paper sculptures in 1972, he said "I think what was also profound about the paper was that you could see the inside and the outside. You couldn't literally see the inside, but you felt the inside because of the nature of the outside. Something like that" (see fig. 58).[36] Like the sculptures he described, his words divide elements only to argue that they are inseparable.

Words were significant for Chamberlain, and his seminal year at Black Mountain College (1955–6) taught him an approach to poetry that was analogous to collage.[37] This, in turn, suggested a new understanding of sculptural practice as fitting. He recently recalled with reference to his Black Mountain years: "If I have a room full of parts, they are like a lot of words and I have to take one piece and put it next to another and find out if it really fits. The poet's influence is there, plus in my titles."[38] Because of this emphasis on language, Chamberlain's own words should never be dismissed, despite their performances of difficulty and shallowness. Through his words, his performed artistic identity mirrors the parataxical formal and strategic operations of his sculpture. He was both forthright and evasive, straight-talking and word-mincing, and if nothing else he mocked the idea that meaning has a single source – in him or elsewhere. That is, beyond being an artistic strategy, oxymoronic coupling also characterized the persona he presented when discussing his work – what Betsy Baker referred to as his "tendency towards evasion and self-camouflage."[39] Chamberlain stated that he did not like interviews, but the interview, more than any other critical genre, has dominated the literature on Chamberlain since he began doing them in the 1970s. Whether he liked them or not – or, rather, because he liked to dislike them – the interviews reveal a parallel strategy to the sculptures. When performing his artistic persona in the staged setting of the formal interview intended for publication, Chamberlain consistently proposed an idea only to amend it with a contradiction, a tangent, or a counter-proposition. For instance, in a telling moment in his widely cited interview with Julie Sylvester, she remarked "One of the strongest elements of your sculpture is stance and attitude," to which Chamberlain replied: "Well, that's just what *I* said. I could have been lying." Sylvester replied, "Were you?" Chamberlain: "I'm not certain. Only time will tell."[40] In such exchanges, neither proposition nor counter-proposition prevails. They are always neatly fitted together, and it is the on-going dance between them

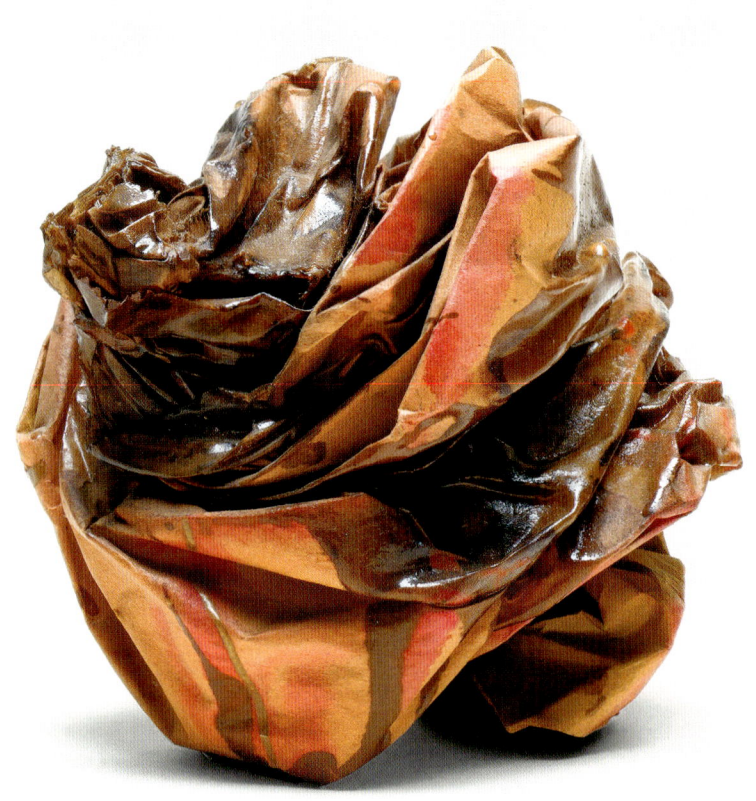

58   John Chamberlain, *Penthouse #46*, 1969. Watercolor and resin on paper, 13.5 × 17.8 × 11.4 cm (5¼ × 7 × 4½ in.). Dia Art Foundation.

that produces the best window into Chamberlain's artistic practice. That is, Chamberlain never explained his work directly nor pinned down its meaning. Instead, he offered his own circular and coupled words as a further example of how his sculptures operate. As he remarked in a late interview, "And I guess I have difficulty being interviewed because I don't want to talk about my work. Like now, we are talking *around* the work."[41]

Consequently, when one reads about Chamberlain, his many interviews seem at first to offer little help. Instead, it has been Judd's writings that have become the key interpretive texts. Judd was a sensitive critic and a long-time advocate of Chamberlain's work. He wrote a great deal about Chamberlain, despite the fact that the latter's art seems, initially, antithetical to the austerity that Judd favored in his own. Compared to Chamberlain's evasiveness and circularity, Judd's writing about the sculptures is strikingly direct, and it is no surprise that Judd's assessments from the 1960s have been reprinted again and again in exhibition catalogues of Chamberlain's work. With his characteristic concision, he attempted to give an account of the slipperiness of Chamberlain's work.[42] There is one statement of his, in particular, that seems to me to summarize Chamberlain's sculpture in all its excess. Discussing some of Chamberlain's lacquer paintings in 1965, Judd wrote, "Another important thing about the reliefs is that they don't have the same kind of generality or objective quality as that in the work of the best of older artists. The reliefs are not austere or whatever the quality is – it's usually intrinsic to paint on canvas. They are extreme, snazzy, elegant in the wrong way, immoderate."[43] "Immoderate": that is, going beyond proper limits, unrestrained in passions or conduct, excessive, wanton.[44] There is too much there. A line has been crossed, and that which is normally kept out of bounds is welcomed in. Not just in his work, Chamberlain seems to relish being immoderate, crossing the line.

I borrow this term from Judd to expose further some of the ways in which Chamberlain operates both in his work and in his evasive and obfuscating statements about it. Immoderation was a tactic for him, like coupling, in which boundaries and distinctions are blurred or folded over each other. Beyond his achievement of immoderation in his work, how did he do this in his statements? Anyone familiar with his remarks and the persona he presented to critics will know that this attitude manifested itself most often – and most strategically – in his use of sex to shock and to disrupt interviews.[45] He relied on sex as a means to break down conventions and to disarm others through his unashamed foregrounding of it. For instance, Larry Bell affectionately recalled,

> When he came into the studio, the first thing he would do was remove his clothes, everything except a tank top, and stand around my place like a tour guide. His schlong was quite prominent. I would have guests come over, and John would just stand there looking at us. I would introduce him and he would nod his head but say nothing; his schlong said it all. He had a rooster and a pig tattoo, one on each foot.[46]

Beyond his discomfiting ways of foregrounding the sexual in his personal interactions and as a disruptive tactic in his interviews, Chamberlain also wove sex and sexual metaphors into his practice and the ways in which he characterized it.

One must take seriously – however immoderate it might seem on our part – how Chamberlain persistently introduced sex into discussions of his work. In addition to the artist's own statements, bodily metaphors are taken up by critics to describe the works, from Judd's mention of "tumescent planes"[47] to Kertess's observation that "The concrete reading of form [in Chamberlain's sculptures] is frustrated, though we are aware of ambiguous sexual references in the mounting, plugging, and hugging that takes place among the individual components."[48] Remember that Chamberlain was the primary origin of this talk. For instance, he said in 1971:

> I found that the particular principle of compression and wadding-up or manipulating with the fingers, so to speak, whether you use a machine or not, has a lot of application to a lot of different materials and I only use materials that deal with that….So it all has to do with if it's sexual, it's squeezing and hugging. And if it's instinctive, it has to do with fit and balance; if it's emotional, it's presence, and I don't know how it gets to be intellectual.[49]

This account of his work deviated little throughout his career. By the 1971 interview just cited, this explanation of his sculptural process through the association with sexuality had become commonplace for him. It continued as his main line from that point onward and is evident in interviews over the span of three and a half decades. For instance, in his oft-used artist's statement, he repeated a similar account of his practice, saying, "I deal with new material as I see fit in terms of my decision making, which has to do primarily with sexual and intuitive thinking."[50] Despite Chamberlain's regular frankness and insistence on this analogy, there remains in the critical record a prevailing reluctance about taking it seriously and saying too much, about being – like Chamberlain – immoderately focused on sex.[51]

The sexual is not a diversion from Chamberlain's art nor is it merely a smokescreen that he came to use. Rather, the sexual emerged as the privileged metaphor for the range of operations of coupling that circulate in Chamberlain's work and public persona. Chamberlain remarked, "What is important for me about this work is what I've learned about assembly. The assembly is a fit, and the fit is sexual. That's a mode I'm working."[52] Since coupling is the persistent formal and artistic strategy for Chamberlain, then it is imperative to investigate why his recurring metaphor for coupling or fitting has been sexual intercourse. This is an artist, for instance, who constantly reminded viewers of the centrality of the sexual for his work, as when he showed a group of participatory foam couches in a 1972 gallery exhibition titled *John Chamberlain/F_____g Couches*, published a series of

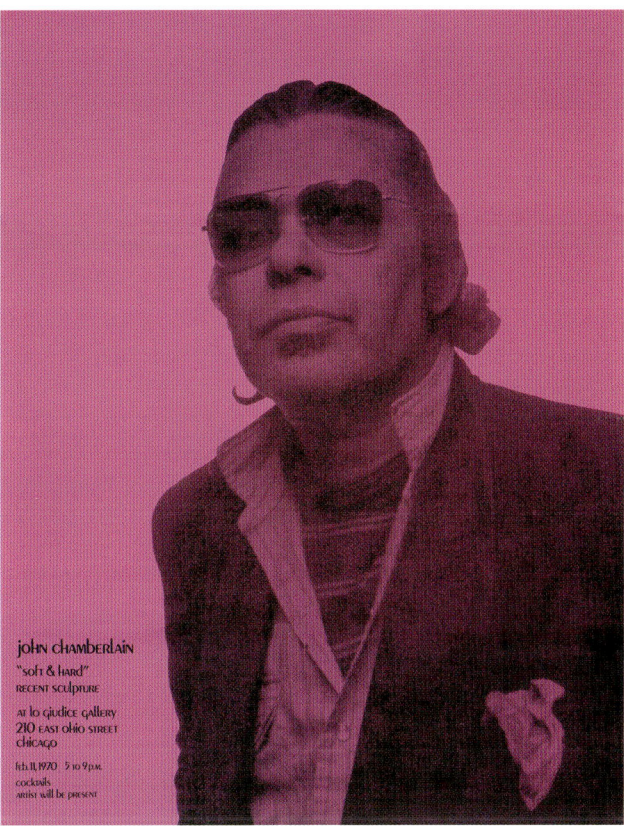

59   Poster for John Chamberlain, *"Soft and Hard": Recent Sculpture*, Lo Giudice Gallery, Chicago, 1970. Photography Archives, Solomon R. Guggenheim Museum, New York.

photographs of Ultra Violet and her genitals, or made his sexually explicit improvised films.[53] If anything, sex was the one recurring element of content in his work. Speaking in general of his practice, he later recalled that "Softness and sexiness has much more to do with my work than automobile crashes" (see fig. 59).[54]

It is clear from his statements that one must not think of coupling and the sexual simply in terms of Chamberlain's personal erotic disposition, and I make no claims about him on this biographical level. While no doubt this comes into play, Chamberlain's work is interesting not because his sculptures might be somehow imprinted by it. My interest, rather, is in Chamberlain's recurring deployment of the analogy of the sexual to works that seem resolutely to resist figuration. This tells us little about Chamberlain the individual, but it points to the ways that his coupling of reference and abstraction (and his concomitant commitment to the sexual metaphor) has wider implications for how his work evokes and unsettles meanings and identifications. That is, if Chamberlain only ever explained his work and practice by analogy (and this analogy has most often been to the "sexual fit"), then a way to understand the operations of his work is to pursue the implications of that analogy.

It is significant that Chamberlain himself was careful to emphasize that the sexual fit is not necessarily between himself and the sculpture but rather that it involves a sexuality of the parts, with each other. For instance, in a 1986 interview, he said: "Each part is different, and each part can fit to some place convenient to itself. In other words, if you have two parts and they fit together, not only do they become much stronger because of their union, but they tend to develop certain lines in relation to each other that suggest a marriage."[55] In other words, what is this marriage if not a coupling of two gendered parts? But the parts are not securely identifiable as male or female, or even penetrative or receptive. As mentioned above, he refers to the sexual fit as "squeezing and hugging," often leaving his description of erotic activity outside of ways that gender might be neatly assigned to parts or activities. As he does repeatedly when talking around his works, he refuses to pin down a specific signification.

Throughout his career, one of Chamberlain's primary concerns was to maintain possibility and openness in the meaning of his works rather than attempt to dictate how a viewer should respond to them. He once explained that "art is the only place left where a person can go discover something and not have to be told by somebody else whether they discovered it or not."[56] This is an important statement, and it reflects Chamberlain's main priorities for his art – transformation and discovery. Accordingly, his refusal to prescribe an essential meaning for his works was central to Chamberlain's artistic priorities (and was, as well, reflected in his frequent evasiveness). Similarly, when making his repeated statements about the sexual fit, he rarely specified its variables through recourse to conventional gender or sexual identities. The fit was generative not prescriptive. By and large he preferred to keep the "sexual" in "sexual fit" deliberately vague, open, and inclusive. Ultimately, it is an unorthodox and unspecified gendered and sexual coupling that emerges from this metaphor that he recurringly conjoined with his abstract sculpture. This characterization of gender as multiple and variable was largely consistent in his statements on the sexual fit. For instance, in a late interview Chamberlain retained such strategic vagueness: "So you have a fit, and you have a form and you have a color. And so all of these three parts are – ...They're having a good time together, if you put them together well."[57] When Chamberlain repeatedly invoked sexuality in his work, his willful unspecificity about its makeup and parameters was significant and, furthermore, entirely in accord with his general avoidance of dictating

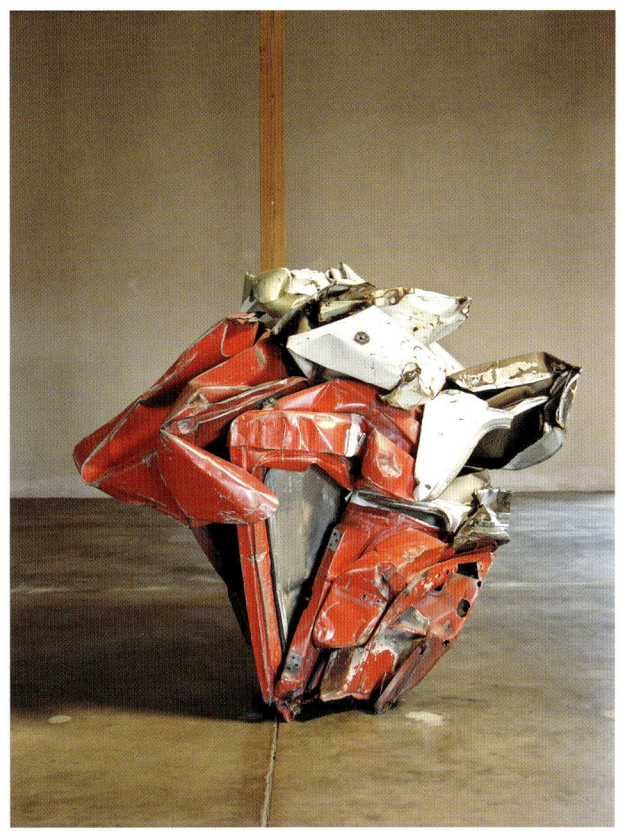 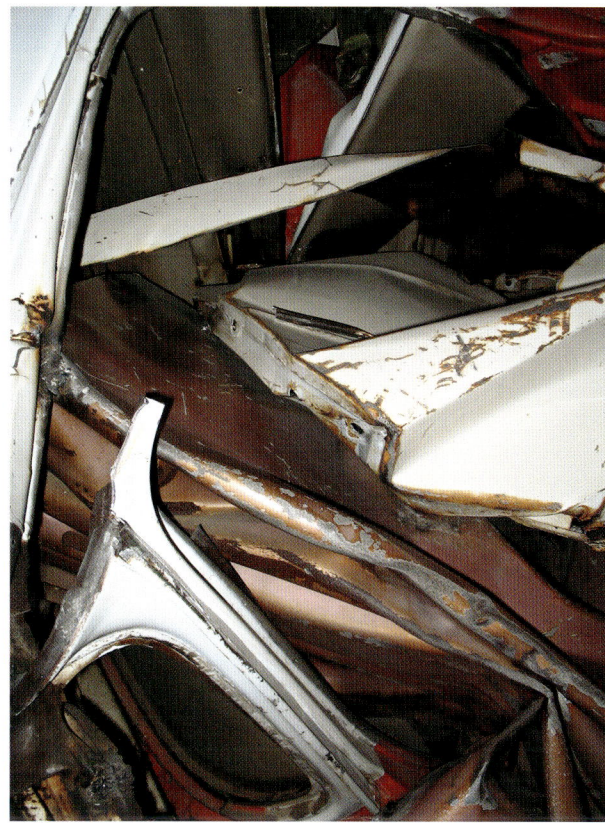

60 John Chamberlain, *Panna-Normanna*, 1972. Painted and chromium-plated steel, 170 × 218.5 × 261.5 cm (67 × 86 × 103 in). Chinati Foundation, Marfa, Texas.

61 Detail of John Chamberlain, *Panna-Normanna*, 1972.

meaning or response for his sculptures. That is, he invoked meaning by referring to the sexual as an analogue for his process but willfully diverted any attempt simply or singularly to define its contours.

The characterization of fit and coupling as sexual, and consequently of his sculptures as summoning multiple but unspecified genders, has been seized on as a descriptive strategy by some commentators. Gary Indiana, writing about *Essex* and other related pieces, remarked:

> The general impetus of the work is consciously sexual, not just in the snug interlocking of parts, but in the repetition of certain allusions, the deployment of unusually (and somewhat inexplicably) libidinal objects. The emphasis on certain elements throughout a sequence of works will

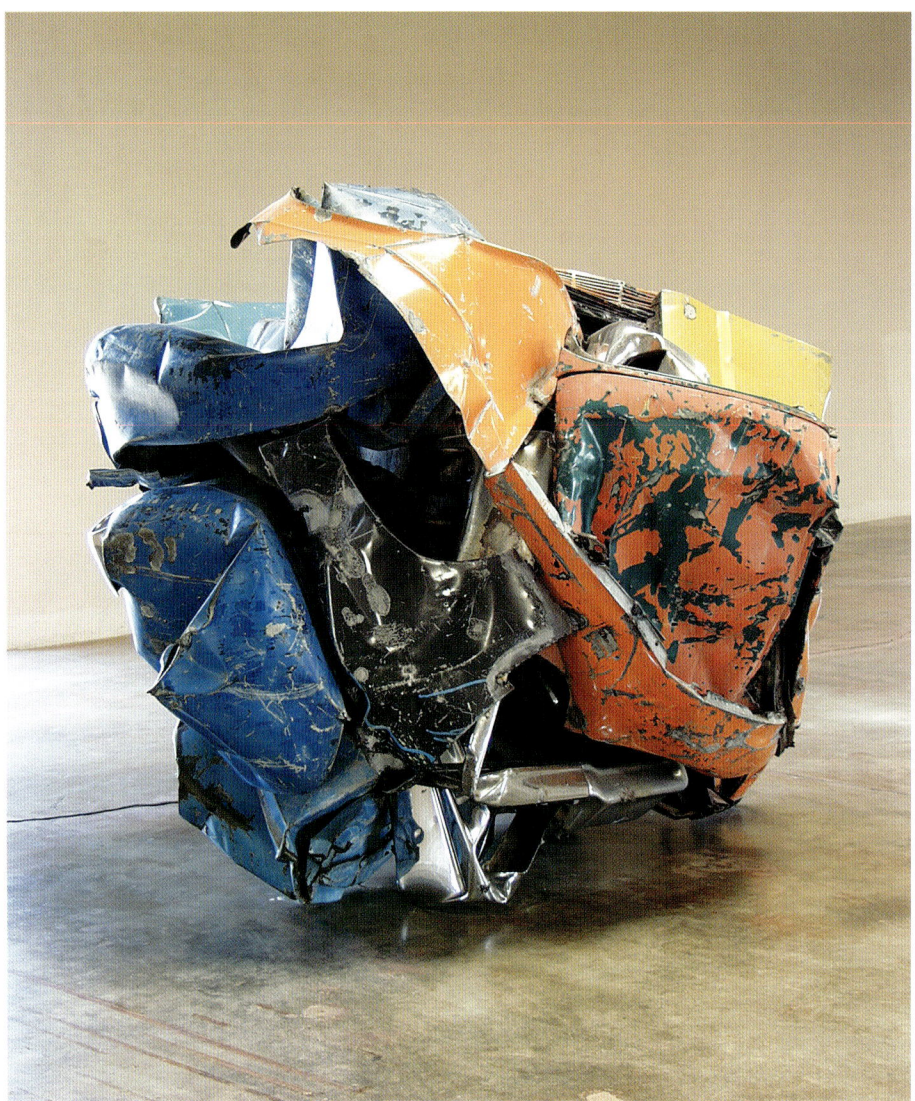

62 John Chamberlain, *Chili Terlingua*, 1972–74. Painted and chromium-plated steel, 176.5 × 208 × 264 cm (69½ × 82 × 104 in.). Chinati Foundation, Marfa, Texas.

stress, say, the erotic lure of crushed door panels, radiator grilles, impacted rear-end assemblies….Consider the eroticism of the massive foam couches: vast, brooding, carnal invitations *designed for one thing and one thing only*.[58]

This persistent invocation of the sexual in accounts offered by Chamberlain and others of his process and of his work makes it imperative to pursue how gender manifests itself in those proposed relations. Sexuality continues to be primarily defined through the genders of its protagonists, and one can barely talk about the sexual without at least questioning what genders might be at play.[59] While gender and sexuality have since the early twentieth century been defined as distinct constellations of cultural and individual traits, they nevertheless implicate each other and are interdependently defined.[60] Most simply, the invocation of sexuality necessarily brings with it the question of genders (regardless of whether that question is answered or deferred). Chamberlain's deployment of the sexual analogies for his fitting is no different. One cannot avoid the fundamental issue of gender and its centrality to how the category of sexuality has itself been defined. What is significant about Chamberlain's rhetoric, however, is how this mutual implication of gender with sexuality interfaced with his own practice of raising the open-ended analogy of the sexual to his otherwise non-figural work.

As the sampling of critical discussions offered earlier attests, the identification of gender in the components and in the fit has proven difficult to pin down. One becomes easily frustrated if one seeks to assign genders securely to the parts, to the sculptures, or to aspects of Chamberlain's process. There is no hidden symbology of sexual organs or body parts.[61] Many of Chamberlain's commentators have found it easier to leave gender indiscriminate while nevertheless calling for a sexualized reading of the work. Indiana, in the passage quoted, calls the parts "libidinal objects," for instance. Jochen Poetter emphasized a similar polymorphous gendering in Chamberlain's process:

> In his work, Chamberlain has spoken repeatedly of the motif of sexuality and eroticism. How this motif might possibly be reflected in the cold metal-works may not be readily apparent. Since the mid-'seventies, Chamberlain has been purchasing car metal directly from the manufacturer. Molded to fit their function, painted and ready for assembly, initially the parts still share an anonymous origin. Only after they have been caught between the metal jaws of the press in the artist's workshop do they metamorphose into living forms.[62]

Poetter's account of the sexual in Chamberlain's work is careful to leave sexes and genders unspecified, even going as far as to consider them emerging variably from the same raw materials. His metaphor of the primordial forging of gendered and sexual forms – always unspecified and new each time – is particularly suggestive. When asking about gender in these sculp-

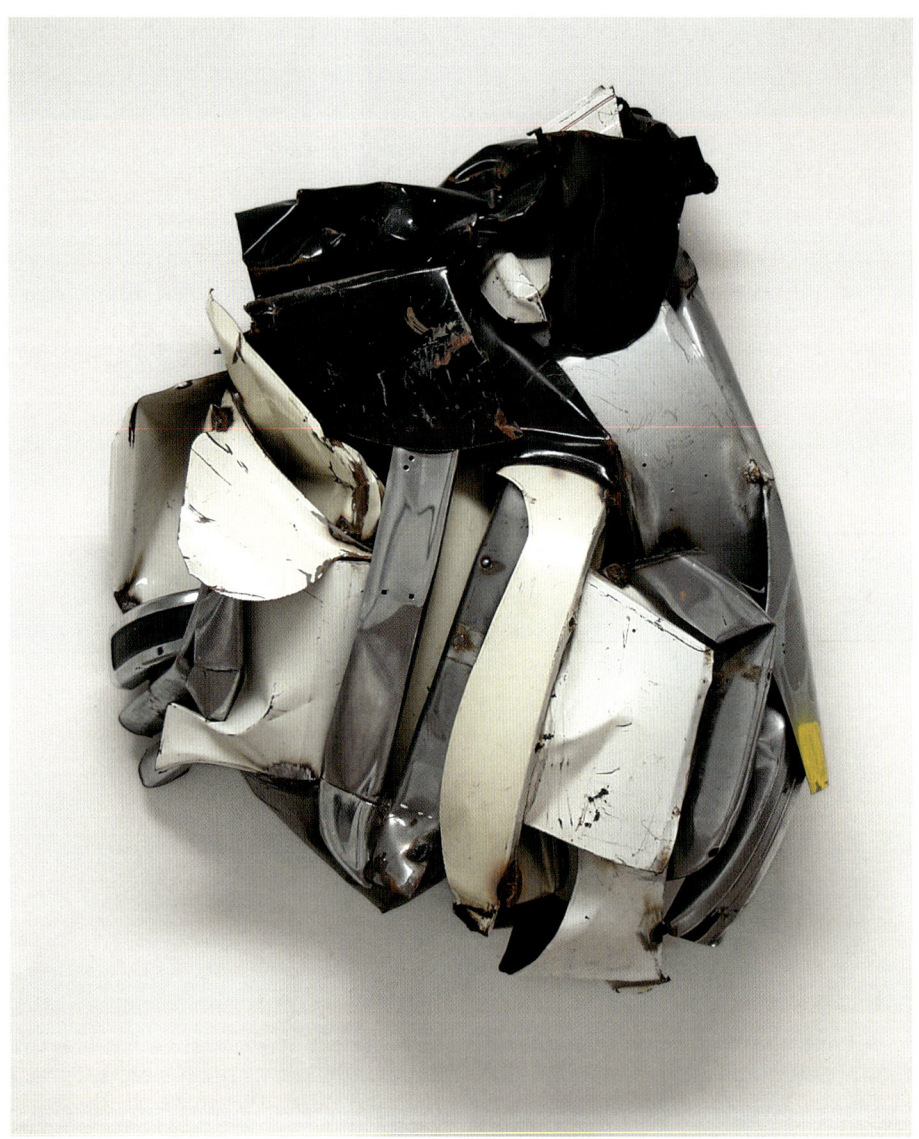

63 John Chamberlain, *Four Polished Nails*, 1979. Painted and chromium-plated steel, 142 × 124.5 × 53.5 cm (56 × 49 × 21 in.). Chinati Foundation, Marfa, Texas.

tures, it is clearly inadequate (and unfruitful) to search for parts that could be nominated as male or female. Stable or static assignments or iconographies are not feasible. Rather, one needs to consider a wider range of possibilities for how the category of gender might be put into play as a result of Chamberlain's process and the analogy he offers for it. Poetter's own metaphor for this is particularly resonant because Chamberlain's work and practice both rely on transformation as a fundamental priority – from the re-use of scrap metal, industrial products, and detritus to the resulting oscillation between abstraction and reference that this recycling fosters (recall Judd's statement about the "successive states of the same form or material").[63] The acts of transformation effected through coupling are what Chamberlain seeks to allude to with his talk of the "sexual fit." However, in order to explicate how his artistic process can support such an analogy to sexuality and, by implication, gender, one needs an account of gender that itself emphasizes material transformations. Required is a definition of gender that incorporates its mutability, its volitional potential, its temporality, and, most of all, the multiplicity of ways it is embodied (fig. 64). In short, Chamberlain's work demands that when pursuing gender one thinks beyond two given, static categories (and, for that matter, those categories' equation with assumptions of dimorphism).

As discussed in the Introduction, a central aim in the emergence of theories and histories of gender in recent decades has been to overturn assumptions that the sexed body is simply dimorphic and that genders are wholly biologically determined, static, and simply binary in scope. Gender identity cannot be assumed to be co-extensive with or deterministically arising from the sexed body.[64] Indeed, as histories of the medical establishment's problematic attempts to manage intersex individuals come to light, it is clear that the boundaries of the sexed body – beyond the complexities of gender at both the personal and the social levels – have never been inflexible or absolute.[65] Genders are contingent and hard-won modes of inhabiting bodies in negotiation with the cultural, historical, and social contexts in which they operate. As Judith Butler has remarked, "Terms of gender designation are thus never settled one and for all but are constantly in the process of being remade."[66] As she has argued, genders may come to seem "natural" or inherent for some, but any sense of "being" a gender is repeatedly subject to the need for its reinforcement. It is, thus, fundamentally temporal rather than static for all individuals, even though many may experience and enact gender identity as consistent. It is this temporal nature of gender that grounds the always-present potential for trans positions. To recall Susan Stryker's definition of trans, it is "the movement across a socially imposed boundary away from an unchosen starting place – rather than any particular destination or mode of transition."[67] Such a movement happens within a temporal register, and all genders are to a degree in transformation and changing, even if it is just the conventional narrative of childhood to adolescence to adulthood. Such transitions require work,

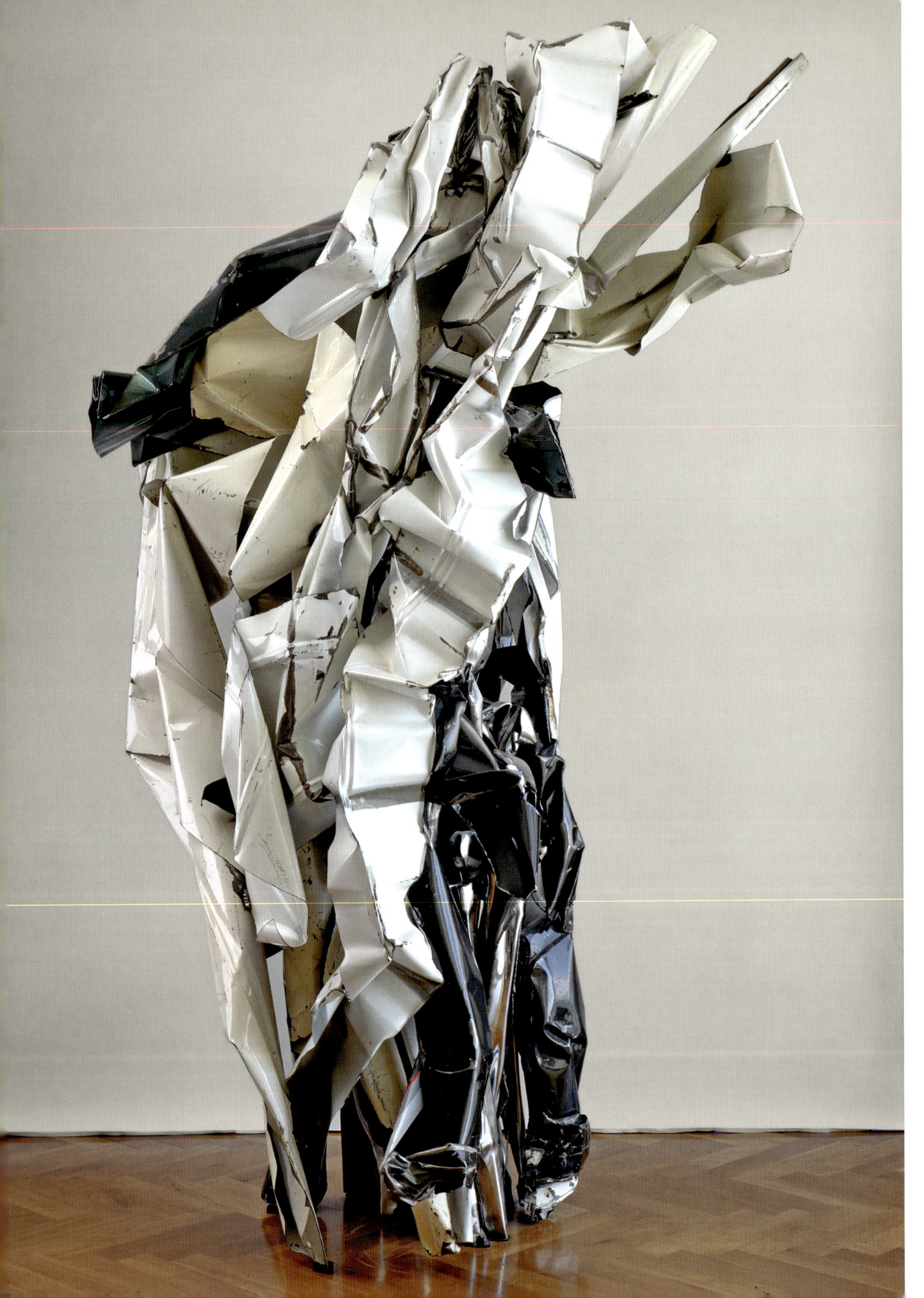

experimentation, and commitment to be and to inhabit a gender, however common or unique.

The understanding of gender as temporally construed is the fundamental epistemological shift for which transgender studies demands recognition. Central to this position is a critical analysis of the "idealization of dimorphism" that underwrites traditional notions of the sexed body.[68] By contrast, transgender histories place value on those many different types of existing genders and bodies that cannot be adequately described through binary, dimorphic, and static categories. The lessons of these accounts of gender are that any all-encompassing and fundamental binary division of humanity into only male and female bodies (and masculine and female genders which are assumed to correspond to those bodies) fails to tell us much about the complexity of individual lives and histories – let alone much about the contingent cultural categories of masculinity and femininity that only sometimes map onto them. Activist movements around transsexual, transgender, and intersex politics have provided the catalysts for such non-dimorphic and temporalized accounts of gender and, importantly, of human bodies. In turn, this more refined interrogation of gender diversity has allowed for the long-standing existences of varieties of transsexual and transgender lives in history to come to light. Ultimately, these critical formulations have deep ramifications not just for how one understands all genders but also for how one conceptualizes sexuality without privileging dimorphism.

While seemingly far from Chamberlain's crushed auto parts, I contend that these understandings of genders via their temporalities and transformations are necessary to recognize the complexity he himself encourages for his work. After all, Chamberlain made transformation, contingency, and synergistic conjunction foundational priorities at both a material and a conceptual level. As Thomas Crow has remarked about these acts of making, "At the inception of [Chamberlain's] process, each potential component circulates in a state of flux, a continuum which its ultimate sculptural destination, if it has one, remains undefined."[69] Chamberlain's best way of characterizing this unforeclosed potential was to make an analogy to the sexual, and it is from this analogy that Chamberlain's work – as he maintained – drew its energy. But it is crucial that his particular overlay of sexuality onto abstraction denies easy identification, standard roles, binary

OPPOSITE 64 John Chamberlain, *F*****g Asterisks*, 1988. Painted chromium and plated steel, 243.8 × 207.6 × 119.3 cm (96 × 81¾ × 47 in.). Martin Z. Margulies Collection.

modes, and simple categorizations. His characteristic evocation and frustration of meaning – present in his titles, his statements, and even in his semi-allusive formal constellations – all demand openness rather than fixity. His deployment of the sexual analogy requires no less. The perspective gained through a recognition of transgender capacities most adequately registers the rejection of foreclosure about meaning, identification, and recognition that he often urged on behalf of his sculpture.

When talking about his own work, Chamberlain repeatedly gave the analogy of the sexual fit to the transformational process that results in each work, composed of multitudes of couplings, conjunctions, and fittings that aggregately make a cohesive whole – a sculpture. When the ramifications of this recurring analogy are pursued in the light of his other concerns over the unfixity of meaning, however, this characterization exceeds the confines of an understanding of genders and of bodies as being simply and irrevocably designated male or female. Most simply put, he always interjects the sexual into discussions of his practice and art in a way that leaves open and unfixed where and how the sexual coupling is located and between whom. In that interjection, gender is offered as a question with an indeterminate answer – one that is never either/or and one that can be posed again and again. It makes little sense to see only male and female in his works when he himself was careful to keep his options from being so limited or static. As many have noted when writing about Chamberlain's works and their relationship to the sexual, far more is going on.

However, it is not precise enough to see the gender operating in Chamberlain's work as fluid. Rather, it is directly rooted in the material possibilities offered by the individual parts and, once coupled with another, how those possibilities are developed or inflected by that new situation. Despite the fact that any assignment of gender to the parts must necessarily be contingent, this does not mean that it is random or arbitrary. It is the temporal process of his fitting of the parts that is significant, for it is one of transforming a material into a particular instance. Just as Judd spoke of the importance of recognizing the "successive states" of Chamberlain's materials and their "oblique imagery," so too must we recognize that the genders that he invokes are also the result of successive transformations – that is, transitioning from one state to another in response to the situations and conjunctions in which they are put.

Chamberlain's statements about ambiguous sexuality could be seen simply in terms of an inclusive definition of the sexual – a kind of "free love" attitude in which the sexual is available to all and any combinations. Such an interpretation of Chamberlain would, itself, be useful, but it would nevertheless fail to embrace the full implications of his mapping of the sexual and, with it, the gendered onto abstraction. His work also implies a multiplication of genders and not just a limitless recombination of conventional or given ones. That is, the generation of semantic openness that Chamberlain claims over and over again for the work under the rubric of the sexual extends to gender beyond and in addition to sexuality.

It is not that Chamberlain necessarily intended to de-classify gender in the terms outlined here, and I am making no claims about any oppositional or critical intent on his part. Instead, it is the complexity of his artistic practice that prompts a need for an interpretative lens focused on the issues he raised for and through his work. While claiming that his sculpture is largely non-signifying and un-mimetic, Chamberlain nevertheless often titled and explained his works with reference to their manifestation of the sexual. Looking back on his career, he remarked, "A lot of my work is very erotic."[70] He urged viewers to find their own meanings in the work but gave them a nudge in the direction of the sexual and the gendered. In short, this is another moment of coupling a trait with its contradiction: his rigorously non-figurative art is couched in a rhetoric that constantly invokes the presence and potentiality of gender in it and in his process.[71] Consequently, his work offers itself as an exemplary theoretical object through which to interrogate the manifestations of genders in a non-figurative register.

We are left to ask how and where genders emerge in Chamberlain's works? Some of his sculptures are, in fact, directly designated as simply female or male. This occurs most often with titles, but also can be coded through materials or colors, like the early works *Miss Lucy Pink* (see fig. 51) or the aforementioned *Huzzy* (see fig. 57). Equally, there are those that are titled as male, like *Son of Dudes* (fig. 65 and see fig. 52). These assignments, however, are never completely stable or unquestionable. One could note, for instance, that *Son of Dudes* is designated as male and as the product of male-male procreation. Titles like these more obvious ones leave little doubt that these figures are intended to be somehow understood in relation to conventional binary genders, yet it is not always clear how viewers are to link up that gender with the formal and artistic elements that are shared, across genders, with other work. In addition, the focus of the sexual fit is on the parts that make up the work as a whole, so no sculpture can be monolithically or simply gendered. Furthermore, when one looks more broadly at Chamberlain's oeuvre, these simply gendered works are only a portion of the whole.

Beyond sculpture labeled male or female, what about the works that seem to evoke more than one body with indeterminate genders, such as

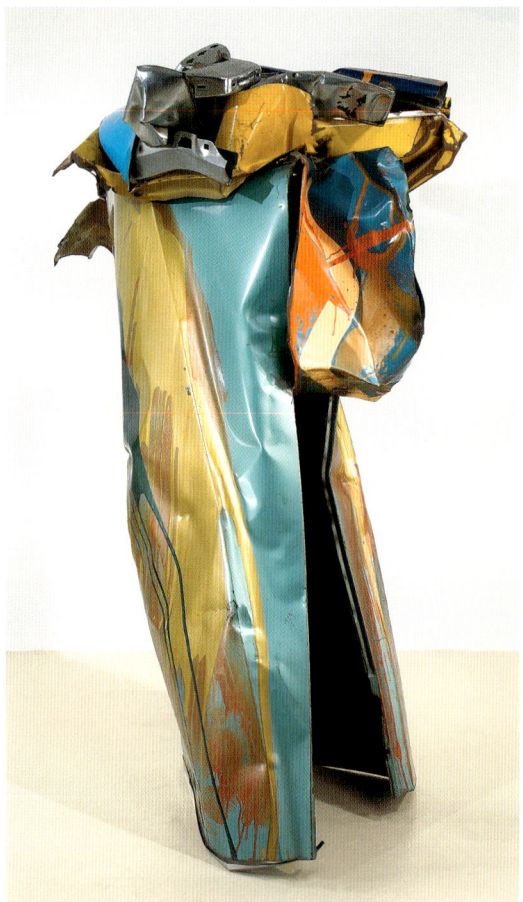

LEFT 65 John Chamberlain, *Son of Dudes* (see also fig. 52).

OPPOSITE 66 John Chamberlain, *Three Cornered Desire*, 1979. Painted and chromium-plated steel, 177.8 × 261.6 × 177.8 cm (70 × 103 × 70 in.). Dia Art Foundation.

Three Cornered Desire (fig. 66), *Crowded Hearts*, and the *Socket* series (see fig. 44)? Just as with his explanations of his work, Chamberlain's titles often invoke genders and couplings without ever fully pinning them down to a color, an iconography, or a formal element. Perhaps this is one of the reasons why the titles often go undiscussed (or suppressed) in the literature on Chamberlain. They are difficult to match up with the works, but they nevertheless can color or direct the viewer's experience of the work.[72] In particular, they often key his sculptures to issues of the figure, the bodily, and the gendered. This is not superfluous to his work, but central to it. Importantly, however, Chamberlain introduces genders in a willfully undefined manner, positing them not as essential traits that simply are or are not there. They are, rather, open to contestation and refiguration in a way analogous to the critique of gender dimorphism and biological determinism

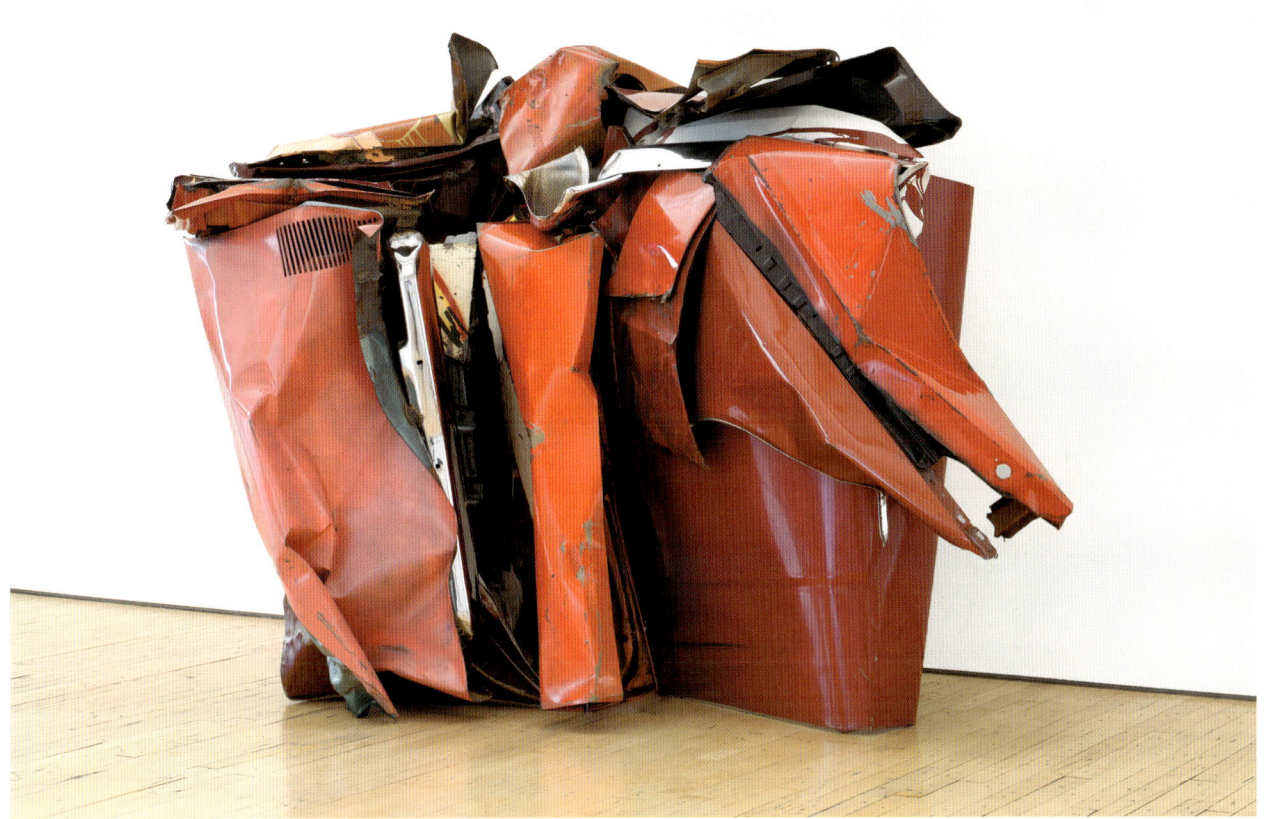

made by transgender theory. This is especially evident in the period when he reinvested his process in working with metal in the 1970s. This retrospective phase coincided with his increasing vocalization of the sexual metaphor for his process and his more explicit and complex staging of genders in the work. When one looks at his body of work as a whole, one can see how this assessment of his own process consistently and repeatedly raises the category of gender only to make its manifestation variable. Again, when talking about making and viewing these works – even the ones identified as a single body – Chamberlain talked about the "sexual fit" within them. For instance, in works from the late 1970s such as *Folded Nude* and *One Twin*, the question of unity and internal division are foregrounded. Both titles ostensibly refer to one body, but one that folds in on itself or is doubled (fig. 67). They are both coupled unities, identified as a body. In

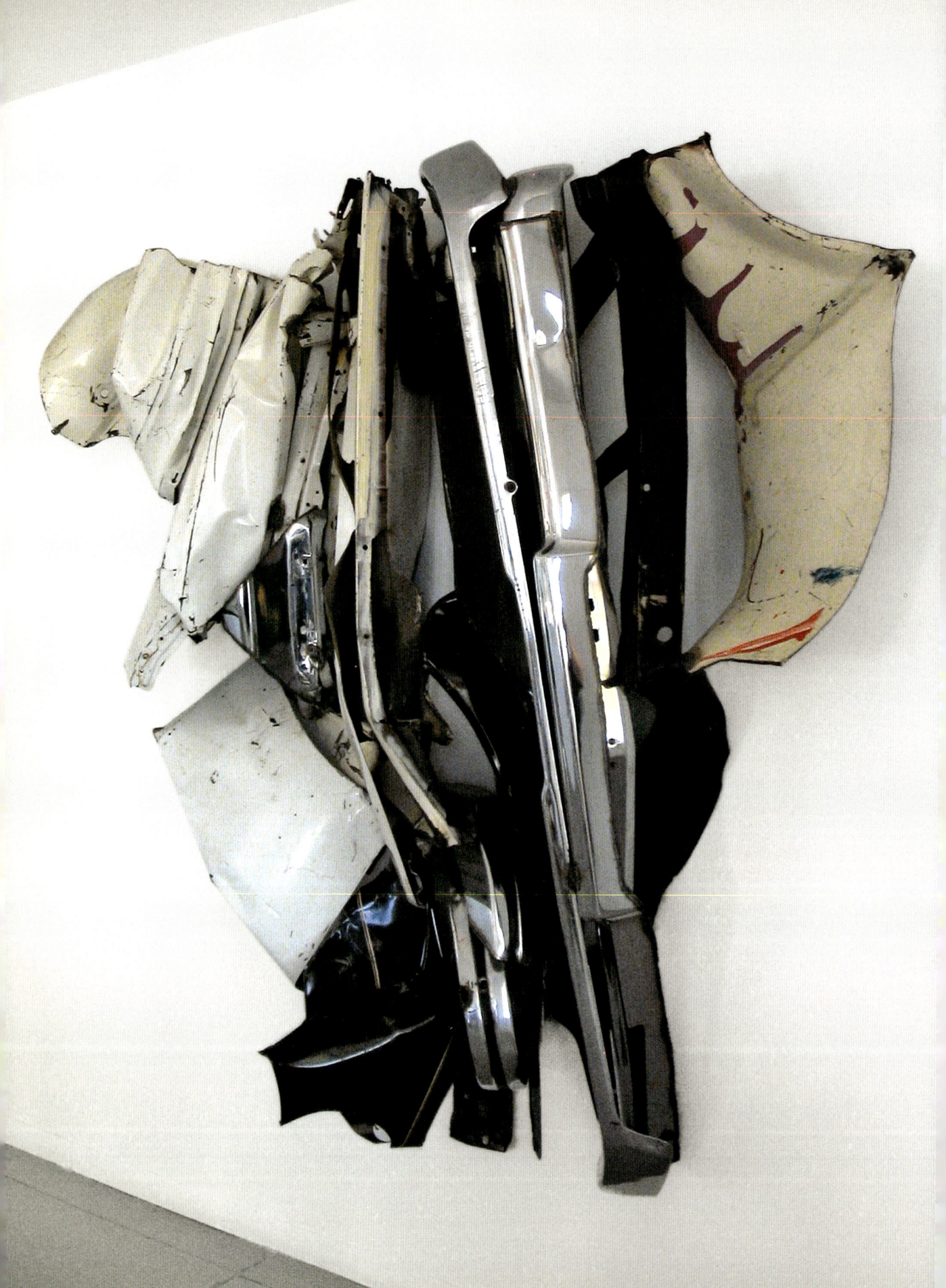

neither, however, do we viewers see a clear identification of gender or any noetic resemblance to a human figure, only Chamberlain's comments about the "sexual fit" within ringing in our ears, prompting us to search for genders both in and of the work. There is no answer to this puzzle, however – no truth of gender there to be recovered once and for all in the sculpture or anchored to its individual parts.

For Chamberlain's most explicit staging of such issues, one could look to the *Kiss* sculptures, also from the late 1970s (figs 68–70; see also figs 72–74). Here, Chamberlain cited a long line of famous sculptures of kissing couples, such as those by Auguste Rodin and Constantin Brancusi (fig. 71), but he left the question open in his works as to who is doing the kissing. The coloring of the works demarcates two halves to each sculpture, implying a kiss between them. As one looks at the series as a whole, it becomes less easy to match up one side with one gender and another side with the other – or even with the same. In some, colors with gendered connotations (pink and blue) are used, but others use different combinations of colors. In all, there is no easy division into halves or segments but, rather, an ambiguity in their generally bilateral compositions. What, from one angle, might be identified as "male" might from another look "female." From yet another perspective, this same element could look like a little bit of both – or neither. Even in Brancusi's paired-down couple, he made sure subtly to indicate sexual difference between the figures with such details as the swelling belly and long hair of his female half. Chamberlain's *Kisses*, however, leave the question willfully open and circulating. The genders, that is, are successive transformations emergent from the same material object (the oil drum). To put it most bluntly, just as transgender theory argues that biology is not deterministic of the infinite variety of genders and the volition of the individuals who enact them, so too can one see in Chamberlain's evocation of the sexual a framing of gender that demands to be seen not as intrinsic or fixed but as the result of particular and unforeclosable transformations.

Perhaps only with a full embrace of this open-endedness and – as Chamberlain put it – "discovery," can one understand the ramifications of his practice. His headlong formal ballet of poised, crushed metal is nothing less than a summary of transformations and metamorphoses. His use of the bodily dynamics of sexuality as his primary metaphor has the effect of

OPPOSITE 67 John Chamberlain, *Folded Nude*, 1978. Painted and chromium-plated steel, 198 × 193 × 53.5 cm (78 × 76 × 21 in.). The Menil Collection, Houston.

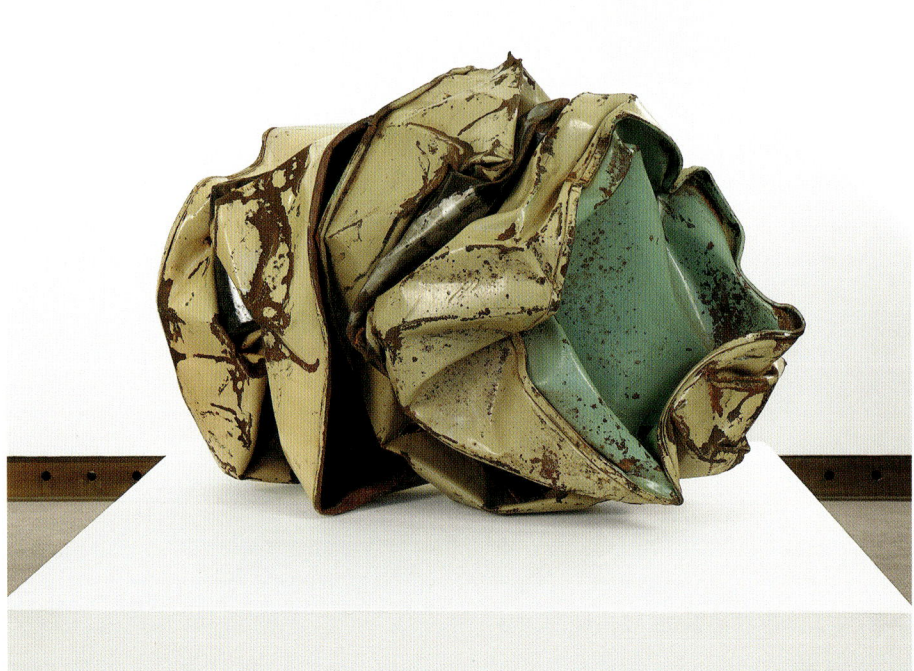

68 John Chamberlain, *Kiss #28*, 1979. Painted steel, 63.5 × 90 × 53.5 cm (25 × 35½ × 21 in.).

injecting a sort of free-floating and unspecified anthropomorphism into his work. This metaphor never resolves into an iconography or attaches itself to the work's forms no matter how much it suffuses his triumphantly lusty accounts of its making. It is this very lack of resolution between the committed non-referentiality of Chamberlain's work and his bodily and erotic allusions that produces an open-ended account of metamorphosis. The work took on a life of its own as Chamberlain adapted to the crushed materials and their balances in order to orchestrate its couplings. This was what he meant when he said, "The completion of the piece is intuitive."[73] Or as he described the job of the sculptor: "first to *see* the pieces, then to *put them together*. He isn't going to take each piece and twist it, bend it, direct it, before he adds it to the ensemble. He's going to choose each piece because he knows in advance it will fit....a sculpture dictates its own form."[74] This was the "discovery angle" that Chamberlain understood his polymorphous couplings producing for him and for viewers.

My concern in this analysis is to draw out from Chamberlain's works this capacity to allegorize the transformability of gender that is made visible and fundamental in transgender theories and histories. It is Chamberlain's long-running insistence on tying the sexual to the non-figural in his particularly open way that seems to me to offer, on the one hand, a way toward a clearer recognition of the conceptual sophistication of his work and aims and, on the other, a way of offering an account of gender as transformed, temporal, and narrativized. This is useful because it is this understanding of gender as narratively construed as a transformation that is itself often difficult to represent, to figure, or to allegorize.[75]

This might all seem far removed from Chamberlain's no-nonsense personality and his stated intentions, however vague. In no way did he espouse a critique of gender when he talked about his work, but he did rigorously attempt to unanchor and multiply meanings in it and in his process. In so doing this under the rubric of the sexual, however, he raised questions about gender in its traditional characterization as static and determined. Sometimes, interviewers posed these questions back to Chamberlain, who appropriately reacted with his characteristic dislike for dictating meanings and intentions. Rather than specify, he preferred openness when it came to his work. This is clearest in a terse but telling response to Henry Geldzahler in a 1992 interview. Geldzahler had remarked:

> Aesthetically, the most amazing thing about your work is the same thing that is amazing about you. In order to do the work, you have to be an engineer on the one hand, and a poet on the other. You have to be a realist and a romantic at the same time. You have to be masculine and not afraid of being feminine all at the same time. Feminine in the sense that such an almost "nail polish-lipstick" aestheticizing is going on, which could embarrass someone who's embarrassed by things like that. I don't know, I just admire the fact that the structure is perfect, and at the same time, the color works. So tender. I know the idea of being feminine doesn't thrill you, but I think it's there.

Chamberlain's reply to him was simple and short: "Well it is. Everybody's both."[76]

In this statement, one can see how fundamental the strategy of coupling was for Chamberlain's understanding of his work and his practice. It is not surprising that when confronted with a question about gender and his work, he would offer an answer that defied the conventional limitations of a binary either/or.

One outcome of this analysis of Chamberlain's deployment of sexuality and gender is to suggest connections between his project and larger contexts

138 ABSTRACT BODIES

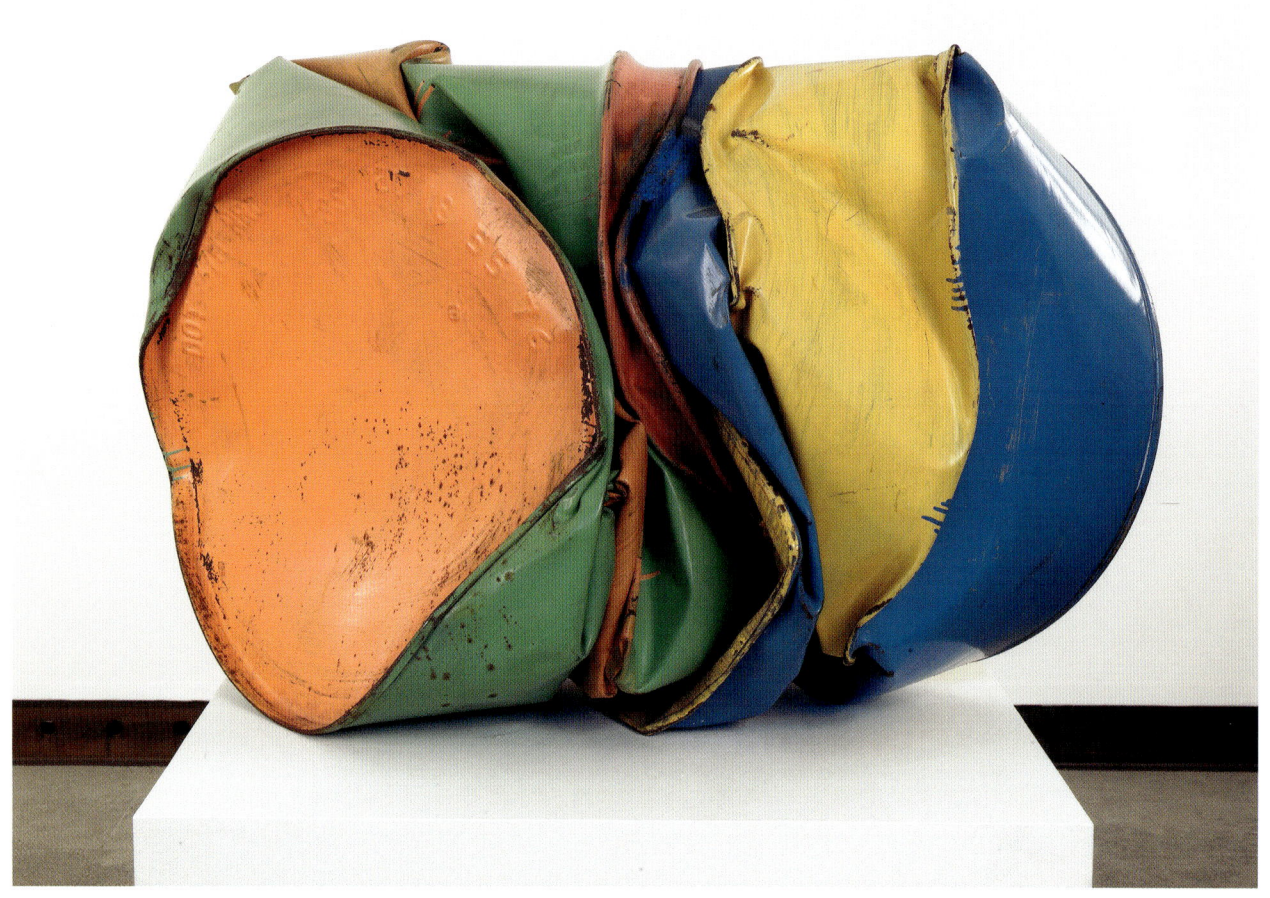

69   John Chamberlain, *Kiss #11*, 1979. Painted steel, 62 × 99 × 51 cm (24½ × 39 × 20 in.).

and currents in postwar art history. He is often consigned to the narrow framework of a latecomer to Abstract Expressionism, and many have uncritically disregarded his work as merely formalist abstraction. This labeling of Chamberlain as an Abstract Expressionist (late or otherwise) has always been inadequate for him, and this taxonomy obscures much of the sophistication of his practice.[77] It is true that he was influenced by painters such as Willem de Kooning and Franz Kline, but what are we to make of an artist who was both a fixture at the Cedar Bar and part of the group that filmed *Lone-*

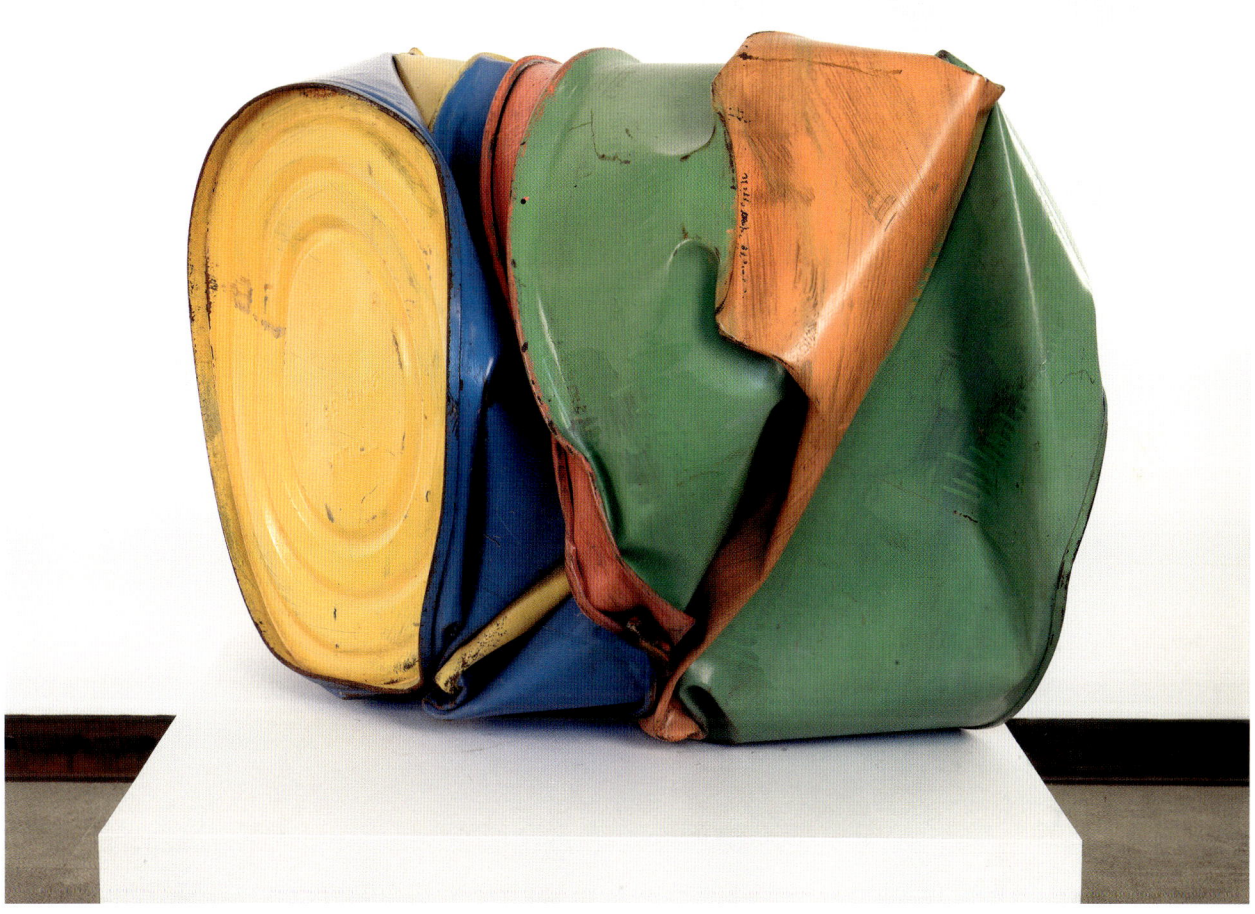

70 John Chamberlain, *Kiss #11*, alternative view.

some Cowboys with Andy Warhol?[78] Chamberlain's tactics are less similar to the heroicism of the Abstract Expressionists to which he is often compared and more akin to the ambivalent and parataxical approach of a contemporary like Larry Rivers.[79] Similarly, Robert Smithson slyly saw in Chamberlain's work a comparison to Kenneth Anger's groundbreaking 1964 film *Scorpio Rising* with its camp take on motorcycle culture.[80] Perhaps the willful unfixity of meaning in Chamberlain's oeuvre is, as well, better compared to the critical engagement with silence and the blocking of direct expression

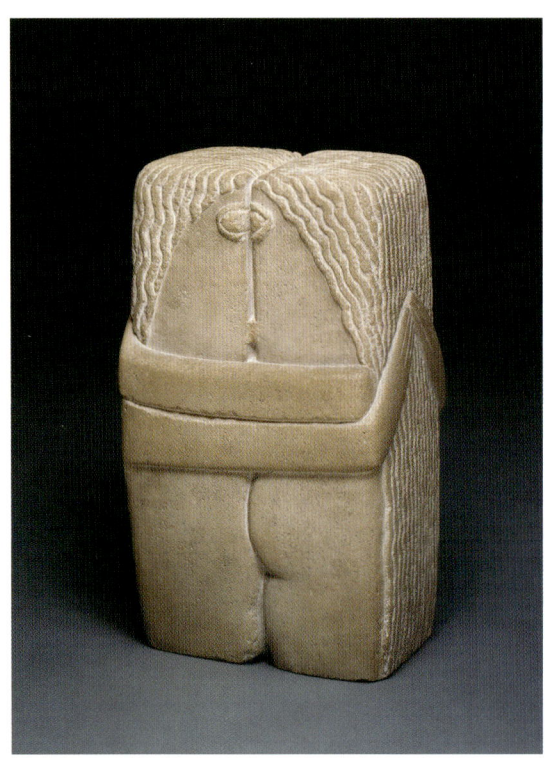

LEFT 71 Constantin Brancusi, *The Kiss*, 1919. Limestone, 58.4 × 33.7 × 25.4 cm (23 × 13¼ × 10 in.). Philadelphia Museum of Art, Louise and Walter Arensberg Collection, 1950-134-4.

BELOW 72 John Chamberlain, *Kiss #12*, 1979. Painted steel, 76 × 78.5 × 68.5 cm (30 × 31 × 27 in.).

OPPOSITE, TOP 73 John Chamberlain, *Kiss #26*, 1979. Painted steel, 63.5 × 73.5 × 51 cm (25 × 29 × 20 in.).

OPPOSITE, BOTTOM 74 John Chamberlin, *Kiss #12*, alternative view.

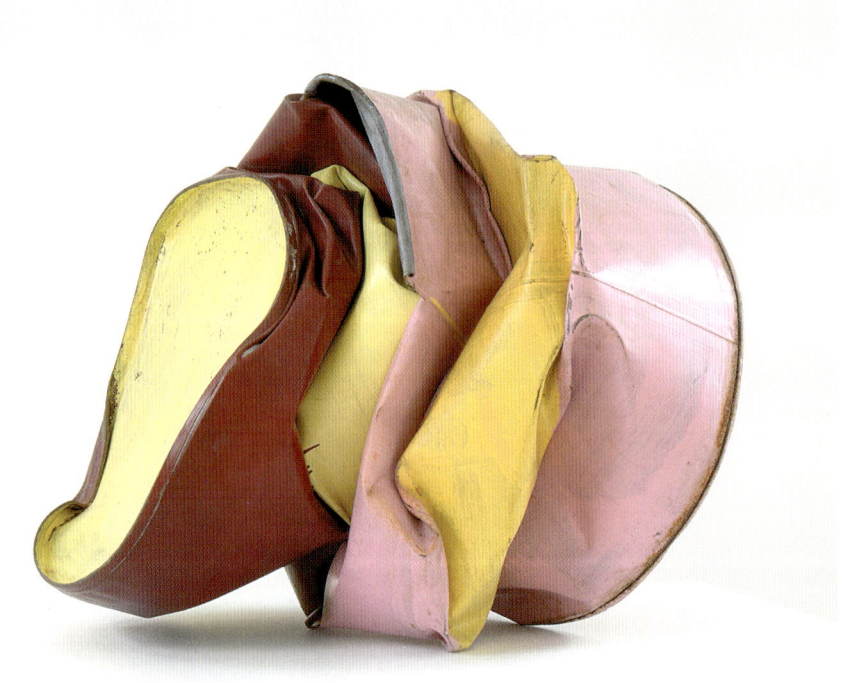

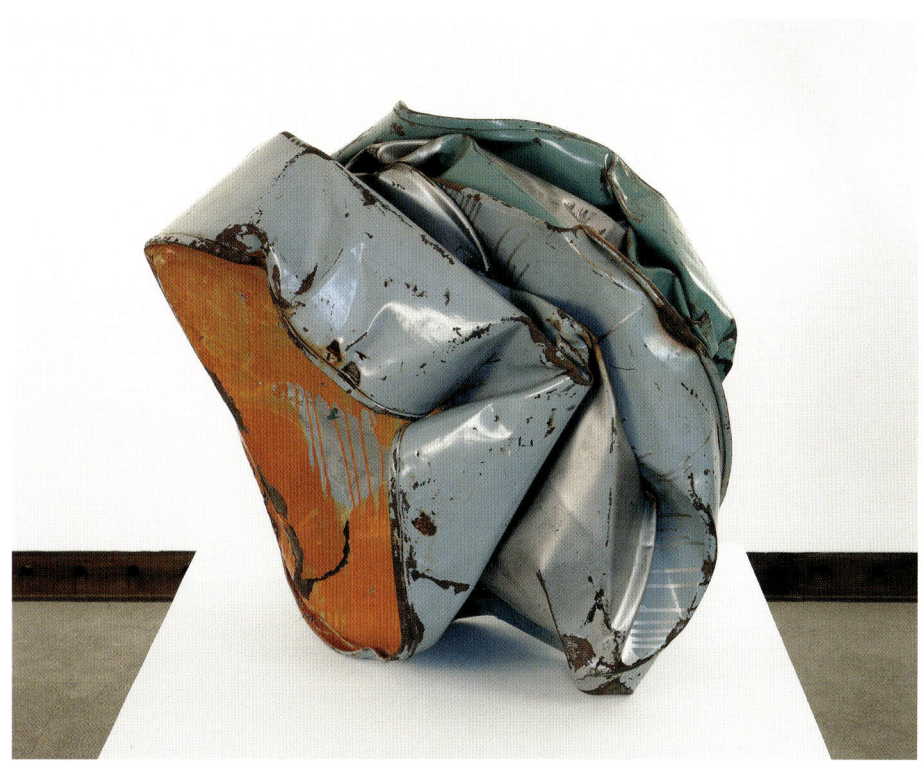
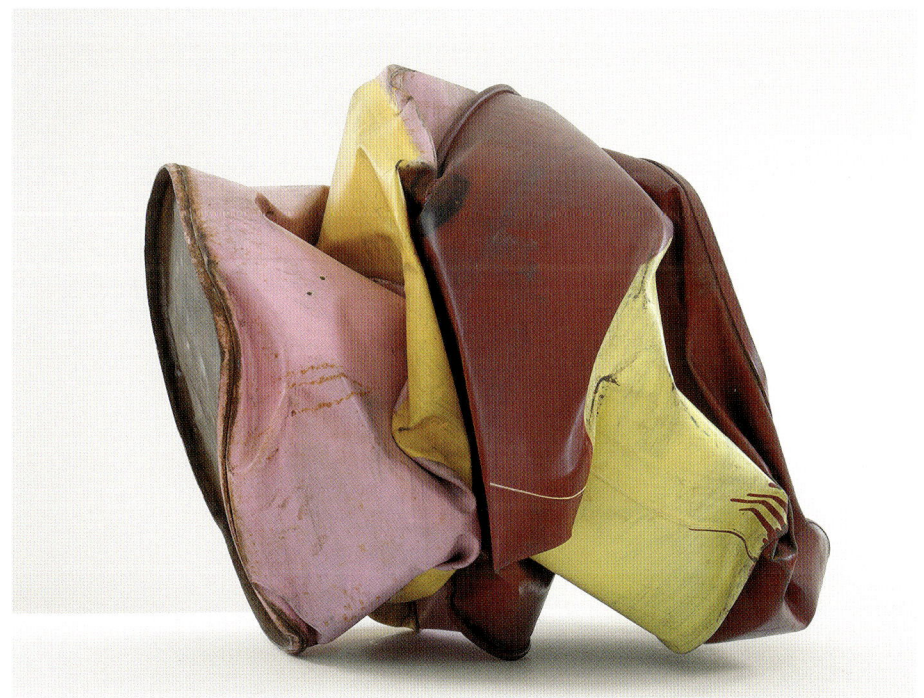

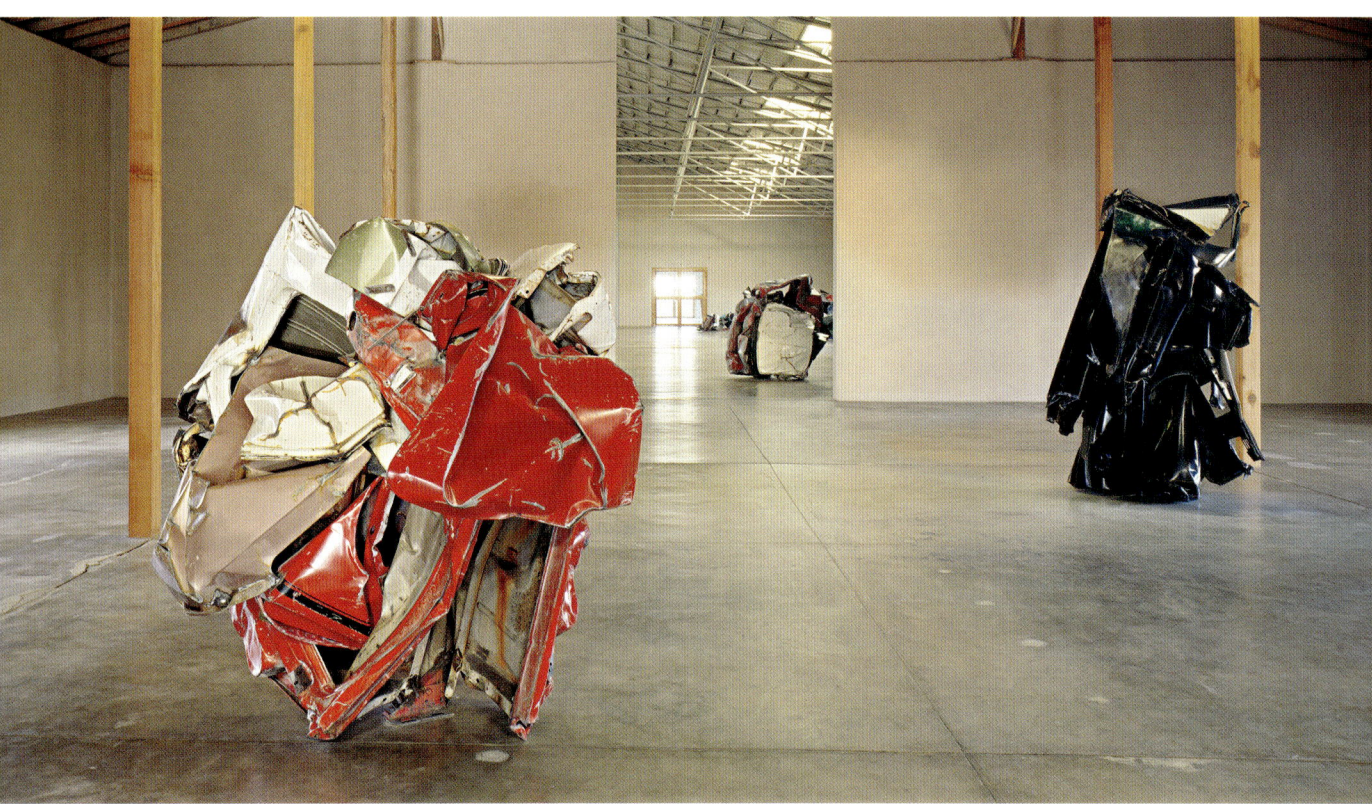

75 Installation view, Chinati Foundation, Marfa, Texas, with *Panna-Normanna*, 1972, in foreground.

characteristic of the work of Jasper Johns or Robert Rauschenberg. Chamberlain works from a different set of starting points from these other artists, with whom he seems to share little stylistic affinity or perspective. Nevertheless, his work – along with Johns, Rauschenberg, Anger, Warhol, and other artists such as Lee Bontecou and Sari Dienes – deployed sophisticated tactics for subverting readability and multiplying meanings that were developed, in part, from a reaction to the dominance of Abstract Expressionism and, significantly, from questions about how and why identity, sexuality, and gender could or should be registered and legible in artwork. In order better to consider Chamberlain's relation to the historical context and art-theoretical debates of his time, it is necessary to look for such connections that may not manifest themselves at the level of stylistic resemblance. One need just remember that Chamberlain's work appealed to a wide variety of his contemporaries – among those who owned his sculpture were Judd, Frank Stella, Johns, Rauschenberg, Cy Twombly, and Warhol.

What I have attempted to outline in this chapter is a way of discussing Chamberlain's works that departs from the tired debate about whether they are about abstraction or about cars. Instead, I have sought to extrapolate larger theoretical issues that his practice manifests and that his rhetoric engenders. He persistently reminded his viewers that the key to understanding his work is in grasping the implications of his artistic process and its sexual fit. At base, gender and sexuality were crucial analogies through which he grappled with the full potential of the fitting of elements and the polyvalence that coupling generates. When Chamberlain spoke of the origins of his attitude, he recalled his time at Black Mountain College:

> So I had this collection of words that I liked to look at. It didn't matter what they meant, I liked the way they looked. I would look at these words and I would put them together and come up with an image that was unlike what you could achieve if you didn't do it this way. I remember one line I wrote in which I put together two words: *blonde day*. I'd never thought of a day being blonde. I still haven't, but I liked the way that connection functioned, and it's a very good example of how I work....I guess that's part of my definition of art. Art is a peculiar madness in which you use other means of communication, means that are recognizable to other people, *to say something they haven't yet heard, or haven't yet perceived, or had repressed.*[81]

Chamberlain claims that the conjoining of the two terms creates new, as yet unimagined meanings. His combination of the words "blonde day" is neither meaningless nor nonsense. The unexpected coupling of the terms draws out their contingency and demonstrates the ability to create something wholly new. Even in this example, the body and gender are invoked but left ambiguous. A "blonde day" may mean something different to each of us, but it nevertheless has different possibilities from a "brunette night" – not to mention a "salt and pepper afternoon". It is openness and the capacity for transformation that Chamberlain stresses. The act of fitting creates new possibilities for seeing the words differently and for seeing in their combination something that could not previously be visualized. One of Chamberlain's own mottos warrants repeating here: "art is the only place left where a person can go discover something and not have to be told by somebody else whether they discovered it or not."[82]

By now, it should be clear that Chamberlain's work is not about sex in any simple or banal way. Rather, to understand why and how the sexual operates for Chamberlain as an analogue to his practice is, on the one hand, to begin to understand how complex his works are with regard to their

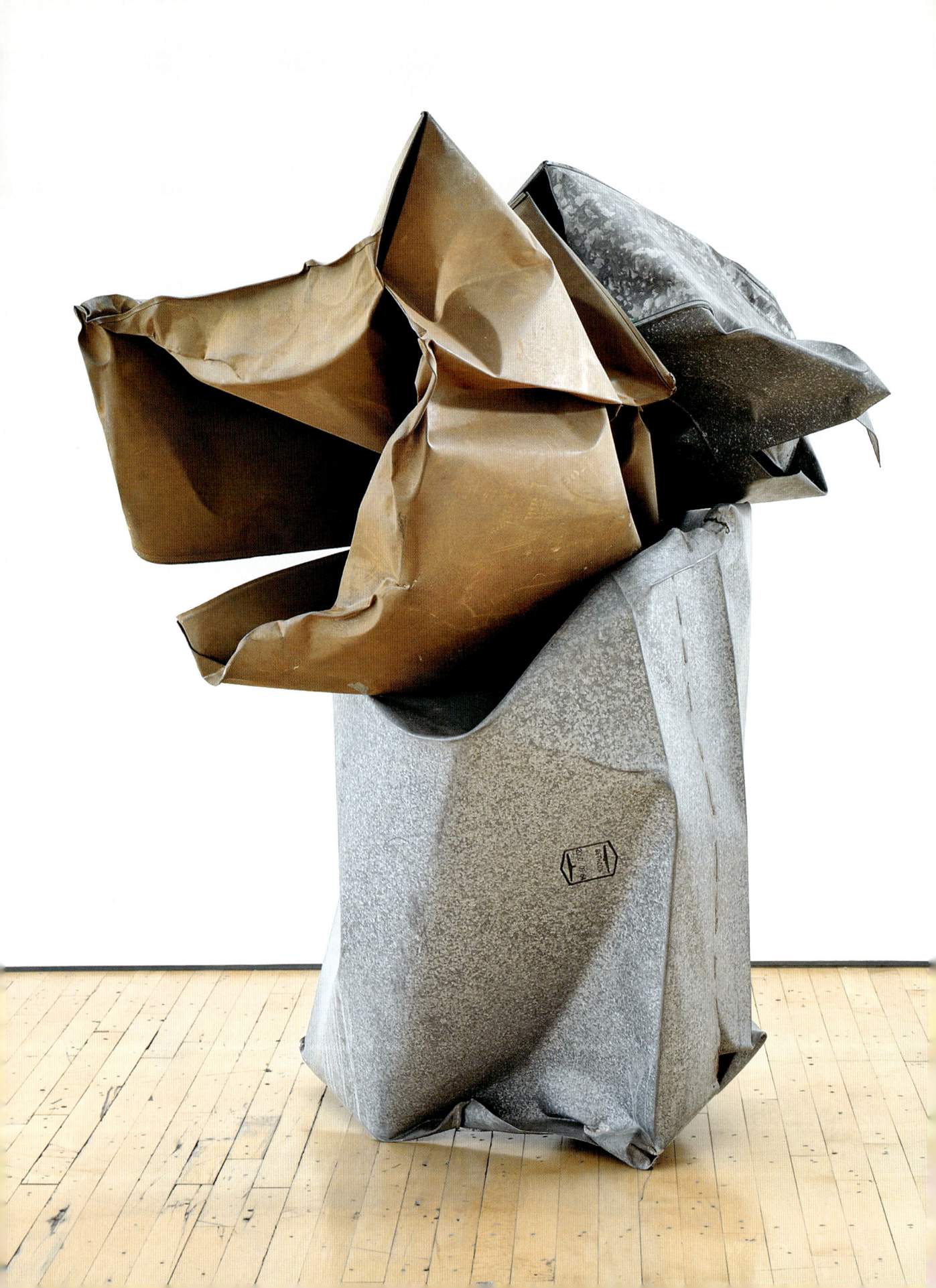

play with meaning and, on the other, to see formulations of both sexuality and gender that are at once both more open and more inclusive. Throughout his statements about his work, Chamberlain left space and time both for coupling and for genders to be imagined otherwise. In this way, Chamberlain's work can be understood to push the long-running issue of abstract anthropomorphism beyond its limits – both in his consistent rejection of mimetic rendering of the human form and in his work's concomitant opening up of the ways in which the human may be located without recourse to resemblance to known bodies. This fostering of potentiality and this allegorization of transformation is precisely why his work is compelling, both visually and conceptually. By underscoring the strategic play in the works and in his words – and specifically the way they persistently call forth sexual and gendered possibilities in spite of the apparent abstraction of his sculptures – I think we can begin to understand how important it is to ask just how Chamberlain fits.

OPPOSITE 76   John Chamberlain, *Ultrafull Private*, 1967. Cor-ten steel and galvanized steel, 169.2 × 138.4 × 146.1 cm (66⅝ × 54½ × 57½ in.) Dia Art Foundation.

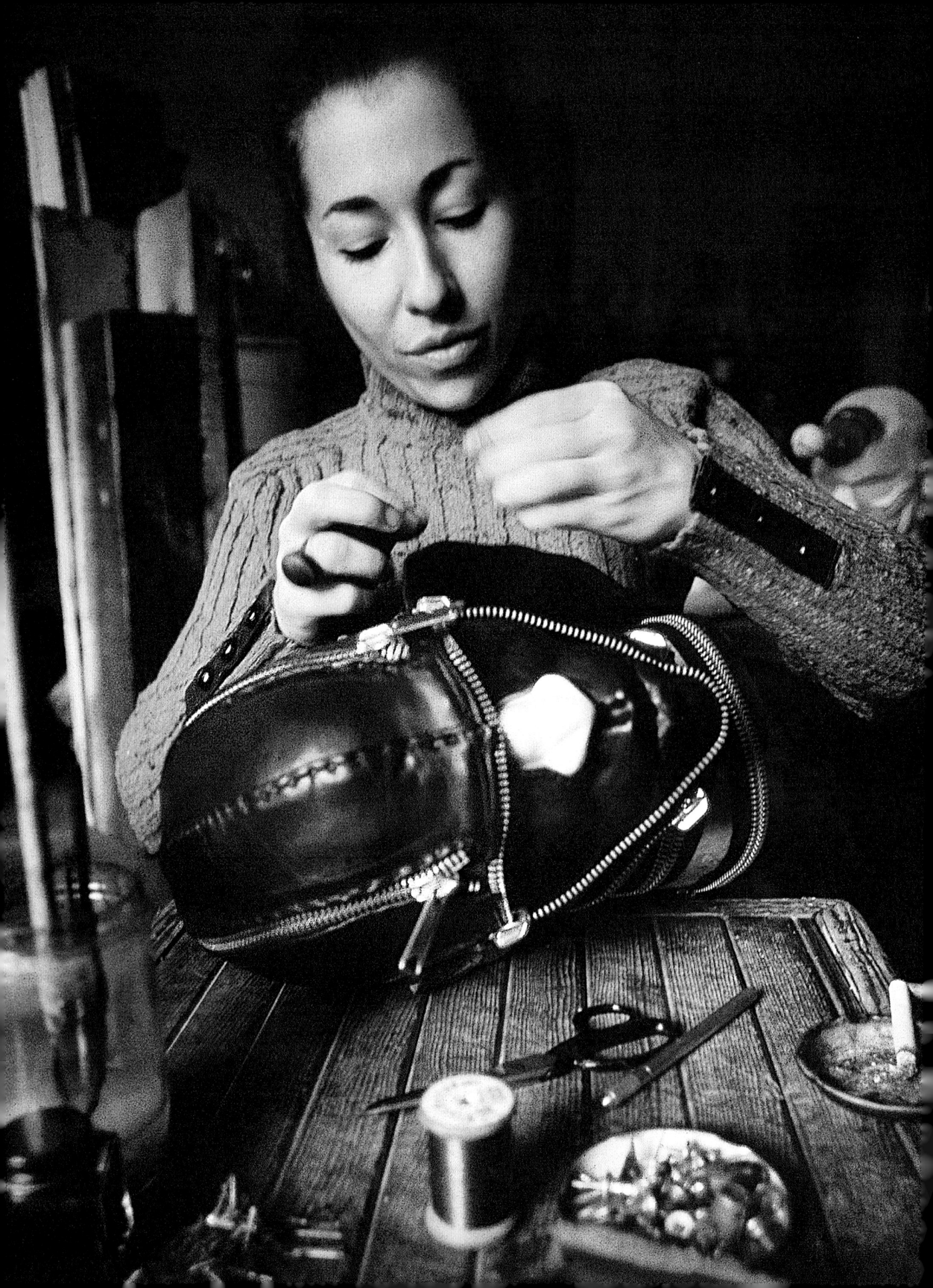

3

SECOND SKINS
THE UNBOUND GENDERS OF NANCY GROSSMAN'S SCULPTURE

"Who are these people? Are they men, women, or generic human beings?" This was the question posed to Nancy Grossman by a group of art students when confronted with the works for which she has become most known – her leather-bound head sculptures. Grossman's long-term partner, the critic Arlene Raven, recounted the artist's response: "She said they were self-portraits. I thought that was an interesting response, because the heads are generally interpreted as male. It got me to thinking about your wanting to delve into masculinity and what happens when women express masculinity, when men do, and what the difference is."[1] This knowing response from Raven – said in a public forum but drawing on their years together – is illustrative of the challenges Grossman's art poses. Bound up with questions of gender, these works evoke but do not image the sexed body. Rather, they vex assumptions about its inhabitations.

Gender is both crucial to and contentious in Grossman's work. While much of the writing on her has dealt exclusively with her iconic head sculptures, I shall instead discuss her engagement with abstraction, assemblage, and practices of re-making in the mid-1960s and then discuss the ways in which this informed her practice and reception in the 1970s. It is through an investigation into her abstract work that one can recognize how Grossman's practice has always offered a complex account of gender's mobility and variability. In her assemblages made from old leather garments, she proposed open accounts of gender's relation to the body and its mutability. In what follows, I shall focus on a handful of these 1960s abstract

OPPOSITE 77 Nancy Grossman in her studio working on *A.F.F.*, 1970.

148 ABSTRACT BODIES

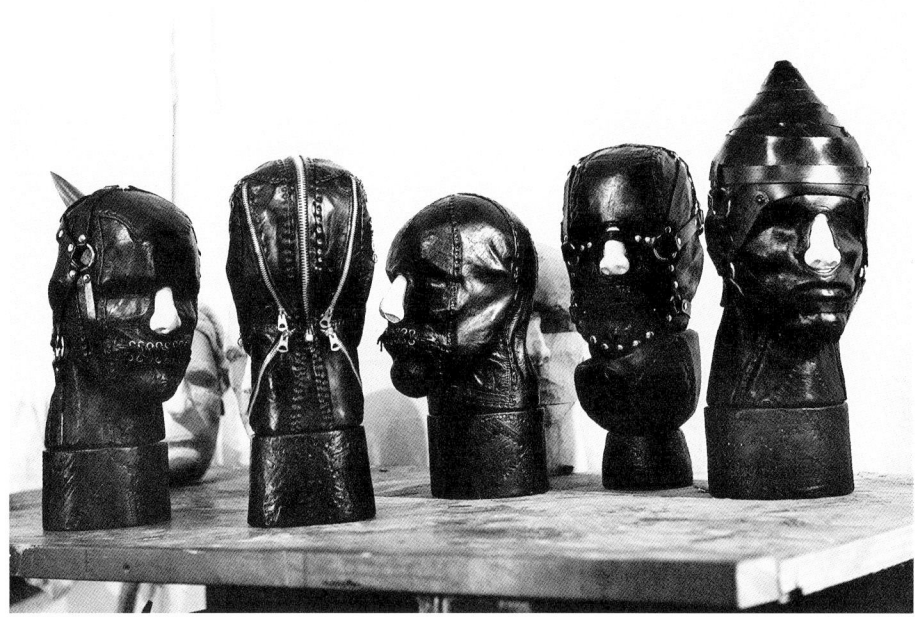

78 Studio view, Eldridge Street, New York, 1968.

works in order to show how she developed an attitude toward the body in which sexual difference was not determining and in which bodily remaking was enabling. In this way, these early works are aligned with the other studies in this book. Grossman's practice used abstraction to propose new ways of understanding the sexed body and to parody our expectations of what we think we know about gender from looking at a body. In the 1960s, Grossman alluded to genital imagery in her abstract assemblages to question playfully its role as sign for gender. She mobilized bodily reconstitution for these works, as well, to remind viewers that what we are looking at now is the result of transformation and remaking. These practices and priorities informed Grossman's work after she turned from abstract renderings of the body to "figurative" sculptures in which the body was absent.[2] Throughout, a recurring question has been how to transcend the limitations of dimorphic sexual difference. For her, the body was nothing but raw material. After all, her sculptures are made from old skins.

Such complexity, however, has not customarily been seen in Grossman's work, which has been chronically misunderstood, parodied, and caricatured. Despite the fact that Grossman was one of the most iconic and recognizable artists of the late years of the 1960s, she has proven to be a problem for later art-historical and art-critical taxonomies. This is both because of the misconception that this work was sexually explicit and because she was one of the first artists to make a "figurative turn" away from abstraction at the end of the decade.[3] She started receiving critical attention in 1964, when Brian O'Doherty wrote in the *New York Times* that "A fabulously talented 23-year-old sprays the results of hard application all over the place in a show that could be the first of a distinguished career....Miss Grossman is a real artist from her fingertips to her subconscious."[4] In 1965, at the age of 25, she was the only painter that year to receive a Guggenheim fellowship, making her one of few women (and one of the youngest) to receive such recognition at the time. Soon after she showed her first head sculpture at the 1968 Whitney Annual, she began having multiple successful one-person shows each year. At the beginning of the 1970s, she was being collected and published widely, in part because her work stood out sharply from that of her contemporaries. During this time, Grossman was also constituted as a feminist forebear, most notably in Cindy Nemser's groundbreaking book of interviews *Art Talk* but also in such varied publications as *Harper's Bazaar* and *Off Our Backs*.[5] As feminism developed in the art world later in the 1970s, however, Grossman's seemingly male-identified representations increasingly sat uneasily with essentialist varieties of feminism that played an important role in the history of the decade. In addition, her commitment to sculptural making and recognizable figurative content kept her at a distance from the mainstream art world as it developed at that time.[6] By the 1980s, Grossman's work was frequently mischaracterized, and her reputation became that of an "artist's artist" known to a devoted few.[7]

These shifts in reputation were, as I discuss shortly, fueled by the mis recognitions of Grossman's head sculptures as sexual, as masculine, and as kink. Indeed, it was because of these presumptions that, for many, Grossman's reputation became difficult to assimilate into versions of feminism from later in the 1970s that understood sexual and gender difference in starkly binary terms. It was during these years that debates began raging about the presence of transwomen in feminism and women-only spaces (a prejudice that continued well after and is still evident today.)[8] Grossman's work, in other words, became increasingly unrecognizable to art histories of the 1970s because the account of gender it offered differed from mainstream feminism during the later years of the 1970s – despite the clarity and conviction of both Grossman and her supporters about the feminist priorities of her work.

The perspective of the abstract assemblages from the mid-1960s allows for a re-reading of the subsequent sculptures that attends to the complexity and mobility of gender that Grossman has claimed for them. Her work – both abstract and representational – prompts projective identifications of gender and sexuality only to complicate and confound them. Remarkably, she does this without representing the body at all.[9] Her head sculptures abstract and suggest the body, and viewers rush to fill in what they think that body should be. For instance, the art students who questioned Grossman themselves struggled to articulate a non-binary answer to the sex of this depicted human head, and the term "generic" was offered as a (literally) neutered version of who this human could be. For Raven's part, she expanded on these students' confusion as a means to address how the works detach gender from sex, pondering "what happens when women express masculinity, when men do, and what the difference is."[10] Keeping this in mind and coupled with Grossman's assertion that these heads are self-portraits, it becomes clear that these sculptures do not rely on an equation of gender with the sexed body.[11] Rather, Grossman's sculptural practice offers an account of the body that is skeptical of its supposed determinism, seeing it instead as open to remaking. From this perspective, Grossman developed a stance in her sculpture in which gender was located variably in ways that are not immediately visible from the exterior.

SUSPENSIONS OF THE BODY

In 1965, the poet and critic Bill Berkson wrote in an early review of Grossman's work that it conveyed "a nostalgia for parts."[12] This enigmatic phrase comes from a dense but short review of Grossman's Spring 1965 exhibition at New York's Krasner Gallery, her first of two that year. Because of the brevity of his one-paragraph commentary on the works, Berkson left this phrase unexplored. Nevertheless, it encapsulates a key issue for the ambitious and intense body of work she created over the next two years – the abstract relief assemblages that immediately preceded the signature mode of her leather-bound head sculptures. Taken as a whole, the relief assemblages from 1965 to 1967 exhibit a mounting tension between their ostensible abstraction and their increasingly recalcitrant figuration. While the early assemblages to which Berkson referred had seemed to him nostalgically to long for their lost parts, the subsequent works located those parts ever more brashly.

Of this group of abstract assemblages, I shall discuss in detail three relief sculptures as exemplary of this body of work that has heretofore received little attention in the literature on Grossman.[13] *For David Smith* (1965; see figs. 81–83), *Bride* (1965–6; see figs. 85 and 86), and *Ali Stoker* (1966–7; see figs. 90–93) each mark different points along Grossman's traversing of abstraction and the accounts of the body that it solicited. In and among the dense and abstract twisted leather strata, discernible body parts start to pop out. Unmistakable, these absurd genitalia signal Grossman's frank and often preposterous confrontation with the sexed body, treating it as raw material to be remade. Increasingly, her relief assemblages detached "parts" from wholes and extended that detachment into areas of black humor and subversion. These works – and their supposed answering of the "nostalgia for parts" through their exposure of sexual organs – were the arena in which Grossman digested the body before leaving it behind to focus on the head.

These relief assemblages moved into three dimensions some of the concerns of her earlier drawings and collages from the early 1960s, becoming the most assertively sculptural and abstract of her works to date. Leather, which became Grossman's signature material, came to be central in these works. The early assemblages such as *Eden* had used leather along with scrap metal, car parts, and rubber, but soon it became her dominant material. In works such as *The Edge of Always* (1964; fig. 79) and *Black Landscape* (1964; fig. 80), brown leather began to be featured. Despite being clearly reused and sutured together, the original objects from which this leather was taken are difficult to ascertain. By contrast, in the works between 1965 and her transition to making head sculptures encased in leather in 1968, Grossman increasingly used repurposed leather that did not wholly disguise the original objects from which it came. Jackets, harnesses, boots, and shoes, though partially broken down, remained visible in the concentrated surfaces. As Raven once wrote of these works, "There were 'ghosts' in the leather jackets, wood, and metal she used that she felt were activated in her work."[14]

Consequently, the source materials for all of these works are important to an understanding of the meanings they put into play. Nowhere is this more evident than in the first major leather relief assemblage Grossman made, *For David Smith* (fig. 81). The year 1965 was a pivotal one for her: with her Guggenheim fellowship, she had recently moved to a larger loft on Eldridge Street on New York's Lower East Side. The financial resources of the fellowship, plus the greater amount of space in her new loft, immediately resulted in these larger, more ambitious works. Grossman experienced a concerted burst of activity and created a heroic number of relief assemblages over the course of the year. She had two one-person shows in 1965, both at Krasner Gallery, that showcased these works. All of this was inaugurated with *For David Smith*, which she created for the sculptor from

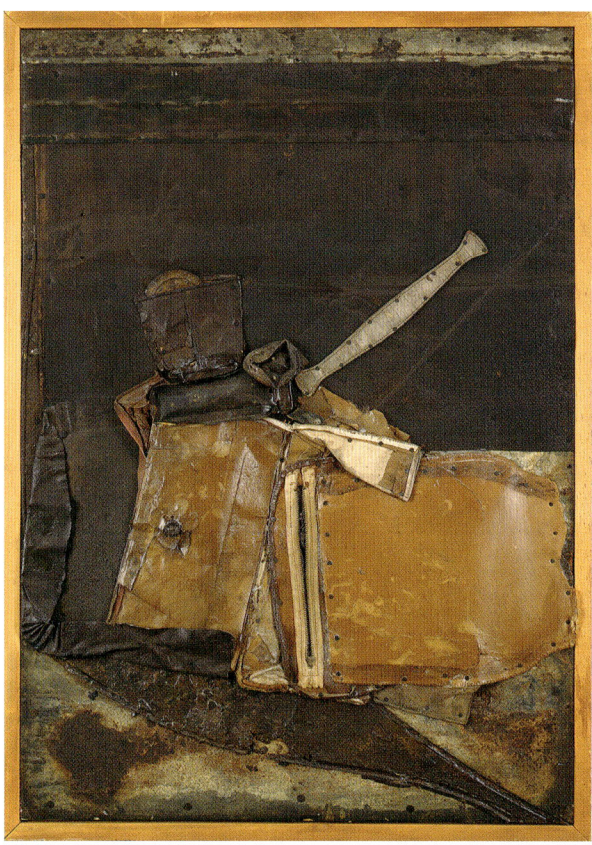 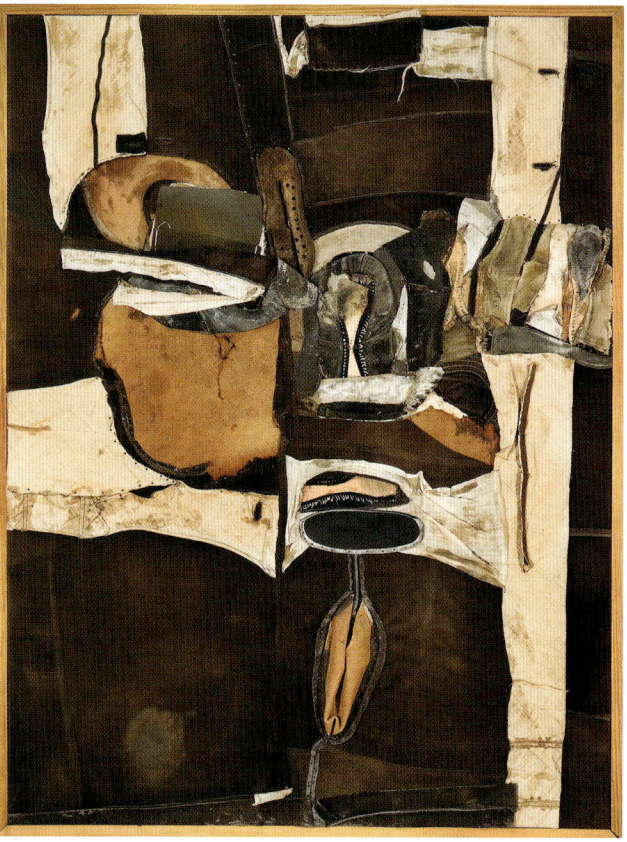

79 Nancy Grossman, *The Edge of Always*, 1964. Leather and metal assemblage mounted on plywood, 78.7 × 55.9 × 5.5 cm (31 × 22¼ × 2½ in.).

80 Nancy Grossman, *Black Landscape*, 1964. Leather, fabric, metal, wood, fur, bristle, paper, nylon, and paint assemblage mounted on plywood, 126.7 × 98.7 × 8.9 cm (49⅞ × 38⅞ × 3½ in.).

materials he had given her, and which established the terms of the relief assemblages she developed over the next two years.

Grossman had met Smith in 1960 while she was still a student at the Pratt Institute, and the two had a sporadic relationship over the next five years. She recalled, "I had such an incredibly pure and simple and lusty relationship with David Smith....What happened between us was totally real and sturdy enough to last a lifetime. It wasn't cynical."[15] Grossman was a regular visitor to Bolton Landing in upstate New York, and she created many of her figure drawings in Smith's drawing studio there. On one of her last trips to Bolton Landing before his death in 1965, Smith gave Grossman a number of leather horse harnesses, purchased in an auction along

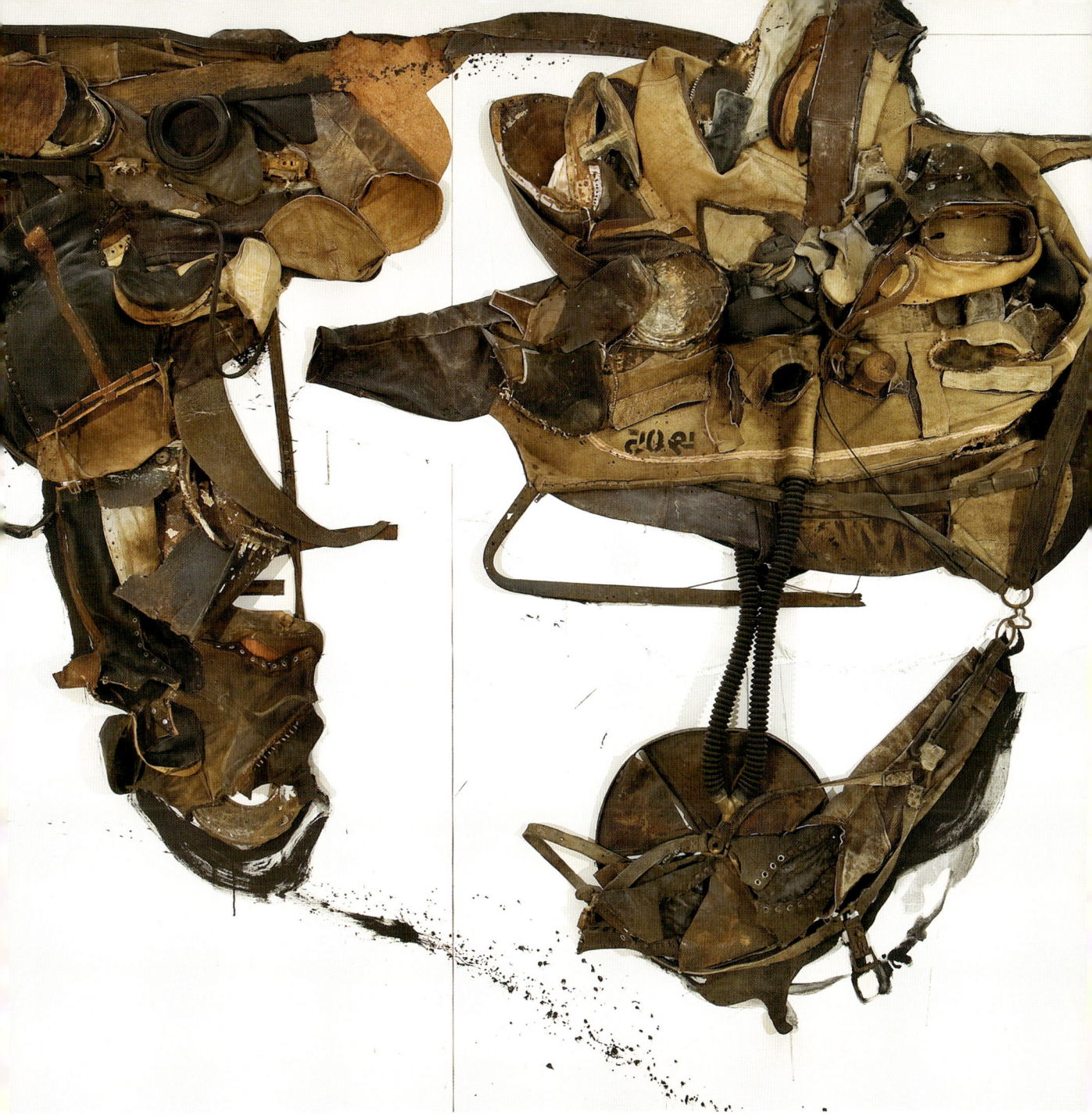

81 Nancy Grossman, *For David Smith*, 1965. Leather, metal, rubber, fabric, and paint assemblage on canvas mounted on plywood, 215.9 × 215.9 × 17.15 cm (85 × 85 × 6¾ in.).

with the rest of the contents of a bankrupt farm. Smith had been interested in the cast-iron tractor wheels and other metal implements, but Grossman admired the horse tack instead. (She had ridden horses since she was a child.) They were Smith's challenge to Grossman, and she took the bundle of leather objects back to New York City to create an ambitious work for him. She completed it before Smith's accident, but, unfortunately, he never saw the final sculpture.

At 7 foot 3 by 7 foot 3 (221 × 221 centimeters), *For David Smith* was the largest relief assemblage Grossman would make and her most extensive use of leather to date. She said of this moment, "I was looking for material I could break down and build up and change midway." The harnesses gave her materials that she could de-construct and remake.[16] More than the found detritus that populated her earlier works, the harnesses needed to be meticulously unstitched and taken apart. A significant component of the labor in this and subsequent works involved the breaking down of these harnesses and garments. Once de-constructed, the odd shapes of these leather components suggested to Grossman new patterns and new ways to combine the elements.

She put these elements into play against a large canvas support where she compressed leather, tubes, and metal. The materials have been torn apart and fused to make the two dense masses floating on the otherwise white canvas. Black paint has been sparingly applied, creating on the left a ragged outline tailed by a splatter. The harness straps are used as lines, connecting and reconnecting within and across the two major shapes. While the masses do not form familiar contours, component objects within them are nevertheless recognizable. In addition to reins and bits, more than one boot is visible (see fig. 83). (One of the opened boots on the upper left is stamped "Endicott Johnson All Leather," referring to the Endicott Johnson Shoe Company, located in upstate New York near Grossman's hometown of Oneonta.) Across the surface of the large relief, tears, zippers, and splayed boots produced openings into the dense forms. In what proved a characteristic move in these reliefs, Grossman furthermore pierced the disassembled leather garments and harnesses with tubes and openings, around which writhes an infernal tangle of horse tack, stirrups, and straps. Wryly, Grossman used elements to suggest other bodily shapes — as with the mask-like form suggested by a folded element from a de-constructed harness at the top of the right figure or the labial allusions in the unlaced boot (on the lower appendage of the right figure) that prefigures the more explicit way she would use this same material in *Bride*, as I shall discuss.

Grossman has said that she worked on these reliefs in an active and often rapid fashion, moving from one element to the next intuitively. "I did them in the same spirit as Abstract Expressionist action painting," she recalled of her energetic and determined process.[17] On the stretched canvas, reinforced

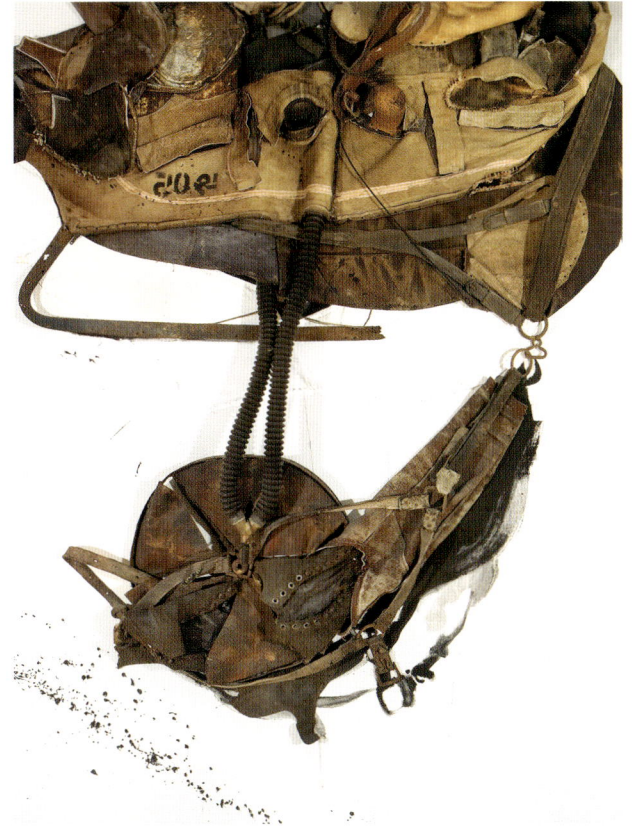 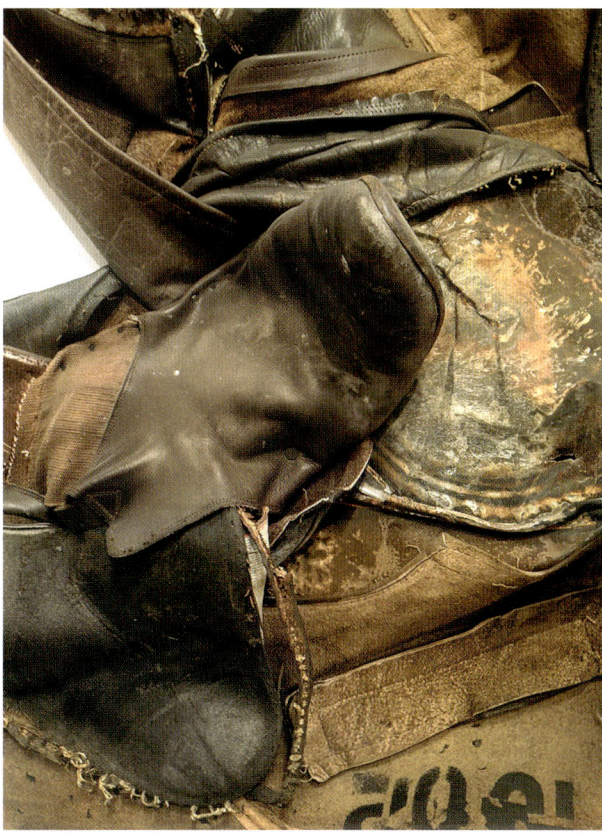

82 Detail of Nancy Grossman, *For David Smith.*   83 Detail of Nancy Grossman, *For David Smith.*

with a wood backing to support the heavy objects, Grossman continued to add density. The work doubled in size and she merged another canvas with the first to give more space. "Sculpture is usually something that is planned and sketched for, but I never did anything like that," she recalled.[18] The result is a concerted and almost frantic layered density within the two masses. These two halves of the work, on separate but conjoined canvases, reflect each other's shapes in a pas-de-deux.

This work is predominantly abstract, but Grossman saw these piled-on masses as figures – part animal, part machine, part human. The vestiges of shoes, the folds of leather skin, the open orifices, and the pliable tubes give the masses a bodily resonance (figs. 82 and 83). In an interview with Cindy Nemser in 1975, Grossman recounted her trajectory from the earlier drawings, collages, and lithographs to these works:

> First I would make the whole figure and then I became more involved with the torso. Then the work became more and more abstract and involved with the visceral and the internal. When I look back on it now, it was always saying the same thing – just where I am in myself is where my work is. At the same time they became more and more like machines. There are animal machine figures and human machine figures. First I made them from the outside. That one is not noisy but they look as if they were yakking or mooing.[19]

Nemser then remarked, with regard to *For David Smith*, "I find it hard to find a figure," to which Grossman replied,

> It is rather like an organic machine. It has insides and an outside. There are two figures in outer space. It's funny because I would [previously] imagine these things in outer space. (This was before the Russians went into outer space and when they did I said, "Oh I know about that.") I saw the space men floating there suspended without gravity. I knew what it would look like. These were done in '65.[20]

With her emphasis on the figures as organic machines, Grossman articulated an account of the body as material and process rather than as a customary morphology. Floating in space, her assembled bodies are rendered as unhampered by gravity and orientation, allowing multiple points of contact and intercourse to be imagined. Indeed, ports, interfaces, and openings are evident across the suspended figures of *For David Smith*, in which the distinction between inside and outside is broken down.

Even though she was working on the scale of monumental painting, Grossman dealt with these assemblage reliefs as if they were drawings. They are formally analogous to the compacted ink on paper drawings she was creating at the same time, such as *Bridey* and *Beever Slats*. Both articulate unorthodox hybrid forms against white grounds, and the narrow chromatic range of *For David Smith*'s source materials reinforced this connection. Grossman later recalled that she wanted to make sculpture from her drawings at this time so that "I could make them more real."[21] Despite their obdurate and heavy materiality, these dark brown and black masses jump out from their white ground as if they were large drawn figures on white paper. This was intentional, and Grossman repeatedly referred to these and related works as representing freefloating and tumbling figures "like spacemen." Raven later reiterated this intention for the work, saying that, "The two figures in this work are bodies in a gravityless outer space."[22] As Grossman indicated in the Nemser interview, images of the Soviet cosmonaut

Yuri Gagarin's 1961 pioneering space journey had been crucial to her as visual analogues to the kind of floating bodies she had wanted to draw and, starting with the reliefs in 1965, sculpt.[23] She had been carrying these images with her well before 1961, however.

It was the bundle of horse straps that Smith had given her that had prompted her to see these long thin pieces of leather as lines with which she could draw in three dimensions.[24] She explained her process to Nemser:

> It seems a funny thing to do with such cumbersome material but when I am working this way those materials are nothing to me. I could draw with straps, I could draw with thirty-pound pieces of steel, if I had to. I set them in place and it becomes a great challenge to me that they be well made and solid. I do it quickly and with no sweat. I was always good with my hands in terms of drawing.[25]

Ultimately, *For David Smith* is a kind of drawing of figures floating in space, made with horse harnesses. As such, it offers a humorously different kind of "drawing in space" from the kind for which Smith had been become famous.[26] While Smith had used repurposed metal, Grossman demonstrated how the straps, harnesses, and boots could be orchestrated as lines capable of making equally "gravityless" forms.

I should pause to note, though, that with its tethered and suspended bodies, *For David Smith* bears an uncanny resemblance to the composition of another work that mapped sexual difference onto alien bodies and objects – Marcel Duchamp's *The Bride Stripped Bare by her Bachelors, Even* (1915–23), which had been reintroduced to American audiences following the influential West Coast retrospective of Duchamp just two years before in 1963. However, when I asked her about this (in relation to *For David Smith* and her subsequent *Bride*), Grossman rebuffed and deflected any such connection, asserting instead that the main intertext for this work was Smith's sculpture.[27] Even without such a direct link, however, a comparison between these two large works nevertheless helps to show how both Duchamp and Grossman sought to render new bodily morphologies by extracting them from conventional representations of gravity and space. This was, as well, one of Smith's tactics for attacking the statuary tradition.

As discussed in Chapter 1, Smith's work of the 1960s had sought to eschew gravity and logical structure, presenting figures that not only vary from every side but that are also often held together in unorthodoxly structured ways solely by the sculptor's fusing of parts. Seen in relation to the importance of action in Abstract Expressionism, Smith's autographic gesture took the form of the weld that held disparate elements in the air without relying on the conventional engineering of structures and bodies. His *Cubi* series, on which he was engaged during the time he knew Grossman, is made up of combinations of simple, regular geometric forms that seemed to have been juggled in the air (fig. 84). While the component forms look as if they are basic geometric building blocks, they are never simply stacked, nor do the masses of the lower forms serve as the structural foundations for the blocks above.[28] The welds hold them up. As noted earlier, these techniques allowed Smith to emphasize the independence of the sculptor from necessary structure and to explore the ways in which he could create previously unseen figures and compositions that varied from every point of view.

Grossman's *For David Smith* exhibits her careful (and irreverent) engagement with the terms of Smith's practice as well as the beginnings of her making of new bodies from the parts of others. It was this assembling of new figures that would drive her work over the next two years.[29] As Raven remarked, "Smith's totemic sculptural *personages* also found an analogy in Grossman's personas."[30] Grossman's personas, at this stage, were categorically dissimilar to the clean, concise statement of the leather heads she came to make. Instead, the bodies floating in space in *For David Smith* are unexpected concatenations of disparate reused parts. They do not resemble the bodies of either horses or humans, but one can see vestiges of both in the "ghosts" of the leather objects that Grossman has broken apart to make them. A boot, straps, laces, and buckles all point back to bodies and muscles, as do the allusive tubes and openings (see figs. 82 and 83). As hybrids of horse, human, and machine made from discernible found objects, these figures refuse to settle into mere abstraction. The bodily shapes of shoes and horse tack, belts, and leather keep all of those possible bodies in proximate suspension, playing the familiarity of their parts against the strangeness of new beings confronting the viewer. In this way, Grossman matched Smith on his own terms while also demonstrating the evocative bodily potential of the leather garments she used. Smith's own use of found or repurposed materials rarely foregrounded so blatantly such a tension between recognizable source objects and the abstract figures they comprise.

The dense constellations of disassembled harnesses, boots, jackets, rubber, and tubes against white canvas in *For David Smith* became the characteristic mode of Grossman's reliefs in 1965. She pursued this idea of using found leather to draw new figures in space. *Hitchcock, Brown and Black*, *Car Horn*, and *Ali of Nostrand* all take up this motif. Made in rapid succession, such works provided an escape for Grossman after Smith's death. "I felt cut off in the middle of my dialogue with David Smith. I worked literally night

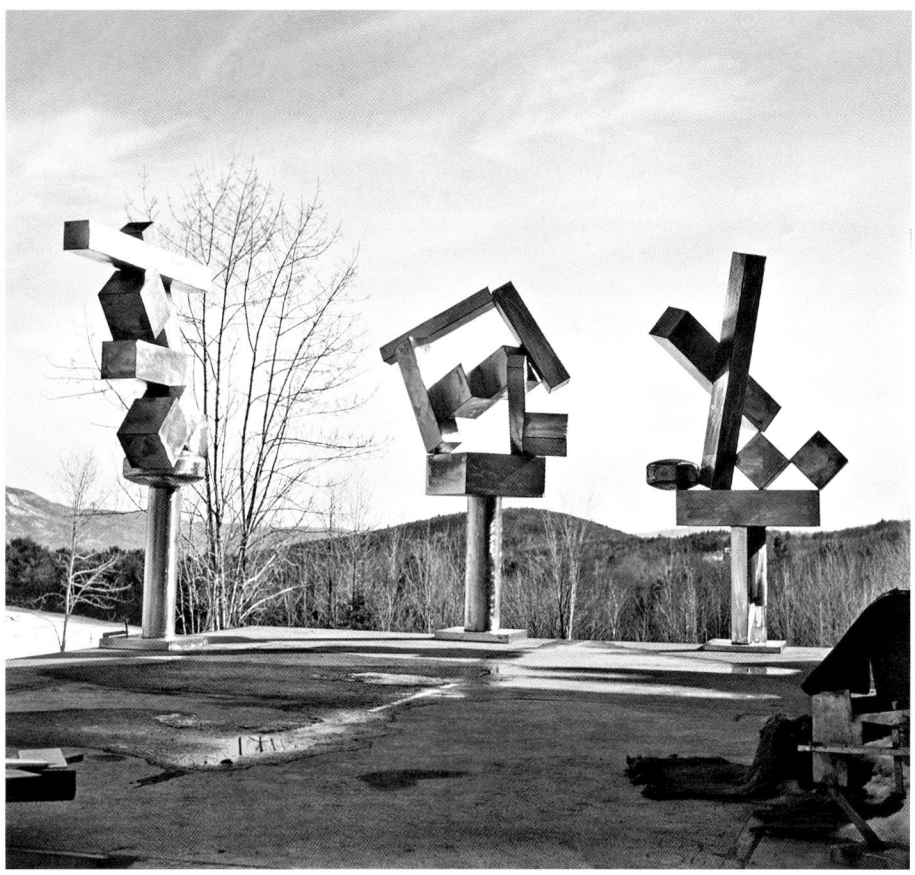

84   David Smith, *Cubi XVIII*, 1964, *Cubi XVII*, 1963, and *Cubi XIX*, 1964.

and day as if trying to finish a sentence that had been cut off."[31] In the series of works after the monumental *For David Smith*, Grossman extended her relief assemblages, creating a number of sculptures that she called "machine-animal hybrids." Slightly smaller than *For David Smith*, these works expanded on her source material of harnesses to create what Raven called "abstract recreations of the horses Grossman owned and rode years earlier."[32] They were never just horses, however. These machine-animal hybrids were new bodies, made from the parts of others.

Jack Halberstam has argued that a central strategy for manifesting transgender issues in contemporary art is "through eccentric and extravagant representations of the body, body parts, neo-organs, and trans bodies."[33] Not uncoincidentally, in the essay from which these words come, Halberstam cites Grossman as one precedent for this practice:

Of course, there is nothing so new in and of itself in the representation of the body as a form of montage, collage, assemblage or aesthetic hybrid. Artists like Hannah Höch, Louise Bourgeois, and Nancy Grossman have all represented the body, and often the female body at that, as a grotesque and beautiful patchwork of the bodily and the machinic, the fleshly and the metallic, the unfinished, the imperfect, and the incomplete.[34]

While Halberstam positions Grossman as a general precedent for the hybrid body rather than her examples of artists (like Eva Hesse) who "address the specific emergence of the transgender body in subcultural terms," I would argue that a closer attention to Grossman's abstract reliefs of the 1960s demonstrates how her work, more directly even than Hesse's, offers an account of transgender capacity and the mutability of both bodies and genders. This is especially evident in the reliefs that followed in the wake of *For David Smith*.

SPARE PARTS: THE *BRIDE* AND RECONSTRUCTIVE ASSEMBLAGE

Grossman's second exhibition at Krasner Gallery, in 1965, included many of the white-background relief assemblages in this mode. Just as the show was going up, however, she was transitioning to a different kind of making. As she zoomed in on the body, the white backgrounds began to disappear, and the subsequent reliefs became claustrophobically packed with materials. Grossman squeezed space out of the reliefs as she went inside the bodies she had been making. Exemplary of this transitional mode is the tondo *Bride* (fig. 85).

In *Bride*, white is not background but layers of repurposed skin. That skin frames what appears, to many, to be an uncompromising representation of a vagina. (For instance, its legibility as such was evidenced in the work's inclusion in an exhibition titled *The Visible Vagina*.[35]) At the center of a compacted circle of leather straps, de-constructed boots, and white paint, a partially laced slit runs up the middle of the work, opened to expose purple folds. "This collage is kind of obscene. It's called *The Bride*," Grossman said to Nemser in 1975. Nemser continued, "I see it's a tondo and it has sewing on it. Did you see it as a woman's sexual organ, a vagina?" Grossman's response was contradictory and reasserted the abstractness of the work: "I was unconscious of that. I have a couple others like that. The others are landscapes – women landscapes."[36] Those related works include the 1964

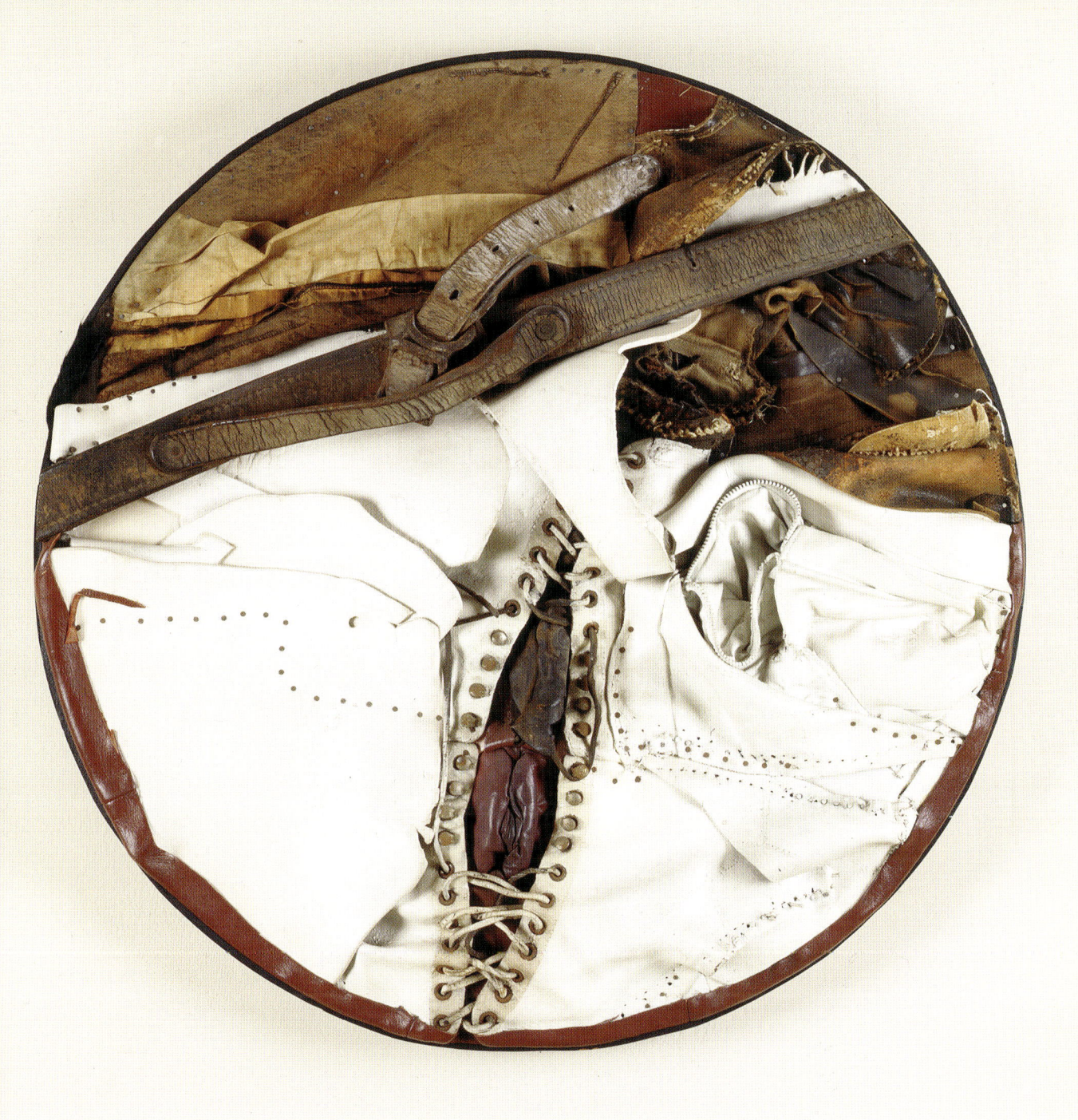

85 Nancy Grossman, *Bride*, 1966. Leather and mixed media assemblage, d. 57.15 cm (22½ in.). Collection of halley k. harrisburg and Michael Rosenfeld.

leather, cloth, and fur assemblage *Black Landscape*, which also showcases a vaginal form in its lower half. Similar motifs are evident in other works from 1964 and 1965 (such as *The Edge of Always*; see fig. 79) and are expanded in slightly later works with multiple zippered and other orifices, such as *Potawatami* (1967) and *Ali Stoker* (1967), discussed in more detail later (see figs. 88–93).

Given these repeated forms, how is one to take Grossman's statement that she was unconscious of the genital imagery that is evident across these otherwise abstract works? Grossman both acknowledged the presence of sexed or sexual imagery while at the same time disavowing its meaning or her full intentionality in showcasing it. I see this less as a contradiction and more as a tactical means of bracketing the all-encompassing sexualized interpretations that her graphic imagery incites. (This dynamic became amplified in the many invested responses to the leather heads.) Grossman's characterization of her own practice drew from the attitudes common to many Abstract Expressionists in which non-representational or semi-abstract forms were mobilized as a means of staging the artist's act of creation, with the meanings of the work being rooted in the artist's struggle to achieve that act. From this perspective, discussions of artistic creation were often cast as being intuitive and partially unconscious, despite the deliberate and highly structured practices developed by Abstract Expressionist artists. Grossman's explanations of her own artistic process often take this form. In a 1975 interview with Kate Horsfield, for instance, Grossman remarked, "When it is happening, there's no consciousness....I can't take the credit."[37] In a discussion with me, she said about her work, "I make it from below the think, and I want you to receive it from below the think."[38]

Grossman's declaration that she was unconscious of the vaginal imagery in *Bride* is a manifestation of this mode of characterizing artistic intention as intuitive or unthought, allowing her both to expose and to detach herself at the same time. She was aware of the image's blatant visibility and readability, as is evidenced by her prefacing the work to Nemser as "obscene." More recently, Grossman told me that she thought she could make such a "female and sexual" work at the time because "Nobody would dare ask about the vagina."[39] However, in her discussion with Nemser, published in the context of a feminist book of interviews with women artists, Grossman's disavowal of conscious intentionality served to call into question the seemingly unambiguous legibility of the image.[40]

In effect, her reliance on abstraction and her deflection of readability offered a different feminist stance on the sexed body – one skeptical of its meanings and determinations. This is not the same as the use of vaginal imagery that became a major resource for feminist art a few years after Grossman's *Bride*.[41] As I discuss later, for all its frankness, *Bride* resists the essentialism that would often be signaled by such imagery in the art of the early 1970s.⁴² Indeed, Nemser and Grossman concluded their 1975 interview by decrying the work of Judy Chicago, whom they characterized as exemplary of this essentialism. Chicago had begun creating her infamous *Dinner Party* earlier in 1974 and had published with Miriam Schapiro in 1973 her theory of the importance of vaginal "central core" imagery for feminist art.⁴³ Nemser remarked, "That's why I resent people like Judy Chicago insisting women are asserting their identity by painting their vaginas. I'm not only a vagina....I have a brain and I have worked hard to learn how to use it," to which Grossman replied, "And the head is where the power is."⁴⁴ Nemser advocated a diversified aesthetic for feminist art, irreducible to a deterministic and single essential image.⁴⁵ Clearly, she understood Grossman's earlier *Bride* (which Nemser illustrated in her 1975 book) to be categorically different from such later uses of vaginal imagery. Perhaps this was because, in its formal organization, *Bride* cultivates multiplicity rather than essentialism through the use of other elements that humorously bracket and question just what it is that we think we have learned from recognizing that genital imagery.

The work, after all, contains much more than just the central form. It is densely packed with material. Its tondo format calls attention to the object-nature of the relief assemblage, and no conventional figure–ground relations occur in its crowded interior. *Bride* offers no image of the human figure among the compacted abstraction created from found and repurposed materials. However, as a "bride," the assemblage's extensive use of white cannot be seen as neutral. A significant portion of the work is composed of leather that Grossman painted white (the painting is most visible on the laces). Given the connections between brides and white, the layered folds of the deconstructed boots mock the ruffles of a wedding dress, one of the most gender-specific of garments. (In a humorous passage, Grossman constructed to the right of the lacing a zippered orifice in white that playfully reprises the purple folds that seem so explicit; fig. 86.) One hostile and apparently uninformed reviewer tried to explain away *Bride*'s use of leather, derisively saying that the work "features mostly white leather, perhaps from a Western bride's outfit. A vagina-like area is exposed by the open bodice laces."⁴⁶ This overly literal and pedestrian reading, however, fails to accept fully that *Bride* and its crowded circular field of repurposed materials are not solely white. The densely packed tondo is bisected into white and brown registers by the other dominant element in the composition – a diagonal strap with a buckle that gives the effect of a belt. The white bride is below the belt, and it is hard not to ask what is above. The belt and the browns above it cannot be simply disregarded but must be understood in dynamic relation to what is

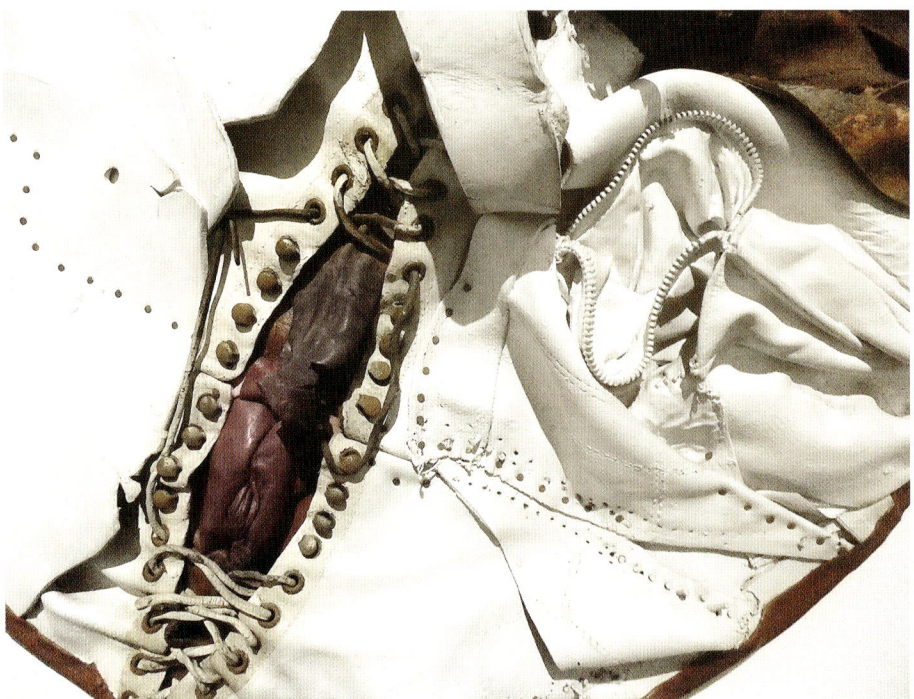

86 Detail of Nancy Grossman, *Bride*.

below. Given the blatant display of vulva-like forms and the title, the work incites a questioning about how consistently or stably gender can be located between these two halves. That is, the frank exposure of the genitals purports to reveal the "truth" of the body as sexed, but Grossman's *Bride* keeps the question of gender – as distinct from anatomical sex – circling.

If the lower register seems to address directly the gendered title with its wedding-dress white folds, what is the "not-bride" of the upper register's dirty browns and blacks? Taken together, they pose at least two different gendered options for the garments that surround the sexed body, rendered frankly through the exposure of genitals. Keeping the upper and lower registers in tension, *Bride* could be read, for instance, as conflating groom and bride or, as one alternative, the bride within (or underneath) the groom. Whatever is above the brown belt, it is in excess of the direct correlation that might be made between the vaginal imagery and the stereotypically feminine garment of the wedding dress. The certainty that the genital display, at first, seems to offer in its agreement with the gendered title and garment increasingly turns to disagreement and ambivalence when the remaining elements of the packed composition are taken into consideration.

Grossman's works often complicate and even collide genders, as I shall discuss. *Bride*'s overall organization is an early manifestation of this. Even though it seems explicit in its revelation of anatomical sex, it nevertheless detaches that bodily part from a one-to-one correlation with genders implied by the different kinds of garments evoked by the work. The uncertain relationship between the upper and lower registers of *Bride* prompts multiple plausible accounts of how gender could be identified in and among its component parts. *Bride* relies on the initial shock of recognition, but then slowly offers complications and inversions of that identification, bracketing its own apparent frankness. That is, the question of gender in *Bride* is more mobile, multiple, and uncertain than one might at first expect when confronted with the blunt flash of the genital imagery. In this, Grossman's work presages later accounts of genders as temporal and successive, sexual difference as unfixed and potentially multiple, and bodies as transformable. As Gayle Salamon has recently argued, "if ones thinks sexual difference in other than bodily terms, the category can become unyoked from determinative bodily materiality in a way that makes it easier to resist the temptation to posit genital morphology as essentially determinative not only of sexual difference but also of the self."[47] Grossman's reliefs, for all their initial reliance on the sexed body, nevertheless treat genital imagery not as self-explanatory or deterministic but as something to be made and remade. Gender here is an open question rather than a fixed (binary) quality, unyoked from the genitals that are often taken to be its determining sign.

The source material Grossman used to make *Bride* was itself tied up with remaking and, in particular, with sex and sexual difference. She made this matrimonial work from an old boyfriend's boots, which she de-constructed and painted white to become the wedding-dress-like layers. She explained: "The joke was that I had this boyfriend who gave me his work boots."[48] The "woman-landscape" of *Bride* was made from a man, just as that man's boots were made from an animal. The logic of taking apart and remaking is crucial to Grossman's process in her found-object reliefs, and it is significant that the only recognizable images to emerge from her otherwise abstract assemblages are suggestions of sexual organs. Genitals might seem to be the least ambiguous of any body part, but Grossman plays with their frank display by making them from other objects that themselves have been made from other bodies. Her use of genital imagery undercuts its authority, instead prompting questions about how multiple genders could circulate – no matter what the parts are. This is why she reminds us that it is

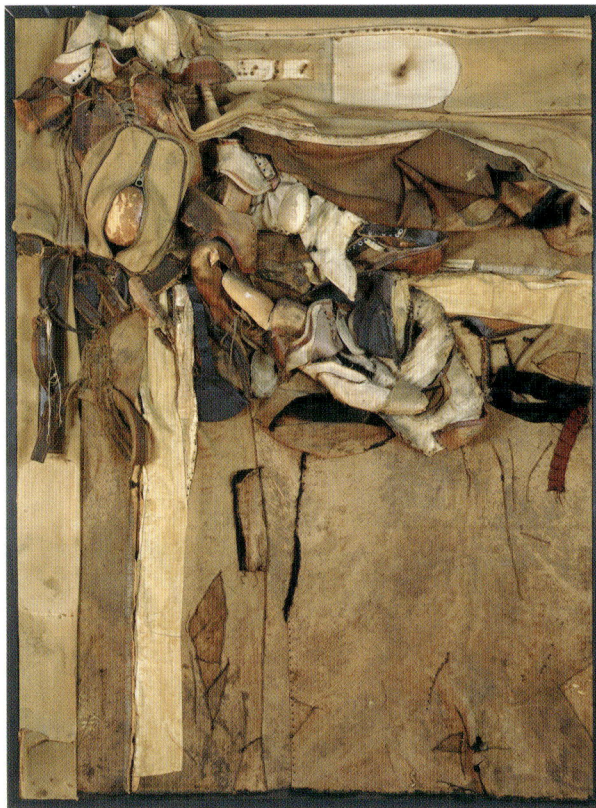

87 Nancy Grossman, *Chiron*, 1966. Mixed media assemblage on cardboard and wood, 123.2 × 91.4 × 16.5 cm (48½ × 36 × 6½ in.). Private collection, Dallas, Texas.

not, simply, a vagina in *Bride*, and nor does that vaginal form delimit the multiplications of meanings and genders in the works. The exposure of the genitals starts rather than stops the question of how gender operates in this intense work of remaking.

Grossman's subsequent relief sculptures further pursue bodily metaphors, though they more playfully combine and recombine possible genital allusions rather than render such explicit and uncompromising imagery. The artist's *Walrus* (1966), for instance, was called by Raven "an emblem of the female."[49] *Chiron* (1966; fig. 87) recapitulates the vaginal imagery found in *Landscape* and *Bride* in the form of a zipper struggling to contain a round form that could be interpreted as the cresting skull of a baby. (This element was made from a man's toiletry bag.[50]) Such readings, however, are never definitive. In Grossman's dense and layered compositions, discernible images emerge and recede. The mythological centaur Chiron, half-man and half-horse teacher of Achilles, again poses an ambivalent and far from fixed question about how gender can be found in the work and further reiterates Grossman's interest in hybrid beings.

The 1967 *Potawatami* (named after the street in Tucson, Arizona where her parents had moved; fig. 88) is strewn with such forms. In addition to partially reconstructed leather garments that have been made to resemble jockstraps, there are a numbered of zippered and other orifices across its surface (such as at the now-vertical light brown pocket that has been given pride of place centered at the top) in addition to stuffed phallic forms (as with the curved light-brown protrusion hidden in the lower left.) Expanding on the more singular statement of *Bride* with its confounding of a reading of a single genital form confrontationally exposed, Grossman's subsequent work began to pile on these parts, detaching them from the body and making them preposterous in their combinations. This is most evident in the work that both summarized Grossman's relief assemblages and signaled the transition to her subsequent work and signature material: the 1967 abstract relief *Ali Stoker*.

RECEPTIVE MACHISMO: *ALI STOKER*'S "ORGY OF INTERCOURSE"

The intense production of the relief assemblages on white backgrounds in 1965 had depleted much of her store of horse harnesses and related objects. In 1966, after the Guggenheim fellowship had run out, Grossman decided to return to illustrating children's books as a means to "give myself a Guggenheim" to keep her production up that year.[51] She took on a number of illustration projects at once, which arrested her production:

> This was a terrible thing for me to do because if there is one concentration of ego in my whole self it is in my work. My work is my worth to myself. I loved it. It was my life. Without it I would have been stepped on, blotted out completely. The illustrations took me about three or four months longer than I had imagined they would. Doing them changed me totally. From being all action and little reflection I was stuck with my legs chained to the table night and day. It changed my metabolism.[52]

Her illustration work was her primary occupation for nine months from 1966 to 1967, followed by another burst of activity in 1967 with the works *Yuma, Potawatami*, her *Slaves* reliefs, and *Ali Stoker*. Ultimately, the imagery of restraint in the leather head sculpture was informed by the experience

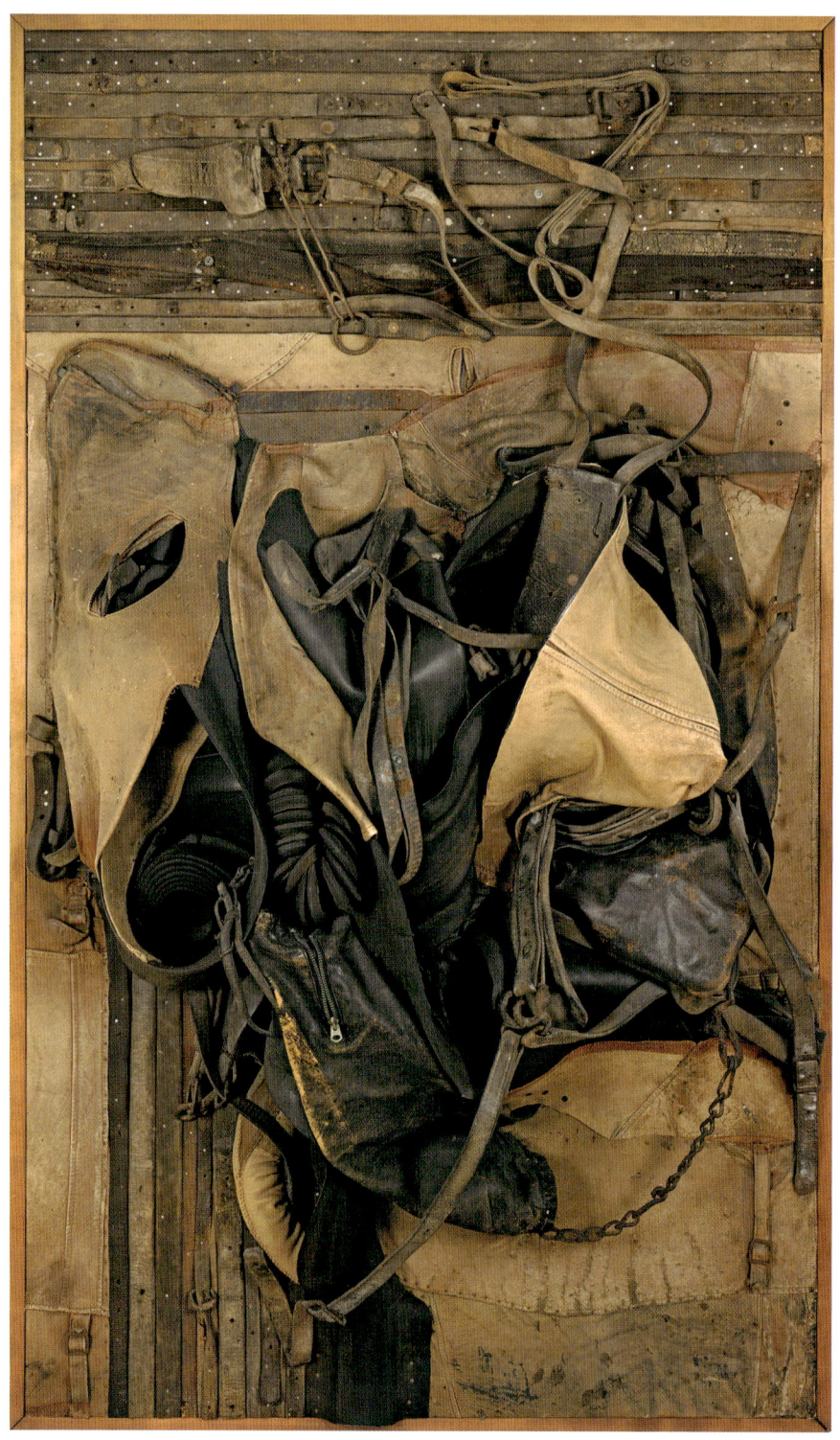

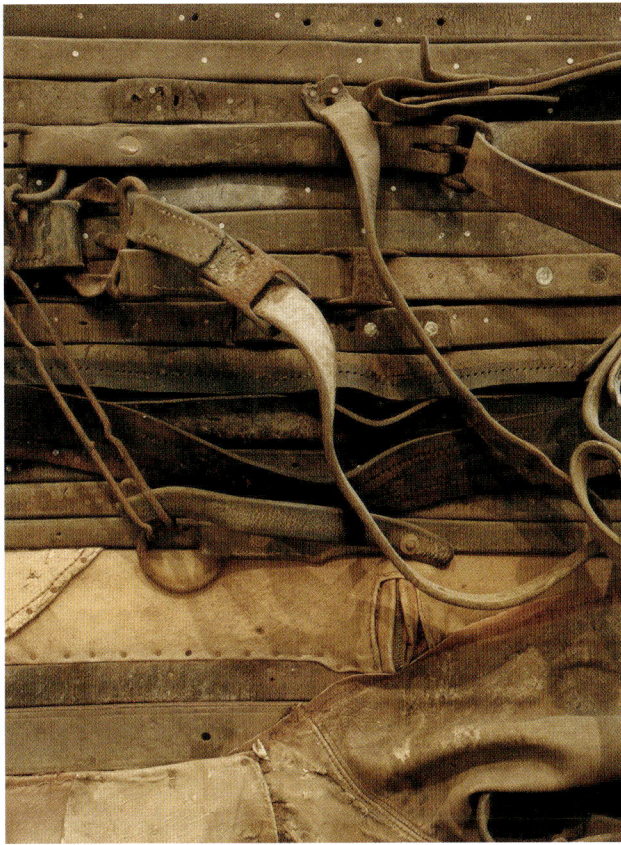

OPPOSITE 88 Nancy Grossman, *Potawatami*, 1967. Leather, rubber, and metal assemblage on plywood, 160.3 × 96.8 × 29.8 cm (63⅛ × 38⅛ × 11¾ in.).

RIGHT 89 Detail of Nancy Grossman, *Potawatami*.

of restriction caused by the need to stop her sculptural practice in order to do the illustrations for hire.[53]

The relief sculptures completed in 1967 reflect the turmoil Grossman attributed to this point in her career. They are even more densely built and claustrophobic, with tortured and twisted forms made in black leather. She made a small group of reliefs titled *Slaves* that referred to Michelangelo's erotically bound and contorted slave sculptures. Works such as these and the conceptually related *Ali Stoker* were, she explained, the "microcosms of the macro-figures" from the 1965 reliefs on white backgrounds.[54] Most dramatically, the abstract assemblage *Ali Stoker* offers an intestinal tangle of black leather, tubes, and zippers (figs. 90 and 91). The metal and rubber tubes predominate, and they emerge out or move into zippered orifices and holes. Nemser said of this piece, "The black tubular piece is even more threatening than the women landscapes. I see them as something torn, as

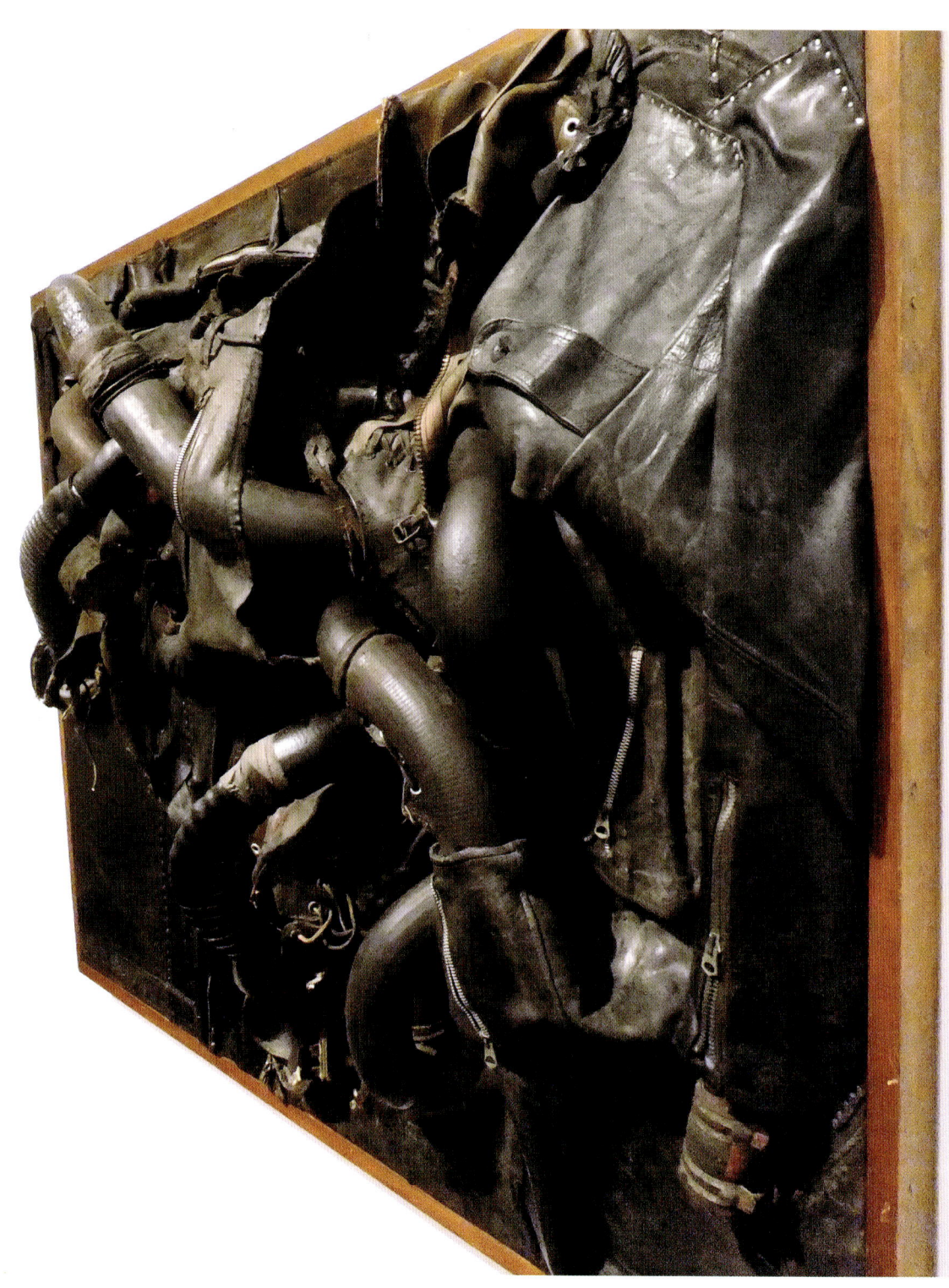

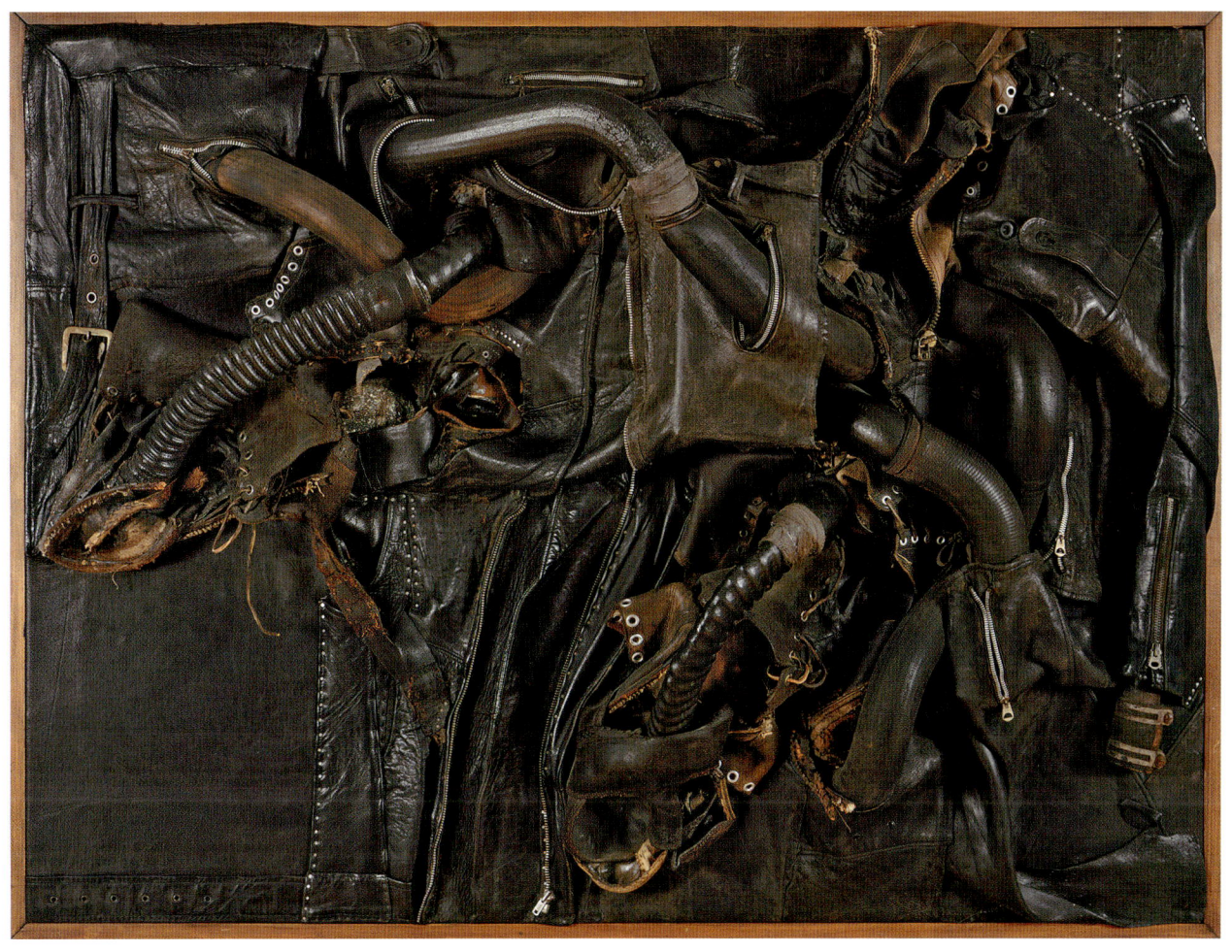

OPPOSITE AND ABOVE 90 and 91   Nancy Grossman, *Ali Stoker*, 1966–7. Mixed media, 94 × 125.7 × 20.3 cm (37½ × 49½ × 8 in. Collection of halley k harrisburg and Michael Rosenfeld, New York.

if someone's insides were being pulled apart."[55] Her response was perspicacious. Unlike the previous works made mainly from harnesses, scraps, and boots, *Ali Stoker* was made from motorcycle jackets shaped like and patterned after the torso. Such garments – even when recombined and partially disassembled – more directly evoked the body in absentia. Grossman remarked that the construction of the jackets was highly influential on her, and she had to take the seams apart meticulously in order to reuse the scraps of material.[56] In this way, the use of the extant jackets (themselves made from the skins of animals) raised the bodily stakes of her work. These works, like all the relief assemblages, were about tearing apart before they were about putting it together. As she later said, "Even when you take apart things that are everyday things, they are kind of shocking."[57]

Around 1966, Grossman managed to buy the mass of black leather motorcycle jackets that gave rise to *Ali Stoker* and the *Slaves*, and she also incorporated this material into the first of the head sculptures the following year. She recounted going to a Bowery loft where she had heard she could buy some leather cheap. She found there bales of old leather jackets, and the seller broke open a large bale for her to pick out the ones she wanted. Some were in fine shape but others were in tatters, she recalled, and she returned home with a duffle bag stuffed with them.[58]

In *Ali Stoker* in particular, Grossman made the most of the black leather jacket. This was one of the most iconic items of fashion in the 1950s and 1960s, becoming in that time a symbol of rebellion, danger, alternative masculinities, and homosexuality. After the Second World War, it was first associated with bikers through movies such as *The Wild One* (1954). In his extensive and affectionate history of the black leather jacket, Mick Farren remarked, "What Marlon Brando didn't know at the time was that his costume from the film would prove to be a codification of a youthful rebel uniform. It would remain fixed, with only the slightest mutation, for the next thirty years."[59] As late as 1974, television network censors refused to allow the producers of the sitcom *Happy Days* to dress the character Fonzie in a leather jacket for the initial episodes of the series. The American Broadcasting Company said it would make him look like a "hoodlum," and he was compelled to wear a windbreaker until the network could be convinced that the appearance of the leather jacket on television would not be misread as criminal.[60]

Throughout the 1950s and 1960s, the black leather jacket had become popularized as a symbol of independence and anti-establishment values (most notably, around the ambivalent figure of James Dean).[61] In the 1960s, it also became increasingly seen as an identifying garment within the ever growing and more visible gay communities in cities such as New York. Such connotations were fueled by its notable presence in underground films such as Kenneth Anger's *Scorpio Rising* (1964) and Andy Warhol's *Blow Job* (1964).[62] In 1964, *Life* magazine clued its readers in to what this uniform meant, saying: "These brawny young men in their leather caps, shirts, jackets and pants are practicing homosexuals."[63] Black leather had a predominant role within the material culture of S/M communities (both gay and straight) by the mid-1960s, but the black leather jacket was not exclusively associated with them. Rather, it had become a somewhat generic symbol of youthful

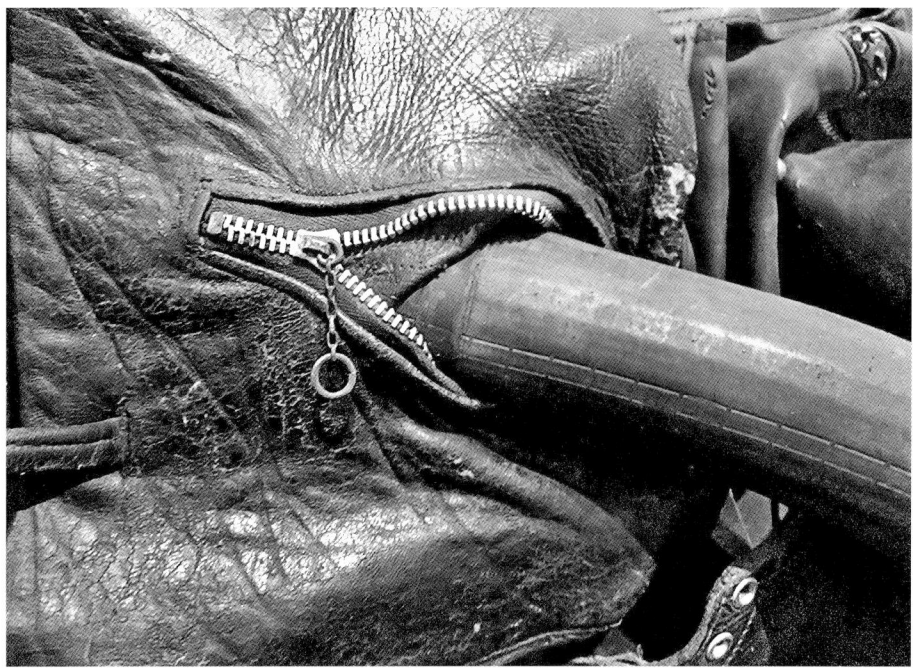

92　Detail of upper left of Nancy Grossman, *Ali Stoker*.

rebellion, outlaw bikers, and gay urbanites. In his remarkable 1968 crossover gay novel about the practice of s/m (loosely based on Pierre Choderlos de Laclos's 1782 *Les liaisons dangereuses*), titled *The Real Thing*, William Carney decried the cheap and plentiful black leather jackets that could be found anywhere in the city. The main character warned his pupil, "I do not think much of the shop where [the leather jacket] is being made, however. It is a new establishment that caters to phonies and to phony tastes."[64] It was exactly such a popularized demand for the black leather jacket that had produced the surplus from which Grossman was able to buy. Based on the details of *Ali Stoker*, that bale of black leather jackets contained items similar to (or cheaper versions of) those made by the New York-based Schott Brothers, one of the major producers at the time.[65]

Just as with her earlier relief assemblages, such source materials influenced the works Grossman made from them. "Everything I used had a connotative relationship," she has remarked.[66] *Ali Stoker* played off the various modifications of masculinity that the black leather jacket had come to stand for (see fig. 91). By 1967, it could be read as rebel, as gay, as outlaw, as poser, and as butch. That is, the black leather jacket signified "macho" – whether hyperbolic, tragic, idealized, inauthentic, homoerotic, or performed. Grossman made sure the jacket was still recognizable in the surface of the otherwise abstract *Ali Stoker*, leaving elements such as the sleeve on the far right or the zippers and buckles that populate the work.

That the highly charged yet contested masculinity of the black leather jacket is key for *Ali Stoker* is most evident in the tentacular tubes that emerge from zippers and pierce holes, which cumulatively read as ludicrously penile. This can be seen, for instance, in the top center of the assemblage in which a thick tube seems to be coming out of a zippered pants pocket. It is not, however, made from leather pants but rather from a jacket that has been turned upside down, as indicated by the direction of the zipper mechanism. The waistlines of the jackets Grossman used regularly incorporated belt loops, belts, and buckles, and she slyly upended the jacket to make it look like pants, splayed open and exposed by the tubes that emerge from it. In this regard, *Ali Stoker* is comparable to *Bride*. Both play off the genders associated with clothing (the wedding dress, the black leather jacket) and set them against ersatz genital imagery, but both mock the supposed brash display that they at first glance seem to promise. In neither is the display of genital imagery as forthright, unambiguous, or explanatory as it first appears. These relief sculptures, after all, offer no rendering of the figure or image of the body. Rather, they use the found object and assemblage to produce a compacted abstract field that evokes garments and body parts only to dilute any meaning one would ascribe to them. Instead, the works offer preposterous allusions to their multiplications and combinations. They intimate but do not image the bodily and the sexual. This is accomplished in an open way, with their non-figuration and bodily allusion combining to solicit successive recognitions and identifications. For instance, Lowery Stokes Sims described *Ali Stoker* as a work that

> ooze[s] a tense, turgid sexuality, reinforced in the allusive shapes and contorted arrangements that make us realize we're not in Kansas anymore. Pipes, vacuum hoses, zippers and studs swirl around one another, connect with one another, penetrate one another, emit one another. It is an orgy of intercourse: raised mounds suggest breasts, concavities vaginas, and the hoses and pipes, of course, penises.[67]

Sims accurately describes the process of looking at *Ali Stoker*'s "orgy of intercourse." The more one examines the work and follows its serpentine auto-penetrations, the more the initial obviousness of its imagery turns in on itself and metamorphoses (fig. 93).

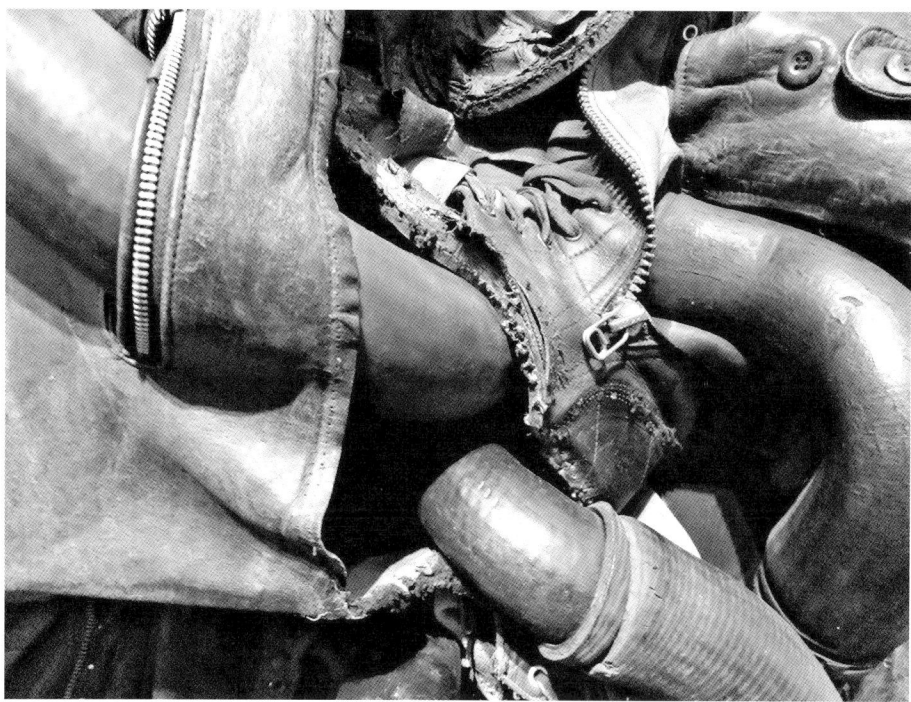

93 Detail of Nancy Grossman, *Ali Stoker*.

Grossman further connected this work explicitly with gender through the obscure title, naming it after a large, unruly German Shepherd she purchased to protect her after she moved to Eldridge Street. Named "Petz Ali Baba," the dog proved to be a headache. "That miserable dog," Grossman has recalled, "he was mopping the floors with me. He was black, and he had these muscular paws. He was practically bursting. Not cute at all."[68] For her, the dog became a competing presence in her studio, full of muscular energy. "Everything that was black and macho I named after that dog," she has said.[69] An earlier relief assemblage on white canvas, *Ali of Nostrand* (1965) also referred to the beast (and humorously gave it noticeable breast-like forms in the upper left). Returning to this motif a year later, Grossman amplified the macho image with "stoker," referring to "stoking coal in the bottom of the world. Black coal. Intestinal."[70]

Combined with the loaded imagery of the black leather jacket, the churning and tentacular *Ali Stoker* was an image of restless masculine energy. She has explained, "It's a coal stoker, it's Ali the dog, it's energy."[71] Mark Daniel Cohen once called it "an assembly of black leather, metal and rubber that is a fury of teeming coils, serpentine and torturous, and tortured in its windings – the writhing intestinal mass of a painful revolt."[72] Nevertheless, the very excess of such imagery and the endless penile looping of the tubes ultimately tempers the flaying and contortions of these skins with absurdity (see fig. 93). Even more so than *Bride*, *Ali Stoker* flouts the exposure of genital imagery as a means of deflating its power and questioning its relationship to gendered behaviors (and garments). Just as the frank exposure of *Bride* fails to limit gender, so too does *Ali Stoker* caricature "macho" in a work that penetrates itself. In so doing, the work relies on the gay male connotations of the black leather jacket to show how exaggerated masculinity is also the receptive object of sexual desires. Nevertheless, the work does not settle on this reading but keeps gender and sexuality transforming through its abstract bodily topographies. Remember, Sims saw this same work's "orgy of intercourse" suggesting breasts and vaginas as well as penises.[73] Both ways of looking at *Ali Stoker* – as many sexes or as the same sex penetrating itself – complicate and caricature the idea that the masculinity one might attribute either to the black leather jacket or to the penis is inviolable. As Catherine Lord has remarked, "Grossman understood earlier than most feminist theorists the performative aspects of masculinity."[74]

Overall, in Grossman's relief assemblages, every revelation that the exposure of the sexed body or the gendered garment seems to promise is undercut, and genitals and genders are made to appear insufficient, exaggerated, unrooted, or ludicrous. "There's always something funny about the assemblages. Something hilariously funny," Grossman has asserted.[75] The reliefs are still tortured, tangled, and dark but their seriousness has been tempered by absurdity. Like black humor, they incite discomfort and laughter at the same time.

This humor is frequently directed at the authority of the genitals in determining who a person is, and Grossman's work mocks their truth-value as supposed primary trait of gendered personhood. In this, she attacks the assumption that the genitals are a natural sign – manifested most baldly with the assignment of a gender to a baby at birth.[76] This presumption is culturally invested as a precursor for assigning personhood, as Susan Stryker has argued. Speaking of the ways in which both the investment in dimorphic reproductive organs and the consequent assignment of binary gender are ideological, she explained:

> [B]odies are rendered meaningful only through some culturally and historically specific mode of grasping their physicality that transforms the

flesh into a useful artifact. Gendering is the initial step in this transformation, inseparable from the process of forming an identity by means of which we're fitted to a system of exchange in a heterosexual economy. Authority seizes upon the specific material qualities of the flesh, particularly the genitals, as the outward indication of future reproductive potential, constructs this flesh as sign, and reads it to enculturate the body. Gender attribution is compulsory; it codes and deploys our bodies in ways that materially affect us, yet we choose neither our marks nor the meanings they carry.[77]

Grossman's abstract assemblages bracket and parody the power of the "construction of this flesh as sign" by detaching these parts from the body and absurdly playing them off cultural artifacts (the wedding dress, the leather jacket) that are themselves hyperbolically but arbitrarily gendered. There is nothing "natural" about the white dress as feminine or the black leather jacket as macho, and Grossman plays with both projections of gender onto them, inverting their terms and forcing other gendered imagery to complicate any one-to-one correlation. Grossman's assemblages compel us to look at the ersatz genitals on display as constructed (as with her ex-boyfriend's boots) and to recognize them as just one more unstable sign of gender circulating in the works, unattached even to bodies themselves. Just as Grossman's abstract works could be seen to contribute to the exploration of the "part-object" in postwar art, her work again aligns with what Halberstam has characterized as the specific use of the part-object (with reference to Hesse) as a central tactic for visualizing transgender through the "fetishistic practice of detaching organs from bodies."[78]

The practice Grossman used to engage with abstraction – that of assemblage – increasingly brought her back to bodily imagery in the form of detached parts. Contrary to Berkson's claim that she had "nostalgia" for them, however, I would argue that the nostalgia was his. Her works do not look backward to a past wholeness from which her parts came. They wryly recombine them into new futures. The items she used, from the horse harnesses to the boots to the clichéd leather jackets, all pointed to the bodies they once clothed and held but also celebrated the new constellations they had become. In turn, her material of leather itself allegorized this process of de-constructing one body to make another, which would play out in her works. During this phase of her work, bodies became visible through their parts, but these parts were opportunities for play, possibility, and humor amid the grave imagery of sex and gender.[79] She has recalled, "In my work, especially in those machine-animal figures, they're both male and female.

And I didn't have to think about it consciously, because maybe it would have made me feel self-conscious, but they're definitely that way."[80]

The mobility of gender and its detachment from the supposed determination of the sexed body are recurring themes in Grossman's discussions of her own practice. For instance, in a diary entry from 1991, Grossman recalled an encounter with one of her abstract assemblages from the 1960s in which she reiterated their openness with regard to gender:

> This afternoon the temperature has reached a humid 100° in New York City. Very uncomfortable. I've been suffering with a headache all day but for an interlude when I opened the door of my un-air-conditioned sculpture studio where, a few days ago, I had begun to remove the mitered one-by-twos which framed a 1960s wall construction. Some of the leather in the piece had become dry and needed to be restored or, perhaps, replaced. Although I had no intention of working on the piece today in the light, airless space, somehow I began to approach it. An hour passed, another – no headache, no worries, no gender, no body. A closed space, a dream space, an ecstatic losing of my care-worn conscious self. That's the way it is sometimes, like going out to play.[81]

The recombinant forms of the Sixties assemblages call for such accounts of potentiality and unforeclosed possibility through their staging of reworking of skins, bodies, and compositions. With their detached, preposterous parts and their humorous play with the signification of gender, these sculptures call for an open-ended account of the body's mutability and gender's inhabitation of it. They evoke the body through garments even as they atomize it into mere components that promiscuously form new constellations.

When she made her figurative turn and started making the head sculptures in 1968, Grossman asserted that she was "reclaiming the body."[82] Not without a touch of humor, her reclaiming of the body left it behind to focus on the head. Moving from the genitals to the head was the next step in taking the body not as a biological given but as something that could be remade and re-inhabited. She told Nemser,

> The figure, male or female, is an erect phallus since it is walking upright on the earth. Its head, which is equivalent to the head of the phallus, is its most aggressive part. After all, your head which is the seat of your hang-ups is also your most powerful organ, not your penis or your vagina. I know male artists experience making art in a so-called very female way. It is not about getting a hard-on. The whole concept of inspiration is

about being filled. Actually in this act of art-making we are really bisexual and it's too bad the word is so distorted and politicized at this point. People feel so fugitive about saying it and will insist everything is black and white while the world is greying all around them.[83]

In her subsequent work, Grossman pursued these grey areas. Her consistent demand that viewers see the leather heads as self-portraits has just that unsettling effect, as I shall discuss. The same thing happens with the reliefs. The unabashed and gleeful toying with genitalia casts them as just parts that explain little. These detached genital forms float among tangles made from the skins of animals that were, themselves, remade as bodily containers (garments, harnesses, boots) before being de-constructed and re-constructed by Grossman. In this process, from cow to human garment to leather scraps to the assembled allusion to a vagina or a penis, Grossman does nothing less than ask us to see the body as raw material, to be remade. Hers is a preposterous account of the body that, in all its earnestness and struggle, ultimately questions sexual difference as determining who we are or can become.

MAKING AND HIDING: GROSSMAN'S PRACTICE OF SELF-PORTRAITURE

The abstract relief assemblages of 1965 to 1967 disrupt gender's identification with the sexed body, mock the importance given to genitals as a determinant of personhood, and stage the body's mutability. Arising from a feminist stance, these works mark Grossman's attempt to wrestle with the body and its supposed determinism. At first, she recast it through the lens of abstraction, leaving only hints of recognizable bodily imagery in the non-figural fields presented by her compounded and layered relief constructions. This process of bodily abstraction, paradoxically, continued as Grossman turned to figuration in 1968 with the works that became her most famous, the leather-bound heads (fig. 94). As one critic summarized it in 1972, "Heads are her figures."[84]

Despite their apparent straightforwardness, the head sculptures are far more complex and compacted than they first appear. In other words, they lend themselves to being "misrecognized," as Nayland Blake has compellingly argued.[85] That is, Grossman's head sculptures have been seen not just as representational but as uncomfortably explicit. Viewers often greet her works with a shock of recognition and a knowing nod. The use of leather and

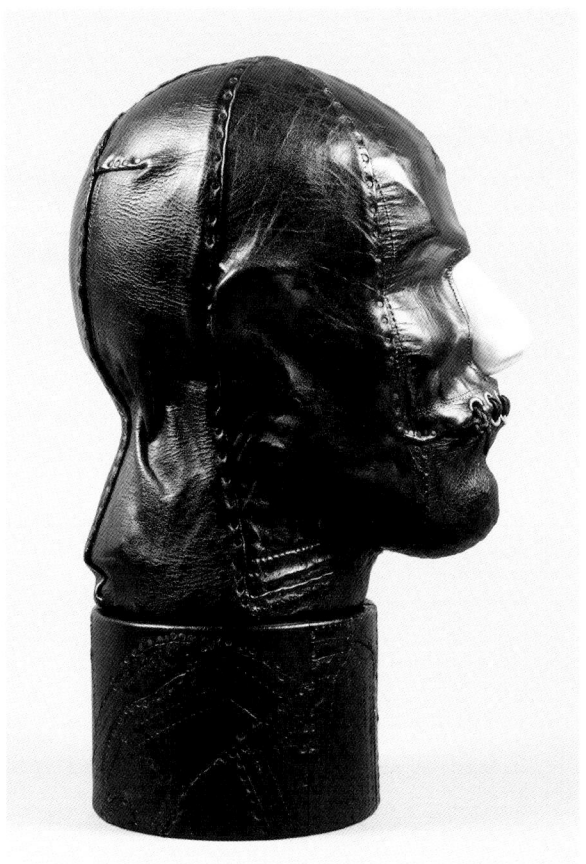

94 Nancy Grossman, *No Name*, 1968. Leather, wood, paint, epoxy, and hardware, 38.1 × 17.8 × 25.4 cm (15 × 7 × 10 in.).

restraints has led many viewers to assume that these works depict s/m practices, which often take black leather as their favored material. At first glance, the works do seem to resemble the world of bondage hoods, ball gags, sensory deprivation gear, and the rest. The buckles and snaps, the evidence of the inner wooden core straining against the tightly bound leather, and the violation of the human head and face could find a place among the material culture developed by communities for whom sexual and erotic practices of domination and submission were the organizing themes. Importantly, however, these sculptures are not these things. Their leather skins are not mere garments. They cannot be removed and replaced. They are integral and formed in direct and intimate contact with the wooden sculptural core. These mere heads do not represent sex, though it is assumed that they scandalously do.

An inquiry into Grossman's process helps to clarify the apparent contradiction between others' assumptions about the explicit content of these works and Grossman's own claims that these are self-portraits that speak to broader human and political themes. While one might think that they are simpler in form than the tangled abstract reliefs of the previous years, Grossman's heads, in fact, rely on an equally intense project of reworking, binding, and transforming. They are meticulously made and are the products of Grossman's extensive, but often hidden, labor.

Grossman's art training was in drawing and illustration, and her early recognition came as a painter. Only when she started "drawing" with leather straps did she more decisively turn to sculpture. This led, as discussed earlier, to the complex re-assemblies of clothing, shoes, and objects for which Grossman drew on knowledge she had gained as a child working in her family's garment factory. Her experience with the patterns and structures of the clothing and shoes fostered her understanding of the shapes and possibilities of the garments that she dismembered and reassembled. She was never really trained in conventional sculptural practices, however. When she decided to make the head sculptures, she taught herself to carve wood.

The first stage of Grossman's making of a sculpture was to create a fully carved wooden head with details and nuances (see fig. 95). Grossman tells stories of using the wrong tools and the wrong materials as she was learning to make these. "When I started to do these head sculpture, I didn't even know how to carve. I was whacking away with carpenter's tools. I didn't even know the difference."[86] In keeping with her attitudes toward remaking, even the wood was repurposed and transformed. For the first years of the heads, the wood was not solid but instead made of planks that were glued together to make a block.[87] Grossman would scavenge two-by-fours and other scraps for this purpose. Sometimes, noses and other protrusions would be made separately and covered in cast shells made from a special mix of epoxy paint that she developed to give them their shiny, sealed surface. As with the leather, this shiny candy-coating layer protects and obscures the underlying wooden sculpture. When there are exposed teeth, dentures are embedded into the wood sculpture, hiding the core as well. The open mouth of *M. L. Sweeney* is even covered in black leather (see fig. 105). Once fully carved and assembled, these elaborate heads would then be covered by not one but two layers of leather. Between the black outer skin and the wooden core, Grossman added a precisely molded layer of thinner leather (usually red, but sometimes tan or purple) that is visible only as it peaks out in details around the nose (figs. 95–97). In this process, the double covering of the initial sculpture has great significance, for it embeds within the final sculpture two reiterative inner layers that are

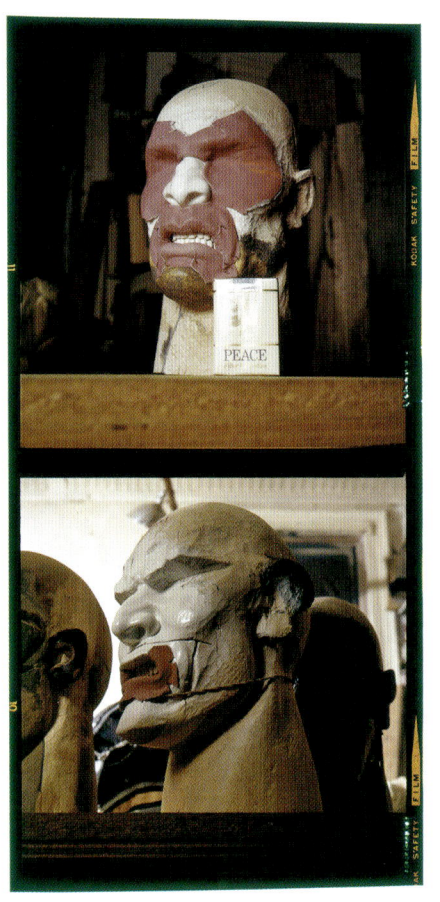 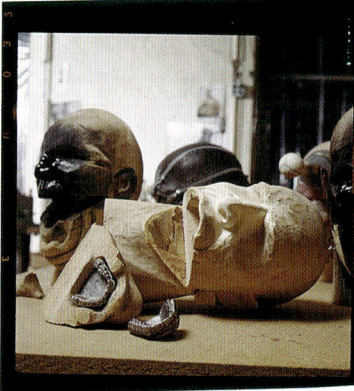 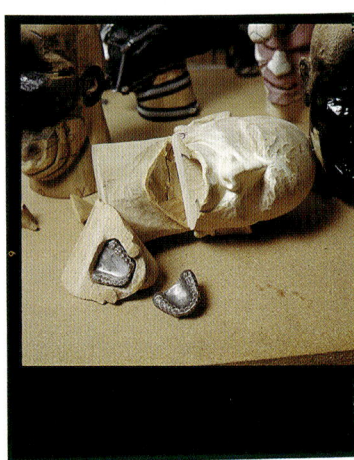 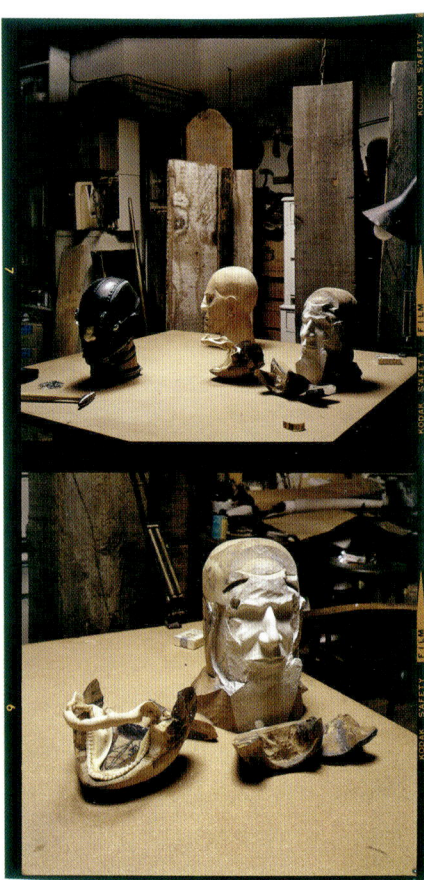

95   Richard Avedon, documentation of Nancy Grossman studio, 13 November 1970.

heavily worked but largely invisible to the viewer. As she said in 1971, "It's the idea of making something, then hiding it again."[88]

After binding colored-leather-clad wooden heads in black leather, Grossman would then create intricate lines of force across the landscape of the head and neck with straps, zippers, and nails hammered in rows through the leather into the wood. She has often talked of these works – that others see as sexual and scandalous – in dynamic material and formal terms, reminding viewers to attend to the variation across the surface of the works established by her invention of lines from her material. Without a doubt, however, these same elements are also read through the intense physicality required to make them. Tightly laced, buckled in, and bound, the surfaces of these works exhibit real material tension as the pliant leather bears the

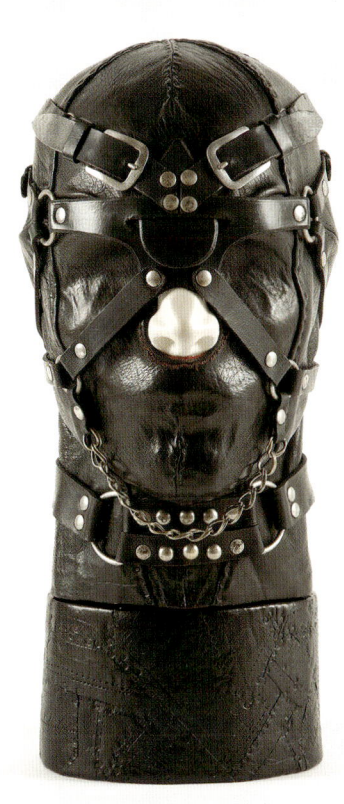 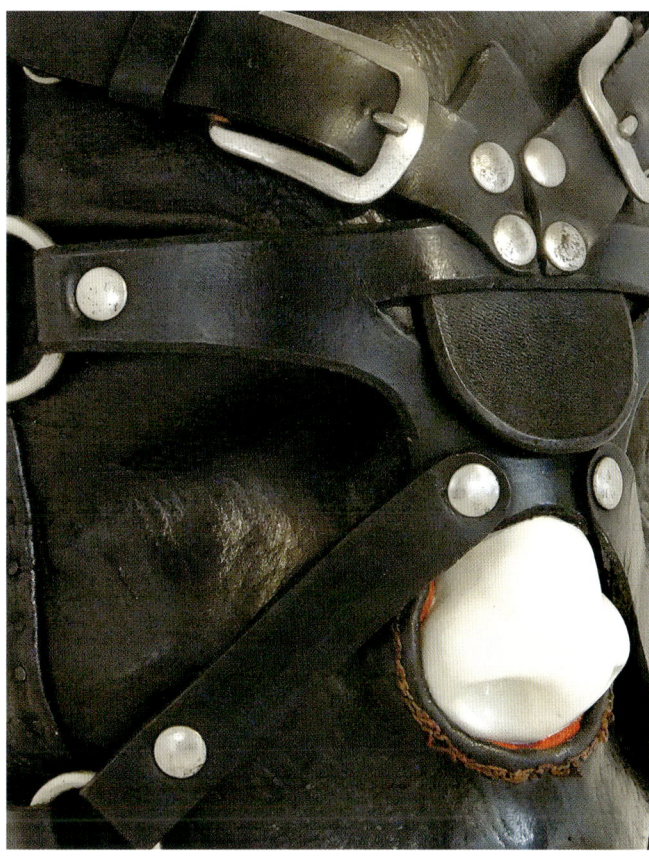

96   Nancy Grossman, *Blunt*, 1968. Leather, wood, hardware, and lacquer, 43.5 × 19.1 × 22.2 cm (17⅛ × 7½ × 8¾ in.). Private collection.

97   Detail of Nancy Grossman, *Blunt*.

evidence of being stretched to take in the head. The denominator for this is Grossman's own physical exertion, the history of which is evident in the perfectly crafted surfaces and their tautness.

Grossman's sculptures (and the full extent of her artistic labor) are never simply or fully visible from the exterior skin. (fig. 98) These works trade on the idea of covering. Cumulatively, her heads problematize visibility, both by blinding her depicted characters and by doubly protecting their faces and her sculpting from our gaze. Despite what many take to be its frankness and blatancy, that is, Grossman's practice reminds us that we should distrust our urge quickly to decode visually and to categorize the exterior. As with the use of recycled and repurposed materials, what is easily visible to us at present never tells the whole story.

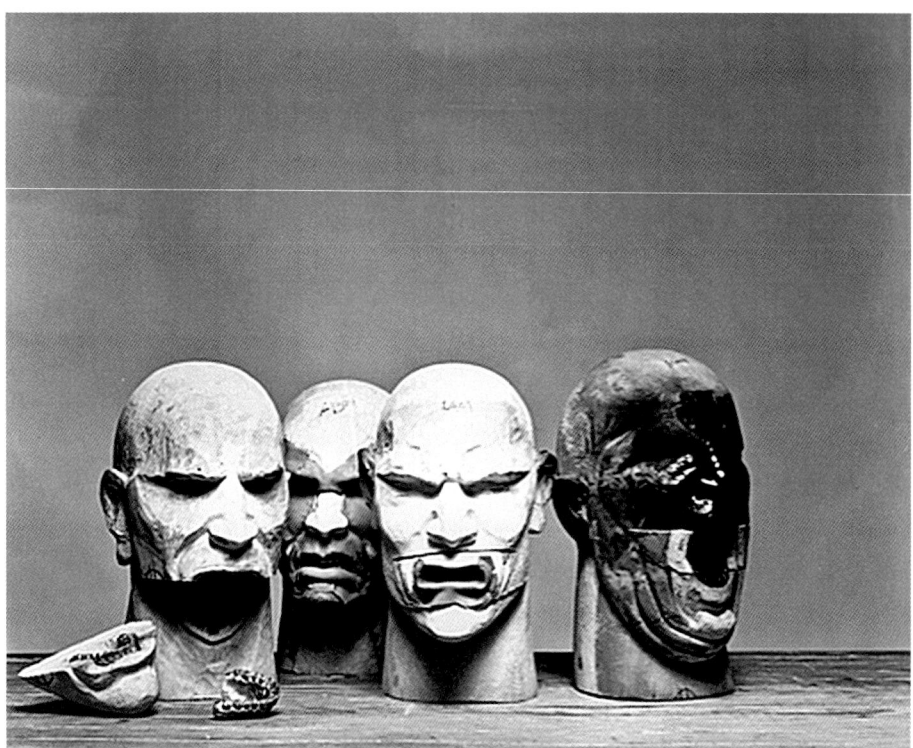

98 Richard Avedon, Nancy Grossman sculptures in progress, 13 November 1970.

The material practice of "making something, then hiding it again" is integral to Grossman's repeated assertion that these works are self-portraits. With the great care it took to make then sheath the deeper layers of the sculptures, she invested in a process resulting in works that were evocative of her identifications, empathies, and thoughts. The head sculptures are, in this way, part of the tradition of conceptual self-portraiture in which the resemblance of the artist's body to the artwork is not assumed.

Grossman's nomination of her head sculptures as self-portraits is neither straightforward nor emotionally singular. In the next section, I shall examine the implications of this with regard to gender, but it is helpful to provide an example of how the works incorporate more than that concern and how they result from complex identifications and emotions on Grossman's part. Although they seem to exhibit relatively small variations to some viewers, the head sculptures often relate to specific moments of her history and life. Many of her titles have autobiographical or anecdotal cues (especially the often unexplained initials attributed to some of the heads). More broadly, she has often spoken of the head sculptures as embodying her own frustrations and emotions. She would spend long hours in her studio while listening to the news on the radio, and many of the early works register her responses to political events of the late 1960s and 1970s, in particular the Vietnam War. This was the case with the sculpture *Mary*, which was named after the disgraced Lieutenant William Calley, as Raven explained in her monograph on Grossman (fig. 99). She reported that Grossman said of this work, "*Mary* was a sissy boy."[89]

To understand this statement and its identificatory complexity, one must think through the implications of a sculpture such as *Mary* both emerging from a political context and being a "self-portrait." Grossman was disgusted by the Vietnam War, and Calley came for many to embody American atrocities in the conflict. He had ordered the killing of unarmed civilians in the infamous 1968 "My Lai Massacre," and he was a recurring topic of discussion in the press following his being charged with mass murder. He was ultimately found guilty of murder of only a small number of those killed (only to have his life sentence reduced to house arrest by a presidential pardon from Richard Nixon in 1971), and the highly publicized trial brought home for the American public the savagery of the conflict. News of the My Lai massacre had prompted outrage but the guilty verdict nevertheless proved divisive, with some defending Calley's role as a soldier (and, by extension, the "good" being done by American intervention in the region) and others decrying the indiscriminate murder of civilians. Debate on questions of guilt and responsibility circled around the coverage of the trial, leaving opinion raw and polarized.

Grossman's work on *Mary* coincided with the trial, which went on from the winter of 1970 through to the spring of the following year. Listening to radio coverage and reading the newspapers, Grossman would have become aware of the reporting on Calley and his personality in which his masculinity and maturity were questioned. Reporters often mentioned his short height (about the same as Grossman's, in fact). There was much speculation about his over-attachment to parental figures (including a transference onto his commanding officer, Ernest Medina). A profile in the *New York Times Sunday Magazine* described him as "altogether too much a pathetic cipher of a man to be anyone's hero, villain or symbol of anything. Five-foot-3, puffy-eyed, lop-eared." The reporter continued: "It is no wonder that Calley craved affection. He told psychiatrists that in the primary grades he always tried to be near his music teacher so he'd be the one she'd choose to sit with her at the piano and turn the pages of the music."[90] As James Olson and Randy Roberts have explained in their history of the massacre, "Most

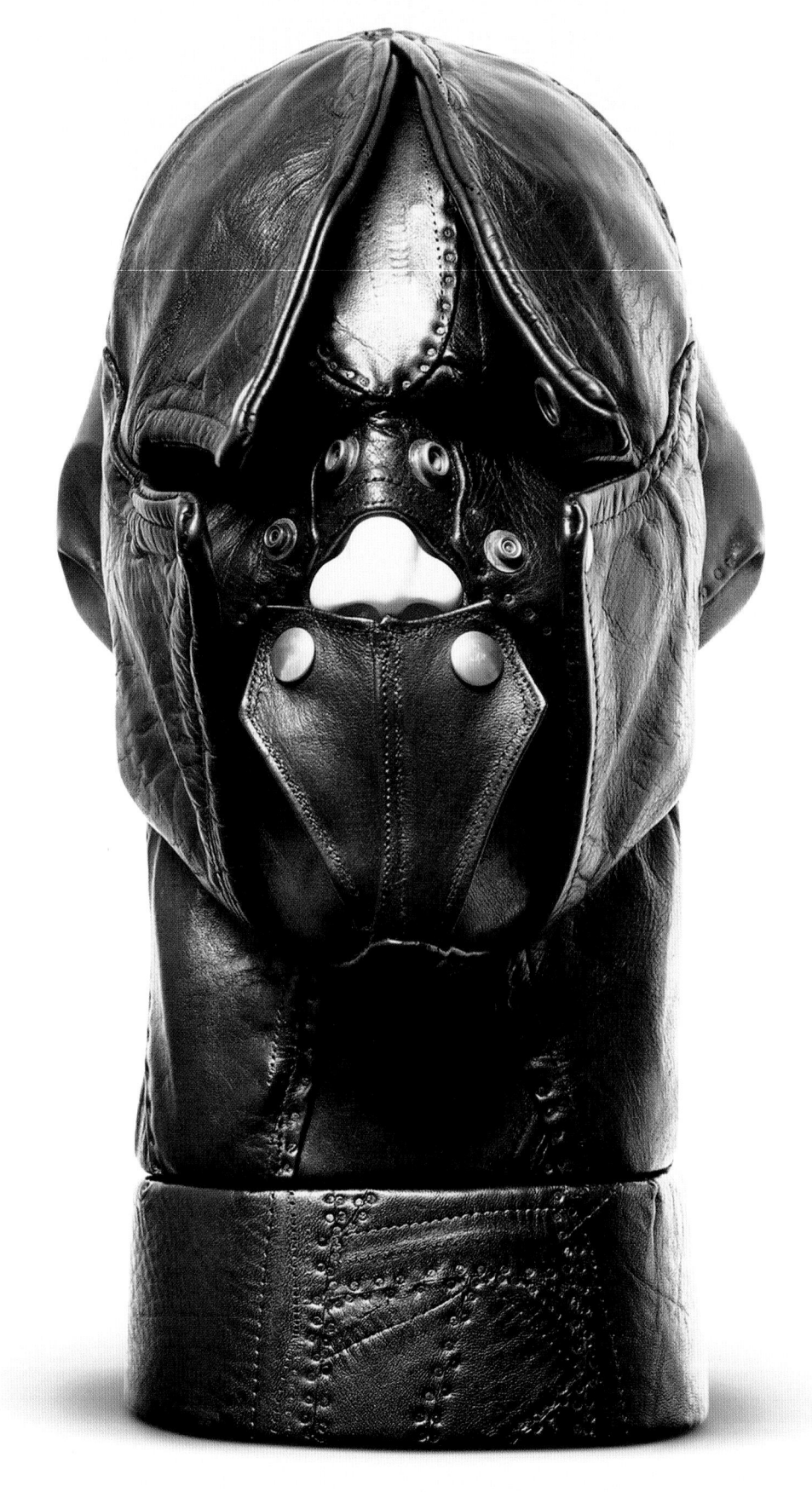

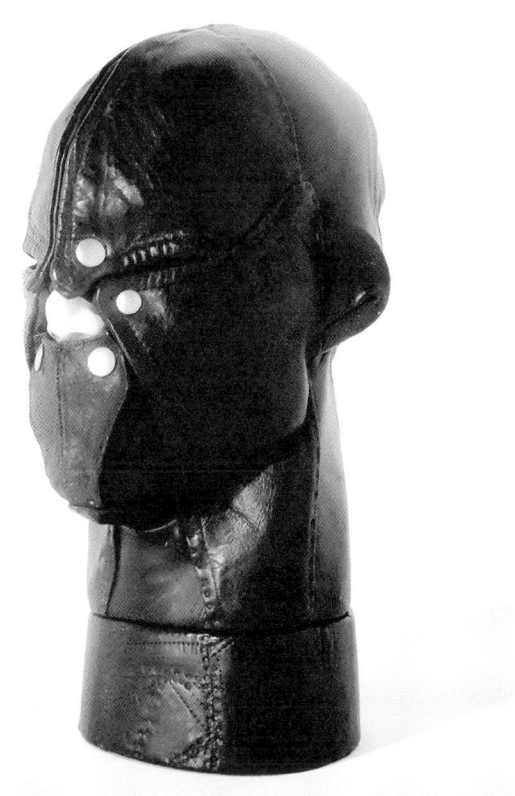

OPPOSITE AND RIGHT
99 and 100
Nancy Grossman, *Mary*, 1970–1. Wood, dyed leather, metal, paint, epoxy, and thread, 33 × 24.1 × 20.3 cm (13 × 9½ × 8 in.). Collection of Mr. and Mrs. Julian Taub.

of [Calley's] men regarded him as something of a pint-sized joke, a Napoleon want-to-be who demanded a level of respect he never earned. He reminded one of his platoon members of 'a little kid trying to play war.'" Medina, they reported, called Calley "Sweetheart."[91] It was this context that informed Grossman's referring to him as a "sissy boy."[92] As Raven explained, "Grossman considered the Vietnam War to be a rank failure of the American Dream, and representative of a pathological stunting of growth – a preadolescent worldview that produced aberrant masculinist behaviors."[93] Probably titling the work with reference to the gay slang term for an effeminate man, "Mary," Grossman created this work as an image of frustrated and stunted masculinity, needing to be contained. She talked about the fact that the leather-clad face was itself under an additional layer of flaps that covered its emotive facial expression and that could be snapped shut over the entire face (see figs. 99 and 100). "The form completely changed when it was snapped shut," she said, indicating how the specific elements of the sculpture related to its themes of containment and disclosure.[94]

While being critical of Calley with her association of this work with him, her description of him as a "sissy boy" nevertheless cast him as lonely child made to compensate for his physical and emotional difference. The brutality of that lifetime of compulsory compensation was evident in his adult atrocities. *Mary* offers a particularly complex case of Grossman's conflicting emotions and identifications with her work. In it, the physical intensity of the binding and (in this case, triple) covering is revealed to be both aggressive and protective as it attacks the adult and registers the frustrations of the misunderstood child. This work, however, is not a portrait of Calley, even though its title encapsulates Grossman's political anger at the Vietnam War (something known only from Raven's insider information). It is, according to Grossman, a self-portrait, and we can see seething within its political critique an empathy with the misunderstood, diminutive boy and the shame he was made to feel for failing to live up the ideal of masculinity that was laid onto him. This work, in other words, fears the policing of "proper" masculinity that stunted this boy. She did not forgive Calley or justify his actions so much as rail against a society that produced this monster. Her political anger and feelings of individual frustration in the face of war – and her rage at the burdens of normalcy laid onto children – make *Mary* both deeply political and deeply personal.

Often, however, we are not given the context for Grossman's titling of the works and she prefers to leave their individual histories opaque. Nevertheless, Raven's disclosure about *Mary* helps to illustrate how Grossman's head sculptures engage with larger political and social contexts while also being vehicles for questions of personal history, self-determination, and identity. Cumulatively, the works speak to such emotional conflicts and frustrations. The carved sculptures sometimes (but not always) have contorted or screaming faces for this reason. As one critic wrote, "Sheathed in anonymity, straining to be free, these make ferocious gestures and a strong, silent bid for human liberation."[95] Again, Grossman linked her practice to a mode of Abstract Expressionism, seeing the work as an evocation of the things for which she could find no words.[96] "The words are used up," she once said.[97] As with the relief sculptures, the intense physical exertion of creating these works was her version of the Abstract Expressionist painters' gestural actions. The wood she chose was intended for building and construction, and it was resistant to being carved. Hacking away these assembled blocks of wood only to obscure them, Grossman directed her thoughts and energies into the process of carving and transforming. The buckles,

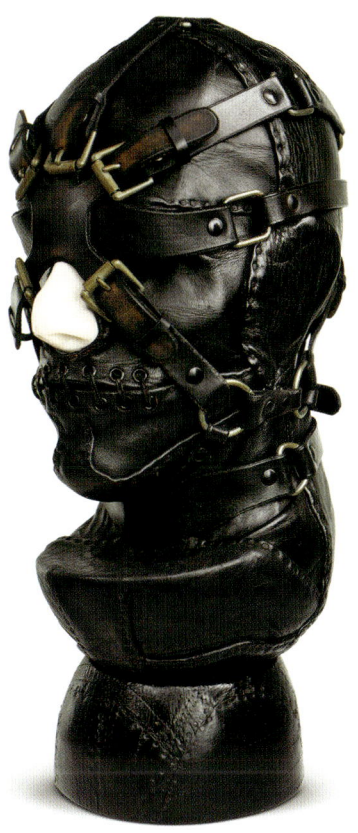

101 Nancy Grossman, M.U.S., 1969. Wood, dyed leather, metal, paint, epoxy, and thread, 40.6 × 17.1 × 20.3 cm (16 × 6 3/4 × 8 in.). Collection of Daniel W. Deitrich II.

straps, laces, and snaps all provide visualization of the two contrasting forces at work in a Grossman sculpture – the struggle to express outwardly and the struggle to hold in (fig. 101).

While most people assume that Grossman's heads are simply and explicitly being tied in and restrained, the heads are also being protected and buffered. "Grossman's pieces come much closer to armor and prosthetic than restraint and fetish," as Nayland Blake has noted.[98] Indeed, Grossman was looking at a wide range of masks and faces, as can be seen in Richard Avedon's previously unpublished 1970 photographs documenting her studio wall (fig. 102). Grossman looked to such disparate sources as Mexican Lucha Libre wrestlers, African facial painting and decoration, protective masks, medical prosthetics, and animals as sources for her exploration of facial

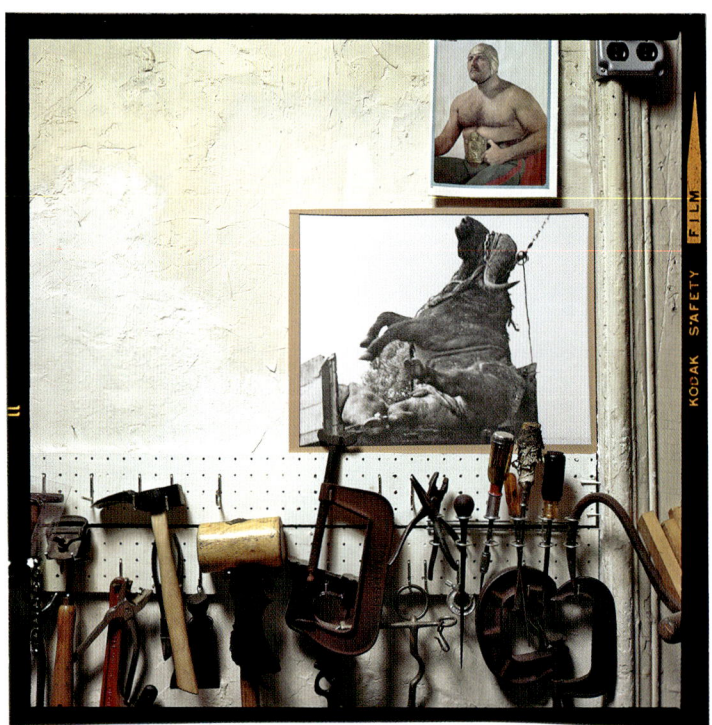

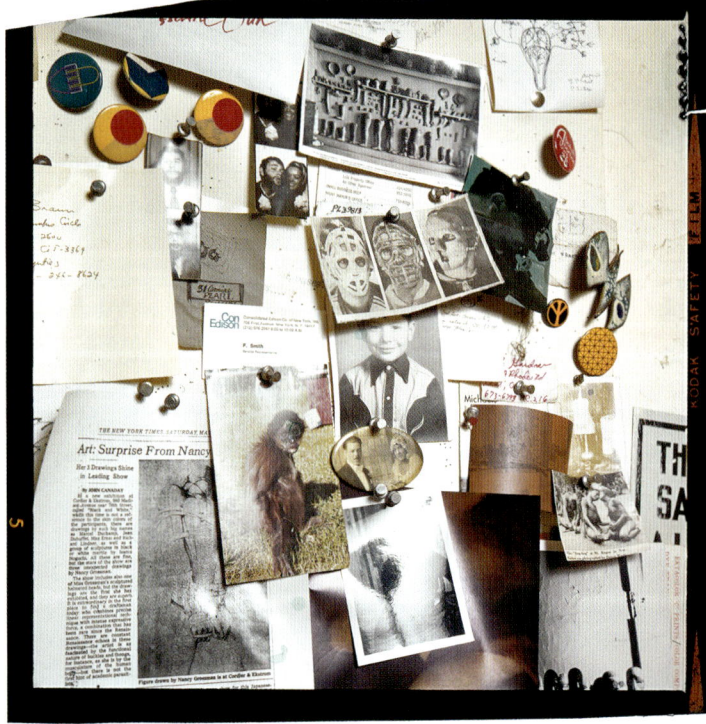

102 Richard Avedon, documentation of Nancy Grossman studio wall, 13 November 1970.

protection and covering. For instance, in one of Avedon's photographs, the corkboard has a range of such materials including a prominently attached triptych showing the evolution of hockey masks (at the right is the famous progenitor of the modern hockey mask designed by Bill Burchmore for the Montreal player Jacques Plante, who became the first goalie to wear a mask when he premiered this invention at a match at Madison Square Garden on 1 November 1959.[99]) This emphasis on protection also informs the physicality of her work, and the bi-directional energy embedded in her protective bindings is crucial. If one takes seriously that these are self-portraits (and one should), then the layers of leather tightly bound to these cores are recognizable as defense from the exterior. The outermost level of leather functions as armor just as much as it functions as restraint, and Grossman is adamant that the wooden core sculptures be completely covered. They are vessels for her identifications. They are for her, and she is their only viewer.[100] The two-ply leather blocks intrusive gazes. Like the use of explicit and confrontational genital imagery in the relief assemblages, the extravagantly buckled, zippered, and strapped exteriors of the head sculptures use extremity and bluster as decoy.

Grossman is not forthcoming about the autobiographical specifics of her works. The complex identifications she has with her head sculptures (which she summarizes through the nomination "self-portrait") are themselves hidden within her technique and in the scene of their creation. Consequently, most viewers of a Grossman sculpture remain arrested by the exterior layer.

EXPLICIT ASSUMPTIONS: S/M AND THE RECEPTION OF GROSSMAN'S SCULPTURE IN THE 1970s

Grossman's head sculptures are confrontational, there is no doubt. The tight laces and the straining zippers spark proprioceptive memories of straining to tie, to zip, to buckle, to hold in. The impact of viewing a Grossman head can activate sense memories and fears in some – whether or not they have ever experienced any degree of restraint or bondage. Recognizing this can help explain the visceral and direct effects these works often have. Understanding the feel and resistance of leather bound so tightly, the viewer is also confronted with an image in which eyes, ears, and sometimes nose and mouth have been covered. This prompts some viewers to imagine themselves as binding or bound in restraints such as those they think they see when looking at a Grossman sculpture.

The affective impact of her work drives many viewers' rush to see Grossman's use of black leather and binding as simply equivalent to s/m devices. Such associations have determined Grossman's reception since the first head sculptures of 1968. Bondage gear was commercially available throughout the 1960s. Leather hoods and masks had become part of the visual vocabulary of illicit erotica propagated in magazines.[101] This is attested by the remarkable tell-all book about the sexual subculture of heterosexual "swinger" couples and fetishists late in the 1950s and early in the 1960s, Michael Leigh's *Velvet Underground*, first published in 1963.[102] In that book, Leigh discussed the mail-order catalogues where leather masks and hoods could be ordered. Such material culture became identified with Grossman's head sculptures soon after they began to be exhibited. John Perreault cited Leigh's book in his 1971 review of Grossman's exhibition in New York at Cordier & Ekstrom, saying "This is and is not a manifestation of the velvet underground." He continued:

> Leather is not a neutral art material. It is a "loaded" material, a fantasy material. The fantasies involved are of a dark sort, fringed jackets and cowboy boots aside. We are in the realm of S.S. uniforms, odd sex. (Come to think of it, all sex is odd if you really think about it.) But leaf through a porno shop or cruise the West Village; visit dark bars, not all of them along the waterfront.[103]

The context for this riff was Perreault's puzzling over Grossman's popularity with collectors. After all, Grossman's turn from abstraction to figuration ran counter to dominant trends of the 1960s.[104] Her sculptures of heads overtook her practice and quickly became a sensation. First shown at the Whitney Annual in 1968, these sculptures soon sold rapidly, and Grossman kept up a frantic pace of production. The success of her 1971 solo show led Perreault to observe:

> Not everyone is having a bad year. A red dot next to an art work in a gallery usually means "sold" (blue means "reserved"). On one level, red dots are the equivalent of grade school stars, and there are red dots all over the place at Cordier & Ekstrom where Nancy Grossman is showing her "leather heads" to full advantage.[105]

While, as mentioned earlier, her work would increasingly sit uneasily in mainstream conceptions of 1970s contemporary art, at the beginning of the decade she had a surge of attention from critics and collectors. Many of these collectors were drawn to her work because they misrecognized it as emblematic of the s/m community (both gay and straight) that was burgeoning in New York, as Perreault's comments attest.

A close study of the heads reveals that few of them would actually function well as bondage gear nor do they resemble the commercially available hoods at the time in any but the most general way (figs. 101, 103–105, 107) It was, however, the association with black leather and the projective inhabitation of the heads by viewers that allowed collectors and critics to jump to that conclusion. This misrecognition overtook Grossman's reputation. In addition to reviews in the art press, her works soon began to be discussed in magazines noted for their erotic content. For instance, in 1971 the German magazine *Twen* published a sensationalist article titled "Nancy Grossman's leather monsters" that played up this content.[106] In 1972, Playboy Enterprises' *Oui* magazine included Grossman in a story about "young s/m artists."[107] This led to errors of association, such as when Gert Schiff put Grossman's *Caracas* (1971) in the "Sex–Sadism" section of his exhibition *Images of Horror and Fantasy* at the Bronx Museum, New York and declared in the catalogue that the sculpture "pays tribute to a recently much publicized elite, the leather scene."[108] As noted earlier, Nayland Blake has succinctly yet decisively refuted such misreadings of Grossman's work in his 2012 essay on the artist. He rightly noted that "The leather heads, in their graphic power and profound isolation, are easily mistaken for artifacts from a sexual community rapidly devolving into a 'lifestyle' as it grew into visibility."[109]

Grossman claims to have been unaware of this flourishing s/m culture when she started making the head sculptures, and she has been consistent in this. While her work evidences a general familiarity with such related aspects as the popular iconography of gay male culture (as in the black leather jacket in *Ali Stoker*; see fig. 91), there is little of the range of s/m's dense and varied material culture such as that catalogued in Leigh's *Velvet Underground* and other contemporary sources. Despite the fact that s/m was neither Grossman's source nor her aim, she was quickly exposed to it when she started exhibiting the head sculptures. Viewers and fans approached her thinking she was "in the know." She has recounted to me a story of an English neighbor who, on seeing her works early on, said "Oh, you're one of those people" and proceeded to invite her over to peruse his catalogues and magazines filled with such material.[110]

Most have followed suit, ignored Grossman's protestations to the contrary, and chosen superficially to associate her work with s/m practices. So, while s/m may not have been central to Grossman's stated or conscious intentions

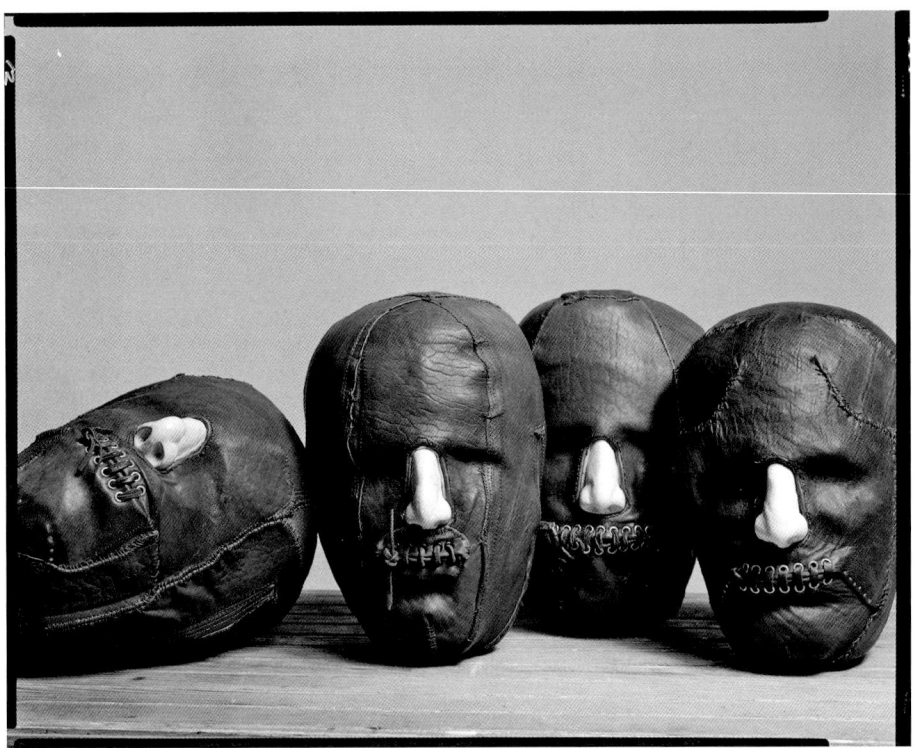

103 Richard Avedon, Nancy Grossman's *Andro* sculptures in progress, 13 November 1970.

at the outset, it was nevertheless crucial to her works' reception history. This is most true in the case of Grossman's many gay male collectors. As Blake observed about Grossman's early reception, "What does it mean when one's work is made emblematic in spite of oneself? Grossman's work was taken up and championed by a group of gay men who misread the ideas and desires in the work through their hunger for the types of representation they lacked."[111] Indeed, within a few years of their debut, the head sculptures could be spotted in interior design articles, such as those in *Home and Garden* and *Connaissance des arts*, where they were set in men's elaborately decorated apartments and houses.[112] As Perreault snarkily commented in reference to this trend in 1971, "Grossman's heads are male. Although it may be irrelevant and a bit insulting, it is amusing to imagine the wooden craniums bound by leather as belonging to male fashion designers."[113] This was registered more than a few times by those who noted the presence of Grossman's sculptures in "designer" houses. A 1977 article in *Residential Interiors*, for instance, illustrated the designer Bill Goldsmith's New York

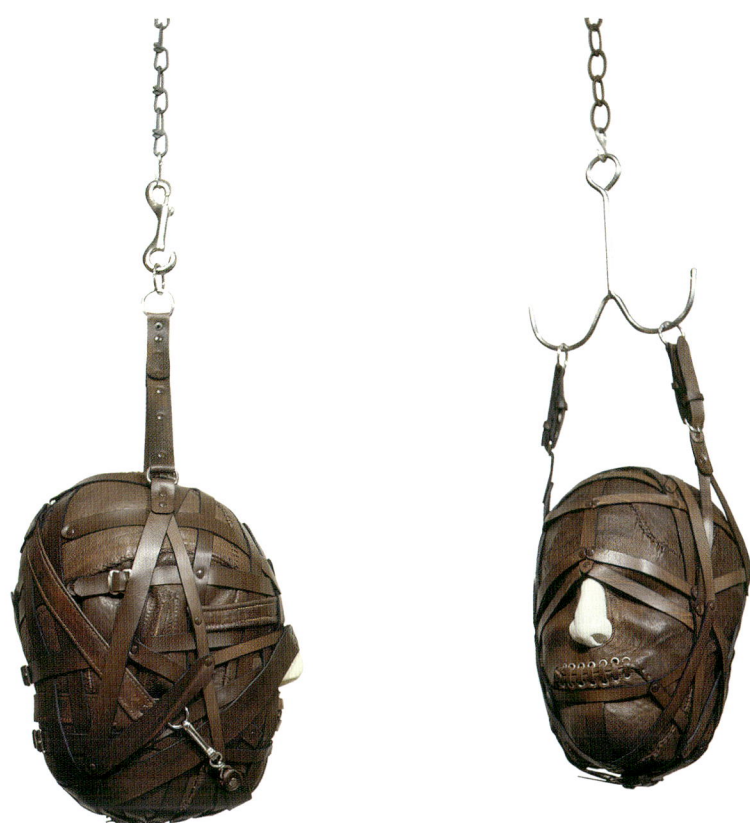

104 Nancy Grossman, *Andro III* and *Andro IV*, 1969–71. Both wood, dyed leather, metal, paint, epoxy, and thread, each 30.5 × 25.4 × 15.2 cm (12 × 10 × 6 in.).

apartment (featuring a Grossman sculpture on the first page of the article) about which the cheeky author reported that it "reflects his enthusiasm for involving and expressing his interests in his personal habitation."[114] Grossman has noted, as well, that during these years the association of her work with gay men also led Jack Smith, Andy Warhol, and Robert Mapplethorpe to ask to visit her studio.[115]

Without a doubt, gay men became central to Grossman's success and were, ultimately, her main patrons in the 1970s. It was during the 1960s and 1970s that an urban, gay male leather culture grew rapidly in New York and other cities. Grossman's heads became quickly absorbed into that iconography. While there had been covert s/m (both gay and straight) net-

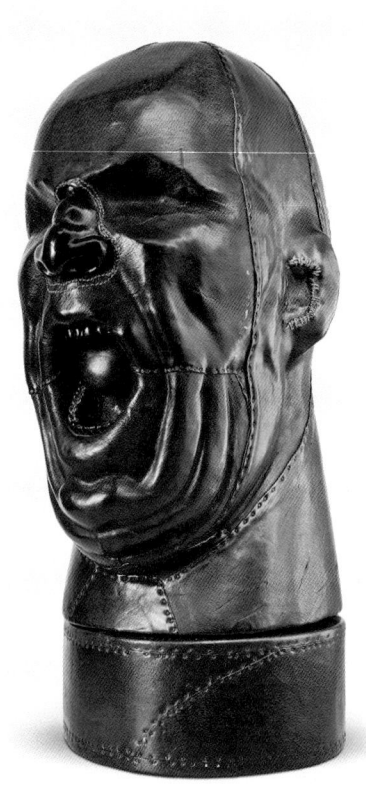

105 Nancy Grossman, *M.L. Sweeney*, 1969–70. Wood, dyed leather, paint, thread, and cast resin, 41.3 × 17.5 × 24.4 cm (16¼ × 6⅞ × 9⅝ in.).

works for decades, gay men in the 1960s began to establish meeting places (bars and clubs) for the s/m community, and leather began to be adopted more widely as a particularly gay male signifier (as discussed earlier in relation to *Ali Stoker*). This expanded and deepened in the 1970s, becoming a general topic of fascination regularly discussed in the press.[116] Highly visible at the start of the decade, Grossman's sculptures became inadvertently iconic of these developments. Jack Fritscher, the editor of *Drummer* magazine, recalled: "Whatever Nancy Grossman intends with her beautiful beheaded sculptures, the Satanic quotient of her existential decapitations exerts a dynamic voodoo pull. Rich, gay, New York leather men particularly respond to her severed male heads in bondage, as if the sculptures are the 'speaking oracles' of some kind of leather fith-fath."[117]

Fritscher was referring to a specific event that he had experienced in 1978 (he mentions it a few times in his voluminous writings). He had been sent to a sex party at a townhouse in Manhattan's Upper East Side by Mapplethorpe (his lover at the time). The gathering was hosted by a well-known television actor (whom he did not name). As Fritscher described it, the party was "scatalogically satanic sadomasochism" and involved a ritualistic scene:

> The afternoon's sensuality centered around artist Nancy Grossman's sculpture of a head wrapped in black leather bondage. A large leather dildo protruded from the head's mouth. I don't know whether that was part of the original sculpture or something added to enhance its powers of conjuration....Under the looming presence of the Grossman totem sculpture, the featured players moved to the heights of ecstasy of flesh and blood.[118]

Telling of the violation and alteration of a sculpture, this sensational anecdote may well be apocryphal. However, the ritualistic scene described by Fritscher (with Grossman's work named each time he repeated this story) attests to the powerful association with S/M culture that her sculptures incited. In other words, even though it is unclear if this was an actual work of hers that had been modified and exploited, its presence in the story attests to the fact that she was, at the very least, iconic enough to have gay S/M scat witches as forgers.

Fritscher would have known about Grossman through Mapplethorpe, and the same associations of her work with S/M had drawn the photographer to her. Grossman and Mapplethorpe developed a friendship, and he was anxious to take photographs of her sculpture. She has recalled: "When I made the heads he was really knocked out. He said, 'I'd love to photograph them. Can I just borrow them? I'd love to photograph them in my basement.' And I said, 'You can't because I don't want them to be actors in your play.' They're full figures. They're already doing their thing. They're already themselves."[119] Nevertheless, Grossman allowed Mapplethorpe to photograph the works (at her studio) and found that he still attempted to make them into characters (fig. 106). "He made the light into a drama....I didn't want them to be anybody's props."[120] Grossman's resistance to Mapplethorpe's taking over of her work was no doubt influenced by the way he and others began to treat her as familiar and experienced with S/M culture (against her own protestations). She recalled that Mapplethorpe was "a sufficiently secure kid, he was a very middle-class kid, so that he could be excited by outrageous things."[121] Much like the English neighbor who showed her his bondage gear catalogues, Mapplethorpe felt enabled by his projection onto her work to show Grossman sexually explicit materials. She continued, "He used to put out the signal – come and talk to me, come and show me everything. He was definitely a voyeur, very excited, but scared too."[122]

A similar confidence was paid by Diane Arbus, with whom Grossman became friends near the end of the photographer's life. (Grossman and her best friend and roommate Anita Siegel were, according to Arbus's biographer, Patricia Bosworth, the last people to see her before she committed suicide in 1971. That year, Grossman titled a head sculpture *Arbus*.[123]) Arbus had started photographing s/m establishments and bringing those photographs to Grossman. As Bosworth recounted, "She'd shown Nancy Grossman a picture of a woman done up in high boots and not much else debasing a naked man on all fours. The image was assaulting, Nancy says. It was like looking at a literal description of the act. Diane seemed a little scared and shocked when she handed it to her, but she said nothing."[124] The stories of Arbus and Mapplethorpe both attest to the ways in which Grossman was understood by many to be familiar with s/m culture. While she was, as she said, not "one of those people," her unjudgmental attitude toward these friends no doubt allowed her to offer a sensitive ear despite their misconceptions of what her work meant about her.

Again, this belief that Grossman was "in the know" affected not just her personal relationships but also the ways in which her work was discussed – and misappropriated. For instance, the *Village Voice* ran a salacious article on s/m in 1975 with a Grossman head sculpture as its central illustration. The contradictory caption dutifully read: "While she is not a part of the leather scene, Nancy Grossman's sculpture of confined males such as the head above, are highly regarded by sm devotees."[125] Problematic as this article was, it contains several interesting details about Grossman. For instance, she is reported as saying about Scott Burton's 1975 *Five Themes of Solitary Behavior*, "that's really sm." His reply: "I guess I'll have to accept that, coming from you."[126] This statement serves to register Grossman's growing awareness of s/m by 1975 as well as the general misapprehension that she was an authority on it. More importantly, the article then went on to explain Grossman's exhaustion at this association. The reporter conveyed Grossman's rejection and discomfort with this narrow view of her work, noting that she asked to be excluded from the article (a request the reporter gleefully conveyed and summarily ignored). Despite his attempt to cast doubt on her, she nevertheless gave the reporter a concise retort to the common misreading of the imagery of confinement in her work: "That's not sm. That's the human condition."[127]

Through such unsolicited encounters (with strangers and friends) and sensationalist appropriations of her sculptures, Grossman's success did, in fact, lead to her growing recognition of the iconography of s/m and the resemblance of her work to its material culture.[128] As her words just quoted indicate, by 1975, she had become familiar with the reasons why her work was misread as s/m. During this time, however, a discernible shift began in her head sculptures. Gradually, the style of the earlier, heavily restrained heads gave way to a less accessorized and more simplified way of working that came to characterize her head sculptures of the 1980s. Starting around 1975, Grossman redirected her work, saying that her newer heads were less autobiographical and not self-portraits in the same way: "These heads, which are much more open, are much more themselves. They become themselves."[129] In the sculptures of the later years of the 1970s, Grossman more often showcased cleaner, uniform surfaces with few (or no) bindings or buckles. (See, for instance, the work *Cob II*, 1977–80, that is on the left of Mapplethorpe's photograph, fig. 106.) They began to have eyes that were open and uncovered. Most significantly, this new phase depicted physiognomies that approximated traits associated with individuals of African descent, though most of the noses continue to be colored white. It seems that the iconography of restraint and resistance so important to Grossman's earlier head sculptures was recast through an empathetic identification with the struggle against racism. This would accord with her support of the Civil Rights movement, which is voiced in some interviews. The black leather now seems less like binding and more like the skin itself. Grossman's late 1970s shift of physiognomy coupled with the abandonment of her bindings and buckles can be understood as her attempt to find an iconography that would not be misread as kink but that nevertheless explored the idea of the struggle for self-determination against resistance and prejudice. However, the contorted faces that characterized the Vietnam-era work no longer dominate. Instead, Grossman gave most of her later heads calm and dignified faces. With their more self-possessed affect and their open eyes, these heads convey a resolve and strength that is different from the conflicted emotional expressions and the restraint/armor of the earlier head sculptures.

Even when looking at this different work of the late 1970s and 1980s, however, critics and the press continued to be happier with their "exposure" of Grossman and with the mischaracterization of her work as bondage iconography. The relationship between Grossman's work and s/m has remained a constant topic in the reviews and writings on the artist. This descended to the point of caricature and an inability to see the works for themselves, as when one *Village Voice* writer tried to win points with her

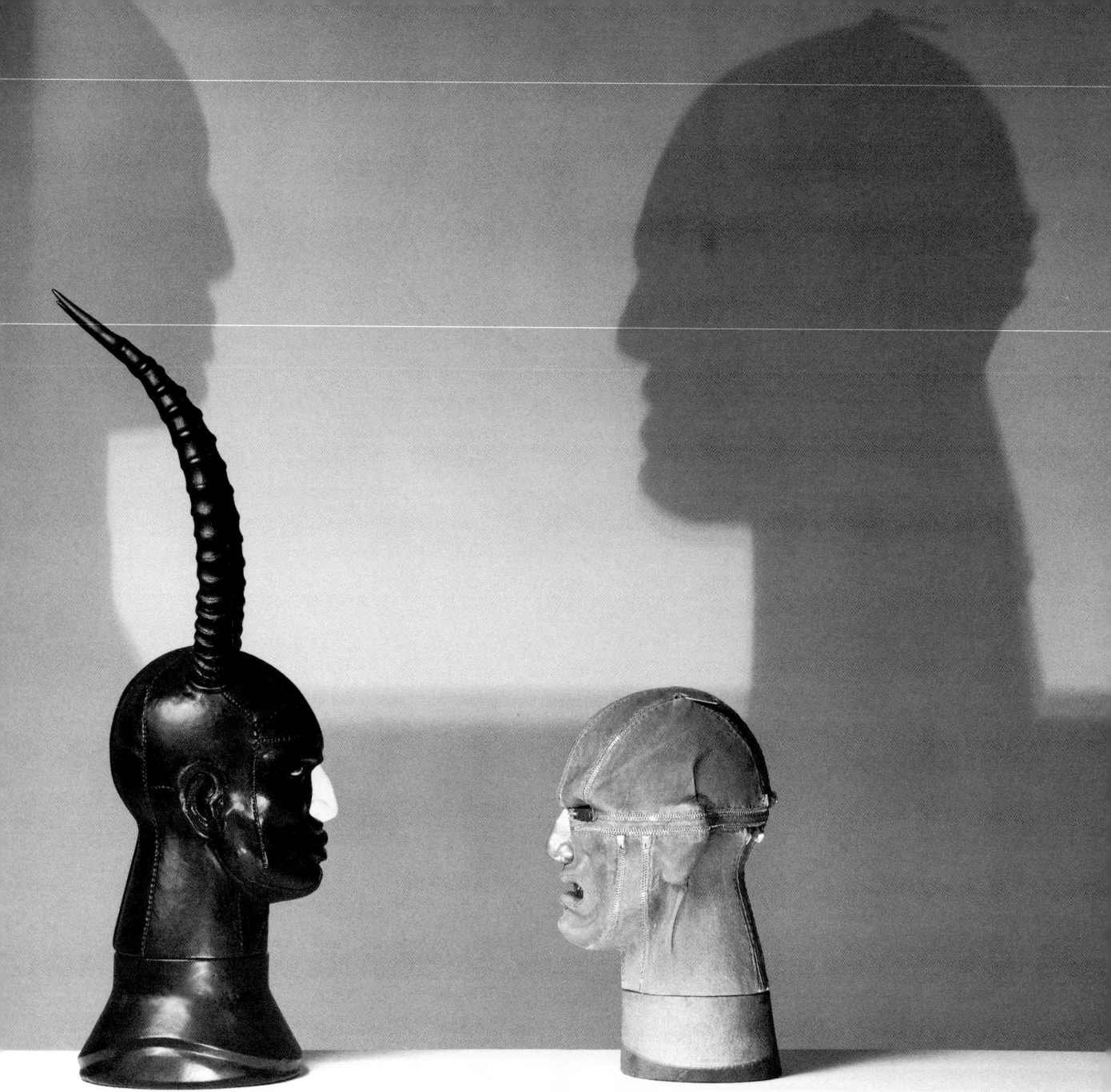

106 Robert Mapplethorpe, *Untitled (Nancy Grossman sculptures)*, 1980.

readers by starting a particularly specious review in 1980 with "I wouldn't want to meet one of Nancy Grossman's figures in a dark alley, but her militia of leather boys can be seen safely at Barbara Gladstone Gallery."[130]

Later, this same author fantasized about Grossman (whom she clearly never met in person) as a dominatrix, saying that the artist "cracks her whip seeking a feminist vengeance." Such viewers imagined that they saw sex in Grossman's heads, despite the fact that there was no representation of it or of the body. As with the more intentionally provocative 1964 film by Andy Warhol, *Blow Job*, the focus on the head and a bit of leather incited viewers to imagine the body and bodily relations not pictured.[131]

Grossman was not silent on this issue, as noted, and she never shied away from the importance of sexual and gendered content in her work, as I shall discuss presently. The heads, however, are not the S/M totems that many have made them out to be. As often happens with intimations of sex or desire, anything seen as evidence of a non-normative sexuality quickly dominates interpretations to the point where viewers claim to have more authentic knowledge about an artist than they themselves do. On this pleasure in assuming knowledge, Eve Kosofsky Sedgwick remarked, "After all, the position of those who think they *know something about one that one may not know oneself* is an excited and empowered one."[132] In Grossman's case, this has proven a constant obstacle, as viewers have chosen to ignore her passionate and committed statements, believing that they know better what this work is *really* about. Grossman's works have been difficult for some museums to collect and display precisely because of this ungrounded fear that these head sculptures explicitly depict deviant sex – not, as Grossman has maintained, "the human condition." Such misrecognitions generate the self-satisfied nod and wink that many viewers and critics have brought and continue to bring to Grossman's sculpture. They have been snared by what they think is an explicit disclosure, never realizing that they are looking at a work that thematizes depth's hiddenness, that grapples with the disjunctions between the inside and outside of personhood, and that allegorizes the struggle for self-determination.

THE POSSIBILITIES OF BODILESSNESS

Grossman emphasized the head because it left the determinations of the sexed body behind while nevertheless consolidating the emotional and psychological aspects of personhood. It was this decision that caused her to refashion her assemblage technique from the covering of relief sculpture's flat planes to the acts of enveloping a psychologically charged and totemic image in three dimensions. The full implications of Grossman's evocation of the body in the absence of its image come into focus when one asks

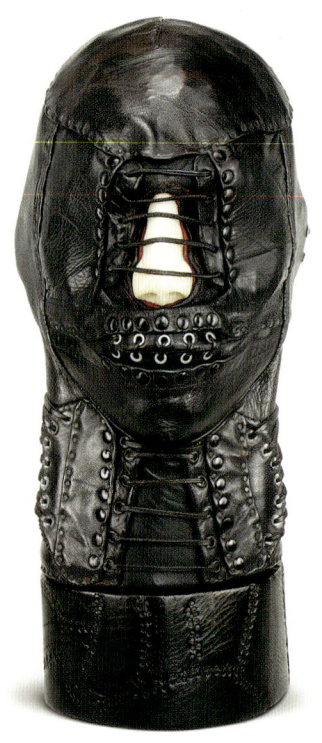

107 Nancy Grossman, *B.Y.K.*, 1969. Wood, dyed leather, metal, paint, epoxy, and thread, 40.6 × 17.1 × 20.3 cm (16 × 6¾ × 8 in.). Collection of Daniel W. Deitrich II.

not about sexuality but about gender. As with her earlier work, the quick read that many give either the assemblages or the head sculptures is eroded when Grossman's statements about the work are taken into consideration. In particular, the claim that the head sculptures are self-portraits disrupts assumptions not just about authorship but also about gender. During the time when Grossman started making the heads, the work of women artists was all too often read solely as if it somehow expressed or reflected femininity. Grossman's style visibly clashed with those expectations but she nevertheless claimed for her works the status of the genre that was most closely tied to biography and self-expression – self-portraiture. When I asked her about this, she reiterated the answer she has given to all interviewers since the early 1970s – "absolutely, they're self-portraits."[133] None seem to resemble her. They are often given obscure initials to evoke different names. Their physiognomies appear, to many, to be those of male-bodied persons – though, on close analysis of the range of head sculptures, there is variation and ambiguity that exceeds such assignments. They seem, based on external appearances alone, to be patently not her. Nevertheless, she absorbs them into the genre that we understand as being most personal, most self-reflective, and most rooted in accounts of the self.

Her assertion that these works are self-portraits is thus a performative speech act. When using a performative, "to say it is to do it," and any artist who nominates one of their works as a self-portrait cannot be refuted. Grossman's consistent claim, then, has iterative force: it affects the ways in which these works can be interpreted. Again, the first look of recognition with a Grossman work is never the whole story, and one must move beyond the decoy of the explicit. Remember, with her 1960s abstract assemblages, she presented supposedly shocking imagery only to complicate the certainty that the exposure of the genitals was said to guarantee. With her head sculptures, she introduced work that resisted being read in relation to her gender (according to the predominant assumptions of the day) while demanding that they be read as self-expressive. What you first see is never what you get with Grossman, and an aim of her works has been to make the viewer nonplussed when attempting to recognize or to nominate gender. One of the central lessons of transgender history is that gender is not always readable as or on the surface; one must resist the impulse to assign gender to others as a predicate for recognizing personhood. Grossman's works demand that one asks about gender beyond (or, more accurately beneath) what one sees on the exterior.

By denying the importance of the body as determining of gender, Grossman's work departed from much 1970s feminism that, increasingly over the course of the decade, rooted its claims in the body as a source of meaning and in an essentialist account of sexual difference. Grossman's divergence from this position was already evident in the abstract assemblages of the 1960s – as was her emphasis on the mutability of the body and of gender. Starting with the head sculptures, the possibilities of multiple identifications with gender became more directly readable through the contradiction produced by the performative nomination of them as self-portraits. For this reason, many increasingly found the leather heads difficult to accommodate fully into the varieties of feminist art-making as they developed in the 1970s.[134] Already by 1972, it was reported that Grossman "has been criticized by women's lib organizations for neglecting the female figure…"[135] Despite Grossman's own feminist statements, her head sculptures seemed to disrupt the aims of mainstream feminist art practice that sought to locate an essential and core femininity in the (securely dimorphic) female body. Grossman's head sculptures, on a cursory glance, offered neither the female nor the body, and her critical engagement with gender's complexity and mobility went unrecognized by many.

The misrecognition of her practice as s/m also pitted her against feminist discourse as it developed in the 1970s. As Gayle Rubin chronicled in the remarkable 1981 essay "The Leather Menace," s/m became a target not just for the popular media who sought to caricature political bids for lesbian and gay rights but also for feminists who saw lesbian s/m communities as unwelcome. Rubin's essay offered a sustained and compelling defense of s/m and its politics, charting how feminist attitudes to lesbian s/m over the previous decade evidenced a move away from a critique of gender and of oppression to a celebration of essential femininity. "Assumptions which now pass as dogma would have horrified activists in 1970. In many respects the women's movement, like the society at large, has quietly shifted to the right."[136] This shift in feminist discourse away from a critique of oppression coincided with the end of the period of "transgender liberation" in 1973 that I discussed in the Introduction.[137] Rubin offered an account of this shift by noting how the term "male-identified" in 1970 meant "a woman lacked consciousness of female oppression." This criticality was lost over the course of the decade:

> By 1980, the term *male identified* had lost that meaning (lack of political consciousness) and became synonymous with "masculine." Now women who do masculine things are accused of imitating men not only by family, church, and the media, but by the feminist movement. Much contemporary feminist ideology maintains that everything female – persons, activities, values, personality characteristics – is good, whereas anything pertaining to males is bad. By this analysis, the task of feminism is to replace male values with female ones, to substitute female culture for male culture. This line of thinking does not encourage women to try to gain access to male activities, privileges, and territories. Instead, it implied that a good feminist wants nothing to do with "male" activities. All of this celebration of femininity tends to reinforce traditional gender roles and values appropriate female behavior. It is not all that different from the sex-role segregation against which early feminists revolted.[138]

Cast as both s/m and male-identified in this latter sense, Grossman became inassimilable to feminist art practices from later in the 1970s that were reliant on essentialist accounts of gender and the body. All the things that many misread in Grossman's sculptures – their being men, their being gay, their being s/m – clashed with the trajectory of feminist debate in the 1970s.

Even into the 1980s, many simply could not see past the binary and dimorphic understandings of gender and sex that Grossman's work problematizes. The perceptive critic and artist Mira Schor, for instance, struggled to overcome this contradiction (based on a misreading of the work as "gay male attire") when she wrote in 1988: "Grossman, as a lesbian artist, is in an interesting position culturally. Her work reflects gay male attire and sensibility, her figures are phallically erect, yet action is prevented by bondage. Whose action, one wonders? That of the male image or of the woman artist?"[139] While Schor was attentive to what she called "the identification of the female artist and the male model," a binary conception of sexual difference disallowed the full sense of what Grossman meant when she called her sculptures "self-portraits."

Over the course of her career, Grossman voiced a feminist stance that called into question the meanings of the body and that posited a mobility of gender and identification.[140] In many ways, the difficulties Grossman faced with her reception have reflected the broader problems of recognition that transgender issues encountered within the politics of gender and sex in the second half of the twentieth century.[141] Early on, Grossman began making work that addressed such issues as nonascribed genders and female masculinity, but these aims were not visible to many owing to the ways in which her work was appropriated and misread.

The significance and sophistication of Grossman's work, in other words, is newly visible when one sees its exploration of genders in relation to transgender politics and transfeminism. This allows for a better understanding of what often goes under-acknowledged in Grossman's discussions of her own work – its emphasis on the mobility and multiplicity of gender. For instance, in an interview from 1972 with an Arizona newspaper, the reporter recounted a conversation in which Grossman responded to the question often posed to her: "People ask her why she doesn't do women (her heads are bald) and [Grossman] asks, 'What is a woman?' What is a man?'"[142] Similarly, she said in 1992, "I think I am specifically female and specifically male. And so is everyone, sometimes less one, and I don't mean just what you're acting out at the time….It's much more arbitrary than people think….I've lived long enough to see both men and women shift."[143] Such statements about her work are, despite changing terminology, consistent. To recall the 1970s interview with Nemser, she said that "we are really bi-sexual and it's too bad the word is so distorted and politicized at this point. People feel so fugitive about saying it and will insist everything is black and white while the world is greying all around them."[144]

Grossman's work demands a more open account of genders' inhabitations of bodies. She confounds the self-evident. What many see as a contradiction – the feminist artist who sculpts work that is misread as male, gay, and fetishistic – is an effect of Grossman's fearless detachment of gender from the sexed body and her thematization of the self's struggle between the interior and the exterior. In response to a question by Nemser about why many of Grossman's works seemed to be male-bodied, Grossman replied: "I don't feel that the male forms are outside of me. I don't feel I have to conform to a political identification, although, naturally, I'm a feminist. But if we have to split hairs, I'm a humanist."[145]

Such statements repeatedly question how others might read (or misread) the body's external traits as signs for an individual's gender. Her performative nomination of the head sculptures as self-portraits serves to disrupt a one-to-one correlation between the reading of bodily or facial characteristics and the mapping of gender onto that body's exterior. As she later remarked in an interview, "It's about how mysterious it is when we move from one gender to the other…We have no way of knowing about the interior, we mark it, we signal it with our exterior inventions and metaphors, there's nothing except metaphor. [It is] a better way [than] male/female, active/passive."[146] With such statements and with her artistic practice, Grossman has articulated a theory of gender that differentiates it both from its bodily determinations and from binary models. This accords with how many in transgender studies call for new accounts of personhood that do not rely on bodily determinations. As Gayle Salamon has argued, "Though it cannot fail to have meaning, the body's morphology does not in any of these instances script either identification or desire, and those who understand bodily morphology to be constitutive of a truth that exceeds ideologies of gender would do well to take seriously some of the ways in which gender is currently being lived."[147] Grossman's heads are not limited to one gender and her statements about them always raise that question of others' assignments. The exterior does not signify the interior in her armored sculptures.

Grossman's sculpture is invested in bodily remaking and in the binding of genders to one another. She makes problematic all that is visible as exterior, and her work refuses the body as a limit to the intellect, to gender, and to a sense of self. In this, both her abstract assemblages and her precise head sculptures abstract the body, leaving it as something suggested and offstage. She saw this refusal of the figure, the body, the genitals, and sexual difference as feminist and argued for a non-binary and mobile account of gender. As she once said about her head sculptures: "This *was*

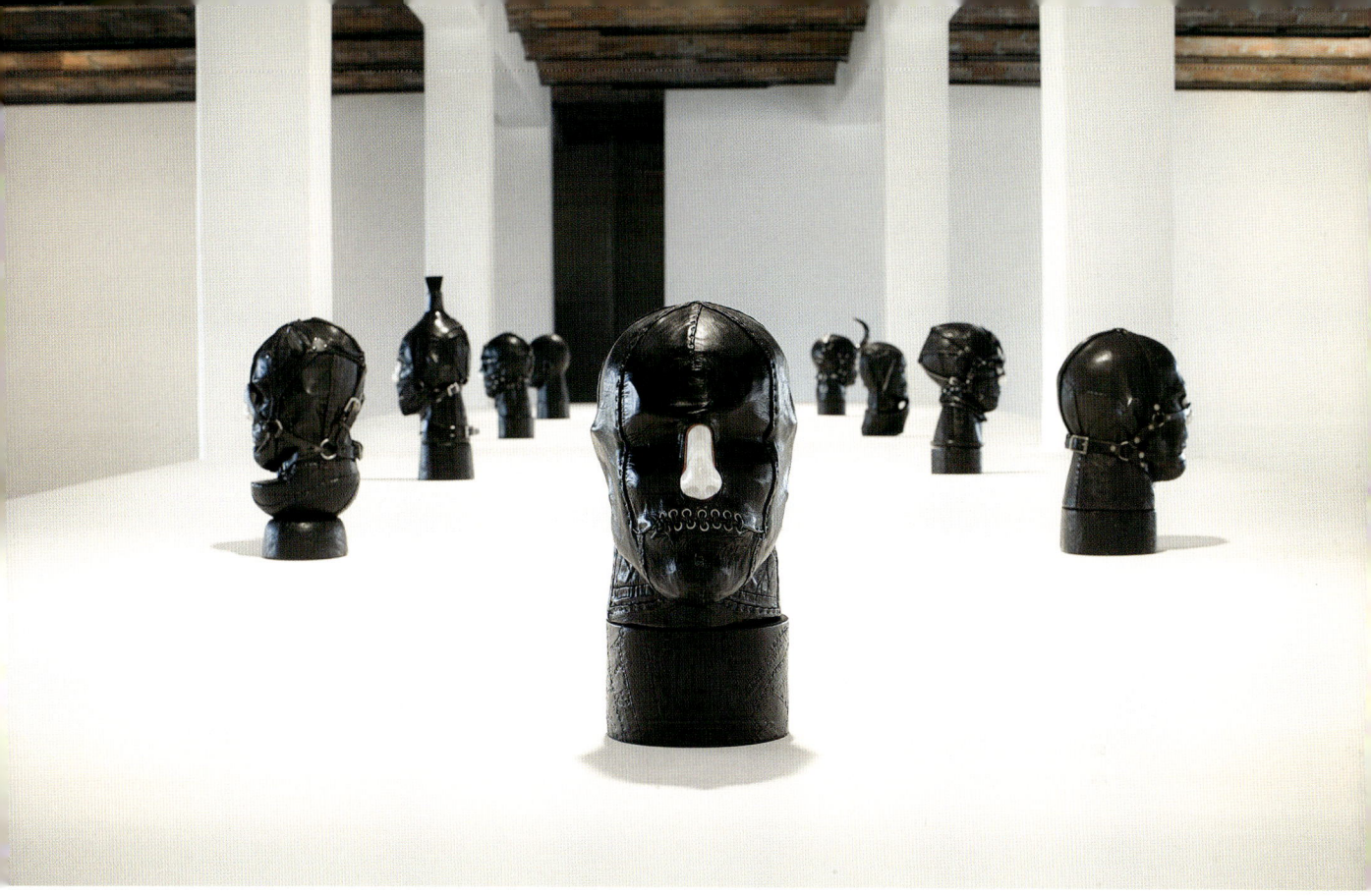

108 Installation view of *Nancy Grossman: Heads* at Museum of Modern Art, New York, PS1, 2011. Foreground: *No Name*, 1968.

the figure – and the most dangerous part of the sculpture. The most sexy part…is between your ears. It's not below your waist."[148] Or, more directly, she declared, "The head was representing the whole body *with all its possibilities*. The head will stand in for the body."[149]

From her abstract reliefs made up of just parts to her hidden heads, Grossman has pursued the possibilities of bodilessness in her work. Her sculptures demand that one think differently about what the body contains and what it can be. As she would often say, "The head is where the power is."[150]

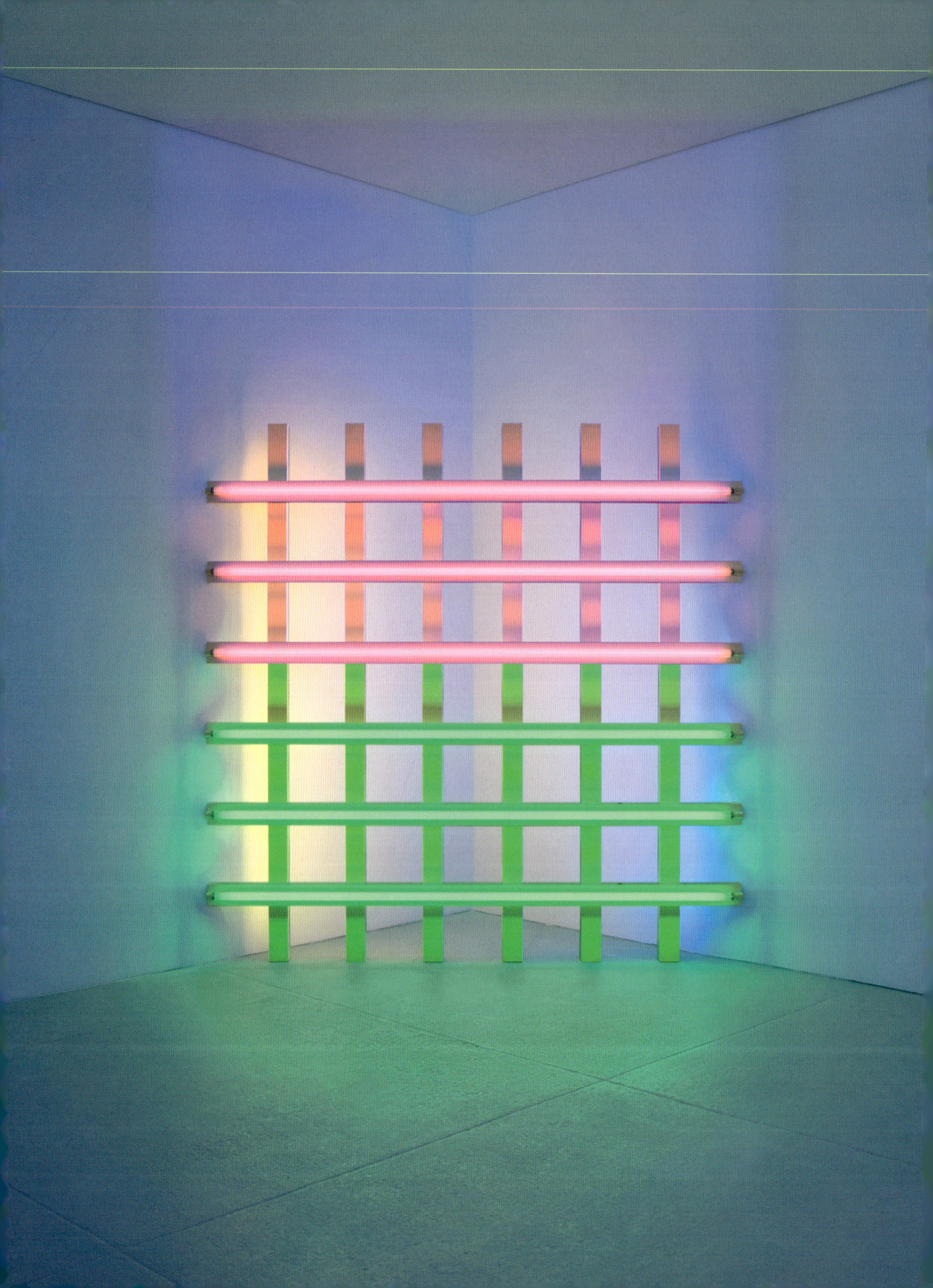

4
DAN FLAVIN'S DEDICATIONS

"Flavin's dedications embarrass me," John Perreault wrote in 1971. "I am consistently annoyed at Flavin's bad habit of dedicating pieces. The motivations behind these gestures are, I am sure, proper, but the effect is sentimental....Flavin is tough-minded in his art and tough-minded in his writings. Why can't he be as tough-minded about his titles as he is about everything else?"[1] Perreault's was a common reaction to Dan Flavin's titles, in which dedications to persons are attached to the artist's combinations of standard units – that is, the fluorescent tubes that, in 1963, he made his signature material. The dedications are often obscure and autobiographical, and they chaff against his literalist art and its supposed refusal of reference. Flavin himself discouraged interest in the titles despite his commitment to them. They were, he said, "mostly extraneous but personal."[2] Consequently, the dedications and their performative effects have rarely been explored in depth in the scholarly literature on Flavin.[3] Nevertheless, Flavin built up a large corpus of titles, consistently dedicating his otherwise untitled works to his friends and interlocutors. They became just as recognizable a part of Flavin's practice as did fluorescent tubes, and he held fast to his naming.[4] After all, the titles are effective. They identify and particularize individual works and allow viewers, critics, and collectors to differentiate one from another of his combinations of industrial light tubes.

The titles also remind viewers how Flavin's work differs from other so-called Minimalists. Although he is often grouped with other artists who pursued literalism, Flavin never sat easily among his peers. Like them,

OPPOSITE 109 Dan Flavin, *untitled (for you, Leo, in long respect and affection) 1*, 1977. Blue, yellow, pink and green fluorescents, 244 × 244 cm (96 × 96 in.).

he came to reject medium categories for his work, though he initially characterized this work in relation to sculpture.[5] Attached to these "image-objects" that flirted with illusionism in the form of colored light, the dedications reinforced a suspicion that too great a sentimentality lurked behind the hard shell of Minimalism. Indeed, Flavin's works produce an instability in the writing about Minimalism and the 1960s. Even though Flavin famously declared about his work, "It is what it is and it ain't nothin' else," the allusive and affectionate titles nevertheless inflect the objects to which they were attached.[6] Perreault's embarrassment was sparked by the fact that, despite the artist's purported hard-nosed literalism, Flavin's dedications forced him to see the mere fluorescent tubes in relation to persons.

Flavin's dedications span his career, but they were particularly important for him in the beginnings of his work with fluorescent light. Indeed, the dedication is one of the few parts of his practice that Flavin kept after his watershed year of 1963 when he developed his signature style. In the years just before and after his fluorescent turn, Flavin used dedications more forcefully and tactically to signal art-theoretical positions as well as his commitments, affections, and identifications. He chose major artists to provide his work with a lineage, such as Constantin Brancusi, Henri Matisse, and Vladimir Tatlin. He offered a work to William of Ockham as a means of alerting viewers to his priorities within the philosophical field of his peers' literalism. Flavin's wife and family appeared in the early dedications, and those artist friends with whom he felt an affinity – such as Donald Judd and Sol LeWitt – also received this gift (fig. 110). In and among these names through which Flavin staked out his position, there are four works with unlikely dedications to men Flavin knew or suspected were homosexual. These are no minor works. They are perhaps the crucial transitional works flanking Flavin's fluorescent turn: his two largest pre-fluorescent *icons* from 1962 and his first two single-tube fluorescents from 1963. As I shall discuss, through his dedications and descriptions of these works, Flavin signaled homosexuality as a metaphor for his exploration of literalism and anti-illusionism. Just as he was attempting to make the ready-made fluorescent tubes into a system of sameness-made-particular, he deployed the homosexual as the figuration of problematic visibility, recognition, and appearance. The homosexual, as Flavin understood him, was characterized by the compulsion to dissemble and to make their difference look the same, and it was through this character that Flavin struggled with questions of visible difference and categorical sameness. By tracking the issues of visible difference and Flavin's figuration of it through homosexual-

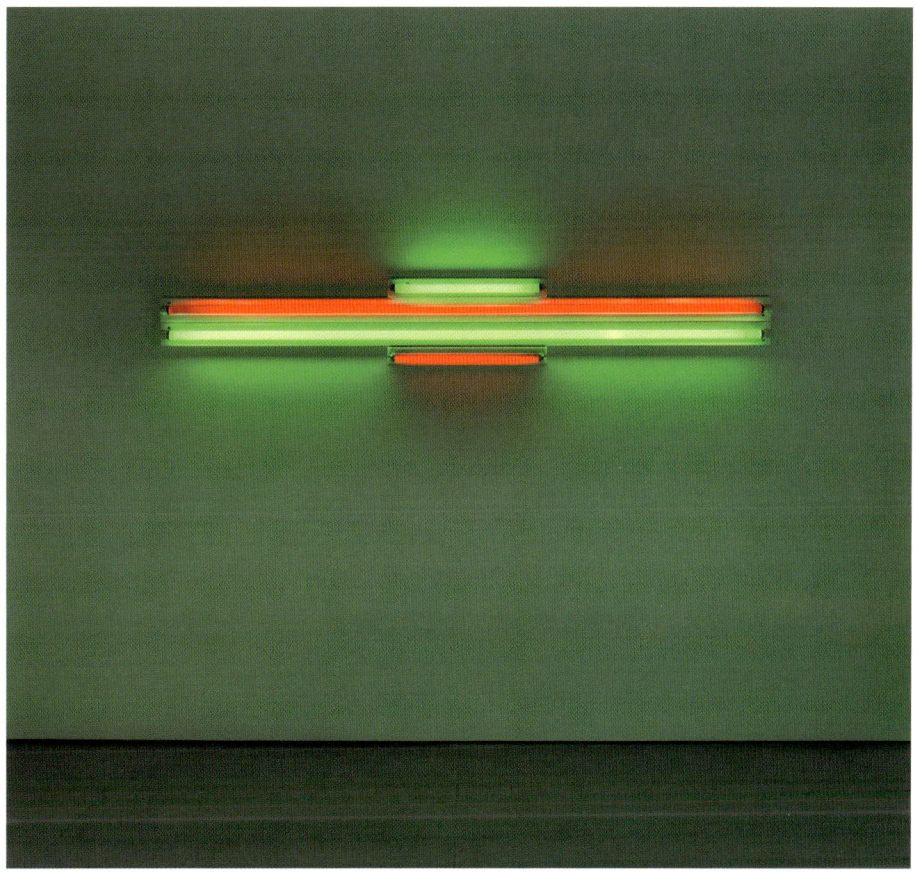

110 Dan Flavin, *red and green alternatives (to Sonja)*, 1964. Red and green fluorescent light, 244 cm w. (96 in.).

ity, I recast his works in light of the accounts of personhood they come inadvertently to demand. From a focused discussion of the works flanking the fluorescent turn, I will examine how they set the terms for Flavin's mature work, with its greater engagement with literalist illusions, interchangeable units, and sameness made particular. Across these changes in his practice, Flavin retained and expanded his pattern of naming, and I shall demonstrate that these titles are not superfluous but a key indicator of his artistic priorities. In turn, these names that he kept attaching to his systematically interchangeable works produce – in excess of Flavin's intentions – a logic of transformational personhood and mutable gender that, like his lights, places value on sameness and interchangeability made particular through naming. Such an account is nascent in his early work and his dedications to homosexual men – who, he knew, might not look different from anyone else.

"IT IS WHAT IT IS": REVELATION, LITERALISM, AND FLAVIN'S FIGURATIONS OF THE HOMOSEXUAL

Flavin led up to his fluorescent turn with a series of transitional works he referred to as "icons" (fig. 111).[7] These works retreated from the found object aesthetic of Flavin's earlier work, replacing it with, as he said, "a hierarchical relationship of an electric light over, under, against and with a square-faced structure full of paint light."[8] The icons all share a flat, uninflected rectilinear plane as their main feature, each one varying in color, placement, and type of electric lights around it. Sidney Tillim called them "reliefless reliefs ringed with light," and Donald Judd reminded readers that "they are things themselves; they are awkward; they are put together bluntly; the materials are considered bluntly – the paint is flat and the lights come that way…they don't involve illusionistic space."[9] The *icons* offered an initial manifestation of Flavin's interest in repeatable, typical form (the monochrome wall box) varied through color and light. He recalled: "I had to start from that blank, almost featureless, square face which could become my standard yet variable icon."[10] They all bear dedications to friends, artists, and cultural figures, though these titles are more cryptic than the familiar ones Flavin later adopted. Consequently, the *icons*' dedications have rarely been analysed in detail. Instead, the works have been seen primarily as merely presaging Flavin's other light works and their literalism. As James Meyer has noted, "Even though they were dedicated to various individuals, the *icons* were legible as abstract art."[11]

By far the most widely discussed of the icons is *icon V*, called *Coran's Broadway Flesh* (1962; fig. 112). This work was important to Flavin, too. He showed it repeatedly in New York, putting it in a group exhibition at Green Gallery in 1963 and in back-to-back exhibitions at Kaymar Gallery in Spring 1964.[12] It was the most often commented on of his *icons* at the time and was illustrated in all the major magazines, including *Arts Magazine* in 1964 and *Art in America* and *Artforum* in 1965.[13] *Coran's Broadway Flesh* is roughly 3½ foot square – a pink square block ringed with commercially available lights in porcelain sockets. Whereas the other *icons* have one, two, or at most four bulbs, *Coran's Broadway Flesh* has 28, echoing the traditional stage lights and theatrical spectacle of Broadway. The bulbs chosen – candelabra or "flame-tipped" lights – were not, however, the kind used for

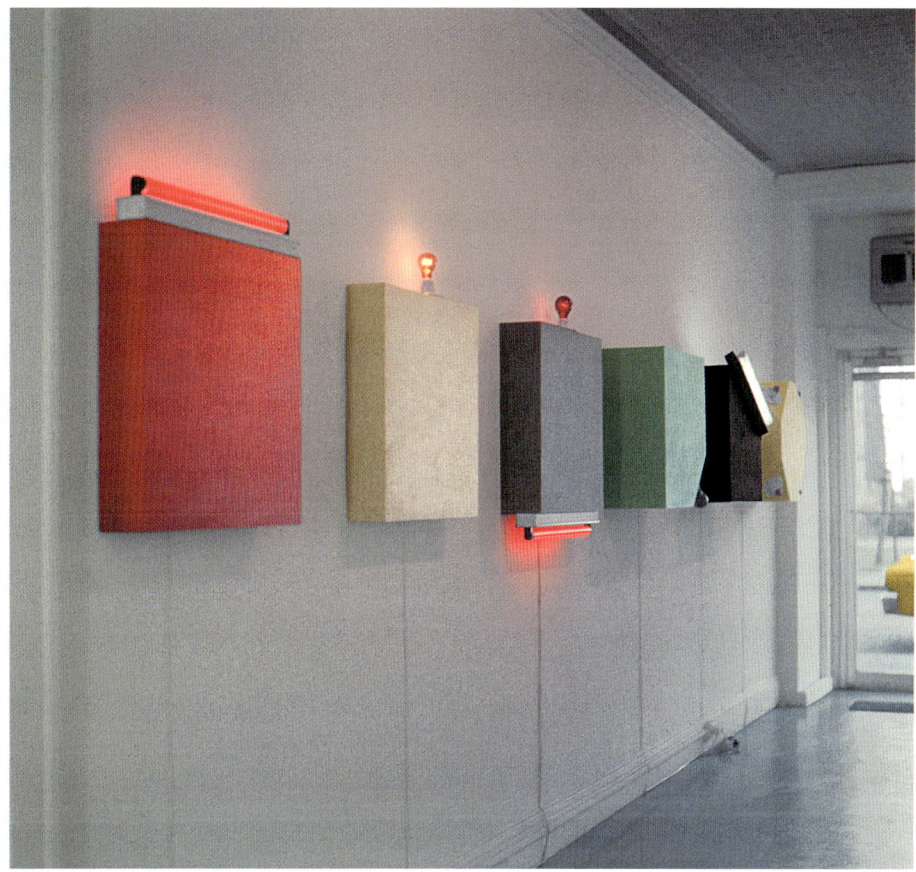

111 Installation view of *Dan Flavin: some light*, Kaymar Gallery, New York, 5–29 March 1964. From left to right: *icons I, II, III, VI, VII*, and *VIII*.

stage lights or indeed for Flavin's other icons, which had rounded bulbs or tubes.[14] This was the only *icon* to be aflame in this way.[15] Lucy Lippard said that with its "sides lined with small pointed bulbs with sparkling filaments; the whole glitters like a jewel case."[16]

For this lighted square, Flavin was deliberate in his choice of the color. He wrote on its verso that it was "flesh tint", and he made sure to repeat this in his statements on the work, starting with a snarky letter to the editor of *ARTnews* written in 1963 in response to what he considered to be a misdescription of his work by Jill Johnston.[17] The phrase "flesh tint" was also part of the caption accompanying *icon V* in Barbara Rose's important article "ABC Art" of 1965.[18] With such comments and with the "flesh" in the title itself, Flavin reminded us that the work was to be understood in

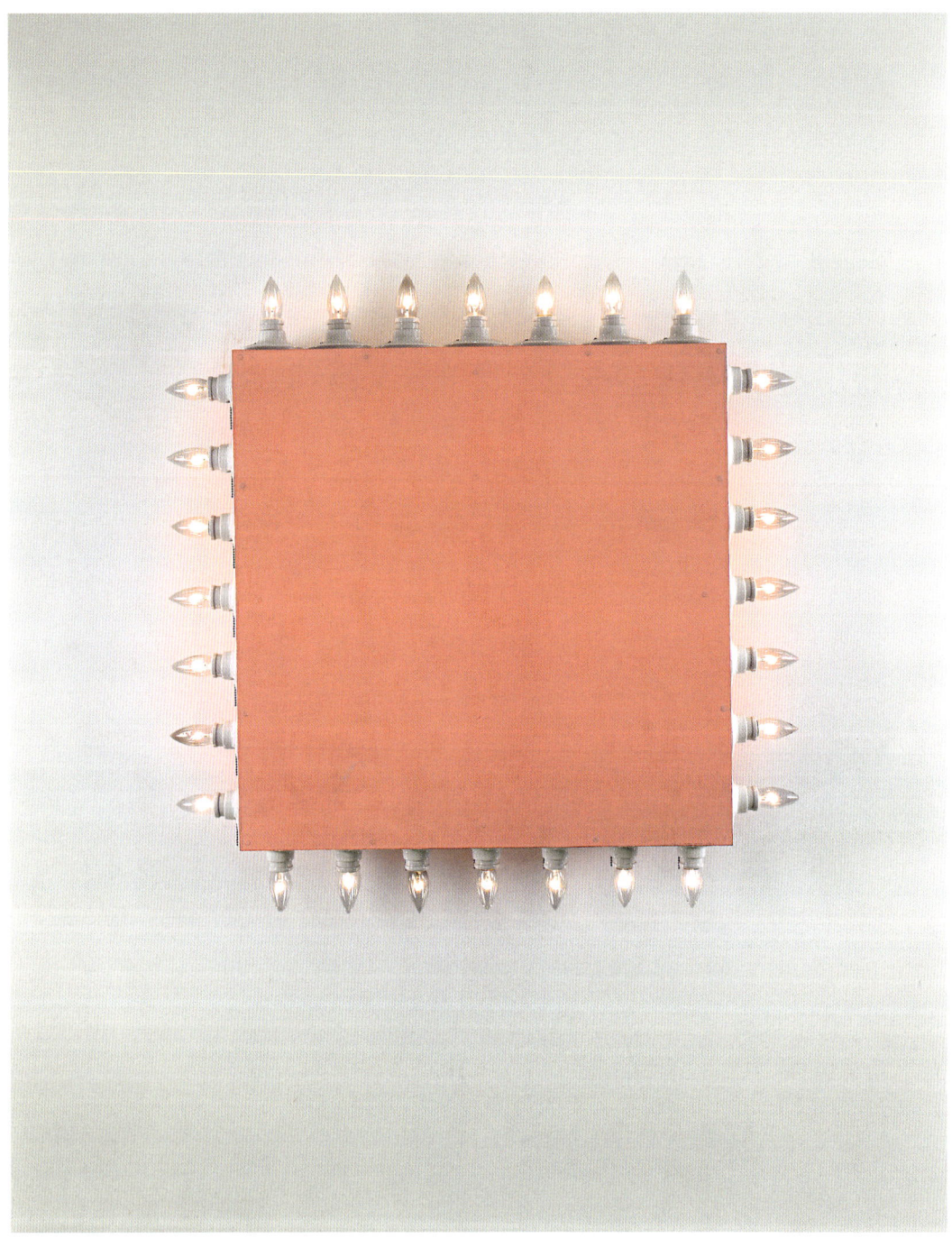

112 Dan Flavin, *icon V (Coran's Broadway Flesh)*, 1962. Oil on cold gesso on Masonite, porcelain receptacles, pull chains, and clear incandescent "candle" bulbs, 105.9 × 105.9 × 25.1 cm (41⅝ × 41⅝ × 9⅞ in.).

relation to the body and carnality. The "Broadway flesh" is exposed, and its ring of stagelike lights implied gratuitous entertainment, erotic display, and theatrical artifice.

Flavin's insistence that the work was "flesh tint" clearly relied on the dominant presumption of whiteness in which the color "flesh" excluded all other skin colors. Even this designation was at issue in 1962, however. Binney & Smith Company, the makers of the famous Crayola-brand crayons, changed the name of one of its colors from "flesh" to "peach" in the same year that Flavin used Winsor & Newton's "flesh tint" oil paint to make *Coran's Broadway Flesh*.[19] (Even after the watershed change of Crayolas' name, referring to this and related colors as "flesh tint," remained in popular circulation for many years.) In this context, Flavin's assignment of "flesh tint" to this work might be less reflex and more specific to its content than it first seems, especially since he dedicated another icon in the series to an African-American Blues musician (see below and fig. 118) and had earlier made works that expressed an advocacy for Africans' resistance to political oppression.[20] Flavin's name for the color of *icon V* not only identifies the bodies of entertainers on display (as I shall discuss). It also points to its dedicatee, Stanley Coran, an English neighbor of Flavin and his wife in East New York. From his initial sketches onward, Flavin developed this work with Coran in mind (fig. 113). He said that he had intended this icon to "stand for" Coran, offering this description of *icon V* to a would-be collector just two months after it was finished (in December 1962):

> *Coran's Broadway Flesh* is my fifth electric light icon. It is an emblem much like Jasper Johns' *Tennyson*. It stands for a young English homosexual who loved New York City. What I have made for him is a square block loaded with flesh tint, mechanized by lamps and bounded by excurrent tips of clear glass glister. But beyond structure and phenomena, I have tried to infect my icon with a blank magic which is my art.[21]

This description became the standard explanation for *icon V*. Flavin would republish versions of it often, including in the catalogue to his major retrospective in Ottawa in 1969 and in the anthology of his writings in 1973.[22]

While this description was frequently quoted by Flavin and by his subsequent historians, the work's dedicatory invocation of homosexuality has largely been passed by with only summary notice – with a few notable exceptions including commentary by Caroline Jones and Alex Potts.[23] One reason for this recurring omission, no doubt, was Flavin's famously irritable personality, which seemed to offer little accord and even less sympathy with the topic of sexuality. Yet, sexuality – particularly homosexuality – is repeat-

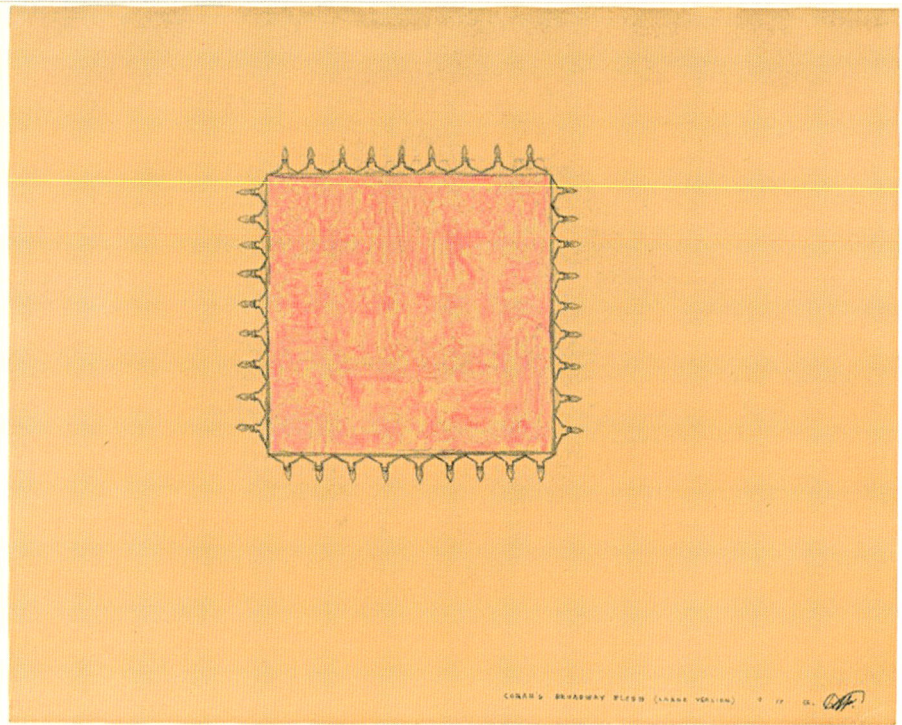

113   Dan Flavin, *final study for Coran's Broadway Flesh* (small version), 1962. Pastel and pencil on paper, 27.9 × 35.2 cm (11 × 13⅞ in.).

edly mentioned by Flavin in the 1960s, but it is most often in the form of the prejudicial and derogatory slur. Calling something or someone homosexual was far from a casual or neutral nomination for Flavin.

Whereas other artists, such as Judd, could write volumes without mentioning homosexuality, Flavin recurrently invoked it in his vitriolic tirades in print against critics, curators, and other artists. Such prejudicial statements were extreme enough to be noted by Flavin's contemporaries. For instance, in 1969, Joe Masheck wrote a letter to the editor of *Studio International* criticizing Flavin for, among other things, his "butcher-than-thou huffs at homosexuals."[24]

One such huff involved Flavin deriding the so-called "anti-form" artists in the *Nine at Leo Castelli* warehouse show by likening their scatter works to the "most preciously effete and affected obviously arty, delicate art decor…[that] appeared to possess the excessively careful compositioning (but sometimes seemingly random-like, of course) of dilettanted dada homosexuals."[25] Or, in 1967, he dismissed MoMA's long-term installation of a piece by the pioneering light artist Thomas Wilfred by saying that it was merely "a rendezvous for boys and girls and boys and boys and so forth. It did not entertain me."[26] Perhaps the most bizarre of such slurs was when, in a snide comment about the critic Barbara Rose (to whom, of course, he had dedicated works and from whom he had benefited), Flavin undercut her credibility through a comparison to "Rudi Gernreich's homosexually transparent undies."[27] Gernreich was a socially engaged fashion designer, co-founder of the pioneering gay and lesbian assimilationist group the Mattachine Society, and one-time partner of the gay activist Harry Hay. He is remembered primarily as the designer of the topless "monokini" bathing suit, which Flavin was citing in his swipe at Barbara Rose. First published in *Women's Wear Daily* in 1962, the monokini was scandalous for its frank exposure of women's breasts. While "transparent" and revealing, such a fashion statement was not "homosexually transparent," as Flavin claimed, unless one was at least partially cognizant of Gernreich's reputation. Flavin's mention of homosexuality was superfluous to his dig at Rose, but it insured that the naming of Gernreich would not be uncoupled from the designer's homosexuality.

It is important to remember that such comments on homosexuality by Flavin were not made only in private. Rather, they were published in Flavin's articles for such magazines as *Artforum* and were anthologized along with the rest of his writings in 1973.[28]

When Flavin mentioned homosexuality in his writings, it was most often accompanied by a concern with its visibility. That is, it was about things or people appearing as homosexual or being recognized as such. A key example can be found in his autobiography, first written in 1964 and published in *Artforum* in 1965. Flavin offered this text as an alternative to the modes of art criticism and theory that were being deployed by his peers such as Judd and Morris. As Stefan Neuner has argued, Flavin asserted his intellectual independence by making his own autobiography stand as the justification for his art, telling it in a narrative modeled on James Joyce.[29] Flavin's inclusions are significant in this oft-cited text, and an anecdote from his time in the army in Korea stands out for its detail and content. Both Flavin and his twin had been stationed in Korea as weather observers, and it was in the soldiers' libraries that Flavin began to read about art. "I drew again for the first time since I was a child," he recalled.[30] His interest in practicing art grew rapidly. In the autobiography, Flavin told the story of how, in 1955, he set up a life-drawing class with a fellow soldier, whom he identified as an unwashed painter who had studied at Oberlin College. He recalled of his joint venture with this hippie G.I., "Within a few weeks, our program was suspended by an Army major whose *obscene eyes* saw the probability of a possibility of an unmanly, immoral disclosure in the posing of fellow G.I.'s stripped to the waist while leaning on brooms."[31] Finding himself on the receiving end of the epistemology of the closet, Flavin decried the "obscene eyes" that saw homosexuality where none was intended. His accuser, the major, was himself suspect in Flavin's eyes for having seen artistic pursuits as erotic ones, hence being labeled "obscene." That Flavin himself could be charged in this way was a particularly difficult recognition for him. This is attested by the edits he made to this passage when it was reprinted in 1969 (which has, since, become the standard version of his autobiography). Flavin removed the phrase "obscene eyes" and replaced it with a tortured backpedalling on the issue of the recognition of homosexuality. In the revised version, the Army major "*presumed* the *probability* of a *possibility* of an unmanly, immoral disclosure."[32]

Clearly, the issue that Flavin identified was of being taken for a homosexual. That Flavin considered this an insult is incontrovertible, as when he wrote despairingly of his time as a visiting artist at the University of North Carolina at Greensboro:

> One comes, a guest, to present himself as an artist to prospective artists and discovers that while so doing he is compelled to confront threats of violence, to be ridiculed publically (to be called a homosexual), to witness the personal intimidation of his graduate students – all of this by one's supposed colleagues in education.[33]

For Flavin it was the insult of the mistaken identification that was further evidence of his colleagues' provinciality and ignorance – rather than any misguided attitude about homosexuality itself. Both Flavin and the bullies who taunted him did not question that to be called a homosexual was a declaration of ridicule.

Flavin's anxious triangulation of the "presumption of a probability of a possibility" of identifying the insult of homosexuality hinged on its visual detection. This concern was carried forward to Flavin's subsequent derogatory comments on gay men, which focus on how they can be spotted or made visible. The "dilettanted dada homosexuals" of the Castelli Warehouse show reveal themselves in their "preciously effete and affected obviously arty, delicate art decor."[34] When it came to *icon V*, Stanley Coran is not just the dedicatee of the flesh-tinted, garishly lit work. Beyond attaching Coran's name to it, Flavin also called him out as homosexual in his repeated published descriptions of the piece. To name someone a homosexual in print in 1965 – as Flavin did with Coran in the Fall issue of *Art in America* – was no everyday act. Such a declaration was not just "ridicule" but could result in legal action, arrest, or castigation. Flavin sacrificed Coran to public scrutiny in order to make certain that the figure of homosexuality that underwrote *icon V* could not be disguised.

At issue in Flavin's autobiography, in his later uses of homosexual as a slur, and in the wider pre-Stonewall culture of the closet that Flavin exposed was the anxious awareness that difference can look like sameness. The politics of visibility that characterize the history of homosexuality in the twentieth century are fueled by the survival tactics of closeting and dissembling – of having difference camouflage itself as the "ordinary" in order to be unidentifiable. Such was Flavin's attitude toward homosexuality: it was something to be called out, spotted, and named. As Nicholas de Villiers has recently argued, such an emphasis on making visible is based in a fear of homosexuality's capacity for duplicity: "it is worth asking, first of all, if homophobia is always a will-to-ignorance and silence, and whether it might in fact include a fear of *not* knowing everything about a person's sexuality. It is important to consider the ways that homophobia often insists on knowing rather than refusing to know about the sexuality of gay people."[35] An insistence on knowing and on naming frames Flavin's comments on homosexuality. Since the difference of the homosexual could remain covert and unrecognized, he became, for Flavin, a figure of problematic visibility. The illusionism of the dissembling homosexual was something to be purged and drawn to the surface – to be made visible.

In 1962, Flavin was struggling to articulate his literalism and to produce work that completely eschewed pictorial illusion and representation. Other artists arrived at literalism from divergent priorities, as was the case with Judd, who emphasized not visibility but credibility.[36] For Flavin, it was the terrain of the visible and the invisible on which he cultivated his literalism, privileging visual self-sameness and clarity. As he later summarized, his aim was to make art where "Everything is clearly, openly, plainly delivered."[37]

He framed such inquiries, especially in his early statements, through questions of what was made visible by light or as light. Indeed, Flavin claimed that a source for his interest in light was the prologue of Ralph Ellison's novel *Invisible Man*.[38] The protagonist of Ellison's book considers himself socially invisible because others refuse to see him as a person owing to his race, and the fantastic mise-en-scène of the prologue uses excessive light (1369 burning light bulbs in an underground chamber) as the metaphor for the narrator's overcoming of this invisibility in the act of telling his own story.[39] Flavin put forth this passage as an analogue for his own practice – including it, for instance, among the quotations he provided to the curator Jan van der Marck for the catalogue of his first solo museum show at the Museum of Contemporary Art Chicago in 1967.[40]

Like Ellison, Flavin saw light as a vehicle for visibility and clarity, and he framed his pursuit of unduplicitous literalism through it. For Flavin, however, the social invisibility of Ellison's African-American protagonist remained too metaphorical and he turned to a different figure for whom social invisibility was a daily and more literal practice – the homosexual. Flavin's anxious concerns with the recognition of homosexuals and others' mistaken identifications of them were both rooted in the compulsory dissemblance and camouflaging practiced by gay men as a survival strategy in an oppressive and discriminatory society. He was not being sympathetic to this struggle so much as using the figure of the passing homosexual as a way to embody a practice of illusionism to be brought to light. With his loaded dedication and his subsequent description, Flavin reinforced the agenda of openness and "revelation" he intended for *icon V*. Flavin made sure of this, and his much quoted description of the piece and its reference to homosexuality served as a recurring performative outing of the work's dedicatee. Flavin's naming of Coran was just as much an assertion of "it is what it is" as his unillusionistic monochrome wall box. Difference was revealed as the "truth" of Coran.

In relation to Flavin's figuration of his neighbor's homosexuality, Coran was also the recipient of one of Flavin's series of expiatory *East New York Shrines* made from flowerpots with electric lights in that same year of 1962. Another was named after the gay painter Edward Plunkett.[41] As James Meyer has noted about the version produced for Plunkett and bearing his name, "[Plunkett's] sins were evidently so dire that he could only be forgiven through the intervention of the Virgin herself," referring to a Virgin Mary light bulb that Flavin substituted in this version of the *Shrines*.[42] Evidence that Coran and Plunkett were linked in Flavin's mind can be found in Flavin's record book entry of 24 February 1963: "Sonja and I made the first version of this shrine for Stanley Coran in the early summer of 1962. We rebuilt it in January for Ed Plunkett who is an artist who makes collage, etc., and teaches in the adult education system for N.Y.U."[43] However, Flavin chose to omit Coran (but not the better known Plunkett) from a list of collectors of his work (dated 25 October 1964). He prefaced that list by saying "In the main, friends and artists have collected my work."[44] Besides Plunkett, the names included Robert Rosenblum, Judd, Frank Stella, Richard Bellamy, and Robert and Ethel Scull. Whether Coran

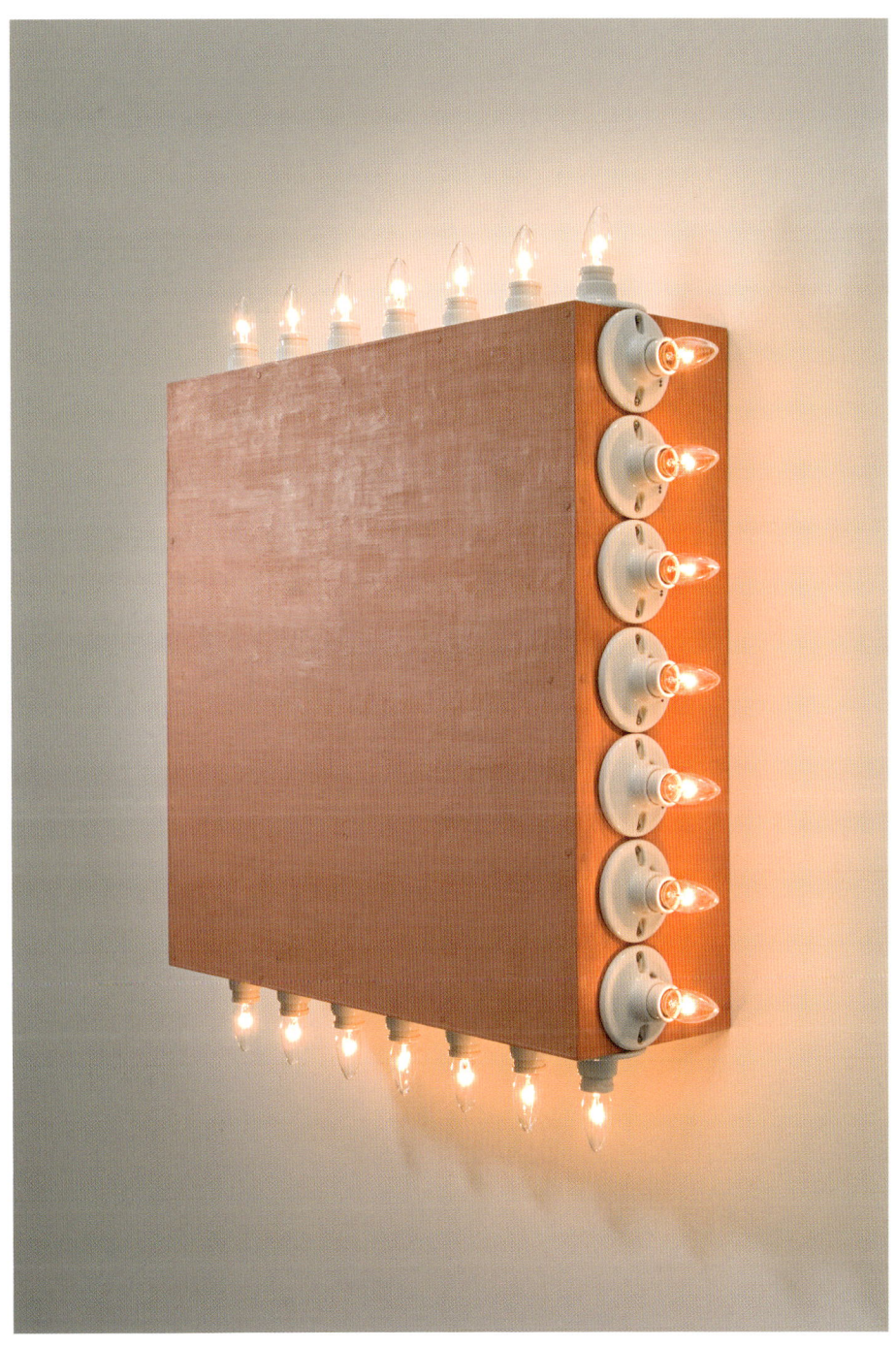

114 Dan Flavin, *icon V (Coran's Broadway Flesh)*, 1962. Oil on cold gesso on Masonite, porcelain receptacles, pull chains, and clear incandescent "candle" bulbs, 105.9 × 105.9 × 25.1 cm (41⅝ × 41⅝ × 9⅞ in.).

was not enough of an artist or not enough of a friend to make that list, it is significant that the slim recounting of sixteen names of collectors did not include his one-time neighbor who received a *Shrine* and from whom his most important *icon* took its name. This is further evidence that Coran had a special, if uneasy, place for Flavin.

That Coran himself stood for the stereotypical visible homosexual in Flavin's eyes is reinforced when one considers the "Broadway" that Flavin also made a central part of *icon V*'s subtitle. The medium of theater has often been singled out (and censored as immoral) for its encouragement of duplicity and the ability to lie – in short, for its illusionism.[45] Nowhere is this clearer than in musical theater, in which scenic or narrative verisimilitude is sacrificed in favor of regular (and spectacular) intervals of song and dance. "Broadway" served as the primary metaphor for American entertainment and theatrical spectacle, emblematized by the musical theater that reigned in the late 1950s and early 1960s. Flavin's conjunction of Broadway and "flesh" surely recalled one of the most famous musicals of all time: *Gypsy: A Musical Fable* by Arthur Laurents, Stephen Sondheim, and Jule Styne, which had just closed on Broadway the year before, in 1961 (fig. 115). Starring the iconic Ethel Merman as the overbearing stage mother Mama Rose, *Gypsy* told the story of the famous striptease artist Gypsy Rose Lee. As Coran could have told him, it was a musical all about the exposure of flesh and the devolution of theatrical artistic ambitions into erotic display.

The genre of the Broadway musical was redefined by *Gypsy* with its self-reflexivity, its frankness, and its psychological complexity. Laurents's book and Sondheim's lyrics interwove meta-commentary on Broadway with nods to drag performance and to thinly veiled crossgender identifications to tell a tale of self-determination, renaming, and outsiderness. This combination has led to *Gypsy* becoming not just one of the most important of musicals in the postwar era but a key text of identification in pre-Stonewall homosexual subculture.[46] In his masterful analysis of *Gypsy*, D. A. Miller has decisively argued that it offered itself as the "fable" of the genre of the Broadway musical, which was "a *gay* genre, the only one that mass culture has ever produced."[47] Flavin's coupling of "Broadway" and "flesh" economically alluded to the culture of the Broadway musical and to its most self-conscious and epochal manifestation in *Gypsy*'s tale of vaudeville turned striptease. This found reinforcement in the named dedication of his *icon V* to the "homosexual who loved New York City." For, the only place where one could live openly (but still beleaguered) as a homosexual was the city, and the opportunities for community and congress afforded by the

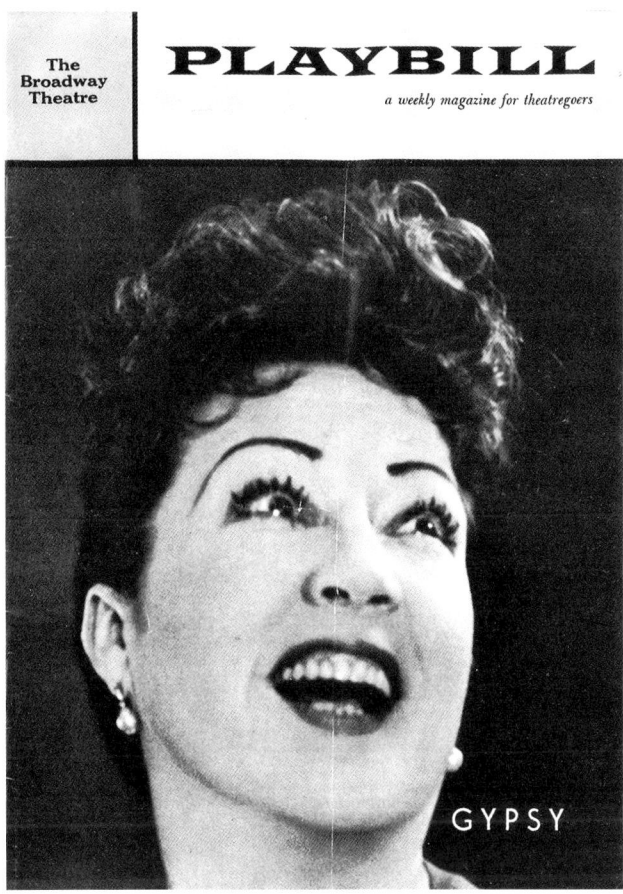

115 Cover of *Playbill* 3, no. 27 (6 July 1959) for *Gypsy*, starring Ethel Merman at the Broadway Theatre, New York, 1959–61.

urban density were liberating for gay men – a theme reinforced in *Gypsy*'s story. This was signaled by Flavin with the over-affected and flamboyant verb "loved" he used to characterize Coran's feelings toward the city.

Invoked in both the title and descriptions of the work, Coran's homosexuality-made-visible functioned for Flavin as a symbol of illusion's defeat and of the uncompromising self-evidence of the "it is what it is" literalist stance he was cultivating. Just as the blank face of the *icons* permitted no sense of illusionistic space or depth, Flavin's choice of flamboyant dedicatee emblematized his nascent literalism in which everything must be seen for what it is. Flavin understood *icon V* as his most important icon. In a letter of February 1963, he singled out *Coran's Broadway Flesh* as being the "summary for more than a year's research," reminding his readers of the work's pivotal significance. He continued, "*I know that this is hard to cope with*, but, if I have succeeded, *Coran's Broadway Flesh* will hold you

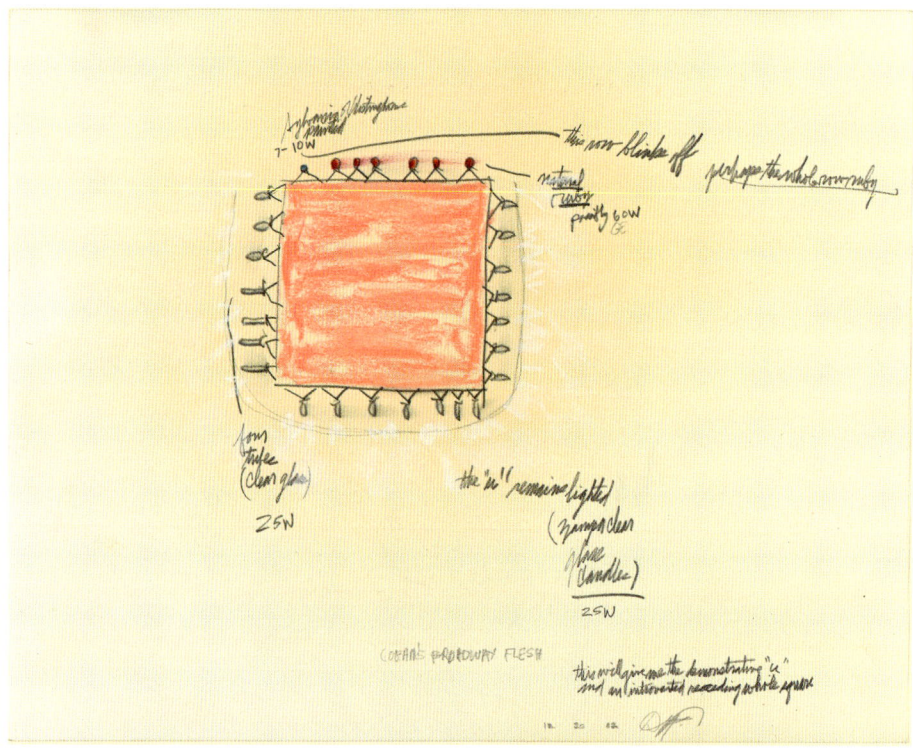

116 Dan Flavin, study for *icon V (Coran's Broadway Flesh)*, 20 December 1962. Graphite, pencil, and pastel on paper, 27.9 × 35.2 cm (11 × 13⅞ in.).

simply, succinctly."[48] *Icon V* owed its succinctness to the coupling of non-illusionist visual form with the reference to the excessive recognizability of the personality of the Broadway-loving homosexual.

The difficult achievement of *Coran's Broadway Flesh* for Flavin can also be seen in the changes he considered for it just after it was finished. Flavin dated the work to 19 December 1962 with an inscription on its verso. The next day, 20 December 1962, he drew up a plan for a more ambitious version with more varied lights (fig. 116). This proposal had different bulbs along the uppermost edge with the top row all in a "ruby" color that were to blink on and off in unison (in contrast to the white lights of the other three sides, which remain constant). As he noted on the drawing, "this will give me the demonstrative 'u' and an introverted receding whole square."[49] In effect, this means that the work would have had two states that it presented to the viewer. The "demonstrative 'u'" in white lights would be altered when the full set of lights were turned on, revealing the "introverted" whole. Although heavily coded, this is a performance of dissemblance itself. The flashy ruby-colored lights, once revealed, would have made viewers see that U-shape differently. The full square would "recede" from view but would never fully disappear since it is a constituent part of the whole. One can see in this alternative plan for *Coran's Broadway Flesh* how much visibility and revelation were at play. In this work already named after Coran and Broadway, Flavin sought ways to give abstract form to the issues of recognition, dissemblance, and revelation – traits associated with the condition of homosexuality. In the end, he did not pursue this plan of increased duplicity, choosing instead to retain the constant, glaring ring of white lights that left no room for illusionism in the work. The realized work, as he implied, was "demonstrative."

All of this emphasis on the recognizability and visibility of Coran's homosexuality is even more striking when one considers the closely linked work that preceded it in Flavin's conception. Flavin began *Coran's Broadway Flesh* just as he was executing a large white *icon* with a single fluorescent tube in the summer of 1962.[50] *Icon IV*, also known as "the pure land," was a memorial work to Flavin's twin brother, David John Flavin, who died of polio that year (fig. 117). The health of Flavin's twin had deteriorated over the months when the artist was working on *icon IV*. On 18 August 1962, some two months before David John Flavin's death on 8 October, Flavin had already referred to the large drawing for *the pure land* as "the prayer drawing."[51] Subsequently, Flavin was explicit in his attachment of this work to his brother's death and to funereal themes.[52] The phrase "the pure land," Michael Govan has argued, refers to the Buddhist "beautiful, blissful way-station on the spiritual journey to complete enlightenment" presided over by Amitabha, the Buddha of Infinite Light.[53]

Flavin bound *the pure land* and *Broadway Flesh* together as an opposing pair. They are the two largest of the series, and both were the first and only *icons* shown when they were exhibited together in January 1963 at the Green Gallery.[54] All of the austerity of the funereal icon was followed by the garish pink work dedicated to "young English homosexual who loved New York." *Icon IV* is solemn while *icon V* is sordid. The succession of these two loaded works cannot be seen as neutral. There is a thoroughgoing inversion of terms from the one work to the next, with *the pure land* being unsullied and spiritual and *Broadway Flesh* being burlesque and carnal. Both emphasize how the invisible can be made visible. Memorials mark the presence of absence, and *icon IV* was rigorously unillusionistic and unpictorial while nevertheless standing for Flavin's no-longer present twin as well as visualizing "the pure land" as an abstraction. The subsequent *icon*

V was blunter in its conjunction of form and reference. With his description of the flesh-tint work and his outing of Stanley Coran, Flavin insured that the homosexuality and carnality that was its content could not be misrecognized. This, too, has an inversion in the *icon* dedicated to his twin brother, which has been – in title and form – purified.

Purified of what, though? In a 2009 interview, Flavin's friend Dan Graham offered a possible explanation for Flavin's negative attitude toward homosexuality: "Dan Flavin was definitely a little [homophobic], because I think his twin brother was gay."[55] This information from Graham helps to bring into focus the inverted relationship between *the pure land* and *Broadway Flesh*. If both of these *icons* negotiated the manifestation of homosexuality, then Flavin made sure that the first was cleansed of its worldly content just as he insured that the second was flamboyant in its form (and that he reminded his readers of the homosexuality of its dedicatee). One could say that this distinction hinged on the *stereotype* of the homosexual, with Flavin displacing all of his concern for his twin's possible difference to the visible flamboyance and telltale exuberance of the foreign, Broadway-loving homosexual. That is, the "purity" of the memorial icon to his twin seemed even more lofty and inviolable next to the company it kept.[56] This pairing, in other words, could be characterized as a rebuttal of suspicion of his twin. The evidence for this denial centered on visibility, with *Coran's Broadway Flesh* being obvious in its difference (but not so obvious that Flavin did not need to call out the homosexual content of this work in print.)

Again, Flavin considered *Coran's Broadway Flesh* a major achievement, and the succession of these two works represents a key episode in his articulation of his "it is what it is" literalism and his aim to make work where "Everything is clearly, openly, plainly delivered." *The pure land* was loaded with overemotional and deeply personal content for Flavin, signaled yet veiled in the symbolic use of white. The meaning of the work was about that which could not be seen again – the whiteness as erasure and as leaving behind of the worldly. By contrast, *icon V* paraded its ostentatiousness and carnality, performing exposure with the self-evident falsity of garish theatrical display and "flesh tint." From one work to the next, Flavin turned away from connotations of the unseen, the vanished, and the cleansed in *the pure land* to explore, in its successor, compulsory visibility.[57] This he allegorized in the figure of the out(ed) and easily identifiable homosexual.

OPPOSITE 117   Dan Flavin, *icon IV (the pure land) (to David John Flavin [1933–1962])*, 1962, reconstructed 1969. Formica and daylight fluorescent light, 122.9 × 113 × 28.6 cm (48$\frac{3}{8}$ × 44$\frac{1}{2}$ × 11$\frac{1}{8}$ in.).

APPROXIMATING INVISIBILITY: HOMOSEXUAL MENTORS AND OTHER ACCEPTABLE ILLUSIONS AT THE FLUORESCENT TURN

Both *icons IV* and *V* resulted from an intense period of artistic research for Flavin centered on his exploration of literalist visibility. Some months earlier in 1961, he had moved his studio to Brooklyn in search of plentiful, cheaper space and further isolation in order to create "more intelligent and personal work."[58] (Within a few years, he made a permanent move out of the city to Cold Springs, New York, furthering this trajectory.) This relocation had spurred the creation of the series of *icons* and his use of electric light, both of which marked significant departures from his earlier assemblage works. He began to pay more attention to the work of Jasper Johns, Frank Stella, and Barnett Newman, and he was befriended by Sol LeWitt and Donald Judd.

After completing *Coran's Broadway Flesh*, Flavin continued to execute a few more *icons*, each of which deployed the dedication as a manifestation of his negotiation of the invisibility of difference (fig. 118). *Icon VI (Ireland dying) (to Louis Sullivan)* dealt directly with questions of the invisibility of heritage, using the flat color of green as a sign for Irishness. He doubly titled the work after Ireland's plight and after the architect Louis Sullivan (whose father came from Ireland). Flavin was Irish Catholic himself (also on his father's side) and would have been familiar with the history of American prejudice against Irish immigrants. His title addressed how Sullivan's Irishness could be easily forgotten or erased when he was constituted as the "father" of American modern architecture. It is possible that Flavin was responding to discussions of Sullivan's Irish heritage that had been sparked by the biography of Sullivan published just two years before he started *icon VI*. Willard Connely's 1960 *Louis Sullivan As He Lived: The Shaping of American Architecture* opened its first chapter by relying on racialized stereotypes to describe how Sullivan's father's "looked" Irish.[59] Much like the problem of social invisibility that drew Flavin to Ellison's protagonist and to the figure of the dissembling homosexual, Flavin was interested in how Sullivan's Irish difference could be made invisible by history. The bright green *icon*, in effect, "outed" Sullivan as Irish. Flavin's next work, *icon VII (via crucis)*, returned to the spiritual and religious context of the works earlier in the series, referring to Christ's carrying of the cross through the streets of Jerusalem. To his persecutors and to the onlookers who mocked him, his divinity was invisible. Flavin's last work to be made in the series, *icon VIII (the dead nigger's icon)(to Blind Lemon Jefferson)*, also conjoined a

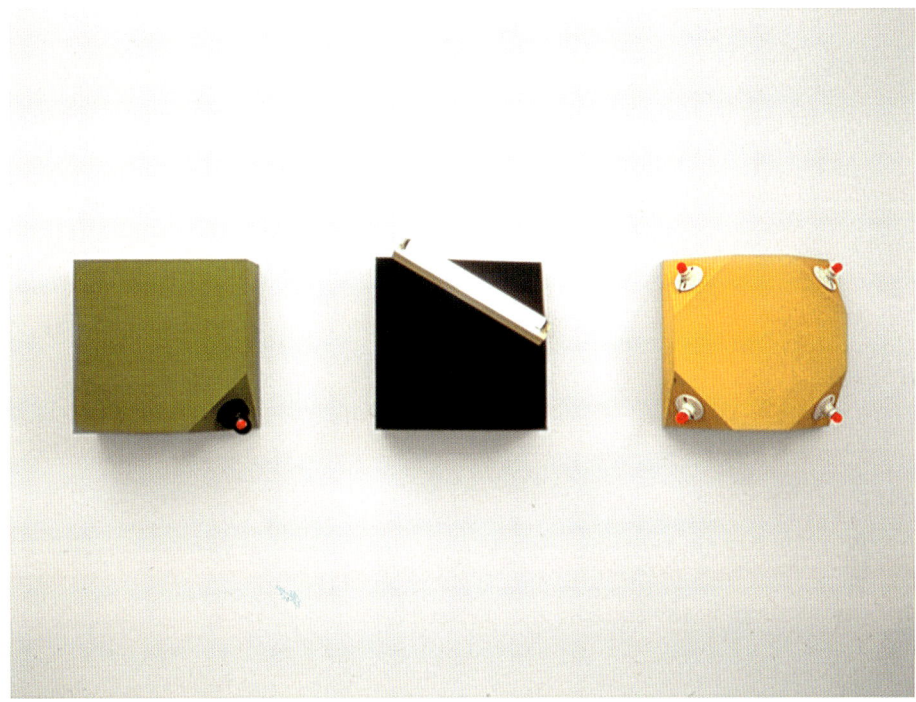

118 Dan Flavin, *icon VI (Ireland dying) (to Louis Sullivan)*, 1962–3, *icon VII (via crucis)*, 1962–4, *icon VIII (the dead nigger's icon) (to Blind Lemon Jefferson)*, 1962–3, installed at Dia Center for the Arts, 1997.

marked identity category with a dedication to an individual. His inflammatory language was probably intended to highlight the disjunction between widespread racial prejudice and the mainstream absorption of African-American musical traditions. Flavin dedicated the work to Blind Lemon Jefferson, a popular blues singer in the 1920s whose songs influenced the development of rock and roll. From the perspective of the early 1960s, Jefferson's style would have been more easily compared to recent mainstream music and its appropriation of African-American traditions of blues. Jefferson's difference, like Sullivan's, could be "overlooked" – especially in the audio format of the record (hence Flavin's title's aggressive reminder of racial prejudice). It is significant, too, that Jefferson was born blind, further tying into Flavin's concerns with visibility.

Flavin worked on these icons simultaneously, and there are sketches with plans for these and more. Only eight were executed during 1962 and the early months of 1963, and he did not exhibit *icons VI, VII,* or *VIII* (or *I, II,* or *III,* for that matter) until his 1964 exhibition at Kaymar Gallery (fig.

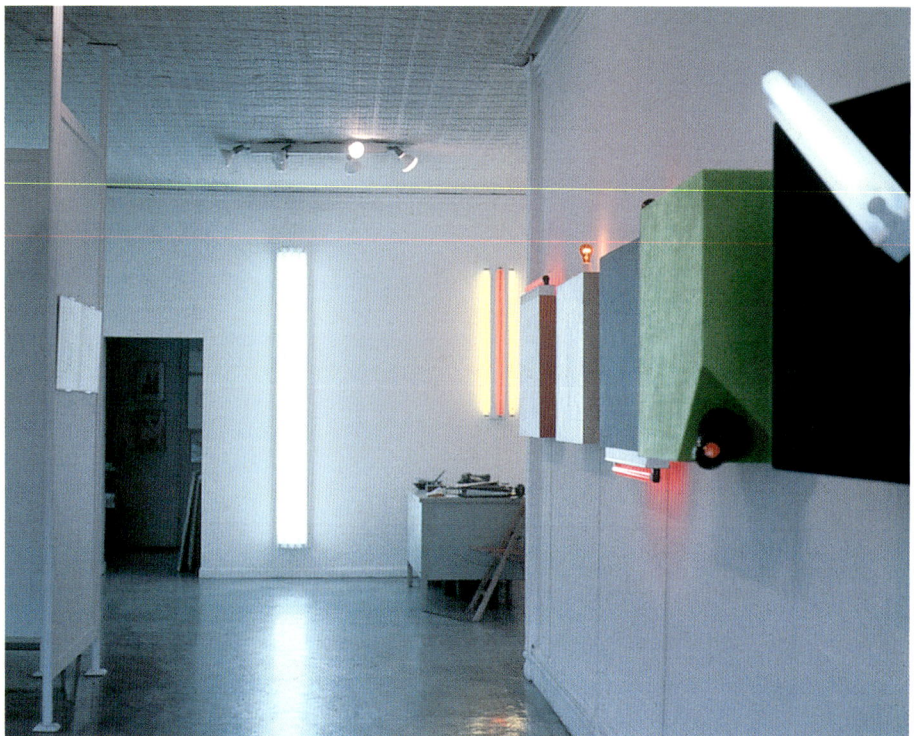

119   Installation view of *Dan Flavin: some light*, Kaymar Gallery, New York, 5–29 March 1964. On facing wall: *daylight and cool white (to Sol LeWitt)*, 1964 and *three fluorescent* tubes, 1963. Right wall, far to near: *icons I, II, III, VI, VII,* and *VIII*.

119). First, Flavin put forth *the pure land* and *Coran's Broadway Flesh* as his exemplary works and summary statements, showing only these two *icons* together in the January 1963 Green Gallery group exhibition and repeatedly providing images of *Coran* for publications, as noted earlier.

During this time, Flavin redoubled his commitment to developing the matter-of-factness he sought for his objects.[60] By February, he had made plans for the last *icon*, and he was executing the later ones almost out of a sense of duty to his initial designs for them. As Flavin later recounted, he then had a breakthrough on 25 May 1963:

> In the spring of 1963, I felt sufficiently founded in my new work to discontinue it. I took up a recent diagram and declared "the diagonal of personal ecstasy" ("the diagonal of May 25, 1963"), a common eight foot strip of fluorescent light in any commercially available color. At first, I chose gold.

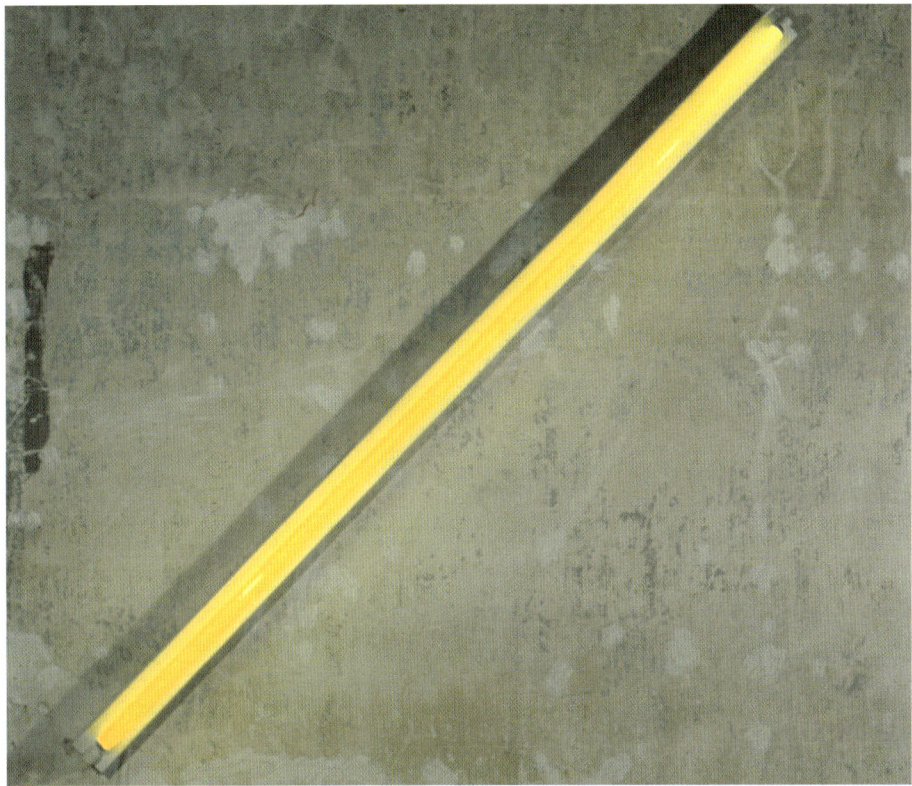

120 Photograph of 1963–4 of Flavin's studio wall with *the diagonal of May 25, 1963 (to Constantin Brancusi)*, 1963.

> The radiant tube and the shadow cast by its pan seemed ironic enough to hold on alone. There was no need to compose this lamp in place; it implanted itself directly, dynamically, dramatically in my workroom wall – a buoyant and relentless gaseous image which, through brilliance, betrayed its physical presence into approximate invisibility.[61]

From this revelatory moment on, Flavin began to redirect his practice to the fluorescent tube exclusively (fig. 120). Restricting himself to the colors and lengths commercially available, he made it his sole material.

The epiphanic account of this moment is a staple of the Flavin literature.[62] As Flavin intended, it succinctly narrated the central theme of his work: the ability to see something for what it was. He had used fluorescent tubes before, but now he let them stand alone. The story of this revelation served to underscore his literalist agenda without recourse to the kind of art-critical theorizing he disdained. In truth, the epiphany was not instantaneous but extended. After deciding to put the unaided tube on the wall in May, Flavin waited months before he could afford and have shipped and wired the proper equipment, not realizing the sculpture until some five months later, in October 1963.[63]

In the story of the epiphany from his 1964 autobiography, Flavin characterized the important leap into using unaided fluorescent light through that same criterion of visibility. However, the literal immediacy of the unaltered light tube was "direct" even as it seemed to disappear behind the light it emitted. Flavin later came to argue that the tube was still recognizable, but in these early years he experienced a conundrum. However literal, readymade, and unaided, the fluorescent tube seemed to him inadvertently to produce illusionism – a "gaseous image" that overtook his studio wall, the material object itself, and its surroundings. In the pursuit of his "it is what it is" visibility, he had arrived at an artistic material that "betrayed" itself into "approximate invisibility." The paradox of the literalist illusion, as I shall discuss, characterized Flavin's subsequent career, and perhaps the main theme of the Flavin literature centers on the parsing of the optical illusions created by his obdurately mundane industrial materials.[64]

Flavin began to pursue the permutations that a standardized system of commercially available fluorescent light tubes made available, and he quickly produced a sizable body of work as well as unexecuted plans for more. With the earliest fluorescents from 1963, Flavin redirected his attitude toward literalism and clarity. As I shall discuss, he came to see value in "approximate invisibility." Indeed, his career starting in the mid-1960s involved increasingly grand installations that altered one's ability to perceive architectural spaces.[65] He worked through the paradox of the literalist illusion in the earliest of his fluorescents – in particular, in two of the works shown in his major one-person exhibition at the Green Gallery in 1964 (fig. 121). Like *icons IV* and *V*, they form a subset within the group of works in which they were created. In his autobiography, Flavin linked the epiphanic *diagonal of May 25, 1963 (to Robert Rosenblum)* to the only other single-tube work he showed at that important manifesto exhibition, *pink out of a corner (to Jasper Johns)*. He grouped these two works in his explanation of his realization that "the actual space of a room could be broken down and played with by planting illusions of real light."[66] As with the polemical *Coran's Broadway Flesh* and its predecessor, Flavin mediated this back-and-forth over visibility (and his realization of the possibility of "real" illusions) through dedicating these transitional works to men known to him as homosexual. These men, Jasper Johns and Robert Rosenblum, were not to be chided and outed like Stanley Coran, however. Flavin admired them

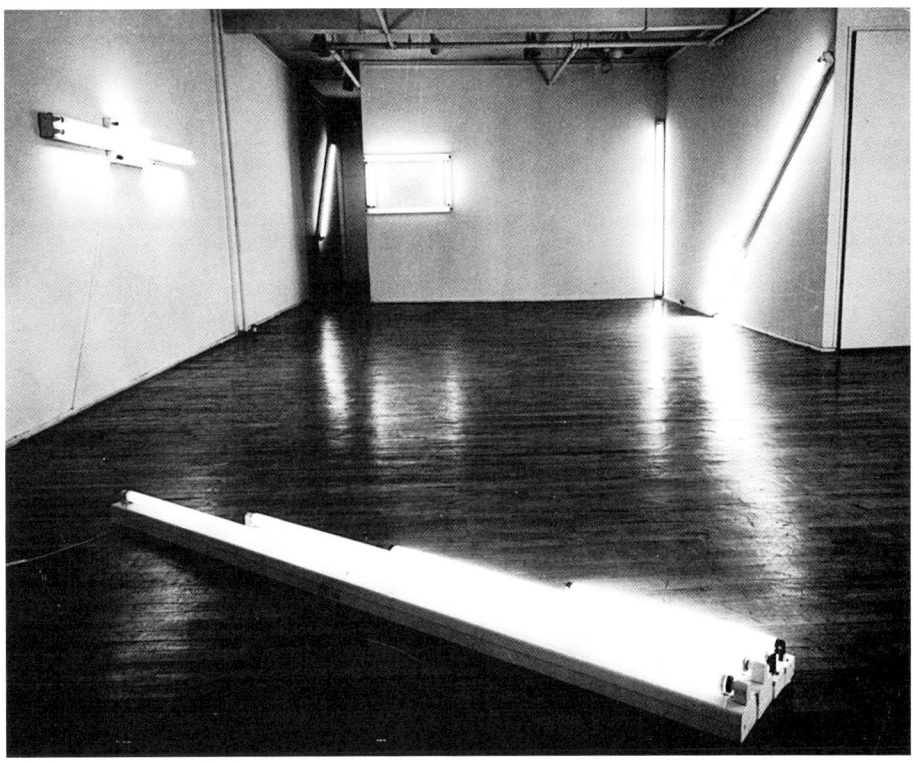

121 Installation view of *Dan Flavin: fluorescent light*, Green Gallery, New York, 18 November–12 December 1964. From left to right: *red and green alternatives (to Sonja)*, 1964, *the diagonal of May 25, 1963 (to Robert Rosenblum)*, *a primary picture*, 1964, *pink out of a corner (to Jasper Johns)*, 1963, *alternate diagonals of March 2, 1964 (to Don Judd)*, 1964; on floor: *gold, pink and red, red*, 1964.

both (and needed their professional support). These citations indicate that Flavin's shift of attitude toward illusionism was shadowed by a renegotiation of the question of homosexuality as a metaphor for visual difference.

Johns, in particular, was on Flavin's mind when he was working on the *icons*, and a clue to the fraught status of homosexuality as a metaphor in Flavin's thinking can be found again in the description he gave of *Coran's Broadway Flesh*. In the original description written in 1963 and published in 1965 (quoted earlier), Flavin named Johns's *Tennyson* as a source for the work in the sentence directly before the one that definitively outed Coran.[67] A few years later, when this statement was republished in 1969 in his retrospective exhibition catalogue, Flavin edited out this comparison, removing *only* the reference to Johns.[68] The words "much like Jasper Johns' *Tennyson*" were replaced with an ellipsis in the 1969 republication. That is, Flavin made

234 ABSTRACT BODIES

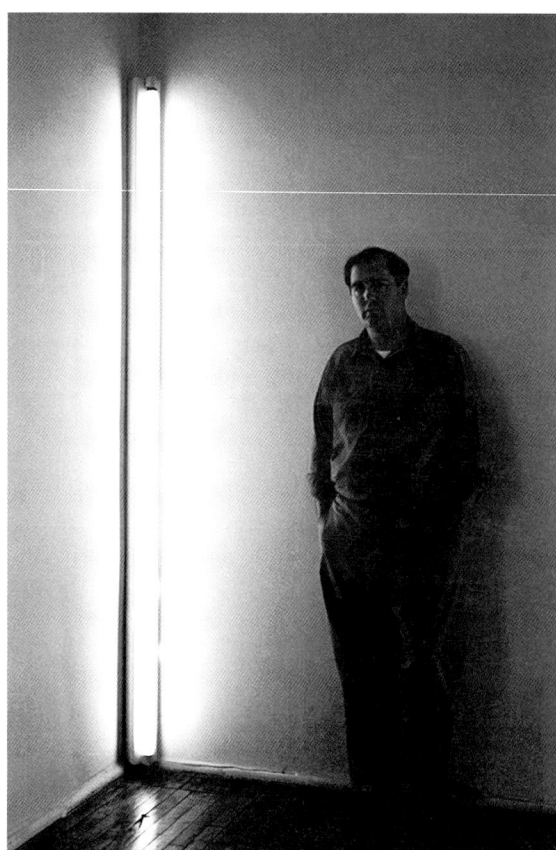

122 Dan Flavin with *pink out of a corner (to Jasper Johns)*, 1963, at Green Gallery, New York, 1964.

sure to excise only the few words that coupled the hyper-visible, flesh-tint *Coran* with Johns. (It might not have helped that Robert Smithson had, as well, connected these two works in print in 1966.[69]) As Govan has remarked, this targeted excision was "Perhaps proof of the uneasy anxiety of Jasper Johns's influence."[70] It was also, I would claim, a retrospective erasure of the connection that Flavin had made at this earlier moment between Johns and visible homosexuality, personified by Stanley Coran.

Flavin was friends with and respected Johns. After Johns visited the Green Gallery exhibition in 1964, Flavin wrote in his journal, "He's on my wavelength. That's clear."[71] Nevertheless, it is significant that, of his friend's paintings, Flavin cited the one he did. A grey painting by Johns from some six years earlier, *Tennyson* (1958; fig. 123) declares its willful obscuring of interiority. Its central component is a painted canvas that has been folded over itself, hiding its contents. Johns, of course, had made dissemblance and code central tactics in his own practice. He was, as Jill Johnston infamously

123 Jasper Johns, *Tennyson*, 1958. Encaustic and canvas collage on canvas, 186.7 × 97.2 cm (73½ × 48¼ in.). Des Moines Art Center, purchased with funds from the Coffin Fine Arts Trust; Nathan Emory Coffin Collection, 1971.4.

argued, "a secret autobiographer."[72] Johns's work of the late 1950s and early 1960s, in particular, incorporated occluded autobiographical content with regard to his same-sex relationship with Robert Rauschenberg.[73] Johns's *Tennyson* was, as James Rondeau has argued, a response to Rauschenberg's 1955 *Bed*.[74] Also, Johns's painting, through its own dedication, harked back to one of Tennyson's widely read works, the 1849 "In Memoriam A.H.H.," in which Tennyson lamented the loss of his friend Arthur Henry Hallam. The deep affection expressed in this work has led many to read this poem as being about the love of two men for each other (whether that be characterized in specific or broad terms).

In short, Flavin's citation of Johns's *Tennyson* was in accord with the themes of the visibility and recognizability of homosexuality that underwrote Flavin's *icons IV* and *V*. Only later in the decade would Flavin edit out and decouple Johns's *Tennyson* from his own *Broadway Flesh*, recognizing perhaps that the common thread of homosexuality among the earlier cita-

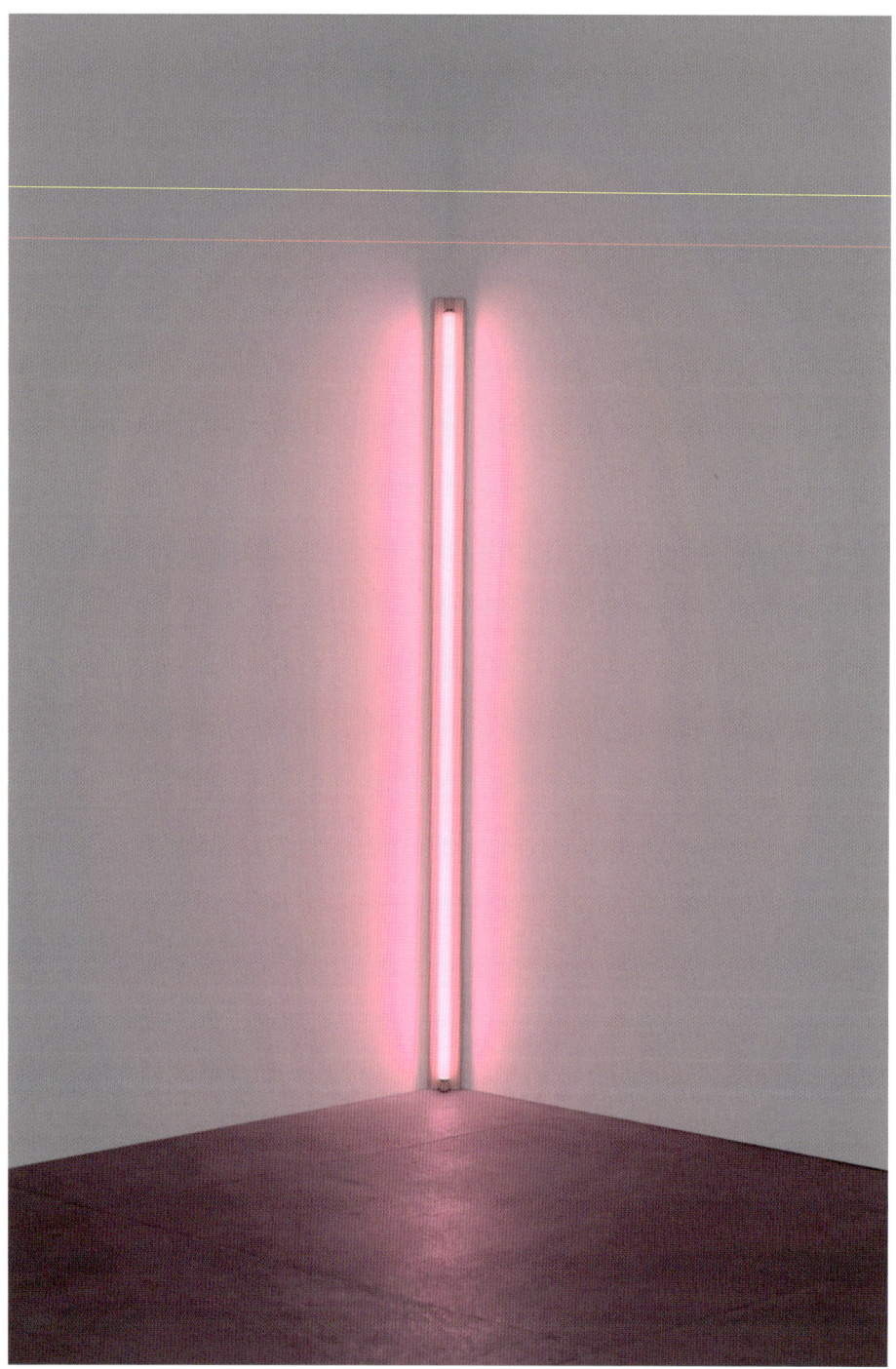

124 Dan Flavin, *pink out of a corner (to Jasper Johns)*, 1963. Pink fluorescent light, h. 244 cm (96 in.).

tions was too clear. Or, more to the point, the "it is what it is" visibility of homosexuality that Flavin attributed to Coran was in contrast to the respect he accorded Johns and his discretion. But early on, in 1963, Flavin likened his work to Johns's painting and to its own loaded dedication to Tennyson as a means of further signaling the homosexual content he made sure to name in his description of *Coran's Broadway Flesh*. As noted above, later that year Flavin himself named one of his most important early fluorescents after Johns – a single tube, in pink, placed in a corner (fig. 124).

Initially, this work was conceived in red, but Flavin shifted it to pink for his 1964 Green Gallery exhibition. That it was conceptually related to the *icons* and to *icon V* in particular is indicated by a unique transitional work, sometimes called *Construction with Red Fluorescent and Incandescent Bulbs* or, according to the date Flavin gave to the work, *one of May 27th 1963* (fig. 125) – two days after the date given to his epiphanic "diagonal of personal ecstasy."[75] Flavin conjoined the vertical red tube that was the original conception of what would become *pink out of a corner* with a row of rounded bulbs that line one side.[76] Flavin executed only two works with such a concentration of bulbs – this one and *Coran's Broadway Flesh*. This work was first shown in a Green Gallery group exhibition in October and November of 1964, just before the important solo exhibition in mid-November that introduced Flavin's use of unaided fluorescent tubes and fixtures. For that show, Flavin shifted the color of his conception of *...out of a corner* to pink and assigned the work to Jasper Johns. Indeed, one might speculate that the shift of *...out of a corner* to pink, like the citation of *Tennyson* from earlier that year, was a way of associating Johns with *Coran's Broadway Flesh* by approximating its pinkish "flesh tint" in fluorescence.[77] These morphological replications and adjustments establish a lineage from *Coran's Broadway Flesh* to the now-pink fluorescent work named after Johns, via the red hybrid fluorescent-incandescent *one of May 27th, 1963* that presaged Flavin's initial red conception of the corner piece.[78] (When *...out of a corner* was finally realized in red fluorescent, in 1970 [fig. 126], Flavin gave it a dedication to the art dealer Annina Nosei, then the wife of the influential John Weber.[79]) These closely linked works before and after Flavin's fluorescent turn further evidence his association of Johns with *Broadway Flesh* and its showcasing of homosexuality as metaphor – even though by the late 1960s he tried to redact this association.

The fluorescent *pink out of a corner* is highly significant for being the first work in which Flavin experimented with the ability of his fluorescent tubes to obscure and alter the perception of the room – to produce illusionary effects. As he enthusiastically wrote in 1964, it was possible to "plant an

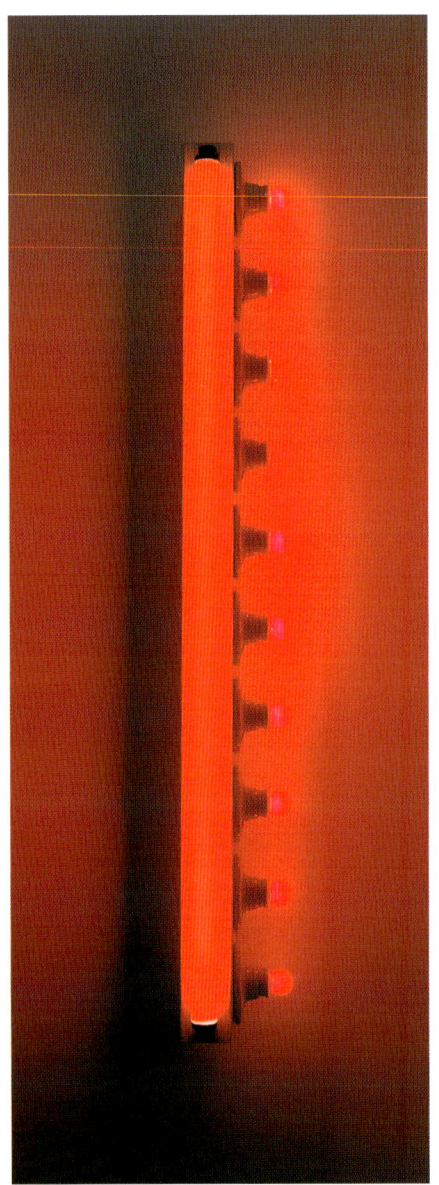 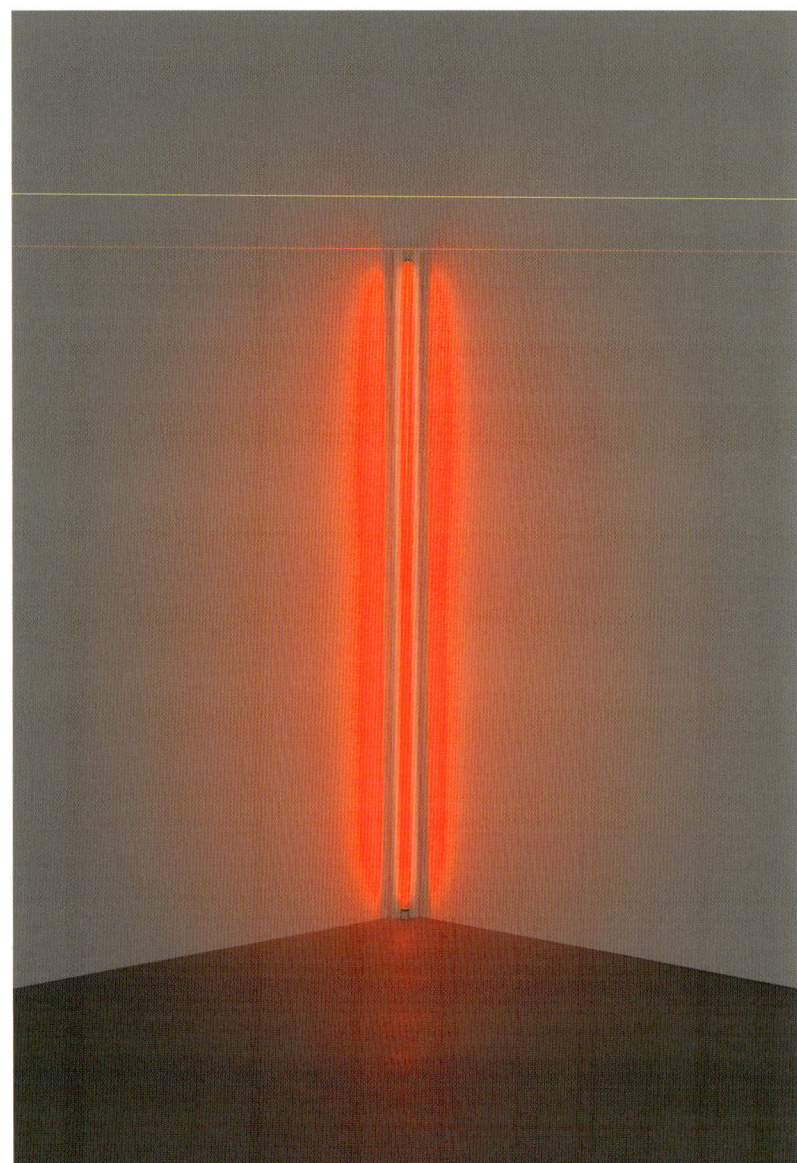

125　Dan Flavin, *one of May 27th, 1963*, 1963. Red fluorescent and incandescent light on acrylic and Masonite and pine, 20 × 122 × 16.5 cm (8 × 48 × 6½ in.). Art Institute of Chicago, promised gift of Donna and Howard Stone.

126　Dan Flavin, *red out of a corner (to Annina)*, 1963/70. Red fluorescent light, 255 cm (96 in.). On view at the Dan Flavin Art Institute, Bridgehampton, New York. Collection of Stephen Flavin.

illusion of real light (electric light) at crucial junctures in the room's composition. For instance, if you press an eight foot fluorescent lamp into the vertical climb of a corner, you can destroy that corner by glare and doubled shadow."[80] In other words, *pink out of a corner* was a work that, like Johns's *Tennyson*, hid just as much as it revealed. The issue of visibility was, again, mediated through a dedication to a gay man although, this time, Flavin chose not to label him as such, preferring Johns's dissemblance over Coran's flamboyance as the new allegory demanded by his turn to unaltered fluorescent tubes that themselves dissembled their readymade status into transformative and immersive light.[81] For the one work that produced an illusion more than any other among his early fluorescents, Flavin chose the artist whom, in print and in his works during these years, he connected directly with *Coran's Broadway Flesh*. Even though this time he respected the other artist, Flavin registered Johns's homosexuality through these citations and chose to tie it to the (now acceptable) emergence of illusionism and dissemblance that Flavin found his works making after his fluorescent turn. Among the loaded dedications of the Green Gallery exhibition that staked out Flavin's art-theoretical position, this one returned to Flavin's use of homosexuality as a metaphor for problematic visibility.[82]

This connection of the illusionism of the fluorescents with homosexuality in these years is also evident in the other work that Flavin discussed in the same paragraph in his 1964 autobiography, in which he talked about the single tubes "planting an illusion." He explicitly linked *pink out of a corner* to his very first fluorescent and the only other single-tube work he initially showed – the *diagonal of May 25, 1963* – a work that, as he put it, "can visually disintegrate" the wall (fig. 127).[83]

This was the epiphanic work he also called the "diagonal of personal ecstasy," and it signaled Flavin's breakthrough in using unaided fluorescent tubes as sufficient in and of themselves.[84] When he placed it on his studio wall in yellow fluorescent, Flavin wrote in his diary that it was a "searing emotional thrust."[85] The *diagonal*'s first year saw it change identity a number of times. When exhibited three months later at the Wadsworth Atheneum, its color was changed to daylight, and it was dedicated to Constantin Brancusi. It was then shown in March of that same year at Kaymar Gallery and later Green Gallery in cool white with a new dedication to the art historian Robert Rosenblum. As with the switch from red to pink for the corner work, the *diagonal*'s history was tied up with shifting dedications and changed appearances.[86]

Just after *Coran* was first exhibited and just before his epiphany that resulted in the *diagonal* in 1963, Flavin asked to audit Robert Rosenblum's

lectures at Columbia University, where Rosenblum was on a visiting professorship.[87] In gratitude, Flavin gave Rosenblum a small drawing of *the pure land* inscribed to him, further linking him to this four-part cadre of works.[88] Over the next year, they became friendly, and Rosenblum responded positively to the diagonal when he saw it in its initial form in gold in Flavin's studio in January 1964.[89] Flavin soon after wrote to the curator and collector Samuel Wagstaff, "Bob Rosenblum on seeing my fluorescent tubes said that I had 'destroyed painting' for him. He was euphoric. He switched the light on and off several times because he wanted to sense 'the difference.'"[90] Soon thereafter, Flavin switched the dedication to Rosenblum.

At this moment, Rosenblum was rising to prominence as an art historian, having published his *Cubism and Abstract Art* in 1960 and the influential article "The Abstract Sublime" the year after. Like Johns, Rosenblum too established a division between his professional practice and his personal life at that time. Rosenblum's then-homosexual identity was common knowledge among his friends and acquaintances. For instance, his friend the art historian Fred Licht wrote in a 1964 letter to him (jokingly or not), "Discussed your Cubism book with Peggy Guggenheim and she said 'I don't mind his being q★eer [sic]. But Jewish, ech!' But I don't mind and am looking forward to getting a 10% rake-off on all the gondoliers I'm going to introduce you to when you and Pierre [Martory] come to Venice."[91] One friend of Rosenblum's later recalled that he was "campy and funny and wonderful [but when he lectured] he was a different person. He spoke differently... And then he finished the lecture and he was back to being the normal Bobby. It was a really marked difference."[92] It is significant that Flavin again chose to dedicate the *diagonal*, his pivotal work, to another friend for whom the visibility of a non-normative sexuality was at issue.[93]

Like the work Flavin came to dedicate to Johns, the *diagonal*, he realized, also "plant[ed] an illusion" despite the literalist use of the single fluorescent light tube. As his words quoted earlier said, "through brilliance, [the *diagonal*] betrayed its physical presence into approximate invisibility." Flavin signaled this very "approximate invisibility" in 1964 by switching the dedications of his two "visually disintegrating" works to friends who transcended, for Flavin, the possibility of their being identified as homosexual. That is, in that loaded group of dedications for his first one-person exhibition, Flavin mediated the illusion that his new literalist practice generated by associating

OPPOSITE 127 Dan Flavin, *diagonal of May 25, 1963 (to Robert Rosenblum)*, 1963. Cool white fluorescent light, l. 244 cm (96 in.).

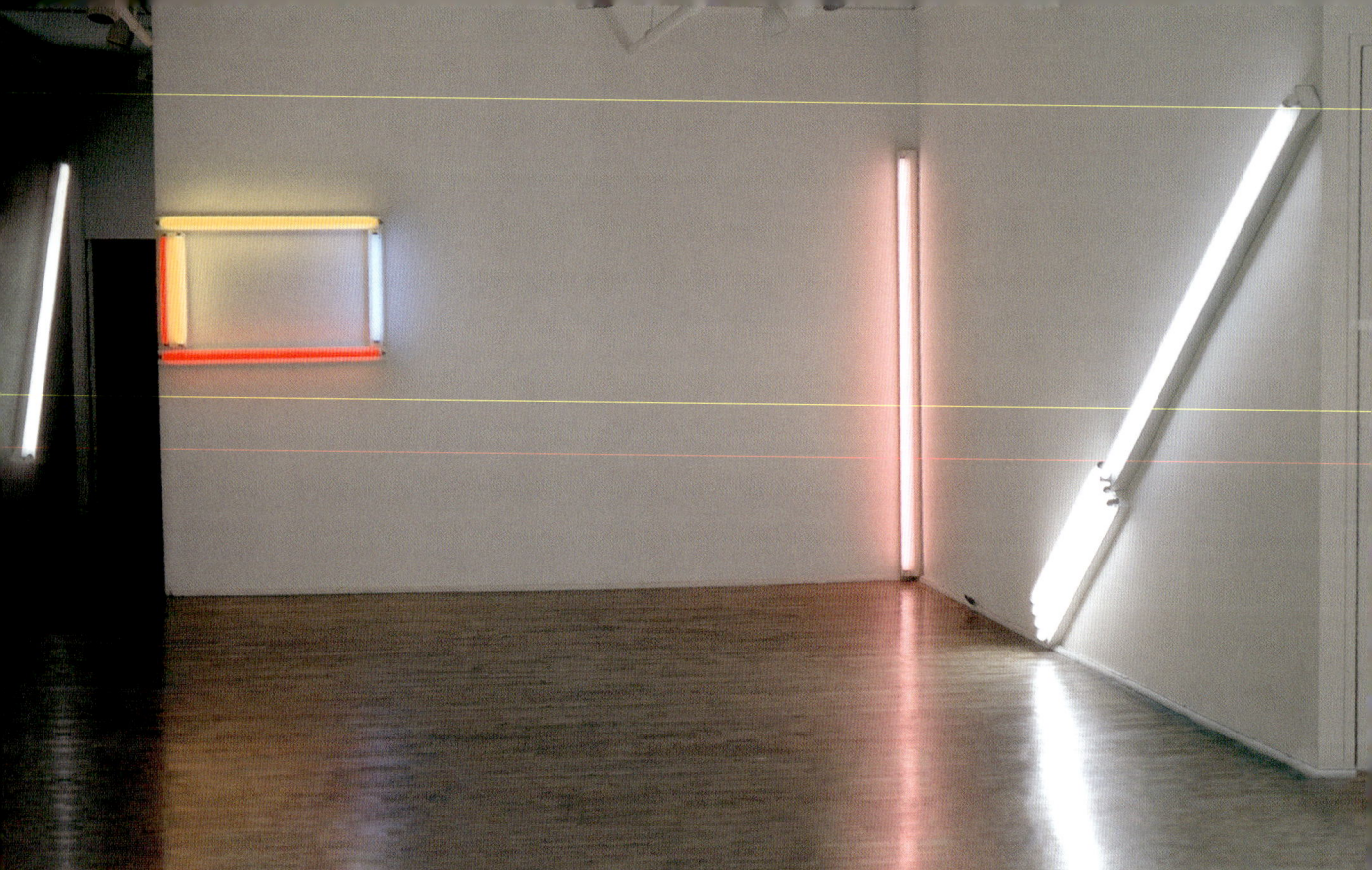

128 Installation view of *Dan Flavin: fluorescent light*, Green Gallery, New York, 18 November–12 December 1964. From left to right: *the diagonal of May 25, 1963 (to Robert Rosenblum)*, *a primary picture*, 1964, *pink out of a corner (to Jasper Johns)*, 1963, *alternate diagonals of March 2, 1964 (to Don Judd)*, 1964.

it with two men he could respect who productively practiced dissemblance. Illusion, couched in literalism, could be lived with. As he recalled in 1967, "I just found over a period of time that illusions are unsolicited but somehow inadvertent, sometimes undesirable and you accept it."[94] Nevertheless, Flavin signaled the presence of literalist illusionary effects in his works by, again, deploying his dedications to lean on homosexuality as the metaphor for illusion. As with the loaded dedications to his twin brother and to Stanley Coran in the pre-fluorescent works, the question of how difference can look like sameness was central to Flavin's formulation of his practice. In these crucial and formative years, Flavin's account of visibility and literalism took sexuality as its organizing figure.[95]

This is especially important because, of all the works in that Green Gallery show (fig. 128), it was *pink out of a corner* that presaged the direction of Flavin's career with his ever grander practice of using light to alter the visibility of architectural spaces (and, often, corners). Again, it is the paradox of the literalist illusion that disturbs critical and art-historical accounts of

Flavin.[96] How could the pursuit of literalism produce that which it set out to deny? I think Flavin's odd but undeniable citation of homosexuality at the outset of his mature practice provides a tool to understand its terms and implications. The *diagonal* and *pink out of a corner* are not singly about homosexuality (unlike *Coran*), but the issues surrounding homosexuality's possible dissemblance underwrote Flavin's canny citations in these works. The dedications – and their shifts – are key in this, and they provide a map of Flavin's thinking at the time. Especially in that 1964 solo exhibition, Flavin used the dedications purposefully as a means to stake out the art-theoretical ground of his works.[97] Flavin derived his practice from many sources and intellectual traditions, and I have only dealt with one layer of the dedications here. Nevertheless, I think it is a crucial one for what it can say about Flavin's later works and their logics. In short, Flavin learned to accept a qualified illusionism for his light effects just as he learned to cope with the possible contradiction of his own attitudes to the homosexuality of two individuals he deeply respected, Rosenblum and Johns. They achieved "approximate invisibility" for their sexual difference, just as the readymade tubes became almost occluded by the light they produced.

OPEN SYSTEMS AND PERFORMATIVE DEDICATIONS ...OR HOW FLAVIN LEARNED TO STOP WORRYING AND LOVE INTERCHANGEABILITY

The acceptance of illusionism, however, demanded a forceful reiteration and expansion of Flavin's "it is what it is" stance. This came to be guaranteed by Flavin's commitment to his "system" of interchangeable, modular units. After the initial experiments of 1963 and 1964, Flavin increasingly pushed his practice to embrace its systematic potential and, by the late 1960s, had developed a mode of work in which architectural spaces were more boldly altered through the light cast by his work.[98] However, viewers of Flavin's work never forget that they are looking at mass-produced tubes, despite the way they marvel at their spectacle. This, I believe, is the more fundamental and productive conjunction at the heart of the practice Flavin went on to develop – the relationship between the multiple interchangeability and the particularity he gave these standard units. That particularity happens in two fundamental ways for Flavin: the room-altering effects of light made from his combinations of units and the parenthetical dedications that give those interchangeable tubes individual names. In short, the illusionism he came to accept (and that is signaled through the shifting dedica-

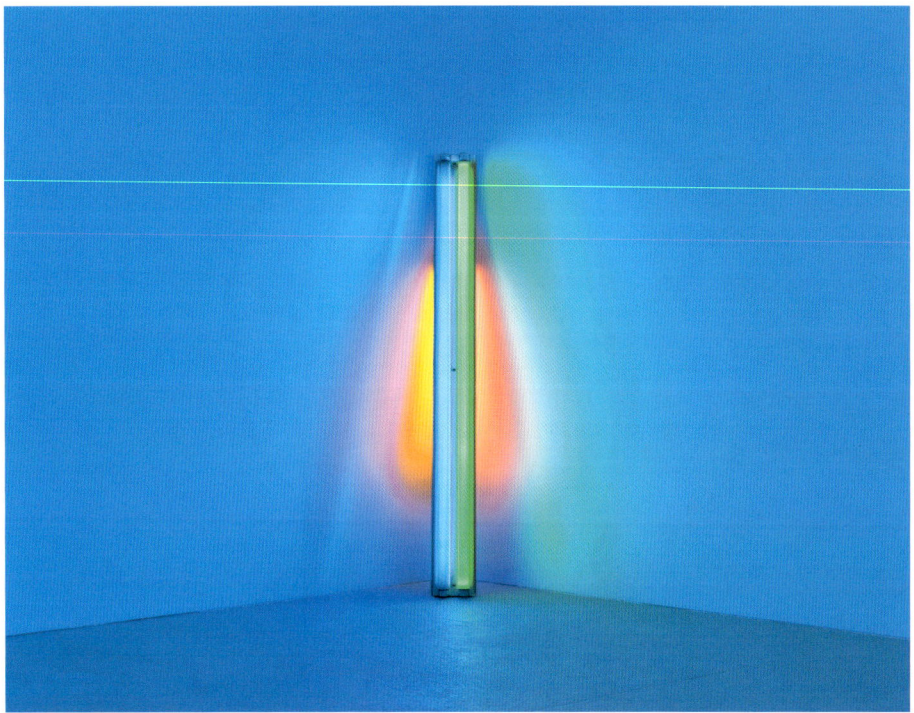

129 Dan Flavin, *untitled (to the real Dan Hill)*, 1978. Blue, green, yellow, and pink fluorescent light, l. 244 cm (96 in.).

tions to Johns and Rosenblum in his earliest single-tube fluorescents) compelled Flavin, on the one hand, to assert more forcefully the sameness and typicality of the mass-produced tubes that allowed for an ongoing system of recombinations and, on the other, to redouble his tactics (such as titling) that guaranteed that these multiply interchangeable components could be understood as nevertheless distinct from each other. As Jack Burnham observed in 1969, "The 'hardware' quality of [Flavin's] proposals and the sentimentality of his titles are again ramifications of a double-edged logic."[99]

Fluorescent tubes cast even light across their length and exhibit little to no coloristic variation in their output. Such consistency was one of the reasons for their widespread use in commercial and industrial settings in which large, open spaces (be they factories or the offices in Modernist skyscrapers) could be flooded with light. Flavin recognized, as well, that for this reason the tubes were interchangeable and typical. They were, by definition, the same. As Craig Kauffman said in 1967, "You can see them in any bar."[100] When commentators would mistakenly refer to his work as neon, Flavin would be quick to correct them. Neon had no similarly restricted shape since it could be bent into any curve or angle. Fluorescents, by contrast, were all straight lines, varying only in the predetermined lengths that allowed them to be fitted modularly into the gridded blocks of Modernist floor plans.

Flavin endlessly explored the limited system of possibilities afforded by standard-length fluorescent tubes. Modularity and interchangeability became, for him, axiomatic. By 1966, he would write: "I know now that I can reiterate any part of my fluorescent light system as adequate. Elements or parts of that system simply alter in situation installation. They lack the look of a history. I sense no stylistic or structural development of any significance within my proposal – only shifts in partitive emphasis – modifying and addable without intrinsic change."[101] This system of interchangeable standard units was mapped out by Flavin in a series of diagrams that were, themselves, considered the generation of the work. The concept of the individual combination or placement could and would be repeated and added to others, but each existed primarily as a concept that might only later be executed. He also wrote: "[T]he system does not proceed; it is simply applied. Incidentally, I have discovered that no diagram is inappropriate for my file. None need be prevented, suspended or discarded for lack of quality. Each one merely awaits coordination again and again."[102] Dan Graham provided his own definition of Flavin's system for Flavin's first one-person museum show, writing in 1967, "Fluorescent light objects in place are re-placeable in various contingently determined interdependent relations with specific environmental situations…The components of a particular exhibition upon its termination are re-placed in another situation – perhaps put to non-art use as part of a different whole in a different future."[103] For Flavin, the limited syntax of his prefabricated tubes proved to be rich enough to be continually applied over his subsequent career, making the fluorescent tube instantly identified with him in art settings. As Barnett Newman remarked, "[Flavin] has turned this thing, this material, into something personal."[104]

Any particularity and variation within Flavin's practice is only gained because of his enforcement of a modular system of the typical and the identical from which any new combinations would emerge. The "gaseous images" created by his tubes were allowed to be illusionistic precisely because he came to argue forcefully that their underlying sameness (not difference) was the source of their literalism and credibility. Whereas his *icons* had sought to make visibility itself manifest as iconographic content

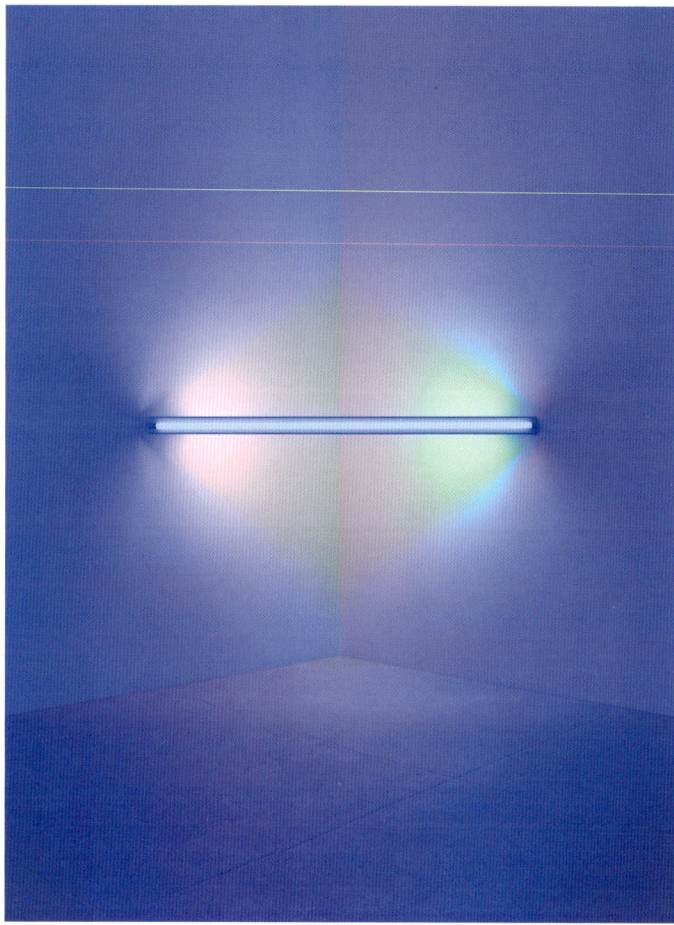

130 Dan Flavin, *untitled (to Janie Lee) one*, 1971. Blue, pink, yellow, and green fluorescent light, w. 244 cm (96 in).

(and expressed an anxiety that difference could look like sameness), his fluorescents were enabled to "plant illusions" because he asserted that his new material was fundamentally the same and without original difference. He wrote to Dan Graham in 1967 about his recent embrace of systematic interchangeability: "Last year, I became fully conscious that I had been deploying an *interchangeable system* of diagrams for fluorescent light held for situation installation. (The system was so thoroughly operative that it could be recorded finally in writing.) This attitude differed greatly from that former sense of development, piece by piece."[105] Significantly, Flavin de-emphasized the individual combination in favor of the ways in which each particular work was more fundamentally an expression of the greater system of identicality and interchangeability. This was effective. We viewers only fully understand Flavin's work when we have seen more than one, and each new experience of a Flavin makes us more aware of the multiple ways in which he achieved contingent particularity making each work distinct. The recognition of the differences among Flavin's art is wholly dependent on our grasp of the fundamental sameness of his components. He relied not only on our experience of fluorescent lights in office buildings and supermarkets but also on the art viewer's cumulative comprehension of his performance of sameness and typicality across the career-long system of his works. This is far more pronounced in Flavin than in the art of his peers who also used industrially fabricated components, such as Carl Andre. The critique Andre offered with his bricks and lead plates relied on the components being read obdurately – and only – as multipliable and generic. Unlike a Flavin, Andre's bricks refuse to transcend their mundaneness and do not inflect or affect an architectural space so much as occupy or impose on it. This was the crux of Flavin's modular system: the generic, massproduced object was interchangeable and uninteresting until it was made to look different from another despite our awareness of its typicality.

This issue of achieving particularity out of sameness is also the key to the practice of dedicating that many find ill-fitting with Flavin's work. Used throughout his career, it evolved from his early use of dedications as citations of ideas and sources to a more generalized system of attaching proper names to his works. At first, the dedication signaled content and affiliation. He said that *Broadway Flesh* "stands for" Coran, that young English homosexual. Similarly, when considering a dedication to Mies van der Rohe for his 1967 installation at the Museum of Contemporary Art Chicago, Flavin said that "It was almost like subject matter" (fig. 131).[106] After these earlier formations, the coded specificity of his dedications to people like Johns, Coran, or Rosenblum transformed into a more open and arbitrary pattern of naming his works after persons.

Without a doubt, the later dedications are arbitrary and seem disjunct from the works to which they are applied. This is why Flavin said in 1972 (some five years after he had embraced systematicity and interchangeability as his modus operandi): "[The dedications are] sentimental, and that's nice. But they're apart.…Some people fret over the dedications. They should just let it go. It's a lovely, incidental thing. It's a very fine sentiment to me. It's the kind of trifling that makes life easier to take from time to time."[107] Here, Flavin demonstrates the importance of the dedications as enunciations of affection just as he attempts to distract his viewers and critics from them. Nevertheless, he was committed and consistent in his pattern of dedicating works, and this titling project was a reiteration of the programmatic interchangeability that became central to his work. In other words, the

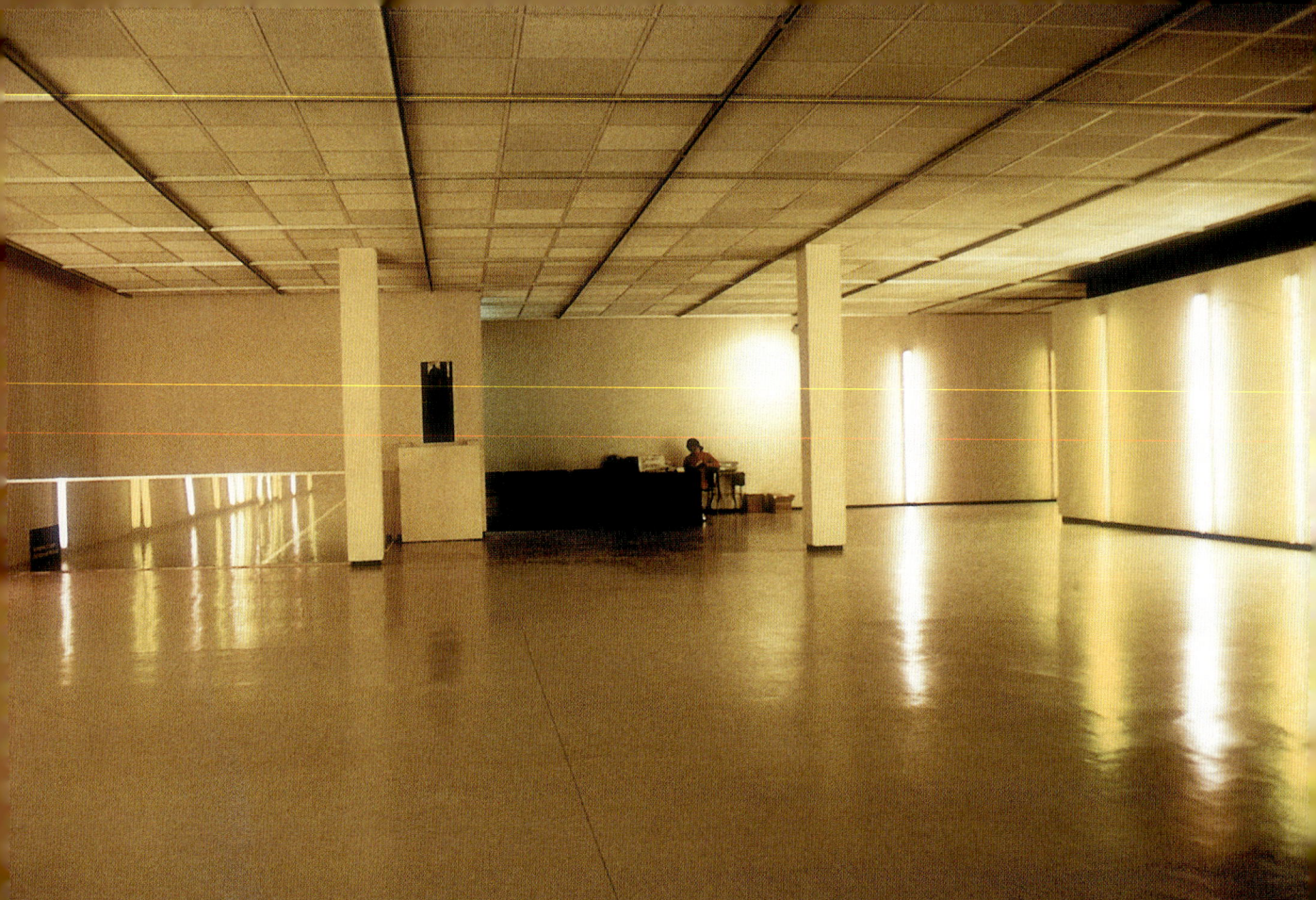

131 Installation view of *Dan Flavin: alternating pink and "gold,"* Museum of Contemporary Art Chicago, 9 December 1967–14 January 1968. Pink and yellow fluorescent light, 54 lamps on 6 walls, h. max. 244 cm (96 in.).

dedications are important because they are extraneous and because they are personal, and they operate alongside his system of modular units as a practice in and of itself. The works mark their fundamental systematicity, sameness, and interchangeability by being all named "untitled" (which is, of course, a title). However, Flavin's works are then made textually distinct among themselves by the parenthetical appending of a name to that title "untitled." These dedications perform as the work's identification, allowing us to differentiate one from the next. All in all, his titling practice affects the works and viewers' engagements with them, especially once it is recognized as having much more than a singular instance. It is, rather, a pattern of nomination and personalization that extends throughout his body of work. Despite his protestations, it is thus productive to fret over the dedications, for an account of them clarifies the terms of Flavin's larger practice. Taking seriously Flavin's pattern of dedicating his interchangeable units also affords an opportunity to see how that practice informs – and indeed offers an unwitting demonstration of – wider discussions of the importance of naming to personhood.

Since Flavin's dedications are efficacious as marks of differentiation and particularity, they come to act as identifiers. This draws on the history of the title in the twentieth century, which John Welchman has charted as a means to analyse the recurring patterns in modern and contemporary artists' reconfigurations of titling practices. As he says, the title "sometimes doubles the image, sometimes blanks it, and sometimes offers it in a transgressive, connotative spin," but it nevertheless assumes an "annunciatory priority or firstness" with regard to the artwork to which it is appended.[108] Welchman argues: "Enmeshed in a complex rapport with the surface or volume to which it relates, the title of a painting or sculpture can be considered the *name* of that object. It is demonstrably implicated in the signifying capacity of the work, providing a lead term in its descriptive articulation and contextual history."[109] In keeping with this, the names of Flavin's dedicatees become, for all intents and purposes, the names of the artworks. Despite Flavin's disavowal of their significance, they nevertheless circulate as the textual sign for each particular combination of interchangeable fluourescent tubes.

Before discussing the particularities of Flavin's titling practice, it is useful to position him in relation to some of his peers and their own attitudes toward the title. The overlay of oblique content onto non-referential and non-mimetic art objects was a tactic used by other artists who embraced abstraction – as, for instance, in the different but not unrelated practice of titling used by John Chamberlain discussed in Chapter 2.

Within Flavin's circle, artists used heavily loaded and obscure titles (as with Johns himself). Alternatively, they insisted on the "untitled" (as with Judd) or less systematically played with titles as ironic or deadpan (as with Carl Andre). Perhaps the most apt comparison for Flavin's "embarrassing" titles might be Frank Stella, who was a significant influence on Flavin (and literalism more broadly) in the early 1960s. Stella's 1959 "Black Paintings," as Brenda Richardson showed, bear obscure titles that append extrinsic content to paintings that performed their matter-of-factness and a concomitant refusal of pictorial signification. Named after events and locations (including one after a gay bar, *Club Onyx*, and one after a lesbian bar, *Seven Steps*), the titles operate cumulatively across the series to create what Richardson referred to as "a virtual catalogue of the dictionary definition of the adjective 'black,' with its myriad, multi-layered connotations."[110] None of the titles, however, are derived directly from the forms of the painting nor is there a necessary correlation between the individual Black Painting and the associative reference attached to it.

Similarly, Flavin's titles share with Stella's their insistence on shadowing the rigorously non-representational artwork with personal, associative content. Even though Flavin retains an allegiance with more ascetic titlers like Judd through the use of "untitled," Flavin's titles are analogous to Stella's in their cumulative and lateral build up of content as a series of repeated nominations. They appear less arbitrary (and more meaningful) when they are seen as instances of a repeated practice – that is, as part of a system of naming. The meaning of the format of the "untitled (dedicated)" emerges not as the result of a correlation between an instance of it and a particular fluorescent artwork. Rather, the pattern of nomination becomes meaningful by virtue of its accumulation and of each title's lateral buttressing of the others in the pattern. To put this another way: if one isolates any one of Flavin's later works to investigate the relation between the untitled dedication and the composition of fluorescent tubes, there will be hardly any observable correlation. Consequently, the title may, at first, seem arbitrary. Any such local and myopic framing of the question yields little, and many have consequently assumed that the titles are therefore meaningless. However, Flavin was insistent that his works were never individual and discrete but were, rather, part of a system of interchangeable modularity. As such, no one instance of the system can ever be seen as autonomous or unrelated to the whole. When one brings this to bear on the insistent pattern of titling, it becomes clear that – as a system – the dedications, too, reinforce each other. Cumulatively, they establish the act of personalization as a central and recurring feature of Flavin's practice. While not all of Flavin's titles embed parenthetical inscriptions to persons, this way of titling nevertheless predominates and has come to be identified with his work. One must, therefore, pay attention to the pattern of nominations that Flavin made a recurrent feature of his systemic practice.

In this practice, the "to" of Flavin's dedications is important, for it invokes a person as the addressee of the title's enunciation of Flavin's affection.[111] That is, the titles are never simply people's names. If this were the case, it would establish too close a relationship between the form of an individual work and the name given to it. Instead, the dedication within the title is an utterance of the name, conjuring that person as the addressee. Flavin wanted to retain openness and interchangeability, and his use of the "to" with a proper name grew with his move to fluorescents. (*Coran's Broadway Flesh*, for instance, had no such respectful address, but it was used for the first fluorescents.) The "to" (or sometimes "for" or other variants) unhinges the necessity of the relation between the work and the proper name appended to it while, at the same time, re-enacting the moment of differentiation in the act of naming. Ultimately, the performativity of the dedications works in tandem with Flavin's open system of interchangeable units to keep the act of naming, itself, open and mobile.

Dedications and other related textual framings of a text affect the text itself. Gérard Genette has called these "peritexts" in his larger analysis of the functioning of paratextual "thresholds." Peritexts (such as the dedication, the title page, or the epigraph) spatially precede, follow, or otherwise surround a text. His discussion of the dedication establishes that it is best understood as performative in the strict sense – it performs what it describes. "Saying it is doing it," as he explained.[112]

To utter, write, or repeat a dedication is to dedicate. This formulation is important when considering the effects of Flavin's titles. The "To X" as opposed to just "X" in his titles, following Genette, "constitutes the act it is supposed to describe."[113] The illocutionary force of that performative affects the works that Flavin names in this way. Whatever else the fluorescent tubes are, they become (via the dedication) an address to another person. The performative act of the dedicating title changes the status of Flavin's works, altering and multiplying the ways in which they are experienced and interpreted.

The form of the dedication requires a person (the dedicatee), and Flavin's pattern of titling insures that persons and affections circulate in the vicinity of the works themselves. Despite Flavin's protests to the contrary, the dedication is thus never wholly "extraneous" or "trifling" because of this performing of an extrinsic address to a person. It is these conjured dedicatees – awkwardly attached to Flavin's non-anthropomorphic and multiply interchangeable units – who establish an "embarrassing" and inescapable context for his artworks. As Joan Lowndes wrote in a 1969 review of Flavin's Vancouver Art Gallery show, "Although Flavin is classed as a minimalist because of the simplicity of means and the concrete 'thereness' of his work, it is also highly charged with emotion."[114]

In addition to the named dedicatee, the performativity of the dedication enfolds the viewer in the scene of nomination. As Genette says, "Whoever the official addressee, there is always an ambiguity in the destination of a dedication, which is always intended for at least two addressees: the dedicatee, of course, but also the reader, for dedicating a work is a public act that the reader is, as it were, called on to witness."[115] Another way to say this is that the reader of the dedication (whether in a frontispiece to a book or on a wall label next to an artwork), becomes implicated in the act. As

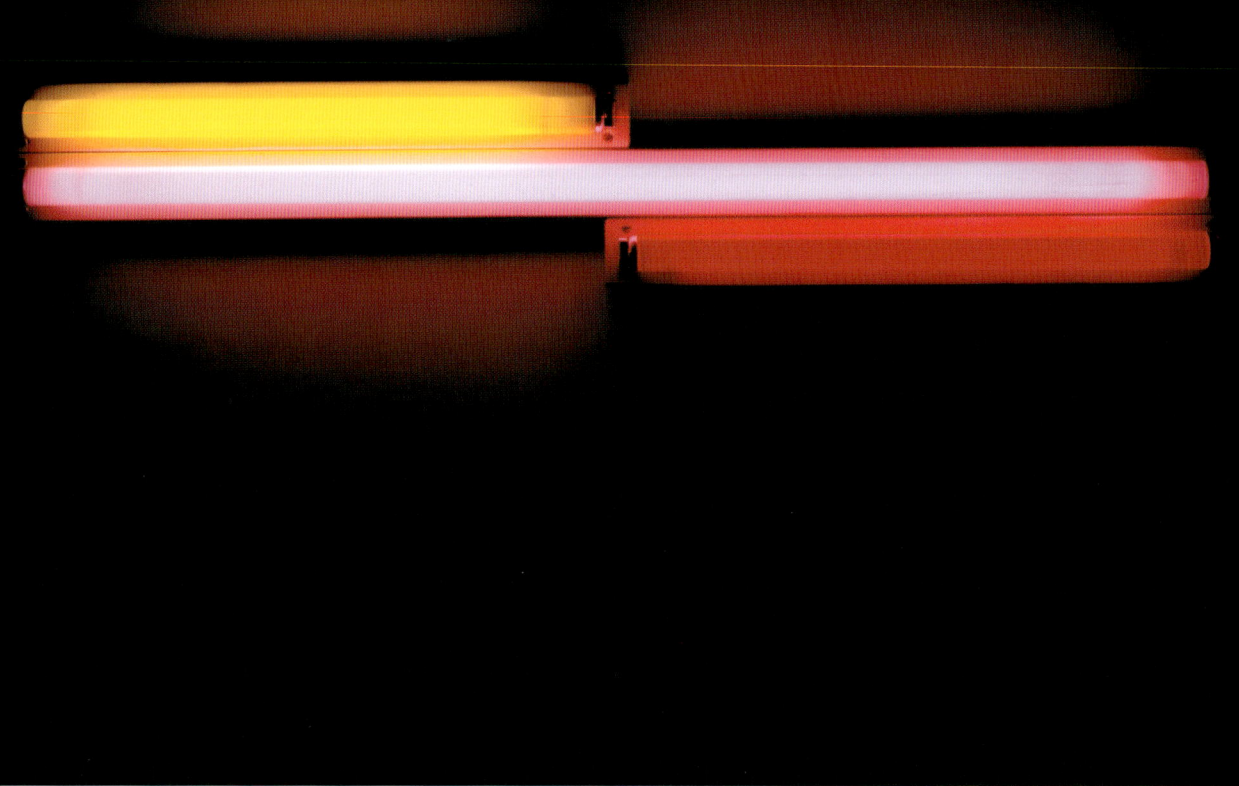

132   Dan Flavin, *untitled (to Ellen Johnson, fondly)*, 1975. Red and yellow fluorescent light tubes, 124.5 × 35.6 × 11.4 cm (49 × 14 × 4½ in.). Allen Memorial Art Museum, Oberlin College, gift of Paul F. Walter, Oberlin College Class of 1957, 1979.7.

the witness to the performative, they are triangulated into an interpersonal relationship with Flavin's affectionate declaration and the absent person (often unknown to them) that they are asked to consider in relation to the work of art. On reading the dedication, the viewer is compelled to witness an affection and to look at the readymade fluorescents as evoking (if not directly imaging) that person who mattered enough for Flavin to bestow this name on this combination of lights. Again, Genette's analysis provides a useful description of how the dedication performs in this way: "one cannot mention a person or thing as a privileged addressee without invoking that person or thing in some way (as the bard of old invoked the muse – who couldn't do anything about it) and therefore implicating the person or thing as a kind of ideal inspirer."[116]

The effects of the dedication are particularly acute in Flavin's case because the dedication's performativity is congruent with the work's title itself – the dedication is *within* the name given by Flavin to the work. This binds the dedication more closely to the work than, say, a dedication page that comes after a novel's title page. A viewer, historian, or critic refers to an artwork by Flavin by repeating the dedication the artist wrote into the title. Consequently, the performative dedication of a Flavin work is not just a past event but one that is re-invoked each time its title is spoken or read. In this way, Flavin repeatedly reminds the viewer of the scene of naming when the artwork became, as well, an address to a specific person.

The cumulative effect of Flavin's pattern of dedication is that the content of his titles is nothing less than the performativity of the act of naming itself – left circling as the capacity of the works to invoke persons despite their refusal of representation and anthropomorphism. Their pattern of arbitrary particularization registers and reinforces Flavin's emphasis on the systematic interchangeability of typical units. Unlike other artists who dedicate (and, furthermore, who make unique art objects), Flavin's use of the dedication is amplified and made more complex by virtue of his works' literalism and mass-produced interchangeability. Flavin made sure to let us know that his artistic materials were fundamentally equivalent, not unique, and part of an ongoing system of modular sameness. Overlaid onto that system, Flavin's committed pattern of dedication replays the potency of naming. It is significant that the performativity of his dedicatory particularizations requires persons, and the scene of naming of Flavin's works is dependent on the specific form of the dedication and its positing of an interpersonal triangulation. The typical and identical unit is proposed as personal and particular through the address that the reader of the title witnesses. That personalization, however, is not made equivalent with the fluorescent work's form so much as nominated anew each time its dedication is considered. The recurring conjunction in Flavin's titles of "untitled" with parenthetical naming is, itself, a manifestation of his desire both to assert the fundamental equivalency of his works and to claim for them particularity and specificity (here through the title's address to a person). Even though his works are not portraits, they evoke persons. More fundamentally, the reliance of Flavin's open system of interchangeable sameness with the performativity of the dedication calls for – beyond Flavin's own design – an account of personhood, based on naming, that is, itself, similarly open and unforeclosed.

"THEY LACK THE LOOK OF HISTORY": TRANSFORMABLE PERSONHOOD AND NAMING IN FLAVIN'S SYSTEM

Perhaps the best way to register the thread of Flavin's logic that I am pursuing is through reference to a later artist who took some of Flavin's strategies as his own – Felix Gonzalez-Torres. Flavin, with his use of the mass-produced, readymade components, was clearly one of his main references, and this is most evident in his use of titles. Gonzalez-Torres also adopted a strategy of parenthetical personalization appended to the word "untitled". He used these titles to refer to works that, like Flavin's, were made up of mass-produced, quotidian components intended to be interchangeable – including light bulbs.

Gonzalez-Torres's practice selectively appropriated from Minimalism. He took the simple, everyday object and made it directly personal by recombining and multiplying it. Some of these are closely autobiographical or directly portraits, such as *"Untitled" (Portrait of Ross in L.A.)*, which takes the form of a replenishable pile of candy whose weight matches the body weight of an adult male (fig. 133). The work is parenthetically titled after his partner, Ross, whom he lost to AIDS. A central concern of Gonzalez-Torres's work was to imbue the everyday with the poetic and the commemorative, and his diminishing stacks of paper or candy have all been taken as figurations of the body and its vulnerability. They are, furthermore, intended to be replenished and maintained by the museum or owner, so that the work "lives" through its dispersal into the world (in the form of the piece of candy or paper) and is kept alive by its caretaker who replaces its components. In this way, it is both a constant and shifting work that relates directly to those who come into contact with it.

This is also the case with his strings of light bulbs that invariably and individually burn out (fig. 134). Even though he attached events and not names to these works, as Andrea Rosen has recalled, "he purposefully decided that each of the light string pieces would be accompanied by a parenthetical title. The light string pieces, in particular, become evidence of Felix' desire, albeit sometimes marginalized desire, to instill *himself* in the work."[117] Such are the effects of the parenthetical title attached to a work that – precisely because of its readymade interchangeability – can be read as open to variation and personalization. The virtue of the readymade, non-anthropomorphic component used in this way is that it opens up – because of its generic quality – to multiple personifications

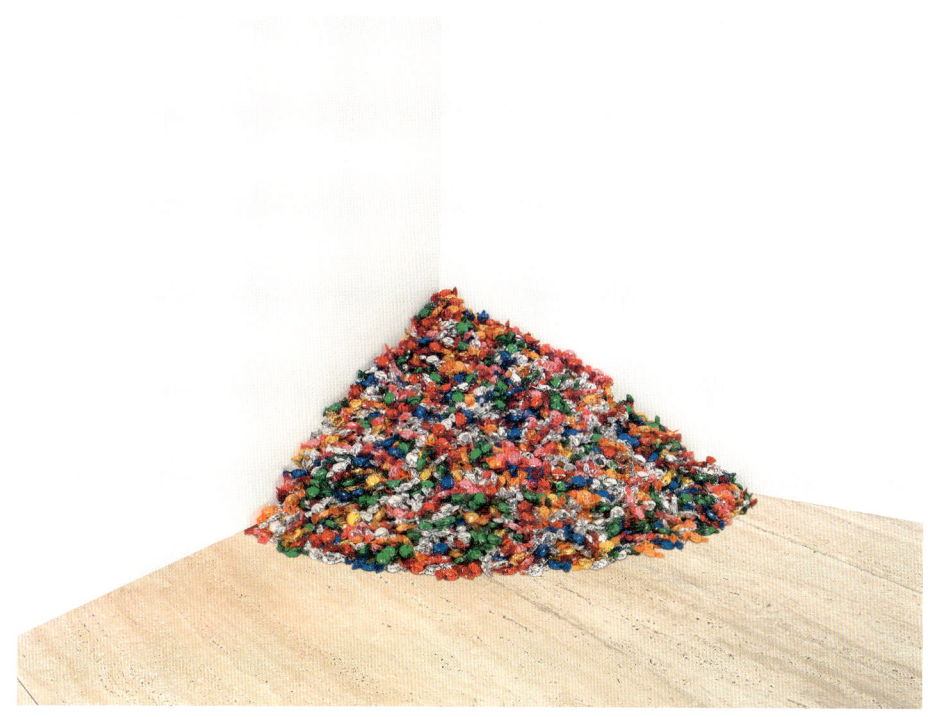

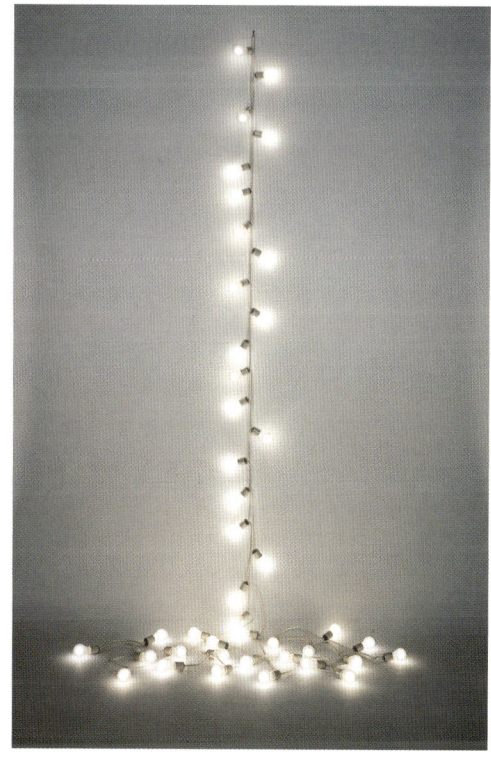

ABOVE 133   Felix Gonzalez-Torres, *"Untitled" (Portrait of Ross in L.A.)*, 1991. Multicolored candies, individually wrapped in cellophane, endless supply, ideal weight 79.4 kg (175 lb); installed dimensions variable, c. 92 × 92 × 92 cm (36 × 36 × 36 in.). Art Institute of Chicago, promised gift of Donna and Howard Stone, 1.1999.

RIGHT 134   Felix Gonzalez-Torres, *"Untitled" (Petit Palais)*, 1992. Light bulbs, porcelain light sockets, and extension cord, overall dimensions vary. Philadelphia Museum of Art, gift of the Peter Norton Family Foundation, 1992-99-1.

and personalizations brought by each subsequent viewer of the work. They are universal and personal at the same time.

This efficacy of the parenthetical dedication to usher in such engagements when coupled with the mass-produced readymade is central to the practice to which both Gonzalez-Torres and Flavin committed themselves. These dedications map an open account of personhood onto these objects without reducing their reference to simple anthropomorphism. Gonzalez-Torres's later appropriation of Flavin's tactics serves to illuminate this capacity that their collisions of non-reference and naming affords. The activated, electrified light, bound to eclipse, is alive like no other Minimal object, and when a name or event is appended to the light bulb, prosopopoeia (if not anthropomorphism) is ushered in with ease. Indeed, the following account of Flavin's works by Grégoire Müller in 1972 could well have been written about Gonzalez-Torres's minimal memorials:

> They *are* only when they are plugged in. They cease to exist when the fluorescent light is *dead*. They can *be* again when the tube is replaced. Within a certain period of time, all the parts of a piece could be replaced. Yet it would still be the same piece, which poses the question of what really 'is' the piece.[118]

Gonzalez-Torres made this aspect of Flavin's personalizations central to his work. Both in the light string works with their mortal bulbs and other works such as *"Untitled" (Perfect Lovers)*, with its battery-powered clocks that are fated to slow to a stop at different rates, Gonzalez-Torres understood how the minimal object could be made to evoke more lucidly the personal as a function of the objects' typicality and simplicity. The titles clue us into how to read the poetics of these objects. As Rosen remarked,

> For those of us that knew Felix, the parenthetical titles are like small gifts left behind: remember when we spoke about this, and remember how I felt about that piece, and remember when we went there…These gifts are welcome, but they are also reminders of just how much one forgets. Do I really know what all of those words meant to Felix? Felix recounted stories to me on a daily basis, stories which were essential to him, often stories were generated by his decision to include or change a particular parenthetical title. They were about defining what was necessary and which memories were infused with meaning.[119]

Flavin's works, some three decades earlier, also opened out to evocations of friends, mentors, and affections in the form of the mortal but changeable light bulb named after a person. As he said, his dedicating "makes life easier to take from time to time."[120]

Such affections motivate the dedication in both Flavin and Gonzalez-Torres's work. They are often obscure and the occasion for them forgotten. Nevertheless, they perform an attachment to objects that seem – because of their mass-produced interchangeability and typicality – unlikely bearers of such meaning. They do, however, convey that meaning through the performativity of the dedication's address and witnessing. It is all too common for viewers of Flavin's works to intersperse their amazed experience of embracing light with their curiosity at the person for whom *this* light is named.

Ultimately, the affections Flavin laid onto his works have the effect of bringing persons into consideration. Whether he denied their importance or not, Flavin's practice engenders an account of personhood hinged on the proper names he appended to his artworks. Even though Flavin's works are decidedly non-referential – and few bear even the slightest anthropomorphism – we know them as "Leo," as "Sandy Calder," as "Annina Nosei." These persons are attached to Flavin's objecthood, and this attachment does not rely on any morphological distinction between his modular units. While they are put in different combinations and contexts, there is nothing intrinsically different from one tube to the next. Flavin made sure one never forgets this. However, his system of modular sameness and interchangeability personalized in the form of the dedication inadvertently produces an account of persons and bodies that are – like his tubes – physically and fundamentally the same just as each, through naming, becomes unique.

Most directly, this openness calls for an account of gender since one often interprets names before anything else in terms of the gender implied by them. Without any other context, "Leo" connotes first and foremost a male gender for its bearer (or "Ellen" female) without offering much other information as forthrightly. For this reason, Flavin's performative dedications and their invocations of personhood directly activate gender as a central category. Whereas Flavin's formative years emphasized sexuality as a key metaphor for establishing literalism, it is gender that emerges as a powerful effect of his expansive pattern of dedicating that went with his embrace of systematicity and interchangeability.

As with the other case studies in this book, it is the collisions of non-reference and metaphors of personhood, the figure, and the body that produce disruptions of conventional accounts of genders as fixed, intrinsic, or binary. Inadvertently, artists such as Flavin who clung to nominations of personhood (while nevertheless pursuing works that eschewed any anthropomorphism) offered works that exhibited capacities for being understood in relation to genders' mutability and proliferation. For Flavin, homosexuality and dissemblance were the issues that spurred the later development of a practice of interchangeable, categorically identical modular units that were allowed to be different depending on the names he gave to them and the situations in which they were placed. Combined with Flavin's insistent system of sameness, the dedications signal Flavin's proliferation of difference and variability among his standard materials that can be recombined, paired, relocated, and exchanged – and that one never forgets are all, fundamentally, the same. The commitments of Flavin's practice do nothing less than call for an account of particularity, a particularity that Flavin derived from and signaled through his assignment of proper names.

Flavin's dedications mattered to him, and they act on viewers of his works. As part of his system, they presage tactics of naming that were increasingly adopted in later decades by individuals who sought to transform the genders assigned to them. Flavin's assertions of sameness and interchangeability rely on a primary gender neutrality of the modular unit that is given a name. It is this fundamental issue that a reframing through transgender theory illuminates.

Transgender history has amply demonstrated that naming is one of the primary tactics for redefining oneself – a redefinition that assumes no deterministic relation between gendered identity signaled in the name and the body to which it is attached. Even though it would be anathema to him, Flavin's system nevertheless arrives at a logic of transformative naming. From the perspective of transgender theory and its accounts of successive states of identity and mutable and multiple genders, Flavin's practice of naming interchangeable units can be extrapolated into an inadvertent account of personhood that shares such priorities with transgender politics and cultures. Both teach us that a name can, after all, make all the difference.

Names function as markers of self-determined identity and personhood. One of the most epochal choices for any trans person is the choice of their proper name, for it becomes the sign expressed to others of who they know themselves to be. Adopting a name can signal a choice of a new gender or a new identity, and for this reason it is one of the forms of self-determination strongly resisted by legal systems and institutional structures. In fact, this potency of renaming is one of the central themes of that primary intertext for *Coran's Broadway Flesh* – the musical *Gypsy*. "Gypsy" was the adopted name of Louise, and her claiming of it marked her self-determination and independence.[121]

The text of *Gypsy* is just one indication of how, even in the 1960s, the power of names was already acknowledged as a means of redefining identity. A name's ability to shift or to call into question gender and sexuality was well known to many, including to that dedicatee of Flavin's first fluorescent, Bobby Rosenblum. He regularly played with names in his correspondence and his circle of friends in the 1960s, and it was an important subcultural practice of gay men at this time (Edward Plunkett, who had with Stanley Coran been a recipient of an *East New York Shrine*, was one of his fellow camp name-playing correspondents). Rosenblum loved to compile drag queen names based on famous people. His personal correspondence of the time is peppered with drag names (both as authors and addressees).[122] According to one friend, Rosenblum kept an annotated copy of the *Encyclopaedia Britannica* in which he would regularly write humorous drag queen names as addenda to the lists of U.S. presidents.[123] As a sequel to his drag presidents, Rosenblum and his friends developed a list of drag names based on famous artists (figs. 136 and 137).[124] There are many funny ones, including "Hello Dalí," "Ann-Magritte," "Twyla Arp," "Stella Stella," "Imogene Caro," "Minnie Andre," "Jasmin Johns," and "Sandy Calder." (Calder went by "Sandy," the standard Scottish diminutive for "Alexander," which Rosenblum thought worked fine on its own as a drag name. Flavin dedicated a work to Calder using this name as well; fig. 135.) One of the youngest on Rosenblum's list was "Connie Edna Flavin" – naming the artist after the electrical power company Consolidated Edison.

Rosenblum's list offers a humorous but illuminating reminder of how names convey aspects of personhood, most importantly gender. It is also a reminder that versions of queer and trans practices of naming were current at the time. The practice of drag is not equivalent to the commitment to transformational genders and successive states of personhood, but both focus on the name as the primary sign of identity and volition. Within the history of transgender experience, one may remember that Christine Jorgensen had made international headlines a decade before, in 1952, as the first publicized case of a successful sex reassignment surgery. Newspapers focused on her former G.I. status and never forgot to tell readers of the male name she had been given at birth. Both these mainstream media representations and the more local practices of dedicatees such as Bobby Rosenblum and Edward Plunkett provide a wider context for Flavin's tendency to want to give different names to his same units.

Naming is never inconsequential, and naming was central to Flavin's practice. Flavin's dedications to his twin, to his neighbor Stanley Coran, to Rosenblum, and to Johns marked the foundational development of Flavin's

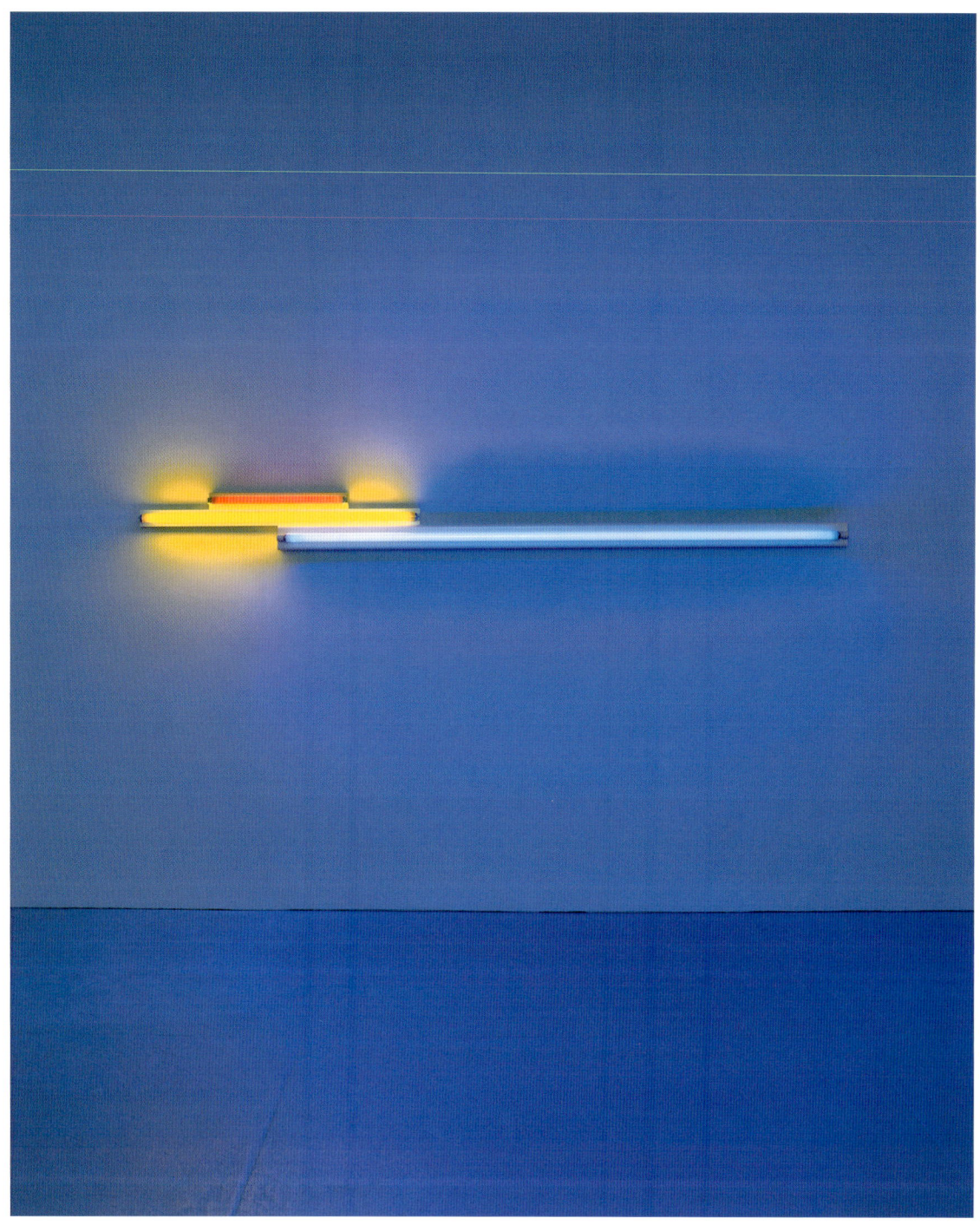

135 Dan Flavin, *untitled (in memory of "Sandy" Calder) V*, 1977. Red, yellow, and blue fluorescent light, w. 305 cm (120 in.).

practice – a development underwritten by his back-and-forth about sexuality being called out, being made visible, being recognized, and being named. These works facilitated his move to embrace fully a modular logic of interchangeable units that could, through the power of naming, be made personal and personifying. That is, despite Flavin's stated prejudicial attitudes, his enabling dedications encoded his work with a poetic account of unforeclosed transformability. He reminds us how each basic unit must be seen for itself. This practice, Flavin's work demonstrates, demands a new proper name for every variation possible.

What the early dedications mark are Flavin's negotiations with how his lights performed. He tried to make *Coran's Broadway Flesh* fully self-evident, and he attached apparent homosexuality to that work to underwrite that aim. Within a year, he stopped manipulating and constructing his lights, letting them be themselves. Despite stepping back from overworking his lights, he found that they themselves performed in a strong way. In their production of illusionistic and architecture-altering effects, they presented a version of the dissemblance he had previously attempted to exorcise in his pursuit of literalism. Buttressed by the readymade, mass-produced nature of his chosen artistic material, he came to accept the ways that they "planted an illusion" or "destroyed a corner" when activated.

This new acceptance of illusion and perceptual effects compelled Flavin to commit to the idea of a system of multiple but standard and interchangeable units. They could create contingent particularity in the form of illusion if they were asserted to be all the more mundane and unspecial in and of themselves. Flavin embraced his systematic approach in the mid-1960s as a counterbalance to the ways in which his works seem easily and readily to produce "gaseous images" and architectural illusions. This same two-step facilitated an expansion of his pattern of dedicating his works. Whereas the early dedications signaled affinities and themes, he expanded and opened up this practice in order to allow the performative dedications to make the generic and interchangeable units "personal" and particular. In their conjunction of "untitled" and dedication, Flavin's titles all replay the formula of particularity as an effect of the systematicity that characterized his practice. The titles are, in this way, reiterations of his art-theoretical priorities and a central point of his practice. Tracking the titles of his works in these early years through the figure of the homosexual helps to illuminate how Flavin developed his particular version of luminary literalism and its paradoxical relationship to illusionism. The cluster of works around the fluorescent turn represent Flavin's acceptance of illusion and "approximate invisibility," figured through the dissembling homosexual. This acceptance,

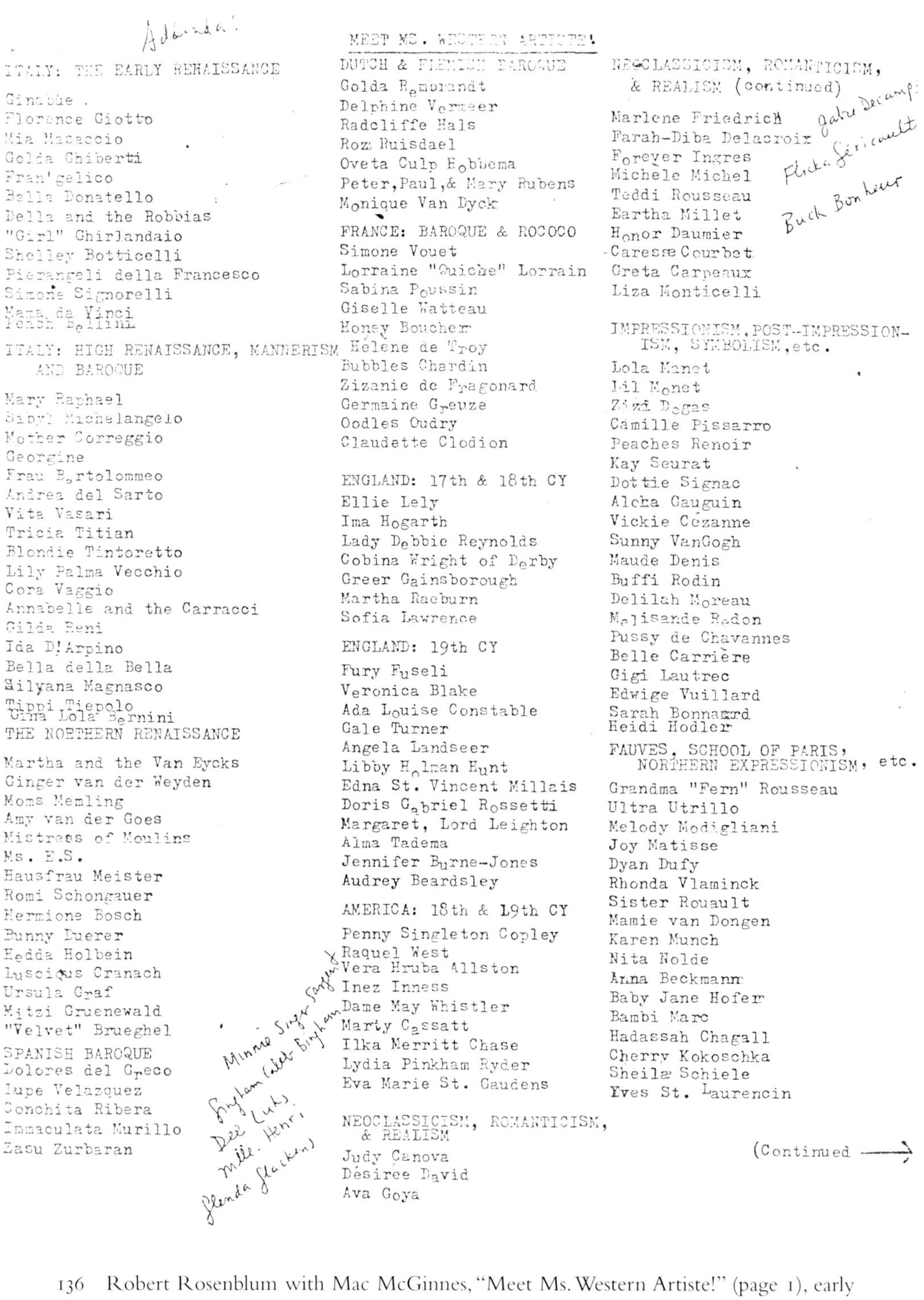

Adorada!

MEET MS. WESTERN ARTISTE!

ITALY: THE EARLY RENAISSANCE

Cimabue
Florence Giotto
Mia Masaccio
Golda Ghiberti
Fran'gelico
Bella Donatello
Della and the Robbias
"Girl" Ghirlandaio
Shelley Botticelli
Pierangeli della Francesco
Simone Signorelli
Mama da Vinci
Peach Bellini

ITALY: HIGH RENAISSANCE, MANNERISM AND BAROQUE

Mary Raphael
Sibyl Michelangelo
Mother Correggio
Georgine
Frau Bartolommeo
Andrea del Sarto
Vita Vasari
Tricia Titian
Blondie Tintoretto
Lily Palma Vecchio
Cora Vaggio
Annabelle and the Carracci
Gilda Reni
Ida D'Arpino
Bella della Bella
Silyana Magnasco
Tippi Tiepolo
Gina Lola Bernini

THE NORTHERN RENAISSANCE

Martha and the Van Eycks
Ginger van der Weyden
Moms Memling
Amy van der Goes
Mistress of Moulins
Ms. E.S.
Hausfrau Meister
Romi Schongauer
Hermione Bosch
Bunny Duerer
Hedda Holbein
Luscious Cranach
Ursula Graf
Mitzi Gruenewald
"Velvet" Brueghel

SPANISH BAROQUE

Dolores del Greco
Lupe Velazquez
Conchita Ribera
Immaculata Murillo
Zasu Zurbaran

DUTCH & FLEMISH BAROQUE

Golda Rembrandt
Delphine Vermeer
Radcliffe Hals
Roz Ruisdael
Oveta Culp Hobbema
Peter, Paul, & Mary Rubens
Monique Van Dyck

FRANCE: BAROQUE & ROCOCO

Simone Vouet
Lorraine "Quiche" Lorrain
Sabina Poussin
Giselle Watteau
Honey Boucher
Hélène de Troy
Bubbles Chardin
Zizanie de Fragonard
Germaine Greuze
Oodles Oudry
Claudette Clodion

ENGLAND: 17th & 18th CY

Ellie Lely
Ima Hogarth
Lady Debbie Reynolds
Cobina Wright of Derby
Greer Gainsborough
Martha Raeburn
Sofia Lawrence

ENGLAND: 19th CY

Fury Fuseli
Veronica Blake
Ada Louise Constable
Gale Turner
Angela Landseer
Libby Holman Hunt
Edna St. Vincent Millais
Doris Gabriel Rossetti
Margaret, Lord Leighton
Alma Tadema
Jennifer Burne-Jones
Audrey Beardsley

AMERICA: 18th & 19th CY

Penny Singleton Copley
Raquel West
Vera Hruba Allston
Inez Inness
Dame May Whistler
Marty Cassatt
Ilka Merritt Chase
Lydia Pinkham Ryder
Eva Marie St. Gaudens

Minnie Singer Sargent &
Bingham (Celeb Bingham
Dee Luks
Mlle. Henri
Glenda Glackens

NEOCLASSICISM, ROMANTICISM, & REALISM

Judy Canova
Désiree David
Ava Goya

NEOCLASSICISM, ROMANTICISM, & REALISM (continued)

Marlene Friedrich
Farah-Diba Delacroix
Forever Ingres
Michele Michel
Teddi Rousseau
Eartha Millet
Honor Daumier
Caresse Courbet
Greta Carpeaux
Liza Monticelli

Gabe Decamps
Flicka Géricault
Buck Bonheur

IMPRESSIONISM, POST-IMPRESSIONISM, SYMBOLISM, etc.

Lola Manet
Lil Monet
Zizi Degas
Camille Pissarro
Peaches Renoir
Kay Seurat
Dottie Signac
Aloha Gauguin
Vickie Cézanne
Sunny VanGogh
Maude Denis
Buffi Rodin
Delilah Moreau
Melisande Redon
Pussy de Chavannes
Belle Carrière
Gigi Lautrec
Edwige Vuillard
Sarah Bonnard
Heidi Hodler

FAUVES, SCHOOL OF PARIS, NORTHERN EXPRESSIONISM, etc.

Grandma "Fern" Rousseau
Ultra Utrillo
Melody Modigliani
Joy Matisse
Dyan Dufy
Rhonda Vlaminck
Sister Rouault
Mamie van Dongen
Karen Munch
Nita Nolde
Anna Beckmann
Baby Jane Hofer
Bambi Marc
Hadassah Chagall
Cherry Kokoschka
Sheila Schiele
Yves St. Laurencin

(Continued →

136 Robert Rosenblum with Mac McGinnes, "Meet Ms. Western Artiste!" (page 1), early 1970s, with Rosenblum's annotations.

MEET MS. WESTERN ARTISTE!
-2-

CUBISM, PURISM, ABSTRACT ART

Dulcinea Malagueña Picasso y Bolero
Coco Braque
Ruth St. Leger
"Pasties" Gris
Glenda Gleizes
Maisie Metzinger
Deanna Herbin   *Faye Delaunay*
Crystal Feininger
Leé Corbusier
Edna May Ozenfant
Alice Kupka
Tempest Kandinsky
Pet Mondrian
"Diamonds" van Doesburg
La Lissitzky   *Anna Mana Albers*
Zsa Zsa Moholy-Nagy
Blanche Malevich
Gwen Nicholson

FUTURISM

Barbarella Balla
Bellissima Boccioni
"Sequins" Severini

DADA, SURREALISM, NEOROMANTICISM

Bridie Duchamp
Yvonne de Chirico
Woman Ray   *Tinkerbelle Klee*
Ann-Magritte
Erna Ernst
Hello Dali
Joan Miró
Maria Tchelitchew
Ethel Berman
Ivy Sutherland
Cruella Bacon
Carmen Morandi
Eva Tanguy

AMERICAN PTG OF THE 20th CY

Paula Prendergast
Christine Sheeler
Iris Dove
Olivia deMuth
Edna Hopper
Jane Stuart Curry
Margie Hart Benton
Natalie Wood
Aqua Marin
Peggy Ann Glarner
Dusty O'Keeffe
Yoko Kuniyoshi
Jane Wyeth
April ? Gorky
Bridie Murphy Tomlin

AMERICAN PTG OF THE 20th CY (continued)

Midge Kline
"Woman" Yvonne de Kooning
Jackson "Miss" Pollock
Jayne Still
Lillian Rothko
Jasmin Johns
Jinx Rauschenberg
Violet Olitski
Stella Stella
Andorra Lichtenstein
Valery Warhol
Jeanne d'Arcangelo
Bobbie Zox
Lilly Poons
Amy Lowell Nesbitt
Azuma Bishop
Bella Button
Naomi Gottlieb
"Cookie" Thiebaud
Jules Freilicher
Happy Hofmann
Bobo Motherwell
Nelson Frankenthaler
Lorna Dine
Clarissa Rivers
"Hell" Blaine
George Hartigan
Knute Rockburne
Georgia Indiana
Loretta Youngerman

20th CY SCULPTURE

Virginia Maillol
Albertine Despiau
Lotte Lehmbruck
Ali Archipenko
Constance Brancusi
Yetta Epstein
Sofia Laurens
Mary Tyler Moore
Greta Gabo
Margo Pevsner
Twiggy Giacometti
Imogene Caro
Minnie Andre
Tammy Grooms
Twyla Arp
Woody Nevelson
Jackie Lipchitz
Connie Edna Flavin
Sandy Calder

EUROPEAN PTG SINCE 1945

Sunset Hockney
Ima Ubac
Kay Y. Vasarely
Joan Fontana

in turn, established the formula for his later, grander practice in which the dedications no longer function as signs for artistic themes but rather become performative enunciations of the making particular on which his systematic practice came to thrive.

It is not the case that all of Flavin's works are about sexuality or closeting or dissemblance or illusionism. These were the themes, however, of the protean years of his practice, and his negotiation of them freed him to accept difference and particularity and compelled him to assert the fundamental sameness and interchangeability of those units that produced that particularity. Conjoined with an engaged pattern of acts of naming, Flavin's practice produces an account of personhood that calls for openness and unforeclosed figurations. In his early statement about systematicity, Flavin said that his works "lack the look of history."[125] That is more than an art-historical assessment on his part. It is also a way of saying that his works are what they are – now. Once combined, the tubes are recognized as particular and as part of a system of sameness. Once dedicated, they become personalized. Another way of saying this is that Flavin's open system relishes the ways in which it can endlessly inaugurate a new particularity out of the endless interchangeability of his system. That inauguration is an embrace of newness. History does not determine. Each naming establishes particularity anew.

It is with this enjoyment of inauguration coupled with proper names that Flavin's practice speaks to and is illuminated by transgender experience and history. The names in Flavin's practice are themselves interchangeable, and there is no determining set of signs that foreclose which gendered names are applied to which works. Rather, they circulate. Once attached to a work, they inaugurate a valence of personhood for the work – not figured by it so much as proposed by it. They lack the look of history in order to inaugurate this personhood. That seems to me a good way to articulate and to espouse personhood and identity not as fixed but as successive and mutable. Transgender lives demand that successive states be embraced as valid and valuable, rather than relying on the past to be deterministic of potential and presence. There is no more replete sign of this in transgender communities, historically, than the adoption of a name for oneself. This is a performative auto-inauguration, and its force is shared with the performative dedications that Flavin gave to works that he asserted were open and interchangeable.

Flavin's system got away from him to create a wild and unpredictable system of naming in which the genders one might assume from his dedications rub up against his modular units that all demand to be seen as part

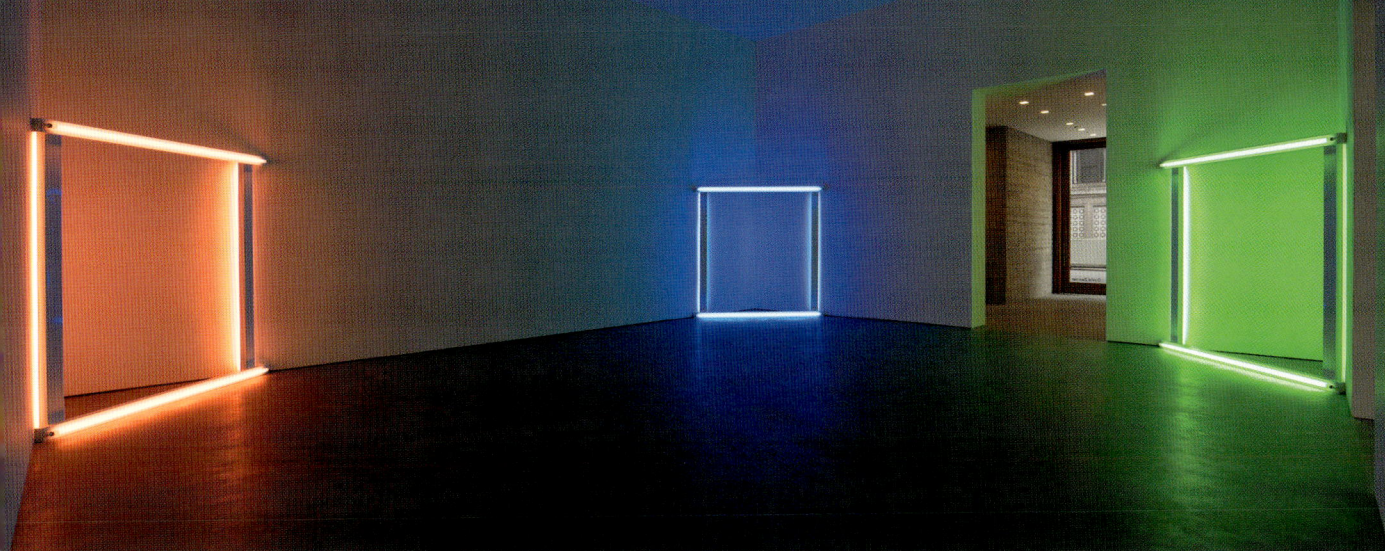

138 Dan Flavin, installation view of *European Couples*, David Zwirner Gallery, New York, 2013.

of his system of literalist sameness. Gonzalez-Torres reminds us how that nascent logic can be enhanced to make the interchangeable object even more deeply personal, but it was Flavin's struggle with visible difference and categorical sameness that compelled him to develop a practice that valued openness and particularity. He reiterated this in his retention of the act of dedication, allowing his works to open up to an account of personhood resonant with the politics and potentials of transgender history's critique of determinism. In this, Flavin's dedications are nothing to be embarrassed about.

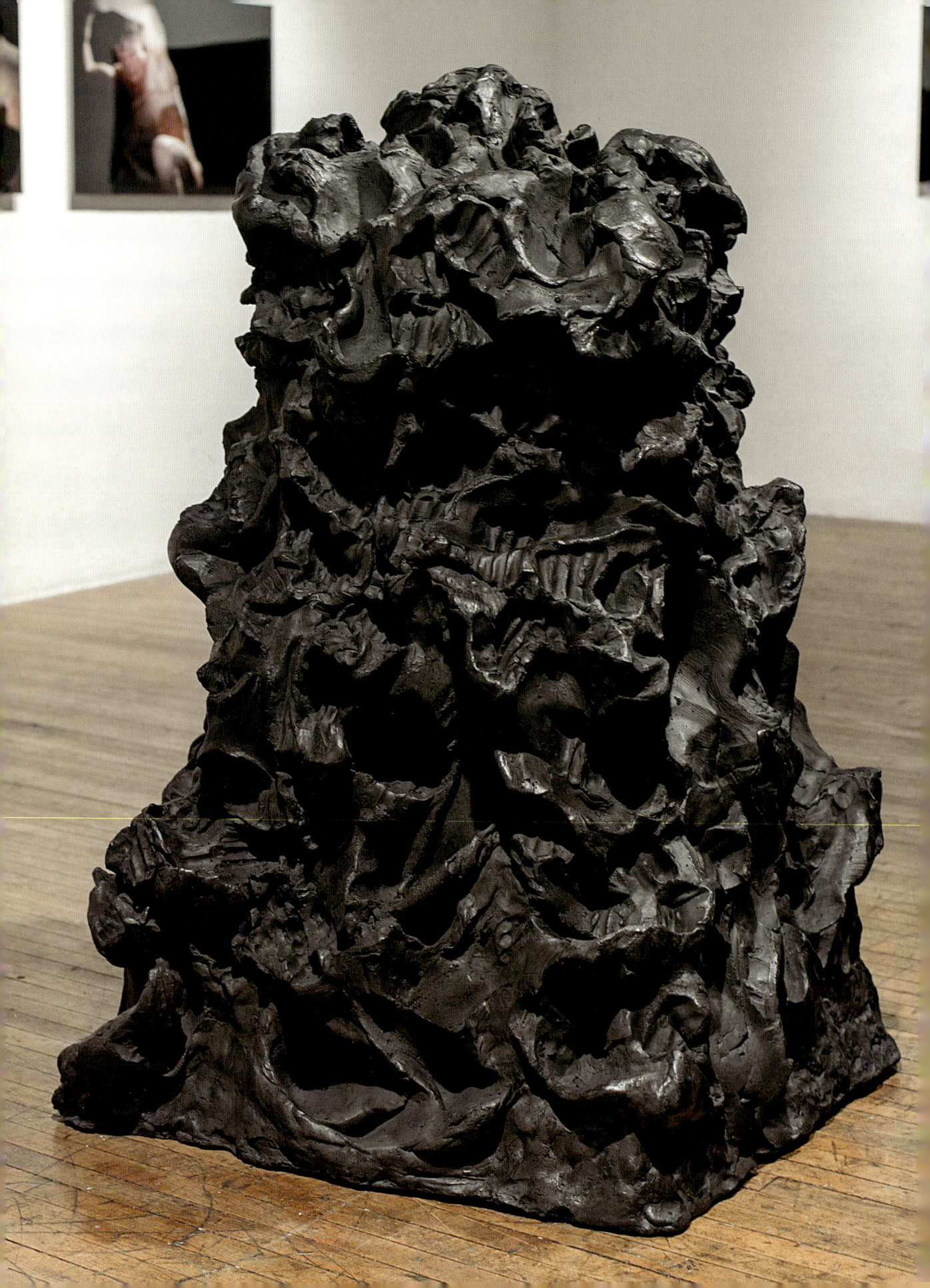

CONCLUSION
ABSTRACTION AND THE UNFORECLOSED

While my aim has been to examine the historical complexity of the practices of the artists in this study, my work has also been motivated by current concerns about gender and art (that themselves find the 1960s as a formative and generative precedent). Ultimately, this book's arguments are directed both at the historical record and at the current artists, critics, viewers, and historians who are grappling with questions of abstraction's usefulness, the politics of transformable personhood, and the recognition of the plurality of gendered inhabitations of the world. To recall Judith Butler's exhortation used in the Preface, my aim has been to offer one "new legitimating lexicon for the gender complexity that we have been living with for a long time."[1] I see abstraction as an especially rich mode through which particularity and difference can be made available, and the four main artists I discuss in this book present historical precedents to those who, more directly, seek to make semantic, cultural, and political space today. In the way of conclusion, I offer two examples of artists who drew on these issues and who speak to the possibilities that Sixties abstraction offered – one near to the time of writing and one immediately following the 1960s. These represent but two of the many and divergent ways in which tactics from abstraction were adapted and used to address more manifestly transgender politics and to call for the need for more pluralistic accounts of persons.

The first comes from the present decade and takes the form of an abstract, seemingly expressionist, sculpture. It appears as a rising mass, about four feet high, covered in indentations, gouges, and extrusions (fig. 139). The dark color of this mottled monolith, a graphite black, flows into the deep shadows created by a surface that is both volcanic and mountainous. Its footprint is regular and rectilinear, three feet wide (90 cm). Along its

OPPOSITE 139 Heather Cassils, *The Resilience of the 20%*, 2013. Poured black concrete cast of clay bash, 122 × 91.5 × 61 cm (48 × 36 × 24 in.).

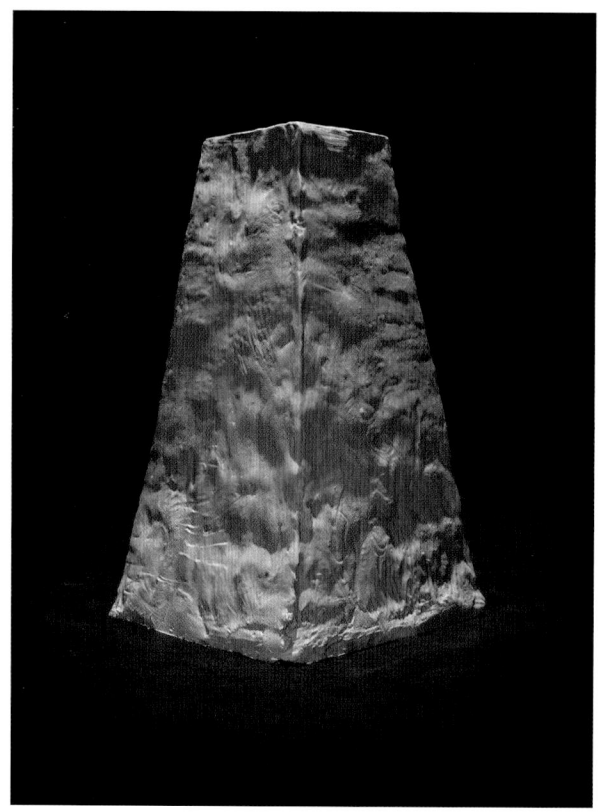
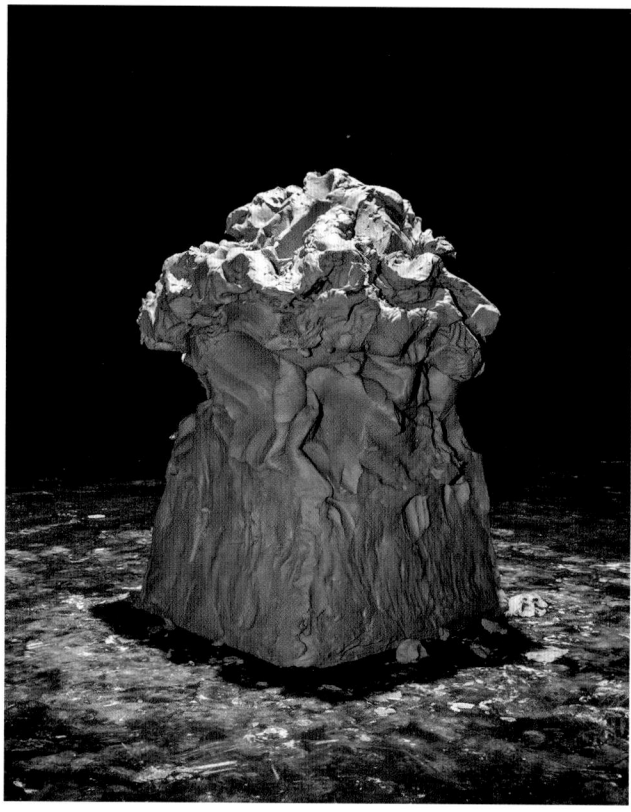

140 Heather Cassils, *Before* from the performance *Becoming an Image*, 2012–present. (This version: 35th Rhubarb Festival, Buddies in Bad Times Theatre, Toronto, 2014.) EM-217 (WED) modeling clay, 907 kg (2000 lbs), 129.5 × 91.4 × 91.4 cm (51 × 36 × 36 in.).

141 Heather Cassils, *After* from the performance *Becoming an Image*, 2012–present. (This version: 35th Rhubarb Festival, Buddies in Bad Times Theatre, Toronto, 2014.) EM-217 (WED) modeling clay, 907 kg (2000 lbs), 103.6 × 91.4 × 91.4 cm (40¼ × 36 × 36 in.).

height, one can see the increasing retreat from this base as the form tapers upward and inward. That retreat (or is it progress?) has been hard-won, and the gouges come into focus as deep impressions of knees, elbows, legs, fingers, and fists that pummeled the material into its present form.

This abstract sculpture by Heather Cassils, titled *The Resilience of the 20%*, is the result of an intensely physical process involving the transformation of the body and its confrontation with materiality. It is a concrete cast of an object created in relation to Cassils's performance *Becoming an Image* (2011 – present), a multi-stage work involving performance, photography, sound, and sculpture. The starting point for this sculpture and the performance was a particular body – Cassils's body – and its athletic exchanges with a rectilinear monolith made of 2000 pounds (some 909 kilos) of modeling clay. Cassils developed this performance in order to speak directly to issues of transgender politics, history, and experience. With this larger project in view, it becomes apparent that *The Resilience of the 20%* uses its final abstraction as a means to evoke the body but leave its visualization open and unforeclosed. It makes explicit the ways in which a non-representational sculptural object in all its physicality can offer a vehicle to realize transgender capacity.

Cassils, who has also competed as a semi-pro boxer, undergoes intense physical training and education for each performance. Much of Cassils's work involves the transformation of their body through athletics and bodybuilding, and they have previously made this a central component of their practice. This is clearest in the work *Cuts: A Traditional Sculpture* (2011). *Cuts* involved photographic documentation of a 23-week performance in which Cassils, through nutrition and training, added 23 pounds (10.4 kilos) of muscle.[2] This performance reinterpreted the canonical feminist work by Eleanor Antin, *Carving: A Traditional Sculpture* (1972), aiming instead at the transformation of the female-assigned body into a conventionally masculine form and ideal.

The somatic work to which Cassils commits is extended, highly considered, and in collaboration with expert trainers. The body serves as the raw material in these life performances, and it is the medium through which Cassils enacts transformation and transition. For *Becoming an Image*, a new kind of advanced training was necessary to ready their body for maximum effect. The modeling clay offered a great deal of resistance to the hits and kicks, and Cassils underwent combat conditioning in order most effectively and safely to prepare their body for the impact. Training with a Muay Thai master at the world-class Glendale Fight Club in Glendale, California, Cassils spent the months leading up to each performance of *Becoming an Image* involved in extensive planning and exercise in order to avoid injury. As they explained,

> I had to shed mass, as mass slows you down. I had to train towards explosive movement, precise form, aligning the skeleton in such a way that it prepares the bones and tendons for impact. I also had to train my heart and lungs to operate at over 170 beats per minute – serious cardiovascular training where I expand the size of both my heart and lungs to work at that capacity for the extended period of 20 to 25 minutes.[3]

Such hard-won reshaping and enhancement are directed at the specific needs for each new live performance, relying solely on intense physical training and nutrition to reorient the body. In this way, the act of sculpting begins with Cassils's own body, which must be remodeled and readied.

Cassils's training and transformation was more than bodily; it was also visual and perceptual. Performances of *Becoming an Image* happen in the dark (figs. 142 and 143). The scene of creation of the final form occurs during a performance in which both Cassils and the audience are together in complete darkness. Light only occurs with the photographer's flash as it documents Cassils's blind combat with the clay form. Visually disorienting for Cassils, the audience, and the photographer, the experience of the performance of 25 minutes is one of retinal burn and glimpses of Cassils's athleticism in an environment of darkness filled with the sounds of exertion. To achieve this performance, Cassils had to incorporate combat training with vertigo, spinning, and extrasensory combat. In addition to being as strong as possible, Cassils also had to establish new ways to deal with the environment.

Such visual disorientation produced by the collective experience of darkness and the flashes of illumination caused by attempts to document the struggle were both ways in which *Becoming an Image* thematized issues from transgender politics and history. The impetus for this work was a commission for a performance work by the ONE National Gay & Lesbian Archives in Los Angeles. To augment the 2011–12 exhibition series *Cruising the Archive: Queer Art and Culture in Los Angeles, 1945–1980*, the ONE Archives created the series "Trans Activation." Rather than draw on the contents of the archives, as others did, Cassils chose to address the omissions of transgender people and the difficulties faced with regard to documentation and archiving. Gay and lesbian communities have a conflicted history of subsuming or ignoring the differences of transgender experience. Consequently, any archive based in gay and lesbian community history will contain partial evidence of transgender history while at the same time appropriating it into narratives of sexual orientation. Cassils recognized that one could speak more strongly by producing a work that complicated the idea of documentation and that embodied transition.

In the *Becoming an Image* performances, the photographer is also blind and unable to frame (and consequently control) the documentary image. While Cassils's photographers have captured some striking pictures of Cassils's process, these were achieved through a struggle between photographer and subject that mirrored the exertion of Cassils's confrontation with the clay. The mastery and objectivity that underwrite the idea of documentation was made more reciprocal and unruly. In this way, the exemplary images that emerged from Cassils's performance remind viewers of their partiality

CONCLUSION 271

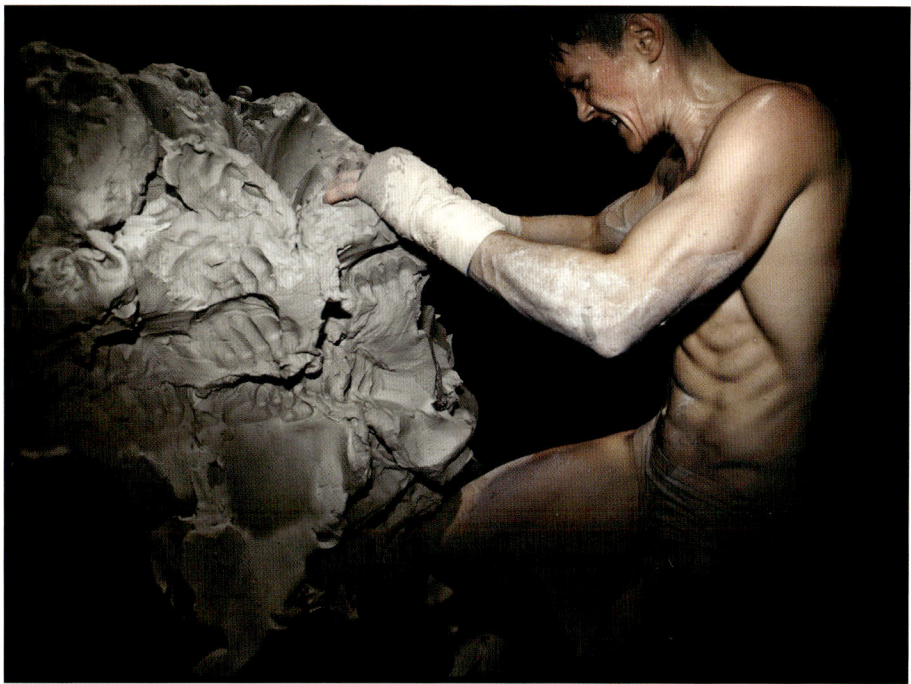

142 Heather Cassils, *Becoming an Image, Performance Still No. 5*, 2013, from the SPILL Festival, National Theatre Studio, London. C-print, 55.9 × 76.2 cm (22 × 30 in.).

and all that they did not capture. The experience of the audience was primarily one of darkness and sound, and their memories, too, were flashes that fade. In fact, because they were just looking and straining to perceive, their experience of the performance was fuller than that of the photographer who wrestled with the environment to make an image. Allegorizing the problem of trans archival presence, this performance both demanded attention to real-time presence (the communal experience of witnessing in the dark an extreme physical encounter) and recognition of the impossibility of adequately remembering that experience (only recorded in retinal burn and images that explicitly render a single moment of that extended encounter).

The resulting objects from the performance include the photographs, a sound installation made from a recording of the impacts between Cassils and the clay, and the hard-won final form of the sculptures. *Becoming an Image* has been performed a few times, and I illustrate documentation and sculptures from some of the different instances. The resulting sculptures are, by definition, unique though they all started from the same geometric

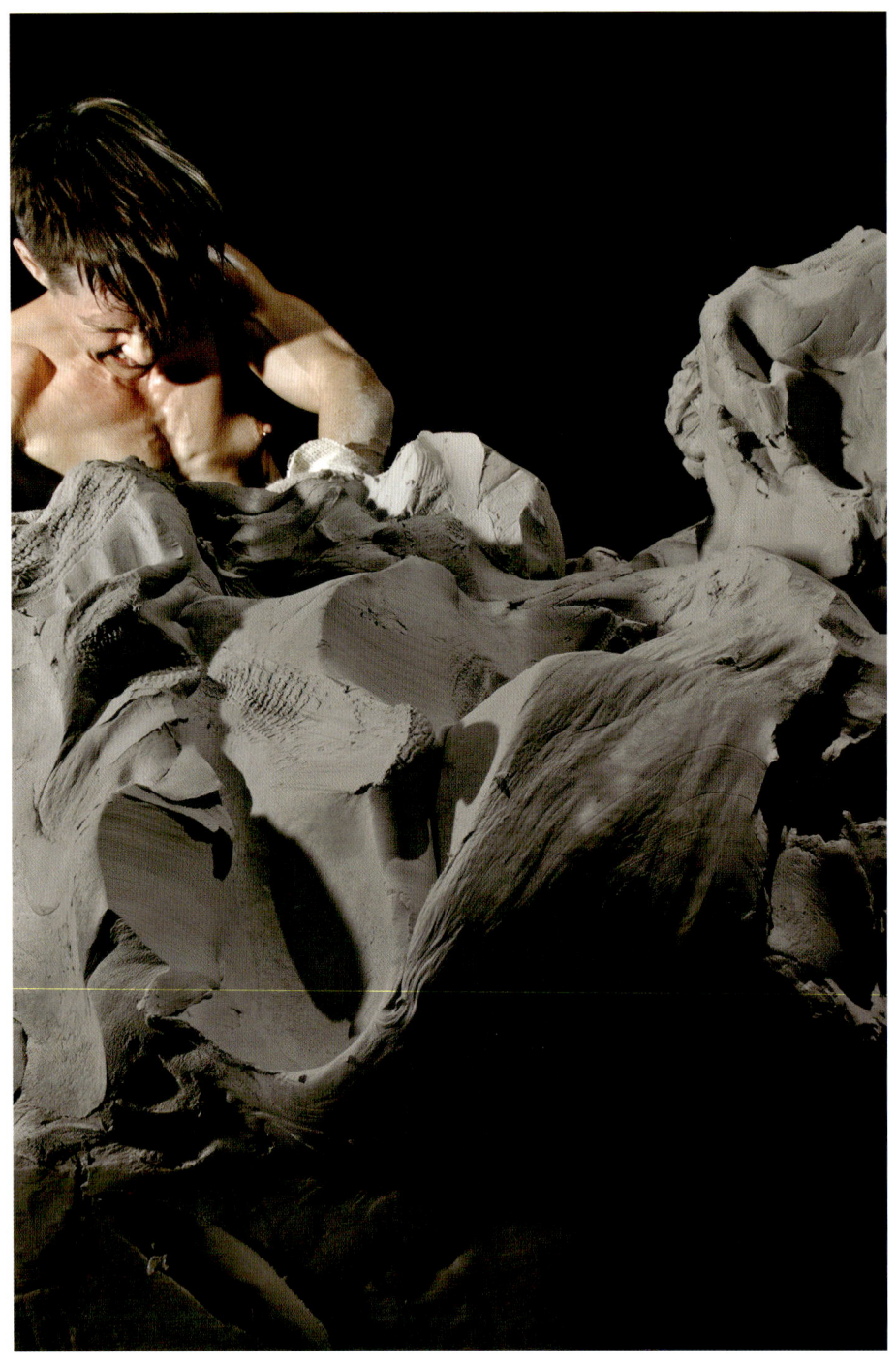

143 Heather Cassils, *Becoming an Image, Performance Still No. 2*, 2013, from Edgy Woman Festival, Montreal. C-print, 91.5 × 61 cm (36 × 24 in.).

form – which Cassils referred to once in conversation as "Juddian," thus signaling its citation of Minimalism's activation of bodily relations.[4]

The clay chosen by Cassils was EM-217 or WED Clay, which is used in the film industry for stop-motion animation and for making elaborate facial sculptures from which latex masks are cast. Named after the most famous of its adopters, Walter Edward Disney, it is now a favorite among special-effects artists who make unorthodox physiognomies, monsters, and new kinds of figures. Disney clay is dense and workable but it cannot be fired. Because of this, it will erode and vanish, and Cassils's resulting sculpture will transform itself as gravity works on its weight. The sculpture itself is thus ephemeral and always in process. This, too, evokes the body as a site of transformation, growth, and age. Not only does this form bear the evidence of work and effort. It also embeds transition into its material substance and into the process whereby the generic and geometric form was made unique, the history of change embedded in its surface.

Cassils's subsequent cast sculpture, *The Resilience of the 20%*, is a monument to this transformational and ephemeral clay sculpture, and it freezes it in a durable form. This secondary casting is a key part of traditional sculptural practice, and through it statues were made into a material that could stand outside as public monument and enduring figure. Auguste Rodin had, in the nineteenth century, made the capture (in bronze) of the fleeting marks of process a key sign for the presence of the artist as maker in works that were made through casting.[5] Cassils's decision to cast the sculpture in a durable form draws on these traditions of the statue, the monument, and Rodin's assertion of the sculptor's acts of making as central to modern sculpture. Furthermore, this object, cast in concrete, has had its surface worked over by Cassils in order to add more variation and transformation into the final form. Areas have been polished smooth and others made rougher.[6] Like the other stages of the work, it has been transformed as it moves into a new state.

The title of the concrete sculpture, *The Resilience of the 20%*, refers to the violence encountered by transgender communities. In 2012, the murders of transgender individuals increased worldwide by twenty percent, and Cassils offered this sculpture as a monument to those lost and as a testament to the hard-won process of becoming. While the title of the work as a whole is *Becoming an Image*, the final monument to the performance is resolutely abstract and offers no image. It refuses to image any one human form, instead allowing the transformations across its surface to call forth bodies no longer present. They are evoked by the partial evidence left. The refusal to image a single body is important, as it opens this monument up to larger accounts of transformation and resilience. This allows it to speak to the openness, determination, and mutability that are central to transgender experience without anchoring (and consequently limiting) that narrative in a single body. No one morphology could be offered as exemplary for all transgender lives. Cassils wrestled with the need to document and the problems of evidence, arriving at a work that refused to image the human form but evoked it as an object of work, transformation, and purpose. As an abstract monument, *The Resilience of the 20%* draws on transgender experience and politics while also standing as an allegory of self-determination and resolve.

Coming some five decades after the earliest sculptures discussed in this book, Cassils's work manifests aspects of the potential which I have been arguing that abstraction carries: its capacity to evoke bodily transformation, mutable genders, and successive states of personhood. Rooted in transgender politics and experience, this work expands on the capacities of abstraction and makes its openness with regard to genders and bodies manifest. While the contexts and issues are vastly different, nevertheless I see such work as Cassils's as being presaged by abstract sculpture's struggle with the bodily in the 1960s. What I have argued for David Smith, John Chamberlain, Nancy Grossman, and Dan Flavin is an account that draws from their own art-theoretical priorities but that nevertheless opens up possibilities that they could not have foreseen. During the decade in which the statuary tradition finally dissolved into the expanded field, these artists grappled with how the body must still be invoked by sculpture even if human morphologies could no longer be taken for granted.

Cassils offers a twenty-first century engagement with the transgender capacity of abstraction – one that is explicit in its politics. At a closer historical time to this book, another artist also developed the issues and tactics that made the 1960s so formative with regard to open accounts of gender. The performance artist, critic, and sculptor Scott Burton also absorbed and rejected ideas from 1960s sculpture to make a case for difference, particularity, and openness.[7] As with Cassils, his work helps to illuminate the stakes of the transgender capacity that Sixties abstraction exhibited. Whereas Cassils attacked a "Juddian" sculpture to transform it, Burton's critical engagement with Minimalism compelled him to develop a more demotic and accessible mode of practice. Consequently, he became one of the progenitors of public art, and it was in this drive towards accessibility and openness that Burton registered the potential of abstract sculpture.

Burton's sculptural practice involved making useful sculpture as furniture. Self-effacing and functional, this work appropriated Minimalist literalism and made it serve the viewer. At the same time, his sculptures are realist. They both are chairs and represent chairs – despite their obdurate "it is what it is" objecthood. For Burton, this work was created both in relation to the human body (in order to be functional) and in allusion to the human form. He once explained, "The human body is central to my work. A piece of furniture, even without the presence of a body, refers to human presence."[8] In this way, Burton created works that overcame the opposition between literalism and figuration.

Many of the furniture works made by Burton in the 1980s embrace their anthropomorphic valences as a means of catering to the bodies of their users. This offering, however, will have different coordinates and meanings based on the particularity of the person or persons who take a seat. Genders vary with each new coupling produced when a participant occupies the seat. Indeed, Burton later remarked about his works, "They take different poses and suggest different genders."[9] As his practice developed, he increasingly made more diverse and ambitious chair sculptures to be used. For his public works, he often relied on a highly geometric style so that the works could operate more anonymously in social spaces (fig. 144). In this way, they were more accessible and useful to the passerby – who may or may not have known that Burton's work was art (a possibility he embraced). Nevertheless, he explored much invention and variation in his seemingly simple chair sculptures. He explained this by saying: "Any chair is useful but a very striking looking chair, something that isn't like a usual chair, can make people perhaps more flexible in their attitudes to accept more things, to become more democratic about what a chair is. *They may even become more democratic about what a person is*. Art can be a moral example."[10] Burton's aim to make art as a moral example – to be *more democratic about what a person is* – derived from his engagement with abstraction's potential to visualize successive openness. His works are also abstract bodies. Indeed, their functionality relies on their successfully being open enough to relate to each subsequent sitter in a different and unique way. Even though most users of his works might have a preconceived notion of what a chair looks like, nevertheless they find themselves seated on something that equally finds a place for them. If participants can be prompted to ask more broadly what a chair is, what art could be, and how they can relate to it, then they might be, as Burton hoped, more open about how they defined persons.

Burton was an astute critic of the debates of 1960s art, and his work sought to draw from it just such an engaged and social version of abstract sculpture that manifested its capacity for more open accounts of personhood. That is, when he turned from a critic of 1960s abstraction to becom-

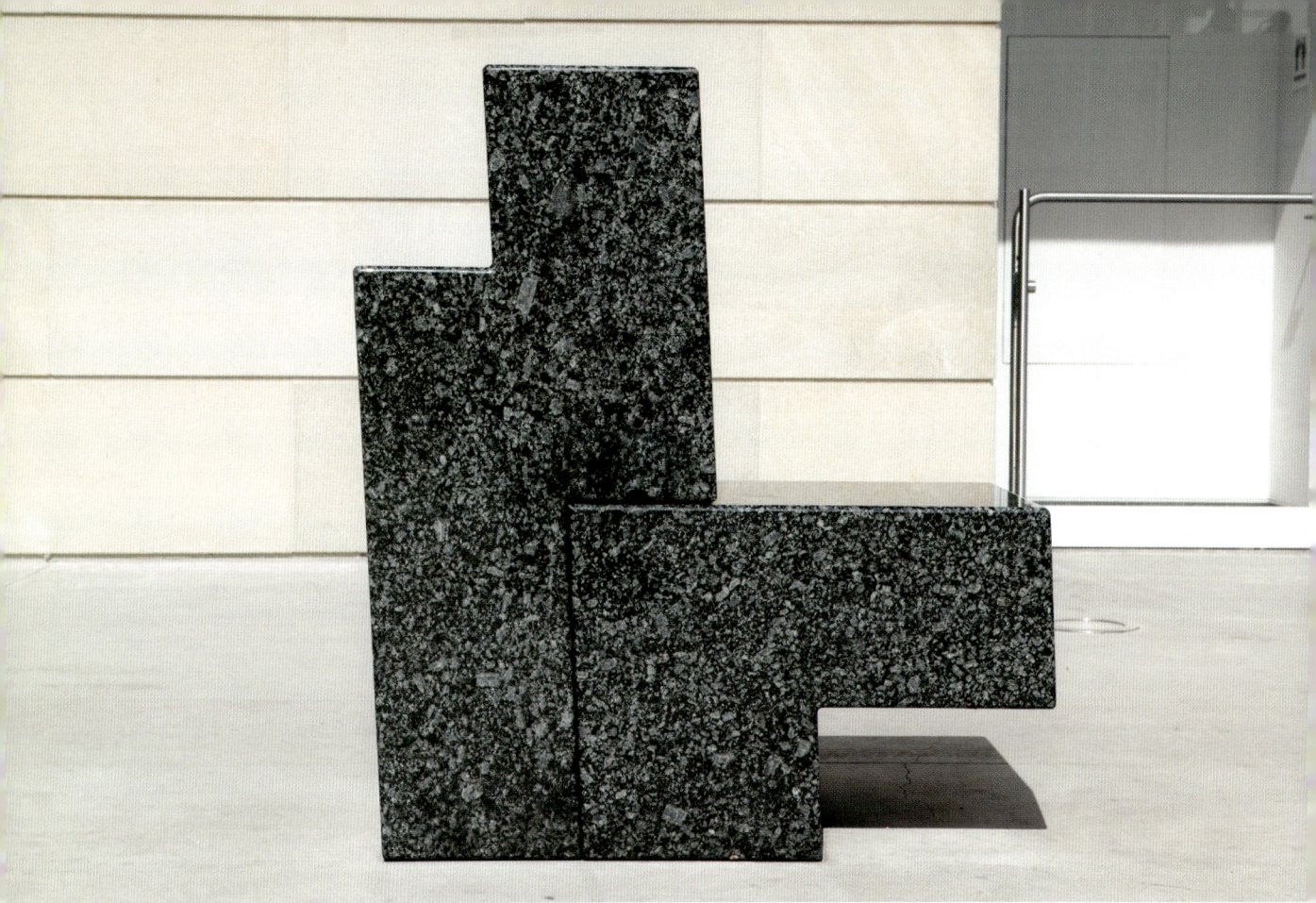

144 Scott Burton, *Two-part Chair*, 1986. Lake Superior Green Granite, 101.6 × 58.4 × 91.4 cm (40 × 23 × 36 in.). Installation view, Art Institute of Chicago.

ing a sculptor in the 1970s, he boldly sought to make work that demanded plural accounts of personhood. This same increasing embrace of expansiveness can be seen in such artists as Grossman, Chamberlain, and Flavin as they developed their work in the 1970s to afford more mobile and multiple ways in which bodily metaphors, names, and genders could be located in their practices. Their work, that is, proposed unforeclosed accounts of "what a person is."

THE UNFORECLOSED

As Cassils, Burton, and the artists discussed in this book suggest, abstraction has capacity. It is productive and proliferative. Rather than an avoidance of representation, it must be considered an embrace of potentiality and a positing of the unforeclosed.[11] Abstraction makes room. Because of this capaciousness, abstraction has emerged as urgent for a growing number of transgender and queer artists in recent years. It offers a position from which to imagine, recognize, or realize new possibilities.

In its earlier moments, abstraction was sometimes characterized as flight – a flight from representation, from narrative, from figuration, from the world, from the mundane, and from the recognizable. In these accounts, abstraction was cast as either distillation or enervation, ghosting the observable world of the everyday that it refuses. Abstraction's early defenders buttressed its flight by declaring its superiority over that which it rejects and purges, be that "literary" content, recognizable representation, or the decorative. That is, whether the argument was spiritual or conceptual, abstraction's "purification" was often defined negatively and oppositionally. Erasure and negation underwrote its rhetorics. Today, about a century beyond when abstraction became an option, such defenses of abstraction's negation ring increasingly hollow. Abstraction and figuration rub shoulders in contemporary art, and many younger artists simply do not understand (or care to understand) the antagonistic rhetoric of the twentieth century that cast them as mutually exclusive opponents. Rather than seeing abstraction as erasure, it appears to many as plenitude. Increasingly, what is called for are more accounts of abstraction that are positively defined, not negatively cast – accounts that ask how abstraction can perform and what it produces.

This is not to say that abstraction is not needful. Abstract art must be motivated by concerns outside of itself, and viewers and artists identify with and engage with abstraction because of the ways in which it spirals out to other associations and allusions. A primary way this happens is with the syntax created by the abstract work of art or practice. What, in other words, are the relations and patterns put forth by an abstract work? These can be internal, spatial, experiential, or otherwise, but the key question is how units establish relationality and organize themselves into iteration. While abstraction does sometimes have an iconography (x form stands for y idea/thing), most abstract artists would never rely on such easy routes as one-to-one symbolizations, decoder rings, map legends, or keys. Instead, investment is put into the relations, where priorities can be played out among forms and materials. Relations are meaningful, ethical, and political, and it is in its syntactical staging of relations that abstract art produces its engagements.

One of the most important of these relations is extrinsic: the embodied presence of the viewer who looks (or the artist who makes and also looks). Abstraction is produced in relation to the bodies of its beholders and creators. Everything has a scale, and we gauge scale through the proprioceptive knowledge of our own bodies and their particularity. Abstraction often accesses bodily scale and suggests memories of corporeal relations through its marshaling of non-depicting form and materials. This is especially the case with abstract sculpture, which even in its most rigorously minimal and unitary versions incites bodily response. In Michael Fried's infamous 1967 critique of Minimalism, he put forth an idea that has proven enduring and infectious when he criticized Tony Smith's *Die* (1962): "One way of describing what Smith was making might be something like a surrogate person – that is, a kind of *statue*."[12] This observation is newly relevant today as artists pursue geometric and reductive abstraction but direct it at bodily evocations and ethical relations. In particular, artists who identify their practice as transgender or queer use this capacity of abstraction to invoke the body without imaging it, offering the abstract form as a receptor to the viewer's own identifications and empathies.[13] Such a practice is generous, as it allows for each viewer to find their own analogies differently and anew. This is one of the lessons that the history of transgender experience teaches: to value mutability, to embrace successive states, and to cultivate both particularity and plurality.

Mobilized by transgender and queer priorities, abstraction has appeared to many today as newly compelling and capacious. It has come to be an important position from which to visualize the unforeclosed. It is for this reason that, in their shift from performance art to sculpture, abstraction became Cassils's mode for evoking the complexity, mutability, and variability of bodies and genders. It is also why Burton, in adapting and superseding Minimalism, played with objecthood to increase the ways in which viewers engaged with his work, in hopes that they would be "more democratic about what a person is."

Abstraction is not the only way to enact or to visualize transgender capacity, but I have attempted to show how it provides a historically rich enabling ground from which to rethink gender's multiplicity and mutability. In its retreat from resemblance and the conventional figure, abstraction offers a position from which to reconsider or to visualize anew the body and personhood. Art-historical debates about the status of the figure or explorations of the evocations of non-figuration both contribute to a history of human morphology's arbitrations and to transgender critique. Again, I have been emboldened by Butler's thinking in my recasting of abstraction in this way. As she has argued, "There is a certain departure from the human that takes place in order to start the process of remaking the human."[14] Abstraction is one such departure, and the artists discussed in this book used non-representational objects to evoke people and bodies in such a way that accounts of remaking and openness were produced.[15]

For the artists in the present study, this often involved the translation of non-representational artworks into words, and I have given weight to the words that were used by the artists themselves, by their critics, and by their viewers. In many ways, the capacity of these works to offer new accounts of the human becomes most immediately evident through the frictions and synergies created when language (especially a language based on a binary gendering) is applied to non-representational artworks. The correlation between abstract objects and the metaphors of the body, implications of sexual coupling, or personifying titles given by the artists all served to produce unruly and expansive capacities. A recurring pattern in the book has been the scene in which artists re-view their work in dialogic situations with others. Seeing the work through others' eyes prompts a reconsideration of the abstract sculpture's openness to multiple identifications. Most evident in the Smith–O'Hara interview, it was also key to Grossman's exchange with the art students and Chamberlain's with Henry Geldzahler. In none of these situations was there a correct way of seeing the works. Far more interesting are the ways in which the works facilitated plurality, prompting even the artists themselves to consider their own productions anew when they saw their abstractions as bodies or persons.[16] As Chamberlain once remarked, "art is the only place left where a person can go discover something and not have to be told by somebody else whether they discovered it or not."[17]

One of the central questions of this book has been how to visualize transformation and its potential. In other words, when we question the limitations of dimorphism or of binaries and when we recognize that personhood is not static, how do we look? The abstract, three-dimensional art object offers an arena in which to work out visualizations and imaginations of new morphologies and successive states. The particular mix of sculpture's physicality, the viewer's three-dimensional engagements, and the refusal to depict simply the human form combine to produce a field in which nominations of the human are dynamic, generative, ongoing, and plural. The collision of abstraction with metaphors of the body or personhood is proliferative, and the four artists discussed in this book each staged such an imbrication between non-reference or non-depiction and allusions to bodies and persons. From their own art-theoretical priorities and concerns, they created works that called for open and unlimited accounts of the body and of personhood. Gender, as the recurring predicate for nominating the human, played a central role in these accounts, and it is in tracking the successive states and plurality of genders that one can begin to grasp the expansiveness of their practices. The perspective of transgender politics and theory not only allows for a more precise articulation of the terms and implications of these artists' output. It also provides a key to understanding how these accounts and these artworks speak directly to broader concerns. From David Smith's anxious realization of his own success in pursuing abstraction's capaciousness to Dan Flavin's fidelity to personalization and naming, an analysis of these four artists also emphatically points to the ways in which we must revise the binary and dimorphic assumptions with which we have heretofore understood the history of figuration and abstraction, the Sixties emphasis on the bodily, and the ways in which the human is nominated.

NOTES

PREFACE

1 From the preface to Gregory Battcock, ed., *Minimal Art: A Critical Anthology* (New York: E. P. Dutton, 1968), 36. Emphases original.

2 Rosalind Krauss, "Sculpture in the Expanded Field," *October* 8 (Spring 1979): 30–44. See the Introduction for further discussion of this text.

3 While the previous decades had seen an increasing disentanglement of gender from a deterministic equation with the sexed body, developments in the 1950s and 1960s propelled it forward. Theories of researchers into intersex conditions such as those of John Money or Robert Stoller filtered from specialist to wider cultural discourses in that period, popularizing the idea of gender identity's multiple determinants. See Elisabeth Reis, *Bodies in Doubt: An American History of Intersex* (Baltimore: Johns Hopkins University Press, 2009); Joanne Meyerowitz, *How Sex Changed: A History of Transsexuality in the United States* (Cambridge, Mass: Harvard University Press, 2002).

4 The report that broke the news first was B. White, "Ex-GI Becomes Blonde Beauty: Operations Transform Bronx Youth," *New York Daily News*, 1 December 1952, 1.

5 "New Sex Switches," *People Today*, 5 May 1954. Clipping reproduced in Meyerowitz, *How Sex Changed*, pl. 8.

6 Harry Benjamin, *The Transsexual Phenomenon* (New York: Julian Press, 1966).

7 Thomas Buckley, "A Changing of Sex by Surgery Begun at Johns Hopkins," *New York Times*, 21 November 1966, 1ff; "A Change of Gender," *Newsweek*, 5 December 1966, 73; "Surgery: A Body to Match the Mind," *Time*, 2 December 1966, 52; "Sex-change Operations at a U.S. Hospital," *U.S. News & World Report*, 5 December 1966, 13; Thomas Buckley, "The Transsexual Operation," *Esquire* 67, no. 4 (April 1967): 111–15, 205–8.

8 While this is the first book-length study to draw extensively on transgender studies as a method for the discipline of art history, there is a growing number of essay-length interventions that have dealt with visual art from a transgender studies perspective, beginning with the formative arguments that can be found in indivdiual chapters in Jay Prosser, *Second Skins: The Body Narratives of Transsexuality* (New York: Columbia University Press, 1998) and J. Jack Halberstam, *In a Queer Time and Place: Transgender Bodies, Subcultural Lives* (New York University Press, 2005). In addition to these and other texts referenced throughout the endnotes to this book, some recent contributions to art-critical writing from a transgender studies perspective include Lucas Crawford, "Breaking Ground on a Theory of Transgender Architecture," *Seattle Journal for Social Justice* 8, no. 2 (May 2010): 515–39; Eva Hayward, "Spider City Sex," *Women & Performance* 20, no. 3 (November 2010): 225–51; Jeanne Vaccaro, "Felt Matters," *Women & Performance* 20, no. 3 (November 2010): 253–66; Gordon Hall, "Object Lessons:

Thinking Gender Variance Through Minimalist Sculpture," *Art Journal* 72, no. 4 (Winter 2013): 47–57; Lucas Crawford, "A Transgender Poetics of the High Line Park," *TSQ: Transgender Studies Quarterly* 1, no. 4 (November 2014): 482–500; Eliza Steinbock, "Generative Negatives: Del LaGrace Volcano's Herm Body Photographs," *TSQ: Transgender Studies Quarterly* 1, no. 4 (November 2014): 539–51.

9 Judith Butler, *Undoing Gender* (New York and London: Routledge, 2004), 11.

10 Susan Stryker discussed this non-consensual gendering that occurs to the infant, arguing that "A gendering violence is the founding condition of human subjectivity; having a gender is the tribal tattoo that makes one's personhood cognizable." Susan Stryker, "My Words to Victor Frankenstein Above the Village of Chamounix: Performing Transgender Rage," *GLQ* 1, no. 3 (1994): 250. The assignment of sex at birth has also been perhaps the central issue for intersex activism. See Reis, *Bodies in Doubt* for the American historical context and, further, Anne Fausto-Sterling, *Sexing the Body: Gender Politics and the Construction of Sexuality* (New York: Basic Books, 2000), 189–211; Cheryl Chase, "Hermaphrodites with Attitude: Mapping the Emergence of Intersex Political Activism," *GLQ* 4, no. 2 (1998: 189–211); Suzanne J. Kessler, *Lessons from the Intersexed* (New Brunswick, N.J: Rutgers University Press, 1998); Katrina Alicia Karkazis, *Fixing Sex: Intersex, Medical Authority, and Lived Experience* (Durham, N.C: Duke University Press, 2008); Sharon E. Preves, *Intersex and Identity: The Contested Self* (New Brunswick, N.J: Rutgers University Press, 2003).

11 For a concise picture of the range of the interdisciplinary critique afforded by transgender studies, see Susan Stryker and Stephen Whittle, eds., *The Transgender Studies Reader* (New York and London: Routledge, 2006) and Susan Stryker and Aren Aizura, eds., *The Transgender Studies Reader 2* (New York: Routledge, 2013).

12 Viviane K. Namaste, *Invisible Lives: The Erasure of Transsexual and Transgendered People* (Chicago and London: University of Chicago Press, 2000), 1.

13 One of the foundational (and widely influential) texts for this usage was a groundbreaking pamphlet by Leslie Feinberg, reprinted as "Transgender Liberation: A Movement Whose Time Has Come" (1992), in Stryker and Whittle, *Transgender Studies Reader*, 205–20. For further discussion of the term "transgender" and its parameters and development, see the Introduction. Useful histories of the term can be found in David Valentine, *Imagining Transgender: An Ethnography of a Category* (Durham, N.C. and London: Duke University Press, 2007) and Susan Stryker, *Transgender History* (Berkeley, Calif: Seal Press, 2008). See also T. Benjamin Singer, "Umbrella," *TSQ: Transgender Studies Quarterly* 1, no. 1–2 (2014): 259–61.

14 Stryker, *Transgender History*, 1.

15 In this, the history of science has played a crucial role. For a recent overview of the relationship among biology, psychology, and social context in the diversity of lived genders, see Anne Fausto-Sterling, *Sex/Gender: Biology in a Social World* (New York: Routledge, 2012). See also the groundbreaking Joan Roughgarden, *Evolution's Rainbow: Diversity, Gender, and Sexuality in Nature and People* (Berkeley: University of California Press, 2004) and Rebecca M. Jordan-Young, *Brain Storm: The Flaws in the Science of Sex Differences* (Cambridge, Mass: Harvard University Press, 2010). For a wide-ranging argument about the biopolitical history of gender as a product of the "pharmacopornographic sex-gender regime," see [Paul] B. Preciado, *Testo Junkie: Sex, Drugs, and Biopolitics in the Pharmacopornographic Era*, trans. Bruce Benderson (New York: Feminist Press, 2013), esp. pp. 99–129. An important theorization of both gender and sex in relation to norms can be found in Judith Butler, *Bodies That Matter: On the Discursive Limits of "Sex"* (New York and London: Routledge, 1993).

16 As the authors of a survey of incidents of intersex traits noted, "Biologists and medical scientists recognize, of course, that absolute dimorphism is a Platonic ideal not actually achieved in the natural world....If one relinquishes an a priori belief in complete genital dimorphism, one can examine sexual development with an eye toward variability rather than bimodality." They concluded that there were one to two intersex infants in every 1000 births. Melanie Blackless et al., "How Sexually Dimorphic Are We? Review and Synthesis," *American Journal of Human Biology* 12 (2000): 151. See also Roughgarden, *Evolution's Rainbow*; Jordan-Young, *Brain Storm*; Fausto-Sterling, *Sex/Gender*.

17 Preciado, *Testo Junkie*, 103–4.

18 Stryker, *Transgender History*, 59–89.

19 Michel Foucault once challenged his readers to take seriously the disruptions that non-ascribed genders presented for conventional understandings, criticizing those who tolerated but did not feel implicated by nonconforming genders and bodies. Decrying their underlying faith in the idea of a "true sex," a natural order, and the politics of mere toleration, he argued: "It is also agreed, though with much difficulty, that it is possible for an individual to adopt a sex that is not biologically his own. Nevertheless, the idea that one must indeed finally have a true sex is far from being completely dispelled....We are certainly more tolerant in regard to practices that break the law. But we continue to think that some of these are insulting to 'the truth': we may be prepared to admit that a 'passive' man, a 'virile' woman, people of the same sex who love one another, do not seriously impair the established order; but we are ready enough to believe that there is something like an 'error' involved in what they do. An 'error' as understood in the most traditionally philosophical sense: a manner of acting that is not adequate to reality. Sexual irregularity is seen as belonging more or less to the realm of chimeras. That is why we rid ourselves easily enough of the idea that these are crimes, but less easily of the suspicion that they are fictions which, whether involuntary or self-indulgent, are useless, and which it would be better to dispel." Gender nonconformity is part of what Foucault terms "sexual irregularity" in his text and it is still often received as a useless "fiction," grudgingly tolerated but not seen to be of general or broad importance. By contrast, I see these issues as central and defining. They allow for new evidentiary accounts of gender's mutability and plurality to be recognized, and they engender reinvigorated accounts of the continued relevance of artistic practices that take bodies or persons as analogues. See Michel Foucault, "Introduction," in *Herculine Barbin: Being the Recently Discovered Memoirs of a Nineteenth-century French Hermaphrodite*, trans. Richard McDougall (New York: Vintage Books, 1980), x.

20 Donald Judd, "Local History" (1964), in *Donald Judd: Complete Writings 1959–1975* (Halifax: Press of the Nova Scotia College of Art and Design, 1975), 152–3.

21 Butler, *Undoing Gender*, 51.

INTRODUCTION: "NEW" GENDERS AND SCULPTURE IN THE 1960S

1 J. Jack Halberstam, *In a Queer Time and Place: Transgender Bodies, Subcultural Lives* (New York: New York University Press, 2005), 97–124.

2 Eve Kosofsky Sedgwick, *Touching Feeling: Affect, Pedagogy, Performativity* (Durham, N.C. and London: Duke University Press, 2003), 150–1.

3 Relief sculpture presents a special case and is best understood as intermedial in its hybridity of three- and two-dimensional systems of representation. It partakes of both actual volume and pictorial depictions of depth. I discuss this further in David Getsy, "Playing in the Sand with Picasso: Relief Sculpture as Game in the Summer of 1930," in *From Diversion to Subversion: Games, Play,*

and Twentieth-century Art, ed. David Getsy (University Park: Pennsylvania State University Press, 2011), 80–93. With regard to the present analysis, assemblage reliefs (such as Grossman's) share many of the same general conditions of freestanding sculpture due to their appropriation of found objects, all of which invoke questions of their past functionality and bodily scale.

4 While there are of course exceptions to this general tendency (such as with the distinct medium of relief sculpture in which architectural and landscape spaces are more readily able to be depicted), the generalization holds true that sculpture has had a primary association with the (often singular) figure. This carries through to *animalier* sculpture, which, though providing an alternative to the representation of the human form, nevertheless often shares the parameters of the discrete freestanding figure. For a useful overview of the predominance of the human form in European and American sculpture, see Ruth Butler, *Western Sculpture: Definitions of Man* (Boston: New York Graphic Society, 1975). Also of interest in this regard is Rudolf Wittkower, *Sculpture: Processes and Principles* (London: Allen Lane, 1977).

5 A detailed history of the modern sculpture that attends to the effects of the spatial and temporal encounter between viewers and sculptural objects can be found in Alex Potts, *The Sculptural Imagination: Figurative, Modernist, Minimalist* (New Haven and London: Yale University Press, 2000). See also Penelope Curtis, *Sculpture 1900–1945: After Rodin* (Oxford University Press, 1999); Penelope Curtis, "After Rodin: The Problem of the Statue in Twentieth-century Sculpture," in *Rodin: The Zola of Sculpture*, ed. Claudine Mitchell (Farnham: Ashgate, 2004).

6 Frances Colpitt, *Minimal Art: The Critical Perspective* (Ann Arbor, Mich: UMI Research Press, 1990), 66.

7 Rosalind Krauss, *Passages in Modern Sculpture* (Cambridge, Mass: MIT Press, 1977).

8 Or, as Henry Geldzahler declared, "But another way of the thinking of the sixties is that perhaps the best work that was done in that decade in America was done by David Smith in the last five years of his life and by Hans Hofmann in the last five years of his life." Henry Geldzahler, "The Sixties: As They Were" (1991), in *Making It New: Essays, Interviews, and Talks* (New York: Turtle Point Press, 1994), 339.

9 A central concern in my own work on the origins and history of modern sculpture has been negotiations of sculpture as both image and object. This relationship between materiality and either representational or abstract modes of sculpture underwrote competing formulations and genealogies of modern sculpture. I offer two different versions of this dynamic – one invested in verisimilitude and the other in its abandonment or subordination – in my two books on the origins of modern sculpture in Britain and in France: David Getsy, *Body Doubles: Sculpture in Britain, 1877–1905* (New Haven and London: Yale University Press, 2004); *Rodin: Sex and the Making of Modern Sculpture* (New Haven and London: Yale University Press, 2010).

10 Lucy Lippard, "As Painting is to Sculpture: A Changing Ratio," in *American Sculpture of the Sixties*, ed. Maurice Tuchman (Los Angeles County Museum of Art, 1967), 32. Emphasis original.

11 Krauss, *Passages*, 279.

12 Lawrence Alloway, "Sculpture as Cliché," *Artforum* 2, no. 4 (October 1963): 26.

13 Ibid.

14 Colpitt provides a useful overview of the debates around anthropomorphism in Minimalist criticism in Colpitt, *Minimal Art*, 67–73. For her, anthropomorphism is strictly defined as mimetic of the human form, and she distinguishes this from "presence" and bodily evocations made through scale. She does, however, chronicle other understandings of the anthropomorphic in her overview.

15 James Meyer, "Anthropomorphism," *Art Bulletin* 94, no. 1 (March 2012): 24.

16 In Oldenburg's case, his avoidance of figural representation permitted viewers to explore their bodily associations with his soft sculpture. Judd, in 1964, devoted a third of his review of Oldenburg's exhibition at the Sidney Janis Gallery, New York, to sorting out how it was that a giant soft light switch made him think of female breasts. He concluded that "Real anthropomorphism is subverted by the grossly anthropomorphic shapes, man-made, not shapes of natural things or people." Donald Judd, "In the Galleries: Claes Oldenburg" (1964), in *Donald Judd: Complete Writings 1959–1975* (Halifax and New York: Press of the Nova Scotia College of Art and Design and New York University Press, 1975), 133. For discussion, see the chapter "Gross Anthropomorphism: Claes Oldenburg" in Jo Applin, *Eccentric Objects: Rethinking Sculpture in 1960s America* (New Haven and London: Yale University Press, 2012), 43–62 as well as Potts, *Sculptural Imagination*, 276–9.

17 Michael Fried, "Art and Objecthood," *Artforum* 5, no. 10 (June 1967): 12–23. For essential commentary on this much discussed text, see James Meyer, "The Writing of 'Art and Objecthood,'" in *Refracting Vision: Essays on the Writings of Michael Fried*, ed. Jill Beaulieu, Mary Roberts, and Toni Ross (Sydney: Power Institute, 2000), 61–96; Potts, *Sculptural Imagination*, 178–206.

18 Fried, "Art and Objecthood," 16. Emphases original.

19 Ibid., 19.

20 In his pivotal 1960 essay "Modernist Painting," Greenberg set up the "sculptural" as the metaphor for all that painting should expunge: pictorial illusionism, figuration, and three-dimensionality. Clement Greenberg, "Modernist Painting" (1960), in *Clement Greenberg: The Collected Essays and Criticism*, ed. John O'Brian, 4 vols (University of Chicago Press, 1993), 4: 88.

21 Fried, "Art and Objecthood," 19.

22 Colpitt, *Minimal Art*, 72.

23 Meyer, "Anthropomorphism," 25.

24 Michael Fried, "Introduction," in *Anthony Caro* (London: Arts Council and the Hayward Gallery, 1969), 9. I am grateful to James Meyer for alerting me to this underappreciated text.

25 Jack Burnham, "On Being Sculpture," *Artforum* 7, no. 9 (May 1969): 44–5. Emphasis original.

26 Briony Fer, *The Infinite Line: Re-making Art After Modernism* (New Haven and London: Yale University Press, 2004), 106.

27 Robert Morris, "Notes on Sculpture, Part I," *Artforum* 4, no. 6 (February 1966): 42–4; "Notes on Sculpture, Part 2," *Artforum* 5, no. 2 (October 1966): 20–3; "Notes on Sculpture, Part III: Notes and Nonsequiturs," *Artforum* 5, no. 10 (Summer 1967): 24–9.

28 Robert Morris, "Notes on Sculpture, Part IV: Beyond Objects," *Artforum* 7, no. 8 (April 1969): 51.

29 Ibid.

30 Lucy Lippard, "Eccentric Abstraction," *Art International* 10, no. 9 (20 November 1966): 28, 34–40.

31 Lucy Lippard, "Eros Presumptive," *Hudson Review* 20, no. 1 (Spring 1967): 91–9; "Eros Presumptive," rev. in *Minimal Art: A Critical Anthology*, ed. Gregory Battcock (New York: E. P. Dutton, 1968), 209–21.

32 Anne Middleton Wagner, "Reading Minimal Art," in *Minimal Art: A Critical Anthology*, ed. Gregory Battcock (Berkeley: University of California Press, 1995), 13.

33 Lippard, "Eros Presumptive," (1967), 94.

34 Ibid., 96. For commentary (and for one of the few extended discussions of "Eros Presumptive"), see Margo Hobbs Thompson, "Agreeable Objects and Angry Paintings: 'Female Imagery' in Art by Hannah Wilke and Louise Fishman, 1970–1973," *Genders* 43 (2006): n.p. See also Rachel Middleman, "Rethinking Vaginal Iconology with

Hannah Wilke's Sculpture," *Art Journal* 72, no. 4 (2013): 34–45.

35   Lippard, "Eros Presumptive," (1967), 91.

36   Lippard, "Eccentric Abstraction," 28.

37   Ibid., 34.

38   Ibid., 39.

39   Of the many discussions of Lippard's text, the primary ones that have informed my thinking are Fer, *Infinite Line*, 101–15; Anne Middleton Wagner, *Three Artists (Three Women): Modernism and the Art of Hesse, Krasner, and O'Keeffe* (Berkeley: University of California Press, 1996); Briony Fer, *On Abstract Art* (New Haven and London: Yale University Press, 1997), 109–30; James Meyer, "Non, Nothing, Everything: Eva Hesse's 'Abstraction,'" in *Eva Hesse*, ed. Elisabeth Sussman (San Francisco Museum of Modern Art, 2002), 57–77; and Applin, *Eccentric Objects*, 7–12. Although it does not discuss the 1960s essays in detail, the insightful essay by Laura Cottingham, "Shifting Ground: On the Critical Practice of Lucy Lippard," in *Seeing through the Seventies: Essays on Feminism and Art* (Amsterdam: G and B Arts, 2000), 1–46, has proven especially helpful. See also Julia Bryan-Wilson, *Art Workers: Radical Practice in the Vietnam War Era* (Berkeley: University of California Press, 2009), 127–71; Judy K. Collischan Van Wagner, *Women Shaping Art: Profiles of Power* (New York: Praeger Publishers, 1984), 99–114.

40   Lucy Lippard, "The Women's Art Movement—What's Next" (1975), in *The Pink Glass Swan: Selected Essays on Feminist Art* (New York: New Press, 1995), 83.

41   Fer, *Infinite Line*, 104–5.

42   Lippard, "Eccentric Abstraction," 40.

43   Lucy Lippard, "Eccentric Abstraction," rev. in *Changing: Essays in Art Criticism* (New York: E. P. Dutton, 1971), 99.

44   Robert Pincus-Witten, "Eva Hesse: More Light on the Transition from Post-minimalism to the Sublime," in *Eva Hesse: A Memorial Exhibition*, ed. Linda Shearer (New York: Solomon R. Guggenheim Museum, 1972), n.p.

45   "Postminimalism" was a retrospective term dubbed by Robert Pincus-Witten in his writings as a good enough catch-all that registered the proliferation of practices and attitudes toward the sculptural object's permanence that began in the late 1960s. See Robert Pincus-Witten, *Postminimalism* (New York: Out of London Press, 1977).

46   The now classic argument about Minimalism's pivotal importance is that of Hal Foster, "The Crux of Minimalism" (1986), in *The Return of the Real* (Cambridge, Mass: MIT Press, 1996), 35–68. See also Rosalind Krauss, "The Cultural Logic of the Late Capitalist Museum," *October* 54 (Fall 1990): 3–17; Hal Foster, "Dan Flavin and the Catastrophe of Minimalism," in *Dan Flavin: New Light*, ed. Jeffrey Weiss (New Haven and London: Yale University Press, 2006), 133–51. These historical views of Minimalism compellingly account for the paradigm shift it signaled, but it was the moves in "Beyond Objects" that seemed, finally, to alter fundamentally the medium of sculpture. This impact of Postminimalism was chronicled in detail in Richard Armstrong and Richard Marshall, eds., *The New Sculpture 1965–1975: Between Geometry and Gesture* (New York: Whitney Museum of American Art, 1990) and is the "after" in Richard J. Williams, *After Modern Sculpture: Art in the United States and Europe, 1965–70* (Manchester University Press, 2000). This marking of a shift is also registered in Lucy R. Lippard, *Six Years: The Dematerialization of the Art Object from 1966 to 1972* (New York: Praeger, 1973).

47   See discussion in e.g. Whitney Chadwick, "Balancing Acts: Reflections on Postminimalism and Gender in the 1970s," in *More Than Minimal: Feminism and Abstraction in the '70s*, ed. Susan L. Stoops (Waltham, Mass: Rose Art Museum, Brandeis University, 1996), 14–25.

48   Recently, Jo Applin's engaging book on Sixties sculpture, *Eccentric Objects*, has taken on some of Lippard's central examples as a means of reconsidering the centrality of Minimalism in the literature on the decade.

49 Of particular use from the extensive literature on these artists have been Anne Middleton Wagner, "Bourgeois Fantasy," in *A House Divided: American Art since 1955* (Berkeley: University of California Press, 2012), 158–82; Mignon Nixon, *Fantastic Reality: Louise Bourgeois and a Story of Modern Art* (Cambridge, Mass: MIT Press, 2005); Potts, *Sculptural Imagination*; Wagner, *Three Artists*.

50 See Josef Helfenstein, *Louise Bourgeois: The Early Work* (Champaign, Ill: Krannert Art Museum, 2002); Ann Gibson, "Louise Bourgeois's Retroactive Politics of Gender," *Art Journal* 53, no. 4 (Winter 1994): 44–7; Mignon Nixon, "'Fantastic Reality': A Note on Louise Bourgeois's *Portrait of C.Y.*," *Sculpture Journal* 5 (2001): 83–9; Nixon, *Fantastic Reality*, 119–63.

51 The implications of this period have been well studied by Mignon Nixon; see e.g. "Bad Enough Mother," *October* 102 (1995): 71–92; "Posing the Phallus," *October* 92 (Spring 2000): 96–127; *Fantastic Reality*, 209–65; "o+x," *October* 119 (2007): 6–20. More broadly, see Helen Molesworth, ed., *Part Object Part Sculpture* (Columbus, Ohio: Wexner Center for the Arts and Pennsylvania State University Press, 2005).

52 Halberstam, *In a Queer Time*, 117.

53 Ibid., 119.

54 Meyer, "Non, Nothing, Everything," 66.

55 For instance, a useful analysis of the organizing example of Bourgeois for feminist art history was offered by Katy Deepwell, "Feminist Readings of Louise Bourgeois or Why Louise Bourgeois is a Feminist Icon," *n.paradoxa* 3 (May 1997): 28–38.

56 Some of that decade's analyses of masculinity in art history produced valuable critiques, e.g. Anna C. Chave, "Minimalism and the Rhetoric of Power," *Arts Magazine* 64, no. 5 (1990): 44–63; Michael Leja, *Reframing Abstract Expressionism: Subjectivity and Painting in the 1940s* (New Haven and London: Yale University Press, 1993), 546–84; Amelia Jones, "Dis/playing the Phallus: Male Artists Perform Their Masculinities," *Art History* 17, no. 4 (December 1994): 546–84; Michael Leja, "Barnet Newman's Solo Tango," *Critical Inquiry* 21, no. 3 (Spring 1995): 556–80; Andrew Perchuk, "Pollock and Postwar Masculinity," in *The Masculine Masquerade: Masculinity and Representation*, ed. Andrew Perchuk and Helaine Posner (Cambridge, Mass: MIT List Visual Arts Center, 1995), 31–42; Caroline Jones, *Machine in the Studio: Constructing the Postwar American Artist* (University of Chicago Press, 1996); Ann Eden Gibson, *Abstract Expressionism: Other Politics* (New Haven and London: Yale University Press, 1997); Terry Smith, ed., *In Visible Touch: Modernism and Masculinity* (University of Chicago Press, 1997); and, for a reprise of these questions in the next decade, Marcia Brennan, *Modernism's Masculine Subjects: Matisse, the New York School, and Post-painterly Abstraction* (Cambridge, Mass: MIT Press, 2004).

57 Halberstam, *In a Queer Time*, 121.

58 Harry Benjamin, *The Transsexual Phenomenon* (New York: Julian Press, 1966), plates. On the hermaphrodite in ancient art, see the useful survey in Aileen Ajootian, "The Only Happy Couple: Hermaphrodites and Gender," in *Naked Truths: Women, Sexuality, and Gender in Classical Art and Archaeology*, ed. Ann Olga Koloski-Ostrow and Claire L. Lyons (London and New York: Routledge, 1997), 220–42.

59 This case about Symbolism is made in the important book by Patricia Mathews, *Passionate Discontent: Creativity, Gender, and French Symbolist Art* (University of Chicago Press, 1999). Other useful discussions of androgyny can be found in Anna Chave, *Constantin Brancusi: Shifting the Bases of Art* (New Haven and London: Yale University Press, 1993); Maud Lavin, *Cut with the Kitchen Knife: The Weimar Photomontages of Hannah Höch* (New Haven and London: Yale University Press, 1993); Susan Fillin-Yeh, "Dandies, Marginality, and Modernism: Georgia O'Keeffe, Marcel Duchamp, and Other Cross-dressers," *Oxford Art*

Journal 18, no. 2 (1995): 33–44; Caroline Jones, "The Sex of the Machine: Mechanomorphic Art, New Women, and Francis Picabia's Neurasthenic Cure," in *Picturing Science, Producing Art*, ed. Caroline Jones and Peter Galison (New York and London: Routledge, 1998), 145–80; Lanier Graham, "Duchamp & Androgyny: The Concept and its Context," *Tout-fait* 2, no. 4 (January 2002): n.p. For a longer view, see also Catriona MacLeod, *Embodying Ambiguity: Androgyny and Aesthetics from Winckelmann to Keller* (Detroit: Wayne State University Press, 1998).

60 See e.g. Amelia Jones, *Postmodernism and the En-gendering of Marcel Duchamp* (Cambridge University Press, 1994); Paul B. Franklin, "Object Choice: Marcel Duchamp's *Fountain* and the Art of Queer Art History," *Oxford Art Journal* 23, no. 1 (2000): 23–50; Helen Molesworth, "Rrose Sélavy Goes Shopping," in *The Dada Seminars*, ed. Leah Dickerman and Matthew Witkovsky (Washington, D.C: Center for Advanced Study in the Visual Arts, National Gallery of Art, 2005), 173–89; David Hopkins, *Dada's Boys: Masculinity after Duchamp* (New Haven and London: Yale University Press, 2007); Deborah Johnson, "Marcel Duchamp, Rrose Sélavy, and Gender Performativity," *International Journal of the Arts in Society* 1, no. 7 (2007): 191–200; Deborah Johnson, "R(r)ose Sélavy as Man Ray: Reconsidering the Alter Ego of Marcel Duchamp," *Art Journal* 72, no. 1 (September 2013): 80–94. A related argument about Duchamp's play with the constructed nature of gender can be found in the useful article by Edward Powers, "Fasten Your Seatbelts as We Prepare for Our *Nude Descending*," *Tout-fait* 2, no. 5 (April 2003): n.p.

61 Chave, *Constantin Brancusi*, 123.

62 The following anecdote from the photographer David Finn about Henry Moore is telling: "The only time Henry acknowledged to me any sexual aspect of one of his sculptures was when I asked him about *Draped Reclining Figure*. It had a skirt around its lower part which showed that it was a female, but coming out of the groin there was what seemed to be an erect phallus. He wasn't happy about the question, but after a moment's pause he did admit rather softly that the figure was 'androgynous.'" David Finn, *One Man's Henry Moore* (Redding Ridge, Conn: Black Swan Books, 1993), 43. For further on gender in Moore and Hepworth, see Anne Middleton Wagner, *Mother Stone: The Vitality of Modern British Sculpture* (New Haven and London: Yale University Press, 2005). On the context of public sculpture and postwar internationalism, see Margaret Garlake, *New Art New World: British Art in Postwar Society* (New Haven and London: Yale University Press, 1998); Christopher Pearson, "Hepworth, Moore and the United Nations: Modern Art and the Ideology of Post-war Internationalism," *Sculpture Journal* 6 (2001): 89–99.

63 See Clare Elliott and Robert Gober, *Forrest Bess: Seeing Things Invisible* (New Haven and London: Yale University Press and the Menil Collection, 2013); Chuck Smith, *Forrest Bess: Key to the Riddle* (Brooklyn, N.Y: powerHouse Books, 2013). For further discussion of the artistic contexts for Bess's work and its reception, see Gregory Tentler, "Painting in a Different Kind of Void," *Studies in Gender and Sexuality* 14, no. 3 (2013): 230–4.

64 Robert Stoller, *Sex and Gender: On the Development of Masculinity and Femininity* (New York: Science House, 1968), 129. Bess had corresponded with Money from 1962 to 1974. Money detailed Bess's case a few years later in John Money and Michael De Priest, "Three Cases of Genital Self-surgery and their Relationship to Transsexualism," *Journal of Sex Research* 12, no. 4 (November 1976): 283–94. Robert Gober has discussed Bess's relationship to Money in Elliott and Gober, *Forrest Bess*, 91, 98.

65 This was a main theme of de Henriquez's work, as discussed in Jan Marsh, *Art & Androgyny: The Life of Sculptor, Fiore de Henriquez* (London: Elliott & Thompson, 2004); for just one of many occurrences of this quotation, see p. 97.

66 Ibid., 151. Here, de Henriquez is also registering the gendered discourse that had sprung from Auguste Rodin's titanic influence as the reputed "father" of modern sculpture. This attitude about modern sculpture as a solely masculine endeavor was common among European and American sculptors in the early part of the twentieth century. For those artists who worked in the traditional sculptural materials of clay and bronze, especially, such limiting characterizations lasted well into the 1960s. I discuss the roots of this formulation of the gendered and sexualized role for the modern sculptor in the conclusion to Getsy, *Rodin*, 173–93.

67 Eva Hesse, from a diary entry of 18 March 1965, quoted in Lucy Lippard, *Eva Hesse* (New York: Da Capo Press, 1976), 34.

68 Oldenburg quoted in Achim Hochdörfer, Maartje Oldenburg, and Barbara Schröder, eds., *Claes Oldenburg: Writing on the Side 1956–1969* (New York: Museum of Modern Art, 2013), 317.

69 Frank O'Hara, "Hermaphrodite," 1st pub. in *Folder* 3 (1955), repr. in Donald Allen, ed. *The Collected Poems of Frank O'Hara* (Berkeley: University of California Press, 1995), 218.

70 Lynda Benglis quoted in Franck Gautherot, Caroline Hancock, and Seungduk Kim, eds., *Lynda Benglis* (Dijon, France: Presses du Réel and the Irish Museum of Modern Art, Dublin, 2009), 171.

71 Louise Bourgeois quoted in *New York Magazine*, 11 February 1974.

72 Jackie Curtis quoted in Raymond Macrino, "Jackie Curtis: The Victory Isn't Vain," *Herald: The Manhattan News and Entertainment Weekly*, 6 June 1971, s.2, 5. I am thankful to Joseph Madura for sharing this reference with me.

73 See e.g. Stuart Byron, "Reactionaries in Radical Drag," *Village Voice*, 16 March 1972, 69.

74 More broadly, see the survey of gender nonconformity in late twentieth-century art provided in Frank Wagner, Kasper König, and Julia Friedrich, eds., *Das achte Feld: Geschlechter, Leben und Begehren in der Kunst seit 1960* (Ostfildern: Hatje Cantz and Museum Ludwig, Cologne, 2006).

75 On transfeminism, see e.g. Gayle Salamon, *Assuming a Body: Transgender and Rhetorics of Materiality* (New York: Columbia University Press, 2010), 95–128.

76 J. Jack Halberstam, *Female Masculinity* (Durham, N.C. and London: Duke University Press, 1998). On this point, see also Gayle Rubin, "Of Catamites and Kings: Reflections on Butch, Gender, and Boundaries" (1992), in *Deviations: A Gayle Rubin Reader* (Durham, N.C: Duke University Press, 2011), 241–53.

77 Elisabeth Reis, *Bodies in Doubt: An American History of Intersex* (Baltimore: Johns Hopkins University Press, 2009).

78 Joanne Meyerowitz, *How Sex Changed: A History of Transsexuality in the United States* (Cambridge, Mass: Harvard University Press, 2002).

79 [Paul] B. Preciado, *Testo Junkie: Sex, Drugs, and Biopolitics in the Pharmacopornographic Era*, trans. Bruce Benderson (New York: The Feminist Press, 2013).

80 This point was made in hir manifesto; Leslie Feinberg, "Transgender Liberation: A Movement Whose Time Has Come" (1992), in *The Transgender Studies Reader*, ed. Susan Stryker and Stephen Whittle (New York and London: Routledge, 2006), 205–20 and then expanded in Leslie Feinberg, *Transgender Warriors: Making History from Joan of Arc to Dennis Rodman* (Boston: Beacon Press, 1997).

81 Susan Stryker, *Transgender History* (Berkeley, Calif: Seal Press, 2008); Susan Stryker, "Why the T in LGBT is Here to Stay," *Salon.com* (11 October 2007), online at www.salon.com/2007/-10/11/transgender_2/ (accessed 26 February 2014).

82 This is a component of all the narratives just cited. Other significant discussions of this co-option of transgender by gay and lesbian histories can be found in Michel Foucault, "Intro-

duction," in *Herculine Barbin: Being the Recently Discovered Memoirs of a Nineteenth-century French Hermaphrodite* (New York: Vintage Books, 1980), vii–xvii; Viviane K. Namaste, *Invisible Lives: The Erasure of Transsexual and Transgendered People* (Chicago and London: University of Chicago Press, 2000); Julian Carter, "On Mother-love: History, Queer Theory, and Nonlesbian Identity," *Journal of the History of Sexuality* 14, no. 1/2 (January 2005): 107–38; Feinberg, *Transgender Warriors*; David Valentine, *Imagining Transgender: An Ethnography of a Category* (Durham, N.C. and London: Duke University Press, 2007).

83 A guiding historiographic and theoretical intervention for me has been Viviane K. Namaste, "The Use and Abuse of Queer Tropes: Metaphor and Catachresis in Queer Theory and Politics," *Social Semiotics* 9, no. 2 (1999): 213–34. An influential founding statement of the rejection of queer theory's appropriation was offered in Jay Prosser, *Second Skins: The Body Narratives of Transsexuality* (New York: Columbia University Press, 1998). See also Viviane K. Namaste, "Tragic Misreadings: Queer Theory's Erasure of Transgender Subjectivity," in *Queer Studies: A Lesbian, Gay, Bisexual, and Transgender Anthology*, ed. Brett Beemyn and Mickey Eliason (New York: New York University Press, 1996), 183–203; Namaste, *Invisible Lives*; Susan Stryker, "Transgender Studies: Queer Theory's Evil Twin," *GLQ* 10, no. 2 (2004): 212–15; Viviane K. Namaste, *Sex Change, Social Change: Reflections on Identity, Institutions, and Imperialism* (Toronto: Women's Press, 2005); Susan Stryker, "(De)Subjugated Knowledges: An Introduction to Transgender Studies," in *The Transgender Studies Reader*, ed. Susan Stryker and Stephen Whittle (New York and London: Routledge, 2006), 1–17. A key point in the early discussions was Judith Butler's work (or, more accurately, the misapplications of Butler's work by her followers). Butler responded to these criticisms in *Bodies That Matter: On the Discursive Limits of "Sex"* (New York and London: Routledge, 1993) and, most productively, in *Undoing Gender* (New York and London: Routledge, 2004). See further the discussion in Cressida Heyes, "Feminist Solidarity After Queer Theory: The Case of Transgender," *Signs* 28, no. 4 (Summer 2003): 1093–120; Viviane K. Namaste, "Undoing Theory: The 'Transgender Question' and the Epistemic Violence of Anglo-American Feminist Theory," *Hypatia* 24, no. 3 (Summer 2009): 11–32; Salamon, *Assuming a Body*, 95–128; J. Jack Halberstam, *The Queer Art of Failure* (Durham, N.C. and London: Duke University Press, 2011); Robyn Wiegman, *Object Lessons* (Durham, N.C: Duke University Press, 2012), 301–43.

84 Stryker, *Transgender History*, 47.

85 Meyerowitz, *How Sex Changed*, 197.

86 Lynda Crawford, "Men Become Women: A Charm School for Transsexuals," *Soho Weekly News*, 16 October 1975, 11.

87 Hubert Selby Jr., *Last Exit to Brooklyn* (New York: Grove Press, 1964); Gore Vidal, *Myra Breckinridge* (New York: Little, Brown & Co., 1968).

88 Harry Benjamin, "Transvestism and Transsexualism," *International Journal of Sexology* 7, no. 1 (August 1953): 12–14.

89 Most notably, John Money, Joan Hampson, and John Hampson, "Imprinting and the Establishment of Gender Role," *Archives of Neurology and Psychiatry* 77 (1957): 333–6.

90 Hedy Jo Star, *"I Changed My Sex"* (Chicago: Novel Books, 1963).

91 On Erickson, see Aaron H. Devor and Nicholas Matte, "One Inc. and Reed Erickson: The Uneasy Collaboration of Gay and Trans Activism, 1964–2003," *GLQ* 10, no. 2 (2004): 179–209.

92 Harry Benjamin, *The Transsexual Phenomenon* (New York: Julian Press, 1966).

93 Thomas Buckley, "A Changing of Sex by Surgery Begun at Johns Hopkins," *New York Times*, 21 November 1966, 1ff; "Surgery: A Body to Match the Mind," *Time*, 2 December 1966, 52;

"A Change of Gender," *Newsweek*, 5 December 1966, 73; "Sex-change Operations at a U.S. Hospital," *U.S. News & World Report*, 5 December 1966, 13.

94 Christine Jorgensen, *A Personal Autobiography* (New York: Paul S. Eriksson, 1967).

95 Susan Stryker, "Introduction," in *Christine Jorgensen: A Personal Autobiography* (San Francisco: Cleis Press, 2000), ix.

96 Thomas Buckley, "The Transsexual Operation," *Esquire* 67, no. 4 (April 1967): 111–15, 205–8.

97 Stoller, *Sex and Gender* (1968). That same year, the term was also the focus of an article by Harry Gershman, "The Evolution of Gender Identity," *American Journal of Psychoanalysis* 28 (1968): 80–90.

98 Esther Newton, *Mother Camp: Female Impersonators in America*, Phoenix ed. (University of Chicago Press, 1979).

99 Richard Green and John Money, eds., *Transsexualism and Sex Reassignment* (Baltimore: Johns Hopkins University Press, 1969).

100 See Leslie Feinberg, "Street Transvestite Action Revolutionaries," *Workers World*, 24 September 2006. See also the recent collection of archival documents by the collective Untorelli Press, *Street Transvestite Action Revolutionaries: Survival, Revolt, and Queer Antagonist Struggle* (Bloomington, Ind. Untorelli Press, 2013). Some of these documents had previously been collected by Reina Gossett; see http://thespiritwas.tumblr.com/post/45275076521/on-untorellis-new-book (accessed 20 April 2014).

101 Stryker, *Transgender History*, 89.

102 This was infamously enacted in the castigation of the transsexual lesbian singer Beth Elliott by a keynote speaker, Robin Morgan, at the 1973 West Coast Lesbian Feminist Conference; ibid., 103–5. A critique of transphobia in feminism became central to the foundational texts for transgender studies, most notably by Sandy Stone in her 1987 "Posttransseuxal Manifesto," which was a direct refutation of Janice Raymond's polemic against transsexuals in her *The Transsexual Empire: The Making of the She-male* (Boston: Beacon Press, 1979). Stone's text went through a series of revisions and republications, but see Sandy Stone, "The *Empire* Strikes Back: A Posttranssexual Manifesto," rev. in Stryker and Whittle, *Transgender Studies Reader*, 221–35. It remains one of the most important texts within transgender studies, and its message continues to be relevant as a retort to the transphobia that is still evident in some recent feminist writing (e.g. Sheila Jeffreys). A critique of transphobia in feminism is also important in the highly influential article by Susan Stryker, "My Words to Victor Frankenstein Above the Village of Chamounix: Performing Transgender Rage," *GLQ* 1, no. 3 (1994): 237–54. For further discussion, see also Feinberg, "Transgender Liberation," 205–20; Heyes, "Feminist Solidarity After Queer Theory," 1093–120. Overviews of the recent debates in this area can be found in Susan Stryker, "Transgender History, Homonormativity, and Disciplinarity," *Radical History Review* 100 (Winter 2008): 145–57; Namaste, "Undoing Theory," 11–32; Patricia Elliot, *Debates in Transgender, Queer, and Feminist Theory: Contested Sites* (Farnham: Ashgate, 2010); Salamon, *Assuming a Body*, 95–128; Raewyn Connell, "Transsexual Women and Feminist Thought: Toward New Understanding and New Politics," *Signs* 37, no. 4 (Summer 2012): 857–81.

103 In addition to the sources cited on feminism's resistance to transgender, see further on "border" disputes among female masculinities in Halberstam, *Female Masculinity*, 141–73; Jacob Hale, "Consuming the Living, Dis(re)membering the Dead in the Butch/Ftm Borderlands," *GLQ* 4, no. 2 (1998): 311–48; Rubin, "Of Catamites and Kings," 241–53; Henry Rubin, *Self-made Men: Identity and Embodiment among Transsexual Men* (Nashville, Tenn: Vanderbilt University Press, 2003).

104 Butler, *Undoing Gender*, 51.

105 Grossman also listed *Myra Breckinridge* as

one of a short list of decade-defining events to an interviewer in Alessandra Codinha, "Working Deep Beneath the Think," *Intermission* 8 (2013): 67.

106   Valentine's account of this is particularly useful; Valentine, *Imagining Transgender*. While not widespread, variations on the term "transgender" did circulate in the 1960s and 1970s. As Valentine notes (261 n. 1), in 1969, *Transvestia* magazine (no. 60) used the term "transgenderal." Cristan Williams has also noted a 1965 usage of the term in John Oliven, *Sexual Hygiene and Pathology: A Manual for the Physician and the Professions*, 2nd ed. (Philadelphia: Lippincott, 1965), 514; www.cristanwilliams.com/b/2012/03/27/tracking-transgender-the-historical-truth/#34 (accessed 22 April 2014).

107   See Feinberg, "Transgender Liberation," 205–20 and discussion in Stryker, "Transgender History, Homonormativity, and Disciplinarity," 146.

108   Stryker, *Transgender History*, 1.

109   See e.g. the early critique of transgender for its effects on the category of transsexual in Prosser, *Second Skins*, 171–205. A recent discussion of the usefulness and limitations of such inclusive categories can be found in T. Benjamin Singer, "Umbrella," *TSQ: Transgender Studies Quarterly* 1, no. 1–2 (2014): 259–61.

110   Stryker, *Transgender History*, 24.

111   Halberstam, *Female Masculinity*, 52–3.

112   Ibid., 162.

113   Salamon, *Assuming a Body*, 95.

114   See the discussion in e.g. Susan Stryker, Paisley Currah, and Lisa Jean Moore, "Introduction: Trans-, Trans, or Transgender?" *WSQ: Women's Studies Quarterly* 36, no. 3–4 (Fall/Winter 2008): 11–22; Trystan Cotten, ed., *Transgender Migrations: The Bodies, Borders, and Politics of Transition* (New York: Routledge, 2011); Susan Stryker, "Biopolitics," *TSQ: Transgender Studies Quarterly* 1, no. 1–2 (2014): 38–42; special issue of *TSQ: Transgender Studies Quarterly* 1, no. 3 (2014) on "Decolonizing the Transgender Imaginary." A revision of biopolitical analysis from a transgender perspective can be found in Preciado, *Testo Junkie*.

115   The core of this section was initially published as David Getsy, "Capacity," *TSQ: Transgender Studies Quarterly* 1, no. 1–2 (2014): 47–9.

116   Again, the concept of "perverse presentism" proposed in Halberstam, *Female Masculinity*, 50–9, offers a defining methodological position on addressing this issue for historical writing.

117   Butler, *Undoing Gender*, 4.

118   While arguing against uncritical and unhistorical acceptance of this distinction as empirical fact, he nevertheless notes that this model has facilitated both politics and cultural theory; David Valentine, "The Categories Themselves," *GLQ* 10, no. 2 (2003): 215–20.

119   Stryker, "Transgender History, Homonormativity, and Disciplinarity," esp. 147–9.

120   As Stryker warned, "all too often *queer* remains a code word for 'gay' or 'lesbian,' and all too often transgender phenomena are misapprehended through a lens that privileges sexual orientation and sexual identity as the primary means of differing from heteronormativity"; Stryker, "Transgender Studies: Queer Theory's Evil Twin," 214. Namaste had earlier asked, "How could we develop a queer politics which presupposes transsexual bodies, but which benevolently accommodates lesbian and gay subject positions?" Namaste, "Use and Abuse of Queer Tropes," 217. Her subsequent book performs a damning critique of queer theory as it was practiced in the 1990s, rightly arguing that its formations did not attend to economic and social conditions in which transgender lives are embedded; Namaste, *Invisible Lives*, 22: "Despite their insistence on the productive nature of power, they do not demonstrate how drag queens or transgendered people of color are produced in different institutional, social, economic, and historical settings. And because they do not offer this type of analysis, they ignore the role their own theories play in creating transgendered people as an object of academic discourse." Namaste's argument was that the specificity and

complexity of transgender lives were erased in these theories, turning them solely into figures for transgression and into theoretical (not political or actual) subjects. Much of the most important subsequent queer theory has been at pains to address this injustice (as with Butler's *Undoing Gender*). See also the history of political activism in Stryker, "Transgender History, Homonormativity, and Disciplinarity," 145–57.

121 Salamon, *Assuming a Body*, 127.

122 Stryker, "Biopolitics," 39; see also Preciado, *Testo Junkie*, esp. pp. 23–54.

123 See Rosalind Krauss, "Sculpture in the Expanded Field," *October* 8 (Spring 1979): 30–44.

124 Krauss's proposition for an expanded field was set in opposition to what she saw as the debased form of historicism that had determined art criticism and history at the time. In particular, it was the teleological explanation of phenomena (new or old) through recourse to a continuous genealogy that the structuralist notion of the expanded field was to supplant as a hermeneutic device. Lurking behind historicism, for Krauss, was Greenberg's Hegelian account of medium specificity. In an essay published concurrently with the expanded field essay, Krauss was even more unforgiving about the limitations of historicism: "Historicism is our intellectual milieu. It affects the way we think and how we act – morally, politically, esthetically. And it must also be seen as a strategic operation, one that works on the strange to make it familiar. Given, say, an ancient civilization, one whose social structures and cultural artifacts are different from our own, historicism acts to construct a developmental model by which the early forms can be seen as the embryonic versions of later ones, which inevitably achieve 'maturity' in the forms of our own time.…This drive to historicize, which amounts to a loathing of the different, is what defines us as an audience for art. And it is that very thing which separates us most profoundly now, in the present, from its makers. For artists, whether they wish it or not, have become the residents of the land of the strange"; Rosalind Krauss, "John Mason and Post-modernist Sculpture: New Experiences, New Words," *Art in America* 67, no. 3 (May–June 1979): 120–1. Krauss developed the model of the expanded field both to recast the medium through a set of its structural coordinates (rather than a lineage) and to offer a more adequate way of accounting for artists for whom medium was no longer a relevant or useful mode of characterizing their practice. Ironically, it is for these two reasons that Krauss's essay has subsequently been seen as the one of the most appropriate and useful of historical descriptions of the previous decade and a half. As she says in the conclusion to the Mason essay (127), "I have been insisting that the expanded field of post-modernism occurs at a specific moment in the recent history of art." Further accounts of Krauss's text, its intentions, and its legacies are discussed in the recently published *Retracing the Expanded Field: Encounters between Art and Architecture*, ed. Spyros Papapetros and Julian Rose (Cambridge, Mass: MIT Press, 2014). Surprisingly, none of the contributors mention the Mason essay despite its informative relation to the *October* article of the same year with which it shares concerns and terms.

125 Eve Meltzer, *Systems We Have Loved: Conceptual Art, Affect, and the Antihumanist Turn* (University of Chicago Press, 2013), 119–36.

126 Krauss, "John Mason and Post-modernist Sculpture," 125.

127 Butler, *Undoing Gender*, 29.

1 ON NOT MAKING BOYS: DAVID SMITH, FRANK O'HARA, AND GENDER ASSIGNMENT

1 David Smith, interview with Frank O'Hara, *The Sculpting Master of Bolton Landing*, aired on WNDT New York, 11 November and repeated 13

November 1964. Recording held in the Department of Film, Museum of Modern Art, New York (hereafter "*Sculpting Master*"). My quotations are taken from the recording itself. In transcribing from the recording, I have been assisted by comparison with the transcript of the program prepared by the Solomon R. Guggenheim Museum for its 2006 exhibition *David Smith: A Centennial*, supplied by the Estate of David Smith, as well as with the original voiceover script for the televised program (Frank O'Hara Papers, Museum of Modern Art Archives, box 4, folder 24).

2   For a useful example of Smith's statements about the inadequacy of words, see e.g. David Smith, "The Language Is Image" (1952) and "The Artist's Image" (1954) in *David Smith*, ed. Garnett McCoy (London: Allen Lane, 1973), 79–81 and 113–16 respectively. For context on Abstract Expressionism and language, see Ann Gibson, "Abstract Expressionism's Evasion of Language," *Art Journal* 47, no. 3 (1988): 208–14.

3   Notable examples of the treatment of this comment, as it was published in 1966, are Rosalind Krauss, *Terminal Iron Works: The Sculpture of David Smith* (Cambridge, Mass: MIT Press, 1971), 93; Candida Smith, *The Fields of David Smith* (New York: Thames and Hudson, 1999), 25; Alex Potts, *The Sculptural Imagination: Figurative, Modernist, Minimalist* (New Haven and London: Yale University Press, 2000), 176.

4   *Art in America* 54, no. 1 (1966).

5   For discussion, see Alex Potts, "Personages: Imperfect and Persistent," in *David Smith: Personage* (New York: Gagosian Gallery, 2006), 7–19.

6   This is part of one of the most often quoted of Smith's statements, which continues: "Rather I would prefer my assemblages to be the savage idols of basic patterns, the veiled directives, subconscious associations, the *image recall* of orders more true than the object itself, resulting in vision, in aura, rather than object reality." David Smith, "Perception and Reality" (1951), in *David Smith*, 78. Emphases original.

7   Potts has perspicaciously discussed the complexity of Smith's image-making in a number of texts; see esp. "Sign," in *Critical Terms for Art History*, ed. R. Nelson and R. Schiff (University of Chicago Press, 1996), 17–30; *Sculptural Imagination*, 158–77; "Abstraction and Image Making in David Smith's Sculpture," in *David Smith: Cubes and Anarchy*, ed. Carol Eliel (Los Angeles County Museum of Art, 2011), 117–41.

8   Jane Gallop, *Anecdotal Theory* (Durham, N.C. and London: Duke University Press, 2002).

9   Brad Gooch, *City Poet: The Life and Times of Frank O'Hara* (New York: Alfred A. Knopf, 1993), 452–3.

10 See e.g. Charles Molesworth, "'The Clear Architecture of the Nerves': The Poetry of Frank O'Hara," *Iowa Review* 6 (Summer/Fall 1975): 61–74, with regard to the Whitman connection and, for O'Hara as postmodernist, see Bruce Boone, "Gay Language as Political Praxis: The Poetry of Frank O'Hara," *Social Text* 1 (Winter 1979): 59–92; Charles Altieri, *Enlarging the Temple: New Directions in American Poetry during the 1960s* (Lewisburg, Penn: Bucknell University Press, 1979), 78–127; Gregory Bredbeck, "B/O – Barthes's Text/O'Hara's Trick," *PMLA* 108, no. 2 (1993): 268–82; Hazel Smith, *Hyperscapes in the Poetry of Frank O'Hara: Difference/Homosexuality/Topography* (Liverpool University Press, 2000); Michael Davidson, *Guys Like Us: Citing Masculinity in Cold War Poetics* (University of Chicago Press, 2003); Maggie Nelson, *Women, the New York School, and Other True Abstractions* (Iowa City: University of Iowa Press, 2007). For assessment and critique of this position, see Micah Mattix, *Frank O'Hara and the Poetics of Saying "I"* (Madison, N.J: Fairleigh Dickinson University Press, 2011).

11 Frank O'Hara, *Jackson Pollock* (New York: George Braziller, 1959). On this monograph, the included poem, and Lee Krasner's reaction to it, see Joe LeSueur, *Digressions on Some Poems by Frank O'Hara: A Memoir* (New York: Farrar, Straus and Giroux, 2003), 197–204. For an overview of

O'Hara and contemporary art, see Russell Ferguson, *In Memory of My Feelings: Frank O'Hara and American Art* (Los Angeles: Museum of Contemporary Art, 1999).

12 The generally accepted publication date of *Lunch Poems* is often given as 1964, but this is contested in Alexander Smith Jr, *Frank O'Hara: A Comprehensive Bibliography* (New York and London: Garland, 1979), 25, where the date of 1965 is given.

13 See Frank O'Hara, "Personism" (1959), in *Standing Still and Walking in New York*, ed. Donald Allen (Bolinas, Calif: Grey Fox Press, 1975), 110–11. On O'Hara and gossip, see Gavin Butt, *Between You and Me: Queer Disclosures in the New York Art World, 1948–1963* (Durham, N.C. and London: Duke University Press, 2005).

14 For general discussion of this context, see John D'Emilio, *Sexual Politics, Sexual Communities: The Making of a Homosexual Minority in the United States 1940–1970* (Chicago and London: University of Chicago Press, 1983).

15 As one reviewer observed about the content of O'Hara's poems, "The material O'Hara worked with looks too often on first glance chichi, dizzy, piss elegant, and faggoty"; John Lowney, "Glistening Torsos, Sandwiches, and Coca Cola," *Parnassus* 6 (Fall/Winter 1977): 242. Marjorie Perloff later remarked, in the new introduction for her book originally published the same year (New York: George Braziller, 1977), that O'Hara's "was a style recognizably gay"; Marjorie Perloff, "Introduction, 1997," in *Frank O'Hara: Poet Among Painters* (University of Chicago Press, 1998), xi. Examples of poems published in O'Hara's lifetime that manifested direct engagement with homosexuality include *Lunch Poems*' "Ave Maria" or, indeed, all of the 1965 *Love Poems (Tentative Title)*. Beyond these published works, there were many, much more explicit, poems that only came to light with ed. Donald Allen, *The Collected Poems of Frank O'Hara* (1971; Berkeley: University of California Press, 1995). On the revelation of this more overt gay content, see Stuart Byron, "Frank O'Hara: Poetic 'Queertalk'" (1974) and Rudy Kikel, "The Gay Frank O'Hara" (1978), in *Frank O'Hara: To Be True to a City*, ed. Jim Elledge (Ann Arbor: University of Michigan Press, 1990), 64–9 and 334–49 respectively. As Gregory Bredbeck noted, "O'Hara's poetry has been simultaneously lauded and marginalized in that it centralizes homosexuality as a linguistic rather than a thematic practice – although the subject is often a theme"; Bredbeck, "B/O," 268. See also the insightful article by Boone, "Gay Language as Political Praxis," and the important observations on camp in O'Hara's work in Andrew Ross, "The Death of Lady Day," in Elledge, *Frank O'Hara*, 380–91.

16 For a useful discussion of both the visibility and invisibility of homosexuality in the art world of the 1950s, see Butt, *Between You and Me*. See also Jonathan D. Katz, "John Cage's Queer Silence or How to Avoid Making Matters Worse," (1999), in *Writings Through John Cage's Music, Poetry, and Art*, ed. David Bernstein (University of Chicago Press, 2001), 41–61.

17 See "The American Artist in a World of Suspicion" in Butt, *Between You and Me*, 23–50; Jonathan D. Katz, "The Art of Code: Jasper Johns & Robert Rauschenberg," in *Significant Others: Creativity & Intimate Partnership*, ed. Whitney Chadwick and Isabelle de Courtivron (London: Thames and Hudson, 1993), 189–207; Jonathan D. Katz, "Passive Resistance: On the Critical and Commercial Success of Queer Artists in Cold War American Art," *L'image* 3 (1996): 119–42; Richard Meyer, *Outlaw Representation: Censorship and Homosexuality in Twentieth-century American Art* (Boston: Beacon Press, 2002), 95–156; Jonathan D. Katz, "'Commiting the Perfect Crime': Sexuality, Assemblage, and the Postmodern Turn in American Art," *Art Journal* 67, no. 1 (Spring 2008): 38–53. See also the important essay by Kenneth Silver, "Modes of Disclosure: The Construction of Gay Identity and the Rise of Pop Art," in

Hand-painted Pop: American Art in Transition 1955–62, ed. Russell Ferguson (Los Angeles: Museum of Contemporary Art, 1992), 178–203.

18   Nelson, *Women, the New York School*, 52–3. Calvin Tomkins, one of the first to discuss this social formation, noted that there was talk in the early 1960s of a "'homintern,' a network of homosexual artists, dealers, and museum curators in league to promote certain favorites." Calvin Tomkins, *Off the Wall: Robert Rauschenberg and the Art World of Our Time* (New York: Doubleday, 1980), 260.

19   Frank O'Hara, "The Sorrows of the Youngman: John Rechy's *City of Night*," (1963), in *Standing Still and Walking in New York*, 160–3. On the minor scandal caused by Rivers's portrait of O'Hara in 1954, see Gooch, *City Poet*, 248.

20   With regard to Johns, Rauschenberg, and Brainard, homosexual affinities grounded the collaborations with O'Hara, but the concerns addressed included far more than that commonality. See Marjorie Perloff, "Watchman, Spy, and Dead Man: Jasper Johns, Frank O'Hara, John Cage and the 'Aesthetic of Indifference,'" *Modernism/Modernity* 8, no. 2 (April 2001): 197–223; Ferguson, *In Memory of My Feelings*; Lytle Shaw, *Frank O'Hara: The Poetics of Coterie* (Iowa City: University of Iowa Press, 2006; hereafter, *Poetics of Coterie*), 189–232, "Coterie and Allegory: Rauschenberg's Raw Materials"; Nick Selby, "Memory Pieces: Collage, Memorial and the Poetics of Intimacy in Joe Brainard, Jasper Johns and Frank O'Hara," in *Frank O'Hara Now: New Essays on the New York Poet*, ed. Robert Hampson and Will Montgomery (Liverpool University Press, 2010), 229–46.

21   John Button, "Frank's Grace," in *Homage to Frank O'Hara*, ed. Bill Berkson and Joe LeSueur (Berkeley, Calif: Creative Arts Book Company, 1980), 43. See also Larry Rivers's comment in Jeffrey Potter, *To a Violent Grave: An Oral Biography of Jackson Pollock* (New York: G. P. Putnam's, 1985), 213.

22   There are many acknowledgments of O'Hara's sexuality among the circle of friends he shared with Smith. For instance, Helen Frankenthaler was one of Smith's close confidants and a frequent correspondent. In a letter to his partner, Vincent Warren, O'Hara wrote in 1961, "Helen Frankenthaler said she thought of us last night while she was crying through the Gershwin hour"; Frank O'Hara to Vincent Warren, 17 January 1961, Donald Allen Collection of Frank O'Hara Letters, Thomas J. Dodd Research Center, University of Connecticut, Storrs. O'Hara's sexual identity, however, exceeded the essentializing category of "gay" in fundamental ways. This is argued in Smith, *Hyperscapes*, 102–35. Similarly, O'Hara's longtime roommate Joe LeSueur said, "As for Frank, I'd say that he was pansexual, a term that better suits him inasmuch as it implies a Whitmanesque grandeur, generosity of spirit, and inclusiveness"; LeSueur, *Digressions*, 103. On the complexities of O'Hara's self-disclosure, see Terrell Scott Herring, "Frank O'Hara's Open Closet," *PMLA* 117, no. 3 (May 2002): 414–27.

23   Byron, "O'Hara: Poetic 'Queertalk,'" 68–9.

24   Frank O'Hara to David Smith, 3 August 1961, David Smith Papers, Archives of American Art, Smithsonian Institution, Washington, D.C., ND Smith 2. O'Hara wrote that he would be coming to Bolton Landing on 8 August and returning to New York the evening of the 10th. He later wrote to Vincent Warren that he was "up at David Smith's Lake George retreat picking sculptures for a show of his work we're doing"; O'Hara to Warren, 17 August 1961, Donald Allen Collection of Frank O'Hara Letters.

25   David Smith to Kenneth Noland, 26 June 1961, Kenneth Noland Papers relating to David Smith, Archives of American Art, Smithsonian Institution.

26   David Smith, postcard to Helen Frankenthaler, July 1961. By the end of August 1961, Smith was writing "I have been depressed since the girls left." David Smith to Helen Fran-

kenthaler and Robert Motherwell, 28/29/30 August 1961. Collection of Helen Frankenthaler and Robert Motherwell Papers relating to David Smith, Archives of American Art, Smithsonian Institution, ND Smith D. For a discussion of Smith as a father, see Paul Tucker, "Family Matters: David Smith's Series Sculptures," in *David Smith: A Centennial*, ed. Carmen Giménez (New York: Solomon R. Guggenheim Museum, 2006), 69–89.

27 "I'm sorry that the notice on the show was short. I had understood from Porter [McCray] that he mentioned it to you in conversation rather vaguely, but we didn't write because up until the week of his leave of absence taking effect, he had still planned to try to get up and see your recent work, as you both had planned"; Frank O'Hara to David Smith, 3 August 1961, David Smith Papers, Archives of American Art, ND Smith 2. McCray, the Director of the International Program, resigned in July 1961 after a two-year power struggle in MoMA. The well-funded International Program operated semi-independently, leading to a movement among other administrative and curatorial departments to pressure the director, René d'Harnoncourt, to rein in McCray and to reintegrate the International Program into the museum's operations. McCray, aware of the problems, insured that O'Hara was promoted and his position placed within the Department of Painting and Sculpture. See Russell Lynes, *Good Old Modern: An Intimate Portrait of the Museum of Modern Art* (New York: Atheneum, 1973), 386–91; Gooch, *City Poet*, 354–5.

28 Frank O'Hara to David Smith, 17 August 1961, David Smith Papers, Archives of American Art, ND Smith 2. The painting remains unidentified. Neither the David Smith Estate nor O'Hara's sister, Maureen Granville-Smith, has been able to identify the painting or determine what happened to it after O'Hara's death; e-mail from Maureen Granville-Smith, 6 May 2010.

29 Emphasis added. David Smith to Helen Frankenthaler, 24 April 1957. He did not, however, have the same respect for Hunter. Written about the same time on an envelope in the Frankenthaler Papers relating to Smith, the sculptor remarked on his "way of choosing and method" and his "old historian arrogance – He doesn't know the elite have been disposed"; Collection of Helen Frankenthaler and Robert Motherwell Papers relating to David Smith, Archives of American Art.

30 Allen, *Collected Poems*, 428, 552.

31 Frank O'Hara and Alfred Leslie, "Transcript of *USA Poetry*," in Berkson and LeSueur, *Homage to Frank O'Hara*, 215.

32 Alfred Leslie with Frank O'Hara, *The Last Clean Shirt* (1964). The film repeats three times identical footage of a conversation between a man and a woman in the front seat of a car driving in New York. The woman speaks gibberish throughout, and O'Hara wrote the subtitles for the second and third repetitions (the first has no subtitles). The line "everyone thinks they're going up / in these here America" occurs in the second segment.

33 Frank O'Hara to David Smith, 17 August 1961; David Smith Papers, Archives of American Art, ND Smith 2.

34 "Biotherm (for Bill Berkson)": "extended vibrations / ziggurats ZIG I to IV stars of the Tigris-Euphrates basin" (formatting original); Allen, *Collected Poems*, 437, 553–4. The title refers to a high-end sunburn ointment used by Berkson's mother.

35 Frank O'Hara, "David Smith: The Color of Steel," *ARTnews* 60, no. 8 (December 1961): 32–4, 69–70.

36 See Rosalind Krauss, "Changing the Work of David Smith," *Art in America* 62, no. 5 (September–October 1974): 30–3 (not to be confused with her 1983 review, of the same title, of the Smith exhibition at the National Gallery of Art). For an insightful account of the debates around Smith's use of color, see Sarah Hamill, "Poly-

chrome in the Sixties: David Smith and Anthony Caro," in *Anglo-American Exchange in Postwar Sculpture, 1945–75* (Los Angeles: Getty Publications, 2011), 91–104.

37 For an astute analysis of O'Hara poetry as criticism, see Lytle Shaw, "Proximity's Plea: O'Hara's Art Writing," *Qui Parle* 12, no. 2 (Spring/Summer 2001): 143–78 and further Shaw, *Poetics of Coterie*.

38 As Sarah Hamill has noted, Smith made photographs of his work outdoors for O'Hara's article that, in turn, probably contributed to its final form; Sarah Hamill, "Picturing Autonomy: David Smith, Photography and Sculpture," *Art History* 37, no. 3 (June 2014): 544–6.

39 For a perceptive account of Smith's early defense of abstraction, see Paula Wisotzki, "Artist and Worker: The Labour of David Smith," *Oxford Art Journal* 28, no. 3 (2005): 347–70.

40 William Tucker, "David Smith," *Studio International* 181, no. 929 (January 1971): 25.

41 The relationship of Smith's abstraction to figuration has been a central preoccupation of Rosalind Krauss's work on Smith; see esp. "The Essential David Smith, Part I," *Artforum* 7, no. 6 (February 1969): 43–9; *Terminal Iron Works*; *Passages in Modern Sculpture* (Cambridge, Mass: MIT Press, 1977), 147–73.

42 Cleve Gray remarked on seeing the paintings, "They were like attacks on womanhood"; Cleve Gray, "Last Visit," *Art in America* 54, no. 1 (January–February 1966): 26. For an analysis of these works, see Michael Brenson, "David Smith's Embrace," in *David Smith: To and From the Figure* (New York: Knoedler, 1995), n.p.

43 Clement Greenberg, "Critical Comment," *Art in America* 54, no. 1 (January–February 1966): 32.

44 O'Hara, "Color of Steel," 32.

45 Ibid., 33.

46 O'Hara to Smith, 17 August 1961, David Smith Papers, Archives of American Art, ND Smith 2.

47 O'Hara, "Color of Steel," 34.

48 Ibid., 69.

49 As Lytle Shaw has observed about the *ARTnews* article, "The theatricality of O'Hara's account has to do, however, not merely with *identities* of the pieces but more importantly with their *interactions* – both among themselves and with the landscape"; Shaw, *Poetics of Coterie*, 224.

50 O'Hara, "Color of Steel," 70.

51 O'Hara to Smith, 17 August 1961, David Smith Papers, Archives of American Art, ND Smith 2.

52 Frank O'Hara to Vincent Warren, 2 March 1962, Donald Allen Collection of Frank O'Hara Letters.

53 Frank O'Hara to David Smith, 16 January 1962, David Smith Papers, Archives of American Art, ND Smith 2.

54 E.g., in an aside on an official MoMA letter regarding an exhibition, O'Hara hand-wrote (so it would not be part of the official museum carbon copy of the typewritten correspondence) a postscript with a personal joke to Smith: "Give an extra pile of corn husks to Horse for me, will you?" which may be a reference to a plaster horse made by Smith's daughters or their real pony, Jo-Jo, which they got that summer; Frank O'Hara to David Smith, 13 September 1963, David Smith Papers, Archives of American Art, ND Smith 2. On the plaster horse, see Rebecca Smith, "Making a Horse with Dad," *Tate Etc* 8 (Autumn 2006): 101. Smith mentioned the new pony, Jo-Jo, in a postcard to Helen Frankenthaler from July 1961 (Collection of Helen Frankenthaler and Robert Motherwell Papers relating to David Smith, Archives of American Art, ND Smith D) and wrote to Kenneth Noland, "My dolls come Thursday for 6 weeks. I've got them a pony and a nice young tutor – not too attractive to be diverting but pleasant to have around – a young college girl well educated and given to house management"; David Smith to Kenneth Noland, 26 June 1961,

Kenneth Noland Papers relating to David Smith, Archives of American Art.

55 Waldo Rasmussen, "Frank O'Hara in the Museum," (1977), in Berkson and LeSueur, *Homage to Frank O'Hara*, 89–90.

56 Gooch, *City Poet*, 449.

57 Frank O'Hara to Joan Mitchell, 15 May 1966, Donald Allen Collection of Frank O'Hara Letters.

58 The catalogue raisonné was eventually completed by Rosalind Krauss, who compiled it as part of the first doctoral dissertation on Smith. This proved to be a contentious issue and there was a tug-of-war about who would be allowed to work on the project: the Harvard curator Jane Harrison Cone (who organized the first American retrospective for the Fogg Art Museum) or Krauss. Krauss was awarded the contract in 1966 and it became a required element of her dissertation. See Helen Franc to Rosalind Krauss, 2 August 1966, Frank O'Hara Papers, Museum of Modern Art Archives, New York. The O'Hara Papers contain extensive correspondence related to this issue. The catalogue was eventually published as Rosalind Krauss, *The Sculpture of David Smith: A Catalogue Raisonné* (New York and London: Garland, 1977). For a discussion of the historiographic significance of Krauss's dissertation with regard to the emerging field of contemporary art history, see Richard Meyer, *What Was Contemporary Art?* (Cambridge, Mass: MIT Press, 2013), 1–10.

59 Erje Ayden, "From *Seven Years of Winter*" (1970), in Berkson and LeSueur, *Homage to Frank O'Hara*, 172. Significantly, this passage ends with an anecdote about O'Hara being a "fag" (172).

60 See the (unauthored) catalogue for the exhibition, *David Smith* (New York: Marlborough-Gerson Gallery, 1964).

61 "Bill Berkson tells me that you are pleased with the idea of a program on your work for Channel 13"; Frank O'Hara to David Smith, 8 September 1964, David Smith Papers, Archives of American Art, ND Smith 2.

62 Bill Berkson to David Smith, 29 October 1964, ibid. "P.S. don't wear a white shirt" is written on the front page of the voiceover script given to O'Hara, and the last has the handwritten "XXXXX B.B."; voiceover script, p. 13, Frank O'Hara Papers, Museum of Modern Art Archives. Smith recorded both Berkson and Channel 13's telephone numbers together in a sketchbook begun in the summer of 1964; David Smith Sketchbook no. 59, Estate of David Smith.

63 O'Hara's comment in a letter about the taping that "I'm very glad that Helen will be on with us" is the only indication of this I have yet been able to find; Frank O'Hara to David Smith, 8 September 1964, David Smith Papers, Archives of American Art, ND Smith 2.

64 This was presumably for the filming of the scenes of O'Hara and Smith walking around Bolton Landing. During the interview, O'Hara remarked, "when I was up at your studio at Bolton Landing a month ago."

65 Frank O'Hara to Michael Goldberg, 16 November 1964, Donald Allen Collection of Frank O'Hara Letters.

66 The 2006 transcription prepared by the Guggenheim Museum missed the word "girls" after "very angular," thus inadvertently tempering O'Hara's disruptive reply to Smith.

67 *Sculpting Master*.
68 Ibid.
69 Ibid.
70 Ibid.
71 Ibid.

72 Voiceover script, p. 13, Frank O'Hara Papers, Museum of Modern Art Archives.

73 Frank O'Hara, "Introduction to Edwin Denby's *Dancers Buildings and People in the Streets*" (1965), in *Standing Still and Walking in New York*, 184. Berkson wrote in 1967: "Attention was Frank's gift and his requirement. You might say it was his message"; Bill Berkson, "Frank O'Hara and His Poems" (1967/69), in Berkson and LeSueur, *Homage to Frank O'Hara*, 164. This

theme is key to the seminal study of O'Hara by Marjorie Perloff, "Frank O'Hara and the Aesthetics of Attention," *boundary 2* 4, no. 3 (Spring 1976): 779–806 and its expansion in her *Frank O'Hara: Poet Among Painters* (1977), "The Aesthetic of Attention," 1–30.

74   By the 1960s, "drawing in space" was a relatively common way of understanding Smith's work. In 1964, e.g., Greenberg called it "the cursiveness of Smith's drawing-in-air"; Clement Greenberg, "David Smith's New Sculpture" (1964), in *Clement Greenberg: The Collected Essays and Criticism*, ed. John O'Brian, 4 vols (University of Chicago Press, 1993), 4: 190. See further discussion in Chapter 3.

75   There is a related line through Smith's practice in his exploration of extreme, almost unsculptural, flatness for his "drawing in space" works. This was of special concern in a cluster of works from 1951 such as *The Letter*, *Hudson River Landscape*, and *Australia*, but it also has later echoes in such works as *Voltri XV*, 1962, or many of the *Wagon* sculptures. For a perceptive account of flatness and faciality in Smith's oeuvre, see Charles Millard, "David Smith," *Hudson Review* 22, no. 2 (Summer 1969): 271–7.

76   This imagery is cut through with his own history with Larry Rivers, for whose plaster statues O'Hara had posed; see e.g. "Two Dreams of Waking" (1957), in Allen, *Collected Poems*, 277.

77   On frontality in the statuary tradition, see David Getsy, *Body Doubles: Sculpture in Britain, 1877–1905* (New Haven and London: Yale University Press, 2004), 30–2. An important analysis of the structuring influence of the human form's faciality on the development of that tradition remains Emanuel Loewy, *The Rendering of Nature in Early Greek Art*, trans. John Fothergill (London: Duckworth, 1907).

78   For discussions of the ways in which modern sculpture departed from the classical and academic traditions' use of the statue as the allegorical image of the unified subject, see Alex Potts, "Male Phantasy and Modern Sculpture," *Oxford Art Journal* 15, no. 2 (1992): 38–47; Potts, *Sculptural Imagination*.

79   As Marjorie Perloff said, "Photographs, monuments, static memories – 'all things that don't change' – these have no place in the poet's world. We can now understand why O'Hara loves the *motion* picture, *action* painting, and all forms of dance – art forms that capture the *present*, rather than the *past*, the present in all its moving, chaotic splendor"; Perloff, "O'Hara and the Aesthetics of Attention," 794.

80   Frank O'Hara, "Having a Coke with You" (1960), in Allen, *Collected Poems*, 360.

81   Paul Carroll, "An Impure Poem About July 17, 1959," in *The Poem in Its Skin* (Chicago and New York: Follett Publishing, 1968), 157–64. More recently, this aspect of O'Hara's late work has been compared to the practices of digital and social media in Todd Tietchen, "Frank O'Hara and the Poetics of the Digital," *Criticism* 56, no. 1 (2014): 45–61.

82   Altieri, *Enlarging the Temple*, 119. For further expansion of these ideas, see Smith, *Hyperscapes* and Alan Feldman, *Frank O'Hara* (Boston: Twayne Publishers, 1979).

83   O'Hara, "Personism," 110.

84   For an extensive analysis of this comparison between O'Hara's poetry and Abstract Expressionism, see Shaw, *Poetics of Coterie* and Lytle Shaw, "Gesture in 1960: Toward Literal Situations," in Hampson and Montgomery, *Frank O'Hara Now*, 29–48. See also Perloff, *Frank O'Hara* (1977); Mattix, *O'Hara and the Poetics of Saying "I"*, 17–26; Anthony Libby, "O'Hara on the Silver Range" (1976), in Elledge, *Frank O'Hara*, 131–55. An intriguing alternative can be found in Stephen Paul Miller's comparison of O'Hara's poetry and the non-relational composition advocated by Donald Judd; Stephen Paul Miller, "O'Hara, Judd and Cold War Accommodation: Perceptions Equalizing Ground and Figure," in *The Scene of My Selves: New Work on*

New York School Poets, ed. Terrence Diggory and Stephen Paul Miller (Orono, Maine: National Poetry Foundation, 2001), 175–86.

85 In addition to Carroll, Altieri, Smith, and Feldman cited above, investigations into the ways in which O'Hara's poetry staged the self as multiple can be found across much of the O'Hara literature. See further James Breslin, "The Contradictions of Frank O'Hara," *American Poetry Review* 12, no. 6 (November/December 1983): 7–16.

86 Frank O'Hara, "In Memory of My Feelings" (1956), in Allen, *Collected Poems*, 252–7. For useful discussions on this poem and O'Hara's positing of multiple selves, see Perloff, *Frank O'Hara*; Mattix, *O'Hara and the Poetics of Saying "I"*, 88–109; Shaw, *Poetics of Coterie*, 86–114.

87 Krauss, "Essential David Smith I," 48–9. A useful account of Krauss's development of these ideas can be found in Judy K. Collischan Van Wagner, *Women Shaping Art: Profiles of Power* (New York: Praeger, 1984), 149–64.

88 Krauss, *Passages*, 158. See further Potts, "Abstraction and Image Making," 117–41 and, for Smith's reiteration of this practice through photography, Sarah Hamill, "What Sculpture Can Never Be: The Photographs of David Smith," in *David Smith Invents*, ed. Susan Behrends Frank (New Haven and London: Yale University Press and the Phillips Collection, 2011), 65–75.

89 O'Hara, "Color of Steel," 69.

90 O'Hara to Smith, 17 August 1964, David Smith Papers, Archives of American Art, ND Smith 2.

91 Shaw, "Proximity's Plea," 147.

92 Richard Howard, *Alone with America: Essays on the Art of Poetry in the United States Since 1950*, enlarged ed. (New York: Atheneum, 1969/80), 471. Emphasis original.

93 "Personages" was sometimes used by various artists of the 1950s to account for abstract bodies and unorthodox morphologies. I am thinking of an artist such as Robert Motherwell (*Personage/Self-portrait*, 1943) or the work of Louise Bourgeois in the 1940s to 1950s. As with Smith, however, the category of "personage" was sometimes modified through titling to indicate or fix a specific gender or identity to the otherwise abstract body; e.g. "Self-portrait" in the case of Motherwell. On Bourgeois's titles, their specificities, and their shifts, see Mignon Nixon, *Fantastic Reality: Louise Bourgeois and a Story of Modern Art* (Cambridge, Mass: MIT Press, 2005), 119–63.

94 Smith's deployment of crass jokes in this regard could be understood as keeping in line with the attitude toward women he displayed regularly. As Cleve Gray reported of a trip to Bolton Landing just before Smith's death, the sculptor used his own paintings of female nudes as an occasion to "joke like a schoolboy." Gray wrote of the paintings: "David, turning around one canvas after another for us to see, was proud of his production, delighted with the fact that there were so many female nudes surrounding him"; Gray, "Last Visit," 26. As Elaine de Kooning once remarked, Smith "tries too hard – it's like people in the Village that beat up gays because they have to act macho"; Potter, *To a Violent Grave*, 214.

95 O'Hara's poetry and criticism, however, evidenced a long history of signaling homosexuality and its communities, often in oblique terms. The dual meanings pursued by O'Hara in his speech, consequently, may have elevated its capacity for being perceived as implication or innuendo. For analysis, see Boone, "Gay Language as Political Praxis" and, earlier, Byron, "O'Hara: Poetic 'Queertalk'" and Feldman, *Frank O'Hara*, 49–53.

96 Brian Massumi, "The Future Birth of the Affective Fact: The Political Ontology of Threat," in *The Affect Theory Reader*, ed. Melissa Gregg and Gregory Seigworth (Durham, N.C. and London: Duke University Press, 2010), 59.

97 Tucker, "Family Matters," 87.

98 Ibid., 89 n. 40.

99 Paraphrased in Joan Marter, "Arcadian Nightmares: The Evolution of David Smith and Dorothy Dehner's Work at Bolton Landing," in *Reading Abstract Expressionism: Context and Critique*, ed. Ellen Landau (New Haven and London: Yale University Press, 2005), 637.

100 Smith said, "Did I tell you I just made 130 or 140 paintings this year from models, all nude models. I don't use drapery. When there's pussy, I put pussy in. And when there's a crack – on some of these girls who are so young you can't even see a definition – I put it in because I think it will be there, sooner or later." A more complete version of this 1964 interview was published as David Smith and Thomas Hess, "The Secret Letter," in McCoy, *David Smith*, 180–81. Smith expressed reservation at this interview's frankness, writing to the collector Lois Orswell, "Here is the catalog. A bit embarrassed about this tape [sic] revelations and bad English"; David Smith to Lois Orswell, n.d., in Marjorie Cohn, *Lois Orswell, David Smith, and Modern Art* (New Haven and London: Yale University Press in association with Harvard University Art Museums, 2002), 289.

101 David Smith, radio interview with Marian Horosko, 25 October 1964, WNCN, Archives of American Art, Smithsonian Institution, transcript, p. 8.

102 Krauss, *Passages*, 148.

103 Smith, "Perception and Reality," 78. Emphases original.

104 This was a general tactic for O'Hara. See Jim Elledge, "The Lack of Gender in Frank O'Hara's Love Poems to Vincent Warren," in *Fictions of Masculinity: Crossing Cultures, Crossing Sexualities*, ed. Peter F. Murphy (New York University Press, 1994), 226–37.

105 Cleve Gray, ed., *David Smith by David Smith: Sculpture and Writings* (London: Thames and Hudson, 1968), 137.

106 David Smith quoted in Belle Krasne, "A David Smith Profile," *Art Digest* 26, no. 13 (1952): 13.

107 David Smith, "Second Thoughts on Sculpture," *Art Journal* 13, no. 3 (Spring 1954): 205.

108 Smith, "Language Is Image," 81.

109 Gene Baro, "Some Late Words from David Smith," *Art International* 9, no. 7 (20 October 1965): 51.

110 Humor was, after all, a key tool for O'Hara in his poetry and his criticism. As Perloff has remarked, "But as so often in O'Hara's writings, the jocular tone masks an underlying seriousness"; Perloff, "O'Hara and the Aesthetics of Attention," 798. On laughter and affect in O'Hara's work, see Josh Robinson, "'A Gasp of Laughter at Desire': Frank O'Hara's Poetics of Breath," in Hampson and Montgomery, *Frank O'Hara Now*, 144–59.

111 Gray, *David Smith by David Smith*. For one of many examples of Gray's rewriting of Smith's words, compare p. 71 to Smith, "The Language Is Image," 81.

112 Cleve Gray, ed. (memorial portfolio for David Smith), *Art in America* 54, no. 1 (January–February 1966): 47.

113 Gray, *David Smith by David Smith*, 87.

114 The only significant voice of skepticism about this statement has been Potts, who followed the literature in accepting the epigram as sincere but rightly notes that "ambiguities are apparent in Smith's own commentary when he feels compelled to envisage his works as gendered presences and yet refuses any fixed associations between them and the viewer"; Potts, *Sculptural Imagination*, 176. At the time of writing his book (it was published in 2000), the only part of the Smith–O'Hara exchange that would have been readily available to Potts continued to be Gray's altered version published more than three decades before and repeated throughout the Smith literature. (The only other variant I have found is not in the Smith literature but in the writing on O'Hara. An entirely idiosyncratic version can be found in Perloff, *Frank O'Hara*, 211 n. 22, which provides another instance of the desire to stabilize gender ambiguity, decon-

textualize Smith's joke, and remove O'Hara's agency in the exchange by casting him as "self-effacing." In Perloff's version, Smith's lines have been rewritten as the assertions "I don't do males. I like the presence of these females.") No full transcript was attempted until the 2006 Guggenheim exhibition, when the recording of the fully televised program was restored and transcribed. The availability of the original program was extremely limited before this. The Guggenheim's full transcript has recently been published in Sarah Hamill, ed., *David Smith: Works, Writings and Interview* (Barcelona: Ediciones Poligrafia, 2011). See further discussion in n. 1 above.

115   Karen Wilkin, "A Sculptor Draws," *Master Drawings* 40, no. 1 (2002): 54. My emphasis.

116   This is also the core argument of Krauss's earlier "Essential David Smith 1," 43–9 and later *Passages*, 147–81.

117   Sigmund Freud and James Strachey, *Totem and Taboo: Some Points of Agreement between the Mental Lives of Savages and Neurotics*, Standard Edition of the Complete Psychological Works of Sigmund Freud (New York: W. W. Norton, 1989).

118   Krauss, *Terminal Iron Works*, 93.

119   Anne Applebaum, "David Smith: Whitechapel Gallery," *Artforum* 25, no. 8 (April 1987): 143.

120   In Krauss's defense, it should be noted that she conveyed her anxiety about such simplifications, however obliquely, at the close of her chapter: "merely to scan his work for the brute recurrence of certain thematic material is to be left with nothing but an endless litany of characterological difficulties and irrelevant private preoccupations"; Krauss, *Terminal Iron Works*, 114.

121   David Smith as quoted in ibid., 93: "the subject is me / the hero is the eye function / the image doesn't lead / the morality is above / the work, or below / but never with."

122   Tucker, "David Smith," 29.

123   Krauss, *Terminal Iron Works*, 114.

124   Judith Butler, *Undoing Gender* (New York and London: Routledge, 2004), 11. See further discussion in the Introduction.

125   Ibid., 28. Such a stance is an expansion of earlier statements such as "the matrix of gender relations is prior to the emergence of the 'human'"; Judith Butler, *Bodies That Matter: On the Discursive Limits of "Sex"* (New York and London: Routledge, 1993), 7.

126   Judith Butler, *Giving an Account of Oneself* (New York: Fordham University Press, 2005), 24. Importantly, however, Butler's use of the term "recognition" goes far beyond the discernment of familiar forms or formats. Instead, it is used with reference to her long-running account of subjectivity (and intersubjectivity) developed from her engagement with the writings of G. W. F. Hegel. See the foundational arguments for these ideas in Judith Butler, *Subjects of Desire: Hegelian Reflections on Twentieth-century France* (New York: Columbia University Press, 1987).

127   David Smith, Sketchbook no. 49, dated 1962–3, Estate of David Smith. Similarly, he said in 1952, "No artist ever finishes a picture. It's up to the person who looks at it to finish it"; quoted in Krasne, "David Smith Profile," 26.

2 IMMODERATE COUPLINGS: TRANSFORMATIONS AND GENDERS IN JOHN CHAMBERLAIN'S WORK

1   This is the foil for an early defense of Chamberlain, e.g., in Barbara Rose, "How to Look at John Chamberlain's Sculpture," *Art International* 12, no. 10 (January 1964): 36–8. Within critical, though not popular, opinion, the denial of reference has remained the dominant position. For a spirited, but ultimately unconvincing, rejoinder, see Duncan Smith, "In the Heart of the Tinman: John Chamberlain," *Artforum* 22, no. 5 (January 1984): 39–43.

2   Elizabeth Baker, "The Chamberlain Crunch," *Art News* 70, no. 10 (February 1972): 26.

3   John Chamberlain, "A Statement," in *John Chamberlain Sculpture: An Extended Exhibition* (New York: Dia Art Foundation, 1982), n.p. This is one of two nearly identical pamphlets prepared by the Dia Art Foundation for its long-term exhibitions of Chamberlain's work, at 67 Vestry Street in New York and also at "Chamberlain Gardens" in Essex, Connecticut. This same text has been used by the Chinati Foundation since 1983 and it regularly distributes it in its permanent installation of Chamberlain's work in Marfa, Texas. Archival copies of the Dia pamphlets can be found in the Richard Bellamy Papers, III.A.11, Museum of Modern Art Archives, New York.

4   Michael Auping, "John Chamberlain: Reliefs 1960–1982," in *John Chamberlain: Reliefs 1960–1982* (Sarasota, Fl: John and Mable Ringling Museum of Art, 1983), 12.

5   Chamberlain, "A Statement," n.p. My emphasis.

6   Parataxis, defined as "The placing of propositions or clauses one after another, without indicating by connecting words the relation (of coordination or subordination) between them" (*OED*), was a fundamental strategy of modernist writers such as Ezra Pound, James Joyce, and William Carlos Williams. At Black Mountain College, Chamberlain developed his artistic practise, in part, out of his reading of such authors. See Julie Sylvester, "Auto/Bio: Conversations with John Chamberlain," in *John Chamberlain: A Catalogue Raisonné of the Sculpture 1954–1985*, ed. Julie Sylvester (New York: Hudson Hills Press, 1986), 11. On the importance of parataxis, see e.g. David Hayman, *Re-forming the Narrative: Toward a Mechanics of Modernist Fiction* (Ithaca, N.Y: Cornell University Press, 1987).

7   Donald Judd, "Chamberlain: Another View," *Art International* 12, no. 10 (January 1964): 39.

8   Rose, "How to Look," 38.

9   Elizabeth Baker, "The Secret Life of John Chamberlain," *Art News* 68, no. 2 (April 1969): 64.

10 Klaus Kertess, "Color in the Round and Then Some: John Chamberlain's Work, 1954–1985," in Sylvester, *John Chamberlain*, 38.

11 Gary Indiana, "John Chamberlain's Irregular Set," *Art in America* 71, no. 10 (1983): 208.

12 "And if it is possible any longer for sculpture to have an expressive as well as a formal content, then it is John Chamberlain, who, uniting the fragile with the massive, the poignant with the brutal, and the gentle with the violent, seeks at the moment its fullest realization"; Rose, "How to Look," 38.

13 Brian O'Doherty related the story of a Chamberlain accidentally hauled away as garbage; Brian O'Doherty, "Chamberlain: Projective Sculpture," in *John Chamberlain: Recent Sculpture* (New York: PaceWildenstein, 1994), 5–6.

14 Rose, "How to Look," 38.

15 Donald Judd, from an August 1964 article repr. as part of Donald Judd, "John Chamberlain," in *John Chamberlain: New Sculpture* (New York: Pace Gallery, 1989), iv.

16 Kertess, "Color in the Round," 38.

17 Ibid., 26.

18 For discussions of Gibson's *Tinted Venus* and of sculptural polychromy in the nineteenth century, see Andreas Blühm, *The Colour of Sculpture 1840–1910* (Zwolle: Waanders Uitgevers for Van Gogh Museum, Amsterdam, and Henry Moore Institute, Leeds, 1996).

19 For a general discussion see David Batchelor, *Chromaphobia: Ancient and Modern, and a Few Notable Exceptions* (Leeds: Henry Moore Institute Essays on Sculpture, 1997). This argument about sculpture was later reprised in David Batchelor, *Chomophobia* (London: Reaktion, 2000).

20 E. C. Goosen, "Two Exhibitions," in *Minimal Art: A Critical Anthology*, ed. Gregory Battcock (New York: E. P. Dutton, 1968), 173.

21 Darby Bannard, "Cubism, Abstract Expressionism, David Smith," *Artforum* 6, no. 8 (April 1968): 32.

22 Fielding Dawson understood Chamberlain's work as a hairdresser and make-up artist to be central to his artistic practice. In a stream of consciousness remark, Dawson declared, "If I had any doubts that his work had somehow emerged from barbering and hairstyling – and painting – the head as foundation, even *lapis*, is not at bottom, but in the center, with all parts around it, to give head body, which in part the Hollywood film did pursue, and was indeed too close, to John"; Fielding Dawson, "Self Portrait in Steel: A Talk with John Chamberlain," *Arts Magazine* 64, no. 8 (April 1990): 56. Such an emphasis on this earlier career is also central to Carl Andre's concrete poem for Chamberlain, which is based on the words "shear" and "thought," with the resulting combination "shearthought" relying on the homonym "sheer"; Carl Andre, "A Word for John Chamberlain" (1961/71), first published in *Artforum* 10, no. 6 (February 1972): 6 and reproduced in Dieter Schwarz, ed., *John Chamberlain: Papier Paradisio* (Winterthur: Kunstmuseum Winterthur, 2005), 44. Chamberlain briefly discussed his work as a hairdresser in Sylvester, "Auto/Bio," 10. See also Michael Auping, *30 Years: Interviews and Outtakes* (Fort Worth, Tex: Modern Art Museum of Fort Worth, 2007), 97, where Chamberlain remarked: "As it turns out, car metal offers me the correct resistance so that I can make a form – not overform it or underform it. At one time, hair offered me the right resistance. I think I probably learned about resistance when I was cutting hair."

23 Phyllis Tuchman, "An Interview with John Chamberlain," *Artforum* 10, no. 6 (February 1972): 40. Chamberlain also ended his artist statement for the Dia Foundation with "As an artist I give away more than I would if I ran a beauty shop"; Chamberlain, "A Statement," n.p.

24 Donald Judd, "Specific Objects," *Arts Yearbook* 8 (1965): 82. In this essay, Judd opposed "sculpture" to "three-dimensional work" (i.e., specific objects) that would be "neither painting nor sculpture" (74). He saw Chamberlain as a central example.

25 Robert Creeley, "John Chamberlain," in *Recent American Sculpture*, ed. Hans van Weeren-Griek (New York: Jewish Museum, 1964), 17.

26 John Chamberlain quoted in Marcia Corbino, "Creating Art from Industrial Waste," *Sarasota Herald Tribune* (18 January 1981): 16. I am grateful to Adrian Kohn for alerting me to this reference. Chamberlain also explained his hiatus from using automobile bodies along these lines: "I was tired of using automobile material, because the only response I ever got was that I was making automobile crashes and that I used the automobile as some symbolic bullshit about society. All of a sudden sculpture was the only thing that was supposed not to have color in our society. The fact that all this material had color had made it very interesting to me. But the more interested I got in it, the more everyone kept insisting it was car crashes"; in Sylvester, "Auto/Bio," 21.

27 This contradiction between a hope for pure formalism on the part of some of Chamberlain's critics and the artist's more promiscuous and wry play with meaning and reference (both in the works themselves and in the modifying titles he gave to them) is evidenced in the recent catalogue to the 2012 retrospective at the Guggenheim. The catalogue paradoxically contains an essay claiming that the titles should by understood as meaningless combinations of words for their visual properties while, at the same time, the book concludes with a lexicon of Chamberlain's titles that traces their references and allusions. See Susan Davidson, ed., *John Chamberlain: Choices* (New York: Solomon R. Guggenheim Museum, 2012).

28 Donald Judd, "Local History," (1964), in *Donald Judd: Complete Writings 1959–1975* (Halifax: Press of the Nova Scotia College of Art and Design, 1975), 152–3. Emphases mine. For a discussion of the importance of this quotation for

Judd, see David Raskin, *Donald Judd* (New Haven and London: Yale University Press, 2010), 42–8.

29 In Chamberlain's late work with aluminum tubes, he came to emphasize compression and twisting as a modification of his practice of fitting. This work, as well, turns on the recognition of the repurposed and transformed material as a signal of art's capacity for "discovery." See discussion in David Getsy, "John Chamberlain's Pliability: The New Monumental Aluminium Works," *Burlington* magazine 153, no. 1304 (November 2011): 738–44.

30 This particular phrase was used in the course of Bonnie Clearwater, "John Chamberlain interview, 1991 Jan. 29–30" (Archives of American Art, Smithsonian Institution, 1991), 38, but the theme of art as transformation and discovery are repeated throughout Chamberlain's statements. See further discussion later in this chapter.

31 John Chamberlain and Viva Auder, treatment for *The Secret Life of William Shakespeare*, n.d., Richard Bellamy Papers III.A.12, Museum of Modern Art Archives. For a discussion of Chamberlain's *Secret Life of Hernando Cortez*, see Angelica Beckmann, "The Roving Eye: On John Chamberlain's Approach to Photography and Film," in *John Chamberlain*, ed. Jochen Poetter (Stuttgart: Edition Cantz and Staatliche Kunsthalle Baden-Baden, 1991), 115–24, with a transcription of the improvised film's lines on pp. 187–205, and Baker, "Secret Life," 48–51, 63–4.

32 Chamberlain and Auder, treatment for *Secret Life of William Shakespeare*, 6–7.

33 Ibid., 20.

34 Ibid., 7. Emphases original.

35 Robert Creeley, "Interview with John Chamberlain, 11/29/1991" (unpublished), 13; original in artist's estate.

36 Tuchman, "Interview," 40.

37 For a useful account of the impact of Black Mountain on Chamberlain, see Dieter Schwarz, "To Create the Flow," in Schwarz, *John Chamberlain*, 8–25.

38 Hans Ulrich Obrist, *John Chamberlain*, The Conversation Series (Cologne: Buchhandlung Walther König, 2006), 69.

39 Baker, "Secret Life," 49.

40 Sylvester, "Auto/Bio," 24. Compare John Chamberlain and Klaus Kertess, "John Chamberlain in Conversation with Klaus Kertess, 8 October 2005," *Chinati Foundation Newsletter* 11 (October 2006): 10. Kertess began: "So can we talk about those urethane [foam] pieces a little? Chamberlain: I thought we would lie a lot."

41 Obrist, *John Chamberlain*, 63. Emphases original.

42 Referring to his attempts to write good art criticism, Judd said: "A little article on John Chamberlain's work long ago is the nearest I've come to this effort"; Donald Judd, "Art and Architecture," (1983), in *Donald Judd: Complete Writings 1975–1986* (Eindhoven: Van Abbemuseum, 1987), 27. On Judd's priorities in his art criticism, see David Raskin, "Judd's Moral Art," in *Donald Judd*, ed. Nicholas Serota (London: Tate Publishing, 2004), 78–95; David Raskin, "The Shiny Illusionism and Krauss and Judd," *Art Journal* 65, no. 1 (Spring 2006): 6–21; Raskin, *Donald Judd*.

43 Judd, "Chamberlain," (1965), 190. This is, in fact, one of the most frequently quoted statements by Judd on Chamberlain.

44 Judd also re-described excess in a positive light when he repeatedly praised Chamberlain for using more metal and space than required. His term for this was "redundancy." See Judd, "Chamberlain: Another View," 39, and further in the collected writings of Judd on Chamberlain in Judd, "Chamberlain" (1989), i–xi.

45 E.g. in response to Fielding Dawson's question as to why he began making independent films, Chamberlain replied, "So I could take Ultra Violet to some secret place and fuck her"; Dawson, "Self Portrait in Steel," 57.

46 Larry Bell, "Perfect Fit," *Artforum* 50, no. 7 (March 2012): 239, 241.

47 Judd, "Chamberlain: Another View," 38.

48   Kertess, "Color in the Round," 30.

49   John Chamberlain in Elizabeth Baker et al., "Excerpts from a Conversation," in *John Chamberlain: A Retrospective Exhibition*, ed. Diane Waldman (New York: Solomon R. Guggenheim Museum, 1971), 17.

50   Chamberlain, "A Statement," n.p.

51   Kertess's sensitive and exemplary essay for the 1986 catalogue raisonné comes closest to a full analysis of this issue, but his commentary was largely limited to a few sentences. In a promising but unfulfilled move, Kertess argued: "And clearly the *motive* of his *auto* is erotics – the erotics of art." Immediately after this sentence, he used this wordplay to jump to a discussion of automobiles. Kertess, "Color in the Round," 30.

52   John Chamberlain, unpublished interview with Michael Auping, 1 October 1981, quoted in Auping, "Chamberlain: Reliefs," 12.

53   *John Chamberlain/F_____g Couches* was at Lo Giudice Gallery, New York, in affiliation with Leo Castelli Gallery, New York, in 1972. Chamberlain had been experimenting with foam couches since the late 1960s. Dan Graham has discussed the "shared body experience [that is] very '60s 'hippie'" afforded by these works in Dan Graham, "John Chamberlain: Conceptual Artist," in *John Chamberlain: New Sculpture*, ed. Kara Vander Weg (New York: Gagosian Gallery, 2011), 140. The Ultra Violet photographs were published in John Chamberlain, "Ultra Violet in Depth," *New York Review of Sex & Politics* 1, no. 2 (1 April 1969): 12–16.

54   Creeley, "Interview with John Chamberlain," 22.

55   Chamberlain in Sylvester, "Auto/Bio," 23.

56   Clearwater, "John Chamberlain interview," 16.

57   Chamberlain and Kertess, "Chamberlain in Conversation," 17.

58   Indiana, "Chamberlain's Irregular Set," 212. Emphasis original.

59   However, sexuality need not be defined exclusively in terms of the sex(es) or gender(s) of participant(s), even though this remains the dominant convention. As Kosofsky Sedgwick remarked, "The definitional narrowing-down in this century of sexuality as a whole to a binarized calculus of *homo-* or *hetero*sexuality is a weighty fact but an entirely historical one"; Eve Kosofsky Sedgwick, *Epistemology of the Closet* (Berkeley: University of California Press, 1990), 31. Similarly, Judith Butler asked: "If a sexuality is to be disclosed, what will be taken as the true determinant of its meaning: the phantasy structure, the act, the orifice, the gender, the anatomy?" Judith Butler, "Imitation and Gender Insubordination," in *Inside/Out: Lesbian Theories, Gay Theories*, ed. Diana Fuss (London and New York: Routledge, 1991), 17. See further discussion in the Introduction above.

60   For a discussion of the effects of the categorical separation of "gender" from "sexuality" in the twentieth century, see David Valentine, "The Categories Themselves," *GLQ* 10, no. 2 (2003): 215–20 and David Valentine, *Imagining Transgender: An Ethnography of a Category* (Durham, N.C. and London: Duke University Press, 2007), 29–65.

61   Some literal-minded critics have attempted to see such elements as paint spatters as ejaculations. This attempt to find obvious iconographies is not only counter to Chamberlain's way of characterizing the work but also fails to account for the ways in which the work is painted before being made into sculpture.

62   Jochen Poetter, "'No leaning on the oars': On John Chamberlain's High-energy Ideograms," in Poetter, *John Chamberlain*, 30.

63   In 1979, Chamberlain remarked, "I think of my art materials not as junk but as – garbage. Manure, actually; it goes from being the waste material of one being to the life-source of another. That is, if you acknowledge that, by their resistance and form, the cars have been re-invested by me with aesthetic power. That attitude – of

recycling – spills over into my other subjects or materials – foam and glass"; repr. in Schwarz, *John Chamberlain*, 92.

64   A recent overview of the complex relationships among biology, psychology, and social context for the emergence of gender is given in Anne Fausto-Sterling, *Sex/Gender: Biology in a Social World* (New York: Routledge, 2012). See also Rebecca M. Jordan-Young, *Brain Storm: The Flaws in the Science of Sex Differences* (Cambridge, Mass: Harvard University Press, 2010).

65   See the important book by Elisabeth Reis, *Bodies in Doubt: An American History of Intersex* (Baltimore: Johns Hopkins University Press, 2009). See also Melanie Blackless et al., "How Sexually Dimorphic Are We? Review and Synthesis," *American Journal of Human Biology* 12 (2000): 151–66.

66   Judith Butler, *Undoing Gender* (New York and London: Routledge, 2004), 10.

67   Susan Stryker, *Transgender History* (Berkeley, Calif: Seal Press, 2008), 1.

68   The phrase "idealization of dimorphism" is Judith Butler's from *Undoing Gender*, 203. On the topic of the body and the cultural inscription of sex, see further her *Bodies That Matter: On the Discursive Limits of "Sex"* (New York and London: Routledge, 1993).

69   Thomas E. Crow, "Figures of Emergence in the Recent Sculpture of John Chamberlain," in Vander Weg, *John Chamberlain*, 6.

70   Obrist, *John Chamberlain*, 115.

71   A related but distinct claim is made about Eva Hesse in Anne Middleton Wagner, *Three Artists (Three Women): Modernism and the Art of Hesse, Krasner, and O'Keeffe* (Berkeley: University of California Press, 1996).

72   In a late interview, Chamberlain remarked about his titles' ambiguity, "And the titling has nothing to do with the object, any more than, for example: Hans is your name, you've had it all your life, you're quite used to it, everybody would know you…But there's nothing specific about the word 'Hans' with the person other than everybody's got used to it"; Obrist, *John Chamberlain*, 111–12. Despite its arbitrariness, however, naming does, as Chamberlain's words reflect, come to affect how we know, recall, and relate to the named person or thing.

73   Chamberlain, "A Statement," n.p.

74   Chamberlain and Auder, treatment for *Secret Life of William Shakespeare*.

75   See discussions in Jay Prosser, *Second Skins: The Body Narratives of Transsexuality* (New York: Columbia University Press, 1998); J. Jack Halberstam, *In a Queer Time and Place: Transgender Bodies, Subcultural Lives* (New York University Press, 2005); Jay Prosser, *Light in the Dark Room: Photography and Loss* (Minneapolis: University of Minnesota Press, 2005).

76   Henry Geldzahler, "Interview with John Chamberlain," in *John Chamberlain: Recent Work* (New York: Pace Gallery, 1992), n.p.

77   Elizabeth Baker urged such a distinction in 1972, when she wrote, "The idea that Chamberlain remains a 'Tenth Street Abstract-Expressionist' dies hard – and it was not much of an insight to begin with. This is the crudest of misconceptions still in circulation about his work today"; Baker, "Chamberlain Crunch," 27.

78   As David Bourdon explained, after Ondine failed to arrive in Arizona for the filming of *Lonesome Cowboys* (1968), Chamberlain was offered his role as "Padre Lawrence, described in the scenario as a 'degenerate and unfrocked priest who tries to hide his addiction to opium-laced cough syrups.'…[He] was also invited to play the father of the cowboy brothers, but declined that part, too, on the grounds that he wasn't old enough"; David Bourdon, *Warhol* (New York: Harry N. Abrams, 1989), 271. See also Andy Warhol and Pat Hackett, *POPism: The Warhol '60s* (New York and London: Harcourt Brace Jovanovich, 1980), 260–2. As Matthew Tinkcom has discussed, *Lonesome Cowboys* explicitly problematized the heteronormative mascu-

linity that was seen as definitional of the Western genre: "Indeed, the hostility towards masculinity voiced at moments in the film would suggest that part of the film's effect is to offer no identificatory pleasure for the straight male spectator, a turnabout from the usual expectations of the Hollywood Western"; Matthew Tinkcom, *Working Like a Homosexual: Camp, Capital, Cinema* (Durham, N.C: Duke University Press, 2002), 112–13. For further discussion of Warhol's relation to Chamberlain, see Edward Leffingwell, "A Box with a Hole in It," in *Wide Point: The Photography of John Chamberlain*, ed. Donna De Salvo (Southampton, N.Y: Parrish Art Museum, 1993), 33–9.

79   See Larry Rivers and Arnold Weinstein, *What Did I Do? The Unauthorized Autobiography of Larry Rivers* (New York: HarperCollins, 1992); Gavin Butt, *Between You and Me: Queer Disclosures in the New York Art World, 1948–1963* (Durham, N.C. and London: Duke University Press, 2005), 74–105.

80   Robert Smithson, "Entropy and the New Monuments," *Artforum* 4, no. 10 (June 1966): 30.

81   Chamberlain in Sylvester, "Auto/Bio," 11. Emphasis mine.

82   Clearwater, "John Chamberlain interview," 16.

3   SECOND SKINS: UNBOUND GENDERS OF NANCY GROSSMAN'S SCULPTURE

1   Transcript of Arlene Raven presentation, Photography Institute, New York, 1999; archived at http://www.thephotographyinstitute.org/www/1999/raven.html, accessed 3 April 2014.

2   Grossman's engagement with abstraction and assemblage (and the shift to "figuration" in the form of head sculptures) could be productively positioned in the narrative about hybrid practices and realist aims for American and European art in the postwar period offered by Alex Potts in his recent book. He compellingly argues that oppositions between abstraction and figuration are not just artificial but have hindered recognition of postwar art's political and social engagements; Alex Potts, *Experiments in Modern Realism: World Making, Politics and the Everyday in Postwar European and American Art* (New Haven and London: Yale University Press, 2013).

3   Much more attention, e.g., has been given to Philip Guston's shift to figuration in 1970, two years after Grossman had also pivoted from abstraction. For a detailed assessment of Guston's "return" to figuration and the context for such shifts, see Robert Slifkin, *Out of Time: Philip Guston and the Refiguration of Postwar American Art* (Berkeley: University of California Press, 2013), 237–54.

4   B[rian] O'D[oherty], "Nancy Grossman (Krasner)," *New York Times*, 23 February 1964, X18.

5   Cindy Nemser, *Art Talk: Conversations with 12 Women Artists* (New York: Charles Scribner's Sons, 1975). Early In the 1970s, Grossman appeared in the pantheons offered in Barbaralee Diamonstein, "100 Women in Touch with Our Time," *Harper's Bazaar*, 3110 (January 1971): 104–16 and Mary Beth Edelson, "Some Living American Women Artists," *Off Our Backs* 4, no. 2 (1974): 10–11.

6   By 1976, one writer was claiming about the artist's mixed success and isolation from the mainstream art world that "She has been in a half-dozen solo shows, been included in group exhibitions around the country, is represented in the collections of some of the most sophisticated art patrons around. But Nancy Grossman, at 35, remains almost unknown to the general public and much of the art world. Her name is not one of the 'musts' automatically included in any big art-now museum survey. Her work is rarely discussed or even listed in new books"; Emily Genauer, "Big 'Unknown' Talent: Drawings by

Nancy Grossman," *International Herald Tribune*, 29 December 1976, 9.

7   See e.g. Norman Kleeblatt's comments in Ann Landi, "The Best Underrated Artists," *ARTnews* (September 2010): 97.

8   See discussion in Susan Stryker, *Transgender History* (Berkeley, Calif: Seal Press, 2008), 103–5 and in Introduction above. See also Leslie Feinberg, "Transgender Liberation: A Movement Whose Time Has Come" (1992), in *The Transgender Studies Reader*, ed. Susan Stryker and Stephen Whittle (New York and London: Routledge, 2006), 205–20; Susan Stryker, "My Words to Victor Frankenstein Above the Village of Chamounix: Performing Transgender Rage," *GLQ* 1, no. 3 (1994): 237–54; Cressida Heyes, "Feminist Solidarity After Queer Theory: The Case of Transgender," *Signs* 28, no. 4 (Summer 2003): 1093–120; Sandy Stone, "The *Empire* Strikes Back: A Posttranssexual Manifesto," rev. in Stryker and Whittle, *Transgender Studies Reader*, 221–35; Viviane K. Namaste, "Undoing Theory: The 'Transgender Question' and the Epistemic Violence of Anglo-American Feminist Theory," *Hypatia* 24, no. 3 (Summer 2009): 11–32.

9   Full-figure imagery does continue in her drawing and collage practice but the focus of this chapter will be on her sculpture and her central artistic theme: the bound head. She experimented with one major figurative sculpture, her 1971 *Untitled* (Israel Museum, Jerusalem). The full range of her practice across her career is discussed in Ian Berry, ed., *Nancy Grossman: Tough Life Diary* (Saratoga Springs, N.Y. and Munich: Frances Young Tang Teaching Museum and Art Gallery at Skidmore College with Prestel Verlag, 2012).

10 In this way, Raven's characterization of Grossman's identifications resonates with what Jack Halberstam has analysed as "female masculinity" in *Female Masculinity* (Durham, N.C. and London: Duke University Press, 1998).

11 A discussion of gender complexity in Grossman's work and its relationship to Surrealist precedents can be found in Anne Swartz, "The Erotics of Envelopment: Figuration in Nancy Grossman's Art," *n.paradoxa* 20 (2007): 64–70.

12 W[illiam] B[erkson], "Nancy Grossman," *Arts Magazine* 39, no. 9 (May–June 1965): 70.

13 The works before 1968 have rarely been discussed in detail. Notable exceptions are Arlene Raven, *Nancy Grossman* (Brookville, N.Y: Hillwood Art Museum, C. W. Post Campus, Long Island University, 1991); Arlene Raven, "True Grit," in *True Grit*, ed. Halley K. Harrisburg and Michael Rosenfeld (New York: Michael Rosenfeld Gallery, 2000), 2–5; Lowery Stokes Sims, "Loud Whispers," in *Nancy Grossman: Loud Whispers: Four Decades of Assemblage, Collage, and Sculpture* (New York: Michael Rosenfeld Gallery, 2000), 6–11; Mark Daniel Cohen, "Review: Nancy Grossman: Loud Whispers: Four Decades of Assemblage, Collage, and Sculpture," *Review: The Critical State of Visual Art in New York* (15 December 2000). Of related interest is Robert C. Morgan's essay on Grossman's return to relief assemblage in the 1990s, Robert C. Morgan, "Nancy Grossman: Opus Volcanus," *Sculpture* 17, no. 6 (July–August 1998): 36–41. A key source for these works is Nemser's interview with Grossman, in Nemser, *Art Talk*, 327–67.

14 Raven, *Grossman*, 105.

15 Nancy Grossman, interview with the author, 30 October 2009. She and Smith initially met at the Museum of Modern Art café. Someone had knocked Grossman's coffee over, and Smith offered to buy her a new one. They struck up a conversation, and Smith was intrigued by the black cigarettes Grossman smoked at the time. She sent him a pack, and he eventually invited her up to Bolton Landing.

16 Nancy Grossman, telephone conversation with the author, 2 December 2011.

17 Grossman, interview with the author, 30 October 2009.

18   Grossman, telephone conversation with the author, 2 December 2011.

19   Nancy Grossman in Nemser, *Art Talk*, 336. In Nemser's book, the last word is "moving," but I think it likely that this is a typographic or transcription error.

20   Ibid., 337.

21   Nancy Grossman, interview by Kate Horsfield, "Art and Artists: Nancy Grossman 1975," video produced by Lyn Blumenthal and Kate Horsfield, 1975, Video Data Bank, School of the Art Institute of Chicago.

22   Raven, *Grossman*, 103.

23   This is mentioned in ibid., 50. Grossman reiterated Gagarin's importance in her visual vocabulary in a telephone conversation with the author, 23 October 2011.

24   Grossman, telephone conversation with the author, 2 December 2011.

25   Grossman in Nemser, *Art Talk*, 340.

26   E.g., in 1956 Clement Greenberg called Smith "the best sculptor of his generation," explaining that "Smith was among the first in this country to practice the art of aerial drawing in metal"; Clement Greenberg, "David Smith," in *Clement Greenberg: The Collected Essays and Criticism*, ed. John O'Brian, 4 vols (University of Chicago Press, 1993), 3: 277. This became a standard appreciation of Smith's practice, which Greenberg called in 1964 "the cursiveness of Smith's drawing-in-air"; Clement Greenberg, "David Smith's New Sculpture" (1964), in ibid., 4: 190.

27   Grossman, telephone conversation with the author, 2 December 2011.

28   As Greenberg described it, "The regularity of contour and surface, the trued and faired planes and lines, are there in order to concentrate attention on the structural and general as against the material and specific, on the diagrammatic as against the substantial; but not because there is any virtue in regularity as such.…The relatively simple and forthright has been put together to form unities that are complex and polymorphous"; Greenberg, "David Smith's New Sculpture," 4: 191.

29   Grossman's *Totem* sculptures from 1966 to 1967 should be considered a further reflection on Smith's practice. "Totem" was a key concept for Smith and it provided a vehicle for a return to figuration in his *Tanktotem* series; see Ch. 1 above; Rosalind Krauss, *Terminal Iron Works: The Sculpture of David Smith* (Cambridge, Mass: MIT Press, 1971), 88–116; Rosalind Krauss, *Passages in Modern Sculpture* (Cambridge, Mass: MIT Press, 1977), 147–73.

30   Raven, *Grossman*, 102. Emphases original.

31   Grossman quoted in ibid. That Smith's death was a catalyst for Grossman was reiterated in Corin Robins, "Man is Anonymous: The Art of Nancy Grossman," *Art Spectrum* 1, no. 2 (February 1975): 36. This early article confused the objects and chronology, erroneously claiming that *Potawatami* (1967) was the first relief sculpture made from the harnesses Smith gave her.

32   Raven, *Grossman*, 100.

33   J. Jack Halberstam, *In a Queer Time and Place: Transgender Bodies, Subcultural Lives* (New York University Press, 2005), 124.

34   Ibid., 117.

35   Francis M. Naumann and David Nolan, *The Visible Vagina* (New York: Francis M. Naumann Fine Art and David Nolan Gallery, 2010).

36   Nemser, *Art Talk*, 340.

37   Grossman, interview by Horsfield, "Art and Artists: Nancy Grossman 1975."

38   Grossman, interview with the author, 30 October 2009.

39   Grossman, telephone conversation with the author, 23 October 2011.

40   Nemser was the outspoken editor of *Feminist Art Journal* from 1972 to 1977 and conducted the interviews that made up *Art Talk* with a purposefully feminist aim. As perhaps the first book about contemporary women's art, it was pioneering in the development of feminist art history and remains a key document of the decade. On

Nemser, see Judy K. Collischan Van Wagner, *Women Shaping Art: Profiles of Power* (New York: Praeger, 1984), 165–79.

41   See e.g. Barbara Rose, "Vaginal Iconology," *New York Magazine* 7 (11 February 1974): 59; Lisa Tickner, "The Body Politic: Female Sexuality and Women Artists Since 1970," *Art History* 1, no. 2 (1978): 236–49; Margo Hobbs Thompson, "Agreeable Objects and Angry Paintings: 'Female Imagery' in Art by Hannah Wilke and Louise Fishman, 1970–1973," *Genders* 43 (2006): n.p; Anna C. Chave, "'Is This Good for Vulva?': Female Genitalia in Contemporary Art," in Naumann and Nolan, *Visible Vagina*, 7–27.

42   Rachel Middleman has also argued that Hannah Wilke's use of vaginal imagery and ambiguity in her work of the 1960s is distinct from the later accounts of 1970s essentialism into which it has often been absorbed; Rachel Middleman, "Rethinking Vaginal Iconology with Hannah Wilke's Sculpture," *Art Journal* 72, no. 4 (2013): 34–45.

43   Judy Chicago and Miriam Schapiro, "Female Imagery," *Womanspace Journal* 1 (Summer 1973): 11–14. For discussion of the *Dinner Party* and its contentious reception, see Amelia Jones, ed., *Sexual Politics: Judy Chicago's Dinner Party in Feminist Art History* (Los Angeles: University of California Press, 1996).

44   Nemser, *Art Talk*, 345–6. Nemser and other co-editors of the *Feminist Art Journal* often decried Chicago's work and its singular reliance on genital imagery. For context, see Christine Rom, "One View: *The Feminist Art Journal*," *Woman's Art Journal* 2, no. 2 (Autumn–Winter 1981–2): 19–24.

45   See Cindy Nemser, "Towards a Feminist Sensibility: Contemporary Trends in Women's Art," *Feminist Art Journal* 5, no. 2 (Summer 1976): 19–23.

46   Virginia Pitts Rembert, "Review: Fiber and Form: The Woman's Legacy," *Woman's Art Journal* 18, no. 1 (Spring–Summer 1997): 65.

47   Gayle Salamon, *Assuming a Body: Transgender and Rhetorics of Materiality* (New York: Columbia University Press, 2010), 138. See further Judith Butler, *Undoing Gender* (New York and London: Routledge, 2004).

48   Grossman, telephone conversation with the author, 23 October 2011.

49   Raven, "True Grit," 5.

50   This was also mentioned in Sims, "Loud Whispers," 10.

51   Grossman, interview by Horsfield, "Art and Artists: Nancy Grossman 1975." She relates in detail in this interview the challenges she faced with publishing companies and reiterates the story told to Nemser.

52   Grossman in Nemser, *Art Talk*, 341.

53   This experience of restriction is discussed at length in Raven, *Grossman*, 106–10.

54   Grossman, telephone conversation with the author, 23 October 2011.

55   Nemser, *Art Talk*, 340.

56   Grossman, telephone conversation with the author, 23 October 2011.

57   Grossman, interview with the author, 30 October 2009.

58   Grossman, telephone conversation with the author, 23 October 2011.

59   Mick Farren, *The Black Leather Jacket* (New York: Abbeville Press, 1985). For further histories of the black leather jacket, see the exhaustive taxonomy in Rin Tanaka, *Motorcycle Jackets: A Century of Leather Design*, 2nd ed. (Atglen, Penna: Schiffer Publishing, 2006) and Lily Phillips, "Blue Jeans, Black Leather Jackets, and a Sneer: The Iconography of the 1950s Biker and its Translation Abroad," *International Journal of Motorcycle Studies* 1, no. 1 (March 2005), online at http://ijms.nova.edu/March2005/IJMS_Art-clPhilips0305.html.

60   Garry Marshall, oral history interview conducted by Karen Herman, 28 August 2000, part 5 of 6, *The Archive of American Television*, Museum of Broadcast Communications, online at

http://emmytvlegends.org/interviews/shows/happy-days. Fonzie's jacket was even dark brown, not black.

61 See Michael DeAngelis, *Gay Fandom and Crossover Stardom: James Dean, Mel Gibson, and Keanu Reeves* (Durham, N.C: Duke University Press, 2001) and Roy Grundmann, *Warhol's Blow Job* (Philadelphia: Temple University Press, 2003).

62 See Juan A. Suárez, *Bike Boys, Drag Queens, & Superstars: Avant-garde, Mass Culture, and Gay Identities in the 1960s Underground Cinema* (Bloomington and Indianapolis: Indiana University Press, 1996); Matthew Tinkcom, *Working Like a Homosexual: Camp, Capital, Cinema* (Durham, N.C: Duke University Press, 2002); Jack Hunter, ed., *Moonchild: The Films of Kenneth Anger* (London: Creation Books, 2002); Grundmann, *Warhol's Blow Job*.

63 Paul Welch, "Homosexuality in America," *Life* (26 June 1964): 66.

64 William Carney, *The Real Thing* (1968; New York: Masquerade Books, 1995), 25.

65 See Tanaka, *Motorcycle Jackets*, 130–1, as well as the related jackets made by Schott and distributed by Beck Motorcycle Distributors (p. 152).

66 Grossman, telephone conversation with the author, 2 December 2011.

67 Sims, "Loud Whispers," 9.

68 Grossman, interview with the author, 30 October 2009.

69 Grossman, telephone conversation with the author, 23 October 2011. I should note that Grossman's comments on the use of black in *Ali Stoker* do not appear to have racial undertones. Given Grossman's lifelong sympathies with the Civil Rights movement and her belief in self-determination, however, one could contend that the work's parady of macho might also be extended as a critique of the cultural cliches of black masculinity. As with her attempts to derail assumptions that the body's exterior seamlessly equates with gender, Grossman mocks such stereotypes for their inadequacies to the complexities of personhood.

70 Ibid.

71 Grossman, interview with the author, 30 October 2009.

72 Mark Daniel Cohen, "Review: True Grit," *Review: The Critical State of Visual Art in New York* (15 April 2000): 20.

73 Sims, "Loud Whispers," 9.

74 Catherine Lord, "Their Memory Is Playing Tricks on Her: Notes Toward a Calligraphy of Rage," in *Wack!: Art and the Feminist Revolution*, ed. Cornelia Butler (Los Angeles: Museum of Contemporary Art, 2007), 448. Lord is here referring not just to Grossman's post-1968 leather heads but also to the "butch sculptures of industrial jetsam [made] during the 1960s."

75 Grossman, interview with the author, 30 October 2009.

76 As Reis has chronicled, however, there is a long history of human bodies' resistance to this binary assignment of gender based on the infant's genitals and on doctors' beliefs that such bodies should be "normalized"; Elisabeth Reis, *Bodies in Doubt: An American History of Intersex* (Baltimore: Johns Hopkins University Press, 2009). See further the discussion in the Preface and Introduction.

77 Stryker, "My Words to Victor Frankenstein," 249.

78 Halberstam, *In a Queer Time*, 118–19. On the part-object in contemporary art, see Helen Molesworth, ed., *Part Object Part Sculpture* (Columbus, Ohio: Wexner Center for the Arts and Pennsylvania State University Press, 2005). On Hesse and the part-object, see Mignon Nixon, "Posing the Phallus," *October* 92 (Spring 2000): 96–127; Mignon Nixon, "o+x," *October* 119 (2007): 6–20. On the part-object as a protofeminist gesture for postwar sculpture, see Mignon Nixon, *Fantastic Reality: Louise Bourgeois and a Story of Modern Art* (Cambridge, Mass: MIT Press, 2005), 248.

79 In this, Grossman's work aligns with other artists who used assemblage as a medium through which to address issues of sex and gender in a

climate where positions of difference or dissent could not be articulated openly. This is compellingly argued in Jonathan D. Katz, "'Commiting the Perfect Crime': Sexuality, Assemblage, and the Postmodern Turn in American Art," *Art Journal* 67, no. 1 (Spring 2008): 38–53.

80 Grossman, interview with the author, 30 October 2009.

81 Nancy Grossman, diary entry, 28 June 1991; facsimile repr. in Michael Rosenfeld Gallery, *Nancy Grossman: Loud Whispers* (2000), 43.

82 Nancy Grossman quoted in Corin Robins, "Nancy Grossman," *Arts Magazine* 51, no. 4 (1976): 12.

83 Grossman in Nemser, *Art Talk*, 345.

84 Barbara Schwartz, "Letter from New York," *Craft Horizons* 32, no. 1 (February 1972): 42.

85 Nayland Blake, "Misrecognized," in Berry, *Nancy Grossman*, 105–7.

86 Grossman, interview with the author, 30 October 2009.

87 In a public conversation with Elizabeth Streb on 18 February 2012 at the opening of her retrospective at the Tang Teaching Museum and Art Gallery at Skidmore College, Saratoga Springs, N.Y, Grossman said that she used PC-7 epoxy to bind the planks into blocks.

88 Nancy Grossman quoted in Grace Glueck, "A 'New Realism' in Sculpture?" *Art in America* 59, no. 6 (November–December 1971): 152.

89 Raven, *Grossman*, 122.

90 Stephan Lesher, "The Calley Case Re-examined," *New York Times Sunday Magazine* (11 July 1971): 14.

91 James Olson and Randy Roberts, *My Lai: A Brief History with Documents* (New York: Palgrave Macmillan, 1998), 13. Such comments often came in the reporting on Medina, who many thought should also have been convicted: e.g. Thomas Buckley reported: "On the advice of his lawyers, Kadish and Truman, who monitored my conversations with him, Medina declined to give his opinion of Calley's performance in Hawaii and in Vietnam, but the statement of other members of the company and of Calley himself indicate that, despite the generally good rating Medina gave him, the opinion could not have been high. Most shavetails are a nuisance to their troops and their superiors, and Calley, with his limited abilities and attainments, his small size and apparently deeply rooted sense of inferiority, made matters worse through a compensating and highly transparent bluster"; Thomas Buckley, "The Captain Who Commanded Lieutenant Calley: Captain Medina," *New York Times Sunday Magazine* (20 June 1971): 26.

92 Most likely, Grossman's relaying of this phrase to Raven (for her 1991 book) was informed by the popular press surrounding the publication, four years before, of the controversial study of homosexual etiology by Richard Green, *The Sissy Boy Syndrome and the Development of Homosexuality* (New Haven and London: Yale University Press, 1987). Terminology and assumptions from Green's book circulated widely in the years following its publication. For a critique of Green, see "How to Bring Your Kids Up Gay: The War on Effeminate Boys," in Eve Kosofsky Sedgwick, *Tendencies* (Durham, N.C: Duke University Press, 1993), 154–66.

93 Raven, *Grossman*, 122.

94 Grossman, interview by Horsfield, "Art and Artists: Nancy Grossman 1975."

95 Schwartz, "Letter from New York," 42.

96 For general context, see Ann Gibson, "Abstract Expressionism's Evasion of Language," *Art Journal* 47, no. 3 (1988): 208–14.

97 Grossman, interview by Horsfield, "Art and Artists: Nancy Grossman 1975."

98 Blake, "Misrecognized," 107.

99 See "The night [Jacques] Plante made goaltending history," *NHL Insider online*, 1 November 2012, http://www.nhl.com/ice/news.htm?id=383063, accessed 23 September 2014.

100 Nancy Grossman has generously allowed

me to reproduce the previously unpublished photographs by Richard Avedon that illustrate some of her process on the core sculptures. I am grateful both to her and to the Richard Avedon Foundation for permitting the publication of this important documentation of her studio in 1970. In particular, Eugenia Bell provided much encouragement and support that helped these to come to light.

101   For aspects of this history, see e.g., David Kunzle, *Fashion & Fetishism: Corsets, Tight-lacing & Other Forms of Body-sculpture* (Stroud, Gloucestershire: Sutton Publishing, 2004); Valerie Steele, *Fetish: Fashion, Sex and Power* (Oxford and New York: Oxford University Press, 1996).

102   Michael Leigh, *The Velvet Underground* (New York: Macfadden Books, 1963).

103   John Perreault, "Leather: Associations For Your Own Good," *Village Voice*, 9 December 1971, 32.

104   Again, see Slifkin, *Out of Time*, on the concern caused by such "returns" to figuration in relation Philip Guston's infamous 1970 Marlborough Gallery.

105   Perreault, "Leather," 32.

106   Thomas Schroeder, "Nancy Grossman Ledermonstren," *Twen* 5 (May 1971): 39.

107   Allan Mankoff, "Ouch Art: The Pain Aesthetic," *Oui* 7 (July 1973): 76.

108   Gert Schiff, *Images of Horror and Fantasy* (Bronx, N.Y.: Bronx Museum of the Arts, 1977), n.p. Not surprisingly, the salaciousness of this error led to it being repeated in reviews of the exhibition, such as in Annette Kuhn, "Horror Hot and Cold," *Village Voice*, 12 December 1977, 88.

109   Blake, "Misrecognized," 106.

110   Grossman, interview with the author, 30 October 2009. See variation of this story in Nemser, *Art Talk*, 342.

111   Blake, "Misrecognized," 106.

112   Grossman's works appear hanging in an opulent bathroom in the home of Valerian Rybar, the famous interior designer to the rich, in "An Apartment That Works Like a Fine Watch with Precision and Beauty," *Home and Garden* 142, no. 4 (1972): 123, or on a hall table next to a mask from Cameroon in R.-J. V., "À Rome: Chez le directeur d'une galerie d'art," *Connaissance des arts* 259 (1973): 99.

113   Perreault, "Leather," 32.

114   Richard Jones, "Living with Change," *Residential Interiors* (November–December 1977): 62.

115   Grossman, interview with the author, 30 October 2009.

116   As evidenced in the passage from the Carney novel *The Real Thing* quoted above, such newfound popularity was a source of distrust for established members of s/m networks. One chronicler lamented the loss of the more clandestine and selective pre-Stonewall s/m community, saying: "Once the lure of s/m was discovered by those outside the ranks of aficionados, the trappings of the scene, stripped of its essence, became fashion. Leather bars, at least for men, proliferated, and publications featuring fetishes and kinks were sold on newsstands. Thousands, then tens of thousands of gay men adopted a carefully studied Tom of Finland look, but the sexual flavor of choice for the vast majority, once out of their clothes, was still plain vanilla"; David Stein, "S/M's Copernican Revolution: From a Closed World to the Infinite Universe," in *Leatherfolk: Radical Sex, People, Politics, and Practice*, ed. Mark Thompson (Boston: Alyson Publications, 1991), 148.

117   Jack Fritscher, *Popular Witchcraft: Straight from the Witch's Mouth*, rev. ed. (Madison: University of Wisconsin Press, 2004), 170; 1st ed. (lacking the reference to Grossman) Bowling Green University Popular Press, 1972.

118   Jack Fritscher, *Mapplethorpe: Assault with a Deadly Camera* (Mamoreneck, N.Y.: Hastings House, 1994), 41–2.

119   Grossman, interview with the author, 30 October 2009.

120 Ibid.

121 Grossman quoted in Swartz, "Erotics of Envelopment," 69.

122 Ibid.

123 Patricia Bosworth, *Diane Arbus: A Biography* (1984; New York: W. W. Norton, 2005), 318–19.

124 Ibid., 311–12.

125 Richard Goldstein, "S&M: The Dark Side of Gay Liberation," *Village Voice*, 7 July 1975, 10.

126 Ibid., 13. This article conflates Chris Burden, whose 1971 *Shoot* is mentioned just prior, with Scott Burton, known in the 1970s for elaborate and slow-moving performances based on body language and movement. Grossman's response was to a performance in which "a woman was compelled to execute a series of awkward and painful body movements." This description does not match Burden's practice but it does resemble Burton's *New Tableaux: Five Themes of Solitary Behavior* performed by Elke Solomon at Idea Warehouse, New York in March 1975. On Burton at this time, see the introduction to David Getsy, ed., *Scott Burton: Collected Writings on Art and Performance, 1965–1975* (Chicago: Soberscove Press, 2012), esp. 1–32. As I shall discuss in a future book, Burton's work (unlike Grossman's) was deeply invested in the culture and politics of s/m in the 1970s.

127 Goldstein, "S&M," 13. Similarly, Grossman later said, "If my figures are closed in, it's a state of being; it isn't perverse entertainment"; quoted in Rosalind Constable, "New Realism in Sculpture: Look Alive!" *Saturday Review* (22 April 1972): 40.

128 It is possible, however, that Grossman's exposure to the imagery of s/m's material culture by others provided her with some ideas about how to imagine the use of her bindings and buckles. This is less the case with the head sculptures than it is with the ambitious figure drawings (but which also incorporate firearms and other elements). Nevertheless, this reactive appropriation of the images foisted on her by others should not necessarily be taken as evidence for any deep involvement with the s/m community or s/m practices.

129 Grossman, interview by Horsfield, "Art and Artists: Nancy Grossman 1975."

130 Elizabeth Hess, "Of Human Bondage," *Village Voice*, 17 December 1980, 111.

131 See Grundmann, *Warhol's Blow Job*.

132 Eve Kosofsky Sedgwick, *Epistemology of the Closet* (Berkeley: University of California Press, 1990), 80. Emphasis original.

133 Grossman, interview with the author, 30 October 2009.

134 In addition to the context discussed in relation to *Bride*, Grossman also does not feature in accounts of alternatives to feminist figurative work. E.g., in a survey of feminist debates in the 1970s, Whitney Chadwick wrote of a division between women-identified figuration and feminist Postminimalism. Her dichotomous account is useful in that it helps to clarify how an artist such as Grossman – despite her success as both abstract and representational artist during the late 1960s and early 1970s – failed to register as sufficiently abstract or sufficiently representational of women. Whitney Chadwick, "Balancing Acts: Reflections on Postminimalism and Gender in the 1970s," in *More than Minimal: Feminism and Abstraction in the '70s*, ed. Susan L. Stoops (Waltham, Mass: Rose Art Museum, Brandeis University, 1996), 14–25.

135 Constable, "New Realism in Sculpture," 40.

136 Gayle Rubin, "The Leather Menace: Comments on Politics and S/M," (1981/82), in *Deviations: A Gayle Rubin Reader* (Durham, N.C. and London: Duke University Press, 2011), 127.

137 The phrase and periodization is drawn from Stryker, *Transgender History*, 59–89. See the discussion in the Introduction above.

138 Rubin, "Leather Menace," 127.

139 Mira Schor, "Representations of the

Penis," *M/E/A/N/I/N/G* 4 (November 1988): 12.

140 An exemplum can be found in the video interview by Horsfield, "Art and Artists: Nancy Grossman 1975."

141 E.g., in addition to the resistance transfolk encountered in some feminist communities, there were also pitched debates on the relationship among FTM, butch, and lesbian. See Halberstam, *Female Masculinity*, 141–73; Jacob Hale, "Consuming the Living, Dis(re)membering the Dead in the Butch/Ftm Borderlands," *GLQ* 4, no. 2 (1998): 311–48; Gayle Rubin, "Of Catamites and Kings: Reflections on Butch, Gender, and Boundaries" (1992), in *Deviations*, 241–53; Henry Rubin, *Self-made Men: Identity and Embodiment Among Transsexual Men* (Nashville, Tenn: Vanderbilt University Press, 2003) and Salamon, *Assuming a Body*, 95–128. More generally with regard to feminism, see Heyes, "Feminist Solidarity After Queer Theory," 1193–120 and Namaste, "Undoing Theory," 11–23.

142 Sheryl Korman, "Nancy Grossman: Doing the Only Thing That's Real," *Tucson Daily Citizen*, 22 January 1972, 9.

143 Grossman quoted in Swartz, "Erotics of Envelopment," 66.

144 Grossman in Nemser, *Art Talk*, 345.

145 Ibid., 344.

146 Grossman quoted in Swartz, "Erotics of Envelopment," 67.

147 Salamon, *Assuming a Body*, 93.

148 Grossman, interview with the author, 30 October 2009.

149 Grossman quoted in Swartz, "Erotics of Envelopment," 64. My emphasis.

150 Grossman in Nemser, *Art Talk*, 346.

4 DAN FLAVIN'S DEDICATIONS

1 John Perreault, "Snotty Remarks," *Village Voice*, 25 March 1971, 17.

2 Dan Flavin in Phyllis Tuchman, "Dan Flavin Interviewed by Phyllis Tuchman" (9 March 1972), in *Dan Flavin: A Retrospective*, ed. Michael Govan and Tiffany Bell (New York: Dia Art Foundation, 2004), 194.

3 However, see the useful discussions in Alex Potts, "Dan Flavin: 'In…Cool White' and 'Infected with a Blank Magic,'" in *Dan Flavin: New Light*, ed. Jeffrey Weiss (New Haven and London: Yale University Press, 2006), 6; and Michael Govan, "Irony and Light," in Govan and Bell, *Dan Flavin: A Retrospective*, 19–107.

4 See e.g. Flavin's defense of his titling in a letter written in response to Corinne Robins, "Object, Structure or Sculpture: Where Are We?" *Arts Magazine* 40, no. 9 (September/October 1966): 33–7. The terms of Flavin's riposte were clearly sexist, as he implied that his titles had "balls," a metalepsis registered and refused in Robins's letter of reply; Dan Flavin and Corinne Robins, "A Poetic Exchange" (Letters to the Editor), *Arts Magazine* 41, no. 4 (February 1967): 8. Flavin did not wait for *Arts Magazine* to publish his letter after he sent it, and he included it in his December *Artforum* contribution, "Some Remarks…Excerpts from a Spleenish Journal," *Artforum* 5, no. 4 (December 1966): 29.

5 In a 1965 letter to Richard Bellamy asking for a reference in support of his application for a Guggenheim fellowship, Flavin summarized his work and its prospects by saying that the support would bring "my use of fluorescent light further into the range of environmental 'sculpture'"; Dan Flavin to Richard Bellamy, 24 August 1965, Richard Bellamy Papers, Museum of Modern Art Archives, New York, III.A.22. Ever the contrarian, Flavin gave a lecture in the Sculpture Department at the Rhode Island School of Design the following year, on 9 March 1966. In an implicit snub to the sculpture faculty who had invited him, he remarked: "Don Judd, who has one of the most deft intellects at work in New York, has claimed that painting on canvas is obsolete. Now, could

you make a similar determination about the sculpture which you are working on or plan to attempt? Parenthetically, my own proposal has become mainly an indoor routine of placing strips of fluorescent light. It has been labeled sculpture by people who should know better"; Dan Flavin, "A Speech for the Senior and Graduate School Students in Sculpture at the Rhode Island School of Design," 9 March 1966, copy in the Robert Smithson and Nancy Holt Papers, Archives of American Art, Smithsonian Institution, B3.76.

6 Dan Flavin quoted in Michael Gibson, "The Strange Case of the Fluorescent Tube," *Art International* 1 (Autumn 1987): 105.

7 For a useful overview and analysis of these works, see Corinna Thierolf and Johannes Vogt, *Dan Flavin: Icons* (Munich: Pinakothek der Moderne and Schirmer/Mosel, 2009).

8 Dan Flavin, "'…in daylight or cool white': an autobiographical sketch," *Artforum* 4, no. 4 (December 1965): 24 n. 1. Flavin later attempted to suppress the implicit anthropomorphism, changing "square-faced" to "square-fronted" in subsequent editions of his autobiography.

9 Sidney Tillim, "Month in Review," *Arts Magazine* 37, no. 6 (March 1963): 61; Donald Judd, "Dan Flavin," *Arts Magazine* 38, no. 7 (April 1964): 31.

10 Flavin, "'daylight or cool white,'" 24.

11 James Meyer, *Minimalism: Art and Polemics in the Sixties* (New Haven and London: Yale University Press, 2001), 95.

12 The exhibitions were "New Work" at Green Gallery, 8 January–2 February 1963; the solo exhibition "dan flavin: some light" at Kaymar Gallery, 5–29 March 1964; "Eleven Artists" at Kaymar Gallery, 31 March–14 April 1964. For discussion of these exhibitions, see Meyer, *Minimalism*, 95–108.

13 Judd, "Dan Flavin," 31; Flavin, "'daylight or cool white,'" 24; Barbara Rose, "ABC Art," *Art in America* 53, no. 5 (October–November 1965): 68.

14 Flavin referred to them as "clear glass candle bulbs" in Dan Flavin, "Letter to the Editor," *ARTnews* 62, no. 2 (April 1963): 6. I am grateful to Hollis Clayson for her suggestions about the specific type of bulbs Flavin employed.

15 Flavin did have unexecuted plans for others, however, as with the drawing for *Martyr's Crown*; see *Dan Flavin Drawing*, ed. Isabelle Dervaux (New York: Morgan Library & Museum, 2012), 102.

16 Lucy Lippard, "New York," *Artforum* 2, no. 11 (May 1964): 54.

17 Flavin, "Letter to the Editor," 6, in response to Jill Johnston, "New Works" [Green Gallery], *ARTnews* 62, no. 1 (March 1963): 50.

18 Rose, "ABC Art," 68.

19 For an account of this change, see Lauren Roth, "Flesh in Wax: Demystifying the Skin Colours of the Common Crayon," in *Visual Communication and Culture: Images in Action*, ed. Jonathan Finn (Don Mills, Ontario: Oxford University Press, 2012), 73–85.

20 E.g. *Africa (to seventy-two negroes)*, 1960, or the drawing *to those who suffer in the Congo*, 1961.

21 Dan Flavin, 19 February 1963 letter to Seymour H. Knox, President of the Albright-Knox Art Gallery (letter's location unknown). Flavin often wrote best when addressing an individual person, and many of his writings from the early 1960s first appeared in personal letters which were then excerpted and copied into his notes for possible publication. This was the passage that accompanied the illustration of this work in Rose's "ABC Art." See further below.

22 Dan Flavin, letter of 19 February 1963, rev. in Brydon Smith, *Dan Flavin: Fluorescent Light, etc.* (Ottawa: National Gallery of Canada, 1969), 152; this version repr. in Evelyn Weiss, Dieter Ronte, and Manfred Schneckenburger, *Dan Flavin: Three Installations in Fluorescent Light* (Cologne: Wallraf-Richartz-Museums and Kunsthalle Köln, 1973), 83.

23 Caroline Jones, "Light Speed: Dan Flavin at the National Gallery," *Artforum* 43, no. 6 (Feb-

ruary 2005): 157. As Potts noted, "there is in Flavin's titling and commentary [on *Coran's Broadway Flesh*] a gratuitous expressiveness – a psychologically charged frisson that straight society would have associated at the time with male homosexuality"; Potts, "Dan Flavin," 4.

24 Joseph Masheck, "Corn-fed Egotism" (Letter to the Editor), *Studio International* 177, no. 911 (May 1969): 209. In the same letter, Masheck later made his own insinuations, saying "It strikes me that prose like Flavin's is a necessary by-product (*waste* product?) of the art. It is the obverse of the anal-retentive coin, a pressure built up which, well, *came out* in words." (210)

25 Dan Flavin, "Several More Remarks…," *Studio International* 177, no. 910 (April 1969): 175.

26 Dan Flavin, "Some Other Comments …More Pages From a Spleenish Journal," *Artforum* 6, no. 4 (December 1967): 21. Thomas Wilfred's *Lumia Suite, Opus 158* had been commissioned by MoMA in 1963 and remained on view throughout the decade "in a small darkened theater in the Auditorium Gallery"; press release for *Thomas Wilfred: Lumia*, 10 August 1971, Press Archives, Museum of Modern Art, New York.

27 "Barbara Rose as muse above the art political wars is as incredible an image as Lady Godiva riding through the countryside in Rudi Gernreich's homosexually transparent undies"; Flavin, "Several More Remarks…," 174.

28 A comprehensive collection of Flavin's published writings (with some additional unpublished notes and passages) was included in Weiss, Ronte, and Schneckenburger, *Three Installations*.

29 In reference to Joyce's *A Portrait of the Artist as a Young Man* (1916), Neuner argues: "This romantic conception of an autarchic artistic identity provides the standard against which Flavin's self-portrait measures itself"; Stefan Neuner, "Dan Flavin on the Path to an Ironic-sublime: Some Remarks on '…in daylight or cool white,'" in *Dan Flavin – Lights* (Vienna and Ostfildern: Museum Moderner Kunst Stiftung Ludwig Wien and Hatje Cantz Verlag, 2012), 35. While I concur about the heavily revised and edited autobiography, it may be overly generous to ascribe such literary aspirations to Flavin's other writings of the 1960s, which were often bilious and dismissive of others. As *Artforum*'s editor-in-chief, Philip Leider recalled of these years: "Flavin wrote me constantly from Valhalla [in New York State]. Really paranoid. I published a lot of it for a while but then I stopped because they kept getting so crazy and Dan was so paranoid"; in Amy Newman, *Challenging Art: Artforum 1962–1974* (New York: Soho Press, 2003), 256.

30 Dan Flavin, Curriculum Vitae for Copley Foundation, 1964, William and Noma Copley Foundation and Collection Records, Getty Research Institute, Los Angeles, Series 1, box 1, folder 6. Flavin scholars might note that this text offers new information about Flavin's early art training. In addition to the information in the Vitae that was not transferred to his published autobiography, the Copley Foundation papers also contain an early version (then untitled) of "daylight or cool white…," dated 11 October 1965 and submitted as part of his Guggenheim Fellowship application, which slightly revises the chronology of Flavin's engagement with art in the early 1950s; Series 1, box 2, folder 6.

31 Flavin, "'daylight or cool white,'" 22. My emphasis.

32 Flavin, "'daylight or cool white,'" my emphasis, rev. version in Smith, *fluorescent light, etc. from Dan Flavin*, 12.

33 Dan Flavin, 18 October 1967 letter to Jan van der Marck, Exhibition Archives, Museum of Contemporary Art Chicago, Flavin 1967, box 2, folder 8. It was this experience that fueled Flavin's invectives against institutionalized art education, most notably his screed "'…on an American artist's education…,'" *Artforum* 6, no. 7 (March 1968): 28–32.

34 Flavin, "Several More Remarks…," 175.

35 Nicholas de Villiers, *Opacity and the Closet: Queer Tactics in Foucault, Barthes, and Warhol* (Min-

neapolis: University of Minnesota Press, 2012), 2–3.

36 See David Raskin, *Donald Judd* (New Haven and London: Yale University Press, 2010).

37 Flavin quoted in Gibson, "Strange Case," 105.

38 See Govan, "Irony and Light," 26.

39 Ralph Ellison, *Invisible Man* (New York: Random House, 1952), 3–14; Flavin's selection from the prologue took from 6–7.

40 Flavin's extract of Ellison's prologue was ultimately not included in the contentious catalogue that was produced for this show. Jan van der Marck's notes include a page with a quotation from the Ellison novel among others from Flavin that went unused for the catalogue; Exhibition Archives, Museum of Contemporary Art Chicago, Flavin 1967, box 2, folder 6.

41 Edward M. Plunkett should not be confused with his contemporary Edward John Carlos Plunkett, the 20th Baron of Dunsany, though both were painters. E. J. C. Plunkett, in the early 1960s, lived in Rio de Janeiro and then Paris and was decidedly not the adult education art teacher to whom Flavin referred in his notebook (see n. 43 below). It is E. M. Plunkett who (as I briefly discuss later in this chapter) was also Robert Rosenblum's correspondent. This is confirmed by the fact that there are letters in the Rosenblum correspondence from New York to Rosenblum in Paris, signed Edward Plunkett, and with a return addressee "E. M. Plunkett" living at 303 East 76th Street in New York; Edward Plunkett, 2 October 1961 letter to Robert Rosenblum, Robert Rosenblum Papers, Archives of American Art, Smithsonian Institution, box 28. For some insight on Plunkett, see Edward M. Plunkett, "The New York School of Correspondence," *Art Journal* 36, no. 3 (Spring 1977): 233–5.

42 Meyer, *Minimalism*, 95.

43 Dan Flavin, "Record Book 1962–63: Excerpts," in Dervaux, *Dan Flavin Drawing*, 61.

44 Dan Flavin, List of Collectors, part of his application for a Copley Foundation Grant, signed and dated 25 October 1964; William and Noma Copley Foundation and Collection Records, Getty Research Institute, Series 1, box 1, folder 6.

45 This was one of the key themes of Jonas Barish, *The Anti-theatrical Prejudice* (Berkeley: University of California Press, 1981).

46 In his study of the musical, John Clum asks, "What is gay about *Gypsy* (except for its lyricist, librettist, and director)? Everything one might say comes out sounding like a stereotype. But there was a time when gay men proudly, if secretly, played to their stereotypes: the time of the diva musicals. There was a lot a gay young man in 1959, used to reading his fantasies through women characters, could read into *Gypsy*"; John M. Clum, *Something for the Boys: Musical Theater and Gay Culture* (New York: St. Martin's Press, 1999), 169–70.

47 D. A. Miller, *Place for Us: Essay on the Broadway Musical* (Cambridge, Mass: Harvard University Press, 1998), 16. Explaining the importance of Broadway for the pre-Stonewall era, Miller writes (26): "'Broadway' denominates those early pre-sexual realities of gay experience to which, in numerous lives, it became forever bound: not just the solitude, shame, secretiveness by which the impossibility of social integration was first internalized; or the excessive sentimentality that was the necessary condition of sentiments allowed no real object; but also that intense, senseless *joy* that, while not identical to these destitutions, is neither extricable from them. Precisely against such realities, however, is post-Stonewall gay identity defined: a declarable, dignified thing, rooted in a community, and taking manifestly sexual pleasures on this affirmative basis." For an extended discussion of the implications and perceptiveness of Miller's reading, see David Halperin, *How to Be Gay* (Cambridge, Mass: Belknap Press of Harvard University Press, 2012, 90–108.

48 Flavin to Knox, 19 February 1963; my emphasis. This line from the letter was not included in the first version of this excerpt published in Rose, "ABC Art," 68 but it was included in the 1969 Ottawa exhibition catalogue, Smith, *fluorescent light, etc.*, 152. As I discuss presently, this version differs in other significant ways from the 1965 publication.

49 Dervaux, *Dan Flavin Drawing*, 99.

50 Flavin had already planned *Coran's Broadway Flesh* on an inventory drawing of 18 July 1962 and he resolved to build it on 17 September, the same day on which he wrote: "icon IV is ready to be painted"; Flavin, "Record Book 1962–63," 52. The wiring for *icon V* was more complex than any he had attempted previously, and the work was not completed for a few months: he dated the back 19 December 1962.

51 Ibid., 51.

52 The catalogue notes for his 1969 Ottawa retrospective (which Flavin edited and approved), noted: "The all-whiteness of this construction suggested to Flavin an intended reference to the use of white in Chinese funerals"; Smith, *fluorescent light, etc.*, 142. In the same article where his description of *Coran's Broadway Flesh* was published, Rose's "ABC Art," Flavin's memorial dedication to his brother was also quoted. She noted, though, how neutral Flavin's mention of his brother's death was; Rose, "ABC Art," 69.

53 Govan, "Irony and Light," 26, 106 n. 25.

54 That *icon IV* and *V* were understood as a pair is evidenced in Virginia Dwan's recollection of the January 1963 show, in an interview: "In any case, what I also saw was a group show, which consisted of early works of Donald Judd and some of Dan Flavin's early work, including a tribute to his brother, his twin brother had died. That would include a peach-colored painting and regular light bulbs"; in Virginia Dwan and Erik La Prade, "Virginia Dwan," in *Breaking Through: Richard Bellamy and the Green Gallery 1960–1965*, ed. Erik La Prade (New York: Midmarch Arts Press, 2009), 180. In that 1963 show, the original *pure land* was damaged. For Flavin's major one-person show at Kaymar Gallery the next year, he made sure to include in its place the five-and-a-half foot square "prayer drawing" for *the pure land*, thus insuring that the work would be seen in some form with *Coran* and the others. See Flavin, "Record Book 1962–63," 51.

55 Dan Graham and Thurston Moore, "The Conceptual Artist and the Sonic Youth Rocker in Conversation," *Time Out New York*, 7 May 2009, n.p; online at www.timeout.com/newyork/things-to-do/dan-graham-and-thurston-moore.

56 In this regard, even if Graham's comments were unfounded (as some will no doubt contend), the co-extensiveness of the memorial *icon IV* and the flesh-tint *icon V* still produces a dichotomy between purity and carnality that hinges on the outed and flamboyant homosexuality that Flavin attributed to half of this pair.

57 The icons that preceded *pure land* and *Broadway Flesh* were also tied up with questions of visible verification and the unseen. The fore-titles of *icon I* and *II* are "the heart" and "the mystery," both of which are abstract qualities that can only be felt or sensed, whereas *icon III* was titled "(blood) (the blood of a martyr)." Blood is the visual indication of harm (especially since, on oxidation, it turns bright red), and a martyr's blood is a definitional requirement of that status.

58 Flavin, "'daylight or cool white,'" 22.

59 "[Sullivan's father's] face was once described as 'excessively Irish,' which meant that in repose it looked like the caricatures in the old comic papers, rather simian"; Willard Connely, *Louis Sullivan As He Lived: The Shaping of American Architecture* (New York: Horizon Press, 1960), 23.

60 In parallel to this practice, Flavin maintained a mode of drawing quite distinct from the anti-illusionism and literalism he sought in his sculptural objects. This is well chronicled in Dervaux, *Dan Flavin Drawing*.

61 Flavin, "'daylight or cool white,'" 24.

62 E.g. Joachim Pissarro, "Dan Flavin's Epiphany," *Yale University Art Gallery Bulletin* (1997/1998): 84–7.

63 In Flavin, "Record Book 1962–63," 64, 65, on 11 September 1963, he wrote: "Saturday (last) Sonja and I brought home the eight foot slimline....Sonja wired the slimline tonight – it's near perfect. I am delighted"; on 4 October, he stated: "The diagonal declared itself – a delight!"

64 Helpful discussions of this issue can be found in Anne Middleton Wagner, "Flavin's Limited Light," in Weiss, *Dan Flavin: New Light*, 108–32; Potts, "Dan Flavin," 1–24; Richard Schiff, "Lumination," in *Dan Flavin: Series and Progressions*, ed. Kristine Bell, Tiffany Bell, and Alexandra Whitney (Göttingen, Germany: Steidl with David Zwirner Gallery, New York, 2010), 83–93.

65 See e.g. Michael Govan, "...Electric Light Defining Space," in *Light in Architecture and Art: The Work of Dan Flavin*, ed. Jeffrey Kopie and Steffen Böddeker (Marfa, Tex: Chinati Foundation, 2002), 65–84; Hal Foster, "Dan Flavin and the Catastrophe of Minimalism," in Weiss, *Dan Flavin: New Light*, 133–51.

66 Flavin, "'daylight or cool white,'" 24.

67 Rose, "ABC Art," 68.

68 See above, nn. 21, 22. Flavin was closely involved with the editing of the Ottawa catalogue (Smith, *fluorescent light, etc.*), as is discussed in Brydon Smith, "Recollections and Thoughts About Dan Flavin," in Govan and Bell, *Dan Flavin: A Retrospective*, 136–8.

69 Robert Smithson, "Entropy and the New Monuments," *Artforum* 4, no. 10 (June 1966): 27.

70 Govan, "Irony and Light," 106 n. 26.

71 Dan Flavin, journal entry dated 26 November 1964, in Kristine Bell, Greg Lulay, and Alexandra Whitney, eds., *Dan Flavin: The 1964 Green Gallery Exhibition* (New York: Zwirner & Wirth, 2008), 30. For the previous day, 25 November, he had written about Johns's declaration, "'It's a joy to see it.' As Jasper Johns burst out of the large room at the Green on his way to the elevator (He usually scurries from people). He beamed and blushed for Sonja and me. He had come away from his island in South Carolina to see my show, Dine's last day, and Warhol's opening. The elevator came and he was gone. (Sat., Nov. 21, 1964)."

72 Jill Johnston, *Jasper Johns: Privileged Information* (New York: Thames and Hudson, 1996), 14.

73 See e.g. Kenneth Silver, "Modes of Disclosure: The Construction of Gay Identity and the Rise of Pop Art," in *Hand-painted Pop: American Art in Transition 1955–62*, ed. Russell Ferguson (Los Angeles: Museum of Contemporary Art, 1992), 178–203; Jonathan D. Katz, "The Art of Code: Jasper Johns & Robert Rauschenberg," in *Significant Others: Creativity & Intimate Partnership*, ed. Whitney Chadwick and Isabelle de Courtivron (London: Thames and Hudson, 1993), 189–207; Gavin Butt, *Between You and Me: Queer Disclosures in the New York Art World, 1948–1963* (Durham, N.C. and London: Duke University Press, 2005); Jonathan D. Katz, "'Commiting the Perfect Crime': Sexuality, Assemblage, and the Postmodern Turn in American Art," *Art Journal* 67, no. 1 (Spring 2008): 38–53.

74 James Rondeau, "Jasper Johns: Gray," in *Jasper Johns: Gray*, ed. James Rondeau and Douglas Druick (Art Institute of Chicago with Yale University Press, 2007), 45–7.

75 Another title given was *no. 1 of May 27, 1963*. See Govan and Bell, *Dan Flavin: Complete Lights*, 220, cat. 23.

76 The *one of May 27th, 1963* was initially shown vertically when it was exhibited at Green Gallery in 1964, thus reiterating the vertical red tube Flavin had planned for *red out of a corner*. It seems that later, Flavin toyed with the idea of showing this work in other orientations; see ibid.

77 It should be remembered that the late-twentieth century association of the color pink with homosexuality emerged as a widespread iconographic sign only in the post-Stonewall era as activists reclaimed the color used to identify homosexuals during the Holocaust. The more common color associated with homosexuality during the 1950s and early 1960s was lavender. The pink of *pink out of a corner* is accordingly not a coded sign for homosexuality, per se, though it may be a more local reference to Flavin's conceptually linked pinkish *Broadway Flesh*.

78 This modifies but reinforces Caroline Jones's observation that "Jasper Johns is everywhere in these early icons...Thus the metamorphosis of early Flavin takes on a special charge when an icon such as *Coran's Broadway Flesh* moves through a figure of martyrdom (in the related drawing [of *the martyr's crown*]) and reemerges as the near-absolute abstraction of *pink out of a corner (to Jasper Johns)*, 1963. Apart from the obvious formal transformation from pink pigment to pink fluorescent tube, the reference to 'icon' returns via the *placement* of the later work. From blank, flesh-colored center in the 1962 work to the 'blankness' of a standard fluorescent fixture in 1963, the distilled and abstracted icon is now installed *in a corner* – a charged position for the Russian abstractionists Tatlin and Malevich, whom Flavin was studying and who both positioned works in the corner, where domestic religious icons had always hung"; Jones, "Light Speed," 157.

79 Govan and Bell, *Dan Flavin: Complete Lights*, 223, cat. 29. Further evidence that the dedication to Annina Nosei was not added until the work was executed and exhibited in 1970 is indicated by the fact that Flavin met Nosei through John Weber, whom he did not know in 1963. Oral History interview with John Weber by James McElhinney, 21 March–4 April 2006, Archives of American Art, Smithsonian Institution.

80 Flavin, "'daylight or cool white,'" 24. As with many of the quotations from this original version, Flavin significantly altered his words when he edited his writings for publication in 1973.

81 On the practice and rewards of dissemblance among Johns and his peers, see Jonathan D. Katz, "Passive Resistance: On the Critical and Commercial Success of Queer Artists in Cold War American Art," *L'image* 3 (1996): 119–42.

82 As an interesting side note, *pink out of a corner* was purchased by a gay patron, Philip Johnson, who installed it in his gallery home in New Canaan, Connecticut. The underground building was built like a bunker and Johnson placed the Flavin work so that it stood just inside the darkened doorway. In this way, the Flavin work acted as solicitation and sentry for this cave-like entrance. Flavin remarked on this installation on a questionnaire given to him by a MoMA curatorial department (in relation to their acquisition of a drawing for *pink out of a corner*). Asked "Were there any exceptional circumstances or incidents in the making of this work or in its subsequent history?" Flavin gave a reply that indicated the "curious" nature of this installation: "Curiously, coincidentally perhaps, 'pink out of a corner' in fluorescent light was positioned in the entrance of the first cave-like gallery either for opening or shortly thereafter"; Dan Flavin, Collection Records Questionnaire, 22 September 1972, Curatorial Files, Museum of Modern Art, Flavin 619.71/acquisition 67.1979. A photograph of this installation was published in *Vogue* 147, no. 9 (1 May 1966), 200.

83 "A piece of wall can be visually disintegrated from the whole into a separate triangle by plunging a diagonal of light from edge to edge on the wall"; Flavin, "'daylight or cool white,'" 24.

84 The phrase "diagonal of personal ecstasy" has been discussed by Anna C. Chave, "Minimal-

ism and the Rhetoric of Power," *Arts Magazine* 64, no. 5 (1990): 45–6; and Jones, "Light Speed," 154–9, 206.

85 Flavin, "Record Book 1962–63," 65.

86 Again, the complexity of the *diagonal* and its logic of interchangeability is evidenced in the discussion of the retrospective catalogue entry for the work in Smith, "Recollections," 136–8.

87 Neuner points out that Flavin's quotation from Kant in his autobiography was taken from a mistranscription borrowed from Robert Rosenblum, "The Abstract Sublime," *ARTnews* 59, no. 10 (February 1961): 38–40, 56–8; Neuner, "Flavin on the Path," 49.

88 The drawing was dated 25 April 1963, one month before the conception of the *diagonal*.

89 The daylight *diagonal* dedicated to Brancusi was on view at the *Black, White, and Gray* exhibition at the Wadsworth Atheneum, which began on 9 January 1964.

90 Dan Flavin, 21 January 1964 letter to Samuel Wagstaff, quoted in James Crump, "Art of Acquisition: The Eye of Sam Wagstaff," *Archives of American Art Journal* 46, no. 3–4 (Fall 2007): 12. See also Robert Rosenblum, "Name in Lights," *Artforum* 35, no. 7 (March 1997): 11–12. Flavin would repeat this story a few times.

91 Fred Licht, 1964 (specific date illegible) letter to Robert Rosenblum; Robert Rosenblum Papers, Archives of American Art, Smithsonian Institution.

92 Mac McGinnes, interview with the author, 2 November 2012. Another friend recalled, "I saw him occasionally in Mac [McGinnes's] apartment in the early '70s […] At the time I was unaware of his professional stature. He was another one of Mac's brilliant gay friends, but operating on a higher level, and he at some point had a cute younger boyfriend who was pretty quiet (as was I in that company)"; email from Michael Harwood to the author, 12 August 2012.

93 In addition to his friends, many in the art world more broadly understood Rosenblum as a gay man through to the 1970s. This is evidenced, in the negative, when Gregory Battcock wrote in 1975 that "Rosenblum's gone straight, didn't you know" in his reporting on the book release party for Rosenblum's *Modern Painting and the Northern Romantic Tradition*, which was, it seems, a who's who of New York art history and criticism at the time. Battcock remarked: "Rosenblum is the youngest and most glamorous of the truly big-time art historians….It was the sort of party that was so impressive that, well, there was hardly a guest that didn't count for something"; Gregory Battcock, "Where the Elite Meet," *Soho Weekly News*, 9 October 1975, 23. The guest list included H. W. Janson, Linda Nochlin, and Henry Russell Hitchcock. Battcock was referring to the fact that Rosenblum had increasingly distanced himself from the identity he had adopted with friends in the previous decade. In the late 1970s, Rosenblum became romantically involved with and eventually married the painter Jane Kaplowitz in 1978. Even after he transitioned out of his relationships with men and into his new sexual identity, Rosenblum retained much of the camp humor that was central to gay male subcultural language of the late 1950s and 1960s. This was implied in the affectionate and respectful memoir of Rosenblum by Jack Bankowsky, the former editor of *Artforum*: "Revisionary History: On Robert Rosenblum," *Artforum* 45, no. 7 (March 2007): 67, 69, 339.

94 Flavin in Barbara Rose, Ronald Davis, Dan Flavin, Craig Kauffman, and John McCracken, transcript of a symposium held on 6 May 1967 in conjunction with the exhibition *A New Aesthetic* at the Washington Gallery of Modern Art, Washington, D.C; Barbara Rose Papers, Archives of American Art, Smithsonian Institution, p. 23. Reiterating the dirtiness of illusion in this context, Craig Kauffman followed Flavin's comment with

"I just said to Dan that as far as I was concerned it was an indiscretion on my part once in a while" and John McCracken said, "It seems to me that illusionism is okay, but trickery is not; deception is not."

95 That Flavin associated the general topic of sexuality to the development of his use of fluorescent tubes is indicated by a note fragment he published in 1973. Like the other revisions and editing of the late 1960s, this odd, undated comment buried within the anthology of his writings served to distance further the conception of the early fluorescents from homosexuality, claiming a straight derivation instead. "Recently, while considering old watercolored sheets and folding books filled with watercolors and poetry, etc. for inclusion in a proposed retrospective examination within The National Gallery of Canada and elsewhere, I was surprised to discover that the aforementioned modular projects for fluorescent light had a painted precedent which dated, at least, from early 1959. These previous examples, entitled 'act of love', were a developmental sequential set of five watercolors with a freely construed quasi-symbolic representation of sexual intercourse"; Flavin in Weiss, Ronte, and Schneckenburger, *Three Installations*, 111.

96 This was well stated in an early review by Jack Burnham: "The nominalism which Flavin asserts is a double-edged logic. On one hand he denies universals (the painter's field and its inherent illusions) by simply setting up three groups of fixtures [in *the nominal three*] – no more, no less; concurrently Flavin creates not only a two-dimensional surface, but a series of hodological spaces within and beyond the work itself. This posits the indivisibility of esthetic experience, not by means of abstractions and universals, but through the immediate experience of concrete objects. Of course these two are contradictory and Flavin is faced with the same dilemma as Ockham, namely how does one intuit a nonexistant thing (unified esthetic experience and/or God) if it is assumed that all knowledge must be based upon intuition gained by direct experience with real objects?" Jack Burnham, "A Dan Flavin Retrospective in Ottawa," *Artforum* 8, no. 4 (December 1969): 52.

97 "Dan's titles always referred to what he was thinking at the time," recalled Barbara Rose in 2008 in reference to Flavin's one-person show at Green Gallery; in Bell, Lulay, and Whitney, *Dan Flavin: 1964 Green Gallery Exhibition*, 18.

98 For critique of this use of space, see Foster, "Catastrophe of Minimalism," 133–51; Anna C. Chave, "Revaluing Minimalism: Patronage, Aura, and Place," *Art Bulletin* 90, no. 3 (September 2008): 466–86.

99 Burnham, "Flavin Retrospective," 55.

100 Kauffman in Rose, et al., transcript of *New Aesthetic* symposium, p. 17.

101 Flavin, "Some Remarks," 27.

102 Flavin, "Some Other Comments," 21.

103 Dan Graham in Jan Van Der Marck, ed., *Dan Flavin: Pink and Gold*, exh. cat., Museum of Contemporary Art Chicago, 1967, n.p., ed. and repr. as "Flavin's Proposal," *Arts Magazine* 44, no. 4 (February 1970): 44.

104 Barnett Newman quoted in Smith, *fluorescent light, etc.*, 144.

105 Flavin, extracted from a 22 June 1967 letter to Dan Graham, repub. in Flavin, "Some Other Comments," 23. My emphasis. For a discussion of this shift, see Meyer, *Minimalism*, 102–5.

106 "I had thought to dedicate the entire installation to Mies van der Rohe, a longtime Chicago resident, because here was this rather formal situation colored pink and yellow in a paradoxical way. I thought of attaching that to his name somewhat in the way I had done with Mondrian. It was almost like subject matter....But he was then old and arthritic, and I couldn't do it"; Flavin in Tuchman, "Flavin Interviewed," 194.

On the exhibition at the Museum of Contemporary Art Chicago, see Alexandra Whitney, "An Illuminating Paradox: Dan Flavin's *alternating pink and 'gold,'* 1967," in Bell, Bell, and Whitney, *Dan Flavin: Series and Progressions*, 17–23.

107 Tuchman, "Flavin Interviewed," 194.

108 John C. Welchman, *Invisible Colors: A Visual History of Titles* (New Haven and London: Yale University Press, 1997), 43.

109 Ibid., 1.

110 Brenda Richardson, *Frank Stella: The Black Paintings* (Baltimore Museum of Art, 1976), 3.

111 I am grateful to Lisa Lee for prompting me to think deeply about the effects of the "to" when she acted as respondent to my presentation of this material in the 30 October 2013 Weissbourd Seminar of the Society of Fellows in the Liberal Arts at the University of Chicago.

112 Gérard Genette, *Paratexts: Thresholds of Interpretation* (1987), trans. Jane E. Lewin (Cambridge University Press, 1997), 11–12. Both my usage of "performative" and Genette's refer to speech act theory and its foundational definition in J. L. Austin, *How to Do Things With Words* (Oxford: Clarendon Press; Cambridge, Mass: Harvard University Press, 1962).

113 Genette, *Paratexts*, 134.

114 Joan Lowndes, "Flavin's 'Mystical' Aura" (1969), in *It Is What It Is: Writings on Dan Flavin since 1964*, ed. Paula Feldman and Karsten Schubert (London: Thames & Hudson, 2004), 65.

115 Genette, *Paratexts*, 134.

116 Ibid., 136.

117 Andrea Rosen, "'Untitled' (The Neverending Portrait)," in *Felix Gonzalez-Torres*, ed. Dietmar Elger (Hannover and Ostfildern-Ruit: Sprengel Museum Hannover and Hatje Cantz Verlag, 1997), 57.

118 Grégoire Müller, *The New Avant-garde: Issues for the Art of the Seventies* (London: Pall Mall Press, 1972), 10.

119 Rosen, "'Untitled' (The Neverending Portrait)," 55.

120 Tuchman, "Flavin Interviewed," 194.

121 *Gypsy* is, in fact, all about acts of naming and renaming, from the repeated "My name's June! What's yours?" to the "gimmick" stage names to Gypsy's declaration: "I am Gypsy Rose Lee! I love her – and if you don't you can clear out now!" Arthur Laurents, Stephen Sondheim, and Jule Styne, *Gypsy: A Musical* (New York: Theater Communications Group, 1960), 101. Furthermore, D. A. Miller has examined the mobility of gender in the book, as when Rose says about her daughter, "Louise can be a boy" (9); Miller, *Place for Us*.

122 Such naming is rife in the personal correspondence of the 1960s into the early 1970s in the Robert Rosenblum Papers, Archives of American Art, Smithsonian Institution.

123 Mac McGinnes said of Rosenblum's list: "A lot of it was compiled on a trip he made to Chicago on an afternoon with me and Dennis Adrian. What you may not know is that its genesis was a list of drag names for American presidents. Bobby went through his copy of the *Encyclopaedia Britannica* and scratched out all the real names. It was a long time ago, but some that I remember are: Cherry Washington, Babe Lincoln, Dawn Adams and Dawn Quincy Adams, Anne of Cleveland, Dot Polk, Liz Tyler, and Tokyo Roosevelt. Name magic was important in those days"; email from Mac McGinnes to the author, 15 August 2012. He expanded on this history in my interview with him on 2 November 2012.

124 The copy of the typewritten transcription of the list with Rosenblum's handwritten annotations (including the addition of Flavin) was sent to Michael Harwood, who generously provided it to me; email from Harwood, 12 August 2012.

125 Flavin, "Some Remarks," 27.

CONCLUSION: ABSTRACTION AND THE UNFORECLOSED

1   Judith Butler, *Undoing Gender* (New York and London: Routledge, 2004), 51.

2   For *Cuts*, Cassils trained with the fitness legend Charles Glass at the famous Venice Muscle Beach in California. As with all of Cassils's preparatory work, a precise regimen of advanced training was developed in consultation with experts such as Glass in order to achieve the transformation required for each performance.

3   Heather Cassils, email to the author, 26 September 2014.

4   Heather Cassils, interview with the author, 1 August 2014.

5   I have discussed at length the implications of Rodin's performative mark-making and its relationship to the multistage process of casting in *Rodin: Sex and the Making of Modern Sculpture* (New Haven and London: Yale University Press, 2010).

6   At the time of writing, Cassils has plans to cast the work in bronze with the aim that, when displayed in public, the cumulative caresses of its viewers will bring shine to certain areas, allowing for a work that is like a durable monument but also bears evidence of repeated bodily engagements.

7   Burton will be the subject of a future book. For an overview of his relationship to the 1960s, however, see the introduction to my volume of his art criticism and writings, David Getsy, ed., *Scott Burton: Collected Writings on Art and Performance, 1965–1975* (Chicago: Soberscove Press, 2012), 1–32.

8   Scott Burton, interview of 10 October 1979, in Michael Auping, *30 Years: Interviews and Outtakes* (Fort Worth, Tex: Modern Art Museum of Fort Worth, 2007), 79.

9   Ibid., 81.

10 Audio recording of interview between Scott Burton and Edward Brooks de Celle, March 1980; Edward Brooks de Celle Papers, Archives of American Art, Smithsonian Institution, Washington, D.C. Emphases mine.

11 Much of this section first appeared in the folio published to accompany the exhibition *FLEX* curated by Orlando Tirando at Kent Fine Art, New York, in 2014.

12 Michael Fried, "Art and Objecthood," *Artforum* 5, no. 10 (June 1967): 19.

13 There are many artists both established and emerging who are, today, exploring abstraction as a resource for engaging with transgender and queer experience. Artists such as Jonah Groeneboer, Math Bass, Gordon Hall, Linda Besemer, Amy Sillman, Ulrike Müller, Sadie Benning, Carrie Moyer, Harmony Hammond, Sheila Pepe, Elijah Burgher, Edie Fake, Prem Sahib, Tom Burr, and Shahryar Nashat have all (very differently) incorporated abstraction of varying degrees into their practices for its capacities and openness.

14 Butler, *Undoing Gender*, 3–4.

15 For a survey of other practices in art since 1960 that have taken gender's mutability and multiplicity as a theme, see Frank Wagner, Kasper König, and Julia Friedrich, eds., *Das achte Feld: Geschlechter, Leben und Begehren in der Kunst seit 1960* (Ostfildern: Hatje Cantz and Museum Ludwig, 2006).

16 In this regard, such scenes turned on the attempt to establish gender agreements, in the sense proposed in Whitney Davis, "Gender," in *Critical Terms for Art History*, ed. Robert S. Nelson and Richard Shiff (University of Chicago Press, 1996), 220–33. While Davis's analysis primarily deals with representation, the method of tracking agreement classes with regard to gender is also suggestive when dealing with abstraction and other forms of non-representational art. The sculptors I have chosen for analysis, from this

perspective, are particularly interesting for the ways in which they confound or defer agreements and invite non-agreements and contestations, as in the dialogic situations discussed in the chapters.

17 Bonnie Clearwater, "John Chamberlain interview, 1991 Jan. 29–30," Oral History Archives, Archives of American Art, Smithsonian Institution, 16.

BIBLIOGRAPHY

ARCHIVES

Richard Avedon Foundation Archives
Archives of American Art, Smithsonian Institution, Washington, D.C.
   Edward Brooks de Celle Papers
   Helen Frankenthaler and Robert Motherwell Papers
   Kenneth Noland Papers
   Oral History Archive
   Barbara Rose Papers
   Robert Rosenblum Papers
   David Smith Papers
   Robert Smithson and Nancy Holt Papers
Thomas J. Dodd Research Center, University of Connecticut, Storrs
   Donald Allen Collection of Frank O'Hara Letters
Getty Research Institute, Los Angeles
   William and Noma Copley Foundation and Collection Records
Nancy Grossman Studio Archives
Museum of Contemporary Art Chicago Exhibition Archives
Museum of Modern Art Archives, New York
   Richard Bellamy Papers
   Scott Burton Papers
   Film Study Center, Department of Film
   Frank O'Hara Papers
   Curatorial Archives, Department of Painting and Sculpture
National Gallery of Art Library, Washington, D.C.
   Department of Image Collections
   Special Collections
School of the Art Institute of Chicago
   Video Data Bank
David Smith Estate Archives
Francis Young Tang Teaching Museum and Art Gallery at Skidmore College Curatorial Archives

PUBLICATIONS

"A Change of Gender." *Newsweek* 5 December 1966, 73.

"Sex-change Operations at a U.S. Hospital." *U.S. News & World Report* 5 December 1966, 13.

"Surgery: A Body to Match the Mind." *Time* 2 December 1966, 52.

Ajootian, Aileen. "The Only Happy Couple: Hermaphrodites and Gender." In *Naked Truths: Women, Sexuality, and Gender in Classical Art and Archaeology*, ed. Ann Olga Koloski-Ostrow and Claire L. Lyons. London and New York: Routledge, 1997, 220–42.

Alloway, Lawrence. "Sculpture as Cliché." *Artforum* 2, no. 4 (October 1963): 26.

Altieri, Charles. *Enlarging the Temple: New Directions in American Poetry during the 1960s*. Lewisburg, Penn: Bucknell University Press, 1979.

Altman, Dennis. *Homosexual Oppression and*

Liberation. New York: Outerbridge & Dienstfrey, 1971.

Andre, Carl. "A Word for John Chamberlain" (1961/71), *Artforum* 10, no. 6 (February 1972): 6.

Anfam, David. "Chamberlain's Gambit: 'Cautious Maniac.'" In *John Chamberlain: Sculpture 1988–2001*. London: Waddington Galleries, 2002, 5–7.

Applebaum, Anne. "David Smith: Whitechapel Gallery." *Artforum* 25, no. 8 (April 1987): 143–4.

Applin, Jo. *Eccentric Objects: Rethinking Sculpture in 1960s America*. New Haven and London: Yale University Press, 2012.

Armstrong, Richard, and Richard Marshall, eds. *The New Sculpture 1965–1975: Between Geometry and Gesture*. New York: Whitney Museum of American Art, 1990.

Auping, Michael. "John Chamberlain: Reliefs 1960–1982." In *John Chamberlain: Reliefs 1960–1982*. Sarasota, Fl: John and Mable Ringling Museum of Art, 1983, 9–13.

—. "An Interview with John Chamberlain." In *John Chamberlain: Reliefs 1960–1982*. Sarasota, Fl: John and Mable Ringling Museum of Art, 1983, 15–18.

—. *30 Years: Interviews and Outtakes*. Fort Worth, Tex: Modern Art Museum of Fort Worth, 2007.

Austin, J. L. *How to Do Things With Words*. Oxford: Clarendon Press; Cambridge, Mass: Harvard University Press, 1962.

Ayden, Erje. "From *Seven Years of Winter*" (1970). In *Homage to Frank O'Hara*, ed. Bill Berkson and Joe LeSueur. Berkeley, Calif: Creative Arts Book Company, 1980, 171–2.

Baker, Elizabeth. "The Secret Life of John Chamberlain." *ARTnews* 68, no. 2 (April 1969): 48–51, 63–4.

—. "The Chamberlain Crunch." *ARTnews* 70, no. 10 (February 1972): 26–31, 60–1.

—, John Chamberlain, Donald Judd, and Diane Waldman. "Excerpts from a Conversation." In *John Chamberlain: A Retrospective Exhibition*, ed. Diane Waldman. New York: Solomon R. Guggenheim Museum, 1971, 15–21.

Bankowsky, Jack. "Revisionary History: On Robert Rosenblum." *Artforum* 45, no. 7 (March 2007): 67, 69, 339.

Bannard, Darby. "Cubism, Abstract Expressionism, David Smith." *Artforum* 6, no. 8 (April 1968): 22–32.

Barish, Jonas. *The Anti-theatrical Prejudice*. Berkeley: University of California Press, 1981.

Baro, Gene. "Some Late Words from David Smith." *Art International* 9, no. 7 (20 October 1965): 47–51.

Batchelor, David. *Chromaphobia: Ancient and Modern, and a Few Notable Exceptions*. Leeds: Henry Moore Institute Essays on Sculpture, 1997.

—. *Chomophobia*. London: Reaktion, 2000.

Battcock, Gregory. "Humanism and Reality – Thek and Warhol." In *The New Art: A Critical Anthology*, ed. Gregory Battcock. New York: E. P. Dutton, 1965.

—. "The Politics of Space." *Arts Magazine* 44, no. 4 (1970): 40–3.

—. "Where the Elite Meet." *Soho Weekly News* 9 October 1975, 23.

—, ed. *Minimal Art: A Critical Anthology*. New York: E. P. Dutton, 1968.

Beckmann, Angelica. "The Roving Eye: On John Chamberlain's Approach to Photography and Film." In *John Chamberlain*, ed. Jochen Poetter. Stuttgart: Edition Cantz and Staatliche Kunsthalle Baden-Baden, 1991, 115–24.

Bedford, Chris. "New Unities." In *David Smith: Cubes and Anarchy*, ed. Carol Eliel. Los

Angeles County Museum of Art, 2011, 89–115.

Bell, Kristine, Greg Lulay, and Alexandra Whitney, eds. *Dan Flavin: The 1964 Green Gallery Exhibition*. New York: Zwirner & Wirth, 2008.

Bell, Larry. "Perfect Fit." *Artforum* 50, no. 7 (March 2012): 239, 241.

Bell, Tiffany. "Working Strategies." In *Light in Architecture and Art: The Work of Dan Flavin*, ed. Jeffrey Kopie and Steffen Böddeker. Marfa, Tex: Chinati Foundation, 2002, 111–26.

Benjamin, Harry. "Transvestism and Transsexualism." *International Journal of Sexology* 7, no. 1 (August 1953): 12–14.

—. *The Transsexual Phenomenon*. New York: Julian Press, 1966.

Benjamin, Jessica. *Like Subjects, Love Objects: Essays on Recognition and Sexual Difference*. New Haven and London: Yale University Press, 1995.

—. *Shadow of the Other: Intersubjectivity and Gender in Psychoanalysis*. New York: Routledge, 1998.

B[erkson], W[illiam]. "Nancy Grossman." *Arts Magazine* 39, no. 9 (May–June 1965): 70.

Berkson, Bill. "Frank O'Hara and His Poems" (1967/69). In *Homage to Frank O'Hara*, ed. Bill Berkson and Joe LeSueur. Berkeley, Calif: Creative Arts Book Company, 1980, 161–5.

Berry, Ian, ed. *Nancy Grossman: Tough Life Diary*. Saratoga Springs, N.Y. and Munich: Frances Young Tang Teaching Museum and Art Gallery at Skidmore College with Prestel Verlag, 2012.

Blackless, Melanie, Anthony Charuvastra, Amanda Derryck, Anne Fausto-Sterling, Karl Lauzanne, and Ellen Lee. "How Sexually Dimorphic Are We? Review and Synthesis." *American Journal of Human Biology* 12 (2000): 151–66.

Blake, Nayland. "Misrecognized." In *Nancy Grossman: Tough Life Diary*, ed. Ian Berry. Saratoga Springs, N.Y. and Munich: Frances Young Tang Teaching Museum and Art Gallery at Skidmore College with Prestel Verlag, 2012, 105–7.

Blühm, Andreas. *The Colour of Sculpture 1840–1910*. Zwolle: Waanders Uitgevers for Van Gogh Museum, Amsterdam, and Henry Moore Institute, Leeds, 1996.

Bois, Yve-Alain. "Dumb." In *Eva Hesse: Sculpture*, ed. Elisabeth Sussman and Fred Wasserman. New York: Jewish Museum, 2006, 17–28.

—, and Rosalind Krauss. *Formless: A User's Guide*. New York: Zone Books, 1997.

Boone, Bruce. "Gay Language as Political Praxis: The Poetry of Frank O'Hara." *Social Text* 1 (Winter 1979): 59–92.

Boorstin, Jonathan. "Art in Process." *Harvard Crimson* 1 October 1966.

Bosworth, Patricia. *Diane Arbus: A Biography* (1984). New York: W. W. Norton, 2005.

Bourdon, David. "Dan Flavin." *Village Voice* 20 November 1964, 11.

—. *Warhol*. New York: Harry N. Abrams, 1989.

Bourgeois, Louise. "A Merging of Male and Female" (1974). In *Louise Bourgeois: Destruction of the Father/Reconstruction of the Father: Writings and Interviews 1923–1997*, ed. Marie-Laure Bernadac and Hans Ulrich Obrist. Cambridge, Mass: MIT Press, 1998, 101.

Bredbeck, Gregory. "B/O – Barthes's Text/O'Hara's Trick." *PMLA* 108, no. 2 (1993): 268–82.

Brennan, Marcia. *Modernism's Masculine Subjects: Matisse, the New York School, and Postpainterly Abstraction*. Cambridge, Mass: MIT Press, 2004.

Brenson, Michael. "David Smith's Embrace." In *David Smith: To and From the Figure*. New York: Knoedler, 1995, n.p.

—. "The Fields." In *David Smith: A Centennial*, ed. Carmen Giménez. New York: Solomon R. Guggenheim Museum, 2006, 39–67.

Breslin, James. "The Contradictions of Frank O'Hara." *American Poetry Review* 12, no. 6 (November/December 1983): 7–16.

Bryan-Wilson, Julia. "Hard Hats and Art Strikes: Robert Morris in 1970." *Art Bulletin* 89, no. 2 (2007): 333–59.

—. *Art Workers: Radical Practice in the Vietnam War Era*. Berkeley: University of California Press, 2009.

Buchloh, Benjamin. "Michael Asher and the Conclusion of Modernist Sculpture" (1980). In *Neo-avantgarde and Culture Industry: Essays on European and American Art from 1955 to 1975*. Cambridge, Mass: MIT Press, 2000, 1–39.

Buckley, Thomas. "A Changing of Sex by Surgery Begun at Johns Hopkins." *New York Times* 21 November 1966, 1, 32.

—. "The Transsexual Operation." *Esquire* 67, no. 4 (April 1967): 111–15, 205–8.

—. "The Captain Who Commanded Lieutenant Calley: Captain Medina." *New York Times Sunday Magazine* 20 June 1971, SM 8–9, 26–30, 34, 40.

Budnik, Dan. "Visits with David Smith." In *Seeing David Smith: Photographs by Dan Budnik*. New York: Knoedler, 2006, n.p.

Burnham, Jack. "On Being Sculpture," *Artforum* 7, no. 9 (May 1969): 44–5.

—. "A Dan Flavin Retrospective in Ottawa," *Artforum* 8, no. 4 (December 1969): 48–55.

Burton, Scott. "Notes on the New." In *When Attitudes Become Form*, ed. Harald Szeemann. Bern: Kunsthalle Bern, 1969, n.p.

—. "Time on Their Hands." *ARTnews* 68, no. 4 (1969): 40–3.

Butler, Judith. *Subjects of Desire: Hegelian Reflections on Twentieth-century France*. New York: Columbia University Press, 1987.

—. *Gender Trouble: Feminism and the Subversion of Identity*. New York and London: Routledge, 1990.

—. "Imitation and Gender Insubordination," in *Inside/Out: Lesbian Theories, Gay Theories*, ed. Diana Fuss. London and New York: Routledge, 1991, 13–31.

—. *Bodies That Matter: On the Discursive Limits of "Sex."* New York and London: Routledge, 1993.

—. "Melancholy Gender/ Refused Identification." In *The Psychic Life of Power: Theories in Subjection*. Stanford University Press, 1997, 132–50.

—. "How Can I Deny That These Hands and This Body Are Mine?" (1998). In *Material Events: Paul De Man and the Afterlife of Theory*, ed. Tom Cohen, J. Hillis Miller and Barbara Cohen. Minneapolis: University of Minnesota Press, 2001, 264–73.

—. *Undoing Gender*. New York and London: Routledge, 2004.

—. *Giving an Account of Oneself*. New York: Fordham University Press, 2005.

Butler, Ruth. *Western Sculpture: Definitions of Man*. Boston: New York Graphic Society, 1975.

Butt, Gavin. *Between You and Me: Queer Disclosures in the New York Art World, 1948–1963*. Durham, N.C. and London: Duke University Press, 2005.

Button, John. "Frank's Grace." In *Homage to Frank O'Hara*, ed. Bill Berkson and Joe LeSueur. Berkeley, Calif: Creative Arts Book Company, 1980, 41–5.

—. "Some Memories" (1980). *No Apologies* 2 (1984): 28–31.

Byron, Stuart. "Reactionaries in Radical Drag." *Village Voice* 16 March 1972, 69.

—. "Frank O'Hara: Poetic 'Queertalk'" (1974). In *Frank O'Hara: To Be True to a City*, ed. Jim Elledge. Ann Arbor: University of Michigan Press, 1990, 64–9.

Califia, Patrick. *Sex Changes: The Politics of Transgenderism*. San Francisco: Cleis Press, 1997.

Cameron, Dan. *Extended Sensibilities: Homosexual Presence in Contemporary Art*. New York: New Museum, 1982.

Canaday, John. "The Least Cruel Artist Alive." *New York Times* 28 November 1971, D21.

Carney, William. *The Real Thing* (1968). New York: Masquerade Books, 1995.

Carroll, Paul. "An Impure Poem About July 17, 1959." In *The Poem in Its Skin*. Chicago and New York: Follett Publishing, 1968, 157–64.

Carter, Julian. "On Mother-love: History, Queer Theory, and Nonlesbian Identity." *Journal of the History of Sexuality* 14, no. 1/2 (January 2005): 107–38.

Chadwick, Whitney. "Balancing Acts: Reflections on Postminimalism and Gender in the 1970s." In *More Than Minimal: Feminism and Abstraction in the '70s*, ed. Susan L. Stoops. Waltham, Mass: Rose Art Museum, Brandeis University, 1996, 14–25.

Chamberlain, John. "Ultra Violet in Depth." *New York Review of Sex & Politics* 1, no. 2 (1 April 1969): 12–16.

—. "A Statement." In *John Chamberlain Sculpture: An Extended Exhibition*. New York: Dia Art Foundation, 1982, n.p.

—, and Klaus Kertess. "John Chamberlain in Conversation with Klaus Kertess, 8 October 2005." *Chinati Foundation Newsletter* 11 (October 2006): 10–17.

Chamberlain, John, and Lawrence Weiner. "Skimming the Water: The Gondolas of John Chamberlain." In *John Chamberlain: Gondolas and Dooms Day Flotilla*. New York: Dia Center for the Arts, 1991, 6–9.

Chase, Cheryl. "Hermaphrodites with Attitude: Mapping the Emergence of Intersex Political Activism." *GLQ* 4, no. 2 (1998): 189–211.

Chave, Anna C. "Minimalism and the Rhetoric of Power." *Arts Magazine* 64, no. 5 (1990): 44–63.

—. *Constantin Brancusi: Shifting the Bases of Art*. New Haven and London: Yale University Press, 1993.

—. "Minimalism and Biography." *Art Bulletin* 82, no. 1 (2000): 149–63.

—. "Revaluing Minimalism: Patronage, Aura, and Place," *Art Bulletin* 90, no. 3 (September 2008): 466–86.

—. "'Is This Good for Vulva?': Female Genitalia in Contemporary Art." In *The Visible Vagina*, ed. Francis M. Naumann and David Nolan. New York: Francis M. Naumann Fine Art, and David Nolan Gallery, 2010, 7–27.

Chicago, Judy, and Miriam Schapiro. "Female Imagery." *Womanspace Journal* 1 (Summer 1973): 11–14.

Clum, John M. *Something for the Boys: Musical Theater and Gay Culture*. New York: St. Martin's Press, 1999.

Codinha, Alessandra. "Working Deep Beneath the Think." *Intermission* 8 (2013): 60–9.

Cohen, Mark Daniel. "Review: True Grit." *Review: The Critical State of Visual Art in New York* (15 April 2000): 19–21.

—. "Review: Nancy Grossman: Loud Whispers: Four Decades of Assemblage, Collage, and Sculpture." *Review: The Critical State of Visual Art in New York* (15 December 2000): 5–8.

Cohn, Marjorie. *Lois Orswell, David Smith, and Modern Art*. New Haven and London: Yale University Press in association with Harvard University Art Museums, 2002.

Collischan Van Wagner, Judy K. *Women Shaping*

Art: Profiles of Power. New York: Praeger, 1984.

Colpitt, Frances. *Minimal Art: The Critical Perspective*. Ann Arbor, Mich: UMI Research Press, 1990.

Connell, Raewyn. "Transsexual Women and Feminist Thought: Toward New Understanding and New Politics." *Signs* 37, no. 4 (Summer 2012): 857–81.

Connely, Willard. *Louis Sullivan As He Lived: The Shaping of American Architecture*. New York: Horizon Press, 1960.

Constable, Rosalind. "New Realism in Sculpture: Look Alive!" *Saturday Review* 22 April 1972, 36–40.

Corbino, Marcia. "Creating Art from Industrial Waste." *Sarasota Herald Tribune* 18 January 1981, 16–21.

Cotten, Trystan, ed. *Transgender Migrations: The Bodies, Borders, and Politics of Transition*. New York: Routledge, 2011.

Cottingham, Laura. "Shifting Ground: On the Critical Practice of Lucy Lippard." In *Seeing through the Seventies: Essays on Feminism and Art*. Amsterdam: G and B Arts, 2000, 1–46.

Crawford, Lucas. "Breaking Ground on a Theory of Transgender Architecture." *Seattle Journal for Social Justice* 8, no. 2 (May 2010): 515–39.

—. "A Transgender Poetics of the High Line Park." *TSQ: Transgender Studies Quarterly* 1, no. 4 (November 2014): 482–500.

Crawford, Lynda. "Men Become Women: A Charm School for Transsexuals." *Soho Weekly News* 16 October 1975, 10–11, 18.

Creeley, Robert. "John Chamberlain." In *Recent American Sculpture*, ed. Hans van Weeren-Griek. New York: Jewish Museum, 1964, 17.

—. "Robert Creeley on John Chamberlain" (1978). In *Chamberlain*, ed. Marianne Schmidt-Miescher and Johannes Gachnang. Kunstalle Bern, 1979, 15–19.

—. "Interview with John Chamberlain, 11/29/1991" (unpublished [1991]). Collection of the Estate of John Chamberlain.

Crow, Thomas E. *Modern Art in the Common Cultures*. New Haven and London: Yale University Press, 1996.

—. *The Rise of the Sixties: American and European Art in the Era of Dissent*. New York: Harry N. Abrams, 1996.

—. "Figures of Emergence in the Recent Sculpture of John Chamberlain." In *John Chamberlain: New Sculpture*, ed. Kara Vander Weg. New York: Gagosian Gallery, 2011, 4–8.

Crump, James. "Art of Acquisition: The Eye of Sam Wagstaff." *Archives of American Art Journal* 46, no. 3–4 (Fall 2007): 5–13.

Curtis, Penelope. *Sculpture 1900–1945: After Rodin*. Oxford University Press, 1999.

—. "After Rodin: The Problem of the Statue in Twentieth-century Sculpture." In *Rodin: The Zola of Sculpture*, ed. Claudine Mitchell. Farnham: Ashgate, 2004, 237–44.

Davidson, Michael. *Guys Like Us: Citing Masculinity in Cold War Poetics*. University of Chicago Press, 2003.

Davidson, Susan, ed. *John Chamberlain: Choices*. New York: Solomon R. Guggenheim Museum, 2012.

Davis, Whitney. "The Subject in the Scene of Representation." *Art Bulletin* 76, no. 4 (1994): 570–5.

—. "Gender." In *Critical Terms for Art History*, ed. Robert S. Nelson and Richard Shiff, University of Chicago Press, 1996, 220–33.

—. *Replications: Archaeology, Art History, Psychoanalysis*. University Park: Pennsylvania State University Press, 1996.

Dawson, Fielding. "Self Portrait in Steel: A Talk

with John Chamberlain." *Arts Magazine* 64, no. 8 (April 1990): 54–7.

D'Emilio, John. *Sexual Politics, Sexual Communities: The Making of a Homosexual Minority in the United States 1940–1970*. Chicago and London: University of Chicago Press, 1983.

de Kooning, Elaine. "David Smith Makes a Sculpture" (1951). In *The Spirit of Abstract Expressionism: Selected Writings*, ed. Rose Slivka and Marjorie Luyckx. New York: George Braziller, 1994, 103–8.

de Villiers, Nicholas. *Opacity and the Closet: Queer Tactics in Foucault, Barthes, and Warhol*. Minneapolis: University of Minnesota Press, 2012.

DeAngelis, Michael. *Gay Fandom and Crossover Stardom: James Dean, Mel Gibson, and Keanu Reeves*. Durham, N.C: Duke University Press, 2001.

DeLong, Marilyn, Kelly Gage, Juyeon Park, and Monica Sklar. "From Renegade to Regular Joe: The Black Leather Jacket's Values for Bikers." *International Journal of Motorcycle Studies* 6, no. 2 (2010): n.p.

Deepwell, Katy. "Feminist Readings of Louise Bourgeois or Why Louise Bourgeois is a Feminist Icon." *n.paradoxa* 3 (May 1997): 28–38.

Dervaux, Isabelle, ed. *Dan Flavin Drawing*. New York: Morgan Library & Museum, 2012.

Devor, Aaron H., and Nicholas Matte. "One Inc. and Reed Erickson: The Uneasy Collaboration of Gay and Trans Activism, 1964–2003." *GLQ* 10, no. 2 (2004): 179–209.

Diamonstein, Barbaralee. "100 Women in Touch with Our Time." *Harper's Bazaar* 3110 (January 1971): 104–17.

Didi-Huberman, Georges. *Confronting Images: Questioning the Ends of a Certain History of Art*. University Park: Pennsylvania State University Press, 2005.

Doyle, Jennifer. *Sex Objects: Art and the Dialectics of Desire*. Minneapolis: University of Minnesota Press, 2006.

—. *Hold It against Me: Difficulty and Emotion in Contemporary Art*. Durham, N.C: Duke University Press, 2013.

Dumbadze, Alexander. "'Can You Hear the Lights?'" In *Art, History and the Senses: 1830 to the Present*, ed. Patrizia Di Bello and Gabriel Koureas. Farnham: Ashgate, 2010, 117–31.

Dwan, Virginia, and Erik La Prade. "Virginia Dwan." In *Breaking Through: Richard Bellamy and the Green Gallery 1960–1965*, ed. Erik La Prade. New York: Midmarch Arts Press, 2009, 180–1.

Edelson, Mary Beth. "Some Living American Women Artists." *Off Our Backs* 4, no. 2 (1974): 10–11.

Eliel, Carol. "Geometry in David Smith." In *David Smith: Cubes and Anarchy*, ed. Carol Eliel. Los Angeles County Museum of Art, 2011, 15–61.

Elledge, Jim, ed. *Frank O'Hara: To Be True to a City*. Ann Arbor: University of Michigan Press, 1990.

—. "The Lack of Gender in Frank O'Hara's Love Poems to Vincent Warren." In *Fictions of Masculinity: Crossing Cultures, Crossing Sexualities*, ed. Peter F. Murphy. New York University Press, 1994, 226–37.

Elliot, Patricia. *Debates in Transgender, Queer, and Feminist Theory: Contested Sites*. Farnham: Ashgate, 2010.

Elliott, Clare, and Robert Gober. *Forrest Bess: Seeing Things Invisible*. New Haven and London: Yale University Press and the Menil Collection, 2013.

Ellison, Ralph. *Invisible Man*. New York: Random House, 1952.

Farren, Mick. *The Black Leather Jacket*. New York: Abbeville Press, 1985.

Fausto-Sterling, Anne. *Sexing the Body: Gender Politics and the Construction of Sexuality*. New York: Basic Books, 2000.

—. *Sex/Gender: Biology in a Social World*. New York: Routledge, 2012.

Feinberg, Leslie. "Transgender Liberation: A Movement Whose Time Has Come" (1992). In *The Transgender Studies Reader*, ed. Susan Stryker and Stephen Whittle. New York and London: Routledge, 2006, 205–20.

—. *Transgender Warriors: Making History from Joan of Arc to Dennis Rodman*. Boston: Beacon Press, 1997.

—. "Street Transvestite Action Revolutionaries." *Workers World* 24 September 2006.

Feldman, Alan. *Frank O'Hara*. Boston, Mass: Twayne Publishers, 1979.

Fer, Briony. *On Abstract Art*. New Haven and London: Yale University Press, 1997.

—. *The Infinite Line: Re-making Art After Modernism*. New Haven and London: Yale University Press, 2004.

—. "Nocturama: Flavin's Light Diagrams." In *Dan Flavin: New Light*, ed. Jeffrey Weiss. New Haven and London: Yale University Press, 2006, 25–48.

—. *Eva Hesse: Studiowork*. Edinburgh: Fruitmarket Gallery, 2009.

Ferguson, Russell. *In Memory of My Feelings: Frank O'Hara and American Art*. Los Angeles: Museum of Contemporary Art, 1999.

Fillin-Yeh, Susan. "Dandies, Marginality, and Modernism: Georgia O'Keeffe, Marcel Duchamp, and Other Cross-dressers." *Oxford Art Journal* 18, no. 2 (1995): 33–44.

—, ed. *Dandies: Fashion and Finesse in Art and Culture*. New York University Press, 2001.

Finn, David. *One Man's Henry Moore*. Redding Ridge, Conn: Black Swan Books, 1993.

Firbank, Maxwell. "Bound and Gagged on Greene Street." *Soho Weekly News* 8 January 1976, 6–7.

Flavin, Dan. "Letter to the Editor." *ARTnews* 62, no. 2 (April 1963): 6.

—. "'…in daylight or cool white': an autobiographical sketch." *Artforum* 4, no. 4 (December 1965): 20–4.

—. "Some Remarks…Excerpts from a Spleenish Journal." *Artforum* 5, no. 4 (December 1966): 27–9.

—. "Some Other Comments…More Pages from a Spleenish Journal." *Artforum* 6, no. 4 (December 1967): 20–5.

——. "Letter to the Editor." *Artforum* 6, no. 6 (February 1968): 4.

—. "'…on an American artist's education…'" *Artforum* 6, no. 7 (March 1968): 28–32.

——. "Letter to the Editor." *Artforum* 6, no. 8 (April 1968): 4.

—. "Several More Remarks…," *Studio International* 177, no. 910 (April 1969): 173–5.

—. "Record Book 1962–63: Excerpts." In *Dan Flavin Drawing*, ed. Isabelle Dervaux. New York: Morgan Library & Museum, 2012, 48–67.

—, and Corinne Robins. "A Poetic Exchange" (Letter to the Editor). *Arts Magazine* 41, no. 4 (February 1967): 8.

Flavin, Dan, and Brydon Smith. "Fluorescent Light, Etc. From Dan Flavin: A Supplement." *Artscanada* 136/137 (1969): 14–19.

Foster, Hal. "The Crux of Minimalism" (1986). In *The Return of the Real*. Cambridge, Mass: MIT Press, 1996, 35–68.

—. "Dan Flavin and the Catastrophe of Minimalism." In *Dan Flavin: New Light*, ed. Jeffrey Weiss. New Haven and London: Yale University Press, 2006, 133–51.

Foucault, Michel. *The History of Sexuality: Vol. 1, an Introduction* (1976). New York: Vintage Books, 1990.

—. "Introduction." In *Herculine Barbin: Being the Recently Discovered Memoirs of a Nineteenth-century French Hermaphrodite*. New York: Vintage Books, 1980, vii–xvii.

—. "Sexual Choice, Sexual Act" (1982). In *Michel Foucault: Politics, Philosophy, Culture*, ed. Lawrence Kritzman. New York and London: Routledge, 1988, 286–303.

—. "Sex, Power, and the Politics of Identity" (1984). In *The Essential Works of Michel Foucault 1954–84, Vol. 1: Ethics: Subjectivity and Truth*, ed. Paul Rabinow. New York: New Press, 1998, 163–73.

Franklin, Paul B. "Object Choice: Marcel Duchamp's *Fountain* and the Art of Queer Art History." *Oxford Art Journal* 23, no. 1 (2000): 23–50.

Freeman, Elizabeth. *Time Binds: Queer Temporalities, Queer Histories*. Durham, N.C. and London: Duke University Press, 2010.

Freud, Sigmund, and James Strachey. *Totem and Taboo: Some Points of Agreement between the Mental Lives of Savages and Neurotics*, Standard Edition of the Complete Psychological Works of Sigmund Freud. New York: W. W. Norton, 1989.

Fried, Michael. "New York Letter." *Art International* 7, no. 2 (1963): 60–4.

—. "Art and Objecthood." *Artforum* 5, no. 10 (June 1967): 12–23.

—. "Introduction." In *Anthony Caro*. London: Arts Council and Hayward Gallery, 1969, 5–16.

Fritscher, Jack. *Mapplethorpe: Assault with a Deadly Camera*. Mamoreneck, N.Y: Hastings House, 1994.

—. *Popular Witchcraft: Straight from the Witch's Mouth* (1972). Rev. ed. Madison: University of Wisconsin Press, 2004.

Fry, Edward, and Miranda McClintic. *David Smith: Painter, Sculptor, Draftsman*. New York: George Braziller in association with the Hirshhorn Museum and Sculpture Garden, 1982.

Gallop, Jane. *Anecdotal Theory*. Durham, N.C. and London: Duke University Press, 2002.

Gamboni, Dario. *Potential Images: Ambiguity and Indeterminacy in Modern Art*. London: Reaktion Books, 2002.

Garlake, Margaret. *New Art New World: British Art in Postwar Society*. New Haven and London: Yale University Press, 1998.

Gautherot, Franck, Caroline Hancock, and Seungduk Kim, eds. *Lynda Benglis*. Dijon, France: Presses du Réel; Dublin: Irish Museum of Modern Art, 2009.

Geldzahler, Henry. "Interview with John Chamberlain." In *John Chamberlain: Recent Work*. New York: Pace Gallery, 1992, n.p.

—. "The Sixties: As They Were" (1991). In *Making It New: Essays, Interviews, and Talks*. New York: Turtle Point Press, 1994, 337–56.

Genauer, Emily. "Art and the Artist." *New York Post* 11 December 1971, 36.

—. "Big 'Unknown' Talent: Drawings by Nancy Grossman." *International Herald Tribune* 29 December 1976, 9.

Genette, Gérard. *Paratexts: Thresholds of Interpretation* (1987), trans. Jane E. Lewin. Cambridge University Press, 1997.

Gershman, Harry. "The Evolution of Gender Identity." *American Journal of Psychoanalysis* 28 (1968): 80–90.

Getsy, David J. *Body Doubles: Sculpture in Britain, 1877–1905*. New Haven and London: Yale University Press, 2004.

—. *Rodin: Sex and the Making of Modern Sculpture*. New Haven and London: Yale University Press, 2010.

—. "Tactility or Opticality, Henry Moore or David Smith: Herbert Read and Clement Greenberg on *the Art of Sculpture*, 1956." In

Anglo-American Exchange in Postwar Sculpture, 1945–75, ed. Rebecca Peabody. Santa Monica, Calif.: J. Paul Getty Museum Online Publications, 2011, 105–21.

—. "John Chamberlain's Pliability: The New Monumental Aluminium Works." *Burlington Magazine* 153, no. 1304 (November 2011): 738–44.

—. "Playing in the Sand with Picasso: Relief Sculpture as Game in the Summer of 1930." In *From Diversion to Subversion: Games, Play, and Twentieth-century Art*, ed. David Getsy. University Park: Pennsylvania State University Press, 2011, 80–93.

—, ed. *Scott Burton: Collected Writings on Art and Performance, 1965–1975*. Chicago: Soberscove Press, 2012.

—. "Acts of Stillness: Statues, Performativity, and Passive Resistance." *Criticism* 56, no. 1 (2014): 1–20.

—. "Capacity." *TSQ: Transgender Studies Quarterly* 1, no. 1–2 (2014): 47–9.

Gibson, Ann. "Abstract Expressionism's Evasion of Language." *Art Journal* 47, no. 3 (1988): 208–14.

—. "Louise Bourgeois's Retroactive Politics of Gender." *Art Journal* 53, no. 4 (Winter 1994): 44–7.

—. *Abstract Expressionism: Other Politics*. New Haven and London: Yale University Press, 1997.

Gibson, Michael. "The Strange Case of the Fluorescent Tube." *Art International* 1 (Autumn 1987): 105–10.

Giménez, Carmen. *Picasso and the Age of Iron*. New York: Solomon R. Guggenheim Museum, 1993.

—, ed. *David Smith: A Centennial*. New York: Solomon R. Guggenheim Museum, 2006.

Glueck, Grace. "A 'New Realism' in Sculpture?" *Art in America* 59, no. 6 (November–December 1971): 150–5.

Goldstein, Richard. "S&M: The Dark Side of Gay Liberation." *Village Voice* 7 July 1975, 10–13.

Gooch, Brad. *City Poet: The Life and Times of Frank O'Hara*. New York: Alfred A. Knopf, 1993.

—. *The Golden Age of Promiscuity*. New York: Alfred A. Knopf, 1996.

Goosen, E. C. "Two Exhibitions." In *Minimal Art: A Critical Anthology*, ed. Gregory Battcock. New York: E. P. Dutton, 1968, 165–74.

Govan, Michael. "…Electric Light Defining Space." In *Light in Architecture and Art: The Work of Dan Flavin*, ed. Jeffrey Kopie and Steffen Böddeker. Marfa, Tex: Chinati Foundation, 2002, 65–84.

—. "Irony and Light." In *Dan Flavin: A Retrospective*, ed. Michael Govan and Tiffany Bell. New York: Dia Art Foundation, 2004, 19–107.

—, and Tiffany Bell. *Dan Flavin: The Complete Lights*. New York: Dia Art Foundation and Yale University Press, 2004.

— and —, eds. *Dan Flavin: A Retrospective*, New York: Dia Art Foundation, 2004.

Graham, Dan. "Flavin's Proposal." *Arts Magazine* 44, no. 4 (February 1970): 44–5.

—. "John Chamberlain: Conceptual Artist." In *John Chamberlain: New Sculpture*, ed. Kara Vander Weg. New York: Gagosian Gallery, 2011, 139–41.

—, and Benjamin Buchloh. "Four Conversations: December 1999–May 2000." In *Dan Graham: Works 1965–2000*, ed. Marianne Brouwer. Porto: Museu de Arte Contemporânea de Serralves, 2001, 69–84.

Graham, Dan, and Thurston Moore. "The Conceptual Artist and the Sonic Youth Rocker in Conversation." *Time Out New York* 7 May 2009, n.p.

Graham, Lanier. "Duchamp & Androgyny: The Concept and its Context." *Tout-fait* 2, no. 4 (January 2002): n.p.

Gray, Cleve. "Last Visit." *Art in America* 54, no. 1 (January–February 1966): 23–6.

—, ed. *David Smith by David Smith: Sculpture and Writings*. London: Thames and Hudson, 1968.

Green, Richard. *The Sissy Boy Syndrome and the Development of Homosexuality*. New Haven and London: Yale University Press, 1987.

—, and John Money, eds. *Transsexualism and Sex Reassignment*. Baltimore: Johns Hopkins University Press, 1969.

Greenberg, Clement. "Review of Exhibitions of David Smith, David Hare, and Mirko" (1947). In *Clement Greenberg: The Collected Essays and Criticism*, ed. John O'Brian. 4 vols. University of Chicago Press, 1986, 2: 140–3.

—. "The New Sculpture" (1949). In *Clement Greenberg: The Collected Essays and Criticism*, ed. John O'Brian. 4 vols. University of Chicago Press, 1986, 2: 313–19.

—. "Cross-breeding of Modern Sculpture (1952)." In *Clement Greenberg: The Collected Essays and Criticism*, ed. John O'Brian. 4 vols. University of Chicago Press, 1993, 3: 107–13.

—. "David Smith" (1956). In *Clement Greenberg: The Collected Essays and Criticism*, ed. John O'Brian, 4 vols. University of Chicago Press, 1993, 3: 275–9.

—. "Sculpture in Our Time (1958)." In *Clement Greenberg: The Collected Essays and Criticism*, ed. John O'Brian. 4 vols. University of Chicago Press, 1993, 4: 55–61.

—. "Modernist Painting (1960)." In *Clement Greenberg: The Collected Essays and Criticism*, ed. John O'Brian. 4 vols. University of Chicago Press, 1993, 4: 85–91.

—. *Art and Culture: Critical Essays*. Boston, Mass: Beacon Press, 1961.

—. "David Smith's New Sculpture" (1964). In *Clement Greenberg: The Collected Essays and Criticism*, ed. John O'Brian. 4 vols. University of Chicago Press, 1993, 4: 188–92.

—. "Critical Comment." *Art in America* 54, no. 1 (January–February 1966): 27–32.

Gruen, John. "Nudes and Other Art Objects." *Soho Weekly News* 15 May 1975, 16.

Grundmann, Roy. *Warhol's Blow Job*. Philadelphia: Temple University Press, 2003.

Halberstam, J. Jack. *Female Masculinity*. Durham, N.C. and London: Duke University Press, 1998.

—. *In a Queer Time and Place: Transgender Bodies, Subcultural Lives*. New York University Press, 2005.

—. *The Queer Art of Failure*. Durham, N.C. and London: Duke University Press, 2011.

Hale, Jacob. "Consuming the Living, Dis(re)membering the Dead in the Butch/Ftm Borderlands." *GLQ* 4, no. 2 (1998): 311–48.

Hall, Gordon. "Object Lessons: Thinking Gender Variance Through Minimalist Sculpture." *Art Journal* 72, no. 4 (Winter 2013): 47–57.

Halperin, David. *Saint Foucault*. Oxford and New York: Oxford University Press, 1995.

—. *How to Be Gay*. Cambridge, Mass: Belknap Press of Harvard University Press, 2012.

Hamill, Sarah. "Polychrome in the Sixties: David Smith and Anthony Caro." In *Anglo-American Exchange in Postwar Sculpture, 1945–75*. Los Angeles: Getty Publications, 2011, 91–104.

—. "What Sculpture Can Never Be: The Photographs of David Smith." In *David Smith Invents*, ed. Susan Behrends Frank. New Haven and London: Yale University Press and the Phillips Collection, 2011, 65–75.

—. "Picturing Autonomy: David Smith, Photography and Sculpture." *Art History* 37, no. 3 (June 2014): 536–65.

—, ed. *David Smith: Works, Writings and Interview*. Barcelona: Ediciones Poligrafica, 2011.

Hampson, Robert, and Will Montgomery, eds. *Frank O'Hara Now: New Essays on the New York Poet*. Liverpool University Press, 2010.

Haskell, Barbara. *Blam! The Explosion of Pop, Minimalism, and Performance, 1958–1964*. New York: Whitney Museum of American Art, 1983.

Hayman, David. *Re-forming the Narrative: Toward a Mechanics of Modernist Fiction*. Ithaca, N.Y: Cornell University Press, 1987.

Hayward, Eva. "Spider City Sex." *Women & Performance* 20, no. 3 (November 2010): 225–51.

Heidenry, John. *What Wild Ecstasy: The Rise and Fall of the Sexual Revolution*. New York: Simon & Schuster, 1997.

Helfenstein, Josef. *Louise Bourgeois: The Early Work*. Champaign, Ill: Krannert Art Museum, 2002.

Herring, Terrell Scott. "Frank O'Hara's Open Closet." *PMLA* 117, no. 3 (May 2002): 414–27.

Hess, Elizabeth. "Of Human Bondage." *Village Voice* 17 December 1980, 111.

Heyes, Cressida. "Feminist Solidarity After Queer Theory: The Case of Transgender." *Signs* 28, no. 4 (Summer 2003): 1093–120.

Hickey, Dave. "The Luminous Body: Sourceless Illumination as a Metaphor for Grace." In *Light in Architecture and Art: The Work of Dan Flavin*, ed. Jeffrey Kopie and Steffen Böddeker. Marfa, Tex: Chinati Foundation, 2002, 147–58.

Hochdörfer, Achim, Maartje Oldenburg, and Barbara Schröder, eds. *Claes Oldenburg: Writing on the Side 1956–1969*. New York: Museum of Modern Art, 2013.

Hopkins, David. *Dada's Boys: Masculinity after Duchamp*. New Haven and London: Yale University Press, 2007.

Howard, Richard. *Alone with America: Essays on the Art of Poetry in the United States Since 1950* (1969). Enlarged ed. New York: Atheneum, 1980.

Hughes, Robert. "Myths of Sensibility." *Time* 99, no. 12 (1972): 72–7.

Hunter, Jack, ed. *Moonchild: The Films of Kenneth Anger*. London: Creation Books, 2002.

Indiana, Gary. "John Chamberlain's Irregular Set." *Art in America* 71, no. 10 (1983): 208–16.

Johnson, Barbara. "Anthropomorphism in Lyric and Law." In *Material Events: Paul De Man and the Afterlife of Theory*, ed. Tom Cohen, J. Hillis Miller and Barbara Cohen. Minneapolis: University of Minnesota Press, 2001, 205–25.

—. *Persons and Things*. Cambridge, Mass: Harvard University Press, 2008.

Johnson, Dan Rhodes. "From 'Statuary' to Sculpture – a Long Haul in a Short Time." *Art Digest* 26, no. 1 (1951): 23–5.

Johnson, Deborah. "Marcel Duchamp, Rrose Sélavy, and Gender Performativity." *International Journal of the Arts in Society* 1, no. 7 (2007): 191–200.

—. "R(r)ose Sélavy as Man Ray: Reconsidering the Alter Ego of Marcel Duchamp." *Art Journal* 72, no. 1 (September 2013): 80–94.

Johnson, Ellen. *Modern Art and the Object*. New York: Harper & Row, 1976.

Johnston, Jill. "New Works" [Green Gallery]. *ARTnews* 62, no. 1 (March 1963): 50.

—. *Jasper Johns: Privileged Information*. New York: Thames and Hudson, 1996.

—. "Dan Flavin." In *It Is What It Is: Writings on Dan Flavin since 1964*, ed. Paula Feldman and Karsten Schubert. London: Thames & Hudson, 2004, 26.

Jones, Amelia. *Postmodernism and the En-gendering*

of Marcel Duchamp. Cambridge University Press, 1994.

——. "Dis/playing the Phallus: Male Artists Perform Their Masculinities," *Art History* 17, no. 4 (December 1994): 546–84.

——, ed. *Sexual Politics: Judy Chicago's Dinner Party in Feminist Art History*. Los Angeles: University of California Press, 1996.

Jones, Caroline. *Machine in the Studio: Constructing the Postwar American Artist*. University of Chicago Press, 1996.

——. "The Sex of the Machine: Mechanomorphic Art, New Women, and Francis Picabia's Neurasthenic Cure." In *Picturing Science, Producing Art*, ed. Caroline Jones and Peter Galison. New York and London: Routledge, 1998, 145–80.

——. *Eyesight Alone: Clement Greenberg's Modernism and the Bureaucratization of the Senses*. University of Chicago Press, 2005.

——. "Light Speed: Dan Flavin at the National Gallery." *Artforum* 43, no. 6 (February 2005): 154–9, 206.

Jones, Richard. "Living with Change." *Residential Interiors* (November–December 1977): 62–5.

Jordan-Young, Rebecca M. *Brain Storm: The Flaws in the Science of Sex Differences*. Cambridge, Mass: Harvard University Press, 2010.

Jorgensen, Christine. *A Personal Autobiography*. New York: Paul S. Eriksson, 1967.

Joselit, David. "Notes on Surface: Toward a Genealogy of Flatness." *Art History* 23, no. 1 (March 2000): 19–34.

Judd, Donald. "Chamberlain: Another View." *Art International* 12, no. 10 (January 1964): 38–9.

——. "Dan Flavin." *Arts Magazine* 38, no. 7 (April 1964): 31.

——. "In the Galleries: Claes Oldenburg" (1964). In *Donald Judd: Complete Writings 1959–1975*. Halifax and New York: Press of the Nova Scotia College of Art and Design and New York University Press, 1975, 133.

——. "Local History" (1964). In *Donald Judd: Complete Writings 1959–1975*. Halifax and New York: Press of the Nova Scotia College of Art and Design and New York University Press, 1975, 148–56.

——. "John Chamberlain" (1965). In *Donald Judd: Complete Writings 1959–1975*. Halifax and New York: Press of the Nova Scotia College of Art and Design and New York University Press, 1975, 190.

——. "Specific Objects." *Arts Yearbook* 8 (1965): 74–82.

——. "Art and Architecture" (1983). In *Donald Judd: Complete Writings 1975–1986*. Eindhoven: Van Abbemuseum, 1987.

——. "John Chamberlain." In *John Chamberlain: New Sculpture*. New York: Pace Gallery, 1989, i–xi.

Karkazis, Katrina Alicia. *Fixing Sex: Intersex, Medical Authority, and Lived Experience*. Durham, N.C: Duke University Press, 2008.

Katz, Jonathan D. "The Art of Code: Jasper Johns & Robert Rauschenberg." In *Significant Others: Creativity & Intimate Partnership*, ed. Whitney Chadwick and Isabelle de Courtivron. London: Thames and Hudson, 1993, 189–207.

——. "Passive Resistance: On the Critical and Commercial Success of Queer Artists in Cold War American Art." *L'image* 3 (1996): 119–42.

——. "Dismembership: Jasper Johns and the Body Politic." In *Performing the Body/ Performing the Text*, ed. Amelia Jones and Andrew Stephenson. London: Routledge, 1999, 170–85.

——. "John Cage's Queer Silence or How to Avoid Making Matters Worse" (1999). In *Writings Through John Cage's Music, Poetry, and*

Art, ed. David Bernstein. University of Chicago Press, 2001, 41–61.

—. "'Commiting the Perfect Crime': Sexuality, Assemblage, and the Postmodern Turn in American Art." *Art Journal* 67, no. 1 (Spring 2008): 38–53.

Kertess, Klaus. "Color in the Round and Then Some: John Chamberlain's Work, 1954–1985." In *John Chamberlain: A Catalogue Raisonné of the Sculpture 1954–1985*, ed. Julie Sylvester. New York: Hudson Hills Press, 1986, 26–38.

Kessler, Suzanne J. *Lessons from the Intersexed*. New Brunswick, N.J: Rutgers University Press, 1998.

Kikel, Rudy. "The Gay Frank O'Hara" (1978). In *Frank O'Hara: To Be True to a City*, ed. Jim Elledge. Ann Arbor: University of Michigan Press, 1990, 334–49.

Kingsley, April. "The Color of Pure Snow." *Soho Weekly News* 3 February 1977, 18–19.

Kopie, Jeffrey, and Steffen Böddeker, eds. *Light in Architecture and Art: The Work of Dan Flavin*. Marfa, Tex: Chinati Foundation, 2002.

Korman, Sheryl. "Nancy Grossman: Doing the Only Thing That's Real." *Tucson Daily Citizen* 22 January 1972, 8–9.

Kozloff, Max. "American Sculpture in Transition." *Arts Magazine* 38, no. 9 (May–June 1964): 19–25.

—. "9 in a Warehouse: An 'Attack on the Status of the Object.'" *Artforum* 7, no. 6 (February 1969): 38–42.

Kramer, Hilton. "David Smith's New Work." *Arts Magazine* 38, no. 6 (March 1964): 28–35.

Krasne, Belle. "A David Smith Profile." *Art Digest* 26, no. 13 (1 April 1952): 12–13, 26, 29.

Krauss, Rosalind. "Boston Letter." *Art International* 8, no. 1 (1964): 32–4.

—. "On Frontality." *Artforum* 6, no. 9 (May 1968): 40–6.

—. "The Essential David Smith, Part I." *Artforum* 7, no. 6 (February 1969): 43–9.

—. "The Essential David Smith, Part II." *Artforum* 7, no. 8 (April 1969): 34–41.

—. "New York" [1969]. In *It Is What It Is: Writings on Dan Flavin since 1964*, ed. Paula Feldman and Karsten Schubert. London: Thames & Hudson, 2004, 52–3.

—. *Terminal Iron Works: The Sculpture of David Smith*. Cambridge, Mass: MIT Press, 1971.

—. "Sense and Sensibility: Reflection on Post '60s Sculpture." *Artforum* 12, no. 3 (November 1973): 43–53.

—. "Changing the Work of David Smith." *Art in America* 62, no. 5 (September–October 1974): 30–3.

—. "How Paradigmatic Is Anthony Caro?" *Art in America* 63, no. 5 (September–October 1975): 80–3.

—. "Objecthood." In *Critical Perspectives in American Art*. Amherst, Mass: Fine Arts Center Gallery, 1976, 25–7.

—. *Passages in Modern Sculpture*. Cambridge, Mass: MIT Press, 1977.

—. *The Sculpture of David Smith: A Catalogue Raisonné*. New York and London: Garland, 1977.

—. "John Mason and Post-modernist Sculpture: New Experiences, New Words." *Art in America* 67, no. 3 (May–June 1979): 120–7.

—. "Sculpture in the Expanded Field." *October* 8 (Spring 1979): 30–44.

—. "Changing the Work of David Smith." Review. *Art Journal* 43, no. 1 (1983): 89–95.

—. "The Cultural Logic of the Late Capitalist Museum." *October* 54 (Fall 1990): 3–17.

—. *Bachelors*. Cambridge, Mass: MIT Press, 1999.

—. *"A Voyage on the North Sea": Art in the Age of the Post-medium Condition*, Walter Neurath

Memorial Lectures. London and New York: Thames and Hudson, 1999.

——. "'Specific' Objects." *Res* 46 (Autumn 2004): 221–4.

——. "A Photo a Day: Recording the Work of David Smith." In *David Smith: A Centennial*, ed. Carmen Giménez. New York: Solomon R. Guggenheim Museum, 2006, 10–15.

——, et al. "The Reception of the Sixties." *October* 69 (Summer 1994): 3–21.

Krens, Thomas, and Rosalind Krauss, eds. *Robert Morris: The Mind/Body Problem*. New York: Solomon R. Guggenheim Museum, 1994.

Kuhn, Annette. "Horror Hot and Cold." *Village Voice* 12 December 1977, 88.

Kunzle, David. *Fashion & Fetishism: Corsets, Tight-lacing & Other Forms of Body-sculpture*. Stroud, Gloucestershire: Sutton Publishing, 2004.

Kuspit, Donald. "Troubled Titan: John Chamberlain's Existential Vernacular." *Arts Magazine* 64, no. 8 (1990): 51–3.

Landi, Ann. "The Best Underrated Artists." *ARTnews* (September 2010): 96–103.

Laurents, Arthur, Stephen Sondheim, and Jule Styne. *Gypsy: A Musical* (1959). New York: Theater Communications Group, 1960.

Lavin, Maud. *Cut with the Kitchen Knife: The Weimar Photomontages of Hannah Höch*. New Haven and London: Yale University Press, 1993.

Lee, Pamela. *Chronophobia: On Time in the Art of the 1960s*. Cambridge, Mass: MIT Press, 2004.

Leffingwell, Edward. "A Box with a Hole in It." In *Wide Point: The Photography of John Chamberlain*, ed. Donna De Salvo. Southampton, N.Y: Parrish Art Museum, 1993, 33–9.

L[eider], P[hilip]. "Reply." *Artforum* 6, no. 6 (1968): 4.

Leider, Philp. "The Flavin Case" (1968). In *It Is What It Is: Writings on Dan Flavin since 1964*, ed. Paula Feldman and Karsten Schubert. London: Thames & Hudson, 2004, 44–7.

Leigh, Michael. *The Velvet Underground*. New York: Macfadden Books, 1963.

Leja, Michael. *Reframing Abstract Expressionism: Subjectivity and Painting in the 1940s*. New Haven and London: Yale University Press, 1993.

——. "Barnet Newman's Solo Tango." *Critical Inquiry* 21, no. 3 (Spring 1995): 556–80.

Lesher, Stephan. "The Calley Case Re-examined." *New York Times Sunday Magazine* 11 July 1971, SM 6–7, 14–23, 26.

LeSueur, Joe. *Digressions on Some Poems by Frank O'Hara: A Memoir*. New York: Farrar, Straus and Giroux, 2003.

Levin, Kim. "Dan Flavin." *ARTnews* 63, no. 1 (1964): 14.

——. "Dan Flavin." *Arts Magazine* 53, no. 1 (1978): 20.

Libby, Anthony. "O'Hara on the Silver Range" (1976). In *Frank O'Hara: To Be True to a City*, ed. Jim Elledge. Ann Arbor: University of Michigan Press, 1990, 131–55.

Lippard, Lucy. "New York." *Artforum* 2, no. 11 (May 1964): 53–4.

——. "Eccentric Abstraction." *Art International* 10, no. 9 (20 November 1966): 28, 34–40.

——. "As Painting Is to Sculpture: A Changing Ratio." In *American Sculpture of the Sixties*, ed. Maurice Tuchman. Los Angeles County Museum of Art, 1967, 31–4.

——. "Notes on a Total Light." In *Focus on Light*, ed. Richard Bellamy, Lucy Lippard, and Leah P. Sloshberg. Trenton: New Jersey State Museum, 1967, n.p.

——. "Eros Presumptive." *Hudson Review* 20, no. 1 (Spring 1967): 91–9.

——. "Eros Presumptive" (rev.). In *Minimal Art:*

A Critical Anthology. ed. Gregory Battcock. New York: E. P. Dutton, 1968, 209–21.

—. "Eccentric Abstraction" (rev.). In *Changing: Essays in Art Criticism*. New York: E. P. Dutton, 1971, 98–111.

—. *Six Years: The Dematerialization of the Art Object from 1966 to 1972*. New York: Praeger, 1973.

—. "The Women's Art Movement – What's Next?" (1975). In *The Pink Glass Swan: Selected Essays on Feminist Art*. New York: New Press, 1995, 80–83.

—. *Eva Hesse*. New York: Da Capo Press, 1976.

Loewy, Emanuel. *The Rendering of Nature in Early Greek Art*, trans. John Fothergill. London: Duckworth, 1907.

Lord, Catherine. "Their Memory Is Playing Tricks on Her: Notes Toward a Calligraphy of Rage." In *Wack!: Art and the Feminist Revolution*, ed. Cornelia Butler. Los Angeles: Museum of Contemporary Art, 2007, 440–57.

Lowndes, Joan. "Flavin's 'Mystical' Aura" (1969). In *It Is What It Is: Writings on Dan Flavin since 1964*, ed. Paula Feldman and Karsten Schubert. London: Thames & Hudson, 2004, 64–5.

Lowney, John. "Glistening Torsos, Sandwiches, and Coca Cola." *Parnassus* 6 (Fall/Winter 1977): 241–57.

Lynes, Russell. *Good Old Modern: An Intimate Portrait of the Museum of Modern Art*. New York: Atheneum, 1973.

MacLeod, Catriona. *Embodying Ambiguity: Androgyny and Aesthetics from Winckelmann to Keller*. Detroit: Wayne State University Press, 1998.

Macrino, Raymond. "Jackie Curtis: The Victory Isn't Vain." *Herald: The Manhattan News and Entertainment Weekly* 6 June 1971, s.2, 5.

Mains, Geoff. *Urban Aboriginals: A Celebration of Leathersexuality* (1984). 3rd ed. Los Angeles: Daedalus Publishing, 2002.

Mankoff, Allan. "Ouch Art: The Pain Aesthetic." *Oui* 7 (July 1973): 76–9.

Marcus, Stanley. *David Smith: The Sculptor and His Work*. Ithaca and London: Cornell University Press, 1983.

Marsh, Jan. *Art & Androgyny: The Life of Sculptor, Fiore de Henriquez*. London: Elliott & Thompson, 2004.

Marter, Joan. "Arcadian Nightmares: The Evolution of David Smith and Dorothy Dehner's Work at Bolton Landing." In *Reading Abstract Expressionism: Context and Critique*, ed. Ellen Landau. New Haven and London: Yale University Press, 2005, 625–45.

Masheck, Joseph. "Corn-fed Egotism" (Letter to the Editor). *Studio International* 177, no. 911 (May 1969): 209–10.

Massumi, Brian. *Parables for the Virtual: Movement, Affect, Sensation*. Durham, N.C: Duke University Press, 2002.

—. "The Future Birth of the Affective Fact: The Political Ontology of Threat." In *The Affect Theory Reader*, ed. Melissa Gregg and Gregory Seigworth. Durham, N.C. and London: Duke University Press, 2010, 52–70.

Mathews, Patricia. "The Politics of Feminist Art History." In *The Subjects of Art History: Historical Objects in Contemporary Perspective*, ed. Mark Cheetham, Michael Ann Holly, and Keith Moxey. Cambridge University Press, 1998, 94–114.

—. *Passionate Discontent: Creativity, Gender, and French Symbolist Art*. University of Chicago Press, 1999.

Mattix, Micah. *Frank O'Hara and the Poetics of Saying "I"*. Madison, N.J: Fairleigh Dickinson University Press, 2011.

McShine, Kynaston, ed. *Primary Structures: Younger American and British Sculptors*. New York: Jewish Museum, 1966.

Meltzer, Eve. *Systems We Have Loved: Conceptual*

Art, Affect, and the Antihumanist Turn. University of Chicago Press, 2013.

Merillat, Herbert Christian. *Modern Sculpture: The New Old Masters*. New York: Dodd, Mead & Co., 1974.

Meyer, James. "The Writing of 'Art and Objecthood.'" In *Refracting Vision: Essays on the Writings of Michael Fried*, ed. Jill Beaulieu, Mary Roberts, and Toni Ross. Sydney: Power Institute, 2000, 61–96.

—. *Minimalism: Art and Polemics in the Sixties*. New Haven and London: Yale University Press, 2001.

—. "Non, Nothing, Everything: Eva Hesse's 'Abstraction.'" In *Eva Hesse*, ed. Elisabeth Sussman. San Francisco Museum of Modern Art, 2002, 57–77.

—. "The Minimal Unconscious." *October* 130 (2009): 141–76.

—. "Anthropomorphism." *Art Bulletin* 94, no. 1 (March 2012): 24–7.

Meyer, Richard. *Outlaw Representation: Censorship and Homosexuality in Twentieth-century American Art*. Boston: Beacon Press, 2002.

—. *What Was Contemporary Art?* Cambridge, Mass: MIT Press, 2013.

Meyerowitz, Joanne. *How Sex Changed: A History of Transsexuality in the United States*. Cambridge, Mass: Harvard University Press, 2002.

Middleman, Rachel. "Rethinking Vaginal Iconology with Hannah Wilke's Sculpture." *Art Journal* 72, no. 4 (2013): 34–45.

Millard, Charles. "David Smith." *Hudson Review* 22, no. 2 (Summer 1969): 271–7.

Miller, D. A. *Place for Us: Essay on the Broadway Musical*. Cambridge, Mass: Harvard University Press, 1998.

Miller, Dorothy. *The 1960's: Painting and Sculpture from the Museum Collection*. New York: Museum of Modern Art, 1967.

Miller, Stephen Paul. "O'Hara, Judd, and Cold War Accommodation: Perceptions Equalizing Ground and Figure." In *The Scene of My Selves: New Work on New York School Poets*, ed. Terrence Diggory and Stephen Paul Miller. Orono, Maine: National Poetry Foundation, 2001, 175–86.

Molesworth, Charles. "'The Clear Architecture of the Nerves': The Poetry of Frank O'Hara." *Iowa Review* 6 (Summer/Fall 1975): 61–74.

Molesworth, Helen, ed. *Part Object Part Sculpture*. Columbus, Ohio: Wexner Center for the Arts and Pennsylvania State University Press, 2005.

—. "Rrose Sélavy Goes Shopping." In *The Dada Seminars*, ed. Leah Dickerman and Matthew Witkovsky. Washington, D.C: Center for Advanced Study in the Visual Arts, National Gallery of Art, 2005, 173–89.

Money, John, and Michael De Priest. "Three Cases of Genital Self-surgery and their Relationship to Transexualism." *Journal of Sex Research* 12, no. 4 (November 1976): 283–94.

Money, John, Joan Hampson, and John Hampson. "Imprinting and the Establishment of Gender Role." *Archives of Neurology and Psychiatry* 77 (1957): 333–6.

Morgan, Robert C. "Nancy Grossman: Opus Volcanus." *Sculpture* 17, no. 6 (July–August 1998): 36–41.

Morris, Robert. "Notes on Sculpture, Part I." *Artforum* 4, no. 6 (February 1966): 42–4.

—. "Notes on Sculpture, Part 2." *Artforum* 5, no. 2 (October 1966): 20–23.

—. "Notes on Sculpture, Part III: Notes and Nonsequiturs," *Artforum* 5, no. 10 (1967): 24–9.

—. "Notes on Sculpture, Part IV: Beyond Objects." *Artforum* 7, no. 8 (April 1969): 50–4.

Motherwell, Robert. "For David Smith" (1950). In *The Writings of Robert Motherwell*, ed. Dore Ashton. Berkeley: University of California Press, 2007, 88.

—. "David Smith: A Major American Sculptor" (1965). In *The Writings of Robert Motherwell*, ed. Dore Ashton. Berkeley: University of California Press, 2007, 218–21.

—. "A Recollection of David Smith and the 1950s" (1971). In *The Writings of Robert Motherwell*, ed. Dore Ashton. Berkeley: University of California Press, 2007, 282–5.

Müller, Grégoire. *The New Avant-garde: Issues for the Art of the Seventies*. London: Pall Mall Press, 1972.

Muñoz, José Esteban. *Cruising Utopia: The Then and There of Queer Futurity*. New York University Press, 2009.

Namaste, Viviane K. "Tragic Misreadings: Queer Theory's Erasure of Transgender Subjectivity." In *Queer Studies: A Lesbian, Gay, Bisexual, and Transgender Anthology*, ed. Brett Beemyn and Mickey Eliason. New York University Press, 1996, 183–203.

—. "The Use and Abuse of Queer Tropes: Metaphor and Catachresis in Queer Theory and Politics." *Social Semiotics* 9, no. 2 (1999): 213–34.

—. *Invisible Lives: The Erasure of Transsexual and Transgendered People*. Chicago and London: University of Chicago Press, 2000.

—. *Sex Change, Social Change: Reflections on Identity, Institutions, and Imperialism*. Toronto: Women's Press, 2005.

—. "Undoing Theory: The 'Transgender Question' and the Epistemic Violence of Anglo-American Feminist Theory." *Hypatia* 24, no. 3 (Summer 2009): 11–32.

Nancy Grossman: Loud Whispers: Four Decades of Assemblage, Collage, and Sculpture. New York: Michael Rosenfeld Gallery, 2000.

Naumann, Francis M., and David Nolan. *The Visible Vagina*. New York: Francis M. Naumann Fine Art and David Nolan Gallery, 2010.

Nelson, Maggie. *Women, the New York School, and Other True Abstractions*. Iowa City: University of Iowa Press, 2007.

Nemser, Cindy. *Art Talk: Conversations with 12 Women Artists*. New York: Charles Scribner's Sons, 1975.

—. "Towards a Feminist Sensibility: Contemporary Trends in Women's Art." *Feminist Art Journal* 5, no. 2 (Summer 1976): 19–23.

Neuner, Stefan. "Dan Flavin on the Path to an Ironic-sublime: Some Remarks on '…in daylight or cool white.'" In *Dan Flavin – Lights*. Vienna and Ostfildern: Museum Moderner Kunst Stiftung Ludwig Wien and Hatje Cantz Verlag, 2012, 29–61.

Newman, Amy. *Challenging Art: Artforum 1962–1974*. New York: Soho Press, 2003.

Newton, Esther. *Mother Camp: Female Impersonators in America* (1972). Phoenix ed. University of Chicago Press, 1979.

Nisbet, James. "Coast to Coast: Land Work between the N. E. Thing Co. and Lucy Lippard." *Archives of American Art Journal* 64, no. 1–2 (2008): 58–65.

Nixon, Mignon. "Bad Enough Mother." *October* 102 (1995): 71–92.

—. "Posing the Phallus." *October* 92 (Spring 2000): 96–127.

—. "'Fantastic Reality': A Note on Louise Bourgeois's *Portrait of C.Y.*" *Sculpture Journal* 5 (2001): 83–9.

—. *Fantastic Reality: Louise Bourgeois and a Story of Modern Art*. Cambridge, Mass: MIT Press, 2005.

—. "o+x." *October* 119 (2007): 6–20.

O'Doherty, Brian. "Chamberlain: Projective Sculpture." In *John Chamberlain: Recent Sculpture*. New York: PaceWildenstein, 1994, 5–15.

—. "Nancy Grossman (Krasner)." *New York Times* 23 February 1964, X18.

O'Hara, Frank. *Jackson Pollock*. New York: George Braziller, 1959.

—. "Personism" (1959). In *Standing Still and Walking in New York*, ed. Donald Allen. Bolinas, Calif: Grey Fox Press, 1975, 110–11.

—. "David Smith: The Color of Steel." *ARTnews* 60, no. 8 (December 1961): 32–4, 69–70.

—. "The Sorrows of the Youngman: John Rechy's *City of Night*" (1963). In *Standing Still and Walking in New York*, ed. Donald Allen. Bolinas, Calif: Grey Fox Press, 1975, 160–4.

—. "Introduction to Edwin Denby's *Dancers Buildings and People in the Streets*" (1965). In *Standing Still and Walking in New York*, ed. Donald Allen. Bolinas, Calif: Grey Fox Press, 1975, 182–4.

—. *Nakian*. New York: Museum of Modern Art, 1966.

—. "David Smith" (1966). In *Art Chronicles 1954–66*. New York: George Braziller, 1975.

—. *The Collected Poems of Frank O'Hara* (1971), ed. Donald Allen. Rev. ed. Berkeley: University of California Press, 1995.

—, and Alfred Leslie. "Transcript of *USA Poetry*." In *Homage to Frank O'Hara*, ed. Bill Berkson and Joe LeSueur. Berkeley, Calif: Creative Arts Book Company, 1980, 215–17.

Obrist, Hans Ulrich. *John Chamberlain*, Conversation Series. Cologne: Buchhandlung Walther König, 2006.

Olson, James, and Randy Roberts. *My Lai: A Brief History with Documents*. New York: Palgrave Macmillan, 1998.

Orton, Fred. *Jasper Johns: The Sculptures*. Leeds: Henry Moore Institute, 1996.

Padgett, Ron. *Joe: A Memoir of Joe Brainard*. Minneapolis: Coffee House Press, 2004.

Papapetros, Spyros, and Julian Rose, eds. *Retracing the Expanded Field: Encounters between Art and Architecture*. Cambridge, Mass: MIT Press, 2014.

Pearson, Christopher. "Hepworth, Moore, and the United Nations: Modern Art and the Ideology of Post-war Internationalism." *Sculpture Journal* 6 (2001): 89–99.

Perchuk, Andrew. "Pollock and Postwar Masculinity." In *The Masculine Masquerade: Masculinity and Representation*, ed. Andrew Perchuk and Helaine Posner. Cambridge, Mass: MIT List Visual Arts Center, 1995, 31–42.

Perloff, Marjorie. "Frank O'Hara and the Aesthetics of Attention." *boundary 2* 4, no. 3 (Spring 1976): 779–806.

—. *Frank O'Hara: Poet Among Painters*. New York: George Braziller, 1977.

—. "Introduction, 1997." In *Frank O'Hara: Poet Among Painters*. University of Chicago Press, 1998, xi–xxx.

—. "Watchman, Spy, and Dead Man: Jasper Johns, Frank O'Hara, John Cage, and the 'Aesthetic of Indifference.'" *Modernism/Modernity* 8, no. 2 (April 2001): 197–223.

—. "'The Ecstasy of Always Burning Forth!': Rereading Frank O'Hara." *Lana Turner: A Journal of Poetry & Opinion* 1 (Fall 2008): n.p.

Perreault, John. "New York." *Art International* 11, no. 3 (1967): 62–6.

—. "Snotty Remarks." *Village Voice* 25 March 1971, 17.

—. "We Applaud the Artist's Good Taste & Exquisite Control." *Village Voice* 4 November 1971, 25.

—. "Leather: Associations for Your Own Good." *Village Voice* 9 December 1971, 32.

Pflanger, Herbert. [Letter to the Editor]. *Arts Magazine* 34, no. 7 (1960): 9.

Phillips, Lily. "Blue Jeans, Black Leather Jackets, and a Sneer: The Iconography of the 1950s

Biker and Its Translation Abroad." *International Journal of Motorcycle Studies* 1, no. 1 (2005): n.p.

Pincus-Witten, Robert. "Eva Hesse: More Light on the Transition from Post-minimalism to the Sublime." In *Eva Hesse: A Memorial Exhibition*, ed. Linda Shearer. New York: Solomon R. Guggenheim Museum, 1972, n.p.

—. *Postminimalism*. New York: Out of London Press, 1977.

—. "Naked Lunches." *October* 3 (1977): 102–18.

—. *Eye to Eye: Twenty Years of Art Criticism*, Contemporary American Art Critics 4. Ann Arbor: UMI Research Press, 1984.

—. *Postminimalism into Maximalism: American Art, 1966–1986*. Ann Arbor: UMI Research Press, 1987.

—. "Receding Horizons: Fading Notes on the Seventies." In *High Times, Hard Times: New York Painting 1967–1975*, ed. Katy Siegel. New York: Independent Curators International, 2006, 143–5.

Piper, Adrian. "Preparatory Notes for *the Mythic Being*" (1973–4). In *Out of Order, Out of Sight, Vol. I: Selected Writings in Meta-art*. Cambridge, Mass: MIT Press, 1996, 91–115.

—. "Notes on *the Mythic Being* I–III" (1974–5). In *Out of Order, Out of Sight, Vol. I: Selected Writings in Meta-art*. Cambridge, Mass: MIT Press, 1996, 117–39.

Pissarro, Joachim. "Dan Flavin's Epiphany." *Yale University Art Gallery Bulletin* (1997/8): 84–7.

Plunkett, Edward M. "The New York School of Correspondence." *Art Journal* 36, no. 3 (Spring 1977): 233–5.

Poetter, Jochen. "'No Leaning on the Oars': On John Chamberlain's High-energy Ideograms." In *John Chamberlain*, ed. Jochen Poetter. Stuttgart: Edition Cantz and Staatliche Kunsthalle Baden-Baden, 1991, 22–37.

Potter, Jeffrey. *To a Violent Grave: An Oral Biography of Jackson Pollock*. New York: G. P. Putnam's, 1985.

Potts, Alex. "Male Phantasy and Modern Sculpture." *Oxford Art Journal* 15, no. 2 (1992): 38–47.

—. "Sign." In *Critical Terms for Art History*, ed. R. Nelson and R. Schiff. University of Chicago Press, 1996, 17–30.

—. *The Sculptural Imagination: Figurative, Modernist, Minimalist*. New Haven and London: Yale University Press, 2000.

—. "Installation and Sculpture." *Oxford Art Journal* 24, no. 2 (2001): 5–24.

—. "Tactility: The Interrogation of Medium in Art of the 1960s." *Art History* 27, no. 2 (2004): 282–304.

—. "Dan Flavin: 'In … Cool White' and 'Infected with a Blank Magic.'" In *Dan Flavin: New Light*, ed. Jeffrey Weiss. New Haven and London: Yale University Press, 2006, 1–24.

—. "Personages: Imperfect and Persistent." In *David Smith: Personage*. New York: Gagosian Gallery, 2006, 7–19.

—. "Abstraction and Image Making in David Smith's Sculpture." In *David Smith: Cubes and Anarchy*, ed. Carol Eliel. Los Angeles County Museum of Art, 2011, 117–41.

—. *Experiments in Modern Realism: World Making, Politics, and the Everyday in Postwar European and American Art*. New Haven and London: Yale University Press, 2013.

Powers, Edward. "Fasten Your Seatbelts as We Prepare for Our *Nude Descending*." *Tout-fait* 2, no. 5 (April 2003): n.p.

Prade, Erik La, ed. *Breaking Through: Richard Bellamy and the Green Gallery 1960–1965*, New York: Midmarch Arts Press, 2009.

Preciado, [Paul] B. *Testo Junkie: Sex, Drugs, and Biopolitics in the Pharmacopornographic Era*, trans. Bruce Benderson. New York: Feminist Press, 2013.

Preves, Sharon E. *Intersex and Identity: The Contested Self*. New Brunswick, N.J: Rutgers University Press, 2003.

Prosser, Jay. *Second Skins: The Body Narratives of Transsexuality*. New York: Columbia University Press, 1998.

—. *Light in the Dark Room: Photography and Loss*. Minneapolis: University of Minnesota Press, 2005.

Raskin, David. "Judd's Moral Art." In *Donald Judd*, ed. Nicholas Serota. London: Tate Publishing, 2004, 78–95.

—. "The Shiny Illusionism and Krauss and Judd." *Art Journal* 65, no. 1 (Spring 2006): 6–21.

—. *Donald Judd*. New Haven and London: Yale University Press, 2010.

Rasmussen, Waldo. "Frank O'Hara in the Museum" (1977). In *Homage to Frank O'Hara*, ed. Bill Berkson and Joe LeSueur. Berkeley, Calif: Creative Arts Book Company, 1980, 84–90.

Ratcliff, Carter. *Out of the Box: The Reinvention of Art 1965–1975*. New York: School of Visual Arts and Allworth Press, 2000.

Raven, Arlene. *Nancy Grossman*. Brookville, N.Y: Hillwood Art Museum, C.W. Post Campus, Long Island University, 1991.

—. "True Grit." In *True Grit*, ed. halley k. harrisburg and Michael Rosenfeld. New York: Michael Rosenfeld Gallery, 2000, 2–5.

Raymond, Janice. *The Transexual Empire: The Making of the She-male*. Boston: Beacon Press, 1979.

Rechy, John. *The Sexual Outlaw: A Documentary*. New York: Grove Weidenfeld, 1977.

Reis, Elisabeth. *Bodies in Doubt: An American History of Intersex*. Baltimore: Johns Hopkins University Press, 2009.

Rembert, Virginia Pitts. "Review: Fiber and Form: The Woman's Legacy." *Woman's Art Journal* 18, no. 1 (Spring–Summer 1997): 64–5.

Ricco, John Paul. "Name No One Man." *Parallax* 11, no. 2 (2005): 93–103.

Richardson, Brenda. *Frank Stella: The Black Paintings*. Baltimore Museum of Art, 1976.

—. *Scott Burton*. Baltimore Museum of Art, 1986.

Rivers, Larry, and Arnold Weinstein. *What Did I Do? The Unauthorized Autobiography of Larry Rivers*. New York: HarperCollins, 1992.

Robins, Corin. "Man Is Anonymous: The Art of Nancy Grossman." *Art Spectrum* 1, no. 2 (February 1975): 33–7.

—. "Nancy Grossman." *Arts Magazine* 51, no. 4 (1976): 12.

Robins, Corinne. "Object, Structure or Sculpture: Where Are We?" *Arts Magazine* 40, no. 9 (September–October 1966): 33–7.

Robinson, Josh. "'A Gasp of Laughter at Desire': Frank O'Hara's Poetics of Breath." In *Frank O'Hara Now: New Essays on the New York Poet*, ed. Robert Hampson and Will Montgomery. Liverpool University Press, 2010, 144–59.

Rom, Christine. "One View: *The Feminist Art Journal*." *Woman's Art Journal* 2, no. 2 (Autumn–Winter 1981–2): 19–24.

Rondeau, James. "Jasper Johns: Gray." In *Jasper Johns: Gray*, ed. James Rondeau and Douglas Druick. Art Institute of Chicago with Yale University Press, 2007, 22–79.

Rose, Barbara. "How to Look at John Chamberlain's Sculpture." *Art International* 12, no. 10 (January 1964): 36–8.

—. "ABC Art." *Art in America* 53, no. 5 (October–November 1965): 57–69.

—. "Sculpture, Intimacy and Perception." In *14 Sculptors: The Industrial Edge*, 7–9. Minneapolis: Walker Art Center, 1969.

—. "On Chamberlain's Interview." *Artforum* 10, no. 6 (1972): 44–5.

—. "Vaginal Iconology." *New York Magazine* 7 (11 February 1974): 59.

—. "John Chamberlain: Painterly Sculpture." In *Autocritique: Essays on Art and Anti-art, 1963–1987*. New York: Weidenfeld & Nicolson, 1988, 170–5.

—, and Irving Sandler. "Sensibility of the Sixties." *Art in America* 55, no. 1 (1967): 44–57.

Rose, Bernice. "Willem De Kooning and John Chamberlain: Displaced Realities." In *De Kooning/Chamberlain: Influence and Tradition*. New York: PaceWildenstein, 2001, 5–13.

Rosen, Andrea. "'Untitled' (The Neverending Portrait)." In *Felix Gonzalez-Torres*, ed. Dietmar Elger. Hannover and Ostfildern-Ruit: Sprengel Museum Hannover and Hatje Cantz Verlag, 1997, 44–59.

Rosenblum, Robert. "The Abstract Sublime." *ARTnews* 59, no. 10 (February 1961): 38–40, 56–8.

—. "Name in Lights." *Artforum* 35, no. 7 (March 1997): 11–12.

Ross, Andrew. "The Death of Lady Day." In *Frank O'Hara: To Be True to a City*, ed. Jim Elledge. Ann Arbor: University of Michigan Press, 1990, 380–91.

Roth, Lauren. "Flesh in Wax: Demystifying the Skin Colours of the Common Crayon." In *Visual Communication and Culture: Images in Action*, ed. Jonathan Finn. Don Mills, Ontario: Oxford University Press, 2012, 73–85.

Roughgarden, Joan. *Evolution's Rainbow: Diversity, Gender, and Sexuality in Nature and People*. Berkeley: University of California Press, 2004.

Rubin, Gayle. "The Traffic in Women: Notes on the 'Political Economy' of Sex." In *Toward an Anthropology of Women*, ed. Rayna R. Reiter. New York: Monthly Review Press, 1975, 157–210.

—. "The Leather Menace: Comments on Politics and S/M" (1981/82). In *Deviations: A Gayle Rubin Reader*. Durham, N.C. and London: Duke University Press, 2011, 109–36.

—. "The Catacombs: A Temple of the Butthole." In *Leatherfolk: Radical Sex, People, Politics and Practice*, ed. Mark Thompson. San Francisco: Alyson Publications, 1991, 119–41.

—. "Of Catamites and Kings: Reflections on Butch, Gender, and Boundaries" (1992). In *Deviations: A Gayle Rubin Reader*, 241–53. Durham, N.C: Duke University Press, 2011.

—. "Sites, Settlements, and Urban Sex: The Ethnography of Gay Communities in Urban North America." In *Archaeologies of Sexuality*, ed. Ellen Lewin and William Leap. New York and London: Routledge, 2000, 62–89.

Rubin, Henry. *Self-made Men: Identity and Embodiment among Transsexual Men*. Nashville, Tenn: Vanderbilt University Press, 2003.

Salamon, Gayle. *Assuming a Body: Transgender and Rhetorics of Materiality*. New York: Columbia University Press, 2010.

SAMOIS Collective. *Coming to Power: Writings and Graphics on Lesbian S/M*. Palo Alto, Calif: Up Press, 1981.

Sandler, Irving. "Gesture and Non-gesture in Recent Sculpture." In *American Sculpture of the Sixties*, ed. Maurice Tuchman. Los Angeles County Museum of Art, 1967, 40–3.

Schiff, Gert. *Images of Horror and Fantasy*. Bronx, N.Y: Bronx Museum of the Arts, 1977.

Schiff, Richard. "Lumination." In *Dan Flavin: Series and Progressions*, ed. Kristine Bell, Tiffany Bell, and Alexandra Whitney. Göttingen, Germany: Steidl with David Zwirner Gallery, New York, 2010, 83–93.

Schor, Mira. "Representations of the Penis." *M/E/A/N/I/N/G* 4 (November 1988): 3–17.

Schroeder, Thomas. "Nancy Grossman Ledermonstren." *Twen* 5 (May 1971): 39.

Schuyler, James. "David Smith." In *James Schuyler: Selected Art Writings*, ed. Simon Pettet. Santa Rosa, Calif: Black Sparrow Press, 1998, 139–40.

Schwartz, Barbara. "Letter from New York." *Craft Horizons* 32, no. 1 (February 1972): 42–5.

Schwarz, Dieter, ed. *John Chamberlain: Papier Paradisio*. Winterthur: Kunstmuseum Winterthur, 2005.

Scott, Bonnie Kime, ed. *The Gender of Modernism: A Critical Anthology*. Bloomington: Indiana University Press, 1990.

Sedgwick, Eve Kosofsky. *Between Men: English Literature and Male Homosocial Desire*. New York: Columbia University Press, 1985.

—. *Epistemology of the Closet*. Berkeley: University of California Press, 1990.

—. *Tendencies*. Durham, N.C: Duke University Press, 1993.

—. *Touching Feeling: Affect, Pedagogy, Performativity*. Durham, N.C. and London: Duke University Press, 2003.

Selby, Jr., Hubert. *Last Exit to Brooklyn*. New York: Grove Press, 1964.

Selby, Nick. "Memory Pieces: Collage, Memorial and the Poetics of Intimacy in Joe Brainard, Jasper Johns and Frank O'Hara." In *Frank O'Hara Now: New Essays on the New York Poet*, ed. Robert Hampson and Will Montgomery. Liverpool University Press, 2010, 229–46.

Shaw, Lytle. "Proximity's Plea: O'Hara's Art Writing." *Qui Parle* 12, no. 2 (Spring/Summer 2001): 143–78.

—. *Frank O'Hara: The Poetics of Coterie*. Iowa City: University of Iowa Press, 2006.

—. "Gesture in 1960: Toward Literal Situations." In *Frank O'Hara Now: New Essays on the New York Poet*, ed. Robert Hampson and Will Montgomery. Liverpool University Press, 2010, 29–48.

Silver, Kenneth. "Modes of Disclosure: The Construction of Gay Identity and the Rise of Pop Art." In *Hand-painted Pop: American Art in Transition 1955–62*, ed. Russell Ferguson. Los Angeles: Museum of Contemporary Art, 1992, 178–203.

Sims, Lowery Stokes. "Loud Whispers." In *Nancy Grossman: Loud Whispers: Four Decades of Assemblage, Collage, and Sculpture*. New York: Michael Rosenfeld Gallery, 2000, 6–11.

Singer, T. Benjamin. "Umbrella." *TSQ: Transgender Studies Quarterly* 1, no. 1–2 (2014): 259–61.

Slifkin, Robert. *Out of Time: Philip Guston and the Refiguration of Postwar American Art*. Berkeley: University of California Press, 2013.

Smith, Jr., Alexander. *Frank O'Hara: A Comprehensive Bibliography*. New York and London: Garland, 1979.

Smith, Brydon. *fluorescent light, etc. from Dan Flavin*. Ottawa: National Gallery of Canada, 1969.

—. "The Art of Dan Flavin – from Water Waves to Light Waves." In *Light in Architecture and Art: The Work of Dan Flavin*, ed. Jeffrey Kopie and Steffen Böddeker. Marfa, Tex: Chinati Foundation, 2002, 85–100.

—. "Recollections and Thoughts About Dan Flavin." In *Dan Flavin: A Retrospective*, ed. Michael Govan and Tiffany Bell. New York: Dia Art Foundation, 2004, 131–44.

Smith, Candida. *The Fields of David Smith*. New York: Thames and Hudson, 1999.

Smith, Chuck. *Forrest Bess: Key to the Riddle*. Brooklyn, N.Y: powerHouse Books, 2013.

Smith, David. "Perception and Reality" (1951). In *David Smith*, ed. Garnett McCoy. London: Allen Lane, 1973, 77–9.

—. "The Language Is Image" (1952). In *David Smith*, ed. Garnett McCoy. London: Allen Lane, 1973, 79–81.

—. "The New Sculpture" (1952). In *David Smith*, ed. Garnett McCoy. London: Allen Lane, 1973, 82–5.

—. "The Artist's Image" (1954). In *David Smith*, ed. Garnett McCoy. London: Allen Lane, 1973, 113–16.

—. "Second Thoughts on Sculpture." *Art Journal* 13, no. 3 (Spring 1954): 203–7.

—. "Memories to Myself" (1960). In *David Smith*, ed. Garnett McCoy. London: Allen Lane, 1973, 148–56.

—. "Notes on My Work." *Arts Magazine* 34, no. 5 (1960): 44.

—, and Thomas Hess. "The Secret Letter." In *David Smith*, ed. Garnett McCoy. London: Allen Lane, 1973, 175–86.

Smith, Duncan. "In the Heart of the Tinman: John Chamberlain." *Artforum* 22, no. 5 (January 1984): 39–43.

Smith, Hazel. *Hyperscapes in the Poetry of Frank O'Hara: Difference/ Homosexuality/ Topography*. Liverpool University Press, 2000.

Smith, Rebecca. "Making a Horse with Dad." *Tate Etc* 8 (Autumn 2006): 101.

Smith, Terry, ed. *In Visible Touch: Modernism and Masculinity*. University of Chicago Press, 1997.

Smithson, Robert. "Entropy and the New Monuments." *Artforum* 4, no. 10 (June 1966): 26–31.

Sontag, Susan. "Fascinating Fascism." In *Under the Sign of Saturn*. New York: Farrar, Straus, Giroux, 1980, 71–105.

Star, Hedy Jo. *"I Changed My Sex."* Chicago: Novel Books, 1963.

Steele, Valerie. *Fetish: Fashion, Sex and Power*. Oxford and New York: Oxford University Press, 1996.

Stein, David. "S/M's Copernican Revolution: From a Closed World to the Infinite Universe." In *Leatherfolk: Radical Sex, People, Politics, and Practice*, ed. Mark Thompson. Boston: Alyson Publications, 1991, 142–56.

Stein, Judith. "Figuring out the Fifties: Aspects of Figuration and Abstraction in New York, 1950–1964." In *The Figurative Fifties*, ed. Paul Schimmel. Newport Beach, Calif: Newport Harbor Art Museum, 1988, 37–52.

Steinberg, Leo. "Reflections on the State of Criticism" (1972). In *Robert Rauschenberg*, ed. Brandon Joseph. Cambridge, Mass: MIT Press, 2002, 7–37.

Steinbock, Eliza. "Generative Negatives: Del LaGrace Volcano's Herm Body Photographs." *TSQ: Transgender Studies Quarterly* 1, no. 4 (November 2014): 539–51.

Stevens, May. "Make a Political Statement: May Stevens." *Art-rite* 6 (1974): 24.

Stoller, Robert. *Sex and Gender: On the Development of Masculinity and Femininity*. New York: Science House, 1968.

—. *Sex and Gender. Vol II: The Transsexual Experiment*. New York: Jason Aronson, 1975.

Stone, Sandy. "The *Empire* Strikes Back: A Post-transsexual Manifesto" (rev.). In *The Transgender Studies Reader*, ed. Susan Stryker and Stephen Whittle. New York and London: Routledge, 2006, 221–35.

Stryker, Susan. "My Words to Victor Frankenstein Above the Village of Chamounix: Performing Transgender Rage." *GLQ* 1, no. 3 (1994): 237–54.

—. "Introduction." In *Christine Jorgensen: A Personal Autobiography*. San Francisco: Cleis Press, 2000, v–xiii.

—. "Transgender Studies: Queer Theory's Evil Twin." *GLQ* 10, no. 2 (2004): 212–15.

—. "(De)Subjugated Knowledges: An Introduction to Transgender Studies." In *The Transgender Studies Reader*, ed. Susan Stryker and Stephen Whittle. New York and London: Routledge, 2006, 1–17.

—. "Why the T in LGBT Is Here to Stay." *Salon.com* (11 October 2007).

—. *Transgender History*. Berkeley, Calif: Seal Press, 2008.

—. "Transgender History, Homonormativity, and Disciplinarity." *Radical History Review* 100 (Winter 2008): 145–57.

—. "Biopolitics." *TSQ: Transgender Studies Quarterly* 1, no. 1–2 (2014): 38–42.

—, and Stephen Whittle, eds. *The Transgender Studies Reader*. New York and London: Routledge, 2006.

Stryker, Susan, Paisley Currah, and Lisa Jean Moore. "Introduction: Trans-, Trans, or Transgender?" *WSQ: Women's Studies Quarterly* 36, no. 3–4 (Fall/Winter 2008): 11–22.

Stryker, Susan, and Aren Aizura, eds. *The Transgender Studies Reader 2*. New York: Routledge, 2013.

Suárez, Juan A. *Bike Boys, Drag Queens, & Superstars: Avant-garde, Mass Culture, and Gay Identities in the 1960s Underground Cinema*. Bloomington and Indianapolis: Indiana University Press, 1996.

Swartz, Anne. "The Erotics of Envelopment: Figuration in Nancy Grossman's Art." *n.paradoxa* 20 (2007): 64–70.

Sylvester, Julie. "Auto/Bio: Conversations with John Chamberlain." In *John Chamberlain: A Catalogue Raisonné of the Sculpture 1954–1985*, ed. Julie Sylvester. New York: Hudson Hills Press in association with the Museum of Contemporary Art, Los Angeles, 1986, 8–38.

—, ed. *John Chamberlain: A Catalogue Raisonné of the Sculpture 1954–1985*. New York: Hudson Hills Press in association with the Museum of Contemporary Art, Los Angeles, 1986.

Tanaka, Rin. *Motorcycle Jackets: A Century of Leather Design*. 2nd ed. Atglen, Penn: Schiffer Publishing, 2006.

Tentler, Gregory. "Painting in a Different Kind of Void." *Studies in Gender and Sexuality* 14, no. 3 (2013): 230–4.

Thierolf, Corinna, and Johannes Vogt. *Dan Flavin: Icons*. Munich: Pinakothek der Moderne and Schirmer/Mosel, 2009.

Thompson, Margo Hobbs. "Agreeable Objects and Angry Paintings: 'Female Imagery' in Art by Hannah Wilke and Louise Fishman, 1970–1973." *Genders* 43 (2006): n.p.

Thompson, Mark. *Leatherfolk: Radical Sex, People, Politics, and Practice*. Boston, Mass: Alyson Publications, 1991.

Tickner, Lisa. "The Body Politic: Female Sexuality and Women Artists since 1970." *Art History* 1, no. 2 (1978): 236–49.

Tietchen, Todd. "Frank O'Hara and the Poetics of the Digital." *Criticism* 56, no. 1 (2014): 45–61.

Tillim, Sidney. "Month in Review." *Arts Magazine* 37, no. 6 (March 1963): 59–62.

—. "The Reception of Figurative Art: Notes on a General Misunderstanding." *Artforum* 7, no. 6 (February 1969): 30–3.

Tinkcom, Matthew. *Working Like a Homosexual: Camp, Capital, Cinema*. Durham, N.C: Duke University Press, 2002.

Tomkins, Calvin. *Off the Wall: Robert Rauschenberg and the Art World of Our Time*. New York: Doubleday, 1980.

Tuchman, Maurice, ed. *American Sculpture of the Sixties*. Los Angeles County Museum of Art, 1967.

Tuchman, Phyllis. "An Interview with John Chamberlain." *Artforum* 10, no. 6 (February 1972): 39–43.

—. "Dan Flavin Interviewed by Phyllis Tuchman" (9 March 1972). In *Dan Flavin: A Retrospective*, ed. Michael Govan and Tiffany Bell. New York: Dia Art Foundation, 2004, 192–4.

Tucker, Paul. "Family Matters: David Smith's

Series Sculptures." In *David Smith: A Centennial*, ed. Carmen Giménez. New York: Solomon R. Guggenheim Museum, 2006, 69–89.

Tucker, William. "David Smith." *Studio International* 181, no. 929 (January 1971): 24–9.

—. *The Language of Sculpture*. London: Thames and Hudson, 1974.

Untorelli Press. *Street Transvestite Action Revolutionaries: Survival, Revolt, and Queer Antagonist Struggle*: Bloomington, Indiana: Untorelli Press, 2013.

V., R.-J. "À Rome: Chez le directeur d'une galerie d'art," *Connaissance des arts* 259 (1973): 99.

Vaccaro, Jeanne. "Felt Matters," *Women & Performance* 20, no. 3 (November 2010): 253–66.

Valentine, David. "The Categories Themselves." *GLQ* 10, no. 2 (2003): 215–20.

—. *Imagining Transgender: An Ethnography of a Category*. Durham, N.C. and London: Duke University Press, 2007.

Van der Marck, Jan, ed. *Dan Flavin: Pink and Gold*. Chicago: Museum of Contemporary Art, 1967.

Vidal, Gore. *Myra Breckinridge*. New York: Little, Brown & Co., 1968.

Wagner, Anne Middleton. "Reading *Minimal Art*." In *Minimal Art: A Critical Anthology*, ed. Gregory Battcock. Berkeley: University of California Press, 1995, 3–18.

—. *Three Artists (Three Women): Modernism and the Art of Hesse, Krasner, and O'Keeffe*. Berkeley: University of California Press, 1996.

—. *Mother Stone: The Vitality of Modern British Sculpture*. New Haven and London: Yale University Press, 2005.

—. "Flavin's Limited Light." In *Dan Flavin: New Light*, ed. Jeffrey Weiss. New Haven and London: Yale University Press, 2006, 108–32.

—. "David Smith: Heavy Metal." In *David Smith: Cubes and Anarchy*, ed. Carol Eliel. Los Angeles County Museum of Art, 2011, 63–87.

—. *A House Divided: American Art since 1955*. Berkeley: University of California Press, 2012.

Wagner, Frank, Kasper König, and Julia Friedrich, eds. *Das achte Feld: Geschlechter, Leben und Begehren in der Kunst seit 1960*. Ostfildern: Hatje Cantz and Museum Ludwig, Cologne, 2006.

Waldman, Diane. "Introduction." In *John Chamberlain: A Retrospective Exhibition*, ed. Diane Waldman. New York: Solomon R. Guggenheim Museum, 1971, 5–11.

Warhol, Andy, and Pat Hackett. *POPism: The Warhol '60s*. New York and London: Harcourt Brace Jovanovich, 1980.

Wasserman, Jeanne. "Introduction." In *Recent Figure Sculpture*, ed. Jeanne Wasserman. Cambridge, Mass: Fogg Art Museum, Harvard University, 1972, 6–9.

Weinberg, Thomas S., ed. *S&M: Studies in Dominance and Submission*. Amherst, N.Y: Prometheus Press, 1995.

Weiss, Evelyn, Dieter Ronte, and Manfred Schneckenburger. *Dan Flavin: Three Installations in Fluorescent Light*. Cologne: Wallraf-Richartz-Museums and Kunsthalle Köln, 1973.

Weiss, Jeffrey. "Blunt in Bright Repose." In *Dan Flavin: New Light*, ed. Jeffrey Weiss. New Haven and London: Yale University Press, 2006, 49–81.

—, ed. *Dan Flavin: New Light*. New Haven and London: Yale University Press, 2006.

Welch, Paul. "Homosexuality in America." *Life* 26 June 1964, 66–80.

Welchman, John C. *Invisible Colors: A Visual History of Titles*. New Haven and London: Yale University Press, 1997.

White, B. "Ex-GI Becomes Blonde Beauty: Operations Transform Bronx Youth." *New York Daily News* 1 December 1952, 1.

Whitney, Alexandra. "An Illuminating Paradox: Dan Flavin's *alternating pink and 'gold,'* 1967." In *Dan Flavin: Series and Progressions*, ed. Kristine Bell, Tiffany Bell and Alexandra Whitney. Göttingen, Germany: Steidl with David Zwirner Gallery, New York, 2010, 17–23.

Wiegman, Robyn. *Object Lessons*. Durham, N.C: Duke University Press, 2012.

Wilchins, Riki. *Read My Lips: Sexual Subversion and the End of Gender*. Ithaca, N.Y: Firebrand Books, 1997.

—. "A Certain Kind of Freedom: Power and the Truth of Bodies – Four Essays on Gender." In *Genderqueer: Voices from Beyond the Sexual Binary*, ed. Joan Nestle, Clare Howell, and Riki Wilchins. Los Angeles and New York: Alyson Books, 2002, 21–63.

Wilkerson, Abby L. "Normate Sex and Its Discontents." In *Sex and Disability*, ed. Robert McRuer and Anna Mollow. Durham, N.C. and London: Duke University Press, 2012, 183–207.

Wilkin, Karen. "A Sculptor Draws." *Master Drawings* 40, no. 1 (2002): 43–56.

Williams, Richard J. *After Modern Sculpture: Art in the United States and Europe, 1965–70*. Manchester University Press, 2000.

Wilson, William S. "Dan Flavin: Fiat Lux." In *Light in Art*, ed. Thomas Hess and John Ashbery. New York: Collier Books, 1971, 137–49.

Wisotzki, Paula. "Artist and Worker: The Labour of David Smith." *Oxford Art Journal* 28, no. 3 (2005): 347–70.

Wittkower, Rudolf. *Sculpture: Processes and Principles*. London: Allen Lane, 1977.

Wood, Jon. "The Small-scale Sculpture of John Chamberlain." In *John Chamberlain: It's His Show*. Berlin: Buchmann Galerie, 2006, 32–7.

Yang, Hanford, and Erik La Prade. "Hanford Yang." In *Breaking Through: Richard Bellamy and the Green Gallery 1960–1965*, ed. Erik La Prade. New York: Midmarch Arts Press, 2009, 137–40.

INDEX

NOTE: Page numbers in italics refer to illustrations. Page numbers followed by *n* and a number refer to information in the Notes. Artists' works appear at the end of their index entries.

abstract eroticism 5, 13–15
  see also Eccentric Abstraction
Abstract Expressionism 24
  and Chamberlain 138–9, 142
  and Grossman 154, 162, 189–90
  and O'Hara, 72
  and Smith 3, 68
abstraction's rejection of human form and invocation in sculpture xii–xiii, xvi, xvii, 1–2, 6–41, 278–9
  anthropomorphism 9–13
    and Minimalism 9–11, 12–13
  Bourgeois's work 17
  Flavin's dedications and personhood 249–53, 256, 257–65
  Flavin's icons and figurations of the homosexual 212–27, 233–5, 237, 241–3, 261
  and genders xiv–xv, 1, 2, 13–19, 44, 279–80
    complication and ambiguity of gender 19–26
  Gonzalez-Torres's dedications and personhood 254, 256, 265
  and Smith's non-figurative art 2–3, 44–5, 54–5, 57–9, 62–8, 70, 80, 81–95
  transgender capacity 2, 4, 34, 38–9, 276–7, 278–80

  and body in Cassils's sculpture 269–74, 278
  Burton's sculpture as furniture 274–6, 278
  Grossman's work 160
  openness of Chamberlain's work 129–42, 145
Acconci, Vito 25
activism and transgender issues xii, 26–7, 28, 29, 30
Adrian, Dennis 326*n*.123
Aestheticism: artists and self-representation 20
Alloway, Lawrence 8
Altieri, Charles 71
ambiguity of gender in art 4, 5, 19
  ambiguity and simplified morphologies in modern sculpture 19–26
    and Brancusi's sculpture 20–2
    Chamberlain's work 131–3, 135
    Smith's non-figurative works 83, 87–95
  and Lippard's discourse 14
  sculpture of Bourgeois and Hesse 17
  and Smith's work 83
  see also androgyny
American Psychiatric Association 30–1
Andre, Carl 247, 249, 259
  "A Word for John Chamberlain" (poem) 305*n*.22
androgyny
  in art 5, 14, 21
    interpretations of Smith's work 83
  artists' self-representation 20, 24
  see also ambiguity of gender in art

anecdotal theory 44
Anger, Kenneth 142
    Scorpio Rising (film) 139, 172
animalier sculpture 283–4nn.4
anthropocentrism critique 9
anthropomorphism 5
    and sculpture 6, 9–13, 145
    Smith's non-figurative work 54–5,
        57–9, 61, 62–8, 70, 80, 81–95
    see also sculpture: relationship with
        human figure
Antin, Eleanor 269
Apollinaire, Guillaume 20
Arbus, Diane 25, 198
art history *see* transgender studies: and
    art history
Artforum: Flavin's autobiography 217–18,
    219
artists and self-representation:
    nonconforming genders 20, 24, 25,
    149, 205
assemblage: Grossman's sculpture 4,
    18–19, 147–8, 149–79, 203
Auder, Viva: *The Secret Life of William
    Shakespeare* (film with Chamberlain)
    114, 116
Auping, Michael 100
Avedon, Richard: Grossman's studio and
    work *182*, *184*, 189, *190*, 191, *194*
Ayden, Erje 61

Baden, Mowry 11
Baker, Elizabeth (Betsy) 97, 102, 117,
    308n.77
Bannard, Darby 106
Bass, Math 327n.13
Battcock, Gregory 324n.93
    Minimal Art (anthology) 13
Bell, Larry 119
Bellamy, Richard 220
Benglis, Lynda: *The Amazing Bow Wow*
    (video) 25
Benjamin, Harry xii, 20, 28, 29
Benning, Sadie 327n.13
Berkson, Bill 61–2, 150, 177

Bernstein, Nancy 27
Besember, Linda 327n.13
Bess, Forrest 24
binary approach to gender and human
    form xiv–xv, 21–2
    fallacy and acknowledgement of
        multiple genders xv–xvi, 14, 23–4,
        31–2, 33, 34, 280
    limitations on human experience 129
        and Grossman 176–7, 179
    see also dimorphism
bi-sexed and inclusive genders in art
    20–1, 24–5
    Grossman on bi-sexed process of art
        178–9, 205
black leather and Grossman's work
    association with S/M 172, 173, 180,
        191–201, 204
    connotations of black leather jacket
        172–4, 176
Black Mountain College and
    Chamberlain 117, 143, 304n.6
Blake, Nayland 179, 189, 193, 194
Blow Job (Warhol film) 172, 201
"bodily"
    and anthropomorphism in sculpture
        9, 11, 13
    and gender and sexuality 13
body
    aesthetics of transgender body 4
    in sculptural work of artists 2–3
        Cassils's use of body in making of
            work 267–74, 278
    see also human figure and shift to
        abstraction; viewer's bodily relation
        with art
bondage *see* S/M community
Bontecou, Lee 142
Bosworth, Patricia 198
Bourgeois, Louise 17–18, 19, 25, 160,
    301n.93
Brainard, Joe 48
Brancusi, Constantin 6, 20–2
    Flavin's dedication of work to 210
    Adam and Eve 20, 21

Golden Bird 23
The Kiss 135, *140*
Leda 20
Princess X 20, 22
Torso of a Young Girl [II] 20, *22*
Torso of a Young Man [I] 20, *21*, 22
Broadway in Flavin's *icon V (Coran's Broadway Flesh)* 212–13, 215, 222–4
Burgher, Elijah 327n.13
Burden, Chris 316n.126
Burnham, Jack 11–12, 244, 325n.96
Burr, Tom 327n.13
Burton, Scott 274–6, 278
  Five Themes of Solitary Behavior 198
  Two-part Chair 276
Butler, Judith xiv, 31, 94, 127, 278, 307n.59
  on acknowledgement of gender complexity xvi, 36, 41, 89–91, 267
Butt, Gavin 47

Calder, Alexander ("Sandy") 259
Calley, Lieutenant William 185, 187–8
capacity *see* transgender capacity
Carney, William: *The Real Thing* 173, 315n.116
Caro, Anthony 11–12
Carroll, Paul 71
Cassils, Heather
  Becoming an Image performance work 268–71, *268*, 271–2, 273, 278
  Cuts: A Traditional Sculpture 269
  The Resilience of the 20% *266*, 267–9, 273–4
Chadwick, Whitney 316n.134
Chamberlain, John xii, xiii, xvi, 2–4, 39, 97–145, *121*, 274, 276, 279
  Black Mountain College 143, 304n.6
    and poet's approach to work 117, 143
  bodies in non-figurative art 2–3, 114
  challenges of describing work 100–2, 138–9, 142
    interviews and evasive attitude to work 117–18, 122–3, 130, 279
    Judd's writing and interpretation 110–11, 118–19
    and "successive states" 110–11, 114, 130
  color and work 105–8, 305n.26
  "fitting" process and coupling in words and work 97–8
    conflicted readings of concrete and abstract 97, 108, 110–12, 143
    coupling and tactics of 100, 102–16, 143
    masculine and feminine in work 137
    sculpture and painting 104–5, 116
    and sexual in work 98, 100, 120–5, 127, 130–1
    volume and mass 103–4, 112, 116
  and gender multiplicity and indetermination 1, 122–42
  Guggenheim retrospective (2012) 305n.27
  John Chamberlain / F_____g Couches exhibition 120–1
  paper sculptures 110, 117
  sexuality
    and personal interactions and interviews 119–20
    and work 38, 98, 100, 120–5, 127, 129–31, 143, 145
  titles and meaning of work 110, 114, 117, 249
    and gender assignment 113–14, 131, 132
  transformative nature of art 112–13, 114, 122, 125, 127, 145
    recycling aesthetic 127
  and transgender perspective 18, 26, 129–42
    open-endedness and transgender capacity 129–42, 145
  Bouquet 99
  Chili Terlingua 124
  Crowded Hearts 132
  Dolores James 112
  Endless Gossip 110

Endzoneboogie 110, *111*
Essex 123–4
F*****g Asterisks 129
Fantail 103
Flavin Flats 3
Folded Nude 96, 133–4, *134*
Four Polished Nails 126
Huzzy 113–14, *115*, 131
Kiss series 135
Kiss #11 138–9
Kiss #12 140, *141*
Kiss #26 *141*
Kiss #28 *136*
M. Junior Love 101
Miss Lucy Pink *108*, 131
Mustang Sally McBright *107*
One Twin 133–4
Panna-Normanna *123*, 142
Penthouse series 110
Penthouse #46 *118*
The Secret Life of William Shakespeare (film with Auder) 114, 116
Socket series *98*, 114, 132
Son of Dudes *109*, 131, *132*
Three Cornered Desire 132, *133*
Tongue Pictures 113
Toy *104*
Ultrafull Private 144
Chave, Anna 20–1
Chicago, Judy: *Dinner Party* 163
Clum, John M. 320*n*.46
Cohen, Mark Daniel 175–6
color and sculpture
　Chamberlain 105–8, 305*n*.26
　critical reservations 105–6
　Smith 48, 54, 105
Colpitt, Frances 6, 10, 284*n*.14
Cone, Jane Harrison 299*n*.58
Conner, Bruce 9
Coran, Stanley 215, 218–19, 220, 222–5, 234, 237, 242, 247
Creeley, Robert 110
Crow, Thomas 129
Curtis, Jackie 25, 30

Dalí, Salvador 20
Darling, Candy 30
Davis, Whitney 327–8*n*.16
Dawson, Fielding 305*n*.22
de Henriquez, Fiore 24, 28
de Kooning, Willem 46, 48
de Villiers, Nicholas 219
dedications *see* Flavin: titles of works and dedications
Dehner, Dorothy 79
Dienes, Sari 142
difference and Flavin's work
　naming of homosexuals and visible difference 210–12, 218–19, 220–7, 233–5, 237, 239, 241–3, 259, 261
　systematic interchangeability and difference and sameness 243–53, 257, 261, 264–5
dimorphism
　fallacy of absolute dimorphism xiv–xvi, 129, 280
　and feminist attitudes 204
　gender assignment and human form in art xiv–xv
　and Brancusi's sculptures 20–2
　and Chamberlain's sculptures 131–2
　and Smith's non-figurative work 44–5, 62–4, 73–86, 89–91, 93
　social insistence on assignment of gender 176–7
　nomination of human gender xiv, 21–2
　see also binary approach to gender and human form
Disney clay (WED clay) and Cassils's work 273
drag/drag queens
　academic study in 1960s 30
　conflict with police 28, 29
　Rosenblum's drag queen names for friends 259, *262–3*
　visibility in Warhol's films 25, 30
Duchamp, Marcel 6, 20
　The Bride Stripped Bare by her Bachelors, Even 157

earthworks as art 7
Eccentric Abstraction exhibition (New York, 1966) 4, 13, 14, 16–17
Ellison, Ralph: *Invisible Man* (novel) 219–20
Erickson, Reed and Erickson Educational Foundation 28–9
erotic in art
   abstract eroticism 5, 13–15
   see also sexuality

Factory (Warhol) films 25, 30
Fake, Edie 327*n*.13
Farren, Mick 172
fashion and black leather jacket 172–3, 176
Feinberg, Leslie 26, 282*n*.13, 289*n*.80
feminism
   binary attitudes to gender 204
   division over transgender participation 31, 291*n*.22
   Grossman and conflicted relationship with 19, 149, 203–5
   Grossman and use of vaginal imagery 162–3
   Lippard on abstraction and sexual difference 15
   and S/M community and practices 204
   transfeminism and gender nonconformism in art 25–6, 149, 205
Fer, Briony 12, 15
figuration *see* human figure and shift to abstraction
film and transsexuality 25, 27, 28, 30
Flavin, Dan xii, xiii, 2–4, 39–40, 209–65, 274, 276
   bodies in non-figurative art 2–3, 213, 215
   and categorization of work 209–10
   as sculpture 2, 6, 210, 317–8*n*.5
   change of direction and use of fluorescent tubes 230–43
      systematic interchangeability and difference and sameness 243–53, 257, 261, 264–5
   homosexuality and attitudes and work 38
      and autobiography in *Artforum* 217–18, 219
      "flesh tint" and carnal nature of *icon V* 213, 215, 225, 227, 234
      homosexual mentors 232–43
      icons and figurations of the homosexual 212–27, 228, 233–5, 237, 241–3, 261
      public offensives and naming of homosexuals 216–17, 218–19, 220, 227, 233–4, 259, 261
   invisibility and art of 228–9
      fluorescent tubes and "approximate invisibility" 232–43, 261, 264
   light and the visible in art 219–20, 239
   titles of works and dedications 40, 209–10, 280
      fluorescent tubes and performative dedications 247–53, 257, 261, 264
      influence on Gonzalez-Torres's naming of works 254–7, 265
      naming of homosexuals and visible difference 210–12, 218–19, 220–7, 233–4, 239, 241–3, 259, 261
      shifting dedication for *diagonal of May 25, 1963* 239, 243
      transformable personhood and naming 254–65
   and transgender perspective 18, 26, 257–65
   alternate diagonals of March 2, 1964 (to Don Judd) 242
   Dan Flavin: alternating pink and "gold" installation *248*
   Dan Flavin: fluorescent light installation 242–3, *242*
   Dan Flavin: some light installation 213, 229–30, *230*
   the diagonal of May 25, 1963 (to Constantin Brancusi / to Robert Rosenblum) 230–1, *231*, 232, 239, *240*, 241, *242*, 243

East New York Shrines 220, 222, 259
European Couples installation 265
icon series 212–27, 228–30
icon IV *(the pure land) (to David John Flavin [1933–1962])* 225, *226*, 227, 228, 230, 241
icon V *(Coran's Broadway Flesh)* 212–16, *214*, 218–27, *221*, 228, 230, 233–5, 237, 239, 247, 261
    final study *216*
    formation of title 250–1
    plan for revised work 224–5, *224*
icon VI *(Ireland dying) (to Louis Sullivan)* 228, *229*
icon VII *(via crucis)* 228, *229*
icon VIII *(the dead nigger's icon) (to Blind Lemon Jefferson)* 228–9, *229*
one of May 27th, 1963 *(Construction with Red Fluorescent and Incandescent Bulbs)* 237, *238*
pink out of a corner *(to Jasper Johns)* 232, *234*, *236*, 237, 239, 242–3, *242*
red and green alternatives *(to Sonja)* 211
red out of a corner *(to Annina)* 237, *238*, 257
untitled *(for you, Leo, in long respect and affection) 208*, 257
untitled *(in memory of "Sandy" Calder) V* 257, *260*
untitled *(to Ellen Johnson, fondly) 252*
untitled *(to Janie Lee) one 246*
untitled *(to the real Dan Hill) 244*
Flavin, David John 217, 225, 227, 242
Flesh (Warhol film) 30
Foucault, Michel 283*n*.19
Frankenthaler, Helen 62
Freas, Jean 48
Fried, Michael 12–13
    "Art and Objecthood" essay 9–10, 278
    on Caro 11–12
Fritscher, Jack 196–7
furniture as art in Burton's work 274–6

Gallop, Jane 44
Gaudier-Brzeska, Henri 6

gay liberation movement xii
    distancing from transgender community and issues 31
    see also homosexuality
Geldzahler, Henry 137, 279, 284*n*.8
gender
    as "expanded field" 40–1
    fallacy of absolute dimorphism xiv–xvi, 129, 280
    feminist attitudes to gender roles 204
    and Flavin's naming of works 257–65
    gender identity
        ascription at birth xiv
        invention of term 28, 30
        shift in understanding in 1960s xi–xii
    historical attitudes and understandings 26–34
    and human figure in art xvi, xvii
        abstraction and genders xiv–xv, 1, 2, 13–19, 279–80
        ambiguity of gender 4, 5, 14, 17, 19–26, 83, 94–5
        assignment of gender xiv–xv, 20–3, 44, 131–2
        assignment of gender and Smith's work 44–5, 62–4, 73–86, 89–91, 93
        Chamberlain's work 114, 122–42
        Grossman's open and disruptive approach to gender 147–8, 149–50, 160–79
        inclusive genders 20–1, 24–5
        nonconforming genders 20, 23–6, 38, 149, 205
    and literature on artists 17–18
    masculine in Grossman's work 150, 188
        connotations of black leather jacket 172–4, 176
    multiplicity xv–xvi, 1, 2, 14, 23–4, 33, 40–1, 279–80
        Chamberlain's work and unspecified gender 1, 122–42
        historical context 31–2
        see also transgender capacity

mutability xvi, 2, 19, 20, 23–4, 40–1, 127
   and Chamberlain's works 131–3, 135
   and Grossman's work 1, 147–8, 149–50, 160–79, 201–7
   historical context 31–2
   temporal nature of gender 127, 129
   see also transgender capacity
and sexuality 36–9
   complexity of Grossman's explicit sculptures 160–76, 179, 203
see also ambiguity of gender in art; binary approach to gender and human form; dimorphism; nonconforming genders; transformation: and gender; transgender
gender research clinics xi–xii, 28–9, 30
Genette, Gérard 251–3
Gernreich, Rudi 217
Gibson, John: *Tinted Venus* 105, *106*
Goldsmith, Bill 194–5
Glass, Charles 327*n*.2
Gonzalez-Torres, Felix 254–7, 265
   "Untitled" (Perfect Lovers) 256
   "Untitled" (Petit Palais) 254, *255*
   "Untitled" (Portrait of Ross in L.A.) 254, *255*
Goosen, E. C. 105
Govan, Michael 225
Graham, Dan 225, 245
Gray, Cleve 82, 86, 301*n*.94
Green, Richard 30
Greenberg, Clement 10, 54, 55, 311*n*.28
Greenson, Ralph 28
Groeneboer, Jonah 327*n*.13
Grossman, Nancy xii, xiii, 2–4, 31, 39, 147–207, 274, 276, 279
   bodies in non-figurative art 2–3
      abstract assemblages 4, 18–19, 147–8, 149–79, 203
   Civil Rights and anti-racism sympathies 199, 313*n*.69
   critical reception and reputation 148–9, 163

   misrepresentations of work 149, 205, 206
   popularity and misreading of "heads" 192–201
drawings
   commercial illustration work 167–8
   and sculpture 151, 152, 155, 156–7, 181
and feminism
   gender nonconformity and uneasy relationship with 19, 149, 203–5
   transgender affinities 19, 26
   and use of vaginal imagery 162–3
figurative art and heads 19, *148*, 172, 178–207, *180*, *183–4*, *186–7*, *189*, *194–6*, *200*, *202*, *207*
   bodilessness and transgender capacity 201–7
   containment and disclosure theme 181–2, 184, 187–8, 191, 201
   earlier abstract assemblages as precursor to 149–50, 167–8
   labor and craft of making 181–3, *182*
   redirection of heads in 1980s 199–201
   S/M association 180, 191–201, 204, 205
   as self-portraits 147, 150, 179–81, 184–91, 202–3, 206
   sources of inspiration and research for 189, 191
friendship with Smith and influence on work 151–60
and gender multiplicity and mutability 1
   bi-sexed process of art 178–9, 205
   bodilessness of heads and transgender perspective 201–7
   disruptive and open approach to gender 147–8, 149–50, 160–79
German shepherd dog 175
leather in work
   black leather and cultural connotations 172–4, 176, 180, 191–201

as repurposed material 151, 152–4, 158, 165, 171–2, 177
"machine-animal hybrids" series 159, 177–8
sexuality and complexity of explicit sculptures 38, 148, 151, 160–76, 179, 203
studio and work in progress *182*, *184*, 189, *190*, *191*, *194*
and transgender perspective 19, 159–60
A.F.F. 146
Ali of Nostrand 158, 175
Ali Stoker 38, 150–1, 162, 167, 169–76, *170–1*, *173*, *175*
Andro sculptures 194–5
Arbus 198
Black Landscape 151, *152*, 161, 166
Blunt 183
Bride 150–1, 154, 160–7, *161*, *164*, 176
Brown and Black 158
B.Y.K. 202
Car Horn 158
Caracas 193
Chiron 166–7, *166*
Cob II 199
Eden 151
The Edge of Always 151, *152*, 161
For David Smith 150–1, 151–60, *153*, *155*
Hitchcock 158
Mary 185, *186–7*, 187–8
M.L. Sweeney 181, *196*
M.U.S. 189
No Name 180, 207
Potawatami 162, 167, *168–9*
Slaves series 167, 169, 172
Totem series 311*n*.29
Walrus 166
Guggenheim, Peggy 241
Gypsy (Broadway musical) 222–3, *223*, 258–9

Halberstam, Jack 4, 17, 18, 26, 33, 159–60, 177
Hall, Gordon 327*n*.13
Hammond, Harmony 327*n*.13

Hampson, Joan and John 28
Harwood, Michael 324*n*.92, 326*n*.124
Henriquez, Fiore de *see* de Henriquez, Fiore
Hepworth, Barbara 23
hermaphrodite statues and ambiguous figures 20
Hess, Thomas 79, 80
Hesse, Eva 17–18, 19, 160, 177
  Ringaround Arosie 24
Höch, Hannah 160
homosexuality
  black leather and clothing 172–3, 176, 195–6
  Flavin's attitudes and work
    homosexual mentors 232–43
    icons and figurations of the homosexual 212–27, 233–5, 237, 241–3, 261
    naming of homosexuals and visible difference 210–12, 215–16, 218–19, 220–7, 233–5, 237, 239, 241–3, 259, 261
    public offensives against homosexuals 216–17, 227
  gay collectors
    Flavin's work 323*n*.82
    Grossman's work 194–5
  and *Gypsy* musical and New York 222–3
  and New York art world 46–8, 241
  see also gay liberation movement; S/M community
Horosko, Marian 79–80
Howard, Richard 73
human figure and shift to abstraction xii–xiii, xvi, xvii, 277
  and genders xiv–xv, 1, 2, 13–19, 279–80
    abstraction and nonconforming genders 20, 23–6, 38, 149, 205
    assignment of gender xiv–xv, 20–3, 44
    assignment of gender and Smith's non-figurative work 44–5, 62–4, 73–86, 89–91, 93

Brancusi's assigned and inclusive genders 20–2
Chamberlain's sculptures 131–2
see also abstraction's rejection of human form and invocation in sculpture; ambiguity of gender in art; body; sculpture: relationship with human figure
Hunter, Sam 49–50

Indiana, Gary 102, 123–4, 125
International Olympic Committee (IOC) 29
intersex
    artists' self-representation 24, 25
    development of history and politics of xv, 26–7, 33–4, 282n.10

Jefferson, Blind Lemon 229
Johns, Jasper 48, 72, 142, 228, 232–5, 237, 249, 259
    and Flavin's *pink out of a corner (to Jasper Johns)* 232, 234, 236, 237, 239, 242–3, 242
    Tennyson 215, 233–5, 235, 237, 239
Johns Hopkins University xi, 29, 30
Johnson, Marsha P. 30
Johnson, Philip 323n.82
Johnston, Jill 213, 234–5
Jones, Caroline 215, 323n.78
Jorgensen, Christine xi, 27, 28, 29–30, 31, 259
Joyce, James 217
Judd, Donald xvi, 9, 12–13, 142, 216, 219, 285n.16
    on Chamberlain 101, 105, 107–8, 110–11, 118–19, 120, 130
    and Flavin 210, 212, 220, 228
    titles of works 249, 250

Kaplowitz, Jane 324
Katz, Jonathan D. 47
Kauffman, Craig 244–5, 324n.94
Kertess, Klaus 102, 105, 120, 307n.51
Kienholz, Edward 9

Kobro, Katarzyna 6
Kosofsky Sedgwick, Eve 4–5, 201, 307n.59
Krauss, Rosalind xi, 13, 16
    on attempts to overcome figuration in sculpture 6–7
    on body in abstract sculpture 7
    "expanded field" term 40–1
    on Smith and work 72, 80, 83–4, 88
        dissertation and catalogue raisonné 299n.58
Kusama, Yayoi 13, 19

language
    nomination of gender at birth xiv
    words and artists' work 279
leather *see* Grossman: leather in work
Leider, Philip 319n.29
Leigh, Michael: *Velvet Underground* 192, 193
lesbian community and feminism 204
Leslie, Alfred: *The Last Clean Shirt* (film with O'Hara) 52
LeWitt, Sol 210, 228
Licht, Fred 241
Linder, Jean 13
Lippard, Lucy
    "Eccentric Abstraction" (essay) 13, 14–15, 16, 17
    Eccentric Abstraction exhibition (New York, 1966) 4, 13, 14, 16–17
    "Eros Presumptive" (essay) 13–15, 16, 17, 38
    on Flavin's *icon V* 213
    on reality of sculpture 7
literalism
    and Flavin's work 209–10
        icons and figurations of the homosexual 212–27, 233–5, 237, 241–3, 261
        turn to fluorescent tubes 230–2, 241–3, 261, 264
    and human form xii, 2, 9, 10, 11, 38
        and Burton's sculpture as furniture 274–5, 278

Flavin's dedications and personhood 249–53, 257–65
Lonesome Cowboys (Warhol film) 138–9
Lord, Catherine 176
Lowndes, Joan 251
Ludlam, Charles: Ridiculous Theater Company 25

McGinnes, Mac 324*n*.92, 326*n*.123
    "Meet Ms. Western Artiste!" (with Rosenblum) *262–3*
Malevich, Kasimir 323*n*.78
Mapplethorpe, Robert 195, 197–8
    Untitled (Nancy Grossman sculptures) 200
Marisol 25
masculine in Grossman's work 150, 188
    associations of black leather 172–4, 176
Masheck, Joe 216
Massumi, Brian 75–6
Matisse, Henri 210
media
    and misrepresentation of Grossman's "heads" 193–5, 198, 199–201
    visibility and understanding of transsexuality xi, xii, 24, 25, 27, 28, 29–30
medicine
    gender reassignment surgery 29
    medical discourse of sex and gender 24
    see also gender research clinics
McCracken, John 324*n*.94
Medina, Ernest 185, 187
Meltzer, Eve 40
Mendieta, Ana: *Untitled (Facial Hair Transplants)* 25
Merman, Ethel 222, *223*
Meyer, James 9, 10–11, 17, 212, 220
Meyer, Richard 47
Meyerowitz, Joanne 26, 27
Mies van der Rohe, Ludwig 247
Miller, D. A. 222

Minimalism 8, 16
    abstraction and human figure 7, 9–13
        anthropomorphism critiques 9–11, 12–13
    and body in Cassils's work 273
    Burton's sculpture as furniture 274–6, 278
    and Flavin 4, 209–10
    and Gonzalez-Torres 254, 256
    see also Postminimalism
Money, John 24, 28, 30
"monokini" and Flavin on Barbara Rose 217
Moore, Henry 23
Morris, Robert 7, 12–13, 16, 25
Motherwell, Robert 301*n*.93
Moyer, Carrie 327*n*.13
Müller, Grégoire 256
Müller, Ulrike 327*n*.13
Museum of Modern Art (MoMA), New York
    Flavin on Wilfred's work at 217
    O'Hara and Smith's work 45–6, 48–50, 59, 61, 62
My Lai Massacre and Grossman's work 185, 187–8

Namaste, Viviane K. xv, 292–3*n*.120
names
    Rosenblum's drag queen names for friends 259, *262–3*
    and self-determination 258–9
    see also titles
Nashat, Shahryar 327*n*.13
Nelson, Maggie 47
Nemser, Cindy 149, 155–6, 157, 160, 162, 163, 169, 171, 311–2*n*.40
Neuner, Stefan 217
New York art world and homosexual networks 46–8, 241
New York School of poets 46, 47
Newman, Barnett 228, 245
Newton, Esther 30
Nine at Leo Castelli warehouse show 216–17, 218

nonconforming genders xvi, xvii
  and abstraction 20, 23–6, 38
    Grossman's work 149–50, 205
  actors and artists 20, 24, 25
  see also transgender; transsexuality
Northwestern University xi–xii, 29
Nosei, Annina 237

Ockham, William of 210
O'Doherty, Brian 149
O'Hara, Frank 47
  homosexuality and New York art world 46–8
  as poet 70–3
    "Having a Coke with You" 70
    "Hermaphrodite" 25
    "In Memory of My Feelings" 72
    Love Poems (Tentative Title) 47
    Lunch Poems 46
    Smith's appearance in "Mozart Chemisier" 50–2
  and social and sexual relationships 46–7, 62
  and visual art and artists 46
  and Smith
    Art New York interview 1, 39, 43–4, 61–8, 63–4, 66, 72, 80, 81–2, 93–5, 279
    ARTnews article 53–4, 57–8, 59
    as curator and role in Smith's career 43, 44–61, 72–3
    response to Smith's sculptures 57–9, 61, 64–8, 70, 72–3, 73–86
    and sexuality 75–7
    visits to Bolton Landing 48–9, 50–3, 57–9, 62, 64–5
Oldenburg, Claes 9, 13
  Drum Set 24–5
Olson, James 185, 187
Olympic Games in Mexico City (1968) xii, 27, 29
ONE National Gay & Lesbian Archives, Los Angeles: "Trans Activation" series 270

Paar, Jack 24, 28
paratextuality *see* peritextuality
Parsons, Betty and gallery 24
part-objects and gender 15, 17, 19, 177
Paterson, Jennifer 24
performativity
  Flavin's titles and dedications 209, 220
    and fluorescent tube works 247–53, 257, 261, 264
  Grossman's heads as self-portraits 203, 206
  nomination of gender at birth xiv
Pepe, Sheila 327n.13
peritextuality and Flavin's dedications 251–3
Perreault, John
  and Flavin's titles and dedications 209, 210
  on Grossman 192, 194
personhood in sculpture 3, 276
  and "expanded field" 41
  and Flavin's naming system
    performative naming of works 249–53, 257
    transformable personhood 254–65
  "successive states" of personhood and gender xvi, xvii, 34, 279–80
  and Chamberlain's work 110–11, 114, 130
Picabia, Francis 20
Picasso, Pablo 105
Pincus-Witten, Robert 16
Piper, Adrian: *Mythic Being* 25
Plunkett, Edward M. 220, 259, 320n.41
Poetter, Jochen 125–7
Pollock, Jackson 46, 48
Pop Art 3–4, 9
Postminimalism 4
  and *Eccentric Abstraction* exhibition 16–17
Potts, Alex 44, 215, 309n.2
Preciado, Paul B. xv, 26
public art: Burton's furniture 274–6

queer studies and queer theory 27, 37

Rasmussen, Waldo 59, 61
Rauschenberg, Robert 48, 142
    Bed 235
Raven, Arlene 147, 150, 151, 156, 158, 166, 185, 187
Rechy, John 28
    City of Night 48
Reis, Elizabeth 26, 27
relief assemblages of Grossman 18–19, 147–8, 149–79, 203
relief sculpture 283–4nn.3&4
reparative readings 4–5
Richardson, Brenda 249
Ridiculous Theater Company 25
Ritchie, Andrew 49–50
Rivera, Sylvia 30
Rivers, Larry 47, 48, 139
Roberts, Randy 185, 187
Rodin, Auguste 135, 273, 289n.66
Rondeau, James 235
Rose, Barbara 101–2, 105, 213, 217
Rosen, Andrea 254, 256
Rosenblum, Robert 220, 232–3, 239, 241, 243
    drag queen names for friends 259
        "Meet Ms. Western Artiste!" (with McGinnes) 262–3
    sexual identity 241, 324n.93
Rubin, Gayle 204

S/M community
    association with Grossman's work 172, 173, 205
    and head figures 180, 191–201, 204
Sahib, Prem 327n.13
Salamon, Gayle 33, 37, 165, 206
Samaras, Lucas 13
Schapiro, Meyer 24
Schapiro, Miriam 163
Schiff, Gert 193
Schor, Mira 205
Scull, Robert and Ethel 220
sculpture
    and color 48, 54, 105–8
    physical relationship with viewer 5–6, 7, 9, 11–12, 14–15, 277–8
    O'Hara's response to Smith's work 57–9, 61, 64–8, 70, 72–3, 73–86
    relationship with human figure 1–41
        abstract sculpture and genders xv, 1, 2, 9–13
        ambiguity and simplified forms 19–26, 83, 87–95, 133–4
        anthropomorphism critiques 6, 9–13
        and distinction as art not object 8
        Smith's non-figurative art 2–3, 44–5, 54–5, 57–9, 62–8, 70, 80, 81–95
        "successive states" of personhood and gender xvi, xvii, 34, 279–80
        and Chamberlain's work 110–11, 114, 130
    transformation in 1960s xi, 2, 6
    see also abstraction's rejection of human form and invocation in sculpture; human figure and shift to abstraction
Sedgwick, Eve Kosofsky *see* Kosofsky Sedgwick
Segal, George 9
Selby, Hubert, Jr.: *Last Exit to Brooklyn* (novel) 27, 28
sex change *see* transsexuality
sexuality
    and Chamberlain's personal interactions and interviews 119–20
    and gender 36–9
    and O'Hara 46–8, 75–7
    in sculpture 3, 37
        abstract eroticism 5, 13–15
        and Chamberlain's work 98, 100, 120–5, 127, 129–31, 143, 145
        complexity of Grossman's explicit art 38, 148, 151, 160–76, 179, 203
        Grossman's association with S/M community 180, 191–201, 204, 205
        and Smith's work 38, 75–7
    see also erotic in art; homosexuality; transsexuality

Shaw, Lytle 72–3
Siegel, Anita 198
Sillman, Amy 327n.13
Sims, Lowery Stokes 174, 176
Smith, David xii, xiii, 2–4, 7, 16, 43–95, 74–5, 89, 274, 280
   bodies in non-figurative art 2–3, 54–5, 57–9, 62–8, 70, 80, 81–95
   and assignment of gender 44–5, 62–4, 73–86, 89–91, 93
   Bolton Landing and sculptures in situ 42, 45, 48–9, 49–53, 50–3, 55–8, 57–9, 61, 62, 64–5, 67, 71, 74–8, 85–6, 88–92, 95
   catalogue raisonné 299n.58
   color and work 48, 54, 105
   composition of work and "drawing in space" 68, 157–8
   daughters and home life and work 48, 51–2, 78–9, 298n.54
   death 59, 61
   friendship with Grossman and *For David Smith* 150–1, 151–60, 153, 155
   and O'Hara
     Art New York interview 1, 39, 43–4, 61–8, 63–4, 66, 72, 80, 81–2, 93–5, 279
     connotations of "I don't make boy sculptures" comment 43–4, 64, 73–84, 86
     and European retrospective (1966) 59, 61
     misrepresentation of Smith's comments and works 81–6, 93
     "Mozart's Chemisier" poem 50–2
     O'Hara at Bolton Landing 48–9, 50–3, 57–9, 62, 64–5
     O'Hara's *ARTnews* article 53–4, 57–8, 59
     O'Hara's response to Smith's sculptures 57–9, 61, 64–8, 70, 72–3, 73–86
     O'Hara's support as curator and role in career 43, 44–61, 72–3
     response to O'Hara's sexuality 75–7

     rejection of words to interpret art 81
   sexuality and work 38, 75–7
     attitudes to women and use of term "girls" 78–80
     female nudes 79
   Tate Modern retrospective 1
   and transgender perspective 18, 26, 87–95
   Agricola I 51
   Black White Forward 77
   Circle and Box (Circle and Ray) 65
   Cube Totem 7 and 6 51, 84, 85
   Cubi series 53, 55, 68, 95, 158, 159
   Cubi VI 65
   Cubi VII xviii
   Cubi VIII 67
   Cubi XI 71
   XI Books III Apples 78
   Fifteen Planes 69–70
   The Five Spring 57
   The Hero (Eyehead of a Hero) 83, 84, 86–7
   Lectern Sentinel 67
   Lonesome Man 76, 78
   March Sentinel (Stainless Steel Planes) 53, 53
   Ninety Father 42, 53, 60, 77, 78
   Ninety Son 42, 53, 60, 77, 78, 91
   Noland's Blues 60
   Personage of August 57, 58
   Pilgrim 57
   Rebecca Circle 60
   Running Daughter 57
   Sentinel series 68, 83
   Sentinel I 56, 57
   Sentinel II 57, 58
   Tahstvaat 51
   Tanktotem series 68, 83
   Tanktotem I 83, 84
   Tanktotem IV 83, 88
   Tanktotem VI 57
   Tanktotem VIII 60
   Tanktotem IX 83, 90
   Two Box Structure 50, 53
   Two Circle Sentinel 50, 53, 53

Zig series 53, 68
Zig II 49, 50, 53, 55
Zig III 49, 50, 53, 77
Smith, Jack 195
Smith, Tony: *Die* 9–10, *10*, 278
Smithson, Robert 139, 234
speech act theory *see* performativity
Stanford University xii, 30
Star, Hedy Jo 27, 28
statue
  assignment of gender in Smith's non-figurative work 44–5, 62–4, 73–86, 89–91, 93
  hermaphrodite statues and ambiguous figures 20
  rejection and transformation in art of 1960s xi, xii, xiii, xvii, 2, 6–7, 8, 10–11, 40
Stella, Frank 142, 220, 228, 259
  titles of "Black Paintings" 249–50
Stoller, Robert 24, 28, 30
Stonewall Riots (New York, 1969) xii, 30
Street Transvestite Action Revolutionaries (STAR) 30
Stryker, Susan xv, 26–7, 32, 36, 127, 282n.10, 292n.120
  on gender and sexuality 37
  on inevitability of gender attribution 176–7
  on "transgender liberation" in 1960s xvi, 30–1
  on use of "transgender" as term 32
"successive states" of personhood and gender in sculpture xvi, xvii, 34, 279–80
  and Chamberlain's work 110–11, 114, 130
Sullivan, Louis 228
Sylvester, Julie 117–18
Symbolism: artists and self-representation 20

Tatlin, Vladimir 6, 210, 323n.78
Tennyson, Alfred, Lord: "In Memoriam A.H.H." (poem) 235, 237

theater and illusionism and Flavin's work 222
Thek, Paul 9
Tillim, Sidney 212
titles *see* Chamberlain: titles and meaning of work; Flavin: titles of works and dedications
Tonight Show (US TV show) 24, 28
transfeminism and gender nonconformism in art 25–6, 149, 205
transformation
  and Chamberlain's work 112–13, 114, 122, 125, 127, 145
  and gender 279–80
    and body in Cassils's work 269–74, 278
    and Flavin's naming practices 257–65
    transformed gender categories xvi, xvii
    transgender experience xv, 35, 273–4
    see also gender: mutability
  sculpture and rejection of statue in 1960s xi, xii, xiii, xvii, 2, 6, 6–7, 8, 10, 40
transgender
  activism and issues xii, 26–7, 28, 29, 30
  aesthetics of transgender body 4
  artists and self-representation 20, 24, 25
  bi-sexed and inclusive genders in art 20–1, 24–5, 178–9, 205
  Cassils's performance and work 269–74, 278
  and Grossman's work 19
  historical understanding and acknowledgement xv–xvi, 25, 26–34
    chronology of 28–30
    in context of gay and lesbian culture 31, 270
  naming and personhood 258, 259, 264
  and temporal nature of gender 127, 129

use of term 32–3
   as inclusive category xv
see also transgender capacity; transgender studies; transsexuality
transgender capacity xvi, 5, 34–6
   and abstract sculpture 2, 4, 34–6, 38–9, 276–7, 278–80
      and body in Cassils's work 269–74, 278
      Grossman's work 160
      openness of Chamberlain's work 129–42, 145
   usefulness as critical tool 34–6
transgender studies
   and art history xiii–xv, xvi, xvii, 33
      application to unexpected artists 18
      and Lippard's "Eros Presumptive" views 14
   development as discipline 27, 33
   and temporal construction of gender 129
Transsexual Action Organization (TAO) 30
transsexuality
   historical understanding and acknowledgement xi–xii, xv–xvi, 25, 27, 28, 29–30
   transgender as umbrella term xv
Tucker, Paul 79
Tucker, William 54, 84
Twombly, Cy 142

Ultra Violet (Warhol actress) 116, 121
universities: gender research clinics xi–xii, 28, 29, 30

University of California Los Angeles xi, 28

Valentine, David 32, 36
van der Marck, Jan 220
Vidal, Gore: *Myra Breckinridge* (novel) xii, 27, 30, 31
Vietnam War: Grossman's response 185, 187–8
viewer's bodily relation with art 2
   abstraction and bodily scale 9–10, 277–8
   sculpture 5–6, 7, 11–12, 278
      Lippard on "Eccentric Abstraction" 14–15
      O'Hara's response to Smith's work 57–9, 61, 64–8, 70, 72–3, 73–86
      Postminimalism and sculpture "beyond objects" 16–17

Wagner, Anne 13
Warhol, Andy 25, 27, 30, 142, 195
   Blow Job (film) 172, 201
   Lonesome Cowboys (film) 138–9
Warren, Vincent 47, 59
Welchman, John 249
Wilfred, Thomas 217
Wilke, Hannah 13, 14
Wilkin, Karen 83
Williams, Cristan 292n.106
Wilson, Phyllis Avon 29
Wood, Ed 28

ILLUSTRATION CREDITS

In most cases illustrative material has been provided by the owners or custodians of the works. Those for which further credit is due are listed below: © Estate of David Smith/Licensed by VAGA, New York: 1, 7, 8, 10, 11, 12, 13, 14, 15, 16, 17, 18, 19, 22, 24, 25, 27, 30, 31, 33, 34, 35, 37, 39, 40, 41, 84; © Fairweather & Fairweather Ltd/Artists Rights Society. Photograph courtesy Staatliche Kunsthalle Baden-Baden, Archiv, and © Philipp Schönborn: 2, 44, 53; © Estate of Tony Smith/Artists Rights Society: 3; © 2014 Artists Rights Society/ADAGP: 4, 5, 6, 71; Photograph: John Jonas Gruen. Hulton Archive, Getty Images: 9; Photograph: Dan Budnik, 1962. © Dan Budnik: 28, 29; Photograph: David Getsy: 26, 36, 43, 61; Image courtesy Department of Image Collections, National Gallery of Art Library, Washington, D.C.: 38; © Fairweather & Fairweather Ltd/Artists Rights Society: 45, 48, 50, 55, 60, 62, 63, 64, 75; © Fairweather & Fairweather Ltd/Artists Rights Society. Photograph courtesy of Allan Stone Projects, New York: 46; © Fairweather & Fairweather Ltd/Artists Rights Society. Photograph: Jerry L. Thompson, courtesy Solomon R. Guggenheim Museum: 47; Courtesy National Museums Liverpool, Walker Art Gallery: 49; © Fairweather & Fairweather Ltd/Artists Rights Society. Photograph: David Heald, courtesy Solomon R. Guggenheim Museum: 51, 58, 66, 78; © Fairweather & Fairweather Ltd/Artists Rights Society. Photograph: Kerry Ryan McFate, courtesy Pace Gallery, New York: 52, 65; © Fairweather & Fairweather Ltd/Artists Rights Society. Photograph: Kristopher McKay, courtesy Solomon R. Guggenheim Museum: 54; © Fairweather & Fairweather Ltd/Artists Rights Society. Courtesy Paula Cooper Gallery, New York: 56; © Fairweather & Fairweather Ltd/Artists Rights Society. Photograph: Jamison Miller: 57; © Fairweather & Fairweather Ltd/Artists Rights Society. Photograph: David Getsy: 67; Photograph: Georges Poncet, courtesy Galerie Karsten Greve, St. Moritz, Paris, Cologne: 68, 69, 70, 73; Photograph: Charles Duprat, courtesy Galerie Karsten Greve, St. Moritz, Paris, Cologne: 72, 74; Photograph: Guido Mangold: 77; Photograph courtesy of the artist and Michael Rosenfeld Gallery, New York: 78, 104; © Nancy Grossman, courtesy of Michael Rosenfeld Gallery, New York: 79, 80, 81, 82, 85, 87, 88, 89, 91, 96; © Nancy Grossman, courtesy of Michael Rosenfeld Gallery, New York. Photograph: David Getsy: 83, 86, 90, 92, 93, 97, 100; © Nancy Grossman. Los Angeles County Museum of Art, courtesy of Michael Rosenfeld Gallery, New York: 94, 101; © Richard

Avedon Foundation: 95, 98, 102, 103; © Nancy Grossman, courtesy of Michael Rosenfeld Gallery, New York. Photograph: Arthur Evans, courtesy Frances Young Tang Teaching Museum and Art Gallery at Skidmore College, Saratoga Springs, New York: 99, 105; © Robert Mapplethorpe Foundation. Used by permission: 106; Photograph: Arthur Evans, courtesy Frances Young Tang Teaching Museum and Art Gallery at Skidmore College, Saratoga Springs, New York: 107; Photograph: Matthew Septimus: 108; © Stephen Flavin/Artists Rights Society, courtesy David Zwirner Gallery, New York/London: 109, 110, 111, 112, 113, 116, 118, 119, 120, 121, 122, 124, 125, 127, 128, 129, 130, 131, 135, 138; © Stephen Flavin/Artists Rights Society Photograph: Haydar Koyupinar courtesy Bayerische Staatsgemäldesammlungen, Pinakothek der Moderne, Munich: 114, 117; © Jasper Johns/licensed by VAGA: 123; © Stephen Flavin/Artists Rights Society, courtesy Dia Art Foundation, New York. Photograph: Billy Jim: 126; © Stephen Flavin/Artists Rights Society, New York: 132; © The Felix Gonzalez-Torres Foundation. Courtesy of Andrea Rosen Gallery, New York: 133, 134; Courtesy of the artist and Ronald Feldman Fine Arts, New York. © Heather Cassils, 2015: 139; Photograph: Heather Cassils and Alejandro Santiago. Courtesy of the artist and Ronald Feldman Fine Arts, New York. © Heather Cassils, 2015: 140, 141, 143; Photograph: Heather Cassils and Manuel Vason. Courtesy of the artist and Ronald Feldman Fine Arts, New York. © Heather Cassils, 2015: 142; © Estate of Scott Burton/Artists Rights Society: 144.